California
HMH SCIENCE DIMENSIONS®

Chemistry
in the Earth System

Watch the cover come alive as you explore how seed crystals grow.

Download the Science Dimensions AR app, available on Android or iOS devices.

This book belongs to

Sindy Hernandez

Teacher/Room

Ms. Herrudora

Houghton Mifflin Harcourt™

ENGINEERING CONSULTANT

Cary I. Sneider, PhD
Associate Research Professor
Portland State University
Portland, Oregon

LAB SAFETY REVIEWER

Kenneth R. Roy, PhD
Senior Lab Safety Compliance Consultant
National Safety Consultants, LLC
Vernon, Connecticut

PROGRAM ADVISORS

Paul D. Asimow, PhD
Professor of Geology and
    Geochemistry
California Institute of Technology
Pasadena, California

Doris Ingram Lewis, PhD
Professor Emerita of Chemistry
Suffolk University
Boston, Massachusetts

Reza M. Mohseni, PhD
Professor of Chemistry/
    Lab Director
East Tennessee State University
Johnson City, Tennessee

Gary E. Mueller, PhD, PE
Associate Professor
Missouri University of Science
    & Technology
Rolla, Missouri

Michael J. Passow, PhD
Adjunct Associate
    Research Scientist
Lamont-Doherty
    Earth Observatory
Palisades, New York

CLASSROOM REVIEWERS

Christopher Becker
Los Altos High School
Hacienda Heights, California

Robert P. Gonzalez
Ocean View High School
Huntington Beach, California

Brandon Good
Shasta High School
Redding, California

Tyler Haglund
Apple Valley High School
Apple Valley, California

Emma Johnson
John F. Kennedy High School
Richmond, California

Brie Lieber-Linn
Highland High School
Palmdale, California

Anthony Palmer
Chemistry Teacher
South Bakersfield High School
Bakersfield, California

Katie Shoff
Enterprise High School
Redding, California

Cover Photo Credits
Cover Images: *crystal* ©HMH; *crystal growing in solution* ©Charles D. Winters/
Science Source

Interior Master Art: *connected dot pattern* ©chuckchee/Shutterstock

Copyright © 2020 by Houghton Mifflin Harcourt Publishing Company

All rights reserved. No part of this work may be reproduced or transmitted in
any form or by any means, electronic or mechanical, including photocopying
or recording, or by any information storage and retrieval system, without
the prior written permission of the copyright owner unless such copying is
expressly permitted by federal copyright law. Requests for permission to make
copies of any part of the work should be submitted through our Permissions
website at https://customercare.hmhco.com/contactus/Permissions.html or
mailed to Houghton Mifflin Harcourt Publishing Company, Attn: Intellectual
Property Licensing, 9400 South Park Center Loop, Orlando, Florida 32819-8647.
Printed in the U.S.A.

ISBN   978-1-328-89613-1

5 6 7 8 9 10   0868   27 26 25 24 23 22 21 20

4500798051   C D E F G

Michael DiSpezio

Global Educator
North Falmouth, Massachusetts

Michael DiSpezio has authored many HMH instructional programs for Science and Mathematics. He has also authored numerous trade books and multimedia programs on various topics and hosted dozens of studio and location broadcasts for various organizations in the U.S. and worldwide. Most recently, he has been working with educators to provide strategies for implementing the Next Generation Science Standards, particularly the Science and Engineering Practices, Crosscutting Concepts, and the use of Evidence Notebooks. To all his projects, he brings his extensive background in science; his expertise in classroom teaching at the elementary, middle, and high school levels; and his deep experience in producing interactive and engaging instructional materials.

Thomas O'Brien, PhD

Professor, Science Teacher Education & Educational Leadership
Department of Teaching, Learning & Educational Leadership
College of Community & Public Affairs
Binghamton University (State University of New York)
Binghamton, New York

Tom O'Brien has directed the graduate-level science teacher education programs at Binghamton since 1987. His scholarly interests include professional leadership development (e.g., co-principal investigator for NYS and national grants); science curriculum development, as related to science-technology-society themes and 5E Teaching Cycles; and K–12 science teacher education as informed by cognitive learning theory. He is the author of *Brain-Powered Science Teaching & Learning with Discrepant Events* and co-author/co-editor of *Science for the Next Generation: Preparing for the New Standards*.

Bernadine Okoro

S.T.E.M. Learning Advocate and Consultant
Washington, DC

Bernadine Okoro is a chemical engineer by training and a playwright, novelist, director, and actress by nature. She went from interacting with patents and biotechnology to the K–12 classroom. A 12-year science educator and Albert Einstein Distinguished Fellow, Okoro was one of the original authors of the Next Generation Science Standards. As a member of the Diversity and Equity Team, her focus on Alternative Education, Community Schools, and now Integrating Social-Emotional Learning and Brain-Based Learning into NGSS is a pathway to support underserved groups from elementary school to adult education. An article and book reviewer for NSTA and other educational publishing companies, Okoro currently works as a S.T.E.M. Learning Advocate & Consultant.

Explosions are chemical reactions that release a lot of energy. If tightly controlled, these reactions can accomplish many things, like taking down an unused building in a matter of seconds.

UNIT 2

Heat and Energy in the Earth System 59

A volcanic eruption transfers large amounts of matter and heat to the atmosphere.

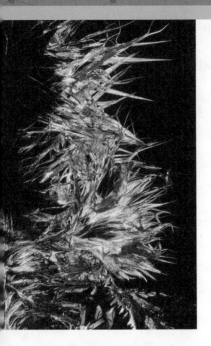

Cholesterol, shown here in crystalline form, is a compound made up of three different elements.

UNIT 4

Chemical Attractions 209

The reaction of copper and nitric acid produces nitric oxide gas and a solution of copper nitrate.

Chemical reactions always involve changes in both matter and energy.

UNIT 6

Human Activity and Earth's Atmosphere 339

City lights can sometimes blur the distinction between day and night.

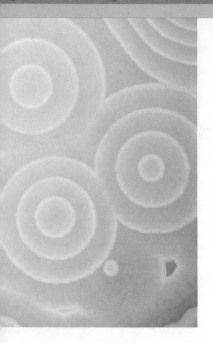

UNIT 7

Chemical Equilibrium Systems

425

Waves of changing equilibrium move across a solution.

Claims, Evidence, and Reasoning

You likely use claims, evidence, and reasoning in your daily life—perhaps without even being aware of it. Suppose you leave a notebook behind in the cafeteria. When you return later, you see a number of similar notebooks on the counter. You say, "I left my notebook here earlier," and pick up one of them.

The cafeteria worker says, "Are you sure that one is yours? They all look pretty much alike."

You say, "Yes, my initials are right here on the cover." To confirm the fact, you open the notebook to show your full name inside. You also present your student ID to prove that it's your name.

This encounter is a claims-evidence-reasoning interaction. You claimed the notebook was yours, and you showed evidence to prove your point.

CLAIM

A *claim* is your position on an issue or problem. It answers the question "What do you know?"

EVIDENCE

Evidence is any data related to your claim that answer the question "How do you know that?" These data may be from your own experiments and observations, reports by scientists or engineers, or other reliable sources. Scientific knowledge is based on *empirical evidence*, or evidence that is derived from observation or experiment. As you read about science, perform lab activities, engage in class discussions, and write explanations, you will need to cite evidence to support your claims.

REASONING

Reasoning is the use of logical, analytical thought to form conclusions or inferences. It answers the question, "Why does your evidence support your claim?" Reasoning may involve citing a scientific law or principle that helps explain the relationship between the evidence and the claim.

Scientists use claims, evidence, and reasoning—or *argumentation*—for many purposes: to explain, to persuade, to convince, to predict, to demonstrate, and to prove things. When scientists publish the results of their investigations, they must be prepared to defend their conclusions if they are challenged by other scientists.

Here is an example of a claims-evidence-reasoning argument.

CLAIM: Ice melts faster in the sun than it does in the shade.

EVIDENCE: We placed two ice cubes of the same size in identical plastic dishes. We placed one dish on a wooden bench in the sun and placed the other on a different part of the same bench in the shade. The ice cube in the sun melted in 14 minutes and 32 seconds. The ice cube in the shade melted in 18 minutes and 15 seconds.

REASONING: We designed the investigation so that the only variable in the setup was whether the ice cubes were in the shade or in the sun. Because the ice cube in the sun melted almost 4 minutes faster, this is sufficient evidence to support the claim that ice melts faster in the sun than it does in the shade.

Construct your own argument below by recording a claim, evidence, and reasoning. With your teacher's permission, you can do an investigation to answer a question you have about how the world works, or you can construct your argument based on observations you have already made about the world.

CLAIM	
EVIDENCE	
REASONING	

 For more information on claims, evidence, and reasoning, see the online **English Language Arts Handbook**.

Lab Safety

Before you work in the laboratory, read these safety rules. Ask your teacher to explain any rules that you do not completely understand. Refer to these rules later on if you have questions about safety in the science classroom.

Personal Protective Equipment (PPE)

- PPE includes eye protection, nitrile or nonlatex gloves, and nonlatex aprons. In all labs involving chemicals, indirectly vented chemical splash goggles are required.

- Wear the required PPE during the setup, hands-on, and takedown segments of the activity.

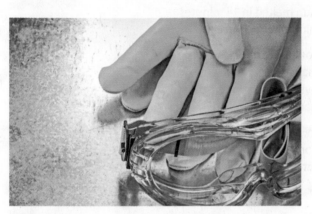

Dress Code

- Secure any article of clothing—such as a loose sweater or a scarf—that hangs down and may touch a flame, chemical, or piece of equipment.

- Wear closed-toe shoes.

- Tie back long hair or hair that hangs in front of your eyes.

- Acrylic fingernails are very flammable and should not be worn when using a flame.

Directions

- Observe all safety icons.

- Know where the fire extinguisher, fire blanket, shower, and eyewash station are located in your classroom or lab, and know how to use them in an emergency.

- Read all directions, and make sure that you understand them before starting the activity.

- Do not begin any investigation or touch any equipment until your teacher has told you to start.

- Never experiment on your own. If you want to try a procedure that the directions do not call for, ask your teacher for permission first.

- If you are hurt or injured in any way, tell your teacher immediately.

Chemical Safety

- If you get a chemical in your eye, use the eyewash station immediately. Flush the eye a minimum of 15 minutes.

- If you get a hazardous chemical on your skin or clothes, use the emergency shower for a minimum of 15 minutes.

- Never touch, taste, or sniff any chemicals in the lab. If you need to determine odor, waft. To waft, hold the chemical in its container 15 cm away from your nose, and use your fingers to bring fumes from the container to your nose.

- Take only the amount of chemical you need for the investigation. If you get too much, ask your teacher how to dispose of the excess. Do not return unused chemicals to the storage container; this can cause contamination.

- When diluting acid with water, always add acid to water. Never add water to an acid.

Heating and Fire Safety

- Keep your work area neat, clean, and free of materials.

- Never reach over a flame or heat source.

- Never heat a substance or an object in a closed container.

- Use oven mitts, clamps, tongs, or a test tube holder to hold heated items.

- Do not throw hot substances into the trash. Wait for them to cool, and dispose of them in the container provided by your teacher.

Electrical Safety

- Never use lamps or other electrical equipment with frayed cords or plugs with a missing ground prong.

- Make sure no cord is lying on the floor where someone can trip over it.

- Do not let a cord hang over the side of a counter or table so that the equipment can easily be pulled or knocked to the floor.

- Never let cords hang into sinks or other places where water can be found.

- Only use a Ground Fault Interrupter (GFI) protected circuit receptacle.

Glassware and Sharp-Object Safety

- Use only clean glassware that is free of chips and cracks.

- Use knives and other cutting instruments carefully. Always wear eye protection, and cut away from yourself.

Animal Safety

- Never hurt an animal.

- Wear gloves when handling animals or preserved specimens.

- Specimens for dissection should be properly mounted and supported.

Cleanup

- Follow your teacher's instructions for the disposal or storage of supplies.

- Clean your work area and pick up anything that has dropped to the floor.

- Wash your hands with soap and water after completing the activity.

Safety in the Field

- Be sure you understand the goal of your fieldwork and the proper way to carry out the investigation before you begin fieldwork.

- Do not approach or touch wild animals. Do not touch plants unless instructed by your teacher to do so. Leave natural areas as you found them.

- Use proper accident procedures, and let your teacher know about a hazard in the environment or an accident immediately, even if the hazard or accident seems minor.

Safety Symbols

Safety is the priority in the science classroom. In all of the activities in this textbook, safety symbols are used to alert you to materials, procedures, or situations that could be potentially hazardous if the safety guidelines are not followed. Learn what you need to do when you see these icons, and read all lab procedures before coming to the lab so you are prepared. Always ask your teacher if you have questions.

 ANIMALS Never injure an animal. Follow your teacher's instructions for handling specific animals or preserved specimens. Wash your hands with soap and water after handling animals or preserved specimens.

 APRON Wear a nonlatex apron at all times in the lab as directed. Stand whenever possible to avoid spilling in your lap.

 BREAKAGE Use caution when handling items that may break, such as glassware and thermometers. Always store test tubes in a test tube rack.

 CHEMICALS Always wear indirectly vented chemical splash goggles when working with chemicals. Stand whenever possible when working with chemicals to avoid spilling on your lap. Tell your teacher immediately if you spill chemicals on yourself, the table, or the floor. Never taste any substance or chemical in the lab. Always wash your hands with soap and water after working with chemicals.

 DISPOSAL Follow your teacher's instructions for disposing of all waste materials, including chemicals, specimens, or broken glass.

 ELECTRIC Keep electrical cords away from water to avoid shock. Do not use cords with frayed edges or plugs with a missing ground prong. Unplug all equipment when done. Only use GFI protected electrical receptacles.

 FIRE Put on safety goggles before lighting flames. Remove loose clothing and tie back hair. Never leave a lit object unattended. Extinguish flames as soon as you finish heating.

 FUMES Always work in a well-ventilated area. Do not inhale or sniff fumes; instead, use your fingers to bring fumes from the container to your nose.

 GLOVES Always wear gloves to protect your skin from possible injury when working with substances that may be harmful or when working with animals.

 HAND WASHING Wash your hands with soap and water after working with soil, chemicals, animals, or preserved specimens.

 HEATING Wear indirectly vented chemical splash goggles, and never leave any substance while it is being heated. Use tongs or appropriate insulated holders when handling heated objects. Point any materials being heated away from you and others. Place hot objects such as test tubes in test tube racks while cooling.

 PLANTS Do not eat any part of a plant. Do not pick any wild plant unless your teacher instructs you to do so. Wash your hands with soap and water after handling any plant.

 SAFETY GOGGLES Always wear indirectly vented chemical splash goggles when working with chemicals, heating any substance, or using a sharp object or any material that could fly up and injure you or others.

 SHARP OBJECTS Use scissors, knives, or razor tools with care. Wear goggles when cutting something. Always cut away from yourself.

 SLIP HAZARD Immediately pick up any items dropped on the floor, and wipe up any spilled water or other liquid so it does not become a slip/fall hazard. Tell your teacher immediately if you spill chemicals.

Measuring Matter and Energy

Explosions are chemical reactions that release a lot of energy. If tightly controlled, these reactions can accomplish many things, such as taking down an unused building in under thirty seconds.

FIGURE 1: Food labels show how many Calories are in each of the ingredients you use to make a meal.

The Calorie is a measure of the stored energy in the food. A food Calorie is actually a kilocalorie, or the amount of heat needed to raise the temperature of 1000 grams of water 1 °C. How can scientists determine how much energy is stored in food, though? Chemists study matter and energy to understand the relationships between them. They make measurements and collect data to describe these relationships. You can use this data every day. By understanding these relationships, chemists measure the chemical energy of foods. Knowing how much energy is in a serving can help you plan a healthy diet.

PREDICT What quantitative measurement and qualitative observations can be made about the interactions of matter and energy?

_____

_____

_____

_____

DRIVING QUESTIONS

As you move through the unit, gather evidence to help you answer the following questions. In your Evidence Notebook, record what you already know about these topics and any questions you have about them.

1. What are some different forms of energy, and how are they measured?
2. How can various properties of matter be measured and described?
3. What happens to the particles and energy of a substance as it changes temperature or changes state?

UNIT PROJECT

Go online to download the Unit Project Worksheet to help plan your project.

Optimizing Toothpaste

What gives a toothpaste its whitening power? Design and produce a home-made toothpaste. Then test its whitening capability by using it to clean a coffee-stained tile, which will serve as a model for teeth. Based on these results, optimize your design by adjusting the toothpaste ingredients.

Language Development

Use the lessons in this unit to complete the chart and expand your understanding of the science concepts.

TERM: potential energy

Definition	Example

Similar Term	Phrase

TERM: kinetic energy

Definition	Example

Similar Term	Phrase

TERM: accuracy

Definition	Example

Similar Term	Phrase

TERM: precision

Definition	Example

Similar Term	Phrase

TERM: matter

Definition	Example

Similar Term	Phrase

TERM: extensive property

Definition	Example

Similar Term	Phrase

TERM: intensive property

Definition	Example

Similar Term	Phrase

TERM: system

Definition	Example

Similar Term	Phrase

Investigating Matter and Energy

A crowd gathers around to get a closer look at a record-setting rice cake. Sixty cooks worked together for almost an hour to prepare the cake.

CAN YOU SOLVE IT?

This giant cake set a new record for the world's largest glutinous rice cake. It was made from over 1300 pounds of a special type of rice and required the work of dozens of cooks to complete. When finished, it measured almost 4 meters (12.5 feet) in diameter! Rice cakes like this one are often made with a special type of rice that has been steamed, mashed, and then toasted. The cakes not only provide energy and nutrients, but they also represent reunion and good luck.

Food such as a rice cake contains matter and energy your body can use. When you eat, a series of chemical reactions helps break down the food and release the energy stored in its molecules. Because different food items have different amounts of energy and nutrients, knowing the content of your food can help you make wise choices. If you wanted to know how many calories were in a food, you might look at the label on the package. But how could you find out the amount of energy in a record-breaking food like this?

PREDICT How might you measure the amount of energy in the world's largest rice cake?

_____

_____

_____

_____

 Evidence Notebook As you explore this lesson, gather evidence to explain how you can measure the matter and energy in food.

Measuring the Energy in Food

FIGURE 1: Food nutrition label

Corn Crunch Cereal

Nutrition Facts / Datos de Nutrición

Serving Size / Tamaño de porción ¾ Cup / ¾ de taza (29g)

		with ½ cup skim milk / com ½ taza de leche descremada
Amount Per Serving / Cantidad por porción	Cereal/Cereal	descremada
Calories / Calorías	110	150
Calories from Fat / Calorías de grasa	0	0

	% Daily Values / % Valor diearie	
Total Fat / Grasa total 0g*	0%	0%
Saturated Fat / Grasa saturada 0g	0%	0%
Trans Fat / Grasa *trans* 0g		
Polyunsaturated Fat / Grasa poliinsaturada 0g		
Monounsaturated Fat / Grasa monoinsaturada 0g		
Cholesterol / Colesterol 0mg	0%	0%
Sodium / Sodio 150mg	6%	8%
Potassium / Potasio 35mg	1%	7%
Total Carbohydrate / Carbohidratos totales 26g	9%	11%
Dietary Fiber / Fibra dietética < 1g	3%	3%
Sugar / Azúcares 10g		
Protein / Proteínas 1g		

Ingredients: Milled corn, sugar, contains 2% or less of malt flavor, salt, BHT for freshness.
Vitamins and Minerals: Iron, vitamin C (ascorbic acid and sodium ascorbate), niacinamide, vitamin B6 (pyridoxine hydrochloride), vitamin B2 (riboflavin), vitamin B1 (thiamin hydrochloride), vitamin A palmitate, folic acid, vitamin D, vitmain B12.
CORN USED IN THE PRODUCT MAY CONTAIN TRACES OF SOYBEANS.
Ingredientes: Maíz triturado, azúcar, contiene 2% o menos de sabor malta, sal, BHT para mantener la frescura.
Vitaminas and Minerales: Hierro, vitamina C (ácido ascórbico y ascorbato de sodio), niainamida, vitamina B6 (clorhidrato de piridoxina),vitamína B2 (riboflavina), ,vitamina B1 (clorhidrato de tiamina), vitamina A palmitato, ácido folico, vitamina D, vitmaina B12.
El MAIZ UTILIZADO EN ESTE PRODUCTO PUEDE CONTENER TRAZAS DE SOYA.

Chemistry involves the study of matter and energy. As matter changes, energy may be released or absorbed. Food nutrition labels show the matter and energy contained in food. Federal and state laws require food makers to place these labels on packages to tell consumers about the nutritional value of the foods they choose to eat. This helps people see the amount of matter and energy in a food or drink they want to consume.

Nutrition labels also contain a variety of other information. For example, these labels include measurements of mass and volume as well as percentages of suggested overall intake. They may even list the specific chemical elements and compounds in the food.

GATHER EVIDENCE Describe some of the units of measurement that you see on this food label. What does each unit measure? What other information do you see?

_____

_____

_____

_____

_____

One important piece of information on nutrition labels is the energy value of the food, as given in nutritional Calories. The Calorie value shown on a nutrition label (with an uppercase C) is different than calories (with a lowercase c). One nutritional Calorie is equal one kilocalorie, or 1000 calories. If nutrition labels gave energy values in calories, the cereal shown here would contain 110 000 calories per serving!

Notice that the Calorie values on this food label are listed on a per-serving basis. To identify the total amount of energy for the entire package, therefore, you must multiply this value by the number of servings in the package.

💡 Data Analysis

SOLVE Use the nutrition label in Figure 1 to answer these questions.

1. A person who eats three servings of the cereal without milk will consume

_____ Calories and _____ grams of carbohydrates.

2. A person who eats two servings of cereal, each with 1/2 cup skim milk, will

consume _____ Calories and _____ % of the daily value of dietary fiber.

Hands-On Lab
Snack-Food Calorimeter

If a food nutrition label says one serving of food is 29 grams, you could use a balance to measure that amount of food. But if the same label stated there were 300 Calories in a serving, how could you verify that value? A calorie is the amount of energy required to raise the temperature of one gram of water by one degree Celsius. So, to measure calories, energy from a food sample must be released and transferred to water. The tool that scientists use to measure energy released by food is called a calorimeter. In this investigation, the primary materials available for constructing a calorimeter are a soda can, a ring stand, water, and an evaporating dish.

Research Questions: How can you use the materials provided to measure the amount of energy released by different types of food? Which food has the most Calories?

MAKE A CLAIM

In your Evidence Notebook, predict how you could use the materials shown to release the energy in a food sample and measure the amount of energy that is transferred to a sample of water. Then, predict which food will have the most calories. Explain your thinking.

MATERIALS

- indirectly vented chemical splash goggles, nonlatex apron, nitrile gloves
- aluminum foil, 30 cm × 30 cm sheet
- balance
- beaker tongs
- evaporating dish

- graduated cylinder, 100 mL
- matches or propane lighter
- ring and clamp
- ring stand
- snack foods with nutrition labels, 2 types (cheese puff, marshmallow, dry cereal, etc.)
- soda can

- spatula
- thermometer
- thermometer clamp
- three-finger clamp
- water
- weighing boat or weighing paper (2)
- wire gauze

SAFETY INFORMATION

- Wear indirectly vented chemical splash goggles, a nonlatex apron, and nitrile gloves during the setup, hands-on, and takedown segments of the activity.

- Note the danger of burning the food samples that have oils, which can splatter and burn skin.

- Notify your teacher of any food allergies, and never eat any food items used in a lab.

- Secure loose clothing, wear closed-toe shoes, and tie back long hair.

- Use only GFI protected circuits when using electrical equipment, and keep away from water sources to prevent shock.

indirectly vented chemical splash goggles

PLAN THE INVESTIGATION

FIGURE 2: Energy from the burning snack food sample warms the water in the soda can calorimeter.

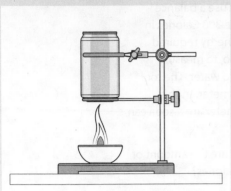

1. Using Figure 2 and the materials list as a guide, write a procedure and safety plan in your Evidence Notebook explaining how you will measure the amount of energy transferred from the food to the water in the calorimeter. Data you should collect include the mass of each food sample, the mass of the water used in the calorimeter, the initial temperature of the water, and the final temperature of the water. Things to keep in mind are:
   - When measuring the temperature of water in a container, the thermometer should only be in contact with the water and not be touching the container itself.
   - Because the density of water is 1.00 g/mL, the volume of water can be used to infer its mass. So, if you were to use a graduated cylinder to measure 50.0 milliliters (mL) of water, this amount of water would have a mass of 50.0 grams (g).

Ask your teacher to approve your procedure and safety plan before you begin.

2. Calculate the change in water temperature by subtracting the initial water temperature from the final water temperature. Then, use this value to calculate and record the amount of energy absorbed by the water. Use the following equation:
   energy in Calories = (mass of water)(change in water temperature)(0.001 Cal/g·°C)

3. Determine the Calories per gram for each food item as shown on the nutrition label. You may need to ask your teacher for these values. Record them for later use.

COLLECT DATA

Food Item	Mass of food (g)	Mass of water (g)	Initial water temperature (°C)	Final water temperature (°C)	Energy (Calories)

ANALYZE

1. Calculate the Calories per gram for each food you tested by dividing the Calorie value by the mass of the food. How do these values compare to the Calories per gram shown on the nutrition label for each food?

2. If you were to measure the mass of a food item after it was burned, you would most likely find that its mass had decreased. What do you think happens to the matter in a food sample as it is burned?

3. Draw a diagram showing how you think energy was transferred from the food to the water in the soda can calorimeter.

DRAW CONCLUSIONS

Claim How much energy per gram did each snack food contain? How do your findings compare with the values shown on the food labels for these foods?

Evidence Use evidence from your data and calculations to support your claim.

Reasoning Explain how the evidence you cited supports your claim. In addition, discuss possible reasons for differences between your measurements and the Calorie values shown on the nutrition label for each food.

_____

_____

_____

_____

_____

_____

_____

EXTEND

How do you think the results of this investigation would have been different if you had used salt water? If time allows, write a procedure in your Evidence Notebook describing how you could investigate this question. With your teacher's permission, carry out your procedure, and analyze your results.

 Evidence Notebook Based on what you have learned so far, how would you measure the amount of energy contained in the world's largest glutinous rice cake?

Using Units of Measurement

FIGURE 3: The Mars Climate Orbiter was lost due to a miscommunication about units of measurement.

Clear communication is a critical aspect of all scientific investigation. In 1999, a miscommunication about units of measurement had devastating consequences for NASA's Mars Climate Orbiter. Part of the landing system was programmed to transmit information in one unit of measurement, and the intended receiving component was programmed to receive information in a different unit of measurement. The resulting miscalculation caused the Orbiter to pass too close to Mars and to disintegrate in the planet's atmosphere. The mathematical mistake cost $125 million, and no data were collected.

> **Collaborate** Talk with a partner about another situation where clear communication regarding measurements could be vital.

Standardizing Measurements

In order to communicate clearly with each other, scientists rely on a standardized system of measurement. In 1960 scientists established a standard set of units based on the metric system called the *Système International d'Unités* (French for the *International System of Units*), or the SI System. This system includes base units to describe physical quantities that have key importance in scientific measurements.

The SI unit for mass is the kilogram (kg). However, the balance you used in the lab most likely reported mass in grams (g). And, many nutrition labels list amounts in milligrams (mg). Because the metric system is based on powers of 10, quantities can easily be converted from one unit to another. The base units shown in the table below are grams, meters, and liters, abbreviated g, m, and L. Prefixes such as kilo- and milli- are added to the name of the base unit to communicate the size of the quantity. For example, 1 kilometer is equal to 1000 meters, and 1 milligram is equal to 1/1000th of a gram.

Kilo (k)	Hecto (h)	Deka (dk)	Base Unit	Deci (d)	Centi (c)	Milli (m)
1000	100	10	g, m, L	1/10	1/100	1/1000

To convert a quantity such as 5 kilograms to grams, you could multiply by 1000 or move the decimal to the right three places and fill in the necessary zeros. To convert a quantity such as 8 milligrams to grams, you would divide by 1000 or move the decimal to the left three places and fill in the necessary zeros.

$$5\text{kg} = 5000 \text{ g} \qquad 8\text{mg} = 0.008 \text{ g}$$

Problem Solving

SOLVE Write the correct quantity for each conversion.

1. 38 000 kg = _____ g

2. 6.5 m = _____ mm

3. 4.3 mL = _____ L

4. 0.02 km = _____ cm

To communicate very large quantities, scientists may use prefixes such as mega- (1 000 000) and giga- (1 000 000 000). For very small quantities, scientists can use prefixes such as micro- (1/1 000 000) and nano- (1/1 000 000 000). For reference, a single bacterium is about 1000 nanometers long, and a strand of human hair is about 80 000 nanometers wide. A single atom ranges in diameter from about 0.1 nanometers to about 0.3 nanometers.

 Scale, Proportion, and Quantity

Communicating the Sizes of Objects

Scientists often work with quantities that are very large or very small. An astronomer might study a solar system that is hundreds of billions of kilometers across. Expressing the distance between two planets in kilometers is impractical. So, scientists use units such as astronomical units (AU) to describe distances between planets and other objects in space. One AU is equal to the distance from Earth to the sun, which is about 150 million kilometers.

A biologist might study structures that are too small to be seen with the human eye. Cells, viruses, and other very small structures are often viewed under a microscope and measured in micrometers or nanometers. Pollen grains, like the one shown in Figure 4, range from about 10 micrometers to about 100 micrometers across.

Chemists study the properties of and interactions between very small objects—atoms. The diameter of an atom ranges from about 0.1 nanometers to about 0.3 nanometers, depending on the type of atom. This means that an atom is about a million times smaller than a strand of human hair.

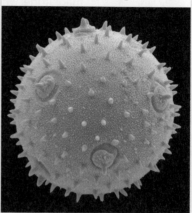

FIGURE 4: A colored scanning electron micrograph (SEM) shows a pollen grain at 353x magnification.

In all of these disciplines, advances in technology help scientists better view and understand large and small objects. Specialized microscopes have allowed us to see tiny objects we could never have pictured in the past. Improvements in telescopes have allowed us to view distant objects in space that have never been seen in such vivid detail. Technology and scientific discovery drive each other to advance.

 Language Arts Connection Research the sizes of a range of objects, from extremely small to extremely large. Then, make a multimedia presentation to illustrate how the sizes of these objects compare. Be sure to communicate the size of each object and how it compares to the others. You may choose to focus on quantities such as mass, length, or volume.

Measuring Mass

In the calorimeter lab, you used a balance to determine the mass of the food samples you tested. But what does mass actually measure? People often use the terms mass and weight interchangeably, but they have different meanings in science. *Mass* is a measure of the amount of matter in an object. *Weight* is the force exerted on an object by Earth's gravitational pull. So, an object's weight changes when the gravitational force changes, but its mass does not. For example, a rocket would have a different weight on Earth than it does on the moon, but its mass would not change. If a rocket were traveling through space, it would be weightless due to the lack of gravity in space. However, its mass would remain the same as it is on Earth and other planets.

Measuring Temperature

When using a thermometer, you might read the temperature in degrees Fahrenheit or Celsius. The Fahrenheit scale is commonly used in the United States, whereas the Celsius scale is used in most other countries and in science.

The Celsius scale defines the temperature at which water freezes as 0 °C and the temperature at which it boils as 100 °C. The degrees are equal increments between these two values. Although most thermometers measure temperature in degrees Celsius or Fahrenheit, the SI unit for temperature is the kelvin. Unlike other temperature scales, which are relative scales, the Kelvin scale is an absolute scale. This is because the kelvin is defined in relation to absolute zero. Absolute zero is the theoretical temperature at which all molecules in a substance have no kinetic energy. That is, they cannot get any colder. Absolute zero is theoretically given as 0 K. This makes the freezing point of water on the Kelvin scale 273 K. As shown in Figure 5, the Kelvin and Celsius scales have the same magnitude, whereas the Fahrenehit scale is based on smaller units. Many physical laws are more easily expressed using an absolute temperature scale, so the kelvin has been adopted as the SI unit of temperature.

FIGURE 5: The Kelvin scale is an absolute scale, whereas Celsius and Fahrenheit are relative scales. The Celsius scale is primarily used to express temperature internationally, but the Fahrenheit scale is used in the United States. Celsius or Kelvin scales are almost always used in scientific measurements.

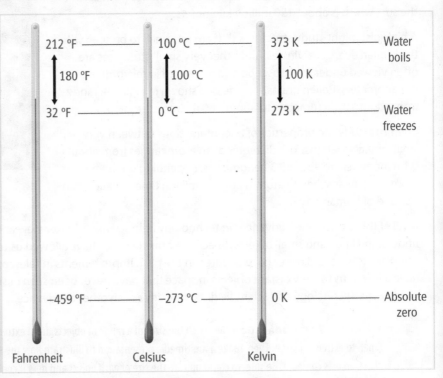

EXPLAIN Room temperature is about 20 degrees Celsius. Explain how you could convert this temperature to kelvin. Use evidence from Figure 5 to support your answer.

_____

_____

_____

Counting Objects

Sometimes it is necessary to quantify the number of particles in a substance, such as atoms or molecules. The mole is a unit of measure used to count particles. It is based on the number of carbon atoms present in exactly 12 grams of pure carbon. This value is called Avogadro's number, and it is equal to 6.02×10^{23}. One mole of a substance is equal to 6.02×10^{23} particles of the substance. You can easily hold 12 grams of carbon in your hand, so this large number implies that atoms must be incredibly small!

Combining Units

You can express mass using a single unit. However, what if you wanted to know how the mass of a substance compares to its volume? Additional units of measure can be made by combining the base SI units into compound units known as *derived units*.

Measuring Volume

When you look at the label on a drink, you might see units of measurement such as milliliters. These units indicate the volume of the liquid. Volume is the amount of space occupied by an object. The units used to express the volume of solids are based on length. Volume can be described in terms of cubic meters (m^3), the amount of space occupied by a cube that measures one meter on each edge. A common unit of liquid volume is the liter (L), which is equal to 1000 cubic centimeters (cm^3). Therefore, 1 milliliter (mL) equals 1 cubic centimeter (cm^3).

When measuring the volume of a liquid, it is important to read the meniscus correctly. The meniscus is a curved upper surface of liquids in thin cylinders. The curve forms due to adhesion between the liquid and the cylinder. To read volume correctly, record the volume that corresponds to the bottom of the meniscus. For example, the volume shown in Figure 6 is 40.0 mL, not 41.0 mL.

The volume of a rectangular solid, such as a block of wood, is the product of its length, width, and height. To determine the volume of an irregular solid, such as a rock, the method of displacement is used. This method involves submerging the object in a known volume of liquid. The difference in the volume of liquid before and after the object was inserted equals the volume of the object.

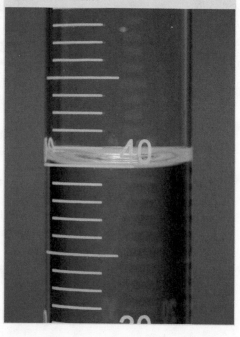

FIGURE 6: A liquid poured into a thin cylinder forms a curved upper surface called a meniscus.

SOLVE Use Figure 7 to calculate the answers needed to complete these statements.

The volume of Object A is _____ cm^3. The volume of water displaced by Object B is _____ mL, so the volume of Object B is _____ mL.

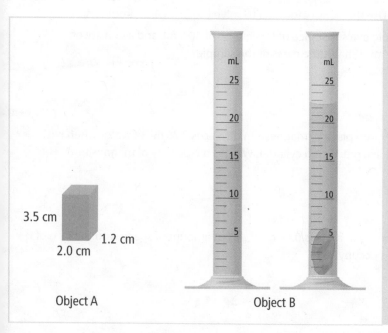

Object A

3.5 cm
1.2 cm
2.0 cm

Object B

FIGURE 7: Two methods for measuring the volume of a solid are shown. For regular solids, volume can be calculated using a formula and measurements. For example, the volume of this regular solid is the product of its length, height, and width. For irregular solids, the displacement method is used. Note that if the displacement method was used for the regular solid, the amount of water displaced would be equal to the calculated volume of the block.

Measuring Density

By comparing a substance's mass to its volume, we can determine how closely packed its particles are. Density is a ratio of a substance's mass to its volume. The SI unit for density is derived from the units for mass and volume (the kilogram and the cubic meter) and can be expressed as kilograms per cubic meter (kg/m^3). Because these units are too large for most laboratory applications, density is often reported in terms of grams per cubic centimeter (g/cm^3) or grams per milliliter (g/mL). Remember that one cubic centimeter is equivalent to one milliliter.

 Problem Solving

Practicing Density Calculations

The formula for density is:

$$density = \frac{mass}{volume}$$

The density formula can be rearranged to solve for mass or volume:

$$mass = density \times volume \qquad volume = \frac{mass}{density}$$

SAMPLE PROBLEMS

1. A metallic substance has a volume of 10.5 cm³ and a mass of 81.9 grams. What is the density of this substance?

$$density = \frac{mass}{volume} = \frac{81.9\ g}{10.5\ cm^3} = 7.80\ g/cm^3$$

2. What is the mass of a liquid with a density of 0.768 g/mL and a volume of 237 mL?

$$mass = density \times volume = 0.768\ \tfrac{g}{mL} \times 237\ \cancel{mL} = 182\ g$$

Notice that the unit milliliters cancels out when it is multiplied by a number with the unit grams/milliliter. Therefore, the unit for the final value is grams.

PRACTICE PROBLEMS

SOLVE Use the density formula to solve the following problems.

1. A sample of a substance has a volume of 60.5 mL and a density of 1.20 g/mL. What is the mass of the sample?

2. A 4.80-gram piece of magnesium displaces 2.76 mL of water when it is placed in a graduated cylinder. What is the density of magnesium?

3. The density of a gas is 0.68 g/mL. What amount of space would 23.8 g of this gas occupy?

When liquids with different densities are combined, the liquid with the lower density floats on top of the liquid with the higher density. In Figure 8, you can see the result of combining several substances with different densities. The liquid with the lowest density is at the top of the column, and the liquid with the highest density is at the bottom.

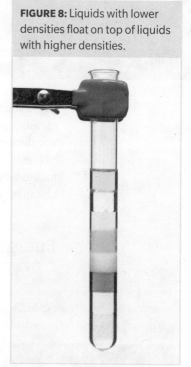

FIGURE 8: Liquids with lower densities float on top of liquids with higher densities.

INFER Select the correct terms to complete the statement.

A student measures properties of two liquids. Liquid 1 has a mass of 107 g and a volume of 102 mL. Liquid 2 has a mass of 106 g and a volume of 125 mL. Therefore, Liquid 1 has a lower | higher density than Liquid 2. As a result, Liquid 1 will float | sink when the two liquids are combined.

A liquid with a lower density will always float on a liquid with a higher density, now matter how much of each sample is present. Because density is the ratio of two quantities, its value does not depend on the size of the sample. This property can be explained mathematically because as the mass of a sample of the substance increases or decreases, its volume increases or decreases proportionately. Thus, the ratio of mass to volume remains constant. A small sample of a substance therefore has the same density as a larger sample of the same substance. For example, gold has a density of 19.32 g/cm^3, whether the sample of gold is very large or very small.

MODEL Use mathematical models, in the form of sketches, example problems, or calculations, to illustrate why density is a quantity that does not depend on the size of the sample tested.

Evidence Notebook Make a graphic organizer to summarize what you have learned about how different quantities are measured. Include the units used for each quantity, as well as other important information. Then, write a statement explaining which of these units would be most appropriate for measuring the amount of mass and energy in the world's largest rice cake.

Describing Changes in Energy

In the snack food calorimeter lab, you used the increase in temperature of water to measure the energy released when food is burned. As the food burned, energy was transferred to the can, increasing the temperature of the water inside it. The transfer of thermal energy is called heat. The amount of energy transferred as heat is usually measured in joules, the SI unit for energy. One calorie equals 4.184 Joules. In some countries, nutrition labels show the energy content of food in kilojoules.

Energy Transformations

FIGURE 9: Examples of materials that store chemical energy include foods, such as carbohydrates, and fuels, such as propane.

Potential energy is stored energy associated with the position, shape, or condition of an object. One form of potential energy is chemical energy, which is the energy stored in the bonds of chemical compounds. Examples of materials that store chemical energy include foods, such as breads and fruit, and fuels, such as propane and petroleum. Energy stored in the bonds of a fuel such as propane is released when the fuel is burned. Other forms of potential energy include nuclear energy, gravitational potential energy, and elastic potential energy. Nuclear energy is the potential energy stored in the nucleus of an atom. When the nucleus of an atom breaks down or when the nuclei of two smaller atoms fuse, energy is released.

Kinetic energy is the energy associated with the motion of an object. Forms of kinetic energy you observed in the lab include thermal energy, sound energy, and electromagnetic energy. Thermal energy is the internal energy of an object due to the motion and vibration of its particles. As thermal energy increases, so does the temperature of the object. Sound energy is caused by the vibration of particles in a medium such as air. Electromagnetic energy is the kinetic energy of electromagnetic waves, which include visible light, x-rays, and microwaves.

EXPLAIN How did energy change form in the calorimeter lab?

As the food burned, thermal | chemical | nuclear energy was transformed into thermal | chemical | nuclear energy. Thus, a form of kinetic | potential energy was converted to a form of kinetic | potential energy.

Any form of energy can transform into any other. The law of conservation of energy states that energy cannot be created or destroyed. Thus, when potential energy decreases in a system, kinetic energy must increase.

 Language Arts Connection Research forms of kinetic and potential energy. Make a pamphlet describing each form of energy and explaining whether it is a form of kinetic or potential energy. Include an example and a visual for each type of energy you describe.

Energy Transfer

An energy transfer is the passing of energy from one object or location to another. You observed an energy transfer during the hands-on lab when energy released from the burning of the food was transferred to the water in the soda can.

MODEL Draw a diagram of the soda can calorimeter as a system with energy inputs and outputs represented by arrows showing the transfer of energy from the chemical reaction. Include labels on the diagram for chemical, thermal, sound, and electromagnetic energy, and specify whether each is a form of kinetic or potential energy.

Thermal energy can be transferred by conduction, convection, or radiation. Conduction is the transfer of energy when objects or substances collide or touch. For example, when a metal pot touches a hot stove, the particles of matter in the metal collide with the faster-moving particles in the stove, and energy is transferred from one particle to another. Convection is the transfer of energy through currents within a fluid, such as a liquid or a gas. For example, warm air is generally less dense than cool air and will be pushed up when the density of the cooler air causes it to sink. The resulting motion produces convection currents that transfer thermal energy throughout the fluid. Radiation is the transfer of energy by electromagnetic waves. Electromagnetic waves can travel through matter and through empty space. Energy from the sun reaches the Earth by radiation. Different types of matter reflect and absorb radiation to greater or lesser degrees.

ANALYZE Think back to the snack food calorimeter. Describe an example of each of these occurring in the lab: conduction, convection, and radiation.

_____

_____

_____

_____

When thermal energy is transferred from one place or object to another, the transfer occurs in a certain direction. Think about how heat was transferred in the hands-on lab.

INFER Select the correct terms to complete the statement.

Based on your observations, you can infer that thermal energy transfers to | from objects with higher temperatures to | from objects with lower temperatures.

Thermal energy is transferred between objects when particles collide. The point at which all particles have the same energy is called thermal equilibrium. You can model the transfer of kinetic energy from one object to another on a macroscopic scale. For example, think about what happens when a rolling ball (which has kinetic energy) collides with a motionless ball of equal size and mass (which does not have kinetic energy). At the point of collision, the speed of the rolling ball decreases as some of its kinetic energy is transferred to the stationary ball. The motionless ball absorbs this energy and begins to move because of the increase in kinetic energy. As the balls collide, some energy is lost to the surroundings in the form of thermal and sound energy. In addition, rarely do two objects collide head-on so that the maximum possible amount of energy is transferred.

Kinetic Energy and Temperature

Temperature is a measure of the average kinetic energy of the particles that make up a sample of matter. The greater the kinetic energy of the particles in a sample, the higher the temperature is and the hotter the substance feels. Increasing the temperature of a substance by warming it provides more energy to its particles, so the particles move more quickly. Decreasing the temperature of a substance by cooling it removes energy from its particles, and the particles move more slowly. Liquid thermometers make use of this fact to indicate different temperatures.

FIGURE 10: As temperature increases, the particles of liquid in a thermometer move faster. At lower temperatures, the particles of a liquid have less energy. At higher temperatures, the particles of a liquid move more energetically. A thermometer is a very thin tube of glass, so the volume of the liquid changes as temperature changes.

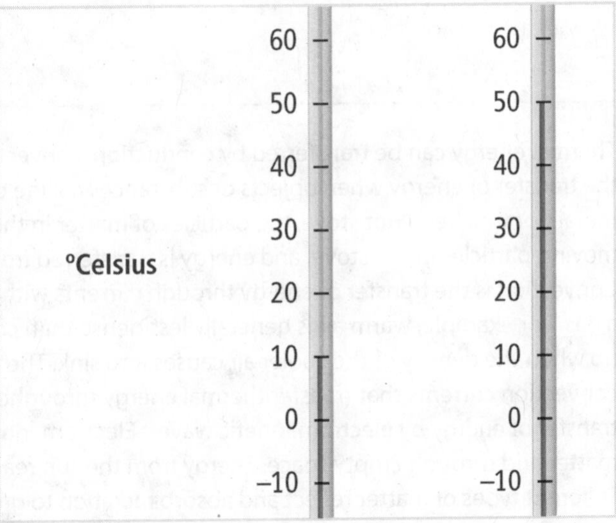

°Celsius

60	60
50	50
40	40
30	30
20	20
10	10
0	0
−10	−10

ANALYZE Explain why the liquid in a thermometer expands as temperature increases. How is this related to the kinetic energy of the particles that make up the liquid?

_____

_____

_____

_____

 Collaborate Share your answer to the previous question with a partner and compare your responses. How did you describe the connections between temperature, kinetic energy, and particle movement?

As the temperature of a liquid or gas increases, its particles move more quickly and collide more frequently. As a result, the substance expands and takes up more space. If volume increases but mass does not, the density of a substance will decrease. This effect is apparent in a two-story house. As you walk to the second floor, you may notice that the air begins to feel warmer. This is because warmer air masses are less dense than cooler ones. Because substances with lower densities float on those with higher densities, the lower-density warm air rises to the top of the house, while the higher-density cool air settles at the bottom. The movement of air in this way is an example of a convection current.

Convection currents are responsible for many of the weather patterns we observe on Earth. When the temperature of air near Earth's surface increases, its density decreases. As a result, the warm air rises to higher levels of the atmosphere, where the temperature is lower. As the air cools, its particles slow down, so its density increases, causing it to sink. Convection currents can even be observed in the sun, where energy in the star's core drives the constant cycling of matter.

 Energy and Matter

Using Density to Measure Temperature

Explore Online ▶

FIGURE 11: Galileo thermometer

Another type of thermometer is a Galileo thermometer. A Galileo thermometer consists of a cylinder filled with a clear liquid. Several glass bulbs of different densities float in the liquid. Each glass bulb is connected to a metal weight indicating the temperature at which it will sink. The lowest floating bulb indicates the current temperature.

APPLY Select the correct terms to complete the statement.

When the temperature outside increases, the temperature of the clear liquid in the thermometer also increases. Therefore, the kinetic energy of the particles of the liquid decreases | increases and the space between particles decreases | increases. As a result, the density of the liquid decreases | increases. As the temperature of the liquid in the tube continues to increase, glass bulbs with higher | lower densities than the clear liquid will begin to sink. When temperature of the clear liquid decreases, its density will decrease | increase, so more bulbs will begin to float.

Because some physical qualities such as density may change under different temperatures and pressures, we must know the conditions under which those qualities were measured in order to compare them. Scientists use a standard temperature and pressure, referred to as STP, to standardize measurements. At STP, air pressure is 1 atmosphere (atm) and temperature is 0 °C (273 K). An atmosphere is the average atmospheric pressure at sea level at 0 °C. Most tables of physical quantities you will see are given at STP.

 Evidence Notebook Think back to the water you used in the calorimetry lab. In your Evidence Notebook, draw a diagram to illustrate how the kinetic energy of the water molecules changed as energy in the form of heat caused the temperature of the water to increase. Then, write an explanation for how this increase in kinetic energy affects the density of the water.

Analyzing Data and Converting Quantities

FIGURE 12: Tools used for cooking may show both metric and customary units.

Think back to the error that led to the loss of the NASA Mars Climate Orbiter. How could such a miscommunication happen? The answer has to do with systems of measurement. In the United States, we use units of measurement such as inches, miles, ounces, and pounds. These are known as U.S. customary units. However, scientists and people in most other countries use the metric system. The existence of two systems of measurement can present a challenge when trying to interpret instructions or use tools. Confusion between U.S. units and metric units is what led to the destruction of the Mars Climate Orbiter.

> **Collaborate** Describe a situation where you might need to convert U.S. units, such as feet, ounces, or pounds, to metric units, such as meters, liters, or grams. What might happen if the units were converted incorrectly?

Dimensional Analysis

You often receive measurements in units other than what you need. For example, you might need to know how many cups of water are required for a recipe in which the amounts are given in milliliters. Similar conversions are often necessary for scientific calculations. The mathematical technique that allows you to use units to solve problems involving different measurements is known as *dimensional analysis*. This technique is often used to convert between scales of the metric system or between non-SI units and SI units. Completing a unit conversion requires that you know how the two units are related. For example, a measurement of 1 foot is equivalent to a measurement of 0.3048 meter.

$$1 \text{ ft} = 0.3048 \text{ m}$$

Conversion factors are ratios relating the value of one unit of measure to another. This equality can be expressed as a conversion factor in two ways. Each of these conversion factors is equal to 1 because the two values in the ratio are equivalent.

$$\frac{1 \text{ ft}}{0.3048 \text{ m}} \text{ or } \frac{0.3048 \text{ m}}{1 \text{ ft}}$$

Unit cancellation is a method of setting up a series of conversion factors so that the units in the numerators "cancel out" the units in the denominators, resulting in a quantity with the desired units. Suppose you know that the distance between your house and an intersection is 215 feet, but you need to convey the information in meters. You can set up an equation using unit cancellation to calculate the conversion:

$$215 \text{ ft} \times \frac{0.3048 \text{ m}}{1 \text{ ft}} \approx 65.5 \text{ m}$$

The conversion factor is written with feet in the denominator so that the units of the given quantity, 215 ft, cancel out. Unit cancellation is often useful for calculating conversions from non-standard units. Suppose you have determined that your average pace length is 2.5 feet, and you would like to know the approximate distance you traveled in kilometers after walking 1200 paces. You can use unit cancellation to set up a chain of conversions:

$$1200 \text{ paces} \times \frac{2.5 \text{ ft}}{1 \text{ pace}} \times \frac{0.3048 \text{ m}}{1 \text{ ft}} \times \frac{0.001 \text{ km}}{1 \text{ m}} \approx 0.91 \text{ km}$$

Practicing Unit Conversion

Use dimensional analysis to solve the following problems.

1. The nutrition label on a package of food gives the serving size in grams. But the amount of food in the container is printed on the label in pounds. If a person eats 0.410 pounds of the food, how many grams of food will the person have consumed?

2. One serving of a drink is 6 ounces (oz) and provides 70 Calories of energy. Jade wants to know how many servings are in one bottle of the drink, but the volume printed on the bottle is in mL. How many Calories will Jade consume if she drinks 350 mL?

ANALYZE

The following are equalities that may be used:

1 gram = 1000 milligrams	1 liter = 4.23 cups
1 kilogram = 1000 grams	1 quart = 4 cups
1 kilogram = 2.2 pounds	1 pint = 2 cups
1 liter = 1000 milliliters	1 cup = 8 ounces

SOLVE

Begin with the quantity you want to convert and arrange conversion factors so that units cancel out. The final answer should have the unit that is requested in the problem.

1. $0.410 \text{ lb} \times \dfrac{1 \text{ kg}}{2.2 \text{ lb}} \times \dfrac{1000 \text{ g}}{1 \text{ kg}} = 186 \text{ g}$

2. $350 \text{ mL} \times \dfrac{1 \text{ L}}{1000 \text{ mL}} \times \dfrac{4.23 \text{ c}}{1 \text{ L}} \times \dfrac{8 \text{ oz}}{1 \text{ c}} \times \dfrac{1 \text{ serving}}{6 \text{ oz}} \times \dfrac{70 \text{ Cal}}{1 \text{ serving}} = 138 \text{ Cal}$

**PRACTICE
PROBLEMS**

SOLVE Use dimensional analysis to solve the following problems. Round your answers to the nearest whole number.

1. Alex buys a drink carton with a volume of 1.00 pint. How many milliliters of the drink will Alex consume if he drinks the whole carton?

2. A recipe calls for 1500 milliliters of water, but Marco only has a pitcher that shows values in pints. How many pints of water should Marco measure out?

3. Eva buys a package of food, and the nutrition label says that one serving is equal to 36 grams and has 110 Calories. However, the box is printed with a label that says 0.150 pounds. If Eva eats the whole package, how many Calories will she have consumed?

Accuracy and Precision

The terms precise and accurate are often used interchangeably in everyday conversation. In science, however, these terms have different meanings. Accuracy is the closeness of a measurement to the correct or accepted value of the quantity measured. Precision is the closeness of a set of measurements of the same quantity made in the same way. If a balance displayed values that were two grams off every time you used it, the scale would be precise but not accurate. Its readings are wrong, but they are consistent.

ANALYZE Below each image, write whether the points on the target are accurate or not accurate, and whether they are precise or not precise.

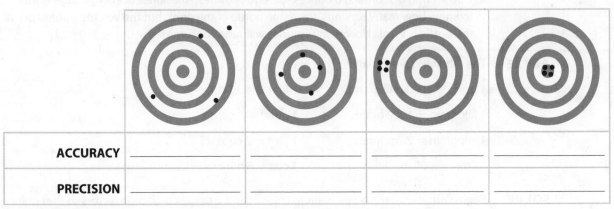

ACCURACY	_____	_____	_____	_____
PRECISION	_____	_____	_____	_____

Explore Online ▶

Hands-On Lab

Estimating Data Accurately
Estimate the number of objects in a jar and evaluate the accuracy of your estimates.

Some error or uncertainty exists in every measurement. This can be due to the conditions under which the measurement was made, the limitations of the measuring instruments themselves, or human error. One way to describe the accuracy of an individual value or the average of a set of experimental values is percentage error. Percentage error is calculated by subtracting the accepted value from the experimental value, dividing the difference by the accepted value, and multiplying the resulting fraction by 100%. Percentage error is an absolute value, so only positive values should be reported.

$$\text{Percentage error} = \frac{|\text{value}_{experimental} - \text{value}_{accepted}|}{\text{value}_{accepted}} \times 100$$

SOLVE The scientifically accepted value of the density of pure ethanol is 0.7893 g/mL. Determine the percentage error of each student's measurement.

Sample	Measured density (g/mL)	Percentage error (%)
1	0.72	_____
2	0.74	_____
3	0.81	_____
4	0.79	_____

EVALUATE Which of the measurements was most accurate? Give evidence to support your claim, and explain your reasoning.

_____

_____

_____

Measuring with Precision

Different pieces of equipment allow for measurements with different levels of precision. For example, a graduated cylinder with 0.1-mL divisions allows for more precise measurements than a graduated cylinder with 1-mL divisions. When recording measurements, the smallest division on the equipment indicates how precise the data you record should be.

It is appropriate to estimate a value that is 1/10th the size of the smallest division on a measurement tool. If using equipment that clearly indicates the tenths place, you could record a value with an estimated digit in the hundredths place. For example, if a volume appeared to be between 36.2 and 36.3 mL, the volume could be recorded as 36.25 mL. The 5 in the hundredths place is the estimated digit.

FIGURE 13: The smallest division shown on a piece of equipment indicates how precise data obtained with that equipment should be.

EXPLAIN From left to right, the name and smallest division marked on each piece of equipment in Figure 13 is: graduated cylinder (2 mL), Erlenmeyer flask (25 mL), beaker (10 mL), and volumetric flask (100 mL).

Which of these pieces of equipment would be the most appropriate for precisely measuring 29 mL of liquid? Explain your reasoning, citing evidence related to the divisions on each tool and the concept of an estimated digit.

_____

_____

_____

_____

 Evidence Notebook Describe an example of a situation when very precise measurements would be important. Then, describe an example of a situation where estimated values would be acceptable. Why are these situations different?

Using Significant Figures

To assure that data is as precise and meaningful as possible, scientists report measured results in terms of significant figures. Significant figures in a measurement consist of all of the digits known with certainty, plus the first uncertain or estimated digit. Knowing which digits are significant prevents a scientist from reporting a value that is more precise than the equipment used to gather the data. For example, a scientist calculating the density of a substance with a mass of 5.90 grams and 3.89 milliters might obtain the following on their calculator: 1.516 709 511 568 12 g/mL. However, this value has more digits than the values used in the calculation. An appropriate result would be 1.52 g/mL. To round values correctly, you first need to know which digits are significant.

Rules for determining significant digits:

- Nonzero integers are always significant. For example, 275 has three significant digits.

- Zeros appearing between nonzero digits (*captive zeros*) are significant. For example, the value 40.7 has three significant figures. The value 87 009 has five.

- Zeros that precede nonzero digits (*leading zeros*) are not significant. For example, the value 0.095 897 has five significant figures. The value 0.0009 has one significant figure.

- Zeros at the end of a number (*trailing zeros*) are significant only if the number contains a decimal point. For example, the value 85.00 has four significant figures, and the value 9.000 000 000 has ten. The value 2000 has only one significant figure. However, the value written as 2000. (with a decimal) has four significant figures.

- *Exact numbers*, such as conversion factors, counted numbers, and defined values, are assumed to have no uncertainty and therefore have infinite significant figures.

ANALYZE Write each measurement in the correct box according to the number of significant figures it has.

| 0.217 L | 30.080 kg | 0.000 09 cm | 23 000 m | 784.000 g | 5.003 mL |

One significant figure	Two significant figures	Three significant figures	Four significant figures	Five significant figures	Six significant figures

Mathematical Operations Using Significant Figures

Calculating experimental results usually requires a variety of mathematical operations, such as adding, subtracting, multiplying, or dividing. Calculations also frequently use several types of measurements, all with varying levels of accuracy. The uncertainty of the final result must be accounted for as precisely as possible. In order to do this, scientists have developed rules for determining the correct number of significant figures that should be included when reporting calculated results. In general, the final reported value should be no more precise than the least precise measurement used in the calculation.

Rules for using significant figures in mathematical operations:

- Multiplication and division: The number of significant figures in the result is the same as the number in the least precise measurement used in the calculation. For example, 3.05 divided by 8.470 will produce a result of 0.360 094 451 on a calculator. The result, however, should only have three significant figures, so the final value should be correctly reported as 0.360.

- Addition and subtraction: The result has the same number of decimal places as the least precise measurement used in the calculation. For example, 25.1 added to 2.03 will produce a result of 27.13 on a calculator. However, the value 25.1 has only one decimal place, so the value in the hundredths place is completely unknown. The final answer should therefore be reported with one decimal place: 27.1.

- Exact numbers, such as the conversion factor between meters and centimeters, do not limit significant figures, as they are considered to have no uncertainty. For example:

$$4.608 \text{ m} \times \frac{100 \text{ cm}}{1 \text{ m}} = 460.8 \text{ cm}$$

Explore Online ▶

Hands-On Lab

Measuring with Precision
Practice using the correct number of significant figures when making measurements and completing calculations.

SOLVE Report the result of each calculation using the correct number of significant figures.

1. A scientist measures 1062 mL of a substance with a density of 0.023 g/mL. What is the mass of the substance?

2. An engineer measures the initial depth of liquid in a reactor vessel as 3.29 m and the final depth as 1.0487 m. What is the difference in depth?

3. The distance between two points on a map is 0.704 kilometers. What is this distance in meters?

4. A student measures the the sides of a cube with a ruler and finds that the length of each side is 2.70 cm. What is the volume of the cube in centimeters cubed?

 Evidence Notebook Explain how neglecting to account for significant figures could lead to major variations when using data from the analysis of a small sample of food to determine the amount of energy in a very large food sample.

As you have seen, scientists may work with measurements that are incredibly small or incredibly large. The range of measurable values in nature is so large that it would be difficult to express many of these values in standard notation. Therefore, scientists often use scientific notation, which is based on powers of 10.

For example, recall that one mole of carbon contains 6.02×10^{23} atoms. If a scientist had to write out this number in standard notation, it would look like this: 602 000 000 000 000 000 000 000. Obviously, reporting numbers this way would be unwieldy and could lead to errors. So, scientists use scientific notation when reporting very small or very large measurements.

Scientific Notation

In scientific notation, numbers are written in the form $m \times 10^{n}$, where the factor m is a number greater than or equal to 1 but less than 10, and n is a whole number. For example, the value 65 000 is reported in scientific notation as 6.5×10^{4}. The value 0.00012 is expressed in scientific notation as 1.2×10^{-4}.

Steps for converting numbers into scientific notation:

· Determine m by moving the decimal point in the original number to the left or right so that only one nonzero digit remains to the left of the decimal point.

· Determine n by counting the number of places you moved the decimal point.

SOLVE Write the missing values to complete the table.

Standard Notation	Scientific Notation
4 800 000	_____
_____	6.219×10^{6}
0.000 158	_____
_____	7.320×10^{-5}
527	_____

Scientific notation makes reporting and comparing very large and very small values easier because it requires fewer zeros. The number of significant figures is also easily indicated using the decimal point because only the significant figures are shown. For example, when rounding the number 236 000 000 to two significant figures, convert it to scientific notation first:

$$2.36 \times 10^{8}$$

Then, round this number to two significant figures:

$$2.4 \times 10^{8}$$

 Evidence Notebook How could you use conversions to calculate the amount of energy contained in the big rice cake shown at the beginning of the lesson? For example, if the mass of the cake were given in pounds, and you used a calorimeter to find the number of calories in one gram of cake, how could you use dimensional analysis to find the number of calories in the entire cake?

Careers in Science

Food Scientist

How many food scientists does it take to make a loaf of bread? It sounds like the beginning of a joke, but the work of many food scientists is involved with nearly every food item you purchase. These scientists play many important roles in food production and preparation.

Take a look at any nutritional information label and you will see data about the nutrients, ingredients, and energy content of the food. Food scientists work at processing plants, government agencies, and universities. These specialists work to make and improve food products, like bread, to make sure that the food is properly prepared and labeled. Food scientists use calorimetry to determine the energy content of foods. But they don't just burn a slice of whole-grain bread to see how much energy it releases. The reason is because some components, such as fiber, are not digested by the body and therefore do not provide usable energy. Instead, scientists determine the amount of protein, carbohydrates, fats, and fiber in the bread. Strictly controlled calorimetry experiments have provided average values of 4 kcal/g for protein, 4 kcal/g for carbohydrate, and 9 kcal/g for fat. (Remember, a Calorie is the same as a kilocalorie.) Food scientists then use these averages along with the analyzed components in the food to calculate the energy content.

Food scientists also use calorimetry to analyze steps of the production process that are temperature sensitive. For example, they might find that the temperatures needed to kill microorganisms also result in proteins breaking down. This could make the food unappetizing or reduce its nutritional value. They may also want to determine if too much oil is being used to fry chips. Testing chips from different batches in a calorimeter can indicate whether too much oil remains on the chips.

Food scientists look for ways to improve the preservation of food and prevent spoilage. They analyze different cooking and baking processes

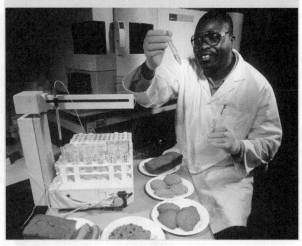

FIGURE 14: A food scientist studies the nutritional content of different foods.

to better understand how these affect different foods. They help develop new products and look for substitutes that can replace potentially harmful additives. Some food scientists even inspect food-processing plants to make sure that they are properly cleaned and maintained.

Whether you're buying food ready to eat or using ingredients to prepare your own meals, you can thank food scientists for helping make the food safe and nutritional, as well as taste good.

 Language Arts Connection Make a pamphlet to hand out at a career fair that describes the work of food scientists. Research examples of work that scientists do in the food industry. Areas of research might include production (pesticides and fertilizers, GMO crops), processing, preservation (methods to reduce spoilage, shelf-stable foods), preparation, or a topic of your choosing. In your pamphlet, give background on your topic, explain what questions scientists are trying to answer, especially related to protecting the environment and public health while enabling a plentiful and available food supply, and describe the methods they use to find those answers.

MORE PRACTICE WITH UNIT CONVERSION | MEASURING WITH PRECISION | DEBATING FOOD LABELING | Go online to choose one of these other paths.

Lesson Self-Check

CAN YOU SOLVE IT?

FIGURE 15: The world's largest glutinous rice cake was prepared in China in 2016 by the work of over fifty cooks.

Imagine the amount of ingredients required to prepare a rice cake that is almost 4 meters (12.5 feet) in diameter. The bakers of this giant rice cake used over 1300 pounds of rice! Packaged foods typically have a nutrition label showing the amount of energy the food contains in a serving. This energy is shown as a number of Calories. But how would you determine the number of Calories in a record-breaking food such as this cake? What types of equipment would you need, and how would you gather data to determine the amount of energy in this massive amount of food?

Evidence Notebook In your Evidence Notebook, make a claim for how you could measure the amount of energy contained in this rice cake. Use evidence and examples to support your claim, and explain your reasoning. In your explanation, address the following questions:

1. How could a scientist determine the number of Calories in a certain mass of this food?
2. How could you determine the number of Calories in the entire rice cake if you knew the number of Calories in a smaller sample? Provide mathematical models in the form of example calculations to illustrate how this could be done.
3. How would the size of the sample tested and the precision of the equipment used affect the number of Calories calculated for the whole rice cake?

CHECKPOINTS

Check Your Understanding

1. Order the units from smallest to largest.

_____ **a.** centigram

_____ **b.** microgram

_____ **c.** kilogram

_____ **d.** milligram

_____ **e.** megagram

_____ **f.** nanogram

2. A student measures the mass of a substance as 1.7132 kg and its volume as 0.65 L. What is the density of the substance in g/mL? Round your answer to the correct number of significant figures. The density of the substance is _____ g/mL.

3. The table lists density calculations based on measurements students made. The accepted value of the density is 1.17 g/mL. Determine the percentage error of each measurement.

Sample	Measured density (g/mL)	Percentage error (%)
1	1.05	_____
2	1.12	_____
3	1.31	_____
4	1.24	_____

4. A beaker contains 0.250 L of liquid. A student pours 0.00385 L of liquid out of the beaker. How much liquid remains in the beaker? Choose the value reported with the correct number of significant figures.

○ **a.** 0.25 L

○ **b.** 0.246 L

○ **c.** 0.2462 L

○ **d.** 0.24615 L

5. Which statement best describes what happens when you hold a cold drink in your hand?

○ **a.** The temperature of the drink decreases, and energy is transferred from the drink to your hand.

○ **b.** The temperature of your hand increases, and energy is transferred from the drink to your hand.

○ **c.** The temperature of the drink increases, and energy is transferred from your hand to the drink.

○ **d.** The temperature of your hand decreases, and energy is transferred from the drink to your hand.

6. Which statement describes what happens inside a liquid thermometer that shows an increase in temperature?

○ **a.** The volume of the liquid decreases because of an increase in kinetic energy.

○ **b.** The movement of the particles decreases because of a decrease in kinetic energy.

○ **c.** The volume of the liquid increases because the movement of the particles decreases.

○ **d.** The movement of the particles increases because of an increase in kinetic energy.

7. Write KE or PE next to each item to show whether it is a form of kinetic energy or a form of potential energy.

_____ **a.** chemical energy

_____ **b.** elastic energy

_____ **c.** electromagnetic energy

_____ **d.** gravitational energy

_____ **e.** light energy

_____ **f.** nuclear energy

_____ **g.** sound energy

_____ **h.** thermal energy

CHECKPOINTS (continued)

8. Describe the changes in energy that occur when a marshmallow is burned over a fire.

_____

_____

_____

_____

9. Students in a class all make measurements and then calculate the density of the same metal block. During analysis, they find that their data are neither accurate nor precise. Explain how several factors may have contributed to these problems.

_____

_____

_____

_____

10. Imagine you need to explain to a friend how to convert a value on a food label to one that is measured in grams. Assume the package of food has a mass of 1.0 pound. Write an explanation for how to use dimensional analysis to convert this value to one expressed in grams.

_____

_____

_____

_____

MAKE YOUR OWN STUDY GUIDE

 In your Evidence Notebook, design a study guide that supports the main ideas from this lesson:

One way to determine the energy content of food is to use the energy released by burning a sample to warm a liquid and measure the liquid's temperature change.

The SI system includes seven base units to describe important scientific measurements. Some quantities are described by derived units using two or more SI base units.

Different types of energy, such as chemical, electrical, and thermal energy, can be classified as a form of either kinetic energy or potential energy. Energy can transfer from one location to another, and it can change from one type to another type.

Dimensional analysis is a method of using conversion factors in calculations that involve changing units.

Remember to include the following information in your study guide:
• Use examples that model main ideas.
• Record explanations for the phenomena you investigated.
• Use evidence to support your explanations. Your support can include drawings, data, graphs, laboratory conclusions, and other evidence recorded throughout the lesson.

Consider how you can describe measurements of matter and energy that flow into, out of, and within a system.

Identifying Physical and Chemical Properties of Matter

Edible spoons are a healthy, nutritious, and eco-friendly alternative to plastic.

CAN YOU EXPLAIN IT?

You buy your take-out lunch and pick up a plastic spoon. After lunch, you throw out the spoon. It may take hundreds of years for that spoon to degrade in a landfill. Even biodegradable plastics made from corn starch do not break down easily. They require controlled composting facilities that aren't readily available. But now, edible spoons may solve the plastic-waste problem. Edible utensils are made of grains—rice, wheat, and sorghum—with a little salt, sugar, and spice added for flavor. They taste like crackers. And if you are too full after lunch to eat your spoon, it will degrade within a few days.

PREDICT What properties do you think a spoon must have for it to be useful as an eating tool? What additional properties must an edible spoon have?

_____

_____

_____

_____

_____

 Evidence Notebook As you explore the lesson, gather evidence to explain how the properties of materials influence what we use the materials for and the ways we use them.

Properties of Matter

Everything around you—your desk, your chair, and the people around you—are all made of matter. Even things you cannot see, such as air, are made of matter. Matter is anything that takes up space and has mass. The mass of an object is the amount of matter the object contains. Although all things are made of matter, the kind and amount of matter in each object varies.

Consider a spoonful of sodium chloride, otherwise known as table salt. The spoonful of sodium chloride has a certain mass. You can change the mass by adding or removing salt. However, any size sample of sodium chloride will always consist of 39.34% by mass of the element sodium and 60.66% by mass of the element chlorine. If you pour the spoonful of sodium chloride into a glass of water, the mass of salt and the matter have not changed. The salt may dissolve, but the amounts of sodium and chlorine do not change. The idea that matter cannot be created or destroyed is known as the *law of conservation of matter*, or the *law of conservation of mass*.

ANALYZE A ball of clay is manipulated into different shapes in each of the images below. Does the amount of mass and matter in each of the images below change as the size and shape of the clay ball is changed? Explain your reasoning.

_____
_____
_____
_____

_____
_____
_____
_____

_____
_____
_____
_____

Physical Properties of Matter

Every substance has characteristic physical and chemical properties that determine its identity. A *physical property* is a property that can be measured or observed without changing the identity of matter. Some recognizable physical properties are shown in Figure 1.

 Collaborate With a partner, make a list of questions you have about the physical properties shown in Figure 1. What other characteristics of matter do you think are physical properties?

FIGURE 1: Examples of some common physical properties of matter

Explore Online ▶

a Density is the amount of mass per volume of a substance. Less-dense liquids will float above liquids of higher density.

b Conductivity is a measure of the amount of electricity, heat, or sound that a substance can carry.

c Magnetic attraction is the ability of a substance to be attracted to a magnet.

d Solubility is the amount of a substance that can dissolve in a given amount of another substance.

When a change occurs without a change in a substance's chemical composition at a molecular scale, that change is a physical change. Table salt is soluble in water. When in the water, however, it is still table salt. It has not changed identity. Attach copper wires between a battery and a light bulb, and the metal will conduct electricity from the battery to light the bulb. Conducting electricity does not change the identity of the metal.

States of Matter

States of matter—solid, liquid, or gas—are the common forms in which matter can exist. When a substance goes from one state of matter to another, the process is a change in state. This is a physical change. During a change in state, the substance changes its physical properties without changing its chemical composition. The water looks different at the macroscopic scale, but its chemical composition has not changed at the molecular scale.

FIGURE 2: Water changes state from solid (ice) to liquid (liquid water) to gas (water vapor).

ASK What questions could you ask about the arrangement of particles in the states of matter shown in Figure 2?

_____

_____

_____

_____

_____

_____

The particles in a solid are packed very close together in a rigid, orderly arrangement. They are held together by the attractive forces that act between all particles of matter. Solids, therefore, have fixed volumes and shapes. In the solid state, particles cannot break away from their fixed position. The particles can only vibrate in place. No matter what container you put a solid into, the solid has its own shape.

The particles that make up a liquid move more rapidly than those in a solid. This causes the particles in the liquid to overcome the strong attractive forces between them. A liquid, therefore, can flow and take the shape of a container.

The particles of a gas are very far apart and move very rapidly compared to solids or liquids. At these distances, the attractive forces between gas particles have a lesser effect than they do at the small distances between particles of liquids and solids. Gases, therefore, have no definite shape or volume. Gases will fill any container they occupy as their particles move apart. In general, the volume of a liquid or solid increases greatly when it forms a gas. Gases exert pressure in all directions.

Plasma is a gas in which the particles have so much energy that they have broken apart and become electrically charged. Plasma is usually considered the fourth state of matter because it is different from the gas state. Most of the matter in the universe is plasma.

 Energy and Matter

Bose-Einstein Condensate

A fifth state of matter, known as a Bose-Einstein condensate (BEC) was identified by scientists. In this state, extremely cold particles just above absolute zero (−273 °C or 0 K) barely move. Condensate particles have so little energy that they clump and behave as a single particle. Satyendra Bose and Albert Einstein predicted the BEC in the 1920s, but the sophisticated equipment needed to produce the matter did not exist until 1995.

 Collaborate With a partner, discuss how the matter in a BEC is different from other states of matter.

Chemical Properties of Matter

Lithium, sodium, and potassium react with water. The products of the reaction include hydrogen gas, which can burn if the reaction takes place in an atmosphere that includes oxygen. The lithium reaction is slow and may only produce a small amount of smoke. Sodium reacts faster, with more smoke and flame. Potassium reacts so fast that it can be explosive.

FIGURE 3: The alkali metals lithium, sodium, and potassium react with water.   Explore Online ▶

a lithium   b sodium   c potassium

Chemical properties are only observed when one attempts to change the identity of a substance. They cannot be determined simply by observing a substance, as physical properties can. Rather, a change (or lack of a change) in a substance must be observed during or after a chemical reaction. For example, the reactivity of alkali metals with water is a chemical property. This property cannot be observed until the metal and water react, and both the metal and the water change in the process.

In a chemical change, the particles of a substance are rearranged, resulting in a change in chemical composition. The substances undergoing the change are the reactants; the new substances formed are the products. When sodium reacts with water, sodium and water are reactants. Sodium hydroxide and hydrogen gas are products.

Explore Online ▶

🧪 **Hands-On Lab**

Performing Physical and Chemical Changes
Gather evidence in a series of experiments to determine whether physical or chemical changes occur.

ANALYZE Determine whether each observation describes a chemical or a physical property.

chemical   physical

When a piece of sodium metal is placed in a test tube with water, the sodium fizzes and bubbles of a gas are produced. _____

When table salt is added to water in a test tube, the table salt dissolves. _____

When water is placed in a freezer at 0 °C it becomes ice. _____

When an iron bicycle is left outdoors and is exposed to moist air, it gets rusty. _____

When a glass marble is heated and then quickly cooled, it shatters. _____

Extensive and Intensive Properties

Scientists describe properties of matter as extensive and intensive. An extensive property is one that depends directly on the amount of a substance present. An intensive property is one that does not depend on the amount of the substance present. All quantities of a substance have the same values of the intensive property.

If you immerse a 12-ounce can of regular cola and an equal-sized can of diet cola in a tub of water, you will notice that the regular cola sinks and the diet cola floats, although both cans contain the same volume. The sweetener in diet cola is hundreds of times sweeter per unit volume than the sugar in regular cola. So, a much smaller mass of sweetener is needed in the diet cola to produce the amount of sweetness sugar produces in regular cola.

FIGURE 4: Cans of regular cola and diet cola behave differently in water.

EXPLAIN What are the extensive and intensive properties described in this experiment? Which properties would change and which would stay the same if you ran the experiment using 7.5-ounce cans instead of 12-ounce cans?

_____

_____

Mass and volume are both extensive properties; they change with the amount of substance, such as cola in the container. Density, however, is an intensive property and is independent of the amount of a substance. Melting points, boiling points, and conductivity are other intensive properties. Two liters of water boil at the same temperature and have the same density as one liter of water does.

ANALYZE Classify each statement as an extensive or an intensive property.

extensive   intensive

A pot of boiling water has more energy than a cup of boiling water. _____

A pot of water boils at the same temperature as a cup of water. _____

Copper wire conducts electricity. _____

A block of ice takes longer to melt than does a small ice cube. _____

Mixtures and Pure Substances

Matter can be either a pure substance or a mixture. A *pure substance* has a fixed composition. A *mixture* is a blend of two or more kinds of matter, each of which retains its own identity and properties.

PLAN How could you determine whether an unknown clear liquid is pure water or salt water? Remember that you should never taste any substance of unknown identity.

_____

_____

_____

_____

_____

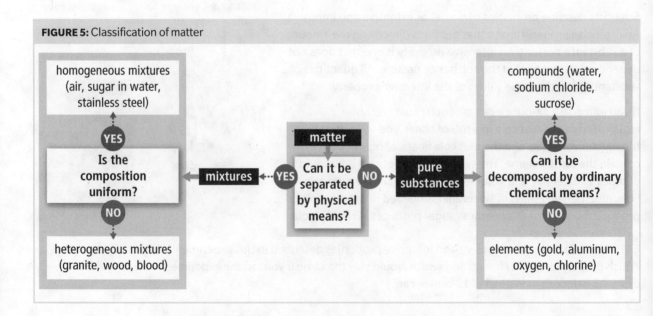

FIGURE 5: Classification of matter

Mixtures

Distilled water is a pure substance. Salt water is a mixture. Every sample of pure water has the same characteristic chemical and physical properties and the same composition. Salt water, however, contains both salt and water, each with different properties, even though the salt cannot be readily seen. Mixtures that have the same composition, or are uniform, are said to be *homogeneous* and are sometimes referred to as *solutions*. Mixtures that are not uniform throughout are said to be *heterogeneous*.

FIGURE 6: Mixtures can be separated into their components based on differences in their physical properties.

a Filtration is often used to separate a solid with larger particles from a liquid with smaller particles.

b Centrifugation can be used to separate certain solid components. The centrifuge spins rapidly, causing the solids to settle at the bottom of the test tube.

c Paper chromatography can be used to separate dyes or pigments. The different substances move at different rates on the paper.

Mixtures can often be separated by using techniques such as filtration, evaporation, distillation, decanting, or centrifugation. These methods take advantage of different physical properties of the components. For example, a mixture of sand and water can be separated by letting the large particles of sand settle to the bottom of a container. Filtration can separate components that have small differences in particle size. Distillation separates components based on differences in the volatility of the components. Components with higher volatility become gases more readily than those with lower volatility. Chromatography separates mixtures by their attraction to the medium.

Pure Substances

Ten samples of a pure substance would all have the same properties and composition. Thus, pure substances are always homogeneous. A pure substance can be either an element or a compound. Elements cannot be broken down into simpler substances by chemical or physical means. The iron and the sulfur shown in Figure 7 are elements. Compounds are substances with constant composition that can be broken down into elements by chemical processes. Iron(II) sulfide is a compound containing the elements iron and sulfur.

FIGURE 7: Iron(II) sulfide (right) is composed of iron (left) and sulfur (center).

 Evidence Notebook Consider the differences between the chemical and physical properties of an edible spoon compared to other types of spoons. How could you investigate the differences in the matter that makes up each spoon?

Engineering Lab

Separating a Mixture

The ability to separate and recover pure substances from mixtures is extremely important in scientific research and industry. Chemists often need to work with pure substances, but naturally occurring materials are seldom pure. Generally, differences in the physical properties of the components in a mixture provide the means for separating them.

Design Challenge: How would you design, develop, and implement your own procedure for separating a mixture containing salt, sand, iron filings, and poppy seeds? All four components are in dry, granular form.

DEFINE THE PROBLEM

In your Evidence Notebook, identify which physical properties will be useful in separating the components of the mixture and criteria and constraints of a successful separation.

POSSIBLE MATERIALS

- indirectly vented chemical splash goggles, nonlatex apron, nonlatex gloves
- components (salt, sand, iron filings, poppy seeds)
- distilled water
- filter funnel and paper
- forceps
- hot plate
- magnet
- mixture sample
- test tubes and rack

SAFETY INFORMATION

- Wear indirectly vented chemical splash goggles, a nonlatex apron, and nonlatex gloves during the setup, hands-on, and takedown segments of the activity.

- Use caution when working with iron fillings, which are hazardous if they are swallowed or inhaled, or enter the eyes, nose, or other body cavities.

- Use caution when working with hot plates, which can cause skin burns or electric shock. Use only GFI protected circuits when using electrical equipment, and keep away from water sources to prevent shock.

COLLECT DATA

Obtain separate samples of each of the four mixture components from your teacher. Use the equipment you have available to make observations of the components and determine their properties. You will need to run several tests with each material, so don't use all of your sample on the first test. Look for things like whether the material is magnetic, if it dissolves, or if it floats. Record your observations in a data table.

TEST

1. In your Evidence Notebook, develop a procedure explaining how you will isolate each material in the mixture. Make sure your teacher approves your plans and safety precautions before proceeding.

2. When your procedure, safety plan, and materials are approved, obtain a sample of the mixture from your teacher and begin separating the mixture.

indirectly vented chemical splash goggles

OPTIMIZE

In your Evidence Notebook, explain how successful your separation process was based on your criteria and constraints. How could you optimize your process?

ANALYZE

1. How could you separate each of the following two-component mixtures?

Mixture	Separation method
Aluminum filings and iron filings	
Sand and finely ground polystyrene foam	
Alcohol and water	

2. One of the components of the mixture in this experiment is in a different physical form at the completion of this experiment than it was at the start. Which one? How would you convert that component back to its original form?

COMMUNICATE

For each of the four components, describe a specific physical property that enabled you to separate the component from the rest of the mixture. Give specific examples and explain how this evidence supports your claim.

 Evidence Notebook An edible spoon is made from a mixture of substances. What properties should the substances have to prevent them from separating from the mixture when the spoon is used to stir or consume liquids?

The Study of Chemistry

Developing an edible spoon will involve a team of scientists, engineers, and specialists, such as nutritionists. This team will need to break down the design challenge into smaller, more manageable pieces to design the edible spoon. The team would determine how the matter in an edible spoon is different from a metal or plastic spoon. They may use this information to find ways to make the edible spoon behave more like a metal or plastic spoon. Since the spoons will be eaten, the team must consider their nutritional value. The team must consider if a design can be produced in large quantities and within a budget. All these design aspects involve chemistry.

What Is Chemistry?

Chemistry is the study of the composition of matter, the physical and chemical changes that matter undergoes, and the energy absorbed or released during those changes. Chemists ask questions such as, What is a material's make-up? and How do different materials react with one another? Many fields of chemistry overlap with other disciplines. For example, chemical engineers study chemistry to learn which material might be the best choice to use for a new product.

FIGURE 8: Analytical chemist

Chemistry is traditionally divided into six major areas of study.

- Physical chemistry—the study of the properties and changes of matter and their relation to energy

- Analytical chemistry—the study of the composition of substances

- Theoretical chemistry—the studies of chemical structure and its dynamics

- Organic chemistry—the study of most carbon-based compounds

- Inorganic chemistry—the study of nonorganic substances

- Biochemistry—the study of the chemistry of living things

Chemists use tools to make observations and take measurements. They develop and use models to study the behavior of matter. A model is a pattern, plan, representation, or description designed to show the structure or workings of an object, system, or concept. Many traditional tools, such as balances, have been replaced by electronic or computer-assisted devices, making the field of chemistry more accurate and precise.

The analytical chemist in Figure 8 is using a computer modeling program to analyze the structure of a complex substance. She may also use gas chromatography to analyze the substance and an atomic absorption spectroscope to burn the sample. This will allow her to study the elements in the compound. Despite all the technology, she also uses standard laboratory glassware, such as beakers and flasks. However, her primary tool is her brain, which allows her to solve problems.

 Collaborate With a partner, make a list of the tools you used, observations you made, and the questions you asked in the Separating a Mixture lab. Discuss your list with your class.

Systems Define Scientific Problems

A system is a set of interacting, interrelated, or interdependent components that form a complex whole. A system can be simple or complex, depending on the number and types of its parts. Every system has boundaries and is influenced by the environment that surrounds it. By setting boundaries between the system and the environment, engineers can examine how the system's components work together. Analyzing and designing chemical systems is usually the job of a chemical engineer, working alongside chemists and engineers with other specialties.

Systems can be categorized according to the changes of energy and matter that flows into, out of, and within the system. In an *open system*, energy and matter flow in and out freely. In a *closed system*, there is little or no exchange of matter with the environment, but energy may be exchanged. In an *isolated system*, neither matter nor energy flows in or out.

ANALYZE Define a system you interact with every day. Is the system open, closed, or isolated? How do matter and energy flow into, out of, or within the system?

_____

_____

_____

FIGURE 9: A syngas methanol plant is a complex system. Its chemical processes use natural gas or coal to make methanol, releasing large amounts of energy.

FIGURE 10: A syngas methanol plant is made of smaller systems, each of which can be isolated. A reactor is an example of a smaller system inside a larger system.

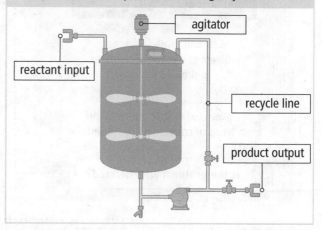

Syngas production is an open system in which the reactants, usually natural gas or coal, enter and methanol leaves as a product. The syngas methanol plant has many components that can each be modeled as its own system. A reactor in the plant can be studied as a single system interacting with other systems inside the plant. The inputs of the system, the reactants, are converted into outputs, the products.

The components of a system include controls to keep the system working properly by monitoring and managing the inputs and outputs. An important control is feedback, the information from one step of a cycle that changes the behavior of a previous step. So, feedback is output that becomes input.

 Evidence Notebook Consider the type of plant in which edible spoons and other disposable spoons would be produced. What systems would have to be included in that location? What models or tools might chemists use to make an edible spoon that functions like a plastic spoon?

Chemistry and the Engineering Design Process

Developing a common product such as toothpaste can be a complex process. Recipes for the abrasives, foaming agents, flavors, fluoride, and other chemicals the toothpaste contains are made first. A nonreactive material for the tube must be chosen and tested. The recipes are then adjusted so large-scale production can occur in a cost-effective way.

Engineering Design Process

Engineering and scientific inquiry both involve a set of principles and a general sequence of events. The scientific process includes steps such as asking questions, making predictions, and investigating the effects of changing variables. The engineering design process includes steps such as defining a problem, developing solutions, and optimizing a solution. Both rely on the continual testing and retesting of results.

FIGURE 11: The engineering design process is a set of steps that lead to designing or improving a solution to a problem.

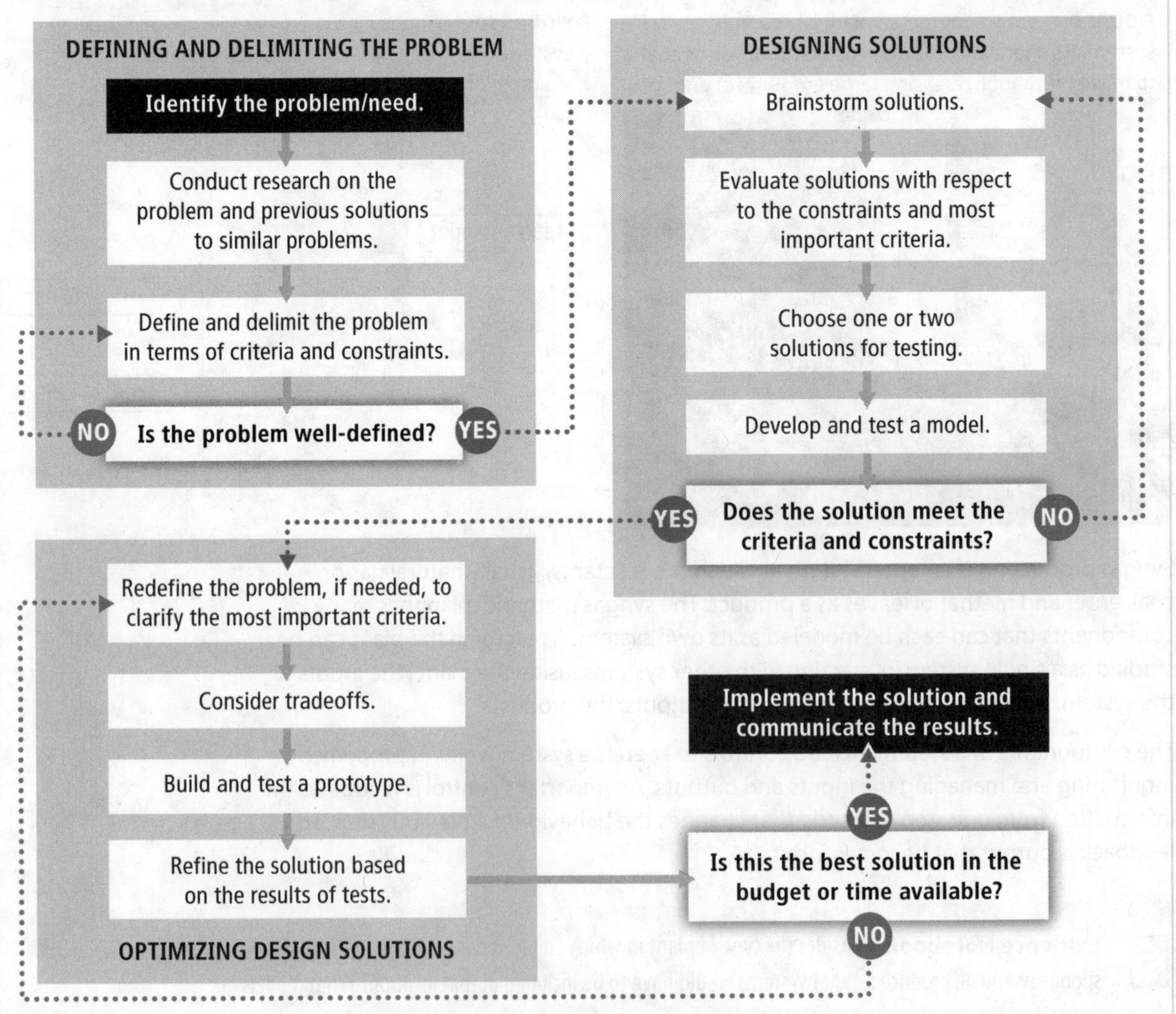

DEFINING AND DELIMITING THE PROBLEM

Identify the problem/need.

Conduct research on the problem and previous solutions to similar problems.

Define and delimit the problem in terms of criteria and constraints.

NO Is the problem well-defined? YES

DESIGNING SOLUTIONS

Brainstorm solutions.

Evaluate solutions with respect to the constraints and most important criteria.

Choose one or two solutions for testing.

Develop and test a model.

YES Does the solution meet the criteria and constraints? NO

Redefine the problem, if needed, to clarify the most important criteria.

Consider tradeoffs.

Build and test a prototype.

Refine the solution based on the results of tests.

OPTIMIZING DESIGN SOLUTIONS

Implement the solution and communicate the results.

YES

Is this the best solution in the budget or time available?

NO

The engineering design process is used to develop or improve technology. Engineers first identify and define the problem. They may perform research or analyze data to identify desired aspects and limits of the solution. Next, engineers design and assess solutions. In the third stage—testing or optimizing—engineers choose one or two options to test, often using computer simulations and prototypes. Based on these test results, the designs may be rejected or accepted. Even accepted designs are often refined. The process is iterative, meaning it repeats steps as often as necessary to obtain an optimal solution. Engineers may decide to choose a different solution and start the process again.

 Engineering

Chemical Engineering

Chemical engineering is the application of chemistry to find solutions to real-world problems. Chemical engineers develop useful products and chemical processes for society in the most efficient, environmentally sound, safe, and cost-effective way. They might need to develop new materials or design new equipment for the production process. Often, chemical engineers are responsible for planning, designing, and optimizing plant processes.

ASK Suppose you are a chemical engineer working with a client who produces toothpaste. The client wants to add a blue stripe with mint flavor to the toothpaste. What questions would you ask to begin to address the design problem?

_____

_____

_____

_____

The advancement of science and technology may provide better solutions with fewer risks in terms of human health and environmental integrity. But today's solutions may lead to unanticipated problems tomorrow. Improving old and developing new products and processes is at the heart of chemical engineering.

Defining and Delimiting the Problem

Engineering problems need to be defined before a solution can be developed. First, they define the problem's system. Next, they identify the groups that must be involved in each portion of the process, any relevant scientific issues, and possible impacts on the environment and society. Once this is done, they can identify the system's major components and their relationships. Finally, the boundaries of the system in which the problem occurs must be defined, clarifying what is and what is not part of the problem.

Identifying criteria further helps engineers define the problem. Criteria (singular *criterion*) are goals that tell whether a solution is successful, and how efficient and economical that solution should be. These are the "wants" for the solution. Criteria can include many different aspects of a design, but often cost, safety, reliability, and aesthetics are considered. For engineers developing the new toothpaste with the blue, mint-flavored stripe, there are several possible criteria they would need to consider. A pleasant taste, enough abrasiveness to clean teeth well, a blue stripe that is visually appealing, and preservatives that will keep the toothpaste safe for use over time are all possible criteria.

After engineers define the problem, they delimit the problem. *Delimiting* is the process of defining the constraints of the solution. Constraints are the limitations of a design and are often, but not always, provided by the client. These constraints can include considerations such as cost, weight, dimensions, available resources, and time. Any solution that does not meet the constraints of the design is generally not considered. For the toothpaste example, some constraints the client might impose include cost of materials, whether or not the blue dye in the stripe could "bleed" into the white toothpaste, a specific thickness for the toothpaste, and a tube of a specific design.

ANALYZE The client told the engineering team that they want their new production cost for the blue, mint-flavored stripe in the toothpaste to be the same as for the old toothpaste. They want to continue to use the same design for the tube, which is made of plastic. Consider whether each of the following statements represents a criterion or a constraint for this engineering problem.

criterion   constraint

The blue stripe must be visually appealing. _____

Adding the blue mint-flavored stripe must be below a certain cost. _____

The chemicals in the blue stripe must not react with plastic. _____

The blue dye cannot cause the toothpaste to foam blue. _____

The mint flavor of the stripe must be refreshing but not too strong. _____

Design Solutions

After identifying the constraints and criteria for solving a problem, engineers continue to work as a team to brainstorm ideas for a solution. Proposed solutions are evaluated against the criteria and constraints. In general, engineers select one or two ideas that best meet the criteria and all constraints and then enter the optimization phase of the design process. Materials scientists often carry out this phase for chemical engineering problems to design solutions that involve the properties and applications of materials.

 Engineering

Considering Tradeoffs

Engineers often must balance criteria and constraints. They may accept some risks in tradeoffs for greater benefits. A tradeoff is an exchange for one thing in return for another. Engineers may give up one benefit in favor of another to avoid a potential risk. For example, the blue, mint-flavored stripe might cause the toothpaste to foam less when brushing than the client prefers. This might be a tradeoff because the amount of foam is less important than the mint flavor. However, if the mint stripe has sugar in it and has the potential to cause cavities, the engineers would not make that tradeoff.

DEFINE Think about some criteria that are important when developing a product such as toothpaste. What tradeoffs would you consider making to ensure that your most important criteria are met in your final design solution?

_____

_____

_____

Optimizing Design Solutions

Chemical engineers often focus on optimizing the design process. This means that they try to adjust the process so that some issues are enhanced without violating a constraint. The most common goals are minimizing cost and maximizing efficiency. To optimize the design process, engineers often build prototypes or scale models. The engineers may run numerous tests and analyze data, and they consider tradeoffs for their optimization.

FIGURE 12: This engineer is working with a model of a complex system.

Engineering One way to optimize and test design solutions is through user testing. Suppose a chemical engineer developed a prototype toothpaste with a blue minty stripe. The prototype is now ready to be user tested. Testers can provide engineers with information about the flavor, the amount of foaming, and the effectiveness of the toothpaste. This information could be reported qualitatively through interviews or descriptions from the user testers. The information could also be reported quantitatively, by having users report their experiences using an opinion scale, say from 1 to 5.

Chemical engineers use the results of their testing to optimize the manufacturing process. Small-scale prototypes may be developed because large-scale manufacturing is expensive. Chemical engineers may run lab experiments, computer simulations, and develop models to test their solutions. If a solution does not solve the problem, criteria and constraints may have to be refined. Engineers then brainstorm new solutions, sometimes combining parts of previous solutions to better solve the problem. They may even test two different prototypes simultaneously to determine which criteria and constraints should be revised.

Most important, however, good engineers never stop trying to think of ways that any design could be further improved. Even a finished design that meets all the criteria and constraints could potentially be made better.

Engineering

Process Design

Syngas is a mixture of carbon dioxide, carbon monoxide, and hydrogen. It is often used to make methanol, an additive in fuel. The production of methanol from syngas is an example of a chemical process. Chemical engineers optimize design solutions to increase the yield from a given quantity of starter material such as coal, natural gas, or biomass. Engineers must design this process for maximum yield at the lowest cost.

FIGURE 13: The production of methanol from syngas is a complex chemical process.

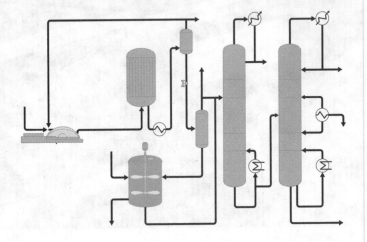

a This chemical engineer is reviewing a process flow diagram.

b This process flow diagram shows the process of making methanol from syngas, which itself is made from natural gas, coal, or biomass.

A process flow diagram helps chemical engineers track energy and matter in the process as a whole, and in the subsystems of the overall process. The diagram has multiple benefits. It might show unnecessary steps or other inefficiencies. Engineers can track the amounts of products and wastes produced. An engineer in a syngas plant can use such a diagram to develop a cost-effective process that produces a maximum yield of methanol from a minimum amount of starter materials. Each subsystem, or step of the process, can be diagrammed with arrows showing the steps from components to finished product.

Heat is important in syngas production, and there are many ways to produce and maintain high temperatures with minimum fuel use. Engineers use models, computers, and prototype plants to determine whether a plant design meets temperature and fuel needs. After full-scale manufacturing begins, temperature, pressure, and input-output data are collected. Computers store and summarize the data. The data may suggest changes in settings or materials to improve efficiency. Further analysis will show the effectiveness of the changes.

Evidence Notebook Think about how the engineering design process could be used to develop an edible utensil. In your Evidence Notebook, explain how a chemical engineer might go through each of the steps of an engineering design process to address the problem.

Engineering

Multiscale Modeling

Systems that are highly complex or difficult to observe directly can be studied using a model. Traditionally, models are designed to represent a system on just one scale. Determining the best scale to use can be a challenge because each scale provides different information about a system.

A more recent approach is *multiscale modeling* in which multiple models are developed to represent a system using various scales. Studying a system with multiple models increases the effectiveness of each individual model. Information obtained from a microscale model of a system can be used to inspire or to alter the design of a macroscale model. Similarly, information from a macroscale model can reveal areas of a system that could best be studied on a smaller scale.

Figure 14 shows a physical model of atmospheric pollution in a city. Observations of the model might reveal how the pollution moves throughout the system. The information gained from the physical model can be used to design a computer model to study pollution on a different scale. For example, they could model the pollution within a larger area or design a model of molecular interactions. Together, the different models can provide information about the system that is both accurate and efficient.

When using multiscale modeling, scientists and engineers must determine the boundaries of the system they are studying. In some cases, physical boundaries are imposed on a system. When studying properties of a substance, chemists might develop a macroscale model of the substance's physical properties. The boundary might include only the substance, or it might also include its surroundings. A computer model of the substance, however, might use a more restrictive boundary to study its molecular structure. By combining information from all the models, scientists and engineers can develop a better understanding of the properties and interactions of the system than they could from a single model.

FIGURE 14: These engineers are using a physical model to study pollution.

Conduct Research

Research ways that scientists and engineers use multiscale modeling. Learn about reasons they might want to use more than one model to solve a problem.

Select Appropriate Models

Identify a simulation that depicts the properties and behavior of matter on a particle level. Design a model that depicts the same behavior on a macroscopic level. Be sure to have your models approved by your teacher before you begin development.

Define the Systems

Define the system that both of your models work within. Consider why defining a system is important when trying to solve a problem.

Language Arts Connection Present your research, the computer simulation you studied, and the model you designed. Explain how using multiscale modeling helped you learn more about the system you investigated and what you learned by modeling a problem on multiple scales.

SALTING OUT | PERFORMING PHYSICAL AND CHEMICAL CHANGES | CRYSTALLOGRAPHER | Go online to choose one of these other paths.

Lesson Self-Check

CAN YOU EXPLAIN IT?

FIGURE 15: Edible spoons may be a preferable alternative to plastic because they do not accumulate in landfills.

Now that you have learned about criteria and constraints in an engineering process, you can apply them to the problem of developing an edible spoon. The properties that an edible spoon must have to be effective can be considered the criteria in the design process. An edible spoon must be shaped so that it can transfer different types of food from plate to mouth without spilling. It must have physical properties that allow it to be used with hot, cold, liquid, or solid foods. It must be chemically unreactive so that it does not react with the many types of food it will come in contact with. If the user chooses to eat the spoon, it must taste good and not harm the user. However, if the user chooses not to eat the spoon, it must decompose in a landfill within a reasonable length of time. All of the evidence you have collected during your study of the properties of matter can be used to understand some of the constraints that might develop during the process of designing an edible spoon.

 Evidence Notebook Refer to your notes in your Evidence Notebook to make a claim about the properties an edible spoon must have to be useful as an eating tool. Your explanation should include a discussion of the following points:

1. What properties should an edible spoon have?
2. What evidence supports the claim that these properties are useful for an edible spoon?
3. How does the evidence you provided support your claim about the properties of an edible spoon?

CHECKPOINTS

Check Your Understanding

1. Which statement best defines matter?
   - ○ **a.** Matter is anything that is a solid at room temperature.
   - ○ **b.** Matter is anything that takes up space and has mass.
   - ○ **c.** Matter is any substance that reacts with another substance.
   - ○ **d.** Matter is any substance that contains carbon.

2. Complete the statement by selecting the correct terms.

   When electricity passes through liquid water, two gases form. This is an example of a physical | chemical change because the identity of the substances changed | stayed the same.

   When liquid water loses energy, a change in state | chemical identity occurs. This is an example of a chemical | physical change.

3. Match the particle description to the correct state of matter.

Particles are packed very close together in a relatively fixed arrangement; has definite volume and shape. ○	○ liquid
Particles are close together but can move past one another; has a definite volume but an indefinite shape. ○	○ plasma
Particles are far apart and move very rapidly; has neither definite volume nor definite shape. ○	○ solid
Particles have a large amount of energy and they become electrically charged. ○	○ gas

4. Complete the statement by selecting the correct terms.

   An intensive | extensive physical property can be used to help identify a substance because it changes | does not change with the amount of matter present. An intensive | extensive property cannot be used to help identify a substance because it changes | does not change with the amount of the substance present.

5. Choose the projects most likely to be worked on by a chemist. Select all correct answers.
   - ☐ **a.** studying the structure of an enzyme
   - ☐ **b.** analyzing the components of petroleum
   - ☐ **c.** analyzing the velocity of planets
   - ☐ **d.** observing the behavior of farm animals
   - ☐ **e.** building a computer model for producing antacids

6. A chemical engineer is developing a manufacturing process for making a new kind of fertilizer. Which factor does she NOT have to consider in her system model?
   - ○ **a.** amount of reactant input
   - ○ **b.** amount of product output
   - ○ **c.** boundaries between the system and the environment
   - ○ **d.** cost of production

7. Categorize each substance as a pure substance or a mixture.

   air   soil   wood

   table salt   aluminum   carbon dioxide

Pure Substance	Mixture
_____	_____
_____	_____
_____	_____

CHECKPOINTS (continued)

8. Is a tossed salad a homogeneous mixture, a heterogeneous mixture, or a pure substance? Explain your reasoning.

_____

_____

_____

_____

_____

9. Many changes occur to a wax candle after it is lit. Which changes are physical? Which changes are chemical? How do you know what kind of change took place?

_____

_____

_____

_____

_____

10. How is iteration used in engineering design? Why is this such an important aspect of the process?

_____

_____

_____

_____

_____

MAKE YOUR OWN STUDY GUIDE

 In your Evidence Notebook, design a study guide that supports the main ideas from this lesson:

Chemistry is the study of matter, which is defined as anything that has mass and occupies space.

Chemists use data to understand how matter and its properties behave and interact. Chemical engineers use the findings of chemistry to define and solve real-world problems. They use an engineering design process to find optimal solutions to these problems.

Remember to include the following information in your study guide:

- Use examples that model main ideas.
- Record explanations for the phenomena you investigated.
- Use evidence to support your explanations. Your support can include drawings, data, graphs, laboratory conclusions, and other evidence recorded throughout the lesson.

Consider how the universe is a vast system in which the same basic laws describe the properties and interactions of matter, whether on Earth, in space, on the sun, or on a planet other than Earth.

Engineering Connection

Nano-measurements High-quality images of "unseeable" objects can be produced using specialized microscopes that can view and measure objects as small as atoms. The image of zinc oxide nanowires was produced using a scanning electron microscope (SEM). This microscope moves an electron beam across a surface to obtain information about the structure of the material. The nanowires in Figure 1 have a diameter of only a few nanometers. A nanometer is 10^{-9} meters or about 1/100 000th the width of a strand of human hair!

> Produce a media presentation, such as a video, a flipbook, or a song, that explains different types of nano-measurements and shows example images. Include in your presentation descriptions of chemistry applications that use the different scales of measurements.

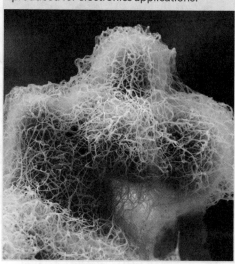

FIGURE 1: These zinc oxide nanowires are produced for electronics applications.

Life Science Connection

Trophic Levels All living things in an ecological system are part of a food web. Producers introduce energy from nonliving sources into the ecosystem. Energy is then transferred to other organisms as consumers eat the producers, and as consumers eat other consumers. The stages of energy transfer are known as *trophic levels*. As little as 10% of an organism's energy may be transferred between levels. The rest of the energy is lost to the environment. Energy and matter are conserved in the Earth system overall.

> Produce an infographic describing a food web in your community. Identify organisms in the food web and what trophic level they occupy. Explain which organisms are key to supporting the energy transfer in the food web. Include images and diagrams in your infographic.

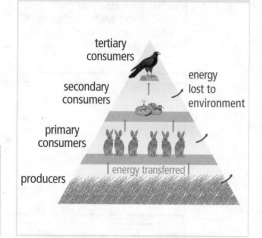

FIGURE 2: A food pyramid models the transfer of energy within an ecosystem.

tertiary consumers

secondary consumers

energy lost to environment

primary consumers

producers

energy transferred

Literature Connection

Drought in California In many ways, the story of California is the story of water. Many stories have been written about droughts in California and people's efforts to maintain their lives and work during them. Novels such as *The Grapes of Wrath*, by John Steinbeck, tell vivid stories of these hardships. Some recent novels even speculate into what the future may be if droughts continue to occur.

> Consider how the variability in water supply has affected the lives of people in the past and in current times. Write a report or make a multimedia presentation about literature that has described the effects of drought on the people of California.

FIGURE 3: Water is an important part of the chemistry of living things. Drought can change the land and the organisms, including humans, who depend on it.

A BOOK EXPLAINING
COMPLEX IDEAS USING
ONLY THE 1,000 MOST
COMMON WORDS

HOW TO COUNT THINGS

A counting system to help people agree with each other

You've learned that scientists all over the world have agreed on a single measurement system called SI. Here's a look at how we use SI to measure the length, velocity, temperature, and mass of things in our world.

RANDALL MUNROE
XKCD.COM

THE STORY OF COUNTING HOW LONG, WARM, FAST, AND HEAVY

TO COUNT HOW HEAVY THINGS ARE, WE PICK A WEIGHT TO CALL "ONE." THEN, IF YOU SAY A WEIGHT IS "TEN," PEOPLE UNDERSTAND IT'S AS HEAVY AS TEN "ONES."

I THINK I LOST THREE ONES.

DO YOU FEEL THINNER?

WE DO THE SAME FOR COUNTING OTHER THINGS, LIKE HOW FAST OR HOT THINGS ARE.

I'M 37. YOU?

YOU DON'T WANT TO KNOW . . .

PEOPLE DON'T ALWAYS AGREE ON HOW MUCH "ONE" IS, WHICH CAN CAUSE A LOT OF PROBLEMS. A SPACE BOAT ONCE MISSED A WORLD BECAUSE PEOPLE GOT CONFUSED ABOUT WHICH "ONE" THEY SHOULD BE USING FOR WEIGHT.

SPACE OFFICE

I THINK IT'S TOO CLOSE!

MOST COUNTRIES HAVE AGREED TO MAKE "ONE" THE SAME THING EVERYWHERE. HERE'S WHAT NUMBERS FROM ONE TO TEN HUNDRED MEAN IN THAT COUNTING SYSTEM.

I WANT ONE!

ME TOO!

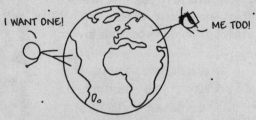

HOW LONG THINGS ARE

In this system, "one" is about half as tall as a tall person.

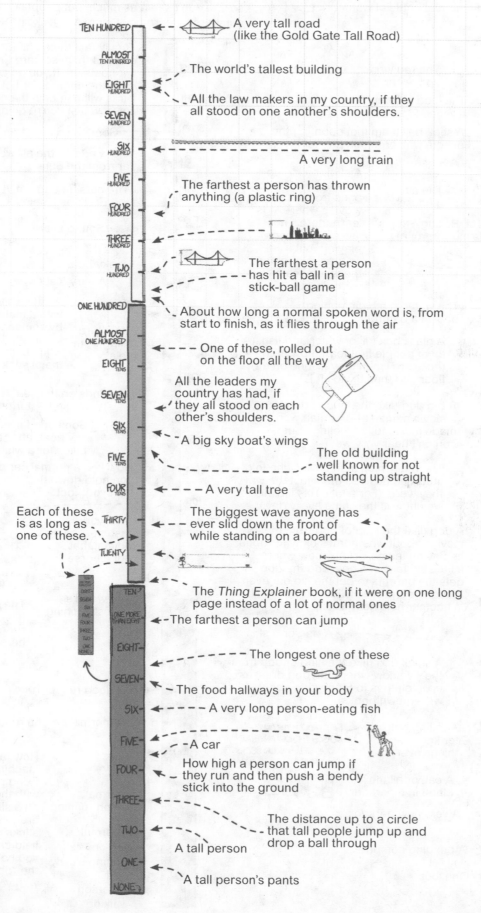

TEN HUNDRED — A very tall road
(like the Gold Gate Tall Road)

ALMOST TEN HUNDRED

EIGHT HUNDRED — The world's tallest building

— All the law makers in my country, if they all stood on one another's shoulders.

SEVEN HUNDRED

SIX HUNDRED — A very long train

FIVE HUNDRED

FOUR HUNDRED — The farthest a person has thrown anything (a plastic ring)

THREE HUNDRED

TWO HUNDRED — The farthest a person has hit a ball in a stick-ball game

ONE HUNDRED — About how long a normal spoken word is, from start to finish, as it flies through the air

ALMOST ONE HUNDRED — One of these, rolled out on the floor all the way

EIGHT TENS

SEVEN TENS — All the leaders my country has had, if they all stood on each other's shoulders.

SIX TENS — A big sky boat's wings

FIVE TENS — The old building well known for not standing up straight

FOUR TENS — A very tall tree

Each of these is as long as one of these.

THIRTY — The biggest wave anyone has ever slid down the front of while standing on a board

TWENTY

TEN — The *Thing Explainer* book, if it were on one long page instead of a lot of normal ones

ONE MORE THAN EIGHT — The farthest a person can jump

EIGHT — The longest one of these

SEVEN — The food hallways in your body

SIX — A very long person-eating fish

FIVE — A car

FOUR — How high a person can jump if they run and then push a bendy stick into the ground

THREE — The distance up to a circle that tall people jump up and drop a ball through

TWO — A tall person

ONE — A tall person's pants

NONE

HOW HEAVY THINGS ARE

In this system, "one" means the weight of a large bottle of water. (In other systems, "one" is the weight of a normal bottle of water.)

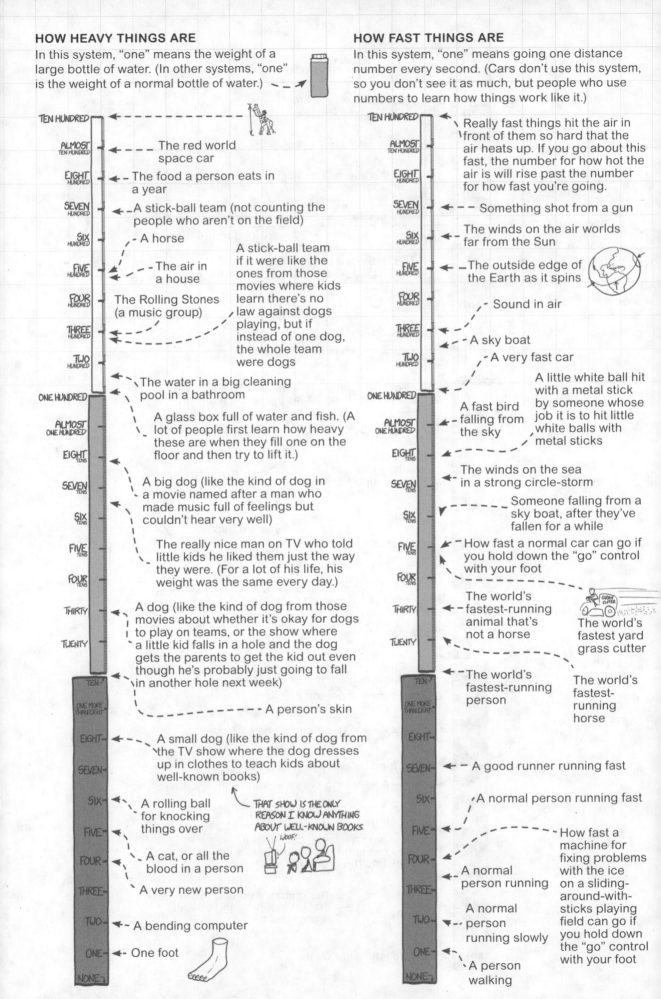

TEN HUNDRED

ALMOST TEN HUNDRED — The red world space car

EIGHT HUNDRED — The food a person eats in a year

SEVEN HUNDRED — A stick-ball team (not counting the people who aren't on the field)

SIX HUNDRED — A horse

FIVE HUNDRED — The air in a house

A stick-ball team if it were like the ones from those movies where kids learn there's no law against dogs playing, but if instead of one dog, the whole team were dogs

FOUR HUNDRED — The Rolling Stones (a music group)

THREE HUNDRED

TWO HUNDRED

ONE HUNDRED — The water in a big cleaning pool in a bathroom

A glass box full of water and fish. (A lot of people first learn how heavy these are when they fill one on the floor and then try to lift it.)

ALMOST ONE HUNDRED

EIGHT TENS

SEVEN TENS — A big dog (like the kind of dog in a movie named after a man who made music full of feelings but couldn't hear very well)

SIX TENS

FIVE TENS — The really nice man on TV who told little kids he liked them just the way they were. (For a lot of his life, his weight was the same every day.)

FOUR TENS

THIRTY — A dog (like the kind of dog from those movies about whether it's okay for dogs to play on teams, or the show where a little kid falls in a hole and the dog gets the parents to get the kid out even though he's probably just going to fall in another hole next week)

TWENTY

TEN

ONE MORE THAN EIGHT — A person's skin

EIGHT — A small dog (like the kind of dog from the TV show where the dog dresses up in clothes to teach kids about well-known books)

SEVEN

SIX — A rolling ball for knocking things over

THAT SHOW IS THE ONLY REASON I KNOW ANYTHING ABOUT WELL-KNOWN BOOKS

WOOF!

FIVE

FOUR — A cat, or all the blood in a person

THREE — A very new person

TWO — A bending computer

ONE — One foot

NONE

HOW FAST THINGS ARE

In this system, "one" means going one distance number every second. (Cars don't use this system, so you don't see it as much, but people who use numbers to learn how things work like it.)

TEN HUNDRED — Really fast things hit the air in front of them so hard that the air heats up. If you go about this fast, the number for how hot the air is will rise past the number for how fast you're going.

ALMOST TEN HUNDRED

EIGHT HUNDRED

SEVEN HUNDRED — Something shot from a gun

SIX HUNDRED — The winds on the air worlds far from the Sun

FIVE HUNDRED — The outside edge of the Earth as it spins

FOUR HUNDRED — Sound in air

THREE HUNDRED — A sky boat

A very fast car

TWO HUNDRED

A little white ball hit with a metal stick by someone whose job it is to hit little white balls with metal sticks

ONE HUNDRED

ALMOST ONE HUNDRED — A fast bird falling from the sky

EIGHT TENS

SEVEN TENS — The winds on the sea in a strong circle-storm

SIX TENS — Someone falling from a sky boat, after they've fallen for a while

FIVE TENS — How fast a normal car can go if you hold down the "go" control with your foot

FOUR TENS

THIRTY — The world's fastest-running animal that's not a horse

The world's fastest yard grass cutter

TWENTY

TEN — The world's fastest-running person

The world's fastest-running horse

EIGHT

SEVEN — A good runner running fast

SIX — A normal person running fast

FIVE — How fast a machine for fixing problems with the ice on a sliding-around-with-sticks playing field can go if you hold down the "go" control with your foot

FOUR — A normal person running

THREE

TWO — A normal person running slowly

ONE — A person walking

NONE

HOW WARM THINGS ARE

In this system, "none" means how cold water has to be to turn to ice, and "one hundred" means how hot it has to be to turn to air.

▶ Go online for more about *Thing Explainer*.

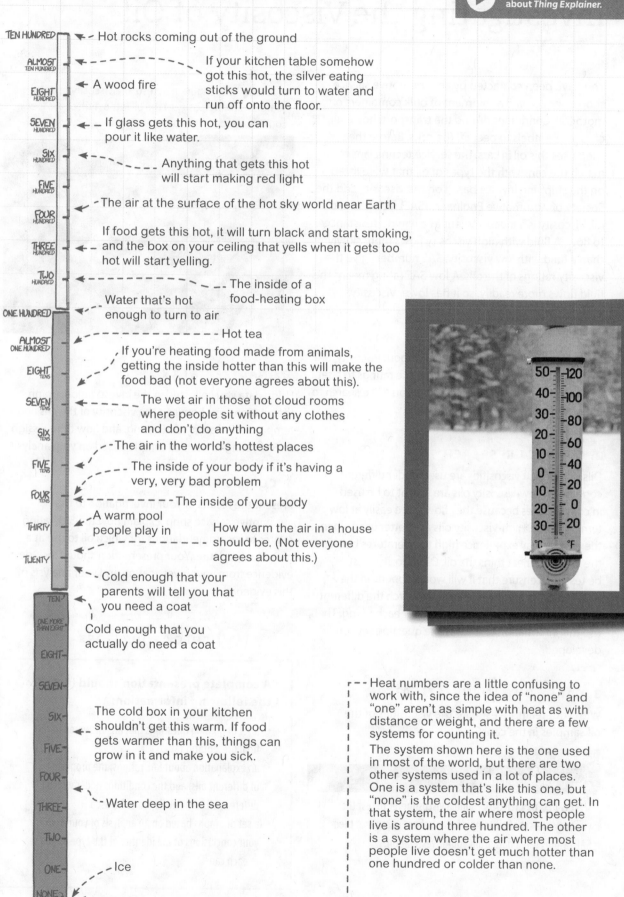

TEN HUNDRED — Hot rocks coming out of the ground

ALMOST TEN HUNDRED — If your kitchen table somehow got this hot, the silver eating sticks would turn to water and run off onto the floor.

EIGHT HUNDRED — A wood fire

SEVEN HUNDRED — If glass gets this hot, you can pour it like water.

SIX HUNDRED — Anything that gets this hot will start making red light

FIVE HUNDRED

FOUR HUNDRED — The air at the surface of the hot sky world near Earth

THREE HUNDRED — If food gets this hot, it will turn black and start smoking, and the box on your ceiling that yells when it gets too hot will start yelling.

TWO HUNDRED — The inside of a food-heating box

ONE HUNDRED — Water that's hot enough to turn to air

ALMOST ONE HUNDRED — Hot tea

If you're heating food made from animals, getting the inside hotter than this will make the food bad (not everyone agrees about this).

EIGHT TENS — The wet air in those hot cloud rooms where people sit without any clothes and don't do anything

SEVEN TENS

SIX TENS — The air in the world's hottest places

FIVE TENS — The inside of your body if it's having a very, very bad problem

FOUR TENS — The inside of your body

THIRTY — A warm pool people play in

How warm the air in a house should be. (Not everyone agrees about this.)

TWENTY — Cold enough that your parents will tell you that you need a coat

TEN

ONE MORE THAN EIGHT — Cold enough that you actually do need a coat

EIGHT

SEVEN

SIX — The cold box in your kitchen shouldn't get this warm. If food gets warmer than this, things can grow in it and make you sick.

FIVE

FOUR

THREE — Water deep in the sea

TWO

ONE — Ice

NONE

Heat numbers are a little confusing to work with, since the idea of "none" and "one" aren't as simple with heat as with distance or weight, and there are a few systems for counting it.

The system shown here is the one used in most of the world, but there are two other systems used in a lot of places. One is a system that's like this one, but "none" is the coldest anything can get. In that system, the air where most people live is around three hundred. The other is a system where the air where most people live doesn't get much hotter than one hundred or colder than none.

Investigating the Viscosity of Oil

You have been contacted by an automotive service shop that received a shipment of bulk containers of motor oil. Conditions during the transport, however, caused the labels to peel off the cans. Before the shop uses this oil in cars, the service technicians must match the cans with the types of oil that were listed on the shipping invoice based on the viscosity and the Society of Automotive Engineers (SAE) rating of each oil. Viscosity is a measurement of a liquid's resistance to flow. A fluid with high viscosity flows more slowly than a fluid with low viscosity. SAE numbers give the viscosity ratings of the oils. A low SAE rating means the fluid flows more readily, so it has lower viscosity.

FIGURE 4: This engineman tests the viscosity of an oil sample. If the viscosity of the oil is too high or too low, it could cause damage to the engine.

1. ASK QUESTIONS

Develop a set of questions you have about viscosity, SAE ratings, and how you could assign these ratings to a set of oil samples. Identify all the factors you will research to answer these questions.

2. CONDUCT RESEARCH

Oils of different viscosities are used under different conditions. Low-viscosity oils are meant to be used in cold climates because they flow more easily at low temperatures. High-viscosity oils are better used when the engine may experience high temperatures because the excessive heat thins the oil. Oil viscosity must be tested to ensure that it will work properly in the conditions the engine must run. Research the different SAE oil ratings and examples of oils for each rating. Then, use this information to answer the question set you developed.

3. CARRY OUT AN INVESTIGATION

With your team, investigate the viscosities of the oil samples in the cans.

Explore Online ▶

🧪 Hands-On Lab

Viscosity of Liquids Build a viscosimeter to test the viscosity of a set of oil samples. Rank them in order of their SAE ratings using data from your investigation.

4. ANALYZE DATA

Using data you collected in the investigation, graph the relationships between the viscosity of the oils and temperature, density, SAE rating, and flow time. Assign an SAE rating to each oil sample based on your analysis.

5. COMMUNICATE

Present the results of your investigation to the automotive service shop. Explain how the SAE rating relates to recommendations for which oil to use at a given temperature. Your presentation should include evidence from your investigation and your analysis of this evidence.

✓ CHECK YOUR WORK

A complete presentation should include the following information:

- a set of guiding questions that are answered in the final presentation
- an explanation about SAE ratings, the properties of different oils, and the conditions under which different oils are developed to be used
- a set of graphs based on an analysis of your data
- your conclusions of the identity of the type of oil in each can

Name _____   Date _____

SYNTHESIZE THE UNIT

In your Evidence Notebook, make a concept map, other graphic organizer, or outline using the Study Guides you made for each lesson in this unit. Be sure to use evidence to support your claims.

When synthesizing individual information, remember to follow these general steps:
- Find the central idea of each piece of information.
- Think about the relationships among the central ideas.
- Combine the ideas to come up with a new understanding.

DRIVING QUESTIONS

Look back to the Driving Questions from the opening section of this unit. In your Evidence Notebook, review and revise your previous answers to those questions. Use the evidence you gathered and other observations you made throughout the unit to support your claims.

PRACTICE AND REVIEW

1. Which of the following are chemical changes? Select all correct answers.
   ☐ **a.** table salt dissolving in water
   ☐ **b.** a liquid evaporating to form a gas
   ☐ **c.** a force causing a sheet of metal to bend
   ☐ **d.** wooden logs burning to form ash
   ☐ **e.** hydrogen and oxygen forming water

2. Complete the statement.

   An example of a pure substance is carbon dioxide | salt water | wood. A mixture is heterogeneous | homogeneous if it has a uniform composition. A mixture is heterogeneous | homogeneous if its composition is not uniform. A mixture | pure substance can often be separated by techniques such as evaporation or filtration.

3. A group of chemical engineers are developing a medication to treat a disease. Which statement describes a possible constraint for the medication?
   ○ **a.** The effectiveness of the medication will be tested during production.
   ○ **b.** The cost of producing the medication will be kept as low as possible.
   ○ **c.** A process for manufacturing the medication will have to be designed.
   ○ **d.** Compounds used in the medication should be easy to obtain or produce.

4. Complete the statement.

   The density of a liquid substance in a container is an intensive | extensive physical property of the substance, so it can be used to help identify it. The volume of the substance is an intensive | extensive property, so it cannot be used in identification because it changes | does not change with the amount of the substance present.

5. An engineer is developing a process to separate a pure substance from a chemical reaction mixture. Which of the following would be considered a constraint on the engineering design process for the separation technique?
   ○ **a.** The final product must have a 99% purity.
   ○ **b.** The budget for the process is $100 000.
   ○ **c.** The separated product will be transferred into 50 kg containers.
   ○ **d.** The remaining contents of the reaction mixture will be recycled.

6. A student determines the density of a substance as 1.536 g/mL. The accepted value of the density is 1.446 g/mL. What is the percentage error in the student's value? Choose the correct answer.

0.9414	1.062	6.224

   _____ %

7. A hot metal block is placed into a beaker of cold water. Explain what happens to the thermal energy of the system.

_____

_____

_____

_____

_____

_____

8. What is scientific notation, and why it is useful for reporting scientific measurements?

_____

_____

_____

_____

_____

_____

_____

9. A block of ice is placed outside on a hot summer day. Describe the changes in particle motion and the corresponding changes in energy as the ice melts and eventually becomes water vapor.

_____

_____

_____

_____

_____

_____

UNIT PROJECT

Return to your unit project. Prepare your research and materials into a presentation to share with the class. In your final presentation, evaluate the strength of your claim, evidence, and conclusions.

Remember these tips while evaluating:

- Was your claim supported by your evidence?
- What are some criteria and constraints of your toothpaste design?

- Look at the evidence gathered from your experiment. Does your evidence support your claim and reasoning regarding which ingredients make a better whitener?
- How could you revise your setup and procedure to further test your prediction, model, or the evidence you collected?

Heat and Energy in the Earth System

A volcanic eruption on Atlasov Island, Russia transfers
large amounts of matter and heat to the atmosphere.

The spread of the California condor's enormous wings enables it to soar almost effortlessly through the air. Whereas birds often flap their wings to stay aloft, once the condor is in flight, its wings hardly move at all. The condor is a glider that uses the upward force of rising currents of warm air called thermals. Riding the thermals enables the condor to move higher and use less energy in its flight.

PREDICT How do you think changes in temperature can cause movement of air and other fluids on Earth?

_____

_____

_____

DRIVING QUESTIONS

As you move through the unit, gather evidence to help you answer the following questions. In your Evidence Notebook, record what you already know about these topics and any questions you have about them.

1. How is the stability of a gaseous system affected by changes in the system?
2. How is energy transferred within and between systems?
3. How do energy and matter cycle in Earth's interior?

UNIT PROJECT

Go online to download the Unit Project Worksheet to help plan your project.

Controlling Energy Transfer

Build a device that will minimize energy transfer. Your device can be a prototype of a small system, or it can be a model of a system that is too large or complex to build as a prototype. Use the engineering design process to improve the device. Prepare a report that describes your design process.

Language Development

Use the lessons in this unit to complete the chart and expand your understanding of the science concepts.

TERM: kinetic-molecular theory

Definition	Example

Similar Term	Phrase

TERM: internal energy

Definition	Example

Similar Term	Phrase

TERM: law of conservation of energy

Definition	Example

Similar Term	Phrase

TERM: specific heat capacity

Definition	Example

Similar Term	Phrase

TERM: entropy

Definition	Example

Similar Term	Phrase

TERM: work

Definition	Example

Similar Term	Phrase

TERM: P-wave

Definition	Example

Similar Term	Phrase

TERM: S-wave

Definition	Example

Similar Term	Phrase

Thermal Energy and the Behavior of Matter

These snorkelers are investigating an iceberg in Greenland.

CAN YOU EXPLAIN IT?

Water exists all over Earth—from oceans to snow-covered mountains, from rivers and lakes to creeks. Although you probably already appreciate the necessity of water for life, you may not be fully aware how large an impact water has on the way that thermal energy is distributed on Earth. Much of Earth's surface is covered in liquid water. This water evaporates to become a gas (water vapor) in the atmosphere. The water in the atmosphere eventually condenses and falls as precipitation. Depending on weather conditions, that precipitation may be either liquid or solid. Snow is a solid form of water that, when it falls, may cover the ground. It may then melt, and the runoff rejoins the liquid bodies of water. Thermal energy has a role in all of these processes.

INFER How is it possible that water can exist in three different states of matter in the same area? How might this be significant for the distribution of thermal energy on Earth?

_____

_____

_____

_____

 Evidence Notebook As you explore the lesson, gather evidence to explain how thermal energy is transferred between substances and how that energy affects each substance.

Systems and Thermal Energy

Energy can be transformed between many forms and to and from systems. Defining systems and analyzing how energy flows in these systems is important for both scientists and engineers. Thermodynamics is the relationship between heat and other forms of energy and the ways energy can be transferred and transformed.

Thermodynamic Systems

FIGURE 1: A hot air balloon burns fuel to heat air in the balloon causing the balloon to float.

Scientists and engineers define systems to help analyze situations and solve problems. A *system* is the portion of the universe they are studying. Everything within the system's boundaries is part of that system, and everything outside of the boundaries is part of the system's surroundings, or its environment. In a closed or isolated system, the system boundaries usually correspond to physical boundaries, such as the glass walls of a beaker. In a closed system, energy may cross the system boundaries, but matter does not. In an isolated system, neither matter nor energy flows into or out of the system. In an open system, both energy and matter can flow into and out of the system through its boundaries. The boundaries of an open system may or may not have a corresponding physical boundary.

ANALYZE A hot air balloon is an example of what type of system?

○ **a.** An open system, because both matter and energy can cross the system boundaries.

○ **b.** A closed system, because energy can cross the system boundaries, but matter cannot.

○ **c.** An isolated system, because neither matter nor energy can cross the system boundaries.

MODEL Draw a sketch of a hot air balloon as a system. Define the system by identifying the system boundaries. Show where matter or energy may cross the system boundaries, if applicable.

Thermal Energy

Temperature is a measure of the average kinetic energy of the particles of a substance. So, the particles in an object with a higher temperature, on average, move faster than the particles in an object made of the same type of matter at a lower temperature. This motion is internal to the system, so this is considered internal energy. Thermal energy is a form of internal energy.

Imagine that two cannonballs are dropped from a tall tower. The cannonballs are made of the same material and have the same mass. One of these cannonballs, however, has been warmed in a fire to a higher temperature than the other. Do both of these cannonballs have the same amount of total energy? Because the cannonballs have the same mass and height above the ground, they have the same amount of gravitational potential energy. Both cannonballs also fall at the same rate, so they have equal amounts of kinetic energy.

PREDICT Do you think warming a cannonball in a fire has any effect on the total energy of the cannonball?

_____

_____

_____

_____

 Energy and Matter

Energy of a System

The total energy of a system depends on its kinetic energy, potential energy, and internal energy. Changing the mass or speed of the system as a whole will change its kinetic energy. Changing certain properties of the system, such as mass or charge, or moving the system in a field may change its potential energy. The internal energy of a system may be changed by adding or removing energy.

EXPLAIN What is one way that the thermal energy of a system can be changed?

_____

_____

_____

_____

_____

FIGURE 2: A thermometer measures the temperature of water.

 Evidence Notebook What type of system is planet Earth? Is the thermal energy within the Earth system distributed evenly? In what type of system are the snorkelers from the beginning of this lesson? Support your claims with evidence and reasoning from the text.

Exploring the Properties of Gases

The state of a gaseous system can be determined by knowing the volume, pressure, temperature, and amount or number of particles of gas in the system. These are all measurable variables, and, for a gaseous system, these variables relate to one another.

Volume

The volume of a gas is the amount of physical space occupied by a gas. Recall that gases will fill any container they occupy. This makes it sometimes easy and sometimes challenging to measure the volume of a gas. One reason for this is that the volume of a certain amount of gas changes when the temperature and pressure change.

The SI unit of volume is cubic meters, m^3. One cubic meter is equal to the volume of a cube whose edges are 1 meter long. This large unit, however, is difficult to use in a chemistry laboratory. A smaller unit, the cubic centimeter, cm^3, therefore, is often used instead. There are 100 centimeters in a meter, so a cubic meter contains $1\,000\,000$ cm^3. Chemists also use liters (L) and milliliters (mL) to measure volume. One liter is equal to 1000 cubic centimeters, so 1 mL is equal to 1 cm^3.

Pressure

A gas consists of many small particles moving very quickly in random directions. When these particles collide with surfaces surrounding the gas, they exert a force on the surface. Many collisions occur on a surface simultaneously, distributing these forces over an area, and creating what is known as pressure. If the pressures on either side of a flexible surface are different, the surface will be forced to move toward the lower pressure side. The force of the impacts "pushes" it there. Many factors affect the pressure exerted by a gas.

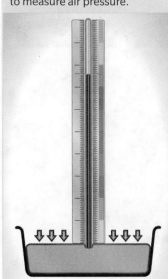

FIGURE 3: Barometers are used to measure air pressure.

PREDICT Select the correct terms to complete the statement.

Particles with more kinetic energy collide with surfaces with a weaker | greater force, which will increase | decrease the pressure of the system. The pressure in a vacuum is zero | infinite because there are no particles in a vacuum.

Different applications commonly use certain units to measure pressure. For example, weather reports often give the pressure of the atmosphere, barometric pressure, in inches of mercury (inHg). Weather fronts move from areas of high pressure to areas of low pressure, so tracking the pressure in an area can help predict the weather in that area. The barometer is the device used to measure atmospheric pressure. Early barometers consisted of an inverted vacuum tube in a pool of liquid mercury, shown in Figure 3. Air pressure pushes on the mercury and forces it up the tube. The height of the column of mercury will vary with the pressure of the air.

The SI unit of pressure is pascals (Pa) which is 1 N/m^2. Other measurements of pressure include pounds per square inch (psi) and standard atmosphere (atm). One atmosphere is equal to the average atmospheric pressure at sea level.

Temperature

As discussed earlier, temperature is a measure of the average kinetic energy of the particles of a substance. Temperature is a property of all states of matter, not only gases. When two systems have different temperatures, thermal energy will transfer between the two systems. If two systems have the same temperature, they are in *thermal equilibrium*, and no energy transfer occurs.

We can extend this observation to say that if two bodies are in thermal equilibrium with a third body, then they are in thermal equilibrium with each other. So, if the systems are in thermal equilibrium with one another, no net transfer of energy will occur. This principle is known as the *zeroth law of thermodynamics*. Using the zeroth law of thermodynamics, we can measure temperature and use it to define the state of a system.

EXPLAIN Complete the statements about cooking with a pressure cooker by selecting the correct terms.

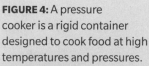

increases   decreases   stays the same

The flame from the stove _____ the thermal energy

of the pressure cooker system, which _____ the

temperature.

The volume of the system _____ .

The pressure of the system _____ .

FIGURE 4: A pressure cooker is a rigid container designed to cook food at high temperatures and pressures.

You may have noticed that cooking instructions for some foods might include different instructions for people living at higher altitudes. At higher altitudes, the air pressure is lower than at lower altitudes. Often, foods need to cook for longer time periods at these high altitudes.

 Engineering

Temperature Scales

As with pressure and volume, there are several different temperature scales. You are probably familiar with the Celsius and Fahrenheit scales. The Fahrenheit scale was one of the earliest widely adopted temperature scales, and it is still commonly used in the United States. In the Fahrenheit scale, water freezes at 32 °F and boils at 212 °F. In the Celsius scale, which is more commonly used worldwide, water freezes at 0 °C and boils at 100 °C. Both of these temperature scales include negative temperatures.

The Kelvin temperature scale has its zero point at *absolute zero*, a temperature at which all particle motion theoretically stops. So for thermodynamic applications, a Kelvin temperature will never be negative. Temperatures on the Kelvin scale, therefore, are not measured using degrees, as it is not a measure between two chosen points. To compare the Kelvin and Celsius scales, 0 °C = 273.15 K.

 Language Arts Connection Each temperature scale has advantages and disadvantages depending on what is being measured. Research experiments where engineers used each of the scales. Explain why that scale was most appropriate to their work.

Hands-On Lab

Investigating Properties of Gases

In this lab, you will investigate the relationships between pressure and volume, pressure and temperature, and volume and temperature in different gaseous systems.

Research Question: How do engineers use these relationships to their advantage when running and optimizing chemical reactions?

MATERIALS

- indirectly vented chemical splash goggles, nonlatex apron
- bottle, thin with small opening
- coin (dime or quarter)
- ice-water bath
- marshmallow, miniature
- paper towels
- syringe, 60 mL (2)
- syringe cap or valve
- thermometer
- warm-water bath

SAFETY INFORMATION

indirectly vented chemical splash goggles

- Wear indirectly vented chemical splash goggles and a nonlatex apron during the setup, hands-on, and takedown segments of the activity.

- Immediately wipe up any spilled water on the floor so it does not become a slip/fall hazard.

Investigate Volume and Pressure

MAKE A CLAIM

In your Evidence Notebook, make a claim about what you think will happen to the marshmallow in the syringe when the pressure in the syringe decreases, but the temperature and amount of gas are held constant.

PLAN THE INVESTIGATION

Using a syringe and marshmallow, develop a safe procedure to determine the relationship between pressure and volume. A marshmallow has air trapped inside it, so it will expand or compress depending on the change in pressure outside of the marshmallow. Before you begin your experiment, have your teacher approve your procedure and safety plan.

COLLECT DATA

Develop a data collection plan in your Evidence Notebook. Identify what variables you are testing in this experiment and what is being held constant. How will you measure the change in the pressure and volume of the system?

ANALYZE

1. Complete the statement using evidence from this investigation.

   When the volume of air in the syringe increased, the pressure on the outside of the

   marshmallow decreased | increased | stayed the same, causing the marshmallow

   to expand.

2. Based on your observations, draw a graph showing how the volume and pressure of a gas are related. Be sure to label all axes of your graph.

Investigate Volume and Temperature

MAKE A CLAIM

In your Evidence Notebook, make a claim about what you think will happen to the volume of air in the syringe when the temperature of the air in the syringe decreases, but the pressure and amount of gas are held constant.

PLAN THE INVESTIGATION

Using a syringe, an ice-water bath, and a warm-water bath, develop a safe procedure to determine the relationship between volume and temperature. Before you begin your experiment, have your teacher approve your procedure and safety plan.

COLLECT DATA

Develop a data collection plan in your Evidence Notebook. Identify what variables you are testing in this experiment and what is being held constant. How will you measure the change in the volume and temperature of air in the syringe?

ANALYZE

1. Complete the statement using evidence from the investigations.

As the temperature of the air in the syringe increased, the volume

decreased | increased | stayed the same.

2. Based on your observations, draw a graph showing how the temperature and volume of a gas are related. Be sure to label all axes of your graph.

Investigate Pressure and Temperature

MAKE A CLAIM

In your Evidence Notebook, make a claim about what you think will happen to the pressure in a bottle when the temperature of the air in the bottle increases, but the volume and amount of gas are held constant.

PLAN THE INVESTIGATION

Using a bottle, an ice-water bath, and a coin, such as a dime or a quarter, develop a safe procedure to determine the relationship between pressure and temperature. Before you begin your experiment, have your teacher approve your procedure and safety plan.

COLLECT DATA

Develop a data collection plan in your Evidence Notebook. Identify what variables you are testing in this experiment and what is being held constant. How will you measure the change in the air pressure and temperature in the bottle?

ANALYZE

1. Complete the statement using evidence from the investigations.

   As the temperature of air in the bottle increased, the pressure

   decreased | increased | stayed the same.

2. Based on your observations, draw a graph showing how the pressure and temperature of a gas are related. Be sure to label all axes of your graph.

EXTEND

Based on your experiments, what do you think would happen to the volume of a gas if the pressure and temperature both increased?

 Evidence Notebook Snorkelers or divers who swim in very cold waters, such as the waters surrounding an iceberg, often wear dry suits. These suits trap a layer of air between the diver's body and the suit, keeping the diver warm in cold waters. If the diver emerges into air that is colder than the water he or she was in, the volume of the air may decrease making the suit uncomfortably tight. Using what you discovered in your investigations, explain this phenomenon.

Describing the Behavior of Gases

There are large numbers of particles in any volume of gas. To make it easier for scientists to compare the number of particles in different substances, they specify the amount of a substance using a unit called a *mole*. A mole (mol) of a substance has 6.022×10^{23} particles. By convention, gases are analyzed at 1 atm of pressure and 273.15 K. This temperature and pressure together are known as *standard temperature and pressure* (STP).

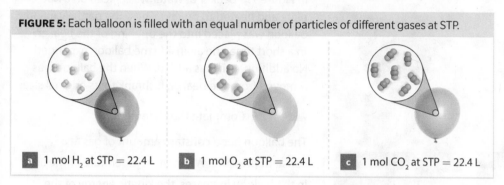

FIGURE 5: Each balloon is filled with an equal number of particles of different gases at STP.

a 1 mol H_2 at STP = 22.4 L   b 1 mol O_2 at STP = 22.4 L   c 1 mol CO_2 at STP = 22.4 L

EXPLAIN All three balloons have the same volume even though the gases contained in the balloons are different. Explain why you think this is possible.

_____

_____

_____

Observing Changes in Gases

Explore Online ▶

Tiny pockets of air are trapped inside the foam-like structure of shaving cream. In the experiment shown in Figure 6, a beaker filled with shaving cream was placed in a sealed bell jar. When the pressure inside the bell jar was decreased, the shaving cream expanded. When the contents of the bell jar returned to the original pressure, the shaving cream collapsed. The temperature and amount of air contained in the shaving cream did not change.

FIGURE 6: When pressure is decreased, the volume of the air bubbles in shaving cream expands.

a Initial pressure   b Decreased pressure

ANALYZE Complete the statement.

Initially, the pressure on the outside of the shaving cream is equal to | different from the pressure on the inside of the shaving cream. When the air pressure in the bell jar decreases, the air particles in the shaving cream continue to push outward with the same force. Because there is less pressure pushing on the outside of the shaving cream, the volume of the shaving cream decreases | increases | stays the same.

When temperature is held constant, the relationship between volume and pressure, demonstrated in the shaving cream experiment, has many important applications. For example, have you ever had your ears "pop" while on a plane or when driving through the mountains? That uncomfortable feeling you experience is due to changes in pressure. Your inner ear contains air, but it is closed off from the outside by the ear drum. As the atmospheric pressure decreases at higher altitudes, the air in your inner ear expands. "Popping" your ears allows the air to return to the same pressure as the atmosphere.

Explore Online ▶

FIGURE 7: When a partially inflated balloon is placed above a beaker of boiling water, the balloon expands.

| a | Initial temperature | b | Increased temperature |

A partially inflated balloon can be used to demonstrate how a gas behaves when temperature is increased and pressure is held constant. During the demonstration in Figure 7, a beaker of water was placed on a hot plate and heated to boiling. Then, the partially inflated balloon was placed into the opening of the beaker. In a short time, the air inside the balloon expanded. No additional air was added. When the balloon was removed from the beaker, it shrank to its original size.

ANALYZE Complete the statement.

The balloon has a constant amount of gas at a constant pressure. When the temperature of the air in the balloon increases, the kinetic energy of the particles in the balloon increases | decreases. The particles collide with each other and the sides of the balloon more | less often, increasing | decreasing the volume of the balloon.

This relationship between volume and temperature explains how a hot air balloon floats. A torch is used to heat the air in the balloon, causing the air in the balloon to be less dense than the air outside the balloon, allowing the balloon to float. This principle is observable on smaller scales, too. For example, you may have noticed that a soccer ball will deflate in cold weather but expand in warmer weather.

Explore Online ▶

FIGURE 8: This can imploded when the temperature of the gas in the can decreased.

| a | Initial temperature | b | Decreased temperature |

A small amount of water was placed inside the open can in Figure 8. The can was then warmed by a flame. When the water began to boil and turn into water vapor, the can was sealed. The sealed can filled with water vapor was then allowed to cool. As the temperature inside decreased, it eventually imploded.

EXPLAIN Describe what happens to the pressure in the open can as it is warmed and then when the can is sealed and allowed to cool.

_____

_____

Have you ever seen a label on an aerosol can saying not to expose to heat? This warning is due to the relationship between temperature and pressure. If the temperature of the sealed can increases, the pressure inside the can could increase so much that it explodes.

APPLY The relationships between volume (*V*), pressure (*P*), and temperature (*T*) can be modeled with graphs or mathematical equations when including a proportionality constant, *k*. Match each graph to the equation that describes the relationship.

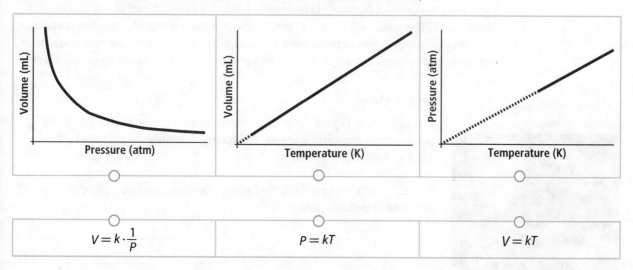

$$V = k \cdot \frac{1}{P}$$

$$P = kT$$

$$V = kT$$

Pressure, Volume, and the Amount of Gas in a System

You have explored how pressure, temperature, and volume of a gas are related given a constant amount of gas. What do you think happens to pressure and volume when the amount of gas in a system changes?

FIGURE 9: Molecules are added to a system held at a constant temperature.

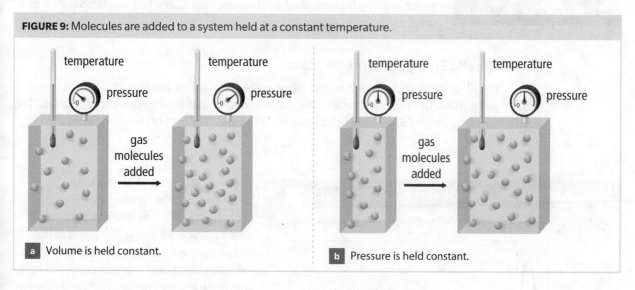

a Volume is held constant.

b Pressure is held constant.

ANALYZE Use the diagrams shown in Figure 9 to complete the statements.

decreases   increases

When the temperature and volume of a gas are held constant and the amount of gas increases, the pressure in the system _____.

When the temperature and pressure of a gas are held constant and the amount of gas increases, the volume in the system _____.

Avogadro's law states that equal volumes of gases at the same temperature and pressure have equal numbers of particles. This relationship explains why the balloons in Figure 5 have equal volumes—they each contain the same number of particles at the same temperature and pressure. Experiments have shown that 1 mol of any gas at STP is about 22.4 L. This volume is known as the standard molar volume of a gas. The particles in a gas may be either atoms or molecules. If pressure and temperature are held constant, it follows from Avogadro's law that volume and amount of a gas are directly proportional.

Molar Mass

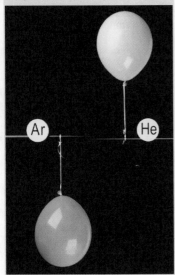

FIGURE 10: Balloons filled with argon and helium

The balloons in Figure 10 have the same number of particles of gas at the same temperature and pressure. Avogadro's law tells you that the balloons will also have equal volumes.

PREDICT Why do you think the helium-filled balloon floats, but the argon-filled balloon sinks?

_____

_____

_____

You know that the balloons have the same number of particles because of Avogadro's Law. The mass of each volume of gas, however, is different because the particles of each gas have a different mass. Molar mass is the mass of one mole of a substance. Argon and helium have different molar masses, which is why a balloon filled with helium may float while one filled with argon sinks, as shown in Figure 10.

Kinetic Energy and Molar Mass

Not all of the particles in a pure gas move at the same speed, but they do all have the same mass. The average speed of the particles determines the temperature of the gas. The kinetic energy of a gas depends on the mass (m) and speed (v) of the particles:

$$KE = \frac{1}{2}mv^2$$

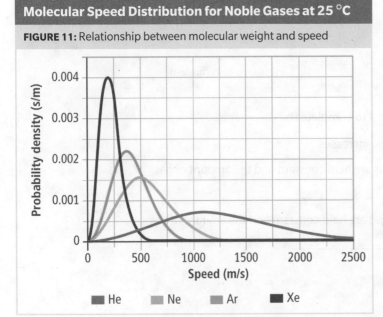

Molecular Speed Distribution for Noble Gases at 25 °C

FIGURE 11: Relationship between molecular weight and speed

ANALYZE Figure 11 shows the relationship between the speeds of particles of different gases at the same temperature. Knowing that gases at the same temperature have the same average kinetic energy and the relationship between kinetic energy, mass, and velocity, what conclusions can you draw based on the data in Figure 11?

_____

_____

_____

_____

_____

_____

Kinetic-Molecular Theory

Consider some of the physical properties of gases you have observed. For one, they do not have a definite shape or volume. Each also can be greatly compressed. More importantly, for all gases, pressure, volume, and temperature are related to each other.

 Collaborate With a partner, discuss other physical properties of gases you have observed. How can the behavior of gas particles explain the macroscopic behavior of gases?

Explore Online ▶

The kinetic-molecular theory is a model that is based on five assumptions that explain the properties of an *ideal gas*. These five assumptions are

FIGURE 12: Ideal gas particles travel in a straight line until they collide with the walls of a container or other particles.

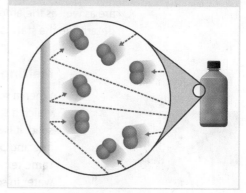

- An ideal gas is composed of constantly moving particles.
- The particles are so far apart that most of a gas is empty space.
- The particles exert negligible forces on each other.
- Collision between particles or between particles and the container wall are elastic, which means there is no loss of total kinetic energy.
- Gas temperature is directly proportional to the particles' average kinetic energy.

Real Gases vs. Ideal Gases

An ideal gas is a hypothetical gas in which the particles have no volume and no attractions for each other. Particles of real gases, of course, do have volume and attract each other. At a low pressure and high temperature, however, a real gas behaves like an ideal gas as described by the kinetic-molecular theory. The attractions between particles and particle volumes do not impact the behavior of gases as much as their kinetic energy. At high pressures and low temperatures this assumption is no longer true. At very low temperatures, the gas particles move at slower speeds and the attractive forces between them affect the motion of the particles more.

MODEL Draw a model that shows what happens to the particles in a real gas when the gas is compressed.

 Evidence Notebook Divers experience increased pressure when under water, so they need to be particularly aware of how gases behave under pressure changes. Research some of the safety considerations divers must be aware of before entering the water.

Thermal Energy and States of Matter

Adding thermal energy to, or removing thermal energy from, a system causes the matter to behave differently. The result, sometimes, can be that it changes state.

Describing Changes of State

The state of a substance is related to how densely packed the particles in that substance are as well as the amount of energy they possess. Both temperature and pressure determine the state of a substance.

FIGURE 13: Ice melting is a change of state of water.

Melting and Freezing

When a solid changes state to a liquid, it is said to melt. The temperature at which a substance melts is its melting point. When a liquid changes state to a solid, it is said to freeze. The temperature at which the substance freezes is its freezing point. At a given pressure, the melting point of a substance has the same temperature as its freezing point. Most life on Earth depends on liquid water in some way. Fortunately, Earth's average climate is ideally suited to allow water to be a liquid, and so a livable environment is maintained. Other substances, however, freeze and melt at different temperatures than water. Steel, for example, melts at a much higher temperature than water. Steel also behaves differently from water as it nears its melting point. While it may remain relatively solid compared to its liquid state, at higher temperatures steel can bend or flow slowly, much like a liquid.

EXPLAIN Select the correct terms to complete the statement.

The particles that make up a substance in its liquid state have less | more kinetic energy than those of the same substance in its solid state. For a solid to melt, energy must be added to | removed from the system. For a liquid to freeze, energy must be added to | removed from the system.

FIGURE 14: Water vapor in the air condenses on a window.

Evaporation and Condensation

Evaporation and boiling are both types of vaporization. Vaporization is the change from a liquid to a gas. Boiling occurs when liquid particles gain enough energy to enter the gas state. While boiling, bubbles of gas form and rise to the surface, but the temperature of the liquid remains constant. This temperature is called the boiling point of the liquid. Evaporation, however, is a process that occurs when particles at the surface of a liquid gain enough energy to become a gas. Evaporation can occur at temperatures below the boiling point. Condensation is the opposite of evaporation and occurs when a gas becomes a liquid.

Engineering Research how evaporative coolers, sometimes known as swamp coolers, use water to cool hot, dry air. What are the advantages of this type of air conditioning? What are the limitations of this type of air conditioning?

Sublimation and Deposition

The process in which a solid changes directly to a gas is called sublimation. The opposite process in which a gas changes directly to a solid is called deposition. Frost is an example of deposition. Water vapor in the air turns directly into ice when a surface is much colder than the air temperature. During sublimation, some particles at the surface of a solid can gain enough energy to enter the gas state without first becoming a liquid.

Explore Online ▶

Hands-On Lab

Dry Ice Sublimation
Observe sublimation of dry ice under various environmental conditions.

ANALYZE How might it be possible for a substance to go directly from a solid to a gas without being liquid in between?

_____

_____

_____

_____

Thermal Energy and Phase Changes

A heating curve shows the temperature of a substance as energy is steadily added to a system. Heating curves are specific to a particular substance at a constant pressure. Notice that the system absorbs more energy as it changes from a liquid to a gas than it does when it changes from a solid to a liquid. Recall that temperature is a measure of the average kinetic energy of the particles in a substance. Thermal energy is the total kinetic energy of the particles in a substance.

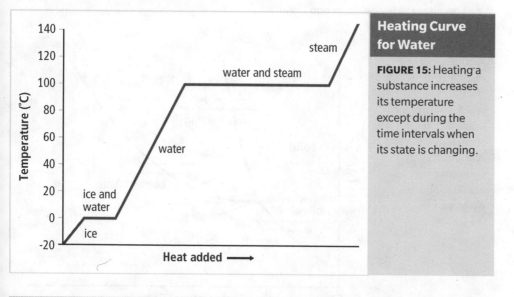

Heating Curve for Water

FIGURE 15: Heating a substance increases its temperature except during the time intervals when its state is changing.

Collaborate With a partner, discuss why you think the heating curve has plateaus instead of being a straight line. Consider what temperature represents. What do you think happens to the added energy during these plateaus?

During a phase change, the two different states coexist in an equilibrium. For example, when a substance is melting, both solid and liquid exist. As energy is added to a system, some particles will gain energy before others. This energy spreads through the system until the phase change is complete.

Consider the structures of a solid, liquid, and gas. How do the motions of particles in these substances and the attractive forces between the particles influence the behavior of each state? As energy is added to a solid and it begins to melt, its particles gain enough energy to break free of their organized structure and transition to the liquid phase. As energy is added to a liquid and it begins to boil, its particles gain enough energy to break free from their attractions in the liquid phase and transition to the gaseous phase.

During these transitions, the internal energy of the substance increases, but the average kinetic energy of randomly moving particles stays the same. Differences in the states of a substance are the result of differences in the internal energy of the substance.

APPLY During a change of state, a material may absorb or release energy instead of changing temperature. How might this characteristic of phase changes be used to solve a problem?

_____

_____

_____

_____

Phase Diagrams

A phase diagram shows the states at which a substance exists under different temperatures and pressures. Lines on the diagram indicate the boundaries between the different states. At a given temperature and pressure on one of the boundaries, the two states on either side coexist in equilibrium.

Explore Online ▶

FIGURE 16: Phase diagrams show the states at which a substance exists at different temperatures and pressures. Each substance has a unique phase diagram.

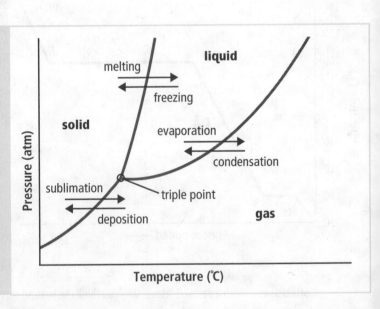

ANALYZE The phase diagram shows that at low temperatures a substance may be either a solid or a gas, but not a liquid. Why might this happen?

_____

_____

_____

_____

Triple Point

The triple point of a substance is the pressure and temperature at which all three states—solid, liquid, and gas—may exist. The triple point of water was one of two points used to define the Kelvin temperature scale. The other point was absolute zero.

 Language Arts Connection Research the phase diagrams of two substances, such as water and carbon dioxide. How can you use a phase diagram to determine if a substance will be solid, liquid, or gas at room temperature? Prepare a blog post that explains how a phase diagram can be used to discover more information about the behavior of a substance. Remember to include sample phase diagrams for the substances you researched.

Pressure and States of Matter

As stated earlier, the heating curve for a substance is for a specific pressure. A heating curve for the same substance at a different pressure may be different. Refer to the phase diagram in Figure 16. If you were to draw horizontal lines at two different pressures, you would see that the substance changes state at different temperatures. Increasing the pressure on a substance in any state pushes its particles closer together. The particles of a liquid, therefore, require more kinetic energy to become a gas. Likewise, solid particles require more kinetic energy to become a liquid. In contrast, less energy must be added or removed to cause a change of state at lower pressures.

The volume of a gaseous substance may be thousands of times greater than the same amount of substance as a liquid. Gases, such as helium or propane, often are compressed, or "liquefied," so they are easier (more compact) to transport and handle. A helium tank, for example, can fill many balloons. The volume of those balloons is much greater than the volume of the tank itself. Propane can be compressed into portable canisters to be used as fuel, such as for the camp stove shown in Figure 17, or for a grill.

FIGURE 17: Propane is often liquefied for easier transportation.

EXPLAIN Select the correct terms to complete the statement.

People often use cans of compressed (liquefied) air to clean electronics. When the nozzle of the can is opened, the high-pressure liquid air changes state to a gas and expands | contracts | does not change into the lower-pressure surroundings. When this happens, condensation | deposition often forms on the can. This is because the liquefied air absorbs | releases energy as it changes state. The water vapor in the air transfers energy to the can of air. In the process it condenses | evaporates on the side of the can.

 Evidence Notebook Many icebergs are melting because of increased global temperatures due to climate change. Explain how increased air temperatures causes this change of state. What affect do melting icebergs have on the oceans?

Engineering

Thermal Pollution and Evaporative Cooling

You may have heard of air and water pollution, but have you ever heard of thermal pollution? Thermal pollution is a temperature increase in a body of water caused by human activity. Thermal pollution can have damaging consequences to the environment around the pollution source. The thermograph in Figure 18 shows an example of thermal pollution produced by a power plant. The red and orange colors on the thermograph indicate warmer water temperatures and blue indicates cooler temperatures.

Power plants, oil refineries, and chemical processing plants generate tremendous amounts of waste energy in their daily operations. If this energy is not removed from the system, the system may be damaged by the excess thermal energy. Water is used as a coolant to prevent the machines in these plants from overheating. The waste energy is transferred from the machines to the water, increasing the temperature of the water.

In the past, this warm water was often released into nearby rivers and lakes. The discharged coolant water would increase the temperature in these bodies of water by several degrees. This sudden change in temperature can disrupt aquatic ecosystems in very damaging ways.

If the temperature of a body of water rises even a few degrees, the amount of dissolved oxygen in the water decreases significantly. Even a small decrease in oxygen levels can result in aquatic organisms suffocating and dying. If the flow of warm water into a lake or stream is constant, it may cause the total disruption of an aquatic ecosystem.

INFER Thermal pollution can cause large numbers of aquatic organisms, particularly fish, to die. Other than affecting the amount of dissolved oxygen in the water, what negative effects might the coolant water have on organisms in the area?

_____

_____

_____

_____

_____

_____

_____

_____

_____

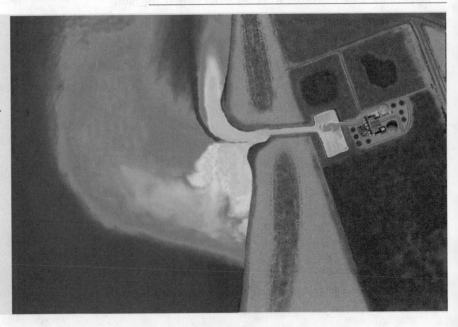

FIGURE 18: This thermogram shows the range of heat released by a power plant into a body of water. Red and orange indicate warmer areas, and blue indicates cooler areas.

FIGURE 19: The thick, white clouds billowing above these cooling towers is steam. The steam is formed when water vapor condenses as it transfers energy to the cooler air in the atmosphere.

The concern about the effect of the warm water on aquatic ecosystems has led to the idea of using cooling towers and cooling ponds to disperse the waste energy safely. Cooling towers at power plants and cooling ponds at industrial plants remove excess thermal energy from the coolant water through evaporation.

Liquid water absorbs energy from the plant and vaporizes. The particles of water vapor then move out of the tower into the atmosphere by convection. As the machines in the industrial plant continue to operate, excess energy continues being transferred to the coolant water, and evaporation continues. This is the principle of evaporative cooling.

ANALYZE Legionnaires' disease can be contracted when a person breathes in water vapor that contains the *Legionella* bacteria. This disease has been connected to bacteria located in water vapor from cooling towers. How do you think this is possible?

_____

_____

_____

_____

_____

Another solution to thermal pollution is combined heat and power (CHP) systems. In these systems, the waste energy generated by industrial processes is used to produce electricity or used to warm homes and factories rather than being discharged into the environment.

DEFINE Describe the problem that engineers used combined heat and power systems to solve.

_____

_____

_____

_____

_____

_____

_____

_____

Language Arts Connection Imagine that you are a particle of coolant water in an industrial plant. Write a short story describing how your movements change as you absorb energy from the machinery, enter the cooling tower, and escape into the atmosphere.

 CONSTRUCTING A HEATING/ COOLING CURVE   **INVESTIGATE THERMOMETERS**   **DRY ICE SUBLIMATION**   Go online to choose one of these other paths.

Lesson Self-Check

CAN YOU EXPLAIN IT?

FIGURE 20: Snorkelers explore icy waters.

Water exists in all three phases on Earth. These snorkelers are swimming in liquid water, next to a large iceberg containing ice, which is solid water. There is even water vapor, a gas, in the clouds above them. Water both absorbs and transfers energy as it moves between these states of matter. Pressure also determines the state water can be in as it cycles.

The ability of water to absorb energy combined with the water cycle greatly affects the way that thermal energy is distributed on Earth. Water that is warmer than its surroundings will transfer thermal energy to its surroundings. Water that is colder than its surroundings will absorb thermal energy from its surroundings. Oceanic and atmospheric currents affect the distribution of water on Earth, which further affects the distribution of thermal energy.

 Evidence Notebook Refer to your notes in your Evidence Notebook to explain how water can exist in three different states in the same area. Your explanation should include a discussion of the flow of energy as heat between a system and the surroundings. Using this information, answer the following:

1. Make a claim explaining how water can exist in three states on Earth.
2. What evidence supports your claim? For example, how does water compare to other substances? Consider the cycling of matter and the flow of energy in your explanation.
3. How does water cycle through different systems on Earth in different states?

CHECKPOINTS

Check Your Understanding

1. You have two flasks of water. You place a thermometer in the first flask and leave it until the temperature no longer changes. The temperature reads 100 °C. When you move the thermometer to the second flask and again leave it, it also reads 100 °C. Select all correct answers for this scenario.

☐ **a.** The thermometer and the first flask of water are in thermal equilibrium.

☐ **b.** The thermometer and the second flask of water are in thermal equilibrium.

☐ **c.** There is no way to tell whether the two flasks are in thermal equilibrium.

☐ **d.** The thermometer can be in thermal equilibrium only with the first flask.

☐ **e.** The zeroth law states that the two flasks are in thermal equilibrium with each other.

2. Choose the correct statement as it relates to the energy of a system and a heating curve.

○ **a.** During a plateau, the internal energy of the system is being lost.

○ **b.** During a plateau, the internal energy of the particles increases.

○ **c.** When the curve rises, the substance changes state.

○ **d.** As the curve rises, energy is not conserved.

3. A known number of moles of gas is placed in a flexible container. What will happen if some of the gas is removed from the container while the pressure and temperature are kept constant?

○ **a.** The volume will increase.

○ **b.** The volume will decrease.

○ **c.** The volume will stay the same.

4. The kinetic-molecular theory states that ideal gas molecules do which of the following?

○ **a.** are in constant, rapid, random motion

○ **b.** slow down as temperature increases

○ **c.** exert forces on each other

○ **d.** lose energy with every collision

5. Two substances have the same temperature. The particles of Substance A have a slower average speed than the particles in Substance B. What can you say about the molar masses of the two substances?

○ **a.** Their molar masses are the same.

○ **b.** The molar mass of Substance A is greater than Substance B.

○ **c.** The molar mass of Substance B is greater than Substance A.

○ **d.** There is not enough information.

6. A puddle of water on a sidewalk evaporates in the hot afternoon sunshine. Complete the statement to describe what is happening.

Before the phase change, thermal energy is
absorbed | released by the water, causing its
temperature to decrease | increase.

7. A scientist is testing the properties of a gas. Before he performs his experiment, he wants to make claims about the way the gas will behave in different situations. Then, he will compare his claims to his results. Complete the claims below based on evidence you gathered in this lesson.

increases   decreases   stays the same

When the temperature of a gas is held
constant, if pressure increases then the volume

_____.

When the volume of a gas is held constant,
if pressure increases then the temperature

_____.

When the pressure of a gas is held constant,
if temperature increases then the volume

_____.

8. Complete the statement.

Solid carbon dioxide changing state to gaseous
carbon dioxide is an example of condensation |
sublimation | evaporation.

CHECKPOINTS (continued)

9. How are evaporation and boiling alike, and how they are different? In your answer, discuss differences in energy and differences in temperature.

_____

_____

_____

_____

10. Describe kinetic-molecular theory and how it applies to the transfer of energy as an ideal gas is heated.

_____

_____

_____

_____

11. During an investigation, you place a gas in a glass syringe and use a moveable plunger to keep the gas inside. You then slightly warm the syringe and the gas inside, causing the gas to expand. You then observe the plunger moving slightly outward. Explain the changes you observed in the system in terms of the kinetic-molecular theory.

_____

_____

_____

_____

_____

_____

MAKE YOUR OWN STUDY GUIDE

 In your Evidence Notebook, design a study guide that supports the main ideas from this lesson:

The energy of a system includes internal energy.

The energy of a substance changes when it changes state.

Pressure, volume, and temperature of gases influence each other.

Remember to include the following information in your study guide:

- Use examples that model main ideas.
- Record explanations for the phenomena you investigated.
- Use evidence to support your explanations. Your support can include drawings, data, graphs, laboratory conclusions, and other evidence recorded throughout the lesson.

Consider how changes in the temperature and state of a substance can be described in terms of the conservation of energy as the energy flows into, out of, and within the system.

Analyzing the Flow of Energy in Systems

Old Faithful Geyser of California in Calistoga, California

CAN YOU EXPLAIN IT?

Imagine walking along on a stretch of seemingly normal ground, when suddenly hot water and steam come spraying several meters high out of it. This spray of hot water and steam is called a geyser. Almost a thousand geysers have been located worldwide. Some geysers erupt at a regular frequency, while others do not. They differ in the height and duration of their water spurts. One of the most well-known geysers in California is known as the Old Faithful Geyser of California. This geyser erupts about every 30 to 40 minutes to a height of about 18 meters. The geology of the area where the geyser is located determines such properties as how frequently and how forcefully it erupts.

PREDICT What do you think is happening within Earth that causes the water of a geyser to erupt so high?

_____

_____

_____

_____

_____

 Evidence Notebook As you explore the lesson, gather evidence to explain how energy flows within and between systems.

Investigating Thermal Energy and Heat

Thermal energy is the total kinetic energy of the particles in a substance. Thermal energy depends on the amount of substance and its temperature. When there is a temperature difference between two systems, thermal energy transfers from one system to the other. The mechanism by which thermal energy is transferred is called *heat transfer*. The flow of energy within and between systems may cause changes to the energy of a system.

Conservation of Energy

When a system loses energy, does that mean the energy is destroyed? No. Recall that all systems are part of the universe. Energy that is lost from a system is not destroyed; it is transferred to the system's surroundings. Similarly, if a system gains energy, the gained energy is transferred from its surroundings to the system. This idea that energy cannot be created or destroyed is known as the law of conservation of energy.

FIGURE 1: A hot piece of metal is submerged in cool water.

Explore Online ▶

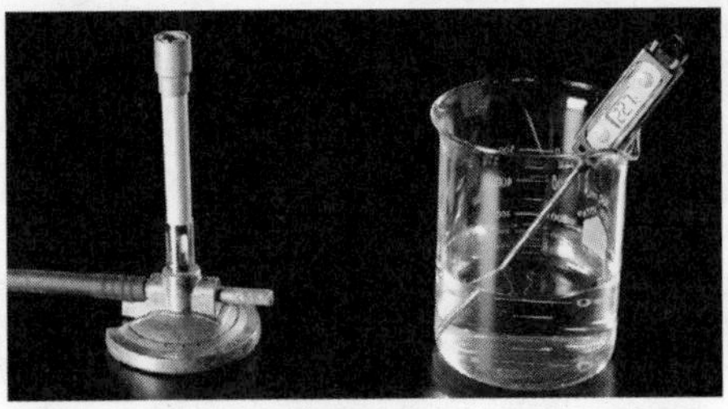

| a | Temperature of the water before the hot metal piece was added | b | Temperature of the water after the hot metal piece was added |

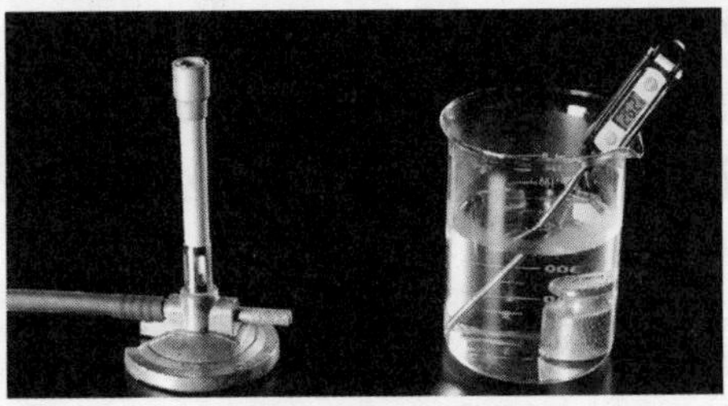

APPLY A small piece of hot metal is placed in cooler water. The metal is left in the water until the metal and water have the same temperature (they are in thermal equilibrium). Based on the conservation of energy, which of the following statements about the energy of the metal and water system is true?

○ **a.** The amount of energy lost by the metal is less than the amount of energy gained by the water.

○ **b.** The amount of energy lost by the metal is equal to the amount of energy gained by the water.

○ **c.** The amount of energy lost by the metal is greater than the amount of energy gained by the water.

In thermodynamics, the conservation of energy is described by the first law of thermodynamics. If you apply the law of conservation of energy to an isolated system, you see that the energy of the system does not change. Energy can be transformed or transferred within an isolated system, but the total amount of energy in the system does not change. The first law of thermodynamics implies that the change in energy of a closed or open system is equivalent to the energy that passes through the system's boundaries. Tracing the transformations and transfers of energy within and between systems can help scientists understand natural processes and engineered processes.

Exploring Thermal Energy and Temperature

The amount of thermal energy in a substance is related to both the temperature and amount of substance. Plan and carry out an investigation to explore the relationship between the thermal energy and temperature of two systems of water.

MAKE A CLAIM

In your Evidence Notebook, explain what you think the resulting temperature will be if you mix two equal volumes of water at different temperatures.

MATERIALS

- indirectly vented chemical splash goggles, nonlatex apron
- beaker, 500 mL (2)
- thermometer (2)
- water

SAFETY INFORMATION

- Wear indirectly vented chemical splash goggles and a nonlatex apron during the setup, hands-on, and takedown segments of the activity.

- Immediately wipe up any spilled water on the floor so it does not become a slip/fall hazard.

CARRY OUT THE INVESTIGATION

Plan and carry out an investigation to investigate your claim. Then, in your Evidence Notebook, explain whether your data does or does not support your claim.

EXTEND

How would you change your procedure to investigate what would happen if both the volumes and temperatures of the water are different before being mixed? What do you think will happen if both the volumes and temperatures are different?

indirectly vented chemical splash goggles

Analyzing Specific Heat Capacity

Think about a large tub of water and a small glass of water. More energy must be added to the large tub than the small glass of water to change the temperature by the same amount. The ratio of the energy needed to change the temperature of a system compared to its change in temperature is known as the system's *heat capacity*. The heat capacity of a system depends on its mass and the type of material from which it is made. Therefore, it is an extensive property.

In order to compare the heat capacities of different materials, scientists compare heat capacity per unit of mass. This is known as the specific heat capacity, often simply referred to as specific heat, of the material. The specific heat capacity is an intensive property defined as the amount of energy required to raise the temperature of one gram of a substance by one kelvin. Values of specific heat capacity are expressed in units of joules per gram per kelvin (J/g·K). Specific heat capacity is also stated in units of joules per gram per degree Celsius (J/g·°C), or as calories per gram per degree Celsius (cal/g·°C).

Different materials have different specific heat capacities. Some materials undergo a large increase in temperature as energy is transferred to them. Other materials exhibit a much smaller change for the same amount of energy transfer. These differences make certain materials more appropriate for different purposes and may impact natural processes.

FIGURE 2: Water is sprayed over newly made steel rods to cool them. The high specific heat capacity of liquid water makes it useful for absorbing excess energy in industrial processes.

PREDICT Liquid water has a very high specific heat capacity value compared to many other substances. How might water's high specific heat capacity affect energy distribution and temperatures on Earth?

_____

_____

_____

Suppose you had three pans made of different materials. One pan is made of iron, another of aluminum, and the third of copper. Each pan requires a different amount of energy to raise the temperature of 1 g of the metal in it by 1 K. The aluminum pan requires 0.897 J of energy, the iron pan requires 0.449 J, and the copper pan requires 0.385 J.

APPLY Assuming these three pans have the same mass, which pan will exhibit the *least* temperature change when 50.00 J of energy are transferred to it?

○ **a.** iron   ○ **b.** copper   ○ **c.** aluminum

Specific heat capacity can vary with pressure. For this reason, specific heat capacity is usually reported at standard pressure conditions, indicated by the subscript p in its variable, c_p. The following equation shows the relationship between the specific heat capacity of a substance (c_p), energy (q), mass (m), and change in temperature (ΔT).

$$c_p = \frac{q}{m \times \Delta T}$$

Using this equation, you can calculate the amount of energy transferred to or from a sample, given its mass, change in temperature, and specific heat capacity.

Evidence Notebook Suppose you are measuring the specific heat capacity of two different substances with the same mass under the same conditions. If ΔT for the first substance is much greater than ΔT for the second substance, how do their specific heat capacities compare? Explain how you know, citing evidence from the equation.

Experimenting with Calorimetry

Sometimes, the specific heat capacity of a substance may be unknown. To calculate the specific heat capacity, scientists use an instrument called a calorimeter. A calorimeter is a device containing a substance with a known specific heat capacity, often water. When another substance at a high temperature is placed into the calorimeter, the change in temperature in the substance of known specific heat capacity is used to determine the amount of energy that was transferred. From this, the specific heat capacity of the other substance can be calculated.

The most important aspect of calorimeter design is to ensure as little energy as possible is lost to the surroundings. Accurate measurements are obtained only if the calorimeter is insulated to isolate the system from its surroundings as much as possible. If the insulation is not adequate, energy flow into or out of the system will affect the measurements. In this lab, you will design a calorimeter and take measurements to determine the specific heat capacity of a sample material.

Design Challenge: Build a calorimeter with materials that will minimize the amount of energy lost to the surroundings.

POSSIBLE MATERIALS

- indirectly vented chemical splash goggles, nonlatex apron
- aluminum foil
- balance
- beakers, assorted sizes
- hot plate or stovetop

- material with unknown specific heat, small sample
- metal can
- metal wire, thin (about 15 cm)
- paper cup

- plastic wrap
- polystyrene cups and lids
- thermometer
- tongs
- water

SAFETY INFORMATION

- Wear indirectly vented chemical splash goggles and a nonlatex apron during the setup, hands-on, and takedown segments of the activity.

- Use caution when working with hot plates, which can cause skin burns or electric shock.

- Use caution when working with glassware, which can shatter if dropped and cut skin.

- Use caution when using sharp materials, which can cut or puncture skin.

- Immediately wipe up any spilled water on the floor so it does not become a slip/fall hazard.

indirectly vented chemical splash goggles

DEFINE THE PROBLEM

Consider the criteria and constraints of an effective calorimeter. In your Evidence Notebook, explain which materials you think will make the most efficient calorimeter. Which of the suggested materials will allow you to most accurately measure the energy lost or gained by a sample?

DESIGN SOLUTIONS

Develop a plan for how you will construct your calorimeter and determine the specific heat capacity of the sample material using some of the materials on the list. Determine which materials you will use and how you will combine them. Remember, the goal is to develop a calorimeter that will lose the least amount of energy to the surroundings. Draw a sketch of your design in your Evidence Notebook.

COLLECT DATA

Write a data collection plan to determine the specific heat capacity of the substance being tested. Remember that the temperature change of the water is what will be used to determine the energy transferred from the substance. This amount and the mass of the substance will be experimentally determined to find the specific heat capacity.

Given this, consider what kind of data you will need to collect and how often you will need to collect it. You may wish to develop a data table in your Evidence Notebook.

TEST

Develop a testing procedure to determine the specific heat capacity of your sample. Determine what safety precautions you will need to take during your experiment. Have your teacher look over the sketch and description of your planned experimental setup, data collection plan, safety plan, and your procedure before you begin.

Use caution when heating your testing sample. Place the sample into a beaker of water and bring the water to a boil. Transfer the sample to your calorimeter using tongs. Do not touch the heated sample or the beaker of water.

CALCULATE

1. In the space provided, calculate the energy transferred from the sample to the water. The specific heat capacity of liquid water is 4.18 J/(g·K).

$$q = c_p \times m \times \Delta T$$

2. Assume the energy transferred to the water (q) is equal to the energy lost as heat by the metal. In the space provided, calculate the specific heat capacity of the metal.

$$c_p = \frac{q}{m \times \Delta T}$$

3. Find the accepted value for the specific heat capacity of the sample you tested. Use this and your experimental value to calculate the percentage error.

OPTIMIZE

How could you modify your calorimeter design to make it more efficient? Recall that a more efficient calorimeter will lose less energy to the environment. Review designs built by your classmates and their percentage error. Did the calorimeters with the lowest percentage error have any details in common? If time allows, make your modifications to your calorimeter and run your test again.

COMMUNICATE

1. **Use a Model** Draw a diagram of your design that shows how energy was transferred between the sample, the water in the calorimeter, and the calorimeter itself. Show where energy was lost to the surroundings.

2. **Evaluate Information** Compare the diagram of your calorimeter and your results to other calorimeter setups. Are the data obtained precise enough to make a conclusion about which structure is best? Explain your answers.

_____

_____

_____

_____

_____

_____

_____

_____

_____

_____

Modes of Energy Transfer

Recall that the kinetic-molecular theory is based on the concept of an ideal gas. The same idea of moving particles and energy transfer between those particles can be applied to solids and liquids. It can also explain different ways that energy can be transferred between and within different systems. Think about sitting in a chair in the sun on a warm sunny day. You may feel warmth from the chair as well as warmth from the sun. A breeze may make you feel cooler. These are all different modes of energy transfer.

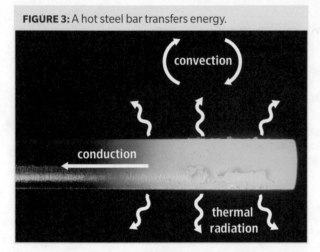

FIGURE 3: A hot steel bar transfers energy.

Conduction

As the steel bar in Figure 3 is warmed, the molecules in the steel bar in contact with the heat source gain kinetic energy. These molecules can transfer that kinetic energy to other molecules with which they collide. When two objects collide, the object with more kinetic energy transfers some of its energy to the object with less kinetic energy. When this happens in a solid, it is known as conduction. *Conduction* is the transfer of thermal energy by the collision of particles when objects or substances are in contact. Thermal conductivity is a measure of the rate at which a system transfers energy via conduction. Thermal conductivity depends on the type of material and temperature difference. When there is a greater temperature difference, conduction tends to occur at a higher rate. Materials with lower thermal conductivities, such as air, make good insulators.

EXPLAIN Give an example of a situation where you would want to minimize conduction. Would a solid, liquid, or gaseous material be best to use to minimize the amount of energy transferred?

_____

_____

_____

Convection

Look again at Figure 3. The air surrounding the steel bar is at a lower temperature than the warmed metal. When energy in the form of heat is transferred to the air around the metal bar, those air molecules then have more kinetic energy than other air molecules. Air molecules with more kinetic energy move faster, spread out, and make the air less dense. The cooler, more dense air falls and displaces, or pushes, the warmer, less dense air upwards. As this cooler air warms, and the warmer air cools, the cycle continues. This cycling of air due to the differences in densities is known as *convection*. Convection may occur in both gases and liquids. Convection driven by natural forces, such as a difference in densities, is called natural convection. When something, such as a fan, causes the liquid or gas to move, this is called forced convection.

ARGUE Why might you feel cooler standing in front of a fan in a warm room?

_____

_____

Thermal Radiation

The light given off by the hot steel bar is an example of radiation. *Thermal radiation* is a mode of energy transfer that occurs when thermal energy is transferred through waves such as visible light, infrared radiation, and other types of electromagnetic waves. Most waves that transfer thermal energy cannot be seen. Unlike conduction and convection, radiation does not require a medium. Radiation is how energy from the sun travels through outer space to Earth across nearly 93 million miles of a near vacuum!

Thermal energy transfer occurs by radiation in many places in your daily life. You may feel the warmth from a fire or a hot pan without having to touch the fire or pan. Incandescent light bulbs, which use electrical energy to generate light, may also get so warm that you can feel heat from the bulb from a short distance away. It is also possible that you may feel colder due to radiation energy transfer.

 Systems and System Models

Energy Transfer in a Lava Lamp

A lava lamp is composed of a sealed glass container with two different substances, which sits on a base that contains an incandescent light bulb. The light bulb gets hot when the lamp is in operation. The waxy substance in the bottom of the container gets warmer and forms blobs that rise to the top of the container where the fluid is cooler. The base of a lava lamp may get so warm that you can feel heat from the lamp without touching it.

MODEL Draw a model showing the conduction, convection, and thermal radiation that occurs in the lava lamp shown in Figure 4. Identify the system boundaries and show particle behavior.

Explore Online ▶

FIGURE 4: A lava lamp demonstrates all three modes of thermal energy transfer.

 Evidence Notebook Describe a way that particle motion could be related to the eruption of water from a geyser.

Describing the Dispersion of Energy

Have you ever been in another room and suddenly smelled what someone else was making for lunch? Or perhaps you have smelled a farm or the beach miles before you saw the source of the smell.

PREDICT Why are you able to smell things across a room or from great distances when you are not near the source of the smell?

_____

_____

_____

_____

Matter and Energy Disperse in Gases

Gases spread out spontaneously and mix with other gases in a process called *diffusion*. Recall that in an ideal gas, particles move in a straight line until they collide with another particle or a boundary. This is why a gas can expand to fill a space. This movement, however, also explains diffusion. Gases diffuse readily into one another and mix together due to the rapid motion of the particles and the empty spaces between the particles.

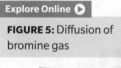

FIGURE 5: Diffusion of bromine gas

ANALYZE When bromine is added to a container, the molecules of its vapor move through the container until they are uniformly distributed. How does this example also represent the movement of energy?

_____

_____

_____

Each particle in a gas has kinetic energy as it moves. So, the particle has both matter and energy. When a more energetic particle collides with a less energetic particle within the gas, an energy transfer occurs. As the random particle motion continues, energy continues to be transferred from particle to particle. In this way, the energy of the particles spreads out from a smaller number of higher-energy particles to a greater number of lower-energy particles.

INFER Think about the differences in particle behavior between a liquid and a gas. Complete the following statement about diffusion.

The diffusion of matter and energy in a liquid will be slower | quicker than diffusion in a gas because the particles in a liquid move less | more quickly than particles in a gas.

Hands-On Lab
Modeling Diffusion

In this lab, you will develop a model of diffusion in a liquid and determine how the rate of diffusion can be increased or decreased.

Research Question: How can models be used to investigate factors that affect the rate of diffusion in everyday substances?

MAKE A CLAIM

In your Evidence Notebook, explain how you think you could increase or decrease the rate of diffusion in a liquid.

POSSIBLE MATERIALS

- indirectly vented chemical splash goggles, nonlatex apron, nitrile gloves
- beaker, 100 mL
- beaker, 250 mL
- food coloring
- hot plate
- ice
- stopwatch
- water

SAFETY INFORMATION

indirectly vented chemical splash goggles

- Wear indirectly vented chemical splash goggles, a nonlatex apron, and nitrile gloves during the setup, hands-on, and takedown segments of the activity.

- Use caution when working with hot plates, which can cause skin burns or electric shock.

- Immediately wipe up any spilled water on the floor so it does not become a slip/fall hazard.

PLAN THE INVESTIGATION

Write a procedure to test diffusion in a liquid, and explain how you will determine the rate of diffusion. Then, describe how you will increase or decrease the rate of diffusion. Develop a data collection plan explaining how you will measure the rate of diffusion, your control, and your variables for the investigation. Be careful to avoid convection currents that may affect the diffusion you are testing. If you have time, develop a procedure to test a different way the rate of diffusion can be affected.

ANALYZE

In your Evidence Notebook, explain how the factor(s) you tested affected the rate of diffusion. Explain how particle motion and energy transfer are related to your observations.

DRAW CONCLUSIONS

In your Evidence Notebook, write a conclusion that addresses each of the points below.

Claim How did the factor(s) you tested affect the rate of diffusion in the liquid?

Evidence Give specific examples from your data to support your claim.

Reasoning Explain how the evidence you gave supports your claim. Describe the connections between the evidence you cited and the argument you are making.

Describing Order in a System

The images in Figure 6 show three different processes. In the first image, an ice cube melts as it absorbs energy from its surroundings. In the second image, a wood log undergoes a chemical reaction (combustion) as it burns. It becomes ash, releasing carbon dioxide gas, thermal energy, and light. In the final image, dyed sugar is added to water. When the water is stirred, the dyed sugar dissolves and evenly distributes within the beaker.

FIGURE 6: Systems undergo processes that result in changes in matter and energy.

a Ice melting   b Wood burning   c Dyed sugar dissolving

PREDICT If the systems in Figure 6 are left alone, would you expect the processes to spontaneously reverse? In other words, would the ice refreeze, the ashes reform into a wood log, and the sugar form crystals again without any external actions being taken?

_____

_____

_____

_____

In each of the systems shown, the system went from a more ordered state to a less ordered state. Entropy (S) is a term used to describe how disordered a system is. A highly ordered system has a low amount of entropy. A disordered system has a high amount of entropy. An audience in a theater, sitting in fixed seats, is an example of a low-entropy system. In this example, you have a high probability of knowing where people will be. Alternately, if you have many people in a field, they can be arranged in many different ways. You are less likely to know where a person will be at any given time. This is an example of a high-entropy system. In each of the processes shown in Figure 6, the entropy of the systems increases. The _second law of thermodynamics_ states that all real processes increase the entropy of the universe. The processes shown will not spontaneously reverse because that would violate the second law of thermodynamics.

Ice has a very regular, organized structure. When energy is added to the system, the ice melts, and the system becomes more disordered—its entropy increases. The particles in the log of wood are organized in a rigid structure. As the wood burns, ash particles and carbon dioxide gas form. These particles are released into the air and spread through the environment. Energy from the combustion is transferred to the environment, making the air more energetic. The sugar dissolves in the water, increasing the entropy of the system as the sugar disperses through the system. A smaller system can be made more ordered by using energy from the outside, creating greater entropy in the larger system.

Entropy and States of Matter

You know that the energy of substances in the different states of matter varies. A substance tends to have more energy as a gas than it does as a liquid. The same substance as a liquid has more energy than it does as a solid. How might entropy relate to the different states of matter?

You know that in a solid, the particles are arranged in a fixed structure. Though the particles still have vibrational energy, they do not move greatly from their fixed positions. We can consider solids as being highly ordered substances. When these substances melt, the particles are able to move relative to each other, which gives a liquid more disorder in comparison. Gases have even more possibilities for disorder, as the particles in a gas move constantly and have no fixed positions relative to the other particles.

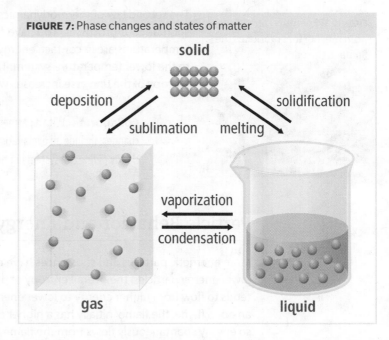

FIGURE 7: Phase changes and states of matter

SOLVE Consider how entropy differs among the different phases of a substance. Complete the inequality by writing the symbols for the entropy, S, for each phase into the correct positions.

S_{solid} S_{gas} S_{liquid}

_____ > _____ > _____

As the energy increases in a system, the entropy also increases. Particles can be arranged in more ways in the gas phase than in the liquid phase and more ways in the liquid phase than the solid phase. The gas phase has the most energy and the least order, so it has the greatest entropy.

EXPLAIN Give an example of a spontaneous natural process involving a change of state. Explain how the process satisfies both the first and second laws of thermodynamics.

_____

_____

_____

_____

Evidence Notebook Explain how the entropy of a geyser system changes as energy is added to the system.

Modeling Heat in a System

FIGURE 8: Energy is transferred from the fuel that produces the flame to the pan.

The second law of thermodynamics helps explain how energy flows in spontaneous processes. You have seen that when two systems with different temperatures are in contact, energy flows from the higher temperature system to the lower temperature system. This flow of energy means that the overall entropy of the universe increases with these processes.

 Collaborate With a partner, describe how the energy of the pan in Figure 8 changes. Include an explanation of energy transfers and transformations, and clearly define the system boundaries.

Particle Behavior and Energy Transfer

More energetic particles and substances have more entropy. By sharing their energy with lower energy particles, the overall entropy of the system increases. This is why energy tends to flow from higher energy to lower energy objects or particles. When cooking on an open flame, the flame initially has a higher energy level than the pan and food within, so energy spontaneously flows from the flame to the pan and food within.

MODEL Draw a model showing the flow of energy for the pan system in Figure 8 after the flame is turned off. Clearly identify the system boundaries.

Recall the different types of systems: open, closed, and isolated. In an open system, both matter and energy cross the system boundaries. Imagine that the system in Figure 8 includes the pan and water within the pan. As the water boils, it changes to a gas and leaves the system. This would be an open system. An example of a closed system would include only the pan. The pan transfers energy to and from its surroundings but does not transfer matter. In an isolated system, energy and matter do not cross the system boundaries. At temperatures above absolute zero, all matter radiates energy.

EXPLAIN Why is it impossible to build a perfectly isolated system in real life? Support your claim with evidence and reasoning.

_____

_____

_____

Matter and Thermal Energy

Scientists and engineers take special care to control the flow of thermal energy during processes. A buildup of thermal energy is a serious problem because it can quickly destroy materials and endanger people. The glass heat exchanger shown in Figure 9 is used as part of a laboratory procedure. In a heat exchanger, cool water inside the container absorbs thermal energy from a fluid flowing through the glass coil. This lowers the temperature of the fluid in the coil. Heat exchangers can also be used to increase the temperature of a liquid or to condense a gas into a liquid.

FIGURE 9: Glass heat exchanger

ANALYZE Consider what you know about the specific heat capacity of water to explain why water is a good substance for this application.

Liquid water has a low | high specific heat capacity compared to many other fluids. This means it has the capacity to absorb less | more thermal energy compared to other liquids.

The flow rate and temperature of the water in the heat exchanger can be controlled. This adjusts the flow of thermal energy to keep the fluid in the coil at a desired temperature.

APPLY A fluid enters the heat exchanger at 98 °C and must be cooled to a temperature of 80 °C. Currently, the fluid exits the heat exchanger at 85 °C. Which of the following would increase the rate of thermal energy transfer from the fluid to the water in the heat exchanger to meet this constraint? Select all correct answers.

☐ **a.** Increase the temperature of the water entering the heat exchanger.

☐ **b.** Decrease the temperature of the water entering the heat exchanger.

☐ **c.** Increase the flow rate of water entering the heat exchanger.

☐ **d.** Decrease the flow rate of water entering the heat exchanger.

Energy Transfer Models

How could you model baking food in an oven? In this system, conduction, convection, and thermal radiation are all occurring simultaneously. The rate of energy transfer by each of these modes, and in each direction, may be different. Accurately modeling the energy transfer in this system requires analyzing many variables, so scientists and engineers often use computational models. In a computational model, a computer performs this analysis or provides a way to model the behavior of matter. Even though the computer will handle the analysis, it is important that the system boundaries are properly specified.

Energy transfer also depends on the types and states of materials, the geometry in which the particles normally arrange themselves, and the temperature and pressure of the system. All of this information must be specified in order for a computational model to give accurate results. As with other models, you must specify any assumptions you made and understand any limitations your computational model may have.

Modeling Energy Transfer

Scientists and engineers use many tools to model the flow of energy through systems, including schematic diagrams, heat-sensitive thermography, physical scale models, computational tools, and sophisticated virtual simulations. Each tool has benefits and drawbacks, ranging from cost to accuracy to efficiency and ease of implementation.

FIGURE 10: This thermograph shows temperature variations as different colors.

Engineers use models to help understand problems involving energy transfer. They can then use their models to investigate possible solutions for their chosen problem. Consider the problem of insulating a building. Engineers may model the energy transfer through the windows, through the walls, or through the roof. They may also investigate the problem of effectively warming or cooling a building. Considering an entire building at once may be too complex to accurately model. Engineers may choose to model and analyze smaller subsystems, and then consider the system as a whole.

Design Challenge: Design or use a simulation to develop a computational model of a system undergoing energy transfer. Your model should be detailed enough to be used to collect meaningful data about the amount of energy that is lost to the surroundings. Then, you will model a solution to limit the energy loss in your system.

- -

CONDUCT RESEARCH

Investigate different ways that energy in the form of heat may be lost in a home, a school, or a single room in a building.

Obtain Information What type of system is a home, school, or room? How can this system be modeled? Where is energy transferred through conduction, convection, and radiation?

_____

_____

_____

_____

_____

_____

Develop a Model Identify the most appropriate computational model to learn more about the energy transfer occurring in your system. There are many energy computational models available that will allow you to simulate your own system. Describe the model you will use in your investigation. Does your model have any limitations that will impact your investigation?

_____

_____

_____

_____

DEFINE THE PROBLEM

Identify a problem that you can solve using the model of your system. Identify the criteria and constraints for your problem and your model.

_____

_____

_____

_____

TEST

Model your system using an energy transfer simulation. Collect data on the conduction, convection, and radiation occurring in the system. Identify the locations that are losing the most energy to the surroundings.

ANALYZE

1. Does your model satisfy the first and second laws of thermodynamics? How is energy conserved in your model?

_____

_____

_____

2. How can you verify that your model is accurate?

_____

_____

_____

OPTIMIZE

Describe any loss of energy that occurs during the process you modeled. Is this a system that might benefit from efforts to improve its efficiency (that is, prevent the loss of energy through energy waste)?

_____

_____

_____

EXTEND

In your Evidence Notebook, develop a plan to decrease the energy loss from the system. Then, adjust your model according to your plan, and record the results.

 Evidence Notebook Describe the dispersion of energy during a geyser eruption. How is energy transferred during the process? How does this energy transfer relate to changes in the entropy of the geyser system and its surroundings?

Describing Work and Heat

Figure 11 shows an air-tight syringe containing a small amount of cotton. The autoignition temperature of cotton, or the temperature at which it will ignite spontaneously, is approximately 400 °C. The air in the syringe is only at room temperature, about 20 °C, well below cotton's autoignition temperature. However, when the syringe is pushed down with considerable force, the cotton ignites.

FIGURE 11: When the plunger is pushed down quickly, the cotton ignites. Explore Online ▶

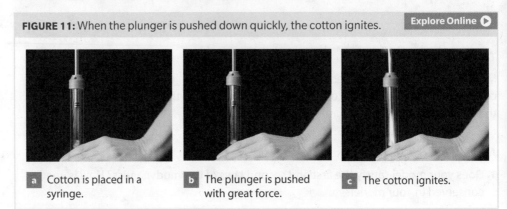

a Cotton is placed in a syringe.   b The plunger is pushed with great force.   c The cotton ignites.

 Collaborate With a partner, describe the changes occurring within the syringe system as the plunger is rapidly pushed down.

Relating Work and Heat

You have seen that transferring energy in the form of heat to or from a system can change the internal energy of a system. Consider the cotton and syringe system shown in Figure 11. The cotton's ignition shows that the energy of the system increased, but how? Work was done on the system. Work is the transfer of energy to a system by the application of force that causes the system to move in the direction of the force.

GATHER EVIDENCE What evidence is there that work was done on the syringe system?

_____

_____

_____

In the syringe example, work is done on the system to increase the internal energy of the system. But, it is more common for engineers to want a system to do work on its environment to solve a problem. In many of these systems, energy is transferred to the system in the form of heat. The system transforms that energy to do work on its surroundings. This type of system is called a heat engine.

EXPLAIN Complete the statement about heat engines.

The amount of work that a heat engine can do on its surroundings cannot be

more than | less than the amount of energy transferred to the heat engine.

In many systems, both energy transfer and work may occur simultaneously. According to the first law of thermodynamics, the change in the total internal energy of a system depends on the energy lost or gained as heat by the system and work done on or by the system. You can write this relationship as an equation:

$$\Delta U = Q + W$$

where ΔU is the change in the system's internal energy, Q is energy absorbed by the system as heat, and W is work done on the system. Work and heat are measured in the same unit, joules (J). Note that energy transfer from a system and work done by the system will be negative in this equation. This equation does not consider wasted energy.

In a perfectly efficient heat engine all of the energy transferred to the system would be converted into work. In reality, as a consequence of the second law of thermodynamics, some of the energy will not be accessible. Instead of performing practical work, it will contribute unusable energy to the engine's surroundings.

Observing Work Performed by a System

Recall that temperature and pressure are proportional in a gaseous system. Volume is also proportional to temperature. This means that as the temperature of a gas increases, the pressure of the gas increases or the gas will expand. This means that a gas does work on its surroundings when its temperature increases. You can also take advantage of a change of state to do work. A substance in its gaseous state has a volume thousands of times greater than the same substance in its liquid state. When a liquid vaporizes, the gas expands and does work.

In Figure 12, a student combines vinegar and baking soda in a flask. He then covers the flask with a balloon. As the reaction proceeds, it produces carbon dioxide gas. The gas increases in pressure and inflates the balloon. Because pressure is force acting over an area, when pressure causes a displacement, work is done.

Explore Online ▶

FIGURE 12: When vinegar reacts with baking soda, the resulting gas inflates a balloon.

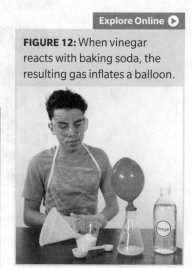

MODEL Draw a model explaining why the balloon in the experiment inflates.

Explore Online ▶

Hands-On Lab

The Relationship Between Work and Heat Design an experiment to determine how the air temperature inside a balloon affects the balloon's ability to do work.

Engineering

Analyzing Engines

Engines are important devices in daily life. An engine is a device that transforms energy into mechanical force or motion. There are many different types of engines, including steam engines, internal combustion engines, and jet engines. Engines, such as an internal combustion engine, use the chemical energy of a fuel to transfer energy in the form of heat to a system so that the system can do work.

Many of the earliest engines created by humans were steam engines. These engines heat water to turn it into steam. The steam expands, causing an increase in the system pressure. This pressure can then do work on the surroundings. Many modern power plants burn a fuel to warm water until it vaporizes. The expanding vapor is used to turn turbines. The spinning turbines use this mechanical energy to generate electrical energy.

A Hero's engine, such as the one shown in Figure 13, was one of the first types of engines ever built. Dating back to first century Roman-occupied Egypt, it was more of a curiosity than a practical machine, but it can demonstrate the transformation from heat to motion. A small amount of water is placed in a container, and the container is then suspended from its top so that it can move freely. When the container is heated, the water boils. The steam then exits through two specially angled holes or tubes such that the container begins to spin around its vertical axis.

FIGURE 13: A Hero's engine uses a phase change to do work.

Explore Online ▶

a Energy is transferred in the form of heat from a flame to water.

b Some of the energy in the system is used to do work as the engine spins.

EXPLAIN Complete the statements about the Hero's engine.

The flame does work on | transfers energy to the system. The water in the system changes to vapor due to the decrease | increase in energy in the system. The system does work on | transfers energy to its surroundings as the vapor expands and the engine turns. If this engine were perfectly efficient (no energy is lost to the surroundings), then the amount of work done on | by the system will equal the amount of energy transferred to | from the system.

Evidence Notebook How is the internal energy of the water in a geyser changed by heat and work?

Engineering

Geothermal Energy

Energy from underground sources is known as *geothermal energy*. Thermal energy within Earth can be used as a renewable energy source. Geothermal energy is more accessible in some locations than others. For example, most homes in Iceland are heated using geothermal energy, and geothermal power plants generate more than 25% of Iceland's electrical energy.

Several meters below Earth's surface, the temperature of the ground stays constant at approximately 10 °C to 16 °C. A *geothermal heat pump* can use the thermal energy from this warm ground to warm a home in winter and cool it in summer. The geothermal heat pump consists of rows of fluid-filled pipes buried in the ground to act as heat exchangers.

In colder seasons, thermal energy from the ground warms the liquid in the pipes, and this liquid travels into the heat pump inside the house. There the energy transfers from the warm liquid to the cooler air in the heat pump. This warm air is then pumped throughout the home. The now cooler liquid then flows back underground where it is again warmed. In warmer seasons, the pump is reversed so that energy from warm air inside the home is transferred to the cooler water in the heat pump. This water then transfers the energy to the cooler rock underground.

Geothermal heat pumps are efficient and clean in operation, but they do have disadvantages. Installing the underground systems can be costly. The geology of the area may mean you must drill deeper to get to a hot spot.

A much more complex method of using geothermal energy is by operating a *geothermal power plant* that uses geothermal energy to generate electrical energy. Often these areas are located along the borders of tectonic plates where magma is closer to the surface. Most geothermal power plants in the United States are located in the western states. California generates the most electricity using geothermal power plants in the nation.

FIGURE 14: Geothermal power plant

Geothermal power plants use either a liquid or steam to drive a turbine. The turbine is part of a generator that produces electrical energy. There are three main designs of geothermal power plants. A *dry steam plant* uses steam from an underground geothermal source to turn a turbine. Water can be pumped underground to recharge the system in order to continue its use. The Geysers geothermal field in northern California is the largest area of dry steam geothermal energy in the world. A *flash steam plant* draws liquid from a geothermal source, uses pressure to convert it to steam to drive a turbine, and returns the water to the ground. A *binary cycle power plant* transfers energy from geothermal water to another liquid. This liquid is then converted to steam to drive a turbine.

Language Arts Connection Research the production and use of geothermal power in California. Develop an informational pamphlet in which you describe why California generates more electricity from geothermal energy than any other state, and explain the importance of California's geography. Include a description of the types and locations of geothermal power plants in California.

| ENTROPY AND LIVING SYSTEMS | PERPETUAL MOTION | THE RELATIONSHIP BETWEEN WORK AND HEAT | Go online to choose one of these other paths. |

Lesson Self-Check

FIGURE 15: Old Faithful Geyser of California periodically erupts, shooting water about 18 meters into the air.

Geysers are an unusual phenomenon throughout the world because conditions must be just right for the water to spew upward with such force. Geysers occur in volcanic areas where a reservoir of water underground is warmed by hot magma. The underground rock must be structured so that a somewhat narrow, vertical opening extends from where the water is warmed up to the surface where the water bursts out. A large amount of energy must be transferred to the groundwater to cause a phase change because it is vapor that does work as the geyser erupts.

 Evidence Notebook Refer to your notes in your Evidence Notebook to construct an explanation about what happens within a geyser that causes the water to erupt so high. Your explanation should include a discussion of transfer of energy, work, heat, internal energy, and entropy. Using this information, answer the following:

1. State a claim about what you think is happening within Earth that causes a geyser to erupt. Explain how a geyser is a system, and identify the system boundaries.
2. What evidence supports your claim? How is energy transferred and transformed throughout the geyser system? How do these transfers and transformations affect the work, heat, internal energy, and entropy of the system?
3. Explain how the evidence you cited supports your claim.

CHECKPOINTS

Check Your Understanding

1. What happens to a cup of water if you place it in a freezer?

   ○ **a.** Work is done on the water, increasing its internal energy.

   ○ **b.** Work is done by the water, decreasing its internal energy.

   ○ **c.** The water transfers thermal energy to the freezer, decreasing the water's internal energy.

   ○ **d.** The water transfers thermal energy from the freezer, increasing the water's internal energy.

2. During an investigation, you connect two containers by a thin tube. A stopcock keeps the tube closed. One container is empty, and the other contains a gas. What will happen if you open the stopcock to connect the containers?

   ○ **a.** The gas will spread out to fill both containers as it does work on the system.

   ○ **b.** The entropy of the gas will increase, and it will spread out to fill both containers.

   ○ **c.** The internal energy of the gas will increase as it all flows into the other container.

   ○ **d.** The gas will all flow into the other container because heat is added to the system.

3. Complete the statements.

   When a hot piece of metal is placed in water, thermal energy is transferred from the metal to the water | water to the metal. The average kinetic energy of the particles in the metal increases | decreases | stays the same, while the average kinetic energy of the water molecules increases | decreases | stays the same. This results in an increase | a decrease | no change in temperature of the metal and an increase | a decrease | no change in temperature of the water. According to the first law of thermodynamics, the overall change in temperature | speed | energy must be zero.

4. Complete the statements.

conduction	convection	thermal radiation

   Energy is transferred by _____ when warm air rises, and cool air moves below it.

   Energy is transferred by _____ when you place a cool metal spoon in a bowl of hot soup, and the spoon becomes warm.

   Energy is transferred by _____ when you feel warm because of sunshine shining through a window.

5. Which describes an example of transfer of energy by conduction? Select all correct answers.

   ☐ **a.** You feel warmth when you stand near a fire.

   ☐ **b.** Warm water rises above nearby cooler water.

   ☐ **c.** Ice melts in a glass of room temperature water.

   ☐ **d.** A coil of a stove warms the bottom of a frying pan.

   ☐ **e.** You touch a hot door handle in summer.

6. In which of these changes does entropy increase? Select all correct answers.

   ☐ **a.** a solid dissolving in a liquid

   ☐ **b.** a substance changing from a liquid to a gas

   ☐ **c.** a gas in which the temperature is decreased

   ☐ **d.** a substance changing from a liquid to a solid

7. How much energy will a sample of aluminum gain when it is warmed from 306 K to 419 K? The specific heat capacity of aluminum is 0.897 J/g·K, and the mass of the sample is 5.00 g. Show your work in the space provided.

   _____ J

CHECKPOINTS (continued)

8. A calorimeter generally uses water as the substance that absorbs energy from the reaction. If the water were replaced by an oil with a lower specific heat capacity than water, how would the temperature change and the total energy measurements be different? Explain your answer.

_____

_____

_____

_____

_____

9. Describe the transfer of energy that occurs when an object with a temperature of 25 °C is placed in water with a temperature of 30 °C. How is the first law of thermodynamics upheld?

_____

_____

_____

_____

_____

_____

_____

MAKE YOUR OWN STUDY GUIDE

 In your Evidence Notebook, design a study guide that supports the main ideas from this lesson:

The change in total internal energy of a system is equal to the heat lost or gained by the system as well as the work done on or by the system.

The second law of thermodynamics states that all real processes increase the entropy of the universe.

Remember to include the following information in your study guide:

- Use examples that model main ideas.
- Record explanations for the phenomena you investigated.
- Use evidence to support your explanations. Your support can include drawings, data, graphs, laboratory conclusions, and other evidence recorded throughout the lesson.

Consider how energy moves between particles when the total internal energy of a system changes as work is done on or by the system.

Energy Transfer in Earth's Interior

Molten rock breaking through to the surface is evidence of the energy inside Earth.

CAN YOU EXPLAIN IT?

In Hawaii, lava from the Kilauea volcano can be seen erupting onto Earth's surface. This extremely hot, molten rock is an example of how energy deep within Earth can affect Earth's surface. Energy inside Earth drives the processes that melt these rocks and shape Earth's landforms. Scientists cannot directly observe what is happening deep inside Earth, so they depend on experiments and inferences from observations to describe Earth's internal structure and composition. By analyzing how energy moves through the planet, scientists are gaining a better understanding of the processes that shape Earth's surface.

INFER Energy within Earth is transferred to the surface and drives geologic processes like this volcanic eruption in Hawaii. How do you think energy might be transferred in Earth's interior?

_____

_____

_____

_____

 Evidence Notebook As you explore this lesson, gather evidence to explain how energy is transferred in Earth's interior.

Processes Driven by Earth's Internal Energy

You may have heard of earthquakes, tsunamis, or volcanic eruptions causing major destruction. These geologic processes are all driven by the movement of tectonic plates, pieces of Earth's very thin and rigid outer shell. Tectonic plates move very slowly—just a few centimeters per year—but as they push, pull, and grind past each other, they cause both sudden and gradual changes. These changes include earthquakes, mountain building, and the formation of ocean basins.

Tectonic plate motion and all of the processes related to it are driven by Earth's internal energy. This energy is the result of events and processes that occurred during the planet's formation. Energy from collisions between Earth and other objects, as well as energy from the breakdown of unstable elements in its interior, is still present inside Earth today. The breakdown of unstable elements continues to occur within Earth, just to a lesser extent.

 Collaborate Earth's core is hotter than its surface. Based on what you have learned about energy transfer, what can you conclude about the energy in Earth's interior? In what general direction should it flow?

Direct Observations

FIGURE 1: The Kola Superdeep Borehole was drilled from 1970 until 1992 to a depth of more than 12 km.

One method to observe Earth's interior involves drilling directly into it. The deepest hole ever drilled is the Kola Superdeep Borehole in Russia. This borehole is more than 12 km deep. The project operated at a high cost and drilled into Earth's crust for more than 20 years. Then, in the early 1990s, the project had to be abandoned because drillers encountered higher-than-predicted temperatures that made the drill no longer operable. At these extreme temperatures, the rock began to behave more plastically, like a putty, making it impossible to maintain the borehole.

PREDICT Why do you think the properties of rock change as temperature and pressure increase? How might this be related to interactions at the particle level?

_____

_____

_____

Although drilling a hole that is more than 12 km deep may seem amazing, this is only about 1/500 the distance to the center of Earth, or one-third of the way through Earth's continental crust.

Today, scientists are working on a project as part of the International Ocean Discovery Program to drill through the much thinner oceanic crust and provide important information about its composition, temperature, pressure, and other properties.

Modeling Earth's Interior

At Earth's center is a solid *inner core* surrounded by a liquid *outer core*. Around that is the mostly solid *lower mantle*, then the mostly solid *asthenosphere*, or upper mantle. The very outermost shell of Earth is the solid and brittle *lithosphere*. Each part is physically different, so energy is transferred in different ways as it makes its way from Earth's interior to its surface.

 Language Arts Connection Conduct research to find the average thickness of these five layers. Then use this information to develop a scale model showing Earth's layers. A scale model accurately reflects relationships between parts of a system. Last, prepare a report that answers the following questions and lists the sources of information you used.

- How did you portray the relative thickness of each of Earth's layers?
- How could this model be used to guide the development of more complex models of Earth's interior?
- What are the benefits and drawbacks of the model you developed?

Because it is so difficult to observe Earth's interior directly, scientists must rely on other methods to study it. In addition to direct evidence from drilling, scientists rely on indirect evidence such as laboratory experiments, chemical analyses, and data from waves of energy that travel through Earth when Earthquakes occur.

Evidence from the Sea Floor

Sea-floor data provide evidence of Earth's internal energy. The mid-ocean ridge is a long volcanic mountain range on the sea floor that forms where tectonic plates move apart. Here, eruptions and hydrothermal vents emit lava and other hot fluids onto the ocean floor. Scientists can study maps of the sea floor and tell where tectonic plates pull apart because the mid-ocean ridge runs along these types of plate boundaries.

Analyzing mid-ocean ridges allows scientists to better understand how processes in Earth's interior are related to their formation. Figure 2 shows the East Pacific Rise, a section of mid-ocean ridge that extends from near Antarctica to the Gulf of California.

ASK What are some questions you would ask to learn more about how mid-ocean ridges form?

_____

_____

_____

_____

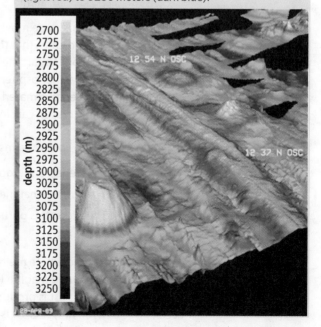

FIGURE 2: This map shows part of a mid-ocean ridge. The colors indicate depth, ranging from 2700 meters (light red) to 3250 meters (dark blue).

Analyzing Sea-Floor Age

The map in Figure 3 shows the ages of sea-floor rock. Boundaries between tectonic plates are indicated by black lines. As you can see, several plate boundaries run along the sea floor. The plate boundaries surrounded by red in Figure 3 are the site of mid-ocean ridges.

FIGURE 3:
This map shows the ages of rocks on the sea floor.

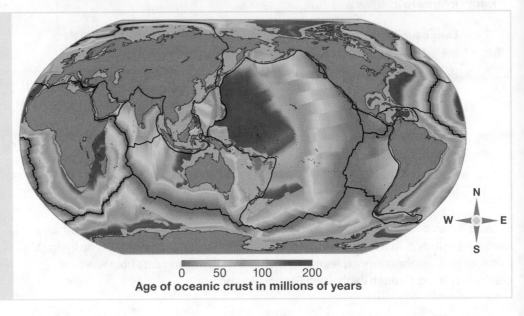

0   50   100   200

Age of oceanic crust in millions of years

ANALYZE Use Figure 3 to complete the statement about rocks in oceanic crust.

Continual eruptions occur along mid-ocean ridges, forming new sea-floor rock. The rocks closest to a mid-ocean ridge are the youngest | oldest. As you move away from a mid-ocean ridge, the rocks get younger | older. This implies that crust is being consumed | produced at mid-ocean ridges.

Earth's surface appears to be moving apart at mid-ocean ridges. But how does this happen? Evidence indicates that the crust undergoes tension, or stretching, at mid-ocean ridges. This tension pulls apart the lithosphere, drawing relatively hotter mantle material from the underlying asthenosphere up toward the surface. Pressure from the rocks above it would normally keep this material from melting. But, as the material rises toward the surface, pressure decreases, causing the rock to partially melt.

EXPLAIN Select the correct terms to complete the statement.

As most solid materials undergo melting, the particles in the material are compressed | spread apart. Thus, the material expands | contracts, and its density increases | decreases. Therefore, this portion of the material will rise | sink relative to the surrounding material.

As rock in the asthenosphere melts, it becomes less dense than the material around it. This causes the newly formed magma to rise to the surface. As molten rock pushes through to Earth's surface, new crust is produced. This crust continually moves away from the mid-ocean ridge as even newer crust is formed and takes its place. This process, called sea-floor spreading, explains the patterns in age shown in Figure 3.

Tectonic Plate Motion

Numerous observations, experiments, and calculations have been put together to map Earth's tectonic plates. Figure 4 shows the name of each plate and he direction of motion along different plate boundaries.

FIGURE 4: The arrows on this map show the direction of movement for tectonic plates.

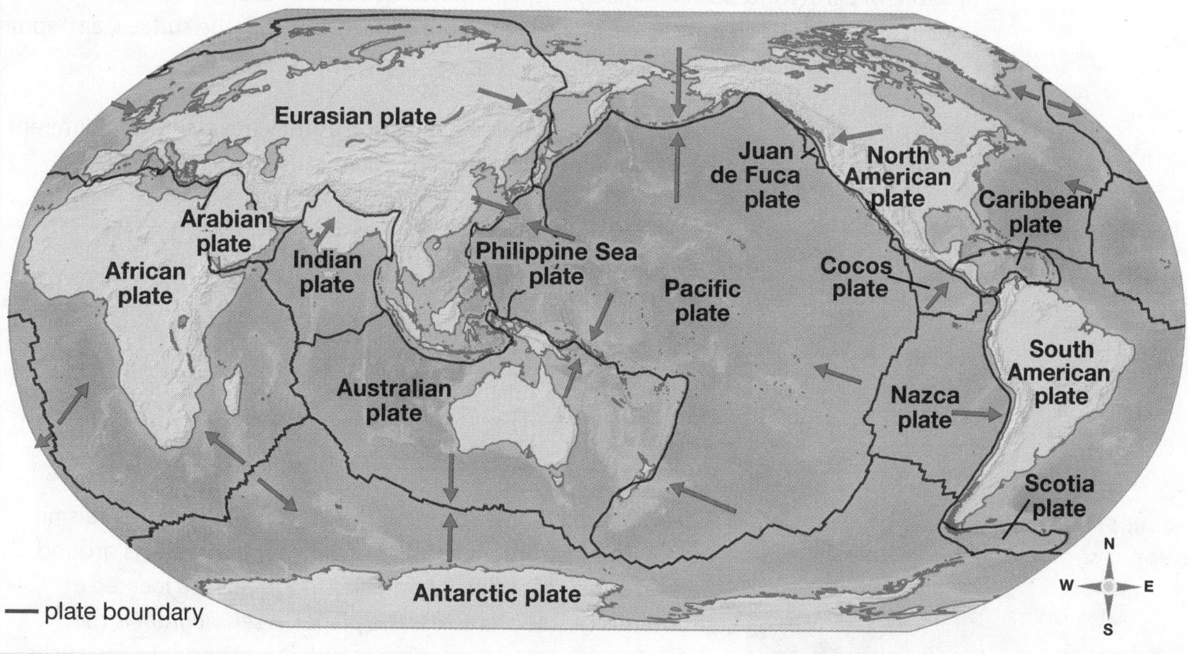

— plate boundary

GPS data tell us how fast and which direction each tectonic plate moves. At plate boundaries, the plates may be pulling apart, pushing together, or grinding past each other, depending on the relative directions of the plates.

 Engineering

Using GPS to Track Tectonic Plates

Scientists track the movement of Earth's plates using GPS measurements. The equipment scientists use to track plate movements is like a more advanced version of the GPS units people use in daily life. GPS instruments use satellites to determine position. This technology was once very expensive and could only deliver data as frequently as once a day. Today, hundreds of GPS units may be placed in a given region, and they can report much more frequent readings. These readings are also very precise, allowing scientists to track ground motions as small as one tenth of a millimeter. GPS networks have revealed a great deal about the movements of tectonic plates.

Language Arts Connection Research GPS equipment and make a presentation explaining how it is used to track the movement of tectonic plates. How are the data collected, stored, and shared? What has been learned from analyzing this data?

The boundaries of tectonic plates are very active regions. They are the sites of mountain chains, active volcanoes, and earthquakes. Earthquakes are happening every day on Earth.

Data from Seismic Waves

Data compiled from earthquakes over the last century have provided scientists a clearer picture of Earth's interior. A single earthquake sends waves of energy called *seismic waves* out in all directions. Seismic waves travel along the surface, beneath the surface, and some go all the way through Earth's interior.

PREDICT Seismic waves can change speed and direction as they travel through different sections of Earth's interior. What factors do you think could cause these changes?

_____

_____

_____

_____

_____

FIGURE 5: The squiggly lines on this drum are a record of vibrations from a distant earthquake.

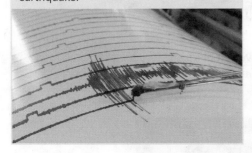

A *seismograph* is an instrument that detects and records seismic waves. This instrument consists of a sensor that detects ground motion and a recording system. Seismographs are located at thousands of stations across the planet. A *seismogram* is the recording produced by a seismograph. An earthquake produces different types of waves, which can be identified on a seismogram.

As Figure 6 shows, P-waves are longitudinal waves that make vibrations in the direction of travel, forming areas of compressions and dilations. P-waves can travel through solids, liquids, and gases. S-waves are transverse waves, so their vibrations are at right angles to the direction of travel. S-waves can only travel through solids.

FIGURE 6: P-waves and S-waves

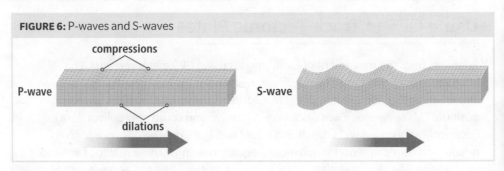

compressions

P-wave

dilations

S-wave

ANALYZE Choose all the materials that S-waves cannot travel through. Select all correct answers.

☐ **a.** water ☐ **b.** solid rock ☐ **c.** sand ☐ **d.** molten rock

The speed and direction of seismic waves changes depending on the properties of the materials that they pass through. Both P-waves and S-waves travel faster through denser and more rigid materials because the energy is transferred through particle to particle collisions. At boundaries where materials change density or rigidity, seismic waves may reflect or refract (bend). Waves refract when the speed and direction of the wave changes.

Figure 7 shows a simplified view of the directions that S-waves (left) and
P-waves (right) travel from a single earthquake. As shown on the left, a
"shadow" zone exists for S-waves where seismographs do not register any
of these waves from the earthquake. From this observation, we can tell that
S-waves do not travel through Earth's core. P-waves have two smaller shadow
zones, which are areas where seismometers do not register any P-waves.
P-waves are bent as they pass through an area where Earth's interior changes
in density. This wave pattern tells us the mantle, outer core, and inner core have different
physical properties, such as density.

Explore Online ▶

Hands-On Lab

Modeling Earth's Interior
Use seismic data to develop a model
of Earth's interior structure.

FIGURE 7: S-waves cannot travel through the liquid outer core. P-waves pass through the
mantle and core, but they change speed and direction when properties change.

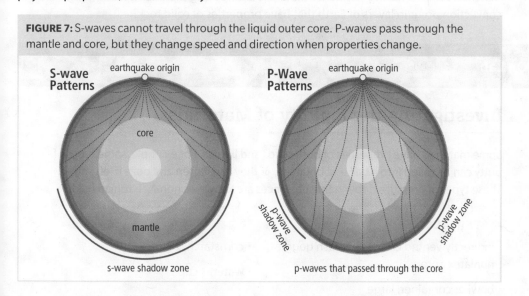

S-wave Patterns — earthquake origin — core — mantle — s-wave shadow zone

P-Wave Patterns — earthquake origin — p-wave shadow zone — p-wave shadow zone — p-waves that passed through the core

INFER Use Figure 7 to complete this statement about Earth's interior.

S-waves do | do not pass through the outer core, so the outer core is most likely

liquid | solid. S- and P-waves do | do not pass through the lithosphere, asthenosphere,

and lower mantle, indicating that they are most likely liquid | solid.

Inge Lehmann, a Danish seismologist, was looking at seismographs after a strong
earthquake in New Zealand in 1929. Lehmann noticed that some seismographs showed
P-waves where they should not appear because they would have been refracted by the
core. She developed a model to explain the pattern she saw in the seismic waves. The
only way her model worked was if the core was a molten outer core and solid inner core.
She published her work in 1936. Additional data collected since then by more sensitive
seismographs support the claim that Earth has a rigid lithosphere, a plastic asthenosphere
and lower mantle, a liquid outer core, and a solid inner core.

EXPLAIN Why does developing a model of Earth's interior require the collaboration of
professionals from many different fields and many different locations around the world?

_____

_____

_____

_____

Evidence Notebook Consider your scale model of Earth's interior. Add to your model by
indicating the properties of each layer. Then, write an explanation that tells how seismic data
support the additional information in your model.

Analyzing Earth's Interior

One way energy is transferred within Earth is by convection. Convection is the movement of material due to density differences and is driven by the force of gravity. Denser materials sink, displacing less dense materials and causing them to rise. But how can convection occur in layers of Earth that have properties of solid rock?

 Hands-On Lab

Investigating the Fluidity of Materials

Some materials have properties of both solids and liquids. For example, some types of putty can be rolled into a ball and bounced, or they can flatten and ooze if left sitting. These types of pressure-dependent substances are known as non-Newtonian fluids.

indirectly vented chemical splash goggles

MATERIALS

- indirectly vented chemical splash goggles, nonlatex apron
- bowl or container, large
- cornstarch, 2 cups
- water, 1 cup

SAFETY INFORMATION

- Wear indirectly vented chemical splash goggles and a nonlatex apron during the setup, hands-on, and takedown segments of the activity.
- Quickly wipe up any spilled water on the floor so it does not become a slip/fall hazard.

FIGURE 8: A mixture of cornstarch and water acts like both a solid and a liquid.

CARRY OUT THE INVESTIGATION

1. Combine 2 cups of cornstarch and 1 cup of water in a container. Mix the ingredients together using your fingers.
2. Apply sudden pressure to the mixture. Then try applying pressure gradually. Record your observations in your Evidence Notebook.
3. Try new ratios of ingredients and repeat the previous step. Record your observations in your Evidence Notebook.

ANALYZE

Answer the following questions in your Evidence Notebook:

1. How did the properties of the mixture change when you applied different types of pressure? Why do you think this is?
2. What happened when you mixed new ratios of ingredients?
3. How do you think observations of this type of material might help in thinking about the behavior of mantle rock?

Earth's asthenosphere and lower mantle are made up of solid rock, but over geologic time, the materials there flow more like a fluid. This behavior is due to the force of gravity and conditions such as high temperatures, as well as density differences throughout the layers of Earth's interior.

More Evidence of Earth's Structure and Composition

The more we know about Earth's interior, the more we can learn about geologic processes driven by energy within Earth. Evidence from drilling, GPS data, the sea floor, and seismic waves tell us the lithosphere is rigid and broken into moving tectonic plates. Seismic wave data also provide evidence of Earth's internal structure beneath the lithosphere including its solid inner core, liquid outer core, and the solid, but plastic, lower mantle and asthenosphere. Additional evidence of Earth's interior come from mantle rocks brought up by eruptions, meteorites, and Earth's density.

Mantle Rocks

Solid chunks of mantle rock can be picked up as deep sources of magma rise to the surface and erupt. These solid chunks are called mantle *xenoliths*. Mantle xenoliths, like the one shown in Figure 9, give scientists actual samples of some of Earth's upper mantle.

FIGURE 9: Mantle xenolith

Meteorites

Meteorites are bodies from space that have crashed onto Earth. Scientists think some meteorites have similar compositions to certain layers in Earth. For example, some rocky meteorites have a similar composition to Earth's lithosphere. Metallic meteorites contain mostly iron and may have a similar makeup to Earth's core.

FIGURE 10: Rocky meteorite

FIGURE 11: Metallic meteorite

Earth's Density

Rocks from Earth's crust—the top part of the lithosphere—have an average density of about 2.8 g/cm^3. Earth's gravitational effect on other bodies in space indicate that Earth's average density is 5.5 g/cm^3. This difference suggests that rock below the crust must be denser than the crust. This information, along with the known densities of specific elements, allows scientists to conclude that the core is composed mainly of iron.

PREDICT How do you think scientists simulate the conditions in Earth's interior to better understand how the properties of iron change under these conditions?

_____

_____

_____

_____

_____

Modeling Conditions in Earth's Interior

FIGURE 12: Two opposing diamonds in a diamond anvil cell exert extreme pressure on tiny rock samples.

One way scientists infer what is happening deep inside Earth is by conducting lab experiments to observe how rocks behave under high pressures and temperatures. A tool that scientists use to measure properties under these extreme conditions is a diamond anvil cell. A diamond anvil cell compresses a tiny piece of material between two diamond tips. Recall that pressure is a force spread over a certain area, and diamond tips have a very small area. Because of the hardness of diamond, high pressure can be exerted on the sample without the diamond breaking. Thermal energy can be added using a laser. This lets scientists observe and analyze the properties of different types of rocks at the pressure and temperatures found deep within Earth.

Diamond anvil cell tests have provided estimated temperatures of Earth's core and mantle. The core has a temperature range of about 4400 °C to 6000 °C. The wide range is due to the fact that temperature changes with depth and that there are uncertainties about the exact composition of the core. As scientists learn more about its composition and improve experimental techniques, more precise determinations can be made. The temperature range for the mantle is about 3700 °C at its base (where it meets the core) and 1000 °C at its top (where it meets the crust). Scientists can better determine temperatures for the mantle because they are not as extreme as the core, and the mantle's composition is better understood.

To understand what happens in the solid inner core, scientists have modeled the three crystalline forms of iron observed at the surface or in diamond-anvil cell experiments: body-centered cubic (bcc), face-centered cubic (fcc), and hexagonal close-packed (hcp). The models used were a series of calculations run on a supercomputer. The results of modeling all three crystal types are compared to seismic data to determine which model best explains the observations.

FIGURE 13: Iron is found in three crystalline forms: body-centered cubic (bcc), face-centered cubic (fcc), and hexagonal close-packed (hcp).

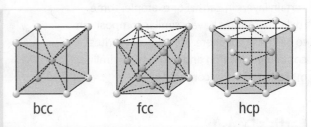

bcc   fcc   hcp

Before the modeling, scientists believed that the bcc structure was most likely to occur in the inner core. However, the computer models simulating the high pressure there showed that hcp is the only structure that fits with the seismic data.

ANALYZE What are the strengths and limitations of using a computer model?

_____

_____

_____

_____

_____

 Evidence Notebook Update your model of Earth's interior by adding information based on lab experiments, meteorites, mantle xenoliths, and density calculations. Explain how each piece of information is evidence for specific compositional or physical characteristics within Earth.

Explaining Energy Transfer in Earth's Interior

Earth's internal energy results in an extremely hot interior. As you go from Earth's surface toward the core, the temperature increases. This is known as the *geothermal gradient*.

Energy Transfer in Earth

Most energy transfer within Earth happens due to the process of convection. The exact nature of convection in Earth's asthenosphere and lower mantle are an important field of study in geology today. Conduction also transfers energy in Earth. For conduction to occur, materials of different temperatures must be in contact with each other. In conduction, kinetic energy moves from one particle to the next particle. Because Earth's core is hotter than the mantle, we can assume heat is transferred from the core to the mantle via conduction.

APPLY Complete the paragraph to explain the transfer of energy between rock particles in contact with one another.

Thermal energy flows from warmer to cooler material. In Earth's interior, solid particles of rock are in contact with one another, so the process of conduction | convection transfers thermal energy from the warmer | cooler interior to the warmer | cooler surface.

Convection occurs when certain materials are unevenly heated. In Figure 14, a candle burns near one corner of a tube filled with water. Yellow dye is added in the opening at the top of the tube. As the candle burns, the temperature of the water increases in the lower right corner, and the density of the water decreases. The yellow dye shows that the cooler, denser water flows in a counter-clockwise direction toward the warmer, less dense water.

As the water moves away from the energy source, its temperature decreases and its density increases. Changes in density caused by uneven heating start a swirling motion that can go on continuously while a heat source is present.

EXPLAIN Complete the paragraph to explain how tectonic plates relate to convection in the mantle.

Where two plates move toward each other and one plate is much denser than the other, the denser | less dense plate sinks beneath the other plate into the asthenosphere. This forces less dense rock in the asthenosphere to rise.

FIGURE 14: A candle warms one corner of a tube, so the water there becomes less dense and rises. This makes the water in the tube circulate, as revealed by the dye.

Modeling Convection in Earth's Interior

Earth's interior can be modeled with a representative slice, as shown in Figure 15. Earth's lithosphere is a rigid solid and is broken into large slabs called tectonic plates. Most of the asthenosphere and lower mantle are also solid but convection occurs in these layers due to high temperatures, gravity, and density differences. The outer core is liquid and the inner core is solid as it is under extreme pressure.

FIGURE 15: Earth's layers

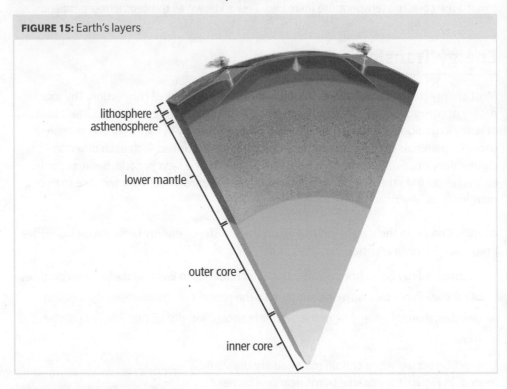

lithosphere
asthenosphere

lower mantle

outer core

inner core

ANALYZE The primary modes of transportation in Earth are conduction and convection. Complete the paragraph to explain how this occurs.

Energy flows from the core toward the surface due to pressure | temperature | density differences. Energy moves through the lower mantle and asthenosphere as rock flows due to density differences. This type of energy transfer is called conduction | convection | radiation. Wherever particles of different temperatures come into contact, conduction | convection | radiation transfers energy from warmer to cooler particles. It can be assumed that this occurs in the lower mantle, asthenosphere, and lithosphere as they are all solid rock.

Convection in the mantle occurs in large convection cells. Where mantle rock is colder and denser, it sinks and pushes up warmer, less-dense rock. This pattern of motion is called mantle convection. Mantle convection is one contributor to the movement of the tectonic plates that make up Earth's thin outer shell. In turn, moving tectonic plates deform Earth's surface, forming landforms and sea-floor features.

 Evidence Notebook Add to your model of Earth's interior to show how energy moves in different parts of Earth's interior and results in geologic processes. Explain what evidence supports the additional information in your model.

Explaining Plate Motion

In a simple model of convection-driven plate motion, the mantle moves by convection, and the plates ride on top like people on a moving walkway. However, this simple model does not fully explain the current data and observations of plate motion and mantle convection. For example, in some places, plates are moving at different speeds than the mantle rock below. Two other mechanisms that cause plate motion are slab pull and ridge push.

Slab Pull

The edges of some tectonic plates are oceanic. When tectonic plates move toward each other, the denser oceanic plate sinks into the mantle beneath the other plate. This is called *subduction*. Deep-sea trenches are formed where an oceanic plate is subducted. When the subducted plate moves down into the mantle, melting occurs that leads to the formation of volcanoes.

FIGURE 16: A deep-sea trench and a chain of volcanoes form at this subduction zone.

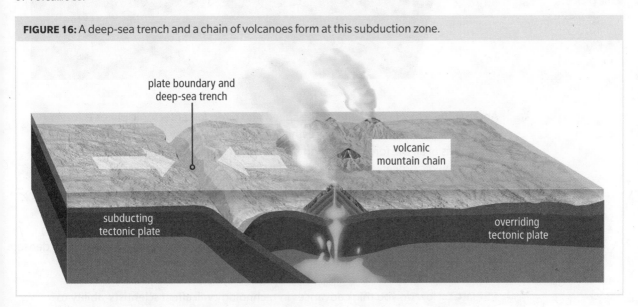

plate boundary and deep-sea trench

volcanic mountain chain

subducting tectonic plate

overriding tectonic plate

The gravitational force on the subducting edge of the plate produces a force called *slab pull*, which pulls the rest of the plate along with it. Most geologists think that this is the main driver of plate motion. This idea is supported by the fact that the speed of the plate is directly correlated to how much of the plate is subducting.

EXPLAIN How could you make a physical model that would demonstrate the process of slab pull? Describe your model and explain how it would demonstrate this process.

_____

_____

_____

_____

_____

Geologists also think that the subducting plate can indirectly exert a force on the other plate, the overriding plate. This is known as trench suction or *slab suction*. As the subducting slab descends, it pulls the overriding plate toward the subducting plate.

Ridge Push

Mid-ocean ridges are mountain ranges that can be thousands of meters higher than the sea floor on either side. At these sites, gravity pulls the newly-formed rock from eruptions downhill, which produces an outward force, called *ridge push*, on the rest of the plate. Some geologists think ridge push may be negligible when considering what drives tectonic plate motion.

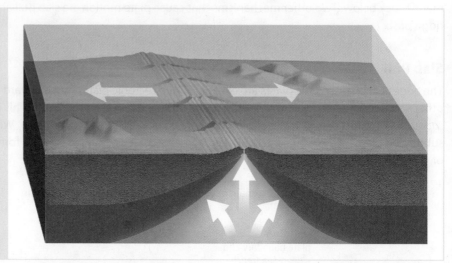

FIGURE 17: New sea-floor rock is formed where two plates pull apart and eruptions occur. This new rock is less dense than the surrounding sea floor, forming an elevated mid-ocean ridge. As rock continually forms and slides down either side of the mid-ocean ridge, it "pushes" the plates.

Another force that contributes to the speed and direction of tectonic plates is friction produced as plates move over the asthenosphere and as they interact with other plates. Regardless of all the forces acting on tectonic plates, we know that plate motion causes many geologic processes that affect society and the environment.

Maps of earthquakes and volcanic eruptions over time show that these processes mostly occur near plate boundaries. Mid-ocean ridges always run along the sea floor where plates are moving apart. The deepest places on Earth, the oceanic trenches, run along boundaries where the denser oceanic edges of lithospheric plates sink beneath less dense plates. At these locations, large earthquakes can occur.

PREDICT How do you think advances in technology will affect scientists' ability to understand processes that change Earth's surface?

_____

_____

_____

_____

_____

_____

_____

 Evidence Notebook Write an explanation summarizing the connections between energy transfer in Earth's interior, plate movements, and changes we see in Earth's surface.

Careers in Science

Geophysicist

Do you enjoy spending time outdoors, carefully observing Earth's features? Do you want to use your knowledge of Earth's interior to help protect people during natural disasters? Do you like using computers to carry out calculations or run simulations? If any of these describes you, you might enjoy a career as a geophysicist. Geophysicists study Earth using different methods, such as seismic, electrical, and magnetic techniques.

The field of geophysics includes many different areas of focus. Careers within this field include seismologist, marine geophysicist, petroleum geophysicist, environmental geophysicist, and magnetic geophysicist, just to name a few.

Seismologists study seismic waves and how they interact with local geology and Earth as a whole. They may study seismic waves generated by earthquakes or by human activities. Some seismologists study how seismic waves are created at different types of faults and the types of stresses that are involved in causing earthquakes.

Seismologists may also locate new faults and identify areas where faults occur to assess them for future earthquakes. These seismologists may work on ways to predict when earthquakes will occur. With warning, the risk to people from earthquakes can be reduced. Seismologists also work with engineers to develop buildings that sustain less damage during earthquakes.

Marine geophysicists use different types of technology to map features of the sea floor and understand the area beneath it. A marine geophysicist might use technology such as sonar, video, and/or a variety of advanced sensors to collect data. These technologies allow scientists to analyze properties of the ocean floor, such as shape, density, and magnetic properties. The data collected by marine geophysicists are used to

FIGURE 18: Seismologists analyze data after an earthquake strikes the coast of El Salvador.

make high-resolution maps. These maps are used for applications in geology, petroleum exploration, marine biology, and transportation.

Geophysicists working for petroleum exploration companies look for specific types of geologic structures where gas or oil may be found. Developing a better picture of what is below Earth's surface helps these geophysicists identify locations where petroleum deposits might be buried. One way these scientists locate petroleum involves using a seismic source to make waves that reflect off of rock layers and then analyzing the data that are collected.

> **Science in Your Community** Research a scientist who is a geophysicist. How did this person's experiences influence them to become a scientist? What does their job entail? How does their research help their community and others? Write an article about the person you researched and include citations for your sources.

| SEISMIC ACTIVITY IN YOUR AREA | MODELING EARTH'S INTERIOR | Go online to choose one of these other paths. |

Lesson Self-Check

CAN YOU EXPLAIN IT?

FIGURE 19: Molten lava erupting through Earth's surface is incredibly hot.

Lava erupting out of a volcano is evidence of the energy inside Earth. Some of the energy in Earth's interior is left over from when the planet formed. Some is the result of the breakdown of unstable elements. The extreme heat and pressures inside Earth make it impossible to directly observe its inner layers. Besides data from mantle xenoliths and from drilling into the uppermost part of the lithosphere, scientists must use indirect evidence to make claims about Earth's structure and composition. Scientists will continue to adjust models of Earth's interior as more data are gathered.

 Evidence Notebook Use the notes in your Evidence Notebook to explain how energy is transferred in different parts of Earth's interior.

1. **Claim** How is energy transferred within Earth? How do the properties of Earth's layers influence the way energy is transferred?
2. **Evidence** Cite evidence to support your claim.
3. **Reasoning** Explain how the evidence you cited supports your claim.

CHECKPOINTS

Check Your Understanding

1. Which of these claims about the way energy is transferred in Earth's interior is supported by evidence?
   - ○ **a.** Convection occurs in the inner core.
   - ○ **b.** Convection occurs in the inner core and crust.
   - ○ **c.** Convection occurs in the outer core and mantle.
   - ○ **d.** Convection occurs in the mantle and inner core.

2. Which of these is true about P-waves?
   - ○ **a.** Their vibrations are at right angles to the direction of travel.
   - ○ **b.** They can only travel through solids.
   - ○ **c.** They travel more slowly through denser materials.
   - ○ **d.** They are longitudinal waves that make areas of compressions and dilations.

3. Which of these are the best evidence that the ocean floors are spreading from oceanic ridges? Select all correct answers.
   - ☐ **a.** The youngest rocks on the ocean floor are found closest to oceanic ridges.
   - ☐ **b.** Deep-sea trenches are found at the mid-oceanic ridges.
   - ☐ **c.** The oldest rocks on the ocean floor are found the farthest from mid-ocean ridges.
   - ☐ **d.** The ocean floor is made up of oceanic crust, which is thinner than continental crust.

4. Which of the following are properties of the mantle? Select all correct answers.
   - ☐ **a.** Only P-waves pass through it.
   - ☐ **b.** P- and S-waves pass through it.
   - ☐ **c.** It is a solid.
   - ☐ **d.** It is a liquid.
   - ☐ **e.** It is made up of mostly gases.

5. Which of the following are properties of the outer core? Select all correct answers.
   - ☐ **a.** It is composed mainly of iron.
   - ☐ **b.** It causes some waves to refract at its boundary.
   - ☐ **c.** Some P-waves are unable to pass through it.
   - ☐ **d.** It is molten.
   - ☐ **e.** It is solid.

6. Scientists look at several pieces of evidence to determine why tectonic plates move. Which of the following do scientists think contribute to plate movement? Select all correct answers.
   - ☐ **a.** mantle convection
   - ☐ **b.** Coriolis effect
   - ☐ **c.** wind currents
   - ☐ **d.** slab pull
   - ☐ **e.** ridge push

7. Select the correct terms to complete the statement.

   A seismograph is located on the other side of Earth from an earthquake. The seismograph records many kinds of seismic waves, but no direct P-waves | S-waves are recorded. This is because S-waves are | are not able to pass through the molten outer core.

8. Select the correct terms to complete the statement.

   Patterns in seismic waves indicate that the outer core is composed of mostly molten iron, and the mantle is a rigid | plastic solid. Therefore, convection can occur in the mantle and inner core | mantle and outer core | mantle only.

CHECKPOINTS (continued)

9. How does a diamond anvil cell help scientists learn more about the behavior of materials in Earth's interior?

_____

_____

_____

_____

_____

10. What happens to P-waves and S-waves when they reach the boundary between the mantle and the outer core? What does this tell us about the outer core?

_____

_____

_____

_____

_____

_____

11. Explain how energy can be transferred through Earth's mantle by convection, even though evidence shows that this layer is made up of solid rock.

_____

_____

_____

_____

_____

_____

_____

MAKE YOUR OWN STUDY GUIDE

 In your Evidence Notebook, design a study guide that supports the main ideas from this lesson:

Energy moves through Earth by conduction, convection, and radiation.

Energy transfer is one factor that causes changes at Earth's surface.

Remember to include the following information in your study guide:
- Use examples that model main ideas.
- Record explanations for the phenomena you investigated.
- Use evidence to support your explanations. Your support can include drawings, data, graphs, laboratory conclusions, and other evidence recorded throughout the lesson.

Consider how modeling allows scientists to better understand the way energy drives the cycling of matter in Earth's interior.

Earth Science Connection

Driving Weather Patterns Along California's coast, atmospheric convection is driven by the interaction between the air and the water of the Pacific Ocean. Convection currents occur when cooler, denser air falls below warmer air, pushing the warmer air above it. This causes the atmosphere to move and mix. This complex system of air and water causes complex weather patterns.

Make a multimedia presentation describing how the interactions between water and air cause convection. How does this interaction drive weather patterns along the California coast? In your presentation, identify the sources of energy that transfers during the convection process.

FIGURE 1: The transfer of energy between the water in the hydrosphere and air in the atmosphere creates constantly changing weather near the coast.

Social Studies Connection

Geothermal Energy A hot spring is a pool of surface water that rises from an underground reservoir warmed by contact with hot rock. The warm spring water at Blue Lagoon, Iceland, is used as a spa, drawing visitors from around the world. The reservoir that provides warm water to the spring is also used at a nearby geothermal power plant. Steam and hot water from the reservoir are used to drive turbines that generate electricity for the country. Nearly 25% of Iceland's electricity comes from geothermal power.

Write an article describing the connection between locations with natural hot springs and geothermal energy. Provide information about how geothermal energy is used in various locations for electricity production, as well as other uses.

FIGURE 2: Blue Lagoon hot spring, Iceland.

Engineering Connection

Studying Volcanoes Scientists have limited knowledge about the conditions inside active volcano craters. It is a place filled with toxic and corrosive gases, extreme heat, and unpredictable shifts of matter—not an easy laboratory to work in. Because scientists cannot enter the volcano themselves, they bring in robots to collect data for them. The challenge for engineers is designing a robot or drone that can withstand those inhospitable conditions that keep humans out of the volcano.

Prepare a poster presentation describing the processes used to engineer robots for extreme tasks, such as collecting data in an active volcano. Pay particular attention to the properties of the materials engineers use to build robots for these extreme tasks.

FIGURE 3: Conditions inside an active volcano crater are not suitable for humans, so research relies on robots and drones.

A BOOK EXPLAINING
COMPLEX IDEAS USING
ONLY THE 1,000 MOST
COMMON WORDS

BIG FLAT ROCKS WE LIVE ON

How the ground under your feet is always on the move

Huge, moving slabs of rock called tectonic plates constantly reshape Earth's surface. Here's how it happens.

RANDALL MUNROE
XKCD.COM

THE STORY OF ROCKS THAT MOVE

THE SURFACE OF THE EARTH IS MADE UP OF BIG FLAT ROCKS MOVING AROUND. THE ROCKS UNDER LAND AREAS ARE USUALLY THICK, SLOW-MOVING, AND LAST FOR A LONG TIME, AND THE ONES UNDER SEAS ARE THIN, HEAVY, AND MOVE FAST.

HARD TO BELIEVE IT'S JUST A BIG PILE OF ROCKS DOWN THERE . . .

YOU COULDN'T JUST ENJOY THE MOMENT, COULD YOU?

(FAST FOR A ROCK, THAT IS. THEY MOVE ABOUT AS FAST AS THE THINGS ON THE ENDS OF YOUR FINGERS GROW.)

WHAT EXACTLY ARE YOU DOING?

COME ON— FASTER, FASTER!

IT'S CLOSE, BUT I THINK I CAN BEAT THIS ROCK!

WHEN A SEA ROCK HITS A LAND ROCK, THE SEA ROCK IS USUALLY PUSHED UNDER IT, DOWN INTO THE EARTH. AREAS WHERE THIS HAPPENS OFTEN HAVE DEEP SEAS RIGHT NEAR LAND, LINES OF MOUNTAINS, SHAKING GROUND, AND BIG WAVES.

YEAH!

YEAH!

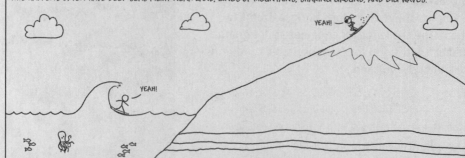

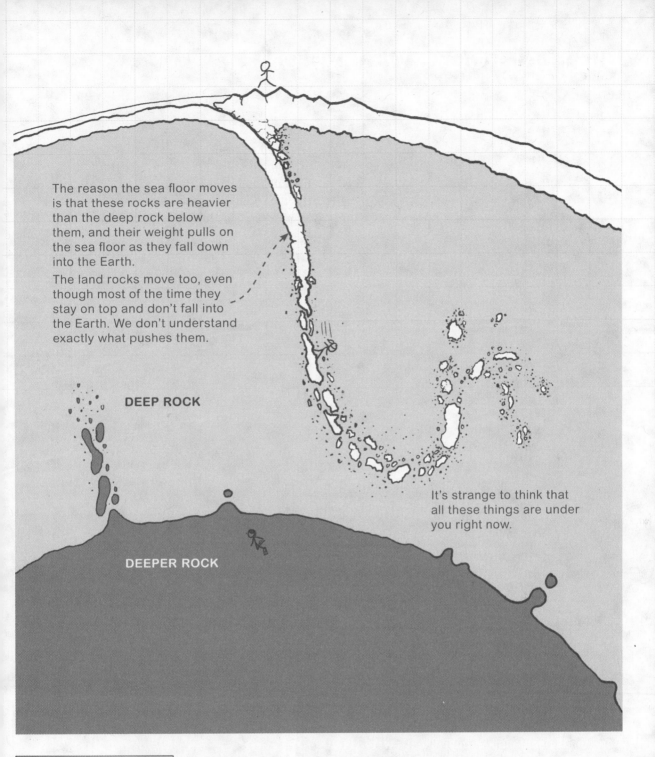

The reason the sea floor moves is that these rocks are heavier than the deep rock below them, and their weight pulls on the sea floor as they fall down into the Earth.

The land rocks move too, even though most of the time they stay on top and don't fall into the Earth. We don't understand exactly what pushes them.

DEEP ROCK

DEEPER ROCK

It's strange to think that all these things are under you right now.

...WHAT ARE YOU DOING?

STOP IT! STOP IT!

AUGH!

WHERE DO ROCKS GO AFTER THEY DIE?

We used to think that when rocks fell into the Earth, they broke up right away from the heat. And even if they stayed together for a little while, it didn't really matter, since they were hidden away forever. That part of our history was gone.

But it turns out they're not quite gone. When the world shakes, we can listen to the sound go around and through the world. By listening very carefully, we can hear the sound hitting things inside the Earth, and learn what it's like in there.

By listening to the Earth, we've learned that the rocks don't all turn to water right away. We can keep track of them, even when they're out of reach of our eyes, as they fall down, down, down into the Earth.

I think that's really cool.

BIG FLAT ROCKS WE LIVE ON

SEA FLOOR

DEEP PART
The sea floor is deeper here because the sea rocks are getting pushed down as they run into the land rocks.

LAND FLOOR

SEA ROCKS
Sea rocks are heavy. They slide along like a moving road, and they move fast! Not as fast as a person, but faster than most kinds of land.

When sea rocks hit land rocks, the sea rocks usually get pushed back down under the land rocks, down into the Earth, where they break down. Because most sea rocks run into land and disappear after a while, most parts of the sea floor aren't as old as the land floor.

WATER-CARRYING ROCKS
Sea water gets carried inside the Earth here. The water changes the rocks in a way that helps the rock go back up through the rocks above it and come out of holes in the ground.

DEEP ROCK
This part of the world can be hard to understand. Sometimes people talk about it like it's watery, but sometimes they talk about it like it's hard.

The real truth is that it's very hard. If you touched a piece of it, it would feel very hard. (You shouldn't touch it, though, because it would also set your hand on fire.) It's harder than the hardest metal, glass, or even stones in a marriage ring. That makes it sound a lot like rock, not water.

But in some ways, it also acts like water. It's sort of like the big rivers of ice that slide slowly down from mountains. The ice is hard up close, and you can walk on it and break pieces off. But if you look at it from far away, and wait a very long time, you'll see that it moves like water.

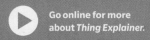
Go online for more about *Thing Explainer*.

LOW AREA

These low areas between mountains sometimes have water in them, and the ground there is usually good for growing things, so people like to live there. Sometimes hot rocks come out of the mountains and cover everyone's houses. But that doesn't happen very often, so people try not to worry about it too much.

Small Soft, the company that makes Windows®, is in a city like this.

HOT ROCK MOUNTAIN

The rocks that get pushed into the Earth get hot and watery, and some of them come up through holes in the rock above them. They come out of those holes and cool down and turn into mountains.

ROCK MOUNTAIN

Not all the mountains in this kind of place are made from hot rock. When a sea plate goes under a land plate, it can make mountains by pushing up on the land plate.

If two land plates hit, it can make very big mountains. The biggest mountains on Earth right now were made this way.

LAND ROCKS

These are like big rock boats that drive around on top of the hotter rocks under them.

WHEN THE EARTH SHAKES, SOMETIMES THERE ARE BIG WAVES. THIS IS THE KIND OF SHAKING THAT MAKES THE BIGGEST WAVES:

There's a place in my country on the edge of the sea. (They once made a game for kids about trying to get to this place. You had to cross rivers and shoot animals for food and sometimes people in your family died. It was supposed to teach you about the past, but I just played the shooting part and never learned very much.)

Right by the water, there's something very strange: dead trees in the sea. There are lots of dead trees in the sea. But what's strange about these trees is that they're not lying down. They're sticking up from the sea floor, like they grew there. That shouldn't be possible, because those trees can't grow in sea water. The sea rises and falls, but the trees only

died 300 years ago, and the sea hasn't risen enough to explain how these trees grew there.

The answer is that the sea didn't rise. The land fell.

On the other side of the sea, 300 years ago, there was a big wave. People who saw it wrote about it. They also wrote that they didn't feel the ground shake before the wave.

The reason they didn't feel the ground shake is that the shaking didn't happen near them. It happened far away, across the sea, in the place from the kids' game. And by the edge of the water, the ground went down a little bit, and the sea came in and covered the trees.

Designing a Convection Model

Convection is the main process by which energy is transferred in fluids, such as the atmosphere, the oceans, and the fluid layers of Earth's structure. A gigantic convection system in the ocean causes worldwide currents that circulate nutrients toward the surface and influence climates throughout the world. Cold, very salty, dense water near the poles sinks and flows toward the equator, displacing other water as it does. Design and build a physical model of convection that represents the flow of materials in convection currents of the world ocean.

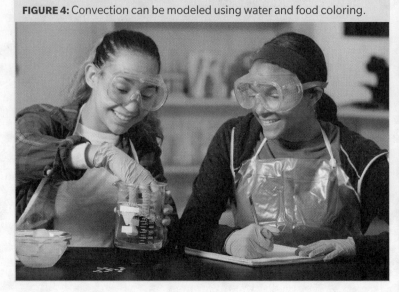
FIGURE 4: Convection can be modeled using water and food coloring.

1. ASK A QUESTION

Write a list of questions you have about the ocean convection process and different ways convection in the ocean can be modeled. Then explain how finding answers to your questions can help you develop your own convection model.

2. CONDUCT RESEARCH

Investigate various types of convection models used by scientists and how these models help them study complex processes. Then investigate simple ways you can model convection. These might include using heated air, liquids with food coloring, or other fluids with differing densities. List at least three methods that you find interesting.

3. DEVELOP A MODEL

Share the modeling methods you found interesting with your team. Decide which type of model you and your team wish to develop. Make a sketch of your convection model and indicate how it will work. Write a procedure, develop a safety plan, and compile a materials list for building your model. Have your teacher check your plans before you build your model.

4. CONSTRUCT AN EXPLANATION

Identify how ocean circulation is driven by convection and how your model could be used to explain the natural processes that drive large currents. Then, make a video of your team using your model to explain how the phenomenon works.

5. COMMUNICATE

Present your video to the class and have them evaluate how well they learned about the phenomenon you modeled. How could you improve your model to be a better teaching tool?

 CHECK YOUR WORK

Once you have completed this task, you should have the following:

- a list of questions about modeling techniques
- research about ways to model convection
- a working model of a convection process
- an explanation of how your model relates to convection within the Earth system
- an evaluation of your model from your classmates

Name _____   Date _____

SYNTHESIZE THE UNIT

In your Evidence Notebook, make a concept map, other graphic organizer, or outline using the Study Guides you made for each lesson in this unit. Be sure to use evidence to support your claims.

When synthesizing individual information, remember to follow these general steps:

- Find the central idea of each piece of information.
- Think about the relationships among the central ideas.
- Combine the ideas to come up with a new understanding.

DRIVING QUESTIONS

Look back to the Driving Questions from the opening section of this unit. In your Evidence Notebook, review and revise your previous answers to those questions. Use the evidence you gathered and other observations you made throughout the unit to support your claims.

PRACTICE AND REVIEW

1. Which observation indicates that the outer core of Earth's interior is in a liquid state?
   - ○ a. P- and S-waves pass through the outer core.
   - ○ b. S-waves do not pass through the outer core.
   - ○ c. All type of waves are reflected when they reach the outer core.

2. Complete the statement.

   | conduction | convection | radiation |

   Energy is transferred by _____ when the soil surface is heated by sunlight on a warm day. As the soil becomes warmer, energy is transferred from the soil to the air touching it by _____. Energy is then transferred by _____ as the warm air mass rises in the atmosphere and is replaced by cooler air.

3. Complete the statement.

   On the ocean floor, the rocks closest to a mid-oceanic ridge are the youngest | oldest, indicating that tectonic plates are moving together | away from each other at the plate boundary. As the plates move away from one another, molten rock | metal flows between them.

4. Which statements describe the melting of an ice cube? Select all correct answers.
   - ☐ a. Entropy decreases as the ice melts.
   - ☐ b. The energy of the water molecules increases.
   - ☐ c. The temperature of the water molecules increases.
   - ☐ d. The system of the ice cube and the air in the room has no change in energy.
   - ☐ e. Work done on the ice causes it to melt.

5. A 14.7-L rigid container is filled with argon gas at 28.7 °C. If the temperature increases by 3.0 °C, how will the volume of the gas change?
   - ○ a. The volume of the gas will decrease.
   - ○ b. The volume of the gas will not change.
   - ○ c. The volume of the gas will increase.
   - ○ d. The volume of the gas will be less than zero.

6. Which of the following best support the claim that the cycling of matter and energy in Earth's interior affects Earth's surface? Select all correct answers.
   - ☐ a. Tectonic plates move together, apart, and past each other.
   - ☐ b. Lava can be observed rising to Earth's surface in some places.
   - ☐ c. The Earth's crust is much cooler than the Earth's interior.
   - ☐ d. The Earth's inner core is composed mostly of solid iron.

7. How are evaporation and boiling alike, and how they are different? In your
answer, discuss differences in energy and differences in temperature.

_____

_____

_____

_____

_____

_____

_____

8. Why does entropy increase during a spontaneous process, such as the process
that takes place when steel wool is placed into vinegar?

_____

_____

_____

_____

_____

_____

_____

9. Along the boundary of the inner and outer core of Earth, there is an interface
between two phases, solid and liquid. Explain how scientists used data from
earthquakes to draw this conclusion about Earth's interior.

_____

_____

_____

_____

_____

_____

_____

UNIT PROJECT

Return to your unit project. Prepare your research
and materials into a presentation to share with
the class. In your final presentation, evaluate the
strength of your hypothesis, data, analysis, and
conclusions.

Remember these tips while evaluating:

- How and where does convection occur within
  Earth systems?

- How is convection related to the transfer of
  energy within a system?

- What does your model demonstrate about
  convection that cannot be conveyed in a verbal
  description?

Patterns in the Properties of Matter

YOU SOLVE IT

Which Planetary-Rover Materials Are Suitable?

 To begin exploring this unit's concepts, go online to investigate ways to solve a real-world problem.

Cholesterol, shown here in crystalline form, is a compound made up of three different elements.

FIGURE 1: Ion traps, such as the one shown here, charge atomic particles and are being developed for use in quantum computers.

Traditional computers use a binary computing language, storing data in defined states as either ones or zeros. Quantum computers rely on particles, which can exist in many states, increasing computing power. While still in development, scientists plan to use quantum computers to solve some of the most complex system analysis challenges, such as artificial intelligence, weather forecasting, and complex molecular modeling.

PREDICT What information would scientists and engineers need to know about particle behavior when designing quantum computers?

_____

_____

DRIVING QUESTIONS

As you move through the unit, gather evidence to help you answer the following questions. In your Evidence Notebook, record what you already know about these topics and any questions you have about them.

1. What are physical and chemical properties of metals, nonmetals, and metalloids?
2. What is the scale and basic structure of an atom?
3. How do patterns in the periodic table predict the behavior and properties of elements?
4. How can different types of bonding affect the properties of substances?
5. How can you use the periodic table to help predict the types of bonds elements will form?

UNIT PROJECT

Go online to download the Unit Project Worksheet to help plan your project.

Designing an Atomic Model

Consider the benefits and drawbacks of different types of atomic models. Are some better suited to certain types of questions? Construct or research two different types of atomic models and explain what could be learned from each.

Language Development

Use the lessons in this unit to complete the chart and expand your understanding of the science concepts.

TERM: orbital

Definition	Example

Similar Term	Phrase

TERM: valence electron(s)

Definition	Example

Similar Term	Phrase

TERM: atomic number

Definition	Example

Similar Term	Phrase

TERM: ionization energy

Definition	Example

Similar Term	Phrase

TERM: electronegativity

Definition	Example

Similar Term	Phrase

TERM: ionic bond

Definition	Example

Similar Term	Phrase

TERM: covalent bond

Definition	Example

Similar Term	Phrase

TERM: metallic bond

Definition	Example

Similar Term	Phrase

Modeling Atomic Structure

This x-ray image shows left and right hands.

CAN YOU EXPLAIN IT?

If you have ever broken a bone, the physician likely confirmed the location and extent of the injury with an x-ray. X-rays are powerful electromagnetic waves often used as a tool to see inside the body and diagnose problems without having to perform surgery. These waves are powerful enough to pass through the softer tissues of the body, but not so powerful that the harder tissues such as bones easily absorb them. The resulting image shows in white the areas where the x-ray waves were absorbed. The areas where the waves passed through appear black.

INFER How can an x-ray image show differences between bones and soft tissues, such as muscles and lungs? How might the atoms that make up bones be different from the atoms that make up soft tissues?

_____

_____

_____

_____

_____

 Evidence Notebook As you explore the lesson, gather evidence to explain why x-rays are powerful enough to pass through some substances but not others.

Analyzing the Behavior of Elements

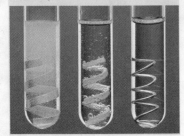

FIGURE 1: Magnesium, zinc, and copper react differently with hydrochloric acid.

Elements are pure substances composed of a single type of atom. No physical or chemical means can break down an element into other substances. The term *atom* means *indivisible* in ancient Greek. The discovery that matter is made of atoms came through a wide range of empirical evidence, especially through experiments on gases. By the early 1800s, scientists had a basic understanding of atoms as solid, indivisible tiny particles that made up all matter.

 Collaborate How is the reactivity of each element in Figure 1 different? Do you think these elements have other properties in common? Discuss your ideas with a partner.

Describing Properties of Elements

Each element has distinct, well-defined properties. Even though each element is unique, certain groups of elements have similar properties and can be classified together. The most general way to classify elements is as metals, nonmetals, and metalloids. Most elements are metals. *Metals* are generally good conductors of electricity and heat, and are shiny. They can be bent or hammered into sheets easily. Almost all metals are solid at room temperature. Magnesium, zinc, and copper are examples of metals.

In contrast, *nonmetals* are generally very poor conductors of electricity and heat. Many, such as nitrogen, oxygen, fluorine, and chlorine, are gases at room temperature. Those nonmetals that are solids at room temperature, such as carbon, phosphorus, sulfur, selenium, and iodine, tend to be brittle and are dull rather than shiny.

Metalloids have characteristics of metals and nonmetals. Metalloids are solids at room temperature. They are less brittle than nonmetals, but less easily shaped than metals. Metalloids do conduct electric current but not as well as metals. The "semiconducting" properties of metalloids such as boron and silicon make them useful in computer chips.

FIGURE 2: Elements are categorized into broad categories based on similar properties.

a Metals   b Nonmetals   c Metalloids

PREDICT How do you think the atoms in metal elements are different from those in nonmetals or metalloids? How might the atoms of different metals vary from one another?

_____

_____

Hands-On Lab

Exploring Reactivity

Reactivity is a measure of how readily an element combines with other elements. By observing the behavior of elements when they react with other substances, chemists can learn about the properties of the element and the atoms that make it. In this lab, you will react three elements with hydrochloric acid and observe the behaviors of each of them.

Research Question: What other types of tests do chemists use to learn about the properties of atoms?

MAKE A CLAIM

Which metal do you think will react most vigorously when placed in hydrochloric acid? What information could you gather to help you make your prediction?

_____

_____

_____

_____

_____

_____

MATERIALS

- indirectly vented chemical splash goggles, nonlatex apron, nitrile gloves
- aluminum, small sample
- hydrochloric acid solution, 1 M
- magnesium, small sample
- test tube rack
- test tubes (3)
- zinc, small sample

SAFETY INFORMATION

- Wear indirectly vented chemical splash goggles, a nonlatex apron, and nitrile gloves during the setup, hands-on, and takedown segments of the activity.
- The reaction between a metal and hydrochloric acid gives off hydrogen gas. Hydrogen gas and fumes from hydrochloric acid should not be inhaled, so these reactions should be completed inside a fume hood or in a well-ventilated room.
- Use caution when working with glassware, which can shatter if dropped and cut skin.
- Hydrochloric acid (HCl) is a strong acid that is highly corrosive to skin and other tissues. Point the test tube away from people and tell your teacher immediately if you spill chemicals on yourself, the table, or floor.

indirectly vented chemical splash goggles

CARRY OUT THE INVESTIGATION

1. Place a piece of aluminum in one test tube, zinc in a second test tube, and magnesium in a third test tube.

2. Place about 5–10 drops of 1 M hydrochloric acid in each test tube.

3. Record the relative reactivity (high, medium, low) of each element in the data table.

4. Pour the hydrochloric acid into a designated waste container, and rinse the test tubes.

COLLECT DATA

Element	Magnesium	Aluminum	Zinc
Relative reactivity			

ANALYZE

1. How did you determine whether a reaction was vigorous or not?

_____

_____

_____

2. Which metal reacted most vigorously when placed in the acid? Give evidence to support your answer.

_____

_____

DRAW CONCLUSIONS

Write a conclusion that addresses each of the points below.

Claim What might the relative reactivities of these elements imply about the structure of the atom?

Evidence Give specific evidence from your data and other observations you have made to support your claim.

Reasoning Explain how the evidence you gave supports your claim. Describe, in detail, the connections between the evidence you cited and the argument you are making.

_____

_____

_____

_____

_____

_____

_____

_____

_____

_____

_____

Arranging Elements by Their Properties

By the mid 1800s chemists had recognized two important facts about elements. The first was that elements could not be broken down into simpler substances. The second was that certain elements had properties similar to others. In other words, not all elements were completely unique.

Through experiments with gases, chemists had even determined the relative masses of atoms of different elements. They noticed there were patterns in the properties of the elements based on these masses. That is, an element with a mass far greater or lower than another often had properties more similar than those with only slightly different masses. For example, lithium, sodium, and potassium all react vigorously with water. Lithium reacts the least vigorously and potassium the most. Lithium's mass is about one-third that of sodium and about one-sixth that of potassium.

 Collaborate With a group, further research the relationship between mass and reactivity. Do other groups of elements show patterns similar to lithium, sodium, and potassium?

The discovery of another type of element, the noble gases, was also curious. Most elements interacted with other elements to form compounds. The noble gases, though, appeared not to combine with any other element. Without any chemical properties by which to compare them, chemists struggled to integrate them into emerging classification schemes. They found that even passing an electric current through these gases did not cause a reaction. It did cause the gases to produce light of different colors, a curious fact that added even more mystery surrounding the behavior of atoms.

FIGURE 3: Each sign spells out the element symbol of the gas with which it is filled.

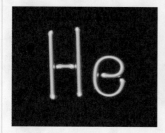 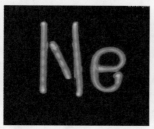 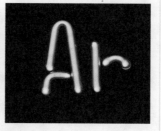

ASK Chemists knew that something other than mass influences the properties of elements. If you were a chemist, what questions would you ask about elements and their atoms that could help you discover more about their properties?

_____

_____

_____

_____

_____

 Evidence Notebook How do you think the structure of atoms that block x-rays differs from the structure of atoms that x-rays pass through?

Modeling the Atom

By the 1800s, most scientists agreed elements were composed of atoms. But what is an atom? Even today, scientists are still asking questions and carrying out investigations to learn more about the structure of atoms.

Investigating Atomic Structure

In the late 1800s, scientists studied gases by passing an electric current through various gases at low pressures inside a cathode-ray tube. A cathode-ray tube consists of a glass tube containing a gas at very low pressure, nearly a vacuum. Particles pass through the tube from the cathode, a metal disk connected to the negative terminal of the energy source, to the anode, a metal disk connected to a positive terminal. When a current is passed through the tube, the surface of the tube opposite the cathode glows. Scientists hypothesized that the glow was caused by a stream of particles they called a *cathode ray*. They then began asking questions about what this cathode ray was made of.

FIGURE 4: Holding a magnet near a cathode-ray tube deflected the particles in the beam.

Explore Online ▶

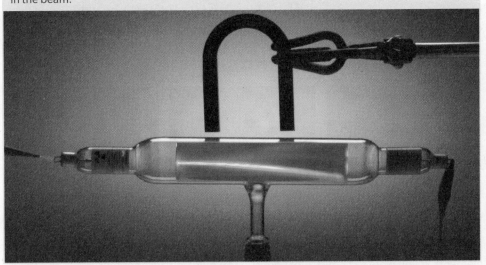

Through many investigations, scientists found that the cathode ray was deflected by a magnet, as shown in Figure 4. They also observed the rays deflected towards the positive plate when placed in an electric field. More importantly, they saw this deflection was always the same, regardless of the type of metal used to make the cathode or the gas in the tube. By measuring the deflection, they even estimated the mass of the particles.

EXPLAIN Based on the findings of these experiments, what could scientists conclude about the particles in the cathode ray?

_____

_____

_____

_____

Discovering Subatomic Particles

Up to the time of the discovery of the particles in the cathode ray, scientists thought of atoms as nothing more than tiny marbles or "billiard balls." Cathode-ray tube experiments showed there were particles even smaller than atoms and that all atoms contain them. These small, negatively charged particles were called electrons. The deflection experiments indicated electrons had a mass of 9.109×10^{-31} kg, or 1/1837 the mass of a hydrogen atom. This discovery was slightly problematic, though. Scientists knew that atoms were electrically neutral. They also realized that the mass of an electron was not large enough to account for the mass of an atom.

ASK What questions might a scientist ask about the structure of the atom based on these discoveries?

_____

_____

_____

These realizations led scientists to develop a new atomic model. It envisioned the negatively charged electrons as being evenly distributed within a mass of positively charged material, much like raisins in a cake. This model was called the "plum pudding" model. It balanced the charge of an atom and accounted for the additional mass of an atom.

FIGURE 5: A plum pudding

In the early 1900s, however, one observation showed that the plum pudding model could not be entirely accurate. Scientists bombarded gold foil with positively charged alpha (α) particles, a byproduct of radioactive decay. They found that most of the particles passed straight through the foil, as if it were not even there. A few, however, were deflected at large angles away from the foil, as shown in Figure 6.

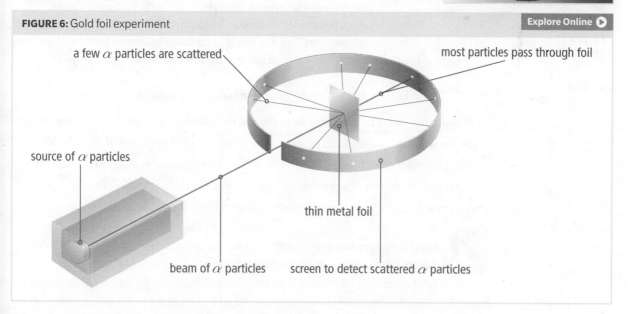

FIGURE 6: Gold foil experiment

Explore Online ▶

a few α particles are scattered

most particles pass through foil

source of α particles

thin metal foil

beam of α particles

screen to detect scattered α particles

ANALYZE Complete the statement by selecting the correct terms.

The fact that only a few particles were deflected at large angles suggested that atoms must have none | most of their mass concentrated in a small | large space. If the plum-pudding model was accurate, all | none of the particles would behave in the same way.

The fact that most of the α particles passed straight through the gold foil suggested that most of the atom consisted of empty space. The wide deflection of a few particles led scientists to conclude that the atom must contain a very small, dense area of positive charge at its center, which came to be called the nucleus.

FIGURE 7: The results of the gold foil experiment led to a new model of the atom.

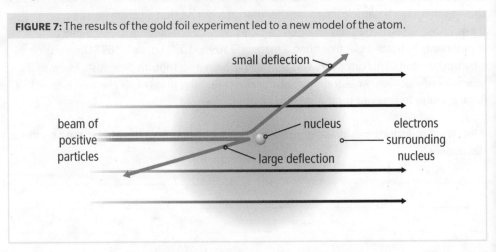

These results were very surprising. They meant that the plum pudding model of the atom was inaccurate, so scientists developed a new model of the atom. In this nuclear model, most of the volume of an atom is occupied by electrons, with the nucleus taking up a small area at the center and accounting for most of the atom's mass.

Scientists measured the number of α particles that were deflected during the gold foil experiment and the angles of deflection. The calculations showed that the nucleus was less than 1/10 000 the size of the entire atom. To have such an effect on the α particles, the nucleus had to contain most of the mass of the atom.

Properties of Subatomic Particles		
Particles	Electric charge	Actual mass (kg)
Electron	−1	9.109×10^{-31}
Proton	+1	1.673×10^{-27}
Neutron	0	1.675×10^{-27}

Scientists eventually came to conclude that the nucleus is composed of two types of particles. One type, called protons, carry a positive charge equal in magnitude to the electron's negative charge. A proton has about 1837 times more mass than an electron. The nucleus also contains neutrons. Each neutron has approximately the same mass as a proton, but no charge.

INFER Complete the statement by selecting the correct terms.

In order for atoms to have no overall charge, the number of protons in an atom must be fewer than | greater than | the same as the number of electrons. If an atom has four protons it must have less than four | four | more than four electrons. Based on experimental results, the number of protons and electrons | protons and neutrons | neutrons and electrons are important in determining the properties of an element.

Scale, Proportion, and Quantity Atoms are extremely tiny, and the parts of which they are composed are even smaller. The models chemists use to study atoms and other particles are often not drawn to scale. Even though these models are not completely accurate, it can make them easier to work with and study. For example, the model of the nuclear atom in Figure 7b is not drawn to scale in terms of the relative sizes of the nucleus to the electrons, and the distance between the nucleus and the electrons. How large would the nuclear atomic model be if it were made to scale?

Analyzing the Energy of Atoms

The nuclear model of the atom was an improvement over previous models, but it did not answer all the questions about the properties of elements. For example, when metal salts are burned, they produce flames of different colors. Each metal produces a specific color. Such "flame tests" are still used today to identify unknown metals.

FIGURE 8: A flame test can be used to identify different metals.

Explore Online ▶

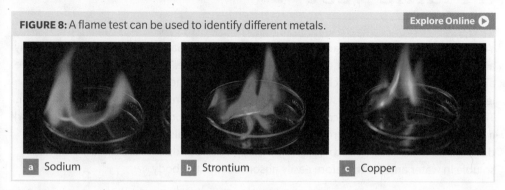

a Sodium   b Strontium   c Copper

PREDICT Why do you think the different metals shown in Figure 8 produce different flame colors? What do these different colors indicate about the metals?

_____

_____

_____

Light is a kind of electromagnetic radiation. The electromagnetic spectrum, shown in Figure 9, is the range of all types of electromagnetic radiation. Each of these types of radiation travels in waves and can be identified based on a certain range of wavelengths. A wavelength is the distance between two wave crests. The shorter the wavelength, the more energy the wave carries.

FIGURE 9: Electromagnetic spectrum

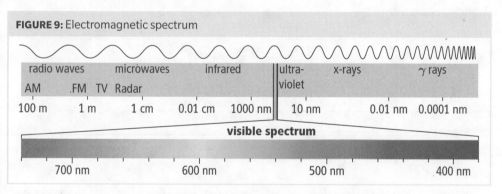

Visible light, the light that we see, is made up of different colors of light—red, orange, yellow, green, blue, indigo, and violet. Passing light through a prism separates light into its different colors because each color has a unique wavelength, and therefore its own energy. Red has the longest wavelength while violet has the shortest. Violet light has more energy than red light. When an atom absorbs energy, the electrons are raised to higher energy "levels." When the electrons return to the normal energy level, energy in the form of light is released. This light has a specific amount of energy and so will appear as a certain color.

 Collaborate The nuclear model of the atom cannot explain how electrons are able to absorb and release energy. With a partner, discuss how the model would need to be changed to explain the colors seen in a flame test.

Identifying Elements Using a Flame Test

Your company has been contacted by Jayden and Sophia Garcia. A construction company abandoned a building project on the lot next to their home. They are worried about some abandoned, rusted barrels of chemicals that were left behind. The barrels have begun to leak a colored liquid that flows through their property before emptying into a local sewer. The Garcia family wants your company to identify the compound in the liquid. Earlier work indicates that it is a dissolved metal compound. Many metals, such as lead, have been determined to be hazardous to our health. Many compounds of these metals are often soluble in water and are therefore easily absorbed into the body.

To determine what metal is contained in the barrels near the Garcia's home, you must first perform flame tests with a variety of standard solutions of different metal compounds. Then you will perform a flame test with the unknown sample from the site to see if it matches any of the solutions you've used as standards. Be sure to keep your equipment very clean and perform multiple trials to check your work.

Research Question: What other tests do chemists perform to determine if unwanted or harmful chemicals are present in the environment, in drinking water, or in food?

MAKE A CLAIM

Why do you think different metals produce unique colors in a flame test? How can you use this phenomenon to identify an unknown metal?

_____

_____

_____

_____

_____

_____

MATERIALS

- indirectly vented chemical splash goggles, nonlatex apron, nitrile gloves
- beaker, 250 mL
- Bunsen burner
- crucible tongs
- distilled water
- flame-test wire, 5 cm
- glass test plate, or microchemistry plate with wells
- hydrochloric acid (HCl) solution, 1 M

Test Solutions

- calcium chloride ($CaCl_2$) solution, 0.05 M
- lithium sulfate (Li_2SO_4) solution, 0.05 M
- potassium sulfate (K_2SO_4) solution, 0.05 M
- sodium sulfate (Na_2SO_4) solution, 0.05 M
- strontium chloride ($SrCl_2$) solution, 0.05 M
- unknown solution

SAFETY INFORMATION

- Wear indirectly vented chemical splash goggles, a nonlatex apron, and nitrile gloves during the setup, hands-on, and takedown segments of the activity.
- Do not touch any of the chemicals used in this experiment. Only touch them with the flame-test wire. If you get a chemical on your skin or clothing, wash the chemical off at the sink while notifying your teacher.
- Secure loose clothing, wear closed-toe shoes, and tie back long hair.
- Do not stare directly into the flames for extended periods of time. Look at the flame for the shortest amount of time needed to determine the color. Run multiple trials to avoid looking at the flame for too long.

indirectly vented chemical splash goggles

PLAN THE INVESTIGATION

In your Evidence Notebook, develop a procedure for your investigation. Make sure your teacher approves of your plans and safety precautions before proceeding. Then, develop a procedure to safely test the unknown solution and identify the metal in the solution. Your teacher should check your procedure before you begin testing.

Carefully consider the controls of your experiment, what the variables are, and that you are only testing one solution at a time. Decide how much solution you will need for each test and how many trials you will need to accurately determine the color of the flame.

COLLECT DATA

In your Evidence Notebook, develop a data collection strategy. How will you record the colors produced in each trial of the flame test? Make sure your data are clear and ordered so you can easily compare the results of the known solutions to the unknown solution.

CARRY OUT THE INVESTIGATION

Before you begin testing your compounds, it is important that you clean your flame-test wire. Clean the test wire by dipping it in 1.0 M HCl solution and then holding it in the flame of the Bunsen burner. Repeat this procedure until the flame is not colored by the wire. Make sure to clean the wire between each test solution to avoid contamination.

ANALYZE

1. Did you notice any differences in the individual trials for the flame tests of each metal solution? Why do you think these differences occurred?

_____

_____

_____

_____

2. How could the level of accuracy of your procedure for the flame test be improved?

_____

_____

CONSTRUCT AN EXPLANATION

Based on the data you gathered from the flame tests, what metal is present in the barrels at the abandoned construction site? How does your data support your findings?

_____

_____

_____

_____

_____

_____

_____

DRAW CONCLUSIONS

Write a conclusion that addresses each of the points below.

Claim Why can a flame test be used to identify different metal elements?

Evidence Give specific examples from your data to support your claim.

Reasoning Explain how the evidence you gave supports your claim. Describe, in detail, the connections between the evidence you cited and the argument you are making.

_____

_____

_____

_____

_____

_____

_____

_____

_____

_____

_____

_____

_____

EXTEND

Some stores sell jars of "fireplace crystals." When sprinkled on a log, these crystals make the flames blue, red, green, and violet. Research how these crystals can change the flame's color. What ingredients would you expect the crystals to contain?

Energy and Matter

Energy of Electrons in Atoms

A tube of hydrogen gas emits a pinkish glow when an electric current is passed through it, as shown in Figure 10a. Passing this pinkish light through a prism or a tool called a spectroscope separates the light into its different wavelengths. Figure 10b shows the results of this test for hydrogen, known as an emission-line spectrum. Hydrogen has four distinct bands of different colors in its emission-line spectrum.

FIGURE 10: The pinkish light emitted by hydrogen can be separated by a spectroscope.

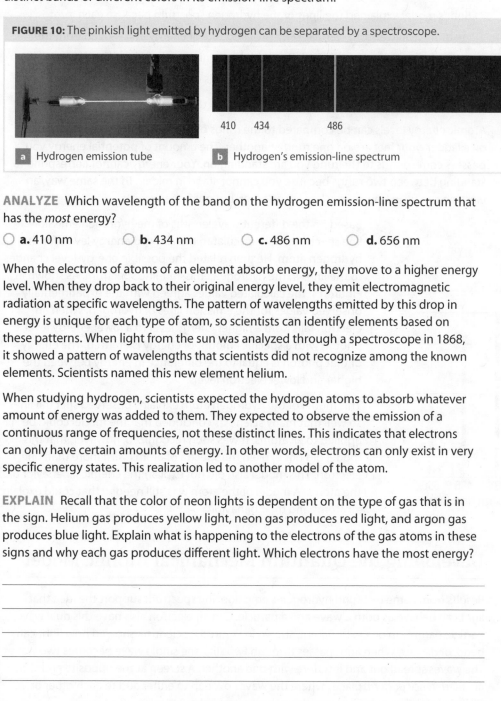

410 434   486   656

a Hydrogen emission tube   b Hydrogen's emission-line spectrum

ANALYZE Which wavelength of the band on the hydrogen emission-line spectrum that has the *most* energy?

○ **a.** 410 nm   ○ **b.** 434 nm   ○ **c.** 486 nm   ○ **d.** 656 nm

When the electrons of atoms of an element absorb energy, they move to a higher energy level. When they drop back to their original energy level, they emit electromagnetic radiation at specific wavelengths. The pattern of wavelengths emitted by this drop in energy is unique for each type of atom, so scientists can identify elements based on these patterns. When light from the sun was analyzed through a spectroscope in 1868, it showed a pattern of wavelengths that scientists did not recognize among the known elements. Scientists named this new element helium.

When studying hydrogen, scientists expected the hydrogen atoms to absorb whatever amount of energy was added to them. They expected to observe the emission of a continuous range of frequencies, not these distinct lines. This indicates that electrons can only have certain amounts of energy. In other words, electrons can only exist in very specific energy states. This realization led to another model of the atom.

EXPLAIN Recall that the color of neon lights is dependent on the type of gas that is in the sign. Helium gas produces yellow light, neon gas produces red light, and argon gas produces blue light. Explain what is happening to the electrons of the gas atoms in these signs and why each gas produces different light. Which electrons have the most energy?

_____

_____

_____

_____

_____

_____

_____

Describing Energy States of Electrons

In 1913, Danish physicist Niels Bohr developed a new model of the atom that accounted for the emission-line spectrum of hydrogen. According to this model, the electron can circle the nucleus only in allowed paths, called *orbits* or atomic energy levels. When the electron is in one of these orbits, the atom has a definite, fixed energy. The electron is in its lowest energy state, or ground state, when it is in the orbit closest to the nucleus. The energy of the electron is higher when the electron is in orbits that are successively farther from the nucleus. These higher energy levels are referred to as "excited" states.

ANALYZE Complete the statement by selecting the correct terms.

Bohr's model explained the lines of the hydrogen spectrum because each proton | electron would absorb certain | any | all amounts of energy as it moved from the ground state to an excited state. It would then emit the same | a different amount of energy as it went back to the ground state. This explains why emission spectra of elements show distinct lines | a continuous range.

Atomic energy levels can be compared to the rungs of a ladder. When you are standing on a ladder, your feet are on one rung or another. The amount of potential energy you possess corresponds to the rung you are standing on. Your energy cannot correspond to standing between two rungs because you cannot stand in midair. In the same way, an electron can be in one energy level or another, but not in between.

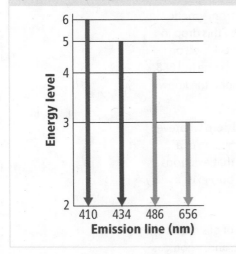

FIGURE 11: An energy-level diagram explains the observed emission-line spectrum of hydrogen.

Based on the different wavelengths of the hydrogen emission-line spectrum, Bohr calculated the allowed energy levels for the hydrogen atom. He then related the possible energy-level changes to the lines in the hydrogen emission-line spectrum. As shown in Figure 11, the calculated values agreed with the experimentally observed values for the emission lines of hydrogen. When an electron falls from a higher energy level to a lower energy level, a photon with a specific amount of energy is emitted. The energy of that photon is equal to the difference in energy between the higher and lower electron levels.

This model of the hydrogen atom explains observed spectral lines so well that many scientists concluded that the model could be applied to all atoms. It was soon recognized, however, that this model did not explain the spectra of atoms with more than one electron. This model also did not explain the chemical behavior of the atoms. A model of the atom was still needed that could explain all atoms and their behavior.

Developing the Quantum Mechanical Atomic Model

Results from flame tests and hydrogen's emission line spectrum support the idea that light can behave as both a wave and a particle. Can an electron also have this dual wave-particle nature? In one experiment, shown in Figure 12, scientists showed how light can bend, or *diffract*. When light passes through two slits, the single wave becomes two waves. The waves spread out and interfere with one another. A screen at the opposite end shows an *interference pattern*, places where the waves overlap to either add to each other or cancel each other out. All waves show this type of behavior.

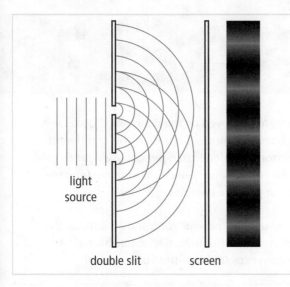

Explore Online ▶

FIGURE 12: When light is diffracted, interference patterns are seen that imply that the light is behaving like a wave.

light source

double slit   screen

INFER When scientists directed a beam of electrons towards a double slit, they found that they produced a similar pattern. What does this say about the nature of electrons?

_____

_____

_____

_____

The idea of electrons having a dual wave-particle nature troubled scientists. If electrons are both particles and waves, then where are they in the atom? An answer to this question came from the study of the detection of electrons using photons, the energy associated with electromagnetic radiation. Because photons have about the same energy as electrons, any attempt to locate a specific electron with a photon knocks the electron off its course. The solution proposed, therefore, was that there is always uncertainty in trying to locate an electron or any other particle. This was a difficult idea for scientists to accept at the time, but it is now fundamental to our understanding of light and matter.

Scientists further developed the idea of the wave properties of electrons and other small particles. The model of the atom that emerged, the one we have today, became known as the quantum mechanical or electron cloud model, shown in Figure 13. This model holds that we can only determine the *probability* of finding an electron at a given place around the nucleus. Electrons, therefore, do not travel around the nucleus in neat orbits, as described by the Bohr model. Instead, they exist in certain regions called orbitals. An orbital is a three-dimensional region around the nucleus that indicates the probable location of an electron. The darker the shading, the greater the probability of finding an electron in that location. Figure 13 shows only a single orbital.

FIGURE 13: The electron cloud model of the atom

Electrons fill orbitals based on how much energy they have. The orbitals closest to the nucleus fill first. As higher orbitals fill, the energy of the electrons in them increases. The outermost electrons in an atom, therefore, are the ones with the most energy. They are also are the ones that interact when atoms come into contact and react.

Evidence Notebook Think about how an atom's electron cloud and the number of electrons an atom has will influence the behavior of electromagnetic waves passing through a substance. How does this relate to the x-ray example?

The Structure of Atoms

The quantum mechanical model of the atom improved on the Bohr model because it better describes the arrangements of electrons in atoms. Because atoms of different elements have different numbers of electrons, a unique arrangement of electrons exists for the atoms of each element. Like all systems in nature, electrons in atoms tend to assume arrangements that have the lowest possible energies.

PREDICT Hydrogen has one electron, helium has two electrons, and lithium has three electrons. Hydrogen and lithium are both reactive, but helium is nonreactive. How could the quantum mechanical model of the atom explain this pattern of behavior?

Describing Electron Orbitals

The atoms of each element have a specific number of electrons arranged in a particular pattern. The greater the number of electrons, the more orbitals get filled and the greater the energy the electrons in these orbitals have. The first energy level can hold a maximum of two electrons. This is the 1s orbital and all elements have one. The electrons around an atom occupy different energy levels, or "shells," each identified by a number, one to seven. Each shell contains subshells of orbitals with a certain shape, identified by a letter. An orbital can hold two electrons. The first shell contains one subshell with one orbital, 1s. The second shell has two subshells, 2s and 2p. While s subshells contain only one orbital, p subshells can contain three. This means the second shell can contain as many as eight electrons, two in the 2s subshell and six in the 2p subshell. The Electron Distribution table shows how electrons are distributed in subshells for the first 20 elements. Figure 14 shows the shapes of the s and p orbitals.

Electron Distribution							
Element	Total number of electrons	Outermost subshell	Number of electrons in subshell	Element	Total number of electrons	Outermost subshell	Number of electrons in subshell
Hydrogen	1	s	1	Sodium	11	s	1
Helium	2	s	2	Magnesium	12	s	2
Lithium	3	s	1	Aluminum	13	p	1
Beryllium	4	s	2	Silicon	14	p	2
Boron	5	p	1	Phosphorus	15	p	3
Carbon	6	p	2	Sulfur	16	p	4
Nitrogen	7	p	3	Chlorine	17	p	5
Oxygen	8	p	4	Argon	18	p	6
Fluorine	9	p	5	Potassium	19	s	1
Neon	10	p	6	Calcium	20	s	2

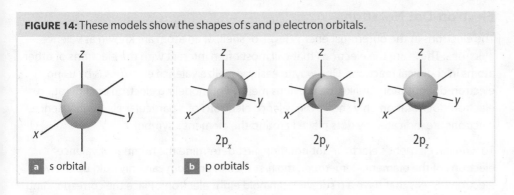

FIGURE 14: These models show the shapes of s and p electron orbitals.

a s orbital

b p orbitals

$2p_x$ $2p_y$ $2p_z$

INFER In terms of the current model of the atom, how is an electron orbital different from an "orbit"? What do the shapes of the orbitals shown in Figure 14 represent?

_____

_____

_____

_____

Electron Configuration

Electrons fill the orbitals that have the lowest possible energies first, and then they fill higher energy orbitals. As the orbitals fill up, the arrangement of electrons in an atom is known as the atom's *electron configuration*.

Figure 15 shows one way to model electron configuration. Each circle represents an orbital, in which two electrons pair up. Each electron is represented by a line drawn through the circle. Each subshell must be completely filled before electrons can be placed in the next subshell. Therefore, the 1s orbital must be filled before electrons can be placed in the 2s subshell. This is represented by two lines through the circle. For a p subshell, one electron is placed in each circle before a second electron is placed in any of the orbitals. The orbitals in the p subshell must be filled before electrons can go in the next s subshell.

FIGURE 15: The electron configuration for sulfur has four electrons in the 3p orbital.

1s   2s   2p   3s   3p

There are other orbital shapes besides s and p. In atoms with many electrons, these electrons occupy d and even f orbitals. The d and f orbitals have more complex geometries than s and p orbitals.

MODEL Using the method shown in Figure 15, draw the electron configuration of argon. Remember to fill the subshells in order.

1s   2s   2p   3s   3p

Electron-Dot Notation

The electrons in the outermost energy level, or shell, of an atom are known as valence electrons. These are the electrons that will most often interact with the electrons of other atoms in chemical reactions. One way to easily visualize valence electrons is by using electron-dot notation. Unlike the previous method of modeling electron configuration, electron-dot notation only shows the valence electrons of a particular element. Valence electrons are indicated by dots placed around the element's symbol.

To write an element's electron-dot notation, first determine the number of valence electrons of the element. Remember, the first shell of an atom can only hold up to two electrons. Shells that have a p subshell can hold eight electrons. Place the corresponding number of dots around the element's symbol. When filling up the four sides of the elements, each side gets one dot until all four sides have a dot. Dots are then added around the sides again until all four sides have pairs. Because the first shell can hold only two electrons, helium is an exception to this rule. For all other atoms, a full outer shell of valence electrons is called an *octet*.

Element	Number of valence electrons	Electron-dot notation	Element	Number of valence electrons	Electron-dot notation
Hydrogen	1	H·	Carbon	4	·Ċ·
Helium	2	He:	Nitrogen	5	·N̈:
Lithium	1	Li·	Oxygen	6	·Ö:
Beryllium	2	Be·	Fluorine	7	:Ḟ:
Boron	3	·Ḃ·	Neon	8	:N̈e:

You can use the previous method of visualizing electron configuration to find the valence electrons. For example, carbon has six electrons. It has two electrons in the 1s subshell, two electrons in the 2s subshell, and two electrons in the 2p subshell. So, carbon does not have a completely filled second shell and so has four valence electrons. Be careful when comparing these models, though. Electron-dot notation does not compare individual subshells, only the valence electrons, those in the highest energy level. This is why carbon has four dots, each on one side of the symbol, and not two dots on each side.

MODEL Using the Electron Distribution table, complete the electron-dot notations for the next eight elements, sodium through argon.

Na   Mg   Al   Si

P   S   Cl   Ar

Describing the Atoms of an Element

Recall that the nucleus of an atom, which contains the majority of the atom's mass, contains two types of particles—protons and neutrons. The number of protons in the nucleus determines the number of electrons a neutral atom can have. By describing the nucleus, we can describe the element.

Atomic Number

The number of protons in an atom defines what element an atom is. The atomic number is the number of protons in an atom of an element. Because the number of electrons must equal the number of protons for the atom to be neutral, the atomic number also indicates the number of electrons in an element's atoms. Oxygen, for example, has eight protons and eight electrons, so its atomic number is 8.

Mass Number

All atoms of an element have the same number of protons, but the number of neutrons can vary within the same element. The mass number of an element is the sum of the protons and neutrons in its nucleus. Atoms of an element that have different mass numbers are *isotopes* of each other. Isotopes of an element have nearly identical chemical properties because an atom's chemistry is due to its electrons. Any sample of an element usually consists of a mixture of different isotopes. As shown in Figure 16, atoms of the element hydrogen have three distinct isotopes.

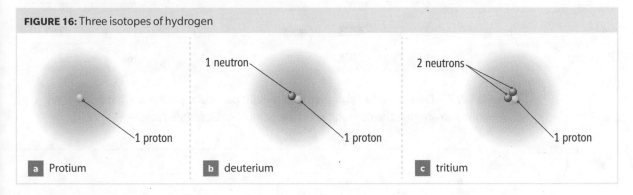

FIGURE 16: Three isotopes of hydrogen

1 neutron
1 proton
a Protium

1 neutron
1 proton
b deuterium

2 neutrons
1 proton
c tritium

Average Atomic Mass

Atoms are very small, but they still have a mass, a mass too small for conventional units. Instead of using kilograms, the SI unit for mass, the mass of atoms is given in unified atomic mass units. The unified atomic mass unit (u) is approximately equal to the mass of one proton or neutron. By convention, this mass is set as 1/12 the mass of the most common isotope of the carbon atom, which contains six protons and six neutrons, and so having an atomic mass of 12 u. The masses of the atoms of all other elements are calculated relative to this.

 Collaborate With a partner, use what you know about the modern atomic model to explain groupings of elements with similar chemical properties. For example, why would lithium, sodium, and potassium have similar chemical properties if they are different elements with different numbers of protons, neutrons, and electrons?

Patterns

Comparing Elements

Data comparing information about elements can be displayed in many ways. The Sample of Elements table lists information about the first twenty elements, listed alphabetically by element name.

Sample of Elements							
Element	Symbol	Atomic number	Atomic mass	Element	Symbol	Atomic number	Atomic mass
Aluminum	Al	13	26.98	Lithium	Li	3	6.94
Argon	Ar	18	39.95	Magnesium	Mg	12	24.31
Beryllium	Be	4	9.012	Neon	Ne	10	20.18
Boron	B	5	10.81	Nitrogen	N	7	14.007
Calcium	Ca	20	40.08	Oxygen	O	8	15.999
Carbon	C	6	12.01	Phosphorous	P	15	30.97
Chlorine	Cl	17	35.45	Potassium	K	19	39.10
Fluorine	F	9	19.00	Silicon	Si	14	28.085
Helium	He	2	4.003	Sodium	Na	11	22.99
Hydrogen	H	1	1.008	Sulfur	S	16	32.07

ANALYZE Data are often arranged to highlight particular patterns. What other ways might you arrange the data shown in the Sample of Elements table?

_____

_____

_____

_____

Comparing Elements in the Body

The soft tissue in your body, such as muscle and lung tissue, is composed mostly of the elements hydrogen, oxygen, carbon, and nitrogen. Bone tissue, however, contains large amounts of calcium and phosphorus in addition to these four elements.

FIGURE 17: Comparison of atomic radii of elements found in the body

hydrogen   carbon   nitrogen   oxygen   phosphorus   calcium

 Evidence Notebook Look at the relative sizes of the atoms making up the human body. Can you think of a reason why x-rays are absorbed by bone but pass through soft tissue more easily?

Language Arts

Mass Spectrometry

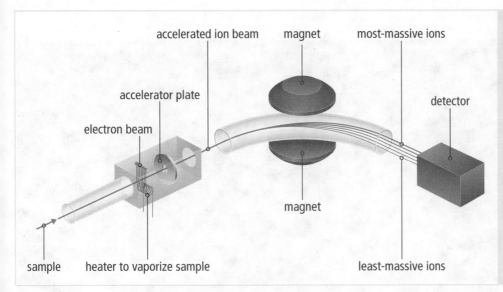

accelerated ion beam   magnet   most-massive ions

accelerator plate

detector

electron beam

magnet

sample   heater to vaporize sample   least-massive ions

FIGURE 18: A mass spectrometer is used to determine the mass of an atom.

Scientists use a method called mass spectrometry to measure the mass of atoms. In a mass spectrometer, shown in Figure 18, atoms pass through a high-energy beam of electrons. This beam knocks off one or more of the particles' electrons, giving them a positive charge. When these charged particles are projected through a magnetic field, it alters their paths. The change in path or deflection of each particle in the sample depends on its mass. The heavier particles have the most inertia and so are deflected the least. The lighter particles are deflected the most. This separates the particles by mass. The positions where the particles hit a detector plate are used to calculate their relative masses.

Mass spectrometry can be used to determine the percentage composition of a sample of particles of known masses. Scientists also use mass spectrometry to identify the chemical composition of a compound based on the mass-to-charge ratio of the particles. Practical applications of mass-spectrometry include medical applications, such as the study of different proteins. It has also been used in space to identify the composition of various planets and moons.

Another important use is in the study of individual elements. For example, scientists can use mass spectrometry to determine the average atomic mass of an element. The average atomic mass of a sample is the weighted average of the masses of all the isotopes of an element. It can also be used to determine the mass of individual isotopes of an element.

For example, carbon has two stable isotopes, carbon-12 and carbon-13. Data from mass spectrometry shows that the ratio of the masses of carbon-12 and carbon-13 is

$$\frac{\text{mass}^{13}\text{C}}{\text{mass}^{12}\text{C}} = 1.0836$$

Because the atomic mass of carbon-12 is exactly 12 u by definition, this ratio can be used to calculate the mass of carbon-13.

$$\text{mass}^{13}\text{C} = 1.0836 \times 12 \text{ u} = 13.0034 \text{ u}$$

> **Language Arts Connection** Write a short blog post about the applications of mass spectrometry. What have scientists learned about the natural world using this tool?

LIGHT WAVE INTERFERENCE   **ELECTRON CONFIGURATIONS**   **CRYO-ELECTRON MICROSCOPY**   Go online to choose one of these other paths.

Lesson Self-Check

CAN YOU EXPLAIN IT?

FIGURE 19: These hands appear in an x-ray image.

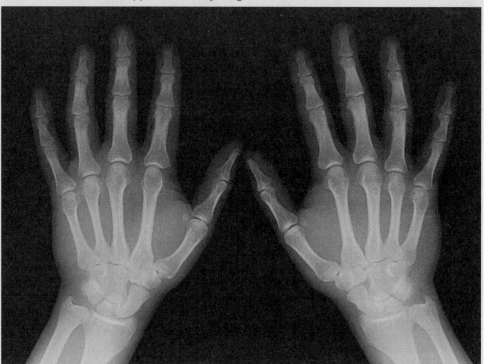

When a technician takes an x-ray of a body part, such as a hand, the bones show up clearly on the film as white images. The muscles and other soft tissues in the hand do not appear. Soft tissues are composed mainly of the elements carbon, oxygen, hydrogen, and nitrogen. These elements have relatively small atoms. X-rays pass through soft tissues because the smaller atoms cannot absorb the high-energy x-ray photons. Bones are made of calcium and phosphorus as well as smaller elements. Calcium and phosphorus have much larger atoms. They are more likely to absorb the x-ray photons and prevent them from reaching the film.

 Evidence Notebook Refer to your notes in your Evidence Notebook to construct an explanation of why some substances interfere with electromagnetic radiation while others do not. Using this information, answer the following:

1. Make a claim that explains how electromagnetic waves carry energy.
2. What evidence supports your claim? How is this characteristic of electromagnetic waves responsible for their energy?
3. How do some atoms block electromagnetic waves?

160   Unit 3 Patterns in the Properties of Matter

CHECKPOINTS

Check Your Understanding

1. A scientist picks up a sample of an element. She thinks it might be a metal. Which of the following properties would support her conclusion? Select all correct answers.
   - ☐ **a.** The element is shiny.
   - ☐ **b.** The element is dull.
   - ☐ **c.** The element partially conducts electricity.
   - ☐ **d.** The element is a good conductor of electricity.
   - ☐ **e.** The element is very brittle.

2. Which of the following statements provides correct evidence that atoms have electrical charges associated with them?
   - ○ **a.** An element is made of a certain kind of atom.
   - ○ **b.** The nucleus of an atom attracts positively charged particles.
   - ○ **c.** Cathode rays are attracted to positively charged atoms.
   - ○ **d.** X-rays produce images of bones.

3. Complete the statement about the gold foil experiment by selecting the correct terms.

   During an experiment, gold foil was bombarded with alpha particles | beta particles | electrons . Most of the particles passed through | were deflected by the gold foil. This implies that most of the space in the atoms in the foil are taken up by electrons | nuclei .

4. Complete the statement by selecting the correct terms.

   | 38 | 50 | 88 |

   Strontium has an atomic number of 38 and an atomic mass number of 88. Therefore, it has

   _____ protons, _____ neutrons, and _____

   electrons.

5. Complete the statement about electron-dot notation by selecting the correct terms.

   Some atoms may have different | the same electron dot notation because this type of notation shows only valence | inner-shell electrons, which take part in emission spectra | chemical reactions .

6. Which of the following can be explained by the nuclear model of the atom? Select all correct answers.
   - ☐ **a.** Atoms have electrical charges.
   - ☐ **b.** Electrons have wave-like properties.
   - ☐ **c.** Electrons exist at specific energy levels.
   - ☐ **d.** Most of the space in an atom is taken up by electrons.

7. Complete the statement about phosphorus by selecting the correct terms.

   Phosphorus has a total of 15 electrons. When showing the electron configuration for phosphorus, the first subshells to be filled are 1s and 2s subshells, with two | four | six | eight electrons each. Then, the 2p subshell is filled with two | four | six | eight electrons. The 3s subshell is filled with two | four | six | eight electrons. This leaves one | three | five | seven electron(s) for the 3p subshell.

8. Chlorine has a total of 17 electrons. How many valence electrons are shown on the electron dot diagram for chlorine?
   - ○ **a.** 17
   - ○ **b.** 8
   - ○ **c.** 7
   - ○ **d.** 1

CHECKPOINTS (continued)

9. What are valence electrons, and why are they important?

_____

_____

_____

_____

10. Draw a model showing the electron configuration of an oxygen atom.

1s   2s   2p   3s   3p

11. A chemist repeats the gold foil experiment, but she uses foil made of aluminum (atomic number 13) instead of gold (atomic number 79). How would you expect her results to compare with the experiment that used gold foil?

_____

_____

_____

_____

_____

_____

_____

MAKE YOUR OWN STUDY GUIDE

In your Evidence Notebook, design a study guide that supports the main ideas from this lesson:

Chemical elements are described by their atomic mass and mass number.

Electrons show both wave and particle behavior.

Valence electrons determine the chemical properties of elements, such as how they react with other substances.

Remember to include the following information in your study guide:

- Use examples that model main ideas.
- Record explanations for the phenomena you investigated.
- Use evidence to support your explanations. Your support can include drawings, data, graphs, laboratory conclusions, and other evidence recorded throughout the lesson.

Consider how different patterns may be observed, and provide evidence for causality both at the scale of atoms in matter and at the smaller scale of electrons within atoms.

Investigating Patterns in the Periodic Table

Silver, gold, and platinum are all metals, but they have different appearances.

CAN YOU EXPLAIN IT?

Some elements, such as silver, gold, and platinum exist in nature, are very stable, and have been used for hundreds of years. By gaining a deeper understanding of what caused these patterns of behavior of known elements, scientists realized ways to create new elements that have never been found in nature. Plutonium, for example, was created at the University of California, Berkeley laboratory and is now used to generate electricity. The scientists working at this laboratory were responsible for the discovery of many transuranic elements—elements with more than 92 protons in their nuclei. Many of these elements are very unstable and last only fractions of seconds. However, based on patterns of behavior and trends in carefully collected data, scientists knew that it was possible to make these elements.

FIGURE 1: The 60-inch cyclotron at the University of California, Berkeley.

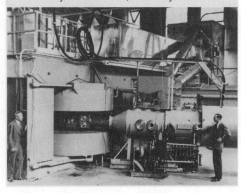

PREDICT How do you think scientists are able to predict that certain elements could be made when the elements do not occur naturally?

_____

_____

_____

_____

Evidence Notebook As you explore the lesson, gather evidence to explain how the periodic table can be used to predict the behavior of elements.

Making Predictions Using the Periodic Table

By 1860, scientists had isolated more than 60 elements. As you've read, various attempts were made to identify patterns in the physical properties, chemical stability, and reactivity of these elements. Using relative atomic mass and knowledge of these properties, chemist Dmitri Mendeleev began ordering the known elements in a systematic way that is still important today—the periodic table.

Organizing the Periodic Table

Mendeleev began by writing element names on separate note cards. He then arranged the cards in different ways. In this way, he could compare atomic mass and other chemical and physical properties of each element. When arranging them by increasing atomic mass, he observed the chemical properties occurred in a repeating pattern.

FIGURE 2: Mendeleev's original periodic table

				Ti=50	Zr=90	?=180.
				V=51	Nb=94	Ta=182.
				Cr=52	Mo=96	W=186.
				Mn=55	Rh=104,4	Pt=197,4
				Fe=56	Ru=104,4	Ir=198.
			Ni=Co=59		Pl=1066,	Os=199.
H=1				Cu=63,4	Ag=108	Hg=200.
	Be=9,4	Mg=24	Zn=65,2		Cd=112	
	B=11	Al=27,4	?=68		Ur=116	Au=197?
	C=12	Si=28	?=70		Su=118	
	N=14	P=31	As=75		Sb=122	Bi=210
	O=16	S=32	Se=79,4		Te=128?	
	F=19	Cl=35,5	Br=80		I=127	
Li=7	Na=23	K=39	Rb=85,4		Cs=133	Tl=204
		Ca=40	Sr=87,6		Ba=137	Pb=207.
		?=45	Ce=92			
		?Er=56	La=94			
		?Yt=60	Di=95			
		?In=75,6	Th=118?			

PREDICT Why do you think Mendeleev left gaps in the periodic table shown in Figure 2?

_____

_____

_____

One thing Mendeleev noticed was that every highly reactive nonmetal was followed by a highly reactive metal. To make the pattern exact, however, Mendeleev had to reverse the atomic mass order of a few elements and leave gaps between others. These changes kept the patterns consistent. Mendeleev inferred that each gap indicated an undiscovered element. By their positions he predicted properties of the undiscovered elements. The discoveries of gallium (1875) and germanium (1886) would prove these predictions accurate.

Recognizing Periodic Patterns

Mendeleev's table of elements revealed a repeating pattern, or *periodicity*, of properties, which is why it is called the *periodic table*. Because of Mendeleev's success in explaining known trends and predicting unknown elements, scientists accepted the table and the idea of periodic trends. Scientists continue to investigate elements and adjust the table in light of new evidence.

In 1913, the British chemist Henry Moseley discovered a new periodic pattern based on nuclear charge. In other words, he discovered atomic number. Organizing the periodic table by the number of protons better fit the patterns of chemical and physical properties Mendeleev had observed. Moseley's work led to our current understanding of atomic number and the order of elements on the modern periodic table.

FIGURE 3: The periodic table showing elements classified as metals, metalloids, and nonmetals

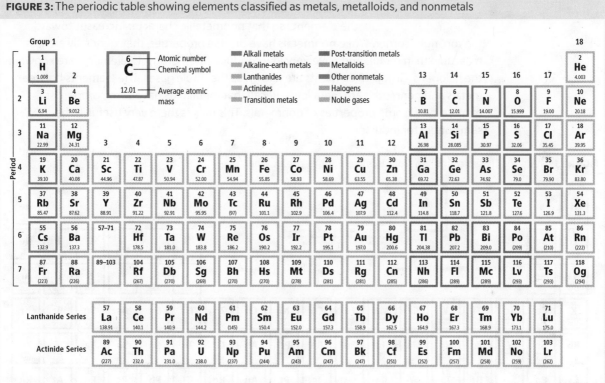

ANALYZE What patterns do you notice in the table in terms of protons, electrons, and valence electrons? How might these relate to an element being a metal or nonmetal?

_____

_____

_____

_____

Over many years scientists continued to study the properties of elements and identified additional patterns that supported what would be known as the *periodic law*. The periodic law states that the chemical and physical properties of elements are periodic functions of their atomic numbers. A row across the periodic table is called a *period*. A column down the periodic table is called a *group* or *family*. Adjacent elements in a period tend to have similar properties. Elements in the same group have similar chemical properties.

Grouping Elements Using Properties

FIGURE 4: Metals and nonmetals

At the time Mendeleev developed the periodic table, most known elements were metals. Scientists knew that metals tended to be solid at room temperature, shiny in appearance, ductile, and malleable. They also observed that metals are good conductors of thermal energy and electricity. Over time, even as new metallic elements were discovered, these properties guided the development of the periodic table. On the modern periodic table, Groups 1 and 2 are known as the alkali and alkaline earth metals, respectively. Groups 3 through 12 in the center of the periodic table are known as the transition metals.

Scientists also observed that some elements are not metallic. Therefore, in developing the modern periodic table, they arranged the elements so that nonmetallic character increases toward the top, right corner. While nonmetals have diverse properties, they generally are less malleable than metals and have very low conductivities. Group 17 elements are known as the halogens. Group 18 elements are known as the noble gases. The elements between metals and nonmetals are metalloids. Recall that metalloids have some properties of metals and some properties of nonmetals. This makes them very useful in the semiconductor industry.

FIGURE 5: This periodic table highlights different categories of elements.

1																	18
1 **H** Hydrogen 1.008	2											13	14	15	16	17	2 **He** Helium 4.003
3 **Li** Lithium 6.94	4 **Be** Beryllium 9.012											5 **B** Boron 10.81	6 **C** Carbon 12.01	7 **N** Nitrogen 14.007	8 **O** Oxygen 15.999	9 **F** Fluorine 19.00	10 **Ne** Neon 20.18
11 **Na** Sodium 22.99	12 **Mg** Magnesium 24.31	3	4	5	6	7	8	9	10	11	12	13 **Al** Aluminum 26.98	14 **Si** Silicon 28.085	15 **P** Phosphorus 30.97	16 **S** Sulfur 32.06	17 **Cl** Chlorine 35.45	18 **Ar** Argon 39.95
19 **K** Potassium 39.10	20 **Ca** Calcium 40.08	21 **Sc** Scandium 44.96	22 **Ti** Titanium 47.87	23 **V** Vanadium 50.94	24 **Cr** Chromium 52.00	25 **Mn** Manganese 54.94	26 **Fe** Iron 55.85	27 **Co** Cobalt 58.93	28 **Ni** Nickel 58.69	29 **Cu** Copper 63.55	30 **Zn** Zinc 65.38	31 **Ga** Gallium 69.72	32 **Ge** Germanium 72.63	33 **As** Arsenic 74.92	34 **Se** Selenium 79.0	35 **Br** Bromine 79.90	36 **Kr** Krypton 83.80
37 **Rb** Rubidium 85.47	38 **Sr** Strontium 87.62	39 **Y** Yttrium 88.91	40 **Zr** Zirconium 91.22	41 **Nb** Niobium 92.91	42 **Mo** Molybdenum 95.95	43 **Tc** Technetium (97)	44 **Ru** Ruthenium 101.1	45 **Rh** Rhodium 102.9	46 **Pd** Palladium 106.4	47 **Ag** Silver 107.9	48 **Cd** Cadmium 112.4	49 **In** Indium 114.8	50 **Sn** Tin 118.7	51 **Sb** Antimony 121.8	52 **Te** Tellurium 127.6	53 **I** Iodine 126.9	54 **Xe** Xenon 131.3
55 **Cs** Cesium 132.9	56 **Ba** Barium 137.3	57–71	72 **Hf** Hafnium 178.5	73 **Ta** Tantalum 181.0	74 **W** Tungsten 183.8	75 **Re** Rhenium 186.2	76 **Os** Osmium 190.2	77 **Ir** Iridium 192.2	78 **Pt** Platinum 195.1	79 **Au** Gold 197.0	80 **Hg** Mercury 200.6	81 **Tl** Thallium 204.38	82 **Pb** Lead 207.2	83 **Bi** Bismuth 209.0	84 **Po** Polonium (209)	85 **At** Astatine (210)	86 **Rn** Radon (222)
87 **Fr** Francium (223)	88 **Ra** Radium (226)	89–103	104 **Rf** Rutherfordium (267)	105 **Db** Dubnium (270)	106 **Sg** Seaborgium (269)	107 **Bh** Bohrium (270)	108 **Hs** Hassium (270)	109 **Mt** Meitnerium (278)	110 **Ds** Darmstadtium (281)	111 **Rg** Roentgenium (281)	112 **Cn** Copernicium (285)	113 **Nh** Nihonium (286)	114 **Fl** Flerovium (289)	115 **Mc** Moscovium (289)	116 **Lv** Livermorium (293)	117 **Ts** Tennessine (293)	118 **Og** Oganesson (294)

6 **C** Carbon 12.01

- Atomic number
- Chemical symbol
- Element name
- Average atomic mass

Values appearing in parentheses do not represent average atomic mass but instead represent the mass number of that element's most stable or most common isotope.

State of Element at STP

Metals | Metalloids | Nonmetals | Solid | Liquid | Gas | Not yet known

Lanthanide Series

57 **La** Lanthanum 138.91	58 **Ce** Cerium 140.1	59 **Pr** Praseodymium 140.9	60 **Nd** Neodymium 144.2	61 **Pm** Promethium (145)	62 **Sm** Samarium 150.4	63 **Eu** Europium 152.0	64 **Gd** Gadolinium 157.3	65 **Tb** Terbium 158.9	66 **Dy** Dysprosium 162.5	67 **Ho** Holmium 164.9	68 **Er** Erbium 167.3	69 **Tm** Thulium 168.9	70 **Yb** Ytterbium 173.1	71 **Lu** Lutetium 175.0

Actinide Series

89 **Ac** Actinium (227)	90 **Th** Thorium 232.0	91 **Pa** Protactinium 231.0	92 **U** Uranium 238.0	93 **Np** Neptunium (237)	94 **Pu** Plutonium (244)	95 **Am** Americium (243)	96 **Cm** Curium (247)	97 **Bk** Berkelium (247)	98 **Cf** Californium (251)	99 **Es** Einsteinium (252)	100 **Fm** Fermium (257)	101 **Md** Mendelevium (258)	102 **No** Nobelium (259)	103 **Lr** Lawrencium (262)

INFER The nonmetals helium, neon, and argon and the metals copper, silver, and gold are among only a few elements that are found in nature in their pure forms. What can you infer about the chemical reactivity of these elements?

_____

_____

_____

Patterns in Chemical Properties

Recall that valence electrons are those in the outermost orbitals of an atom. They are the ones most easily gained or lost when atoms interact. Valence electrons play an important role in determining the properties of an element. As a result, an element's number of valence electrons influences its location in the periodic table.

INFER What trend do you think exists between the number of valence electrons an element has and its placement in the periodic table?

_____

_____

_____

 Engineering

The Noble Gases

As chemists were isolating different elements, they noticed that some gaseous elements showed no apparent reactivity at all. They called these the noble gases. The extremely low reactivity of the noble gases makes them ideal for applications when reactions with other elements must be avoided. For example, noble gases are used in the space between double-pane windows, in medical imaging equipment, in gas-discharge tubes for decorative signs, and in automobile headlamps. They are also frequently used in manufacturing when an air-free environment is required.

EXPLAIN Noble gases have extremely low reactivity because of their valence shell electron configuration. Which properties do the valence shells of every noble gas have in common? Select all correct answers.

☐ **a.** All electrons are paired.   ☐ **c.** All electrons are unpaired.

☐ **b.** It is filled with electrons.   ☐ **d.** It has exactly two electrons.

Helium has two valence electrons, and the other noble gases have eight valence electrons. This filled outer shell is the reason noble gases are stable and have such low reactivity. Other main-group elements can become more stable by gaining, losing, or sharing electrons so they also have full valence shells.

APPLY Complete the statement by selecting the correct terms.

Sodium, a Group 1 element, has one | two | seven | eight valence electron(s). It can easily react with chlorine, a Group 17 element, which has one | two | seven | eight valence electron(s). During bonding, each sodium atom gains one | gains seven | loses one | loses seven electron(s) to become stable, and each chlorine atom gains one | gains seven | loses one | loses seven electron(s) to become stable.

 Evidence Notebook How could modern scientists use the periodic table to predict the properties of newly synthesized elements? Assume the synthesized elements are stable enough for their properties to be observed.

Modeling Periodic Trends

FIGURE 6: A wall of paint samples

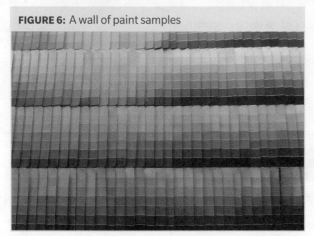

When trying to decide what color to paint a wall, you might view paint samples to compare your choices. Samples on a palette, such as those shown in Figure 6, might have a similar color but vary by color shade or intensity. For instance, samples on a palette containing different shades of red might be arranged from pink to maroon. Another palette may arrange shades of blue in a similar way. Figure 6 shows just a small selection of paint palettes a store may carry. You can also obtain paint chip cards from stores, which are individual cards that have just one paint color on them.

Imagine that you work in a paint store and you receive a shipment of paint chip cards from your supplier. You have a box full of paint chip cards of different colors and hues, but the supplier failed to inform you how many cards there should be. You first need to determine if any cards are missing. Then, you need to find the best way to display the paints so your customers can easily find the color and hue they're looking for.

Research Question: Recognizing patterns is an extremely important skill for scientists. How can this skill be useful in other careers?

- -

MAKE A CLAIM

What patterns will help you determine if any paint chip cards are missing from the set? Can these same patterns be used to display the paints for customers?

_____

_____

_____

_____

- -

MATERIALS

• set of paint chip cards

- -

PLAN THE INVESTIGATION

Obtain a set of paint chip cards from your teacher. Lay out all the cards so you can see the colors. Make a list of all the potential ways you can arrange your cards. For each arrangement, take notes on how it will help you find any missing cards. Also note how easily customers would be able to find the paint they want with each arrangement.

CARRY OUT THE INVESTIGATION

Choose the three arrangements you think will work best, and set your paint chip cards according to each plan. Develop a data table to record any missing cards. Take a picture or make a sketch of each arrangement before you set up the next one.

ANALYZE

Were any paint chip cards missing from your set? How did you determine they were or were not missing? How would you describe the missing cards to someone?

_____

_____

_____

_____

DRAW CONCLUSIONS

Write a conclusion that addresses each of the points below.

Claim What patterns helped you determine whether paint chip cards were missing? Could you use these same patterns to display paints for customers?

Evidence Give specific examples from your data to support your claim.

Reasoning Explain how the evidence you gave supports your claim. Describe, in detail, the connections between the evidence you cited and the argument you are making.

_____

_____

_____

_____

_____

_____

_____

_____

_____

_____

_____

_____

_____

 Evidence Notebook Based on your observations in this investigation, how can scientists use patterns in the properties of elements to predict whether or not undiscovered elements exist?

Patterns in Ionization Energy

Neutral atoms have an equal number of protons and electrons. These oppositely charged particles are electrically attracted to each other. The greater the number of each, the greater the attraction will be. The energy required to remove an electron from a neutral atom is known as ionization energy. This is the energy required to overcome the attraction, remove an electron, and produce a charged atom, called an *ion*.

Analyzing Ionization Energy

As Figure 7 shows, the force to remove an electron is greater on inner electrons than on outer electrons. This is because electrons closer to the nucleus partially shield the outer electrons from the attraction of the positive charge. Also, a repulsive force exists between the inner and outer electrons, pushing the outer electrons outwards. As a result, the outermost, valence electrons are held more loosely than inner electrons and require less energy to break free. Ionization energy depends on this net force that keeps an outermost electron in an atom.

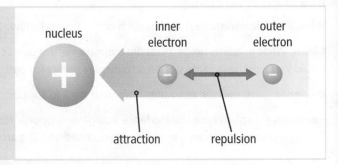

FIGURE 7: Inner electrons partially shield outer electrons from the attraction of protons in the nucleus. They also repel the outer electrons, further weakening the nucleus's hold on them.

nucleus   inner electron   outer electron

attraction   repulsion

Nuclei with a greater number of protons more strongly attract electrons in all energy levels. Not surprisingly, therefore, as atomic number increases, so does ionization energy. Atoms whose outermost electrons occupy higher energy levels, however, are farther from the nucleus. The increased distance and shielding from inner electrons weakens the attraction of the electrons to the nucleus. This causes ionization energy to decrease. Consider these two factors as you answer the following question.

ANALYZE Which elements have an ionization energy greater than that of silicon?

Magnesium and aluminum | Phosphorus and sulfur have a greater ionization energy because their atoms have more protons than silicon has. The additional electrons do not increase shielding because their valence shells are the same as | different from those of the outer electrons of silicon. Magnesium and aluminum | Phosphorus and sulfur have a smaller ionization energy because their atoms have fewer protons than silicon. Germanium has a smaller | larger ionization energy because the shielding effect on its outermost electron is greater than that of silicon.

With sufficient energy, electrons can be removed from positive ions as well as from neutral atoms. The energies for removal of additional electrons from an atom are referred to as the second ionization energy, third ionization energy, and so on.

Patterns in Ionization Energies

To avoid the influence of nearby atoms, measurements of ionization energies are made on isolated atoms in the gas phase. A sample of the element is heated to produce a gas. A beam of light or a stream of electrons is used to eject an electron from the atom.

Ionization Energy

FIGURE 8: Ionization energy can be graphed as a function of an element's atomic number.

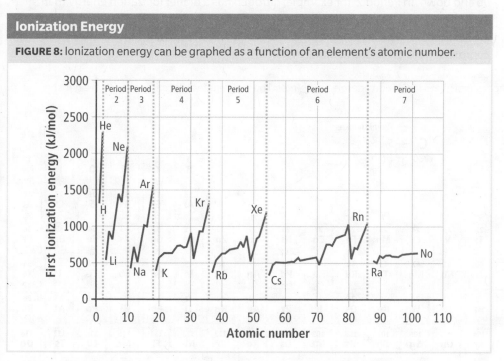

Figure 8 shows the ionization energy required to remove a single electron from a neutral atom of an element as a function of the atomic number of the element, shown on the horizontal axis. The dotted lines note the beginning of a period.

ANALYZE How does ionization energy change with atomic number? Use evidence from the graph to support your claim.

_____

_____

EXPLAIN How does ionization energy change across periods and down groups on the periodic table? Use evidence from the graph to support your claim.

_____

_____

INFER Why do noble gases have high ionization energy? What does this suggest about their chemical stability?

_____

_____

_____

Explaining Trends in Ionization Energy

The graphical representation of ionization energies of the elements reveals some clear patterns. It shows that the Group 1 metals have the lowest ionization energies in their respective periods. They lose electrons most easily. The noble gases, have the highest ionization energies in each period. They do not lose electrons easily. In general, ionization energy generally decreases down a group and across a period.

Within each period and within some groups the individual ionization values do go up and down. In Period 2, for example, nitrogen has a higher ionization energy than oxygen. In Group 14 the ionization of germanium is higher than that of tin, just below it. These inconsistencies in the trends remind us that all scientific models are limited approximations of nature's ultimate reality.

FIGURE 9: This periodic table displays ionization energies in kJ/mol. The lanthanide and actinide series are not shown.

Group 1	2	3	4	5	6	7	8	9	10	11	12	13	14	15	16	17	18
1 H 1312																	2 He 2372
3 Li 520	4 Be 900											5 B 801	6 C 1086	7 N 1402	8 O 1314	9 F 1681	10 Ne 2081
11 Na 496	12 Mg 738											13 Al 578	14 Si 787	15 P 1012	16 S 1000	17 Cl 1251	18 Ar 1521
19 K 419	20 Ca 590	21 Sc 633	22 Ti 659	23 V 651	24 Cr 653	25 Mn 717	26 Fe 762	27 Co 760	28 Ni 737	29 Cu 746	30 Zn 906	31 Ga 579	32 Ge 762	33 As 944	34 Se 941	35 Br 1140	36 Kr 1351
37 Rb 403	38 Sr 550	39 Y 600	40 Zr 640	41 Nb 652	42 Mo 684	43 Tc 702	44 Ru 710	45 Rh 720	46 Pd 804	47 Ag 731	48 Cd 869	49 In 558	50 Sn 709	51 Sb 831	52 Te 869	53 I 1008	54 Xe 1170
55 Cs 376	56 Ba 503	57–71	72 Hf 659	73 Ta 728	74 W 759	75 Re 756	76 Os 814	77 Ir 865	78 Pt 864	79 Au 890	80 Hg 1007	81 Tl 589	82 Pb 716	83 Bi 703	84 Po 812	85 At —	86 Rn 1037
87 Fr —	88 Ra 509	89–103	104 Rf	105 Db	106 Sg	107 Bh	108 Hs	109 Mt	110 Ds	111 Rg	112 Cn	113 Nh	114 Fl	115 Mc	116 Lv	117 Ts	118 Og

Legend:
- 6 — Atomic number
- C — Symbol
- 1086 — First ionization energy

EXPLAIN In a previous lesson, you performed an experiment where you reacted magnesium and aluminum with hydrochloric acid. How does ionization energy explain why magnesium reacted more vigorously than aluminum?

_____

_____

_____

_____

As we move left to right across a period on the table, one proton and one electron are added to each element. These electrons are added to the same energy level so they are the same distance from the nucleus. It requires more energy to remove a single electron as more electrons are added, so the ionization energy increases. The opposite trend occurs when moving down a group. More protons are added, but the electrons are in orbitals farther and farther away from the nucleus. The shielding effect is greater, and it requires less energy to remove an electron. The ionization energy decreases.

 Evidence Notebook How can scientists use ionization energy to learn more about elements that have not been discovered yet?

Patterns in Atomic Size

The exact size of an atom is hard to define because the positions of the electrons cannot be not exactly identified. One way to express an atom's radius is to measure the distance between the nuclei of two identical atoms that are chemically bonded, and then divide this distance by two. Therefore, the atomic radius is often expressed as half the distance between the nuclei of identical atoms that are bonded together. Figure 10 shows the atomic radius of chlorine is about 99 picometers (pm). A picometer is 1×10^{-12} meters.

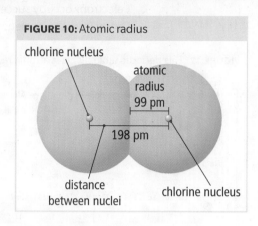

FIGURE 10: Atomic radius

Analyzing Trends in Atomic Radii

Electrons move in the area surrounding an atom's nucleus, the electron cloud. The atomic radius cannot be described by the size of the electron cloud because its outer boundary is not well defined. Instead, scientists can measure the atomic radius using techniques such as x-ray imaging and spectroscopy. The data from these measurements can be graphed against atomic number, as shown in Figure 11.

Atomic Radius

FIGURE 11: A graph of atomic radius versus atomic number reveals a pattern in the data.

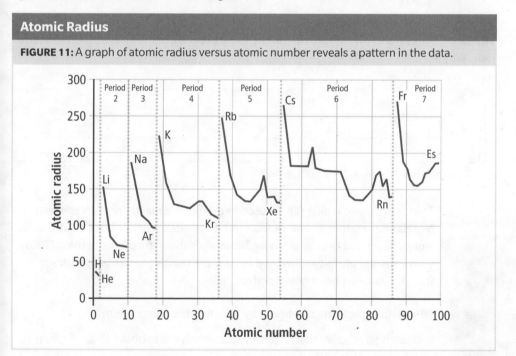

ANALYZE Use the graph of atomic radii to complete the statement.

Within a period, the element with the lowest atomic number tends to have the largest | smallest atomic radius. As the number of the period increases, the element with the largest atomic radius within a period has a higher | lower value than the previous group. Therefore, atomic radius increases | decreases as you move from left to right across a period of the periodic table and increases | decreases as you move down a group.

Explaining Trends in Atomic Radii

Moving across a period, as electrons are added to the same energy level, they are pulled closer and closer to the nucleus as its charge increases. This increased pull results in a decrease in atomic radii. Atomic radius increases as you move down a group because electrons occupy successively higher energy levels farther from the nucleus. The farther away from the nucleus electrons are, the less tightly they are held.

FIGURE 12: This periodic table displays atomic radii. The lanthanide and actinide series are not shown.

Group 1																	18
H 1 37	**2**											**13**	**14**	**15**	**16**	**17**	**He 2** 31
Li 3 152	**Be 4** 112											**B 5** 85	**C 6** 77	**N 7** 75	**O 8** 73	**F 9** 72	**Ne 10** 71
Na 11 186	**Mg 12** 160	**3**	**4**	**5**	**6**	**7**	**8**	**9**	**10**	**11**	**12**	**Al 13** 143	**Si 14** 118	**P 15** 110	**S 16** 103	**Cl 17** 100	**Ar 18** 98
K 19 227	**Ca 20** 197	**Sc 21** 162	**Ti 22** 147	**V 23** 134	**Cr 24** 128	**Mn 25** 127	**Fe 26** 126	**Co 27** 125	**Ni 28** 124	**Cu 29** 128	**Zn 30** 134	**Ga 31** 135	**Ge 32** 122	**As 33** 120	**Se 34** 119	**Br 35** 114	**Kr 36** 112
Rb 37 248	**Sr 38** 215	**Y 39** 180	**Zr 40** 160	**Nb 41** 146	**Mo 42** 139	**Tc 43** 136	**Ru 44** 134	**Rh 45** 134	**Pd 46** 137	**Ag 47** 144	**Cd 48** 149	**In 49** 167	**Sn 50** 140	**Sb 51** 140	**Te 52** 142	**I 53** 133	**Xe 54** 131
Cs 55 265	**Ba 56** 222	57–71	**Hf 72** 159	**Ta 73** 146	**W 74** 139	**Re 75** 137	**Os 76** 135	**Ir 77** 136	**Pt 78** 139	**Au 79** 144	**Hg 80** 151	**Tl 81** 170	**Pb 82** 175	**Bi 83** 150	**Po 84** 168	**At 85** 140	**Rn 86** 141
Fr 87 270	**Ra 88** 220	89–103	**Rf 104** —	**Db 105** —	**Sg 106** —	**Bh 107** —	**Hs 108** —	**Mt 109** —	**Ds 110** —	**Rg 111** —	**Cn 112** —	**Nh 113** —	**Fl 114** —	**Mc 115** —	**Lv 116** —	**Ts 117** —	**Og 118** —

Atomic symbol — **C** 6 — Atomic number
• — Relative atomic size
77 — Atomic radius

EXPLAIN Sodium and phosphorus are in the same period, but they have different atomic radii. Why is this?

_____

_____

_____

_____

FIGURE 13: Sodium metal rusts quickly when exposed to air.

Trends in atomic radius can be used to predict the reactivity of an element. Metals with a larger atomic radius tend to be more reactive because the outer electrons are not held as strongly. Nonmetals show the opposite trend. Those with a smaller atomic radius tend to be more reactive because the attraction from the nucleus has a greater effect.

INFER Complete the statement by selecting the correct terms.

Sodium is so reactive that is quickly rusts when it is exposed to air. Sodium has a relatively large | small atomic radius because it has one | two | three valence electron(s). Other metals below sodium on the periodic table have a larger | a smaller | the same atomic radius. These metals must be more | less reactive than sodium.

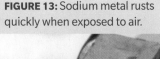 **Evidence Notebook** Explain how chemists could use trends in atomic radius to predict the size of a new element that has not yet been discovered.

Patterns in Electronegativity

When atoms combine to form compounds, electrons may be lost, gained, or shared between the atoms. When two identical atoms bond, electrons are shared equally. When different types of atoms bond, one atom in a compound usually attracts electrons more strongly than the other atom. You can imagine this as a sort of "tug of war" for the electrons being shared or transferred in a compound.

APPLY With a partner, discuss how the dogs playing tug of war in Figure 14 is a good analogy for the sharing of electrons in a compound. Write your own analogy for this phenomenon in the space provided.

FIGURE 14: In a game of tug of war, one player may exert a stronger pull on the rope.

_____

_____

_____

_____

Analyzing Electronegativity

In Figure 14, think of the knot in the center of the rope as an electron. If the dog on the right "tugs" more strongly than the dog on the left, the dog on the right will be slightly more negative than the one on the left. This uneven concentration of charge has a significant effect on the chemical properties of a compound. Electronegativity is a measure of the attraction that an atom has for the electrons it shares in a molecule.

Atoms with more protons tend to have a greater attraction for shared electrons because of the greater positive nuclear charge. Atoms with a large atomic radius tend to have a weaker attraction for shared electrons because the distance between the nucleus and the shared electrons is larger. So, electronegativity is greater for smaller atoms with a larger number of protons. It is smaller for larger atoms with a smaller number of protons.

EXPLAIN Using this information, explain how the electronegativities of the following elements compare to that of phosphorus.

higher   lower

Sulfur is to the right of phosphorus on the periodic table. It has _____

electronegativity than phosphorus because a sulfur atom has more protons. Silicon

is to the left of phosphorus on the periodic table. It has _____

electronegativity because its atoms have fewer protons than phosphorus.

Nitrogen is above phosphorus on the periodic table. It has _____

electronegativity than phosphorus because its atomic radius is smaller. Arsenic is

below phosphorus on the period table. It has _____ electronegativity

because it has a larger atomic radius than phosphorus.

Patterns in Electronegativity

Electronegativity cannot be measured directly. It is calculated using the average energy required to remove an electron from an atom and the energy given off when an electron is added to an atom. Both methods express electronegativity as a quantity without units on a relative scale. The most electronegative element, fluorine, is arbitrarily assigned an electronegativity of 4.0. Other values are calculated in relation to this value. The results of the calculations are shown in Figure 15 as a function of atomic number.

Electronegativity

FIGURE 15: Electronegativity can be described as a function of an element's atomic number.

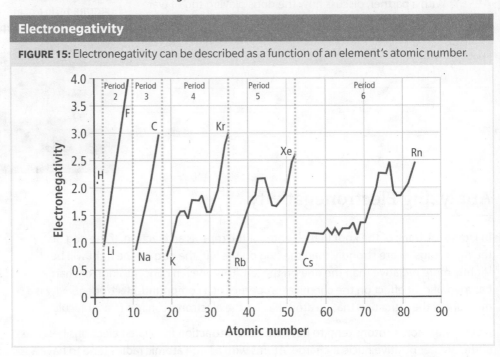

ANALYZE How would the pattern of electronegativities shown in Figure 14 appear across a period and down a group on the periodic table?

_____

_____

_____

EXPLAIN How does the trend in electronegativity in the periodic table compare with the trend in atomic radius? Explain why this relationship makes sense.

_____

_____

_____

EXPLAIN How does the trend in electronegativity in the periodic table compare with the trend in ionization energy? Explain why this relationship makes sense.

_____

_____

_____

Explaining Trends in Electronegativity

Electronegativity on the periodic table generally increases across a period and decreases down a group. Group 1 metals are the least electronegative elements because they have only one valence electron. Their atoms have a low attraction for electrons in compounds. The Group 17 elements are the most electronegative elements of each period. These atoms need only one electron to fill their valence shells, so they attract electrons strongly. Group 18 noble gases are unusual in that some of them do not form compounds and therefore cannot be assigned electronegativities. Among the transition metals, there is little variation across the period and up and down a group. This is because their metallic properties affect their ability to attract electrons as easily as the other elements.

As Figure 16 shows, the combination of the period and group trends in electronegativity results in the highest values belonging to the elements in the upper right of the periodic table. The lowest values belong to the elements in the lower left of the table.

FIGURE 16: This periodic table displays electronegativity. The lanthanide and actinide series are not shown.

Group 1	2	3	4	5	6	7	8	9	10	11	12	13	14	15	16	17	18
1 **H** 2.1																	2 **He** —
3 **Li** 1.0	4 **Be** 1.5											5 **B** 2.0	6 **C** 2.5	7 **N** 3.0	8 **O** 3.5	9 **F** 4.0	10 **Ne** —
11 **Na** 0.9	12 **Mg** 1.2											13 **Al** 1.5	14 **Si** 1.8	15 **P** 2.1	16 **S** 2.5	17 **Cl** 3.0	18 **Ar** —
19 **K** 0.8	20 **Ca** 1.0	21 **Sc** 1.3	22 **Ti** 1.5	23 **V** 1.6	24 **Cr** 1.6	25 **Mn** 1.5	26 **Fe** 1.8	27 **Co** 1.8	28 **Ni** 1.8	29 **Cu** 1.9	30 **Zn** 1.6	31 **Ga** 1.8	32 **Ge** 1.8	33 **As** 2.0	34 **Se** 2.4	35 **Br** 2.8	36 **Kr** 3.0
37 **Rb** 0.8	38 **Sr** 1.0	39 **Y** 1.2	40 **Zr** 1.4	41 **Nb** 1.6	42 **Mo** 1.8	43 **Tc** 1.9	44 **Ru** 2.2	45 **Rh** 2.2	46 **Pd** 2.2	47 **Ag** 1.9	48 **Cd** 1.7	49 **In** 1.7	50 **Sn** 1.8	51 **Sb** 1.9	52 **Te** 2.1	53 **I** 2.5	54 **Xe** 2.6
55 **Cs** 0.7	56 **Ba** 0.9	57–71	72 **Hf** 1.3	73 **Ta** 1.5	74 **W** 1.7	75 **Re** 1.9	76 **Os** 2.2	77 **Ir** 2.2	78 **Pt** 2.2	79 **Au** 2.4	80 **Hg** 1.9	81 **Tl** 1.8	82 **Pb** 1.8	83 **Bi** 1.9	84 **Po** 2.0	85 **At** 2.2	86 **Rn** 2.4
87 **Fr** 0.7	88 **Ra** 0.9	89–103	104 **Rf** —	105 **Db** —	106 **Sg** —	107 **Bh** —	108 **Hs** —	109 **Mt** —	110 **Ds** —	111 **Rg** —	112 **Cn** —	113 **Nh** —	114 **Fl** —	115 **Mc** —	116 **Lv** —	117 **Ts** —	118 **Og** —

Key: 6 — Atomic number; C — Symbol; 2.5 — Electronegativity

Trends in electronegativity on the periodic table can be used to predict the reaction between elements. When elements have a large difference in electronegativity, the element with greater electronegativity has a much stronger attraction for shared electrons. These elements bond by one atom donating one or more electrons to the other atom. Elements that have similar electronegativities are more likely to share valence electrons because their attraction for the electrons is similar.

APPLY Sodium bromide can be used as a disinfectant when a chlorine-based disinfectant is not wanted. When elemental sodium and bromine react, the reaction can be explosive. Complete the statement to explain why sodium and bromine react.

Sodium has a high | low electronegativity, so it has a strong | weak attraction for shared electrons. Bromine has a high | low electronegativity, so it has a strong | weak attraction for shared electrons. Their reaction transfers one electron | two electrons | three electrons from bromine to sodium | sodium to bromine.

FIGURE 17: Sodium reacts with bromine to form sodium bromide.

Engineering
Developing Halogen Bulbs

FIGURE 18: Halogen bulb

A halogen bulb consists of a tungsten filament surrounded by halogen gas inside a clear bulb. Typical incandescent light bulbs also have a tungsten filament, but they are surrounded by argon, a noble gas, that prevents oxygen in the air from corroding the metal filament and shortening the life of the bulb. In contrast, the gas in a halogen lamp is a highly reactive Group 17 element, such as bromine or iodine. As electricity begins to flow through the bulb, the filament becomes extremely hot and begins to vaporize. The halogen gas readily reacts with the tungsten vapor. A cyclic process occurs in which tungsten is redeposited onto the filament, extending the lifetime of the bulb.

The earliest halogen bulbs had a carbon filament surrounded by chlorine gas. Tungsten soon replaced carbon because it could operate at a higher temperature, emitting more light. Chlorine was replaced by iodine to avoid the blackening of the bulb that occurred with previous designs. Later, bromine was used instead of iodine to improve efficiency.

Halogen bulbs are often used in workplaces, overhead lighting, car lights, and spotlights because of their brightness. They also have a longer lifetime than other types of incandescent bulbs. A drawback, however, is that halogen bulbs are extremely hot, and the glass bulb must be kept clean to avoid breakage when the bulb reaches high temperatures.

DEFINE Engineers are evaluating a halogen bulb as a possible solution to lighting a reading workspace. What criteria might they consider?

_____

_____

_____

_____

Both standard incandescent and halogen bulbs are inefficient. They convert more electricity into energy in the form of heat than light. They are increasingly being replaced by LED bulbs that use much less energy to produce the same amount of light. An LED is a light-emitting diode, a solid state electronic device similar to the devices used in computers and calculators. When electric current passes through the LED, it emits light.

 Language Arts Connection Research the benefits and drawbacks of a halogen bulb and an LED bulb. For a given amount of light produced, how do the halogen bulb's cost of production, bulb life, and cost of electricity needed to operate compare with those of the LED bulb? Develop a visual guide that an engineer could use to decide which type of bulb is most appropriate for a given situation.

 Evidence Notebook Suppose chemists attempt to produce an element with atomic number 119. Based on its likely position on the periodic table, what would you expect its electronegativity to be? Explain how you can make this prediction.

Careers in Science

Analytical Chemist

Have you ever read a mystery novel or watched a detective show where a scientist solved a case by analyzing a sample? These movie scientists are sometimes based on analytical chemists, though the portrayal is not always accurate. The work of analytical chemists often does require "detective" work, careful analysis of samples, and the use of precise equipment. Some of the most important skills of analytical chemists are their ability to ask questions and identify patterns.

This drive to solve mysteries about why a product or a process is not working the way it should is part of the reason Barbara Belmont became an analytical chemist. She uses many different types of analytical methods, such as gas chromatography-mass spectrometry and gas-chromatography-flame ionization, to determine if a client's products meet regulation standards. Part of this work is asking questions about what portion of the materials could be causing a failure, and then giving recommendations based on evidence for how to fix the problem.

Barbara Belmont identifies as a member of the LGBTQ+ community and takes on an active role increasing the visibility and inclusion of LGBTQ+ peoples in STEM programs. She performs this work through memberships in the American Chemical Society, the American Association for Advancement of Science, and the National Organization of Gay and Lesbian Scientists and Technical Professionals (NOGLSTP).

Among Barbara Belmont's most important work is her teaching career where she brings her real-life experience to the classroom. She mentors student-driven research projects and has created a safe space on campus for students to discuss LGBTQ+ issues.

FIGURE 19: Barbara Belmont is an analytical chemist who works and teaches in California.

She is also focusing on ways to re-design her course to be more environmentally friendly and cost-effective. This is an important task that all scientists, including analytical chemists, must consider on any project.

Chemistry in Your Community Research an analytical chemist or a company that performed a chemical analysis on a project in your community. For example, you may research a company that analyzed building materials for a construction project. Consider the following to guide your research:

- What materials were tested by the analytical chemist, and what equipment was used to run the tests?
- What kinds of questions do you think the chemist asked before analyzing the materials?
- Were any tests run to determine the effect the materials might have on the environment?

Write a magazine article about the findings and contributions of the chemist. You may wish to conduct an interview with the chemist or group of chemists to gather this information.

| PERIODIC TRENDS IN HISTORY | | THE MENDELEEV LAB OF 1869 | DISCOVERING NEW ELEMENTS | Go online to choose one of these other paths. |

Lesson Self-Check

CAN YOU EXPLAIN IT?

FIGURE 20: Certain elements occur naturally and have been known about for a very long time. Other elements were created in laboratories. Some of these elements only exist for a moment.

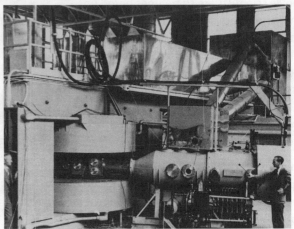

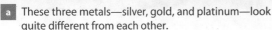 These three metals—silver, gold, and platinum—look quite different from each other.

b The 60-inch cyclotron at the University of California, Berkeley.

The periodic table lists 118 elements. Ninety-two of these are naturally occurring elements, and 29 are transuranium elements that have been produced in laboratories. With some exceptions, the arrangement of the elements on the periodic table reveals patterns in the properties of the elements. Scientists can use these patterns when searching for new elements.

The newest elements on the periodic table have high atomic numbers and can only be produced in high-energy accelerators, such as the 60-inch cyclotron at the University of California, Berkeley. These elements are so unstable that only tiny amounts are produced, and they may last only for a few microseconds. So, most of these elements have no practical, commercial use outside of research labs. Nevertheless, scientists continue the effort to develop elements with even higher atomic numbers.

 Evidence Notebook Refer to the notes in your Evidence Notebook to explain how scientists are able to predict that certain elements could be made when the elements do not occur naturally. Your explanation should include a discussion of periodic table trends. Consider the following when constructing your explanation:

1. How can scientists predict that certain elements can be made?
2. How can scientists use trends in the periodic table to predict a new element? What other information helps scientists predict how an element could be made?
3. How does the evidence you cited support your claim?

CHECKPOINTS

Check Your Understanding

1. Rubidium is an element located below sodium in Group 1 on the periodic table. Which of the following statements is correct?
   ○ **a.** Rubidium has lower electronegativity and a lower ionization energy than sodium.
   ○ **b.** Rubidium has a higher electronegativity and a higher ionization energy than sodium.
   ○ **c.** Rubidium and sodium have the same electronegativity and ionization energy.
   ○ **d.** Rubidium has a lower electronegativity but the same ionization energy as sodium.

2. Which element would you expect to have the highest electronegativity?
   ○ **a.** calcium
   ○ **b.** cesium
   ○ **c.** fluorine
   ○ **d.** phosphorus

3. A scientist determines that an element has a high reactivity and a large atomic radius. What other properties does the element most likely have?
   ○ **a.** high electronegativity and high ionization energy
   ○ **b.** high electronegativity and low ionization energy
   ○ **c.** low electronegativity and high ionization energy
   ○ **d.** low electronegativity and low ionization energy

4. According to periodic trends, at which position on the periodic table would an element most likely have an electronegativity higher than that of calcium? Select all correct answers.
   ☐ **a.** just above calcium
   ☐ **b.** just below calcium
   ☐ **c.** just to the left of calcium
   ☐ **d.** just to the right of calcium

5. What statement best explains why fluorine has a smaller atomic radius than oxygen?
   ○ **a.** Fluorine has fewer electrons than oxygen.
   ○ **b.** Fluorine has one more proton than oxygen.
   ○ **c.** Fluorine has low electronegativity.
   ○ **d.** Fluorine forms bonds readily with oxygen.

6. Put these elements in order of decreasing electronegativity, with the highest electronegative element as number 1.

   _____ **a.** tin (Sn, Group 14, Period 5)

   _____ **b.** rubidium (Rb, Group 1, Period 5)

   _____ **c.** bromine (Br, Group 17, Period 4)

   _____ **d.** lithium (Li, Group 1, Period 2)

   _____ **e.** cadmium (Cd, Group 12, Period 5)

7. Complete the statements.

   As you move from left to right across a period, the size of an atom increases | decreases. This is because the increasing | decreasing charge of the nucleus pulls on the electrons more strongly | more weakly. As you look down a group, the size of an atom increases | decreases. This is because outer electrons are farther from | closer to the nucleus.

8. A sample of potassium (K, found in Group 1) and a sample of iodine (I, found in Group 17) react, forming potassium iodide (KI), which is used to treat thyroid conditions. Complete the statements to describe this reaction.

   The reaction occurs because electrons are pulled away from the more | less electronegative element by the more | less electronegative element. The more electronegative element is found in Group 1 | Group 17. The less electronegative element is found in Group 1 | Group 17.

CHECKPOINTS (continued)

9. Explain how the pattern in ionization energy across a period of the periodic table compares to the pattern in atomic radius across a period.

_____

_____

_____

_____

_____

10. Suppose you have a sample of potassium. Describe several ways you could use periodic trends and a knowledge of valence electrons to predict the element's reactivity and how the element will behave in a chemical bond.

_____

_____

_____

_____

_____

_____

_____

11. Describe generally how the trends in ionization energy and atomic radius apply to the noble gases, and explain the reason for these trends.

_____

_____

_____

_____

_____

_____

MAKE YOUR OWN STUDY GUIDE

 In your Evidence Notebook, design a study guide that supports the main ideas from this lesson:

Patterns in ionization energy, atomic size, and electronegativity can be used to make predictions about the properties and interactions of elements on the periodic table.

Remember to include the following information in your study guide:

• Use examples that model main ideas.

• Record explanations for the phenomena you investigated.

• Use evidence to support your explanations. Your support can include drawings, data, graphs, laboratory conclusions, and other evidence recorded throughout the lesson.

Consider the organization of elements on the periodic table and how patterns in properties such as ionization energy and electronegativity can be used to predict the way elements bond and react in nature and in everyday applications of the elements.

The Arrangement of Atoms in Compounds

A fiery reaction occurs when sodium metal is exposed to chlorine gas.

CAN YOU EXPLAIN IT?

Sodium is an essential metal required by the human body to function. In the United States, about 11% of a person's daily sodium intake comes from adding the mineral table salt to food. Table salt is the common name for sodium chloride, a compound made of sodium and chlorine atoms. While people can safely ingest sodium chloride, the individual elements of the compound are hazardous by themselves. Sodium metal is toxic, corrosive, and reacts vigorously with water to produce hydrogen, a flammable gas. Sodium salts are used in a variety of ways, including deicing roads in the winter. Exposure to elemental chlorine gas can result in poisoning and health complications. Chlorine was weaponized during World War I. Today, chlorine is a commonly manufactured chemical in the United States and is a key component of bleach.

FIGURE 1: Sodium chloride (left) results from the reaction of sodium metal (center) and chlorine gas (right).

PREDICT Pure sodium and chlorine are extremely dangerous, but when combined they result in a substance that we use every day. How do you think the properties of sodium and chlorine change when they are combined to make sodium chloride?

_____

_____

_____

_____

 Evidence Notebook As you explore the lesson, gather evidence to explain how patterns in the periodic table can be used to predict the properties of chemical compounds.

Hands-On Lab

Analyzing the Properties of Compounds

Differences in the structures of compounds at the atomic level cause the differences that are observed at the macroscopic scale. One physical property that varies widely among different materials is melting point.

Research Question: How do the structures of compounds influence the functional uses of compounds in natural or human-designed systems?

MAKE A CLAIM

Which of the substances being tested do you think will have the highest melting point?

MATERIALS

- indirectly vented chemical splash goggles, nonlatex apron, nitrile gloves
- aluminum foil
- Bunsen burner
- citric acid, small amount
- paraffin wax, small amount
- permanent marker
- ring stand, ring, and clamp
- salt, small amount
- spatula or scoop
- striker
- wire gauze

SAFETY INFORMATION

indirectly vented chemical splash goggles

- Wear indirectly vented chemical splash goggles, a nonlatex apron, and nitrile gloves during the setup, hands-on, and takedown segments of the activity.

- Use caution when working with Bunsen burners, because this heat source can seriously burn skin and clothing. Secure loose clothing and tie back long hair.

FIGURE 2: Experimental setup

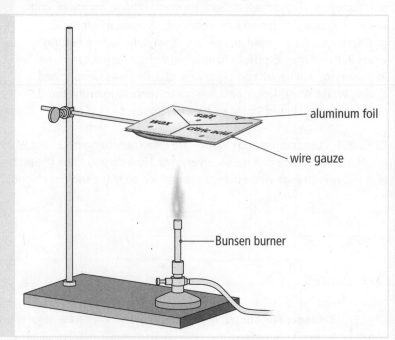

CARRY OUT THE INVESTIGATION

1. Use a marker to divide a square piece of aluminum foil into three sections. Label the sections *salt, wax,* and *citric acid*. Fold the edges up to keep melted wax from spilling.

2. Use a spatula to transfer a very small (less than pea-sized) amount of each substance onto the foil. Be sure to clean and dry the spatula between each substance.

3. Set up a ring stand as shown in Figure 2. Adjust the ring to the appropriate height so the Bunsen burner can fit under it.

4. Place a piece of wire gauze on top of the ring, and carefully place the aluminum foil on top of the gauze.

5. Secure loose clothing and tie back hair. Light the Bunsen burner, and carefully place it under the wire gauze. Observe the order in which the substances melt. Record the melting order in the data table.

6. Turn off the Bunsen burner immediately after the first two substances have melted. Dispose of your materials as instructed by your teacher.

COLLECT DATA

Substance	Salt	Wax	Citric Acid
Melting Order			

DRAW CONCLUSIONS

The melting point of substances is related to the strength of forces between the particles that make up a substance. Write a conclusion that addresses each of the points below.

Claim Which substance tested in this experiment has the strongest attractive forces between its particles? Which substance has the weakest?

Evidence Give specific examples from your data to support your claim.

Reasoning Explain how the evidence you gave supports your claim. Describe, in detail, the connections between the evidence you cited and the argument you are making.

_____

_____

_____

_____

_____

_____

_____

_____

 Evidence Notebook As you have seen, sodium metal, chlorine gas, and sodium chloride have different properties. What conclusion can you make about the forces holding the atoms of these substances together? What tests could you run to learn more about each substance?

Describing Chemical Bonds

The electron arrangement of most atoms causes them to have a high potential energy. Recall that a chemical bond forms when atoms gain, lose, or share valence electrons and end up with a full outer shell, or octet. A full outer shell has less potential energy than a partially filled shell, so the full shell is a more stable arrangement. Therefore, when atoms form chemical bonds, the compound formed typically has a lower potential energy than the total potential energy of the individual atoms. Like a ball rolling down a hill, systems tend to naturally change toward lower, more stable energy states.

Making Predictions about Bonding

Electronegativity is a measure of the tendency of an atom to attract electrons. Differences in electronegativity can be used to predict the types of chemical bonds atoms will form.

 Collaborate With a partner, review the electronegativity trends of the periodic table. Where are the most and least electronegative elements found?

When there is a large electronegativity difference between two atoms—between about 1.7 and about 3.3—electrons tend to transfer from the less electronegative atom to the more electronegative atom. The bond formed by this transfer is called an ionic bond. The greater the electronegativity difference, the stronger the ionic character of the bond and the more completely the electrons move from one atom to the other.

FIGURE 3: Bond types fit into a continuous range of electronegativities.

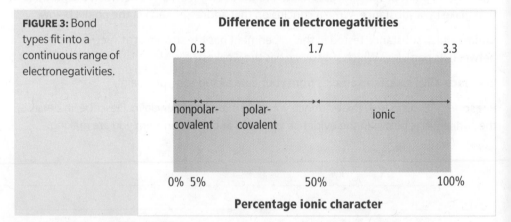

As the electronegativity difference decreases, however, neither atom can attract or "let go" of valence electrons. The two atoms share their valence electrons, forming what is called a covalent bond. If two atoms are from the same element, their electronegativity difference is 0, and a *nonpolar covalent bond* forms. The diatomic elements of hydrogen, nitrogen, oxygen, and the halogens are examples of this type of bond and the electrons are shared equally between the atoms. If there is a small difference in electronegativity, atoms share electrons unevenly, forming a *polar covalent bond*. There is a spectrum of bond types between completely ionic and nonpolar covalent bonds, as shown in Figure 3. All bonds result from the mutual attraction between positively charged and negatively charged particles across two atoms.

ANALYZE Using Figure 3 and the periodic table of electronegativities, fill out the table to describe how the listed elements will interact with one another in a chemical bond.

Elements Bonded	Electronegativity Difference	Bond Type	More Electronegative Atom	Example Compound
C and H				
C and S				
O and H				
Na and Cl				
Cs and F				

 Patterns

You can make generalizations about how each element's value relates to other elements. In general, metal elements do not attract electrons and they have low electronegativities. The electronegativity of nonmetals is much higher, and it increases toward the top right of the periodic table. The exceptions to this pattern are the noble gases, which do not attract electrons. These patterns allow you to make predictions about the type of bond any two elements will form.

INFER Complete the statement about how different elements bond.

Metals tend to have relatively high | low electronegativities, and nonmetals have relatively high | low electronegativities. When a metal bonds with a nonmetal, electrons will most likely be transferred, and a covalent | an ionic bond will form. When a nonmetal bonds with a nonmetal, the difference in electronegativity values is relatively low. Therefore, electrons will be shared between the two nonmetals, and a covalent | an ionic bond will be formed.

Notice that none of the examples involve bonds between the metal atoms. Metal atoms do not interact with one another to form ionic or covalent bonds. The interactions between particles in metals will be discussed in another section.

Describing Ionic Bonding

Elements with very different electronegativity values generally form ionic bonds. Sodium chloride is an example of an ionically bonded compound. Recall that a mixture of sodium metal and chlorine gas reacts to form sodium chloride. Each sodium atom loses an electron, and each chlorine atom gains an electron. The attraction between positive and negative ions holds the ions together in an ionic bond. The ionization of the atoms and the formation of the ionic bond increase the stability of the system. The reaction releases a large amount of energy as light and heat, resulting in a much lower overall energy state. The product of the reaction is very stable relative to the reactants, and the product does not tend to react vigorously with other substances as sodium and chlorine do.

When an atom loses one or more electrons, it becomes a positive ion, or *cation*. Cations have more protons than electrons, and so the atom has an overall positive charge. When an atom gains electrons, it becomes a negative ion, or *anion*. Anions have a greater number of electrons than protons, and so have an overall negative charge. A sodium atom has one valence electron, and chlorine has seven valence electrons. When sodium donates one electron to chlorine in an ionic bond, both ions are left with stable octet configurations. This makes the compound more stable than either of the highly reactive elements.

ANALYZE Sodium transfers an electron to chlorine when forming sodium chloride. Write either a positive sign or a negative sign as a superscript by each ion formed in this bond. Then, label each as either a *cation* or an *anion* below the chemical symbol.

$$\left[\text{Na}\right] \qquad \boxed{} \qquad\qquad \left[:\overset{\cdot}{\underset{\cdot\cdot}{\text{Cl}}}:\right] \qquad \boxed{}$$

sodium ion   chloride ion

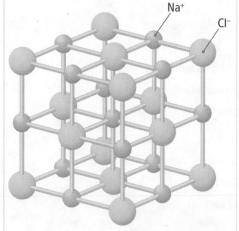

FIGURE 4: Sodium ions and chloride ions arrange to form a network.

Na⁺

Cl⁻

Although an ionic bond forms between two atoms, the ionic components of the compound are not isolated in pairs of ions with opposite charges. As shown in Figure 4, an ionic compound consists of many bonds between positive and negative ions that form predictable, repeating patterns. This arrangement gives the compounds regular, geometric shapes.

The structure of any ionic compound is a *crystal*, a three-dimensional network of positive and negative ions mutually attracted to one another. Each ion forms bonds with all of the adjacent ions of the opposite charge. This arrangement is called a crystal lattice. In the model of an ionic compound in Figure 4, each ionic bond is represented with a solid line. As solid crystals, ionic compounds do not conduct electricity but they do conduct electricity when dissolved in water.

Notice that each ion is attracted to more than one ion of opposite charge. The chemical formula of an ionic compound represents the simplest ratio of the ions in an electrically neutral crystal. A neutral compound always has equal amounts of positive and negative charge.

GATHER EVIDENCE How is the relatively high melting point of sodium chloride related to its structure at the atomic scale? Observe sodium crystals with a hand lens. Use your observations and the model in Figure 4 to support your claim.

_____

_____

_____

_____

Producing Salts

Salts are ionic compounds made of metal and nonmetal atoms. They are important for human life and activities. Salts can be produced by removing water from seawater using evaporation. Salt deposits left by natural evaporation of ancient oceans can also be mined. As the water is removed, the ions in solution form new ionic bonds, producing a crystalline ionic compound. For example, the lithium metal used in batteries is harvested from lithium salts by evaporation of brine deposits.

FIGURE 5: Lithium salts are isolated by solar evaporation of water from brine.

Long-lasting, recyclable lithium batteries are essential to many consumer products. They are also used to store renewable energy from sources such as solar and wind power. Chemical engineers must weigh tradeoffs to minimize the economic and environmental costs of producing lithium salts which maximize the benefits.

Language Arts Connection Companies in California's Silicon Valley have been instrumental in developing devices that rely on lithium batteries. Research the development of lithium batteries, the increased demand for lithium, and how this demand is currently being met. Make a brochure explaining how the need for lithium is related to modern technologies.

Describing Covalent Bonding

In a covalent bond, neither atom exerts sufficient attractive force to cause an electron to transfer between atoms, so electrons are shared. A molecule is a neutral group of atoms that are held together by covalent bonds. A fluorine molecule is shown in Figure 6.

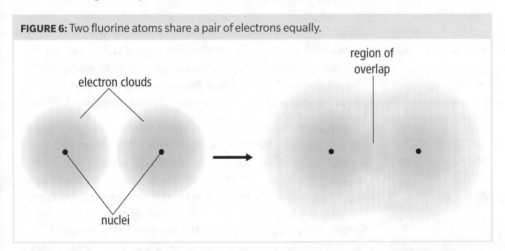

FIGURE 6: Two fluorine atoms share a pair of electrons equally.

electron clouds

region of overlap

nuclei

A single molecule of a chemical compound is an individual unit that acts in many ways as a single particle. A molecule consists of two or more atoms bonded together. Some molecules, such as a fluorine molecule or an oxygen molecule, are made up of atoms of only one element. Other molecules, such as water or sugar, combine atoms of two or more elements, each involved in one or more covalent bonds to form a compound. A chemical compound in which the simplest units are molecules is called a *molecular compound*. Molecules have different properties from ionic compounds.

FIGURE 7: Molecules consist of two or more covalently bonded atoms.

a Oxygen molecule, O_2

b Water molecule, H_2O

c Sucrose molecule, $C_{12}H_{22}O_{11}$

EXPLAIN In general, the melting and boiling points of molecular compounds are much lower than those of ionic compounds. What can explain this difference?

Molecular compounds such as those in Figure 7 are formed when one or more atoms transfer | share | release electrons to form molecules. The covalent bonds *within* a molecule are very strong | weak. However, it requires more | less energy to melt a molecular compound than an ionic compound such as the one in Figure 4. This is because the attractive forces *between* individual molecules are weaker | stronger than the forces between ions in an ionic compound.

Explore Online ▶

Hands-On Lab 🧪

Types of Bonding in Solids
Analyze conductivity, solubility, and melting point to determine the bonding type present in solids.

The general properties of molecular compounds result from their structure as molecules. In general, the melting and boiling points of molecular compounds are much lower than those of ionic compounds. Some of them are gases at room temperatures. Because molecules are neutral, covalently bonded compounds do not conduct electric current in either their solid or liquid state.

Describing Metallic Bonding

Metal atoms have low electronegativity values. They do not attract additional electrons, and their own outer electrons are loosely held. Inside a sample of metal, the positive metal ions are surrounded by delocalized electrons. These electrons are not tightly held by any one atom, so they are free to move about within the sample. The chemical bonding that results from the attraction between metal atoms and the surrounding sea of electrons is called metallic bonding.

Explore Online ▶

FIGURE 8: Electrons are able to move freely within a metal substance.

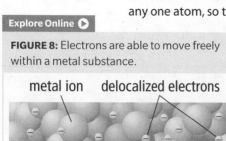
metal ion   delocalized electrons

As with all substances, the properties of metals are related to the bonds they form. Metals are malleable, or easily hammered into sheets. The delocalized electrons around the positive ions form relatively weak links within the substance, making it easy to bend and shape metal. The mobile electrons moving easily throughout the substance allow metals to conduct electricity and contribute to their ability to conduct heat. The strength of the metallic bonds varies depending on atomic structure. While some metals have extremely high melting points, mercury is a liquid at room temperature, and gallium will melt in your hand.

 Evidence Notebook What types of bonds form within a sample of sodium metal, chlorine gas, and sodium chloride crystals? How does the electron structure of each substance affect the properties of compounds that it forms?

Predicting the Structure of Compounds

Every molecule of a covalently bonded substance has the same number and type of atoms in the same arrangement as other molecules of the substance. The number of atoms in the crystal lattice of an ionic compound, however, can vary. Although the number of atoms of each element in the compound is not fixed, the ratio of each type of atom is a characteristic of the compound. For example, calcium and fluorine always combine in a ratio of one calcium ion to two fluoride ions. In ionic compounds, this ratio determines the three-dimensional arrangement of ions within the substance.

 Collaborate With a partner, research other compounds formed when Group 2 and Group 17 atoms combine. What do you notice about the ratio of atoms in the compound? Research how other groups combine, such as Group 1 and Group 16. Do they also show a pattern?

Analyzing Chemical Formulas for Ionic Compounds

The periodic table provides the information needed to determine the ratios of elements in an ionic compound. The number of valence electrons of groups of elements follows a pattern across the table. The metallic elements in Group 1 each have one valence electron, those in Group 2 have two valence electrons, and so on. This pattern continues in the main group elements to the noble gases, which have completely filled outer orbitals. When an ionic bond forms, metal atoms transfer electrons to nonmetal atoms. The outer orbital of the metal is empty, but the next lower orbital has an octet of eight electrons. Nonmetal atoms in ionic bonds accept enough electrons from other atoms to fill their octet.

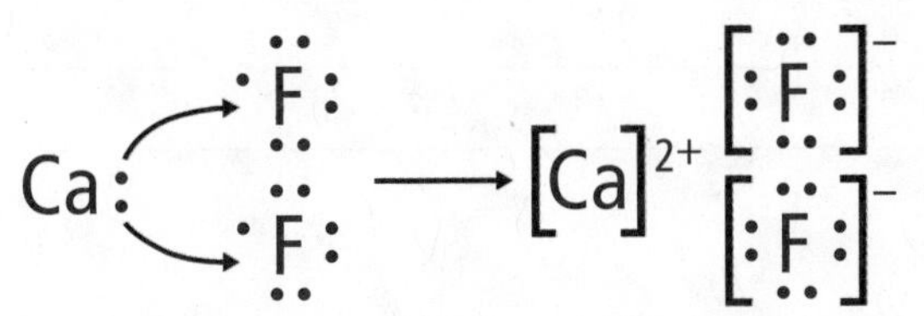

Ca: → F: F: → $[Ca]^{2+}$ $\begin{bmatrix} :F: \end{bmatrix}^{-}$ $\begin{bmatrix} :F: \end{bmatrix}^{-}$

FIGURE 9: Two valence electrons transfer from calcium to fluorine.

As shown in Figure 9, a calcium atom has two valence electrons and a fluorine atom can accept one extra valence electron. Calcium fluoride always combines in a 2 to 1 ratio, with each calcium ion transferring two electrons to two fluoride ions. In the crystal, however, the ions interact with all of the oppositely charged ions around them, not just those that provided or received their electrons.

APPLY Complete the statement about the chemical formula of calcium fluoride.

Calcium is located in the second column of the periodic table, so a calcium atom has one | two | three valence electron(s), which it loses to form a calcium ion. Each fluorine atom has seven valence electrons, so it accepts one | two | three electron(s) to form a fluoride ion. Therefore, the formula for calcium fluoride, CaF_2, represents the exact number | overall ratio of ions present in a crystal of the compound.

The chemical formula of an ionic compound indicates the relative numbers of atoms of each element, using atomic symbols and numerical subscripts. A *formula unit* is the simplest expression of this ratio. In the chemical formula, the metal is always written first, followed by the nonmetal. Subscripts show the number of atoms in the formula unit. The formula unit of calcium fluoride is CaF_2. Because there is only one calcium atom in the formula unit, no subscript is used.

Patterns

Ionic Formulas

The table below shows some chemical formulas for binary ionic compounds, which are compounds containing one metal and one nonmetal element. The elements are all found in Period 3 of the periodic table.

Compounds containing sodium	Na_3P	Na_2S	NaCl
Compounds containing magnesium	Mg_3P_2	MgS	$MgCl_2$
Compounds containing aluminum	AlP	Al_2S_3	$AlCl_3$

EXPLAIN Describe the patterns you see among the chemical formulas. How does the placement of the elements on the periodic table appear to relate to the numbers in the chemical formula?

_____

_____

_____

_____

_____

_____

_____

Writing Chemical Formulas for Ionic Compounds

The patterns in ionic formulas result from the charges of the ions of an element. Because the most stable ions have either a completely empty or a completely filled outer orbital, the charges on ions are related to their group on the periodic table. The charges formed follow the octet rule. Metal elements in Group 1 lose an electron to form a 1+ charge. Metal elements in Group 2 lose two electrons to form a 2+ charge. The chemical symbol of an ion consists of its element symbol followed by its charge as a superscript. For example, a magnesium ion has the symbol Mg^{2+}.

PREDICT Aluminum is a metal with three valence electrons. What is the correct symbol for an aluminum ion?

○ **a.** Al^{5+} ○ **c.** Al^{3-}

○ **b.** Al^{3+} ○ **d.** Al^{5-}

Nonmetals typically have 5, 6, 7, or 8 valence electrons, and nonmetals have higher electronegativities than metals. The most stable arrangement occurs when these elements gain electrons when forming ionic bonds. For example, nitrogen has five valence electrons. A nitrogen atom gains three electrons, forming an octet. The resulting charge on the nitrogen ion is 3−, so the ion formed is written as N^{3-}. Noble gases in Group 18 beyond helium, such as neon and argon, do not typically bond with other elements because they already possess a full outer orbital.

ANALYZE Write in the charges you would expect elements in each group to form. Then, choose an example element from that group, and write its ion symbol in the next row.

Group	1	2	13	14	15	16	17	18
Charge	_____	2+	_____	4+/4−	_____	2−	_____	0
Example ion	_____	_____	Al^{3+}	Si^{4+}	N^{3-}	_____	_____	N/A

The transition metals, Groups 3–12 of the periodic table, do not follow the same predictable pattern of ion formation as do the main group elements. The valence electron structure of transition metals is more complex than those of the metals in the main groups. Many of the transition metal elements can form several different stable cations, depending on the number of electrons lost.

An iron atom can lose two electrons to form Fe^{2+}, or it can lose three electrons to form Fe^{3+}. The ratio of iron ions to nonmetal ions in an ionic iron compound depends on which iron ion is present. For example, iron and oxygen form iron oxide in two different forms, FeO and Fe_2O_3. When you write the name of a compound of a metal that can form more than one ion, the charge on the metal is indicated by a roman numeral. Therefore, the reddish-brown compound that is familiar as rust is designated as Fe_2O_3, or iron(III) oxide, because the iron ion has a 3+ charge.

FIGURE 10: Iron and oxygen can combine to form two different compounds with different chemical and physical properties.

a Iron(II) oxide, FeO, is found in Earth's mantle and is used as a pigment.

b Iron(III) oxide, Fe_2O_3, is the rust that forms when iron is exposed to air.

APPLY What differences do you notice between iron(II) oxide and iron(III) oxide? How does the charge of the iron ions result in different chemical formulas? How does this affect the properties of each substance?

_____

_____

_____

_____

Writing Ionic Formulas

FIGURE 11: Crisscross method

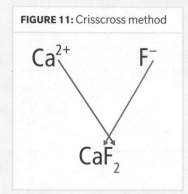

The crisscross method is a shortcut for determining the formula of an ionic compound. Using this method, the charge for each ion becomes the subscript for the other ion in the formula. For example, to write the formula for calcium fluoride, first determine the charges on each ion. Calcium has a 2+ charge and fluorine has a 1− charge. Using this method, calcium has a subscript of 1, which is not written, and fluorine has a subscript of 2. This shortcut is useful, but the chemical formula might need to be reduced to its simplest ratio. For example, the formula for iron(II) oxide obtained by the shortcut is Fe_2O_2. This formula can be reduced to FeO.

ANALYZE Write the ion of each element in the combination. Then use the crisscross method to determine the chemical formula.

Elements	Positive ion	Negative ion	Chemical formula	Chemical name
Magnesium and chlorine	Mg^{2+}	Cl^-	$MgCl_2$	magnesium chloride
Lithium and phosphorus	_____	_____	_____	lithium phosphide
Calcium and sulfur	_____	_____	_____	calcium sulfide
Aluminum and oxygen	_____	_____	_____	aluminum oxide
Aluminum and nitrogen	_____	_____	_____	aluminum nitride

A polyatomic ion is a molecule bound together by covalent bonds that has a charge and acts as an ion. To determine the chemical formula for compounds containing a polyatomic ion, follow the same rules about making the compound neutral as with a single atom ion. For example, when ammonium (NH_4^+) bonds with sulfate (SO_4^{2-}), the resulting compound is ammonium sulfate, $(NH_4)_2SO_4$.

Analyzing Covalent Compounds

Working with formulas for covalent compounds is more complex than for ionic compounds. Many covalent compounds have large and complex molecules, and the arrangement of atoms affects the properties of the molecules. We start our formula work by considering how many electrons atoms must share in order to obtain full energy levels.

FIGURE 12: These models show that four pairs of electrons are shared in a methane molecule.

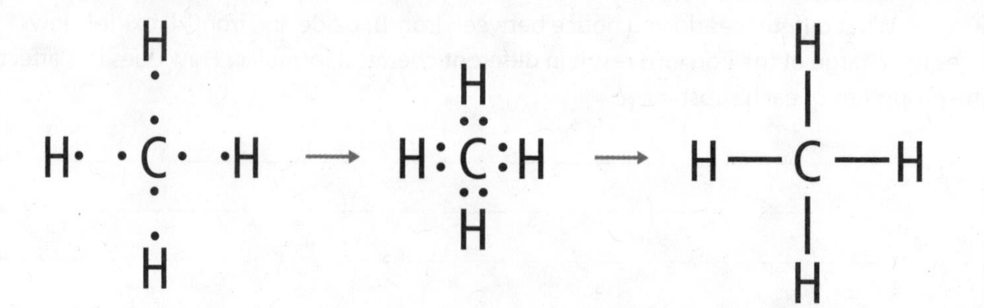

As in ionic bonding, each atom in a covalent molecule obtains an octet. For example, the carbon atom in Figure 12 shares its four valence electrons with four hydrogen atoms that each contribute one electron. Each shared pair of electrons forms a single covalent bond, represented by two dots or a line. This way, the carbon atom obtains an octet. Hydrogen is an exception to the octet rule because a hydrogen atom only needs two electrons to fill its outer orbital.

In some cases, covalent bonds occur as double or triple bonds. A double bond represents four shared electrons, and a triple bond represents six shared electrons. Figure 13 shows the covalent bond formed between two oxygen atoms. Each oxygen atoms has six valence electrons. In order to obtain an octet, the atoms must share four electrons. This results in a double covalent bond, represented by two lines between the atoms. A triple bond is represented by three lines. Triple bonds are the strongest and shortest type of covalent bond, while single bonds are the weakest and longest.

FIGURE 13: Each oxygen atom obtains an octet by forming a double covalent bond.

$$:\ddot{O}\cdot\cdot\ddot{O}: \longrightarrow :\ddot{O}::\ddot{O}: \longrightarrow :\ddot{O}=\ddot{O}:$$

 Evidence Notebook Model the structure of carbon tetrafluoride, a low temperature refrigerant and greenhouse gas. It contains one carbon atom and four fluorine atoms. Explain how your model shows that all the atoms obtain octets by sharing electrons.

The Three-Dimensional Structure of Molecules

The properties of molecules depend on the elements in the compound as well as on the molecular geometry, or three-dimensional arrangement of the atoms in space. The atoms of a molecular compound are arranged in a very specific way based on how the valence electrons are arranged. There may be valence electrons that are left unshared, known as lone pairs, and these also affect the shape of molecules. Differences in electronegativity between the atoms, the shape of the molecule, and the presence of lone pairs all influence the properties of the compound. Consider the electron-dot structures shown in Figure 14. Each molecule has a full octet, but that does not mean they will have the same shape.

FIGURE 14: Electron- dot structures for methane, ammonia, and water

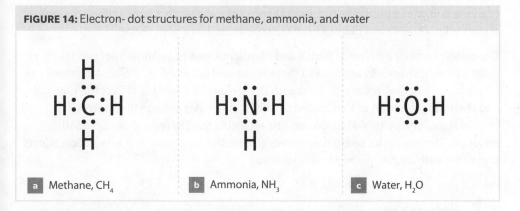

a Methane, CH_4 b Ammonia, NH_3 c Water, H_2O

Electrons in a covalent compound tend to exist as pairs sharing a common orbital. Each pair of electrons, whether in a bond or not, repels all other pairs of valence electrons in the molecule. This is known as VSEPR theory, which stands for "valence-shell electron-pair repulsion." Lone pairs may not be involved directly in bonding, but they do occupy space and so do affect the shape of a molecule. Electron pairs tend to be oriented as far apart as possible. You can predict the shape of a molecule by looking at the number of atoms bonded to the central atom and the number of lone pairs of electrons.

FIGURE 15: Three-dimensional geometry of methane, ammonia, and water

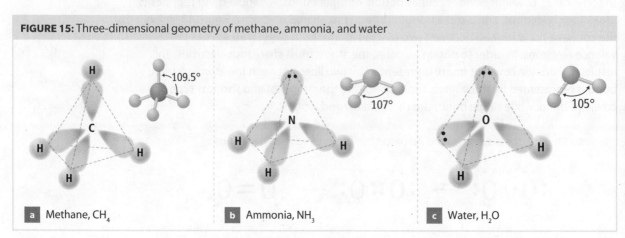

a Methane, CH_4 b Ammonia, NH_3 c Water, H_2O

ANALYZE Models are simplified representations that focus on aspects of more complex systems. Although the electron-dot structure for water looks like a straight line, the molecule actually has a "bent" shape. Why is this molecule bent instead of linear?

_____

_____

INFER Why are the bond angles different between the molecules in Figure 15?

_____

_____

In methane there are four pairs of electrons, each part of a single covalent bond. The result of electron repulsion is that the hydrogen atoms separate as much as possible in three-dimensional space and the molecule has a tetrahedral shape. A molecule of ammonia has one lone pair of electrons. The resulting shape of the molecule is a pyramidal shape. A water molecule, with two pairs of unshared electrons, has a bent shape.

Depending on their number of bonds and number of lone pairs, molecules can take on many different shapes. In addition to those illustrated in Figure 15, molecular shapes can be planar, octahedral, square, or T-shaped. The shape of a molecule affects the physical and chemical properties of that molecule. When molecules arrange themselves in a liquid or solid state, lone pairs of electrons on one molecule tend to repel those on another molecule. The molecules orient themselves to limit this repulsion. This orientation affects properties such as melting and boiling points.

 Evidence Notebook Determine the chemical formulas for sodium metal, chlorine gas, and sodium chloride. How does the structure of each substance affect the chemical and physical properties of that substance?

Guided Research

Asking Questions about Minerals

If you pick up a rock and look at it closely using a hand lens, you can often detect crystal shapes in its structure. Occasionally, you might even find a rock that is itself a single crystal. Rocks are made up of one or more minerals. Minerals are naturally occurring solid materials with a definite chemical composition and a crystalline structure.

What kind of chemical compounds would you expect minerals to be composed of? In general, minerals are composed of ionic compounds. Most minerals consist of compounds of one or more metallic elements bonded to nonmetallic elements, or polyatomic ions composed of nonmetallic elements.

A familiar use of minerals is for decoration. Gems are minerals that are particularly pleasing to look at. A key part of the attractiveness of many gems is their color. The color is caused by the way the mineral reflects or absorbs light. In many cases, the color of a mineral is determined by which metal atoms it contains. The addition of a small amount of different metal atoms into the crystal lattice can change the appearance of the mineral. This occurs because the electrons of each element interact with other atoms in specific ways. Differences in electron interactions affect how the mineral interacts with light.

Quartz, for example, is an ionic compound of silicon and oxygen that is colorless and transparent. However, the addition of a small amount of iron atoms to the quartz forms amethyst, a mineral with a violet color.

Transition metals generally produce minerals with strong colors. Minerals containing copper ions are blue or green. Chromium causes red and green colors, depending on other components. For example, red rubies consist mostly of aluminum oxide, but their color comes from small amounts of chromium compounds in the crystal. Small amounts of iron and titanium compounds in sapphires give them a rich blue color. In other minerals, iron imparts a reddish color.

> **Language Arts Connection** Write a list of questions you have about minerals that are prevalent in your area. Consider the following when writing your list:
>
> - What features about different minerals stand out to you?
> - How are the features related to the chemical composition of the mineral?
> - How have people manipulated mineral structure for their own needs?
>
> Present your information as a slide show, photo gallery, or live presentation. Prepare a list of sources used in your research.

FIGURE 16: The color of a mineral is often determined by metal ions in the crystal.

a Quartz is a colorless compound, but iron gives it a lavender color.

b Copper causes the green bands in malachite.

c The transition metal vanadium makes vanadinite red.

 PRACTICE WITH FORMULAS   **TYPES OF BONDING IN SOLIDS**   **MODELING THE SHAPES OF MOLECULES**   Go online to choose one of these other paths.

Lesson Self-Check

CAN YOU EXPLAIN IT?

FIGURE 17: The reaction between sodium metal and chlorine gas produces sodium chloride.

a Sodium reacting in a beaker of chlorine gas

b Samples of sodium chloride, sodium metal, and chlorine gas

Chlorine is a versatile element. It is used as a disinfectant and to make many household products, and it has even been developed as a chemical weapon. Sodium metal is used in nuclear reactors, but sodium salts are more commonly used than the metal itself. Sodium salts are used in a variety of applications, including deicing roads and softening water. One of the most common sodium salts is sodium chloride, also known as table salt. Unlike its individual components, sodium chloride is extremely stable and does not readily react with other compounds.

Evidence Notebook Refer to your notes in your Evidence Notebook to explain why sodium metal and chlorine gas are dangerous and reactive on their own, but combine to form the stable compound sodium chloride. Your explanation should include a discussion of the electrical forces within and between atoms in each compound. Using this information, address the following:

1. Make a claim about why sodium chloride is more stable than sodium metal or chlorine gas.
2. What evidence supports your claim? For example, what difference in chemical structure could explain the difference in reactivity between the three substances?
3. Explain how the evidence of the properties of the materials supports your claim about the differences between the substances.

CHECKPOINTS

Check Your Understanding

1. Which of the following best explains why ionic crystals are brittle?
   - a. They have low melting points.
   - b. They have high melting points.
   - c. The attraction between positive and negative ions resists motion, so if the ions have shifted at all, repulsive forces build up and cause the bonds to shatter.
   - d. The forces of attraction between positive and negative ions are weak, so they break easily.

2. Categorize each compound as exhibiting ionic bonding or covalent bonding.

   a. LiF _____

   b. Cl_2 _____

   c. NH_3 _____

   d. $CaCl_2$ _____

   e. NaOH _____

   f. FeO _____

   g. NO_2 _____

   h. H_2O _____

3. A student tests a solid sample of a compound and determines that it does not conduct electric current. When the compound is dissolved in water, the solution does conduct an electric current. What type of bonding does the compound have?
   - a. covalent
   - b. ionic
   - c. metallic

4. A long thin sample of a substance is easily bent. When the substance is placed in an electric circuit and the switch is closed, an LED light turns on. What type of bonding holds the particles of the substance together?
   - a. covalent
   - b. ionic
   - c. metallic

5. Complete the statement about bonding by selecting the correct terms.

   A nitrogen molecule, N_2, has less | more potential energy than two separate nitrogen atoms, so the molecule is less | more stable. Each nitrogen atom has five valence electrons, so a nitrogen atom needs one | two | three electron(s) to reach maximum stability. Therefore, the diatomic nitrogen molecule has three | six electrons that are shared between the atoms, forming a triple covalent bond.

6. Use the crisscross method and the periodic table to determine the value of x and y in the formula for aluminum sulfide, Al_xS_y.

   $x = $ _____

   $y = $ _____

7. Which statements correctly describe the compound potassium bromide? Select all correct answers.
   - ☐ a. The compound is considered a salt.
   - ☐ b. It contains potassium and bromide ions in a one-to-one ratio.
   - ☐ c. Potassium bromide likely has a higher melting point than that of candle wax.
   - ☐ d. The electronegativities of the two component atoms are very similar.

8. The electronegativities of carbon and sulfur are almost the same. Both elements form covalently bonded compounds with hydrogen. Why is hydrogen sulfide a polar compound while methane is a nonpolar compound?
   - a. Sulfur has a stronger attraction for electrons than does carbon.
   - b. A hydrogen sulfide molecule has lone pairs of electrons.
   - c. Sulfur forms ionic bonds with hydrogen while carbon forms covalent bonds.
   - d. Sulfur ions are larger than carbon ions.

CHECKPOINTS (continued)

9. Which compound likely has a higher melting point, aluminum trichloride, $AlCl_3$, or phosphorus trichloride, PCl_3? Use the periodic table to support your claim.

_____

_____

_____

10. Formaldehyde, CH_2O, consists of a central carbon atom that has two covalent bonds with hydrogen atoms and a double covalent bond with an oxygen atom. Draw an electron-dot structure of formaldehyde. In the space provided, explain how many unpaired electrons formaldehyde has, if any, and their location in the molecule.

_____

_____

_____

_____

_____

11. Carbon and chlorine have different electronegativity values, so they form polar covalent bonds. However, carbon tetrachloride, CCl_4, is a nonpolar compound. How can a molecule with polar bonds form a nonpolar compound?

_____

_____

_____

_____

_____

MAKE YOUR OWN STUDY GUIDE

In your Evidence Notebook, design a study guide that supports the main ideas from this lesson:

Patterns in the periodic table can be used to predict the type of bond that will form between atoms.

The properties of substances are related to the atomic structure of the substances.

Patterns in valence electrons can be used to predict the structure of substances.

Remember to include the following information in your study guide:

- Use examples that model main ideas.
- Record explanations for the phenomena you investigated.
- Use evidence to support your explanations. Your support can include drawings, data, graphs, laboratory conclusions, and other evidence recorded throughout the lesson.

Consider how patterns of atomic structure, as shown in the periodic table, can provide evidence for explanations of properties of chemical compounds at the bulk scale.

Physical Science Connection

Subatomic Particles The properties of subatomic particles smaller than protons, neutrons, and electrons can be studied by observing high-energy interactions of particle beams at large accelerator facilities such as CERN, the European Organization for Nuclear Research. Over 600 institutes use the equipment at CERN to run studies. CERN employs over 2500 people to build and maintain equipment, run experiments, and interpret data.

Research recent discoveries about subatomic particles and the scientists and engineers that work at facilities such as CERN. Write a news article explaining the importance of one of the discoveries you researched and the team responsible for the discovery.

FIGURE 1: The CMS detector at CERN

Social Studies Connection

Pigments Pigments are substances used for coloring. They have the ability to absorb and emit light at certain wavelengths, giving them distinct colors. Pigments derived from natural sources, such as plants or minerals, often have special significance for cultures where the natural source is located.

Research ways that pigments are used in various cultures around the world. Write a report explaining how the pigments are used, how they are derived, and how their production has become more environmentally friendly and safe over time.

FIGURE 2: An array of different pigments

Technology Connection

Imaging Molecules Light microscopes were an important step forward in allowing scientists to research cells whose size scales range from 10^3–10^5 nanometers and therefore can reflect visible light. But molecular structures that range in size from 0.1 to 10 nanometers are so much smaller that new imaging techniques had to be developed. Today scientists have a variety of techniques for imaging molecules. For example, the atomic force microscope can produce a three-dimensional image with a resolution less than one nanometer by measuring the force between a probe and the sample surface.

Make a multimedia presentation about a molecule that was imaged using a molecular imaging technique. Explain what scientists and engineers learned from being able to image the molecule you researched.

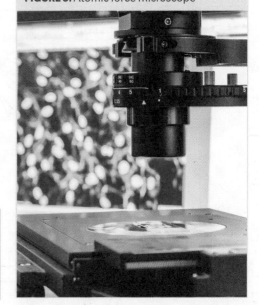

FIGURE 3: Atomic force microscope

A BOOK EXPLAINING COMPLEX IDEAS USING ONLY THE 1,000 MOST COMMON WORDS

THE PIECES EVERYTHING IS MADE OF
A table for putting small pieces in order

You know that the periodic table is an arrangement of the elements in order of their atomic numbers so that elements with similar properties fall in the same column. Here's a look at how this arrangement of elements helps us understand the world on an atomic scale.

RANDALL MUNROE
XKCD.COM

THE STORY OF PUTTING THINGS IN ORDER

PIECES OF PIECES

These pieces are made of even smaller pieces. Different kinds of pieces have different numbers of those smaller parts. There are three main kinds of these smaller parts—two heavy ones and a light one.

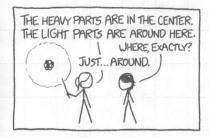

Over the past hundred years, we've learned that the idea of "where" doesn't always work well for very small things.

Light pieces

Heavy pieces

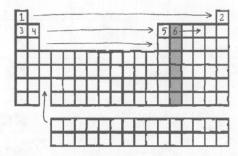

TABLE SHAPE

The boxes in this table are in order from left to right and top to bottom. It has this strange shape because pieces are in groups with other pieces that are a lot like them.

(The reason those groups are like each other has to do with the number of light parts around the outside of the piece—which is mostly the same as the piece's center number—and the way different numbers of light parts sort themselves around the outside of the piece.)

CENTER NUMBER

We number the pieces by counting how many of one kind of heavy part they have in their center, and use that number to put pieces in boxes in the table. The other heavy part doesn't matter to the count, so pieces with different numbers of that part may share the same box in the table.

SHORT LIVES, STRANGE HEAT

Some kinds of pieces don't last very long, slowly breaking down into other pieces over time by throwing away bits of their centers in all directions, which makes them give off a kind of strange heat.

We count how long a kind of piece lasts by timing how long it takes for half of it to break down. We call this the piece's "half-life."

NAMES

Some of the things on this table have had names for a long time (like gold) but some of them were only found in the last few hundred years.

Many of the pieces in this table are named after people or places—and especially for people who helped to learn about them or the places where those people worked.

Here are a few of the things these pieces are named after.

THE PIECES EVERYTHING IS MADE OF

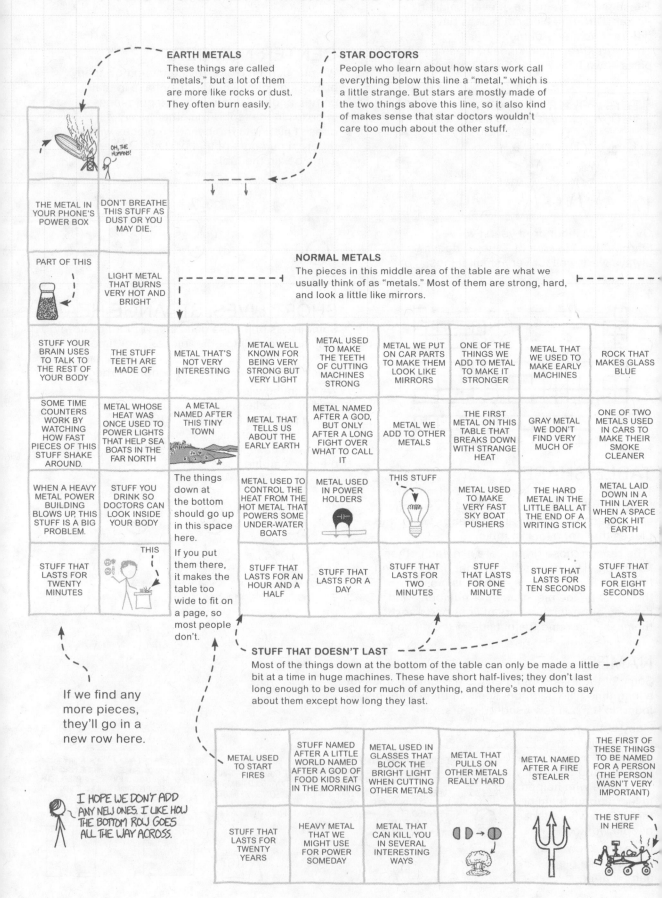

EARTH METALS
These things are called "metals," but a lot of them are more like rocks or dust. They often burn easily.

STAR DOCTORS
People who learn about how stars work call everything below this line a "metal," which is a little strange. But stars are mostly made of the two things above this line, so it also kind of makes sense that star doctors wouldn't care too much about the other stuff.

OH, THE HUMANS!

THE METAL IN YOUR PHONE'S POWER BOX

DON'T BREATHE THIS STUFF AS DUST OR YOU MAY DIE.

PART OF THIS

LIGHT METAL THAT BURNS VERY HOT AND BRIGHT

NORMAL METALS
The pieces in this middle area of the table are what we usually think of as "metals." Most of them are strong, hard, and look a little like mirrors.

STUFF YOUR BRAIN USES TO TALK TO THE REST OF YOUR BODY	THE STUFF TEETH ARE MADE OF	METAL THAT'S NOT VERY INTERESTING	METAL WELL KNOWN FOR BEING VERY STRONG BUT VERY LIGHT	METAL USED TO MAKE THE TEETH OF CUTTING MACHINES STRONG	METAL WE PUT ON CAR PARTS TO MAKE THEM LOOK LIKE MIRRORS	ONE OF THE THINGS WE ADD TO METAL TO MAKE IT STRONGER	METAL THAT WE USED TO MAKE EARLY MACHINES	ROCK THAT MAKES GLASS BLUE
SOME TIME COUNTERS WORK BY WATCHING HOW FAST PIECES OF THIS STUFF SHAKE AROUND.	METAL WHOSE HEAT WAS ONCE USED TO POWER LIGHTS THAT HELP SEA BOATS IN THE FAR NORTH	A METAL NAMED AFTER THIS TINY TOWN	METAL THAT TELLS US ABOUT THE EARLY EARTH	METAL NAMED AFTER A GOD, BUT ONLY AFTER A LONG FIGHT OVER WHAT TO CALL IT	METAL WE ADD TO OTHER METALS	THE FIRST METAL ON THIS TABLE THAT BREAKS DOWN WITH STRANGE HEAT	GRAY METAL WE DON'T FIND VERY MUCH OF	ONE OF TWO METALS USED IN CARS TO MAKE THEIR SMOKE CLEANER
WHEN A HEAVY METAL POWER BUILDING BLOWS UP, THIS STUFF IS A BIG PROBLEM.	STUFF YOU DRINK SO DOCTORS CAN LOOK INSIDE YOUR BODY	The things down at the bottom should go up in this space here.	METAL USED TO CONTROL THE HEAT FROM THE HOT METAL THAT POWERS SOME UNDER-WATER BOATS	METAL USED IN POWER HOLDERS	THIS STUFF	METAL USED TO MAKE VERY FAST SKY BOAT PUSHERS	THE HARD METAL IN THE LITTLE BALL AT THE END OF A WRITING STICK	METAL LAID DOWN IN A THIN LAYER WHEN A SPACE ROCK HIT EARTH
STUFF THAT LASTS FOR TWENTY MINUTES	THIS	If you put them there, it makes the table too wide to fit on a page, so most people don't.	STUFF THAT LASTS FOR AN HOUR AND A HALF	STUFF THAT LASTS FOR A DAY	STUFF THAT LASTS FOR TWO MINUTES	STUFF THAT LASTS FOR ONE MINUTE	STUFF THAT LASTS FOR TEN SECONDS	STUFF THAT LASTS FOR EIGHT SECONDS

If we find any more pieces, they'll go in a new row here.

STUFF THAT DOESN'T LAST
Most of the things down at the bottom of the table can only be made a little bit at a time in huge machines. These have short half-lives; they don't last long enough to be used for much of anything, and there's not much to say about them except how long they last.

I HOPE WE DON'T ADD ANY NEW ONES. I LIKE HOW THE BOTTOM ROW GOES ALL THE WAY ACROSS.

METAL USED TO START FIRES	STUFF NAMED AFTER A LITTLE WORLD NAMED AFTER A GOD OF FOOD KIDS EAT IN THE MORNING	METAL USED IN GLASSES THAT BLOCK THE BRIGHT LIGHT WHEN CUTTING OTHER METALS	METAL THAT PULLS ON OTHER METALS REALLY HARD	METAL NAMED AFTER A FIRE STEALER		THE FIRST OF THESE THINGS TO BE NAMED FOR A PERSON (THE PERSON WASN'T VERY IMPORTANT)
STUFF THAT LASTS FOR TWENTY YEARS	HEAVY METAL THAT WE MIGHT USE FOR POWER SOMEDAY	METAL THAT CAN KILL YOU IN SEVERAL INTERESTING WAYS				THE STUFF IN HERE

Go online for more about *Thing Explainer*.

NOT METAL

The things toward the top right part of the table are things that aren't metal. Most of these things are very different from each other. Many of them come in the form of air. A few of them look like a kind of rock or water instead of air. They usually turn to air easily, and most of them are not very strong.

THE LINE

People don't agree exactly where the line between "metals" and "not metals" is, but it's somewhere around here, and runs down and to the right.

AIR, WATER, AND FIRE

The things in this area of the table do a lot of things. When you put them near things from the other end of the table, they can turn to different kinds of water, start fires, or make everything blow up.

QUIET AIR

This end of the table is pretty quiet. When you put these kinds of air with other things, they usually don't seem to notice.

		THE STUFF THAT KEEPS KITCHEN GLASS FROM BREAKING WHEN HOT	THE STUFF ALL KNOWN LIFE IS MADE FROM	THE PART OF AIR WE DON'T NEED TO BREATHE TO STAY ALIVE	THE PART OF AIR WE DO NEED TO BREATHE TO STAY ALIVE	GREEN BURNING AIR THAT KILLS	AIR IN BRIGHT SIGNS MADE FROM COLORED LIGHT
		THIS METAL	THE ROCK THAT MAKES UP BEACHES, GLASS, AND COMPUTER BRAINS	BURNING WHITE ROCKS	SMELLY YELLOW ROCKS LIKE THIS	THE STUFF THEY PUT IN POOLS SO NOTHING BAD CAN GROW IN THEM	AIR THAT DOESN'T DO MUCH OF ANYTHING
THE GRAY METAL AT THE CENTER OF THE EARTH	BROWN METAL WE USE TO CARRY POWER AND VOICES	METAL USED TO MAKE THE BROWN METAL STRONGER (NOW USED FOR MANY OTHER THINGS)	WATERY METAL THAT MAKES DRINK CANS TEAR LIKE PAPER	METAL NAMED AFTER THIS PLACE	THE ROCK MOST WELL KNOWN FOR KILLING YOU IF YOU EAT IT	A ROCK THAT CAN CHANGE ONE KIND OF POWER INTO ANOTHER	RED WATER	AIR USED BY DOCTORS TO MAKE THIN BRIGHT LIGHTS FOR CUTTING EYES
ONE OF TWO METALS USED IN CARS TO MAKE THEIR SMOKE CLEANER		METAL USED IN PAINT UNTIL WE REALIZED IT MADE PEOPLE SICK	PART OF THE SILVER METAL YOU CAN HEAT UP AT HOME TO STICK PARTS TOGETHER	METAL PUT ON FOOD CANS TO KEEP WATER FROM MAKING HOLES IN THEM	METAL PUT IN THINGS TO KEEP THEM FROM BURNING	METAL THAT CAN BE FOUND IN LOTS OF PLACES, BUT MOST OF THEM AREN'T EARTH	STUFF THEY ADD TO THIS SO YOUR BRAIN GROWS RIGHT	AIR USED IN CAMERA FLASHES
A ROCK THAT PEOPLE WILL PAY AS MUCH FOR AS GOLD	GOLD	THIS	METAL WE USED FOR KILLING ANIMALS BUT STOPPED USING BECAUSE IT WAS TOO GOOD AT IT	METAL WELL KNOWN FOR BEING HEAVY	ROCK THAT LOOKS LIKE A COOL TINY CITY	THIS	STUFF NO ONE HAS SEEN CLEARLY BECAUSE IT BURNS UP TOO FAST	AIR THAT COMES FROM ROCKS UNDER HOUSES AND CAN MAKE YOU SICK
STUFF THAT LASTS FOR TEN SECONDS	STUFF THAT LASTS FOR HALF A MINUTE		STUFF THAT LASTS FOR A THIRD OF A MINUTE	STUFF THAT LASTS THREE SECONDS	STUFF THAT LASTS FOR LESS THAN A THIRD OF A SECOND	STUFF THAT LASTS FOR THE TIME IT TAKES YOU TO CLOSE AND OPEN YOUR EYES		STUFF THAT LASTS FOR THE TIME IT TAKES SOUND TO TRAVEL ONE FOOT

THE AIR IN HERE

MONEY METAL

We use a lot of the things in this group as money—although not the bottom one, since it disappears very fast.

(Some people who know a lot about money actually think that having money that disappears over time could be good, but they probably don't mean quite this quickly.)

FEEL BETTER

This stuff is made from the rock that looks like a tiny city. If you feel like food is going to come out of your mouth, you can eat or drink some of this, and it might help you feel better.

SO MANY DIFFERENT PARTS OF THE WORLD!

METAL NAMED AFTER THIS PLACE

METAL THAT PULLS ON OTHER METALS WHEN IT GETS JUST A LITTLE COLDER THAN NORMAL AIR

ANOTHER METAL NAMED AFTER THIS TINY TOWN

METAL WHOSE NAME MEANS "HARD TO GET"

METAL NAMED AFTER THIS PLACE

ANOTHER METAL NAMED AFTER THIS TINY TOWN

THE NAME PEOPLE HERE USED FOR PEOPLE HERE

I'M SURE THIS IS A NICE TOWN, BUT COME ON.

METAL NAMED AFTER THIS PLACE.

STUFF IN THE BOXES THAT TELL YOU WHEN YOUR HOUSE IS ON FIRE

NAMED FOR THIS PLACE

METAL NAMED FOR HER

METAL NAMED AFTER THIS PLACE

METAL NAMED AFTER THIS PLACE

METAL NAMED FOR HIM

METAL NAMED FOR A MAN WHO HELPED BUILD THE FIRST HEAVY METAL POWER BUILDING

METAL NAMED FOR HIM THIS WAS MY IDEA.

METAL NAMED FOR HIM

METAL THAT LASTS FOR FOUR MINUTES

Identifying Elements Using Patterns

You are an analytical chemist for a company that provides reference materials for industrial analytical labs. During a company financial audit, the auditors bring samples from stock supplies to confirm that the inventory is correct. You analyze the samples to confirm that the products are correctly labeled and accounted for. The table shows some information you collected about properties for each sample. Your job now is to use the periodic table to infer the identity of each sample based on its description. Then, present the auditors with a report identifying each of the samples.

Unknown	Description	Element Identity
1	It is an alkaline earth metal with two valence electrons and relatively low electronegativity. It has the same number of electron energy levels as iodine.	
2	It is a highly reactive metal in Period 4 of the periodic table. Its atoms bond in a one-to-one ratio with elements in the group that have the highest electron affinities of any elements on the periodic table.	
3	It is a highly reactive nonmetal with two isotopes. One has a mass of 35 u and an abundance of 75.78%. The other has a mass of 37 u and an abundance of 24.22%.	
4	It is a metalloid with five valence electrons. It has the same number of electron energy levels as calcium.	
5	Its electron dot structure has six dots, and its atoms bond in a one-to-one ratio with magnesium. It has the highest electronegativity in its group.	

1. DEFINE THE PROBLEM

Write a statement describing the problem you will solve in this investigation. Include information you will need to solve the problem.

2. CONDUCT RESEARCH

With your team, research ways that scientists identify unknown elements in samples. Consider the types of questions they ask about the element, the instruments they use to test the sample, and the approaches they use to analyze the data collected.

3. EVALUATE DATA

With your team, analyze the description of each unknown element in the table. Compare the descriptions to the information in the periodic table as well as trends in the periodic table.

4. CONSTRUCT AN EXPLANATION

Describe the location of each unknown element on the periodic table. Explain how you inferred the identity of each element. Then, record the identity of each element in the table.

5. COMMUNICATE

Make a multimedia presentation to describe the process you and your team used to identify each unknown element. Explain how your approach is similar or different to how a scientist in a lab would determine the identity of an unknown element.

 CHECK YOUR WORK

Once you have completed this task, you should have the following:

- a problem statement that was addressed in the final presentation
- a completed table identifying the location on the periodic table of the five unknown elements.
- a presentation explaining the process used to determine the unknown elements
- images and data that further support your explanation

Name _____ Date _____

SYNTHESIZE THE UNIT

In your Evidence Notebook, make a concept map, other graphic organizer, or outline using the Study Guides you made for each lesson in this unit. Be sure to use evidence to support your claims.

When synthesizing individual information, remember to follow these general steps:

- Find the central idea of each piece of information.
- Think about the relationships among the central ideas.
- Combine the ideas to come up with a new understanding.

DRIVING QUESTIONS

Look back to the Driving Questions from the opening section of this unit. In your Evidence Notebook, review and revise your previous answers to those questions. Use the evidence you gathered and other observations you made throughout the unit to support your claims.

PRACTICE AND REVIEW

1. Complete the statement.

   The atomic number | atomic mass | mass number of an atom identifies the element it is and the number of electrons | neutrons | protons it has. The atomic number | atomic mass | mass number is the sum of the number of electrons and protons | electrons and neutrons | protons and neutrons. Two atoms are isotopes if they have the same number of electrons | neutrons | protons and different numbers of electrons | neutrons | protons.

2. Hydrogen's emission spectrum has bright lines at certain wavelengths. How are these bright lines produced?

   a. The electrons of an atom strike the protons.

   b. Two atoms combine to form a new molecule.

   c. Excited electrons move to the ground state.

   d. Photons of light are absorbed by the atomic nucleus.

3. Based on periodic trends, which of the following elements has the largest electronegativity?

   a. arsenic   c. sodium

   b. oxygen   d. strontium

4. Complete these statements about trends in ionization energy on the periodic table.

   As you move from left to right across a period, the ionization energy tends to increase | decrease.
   As you move down a group, the ionization energy tends to increase | decrease.
   For example, lithium is in Group 1, Period 2, and boron is in Group 13, Period 2. Based on these locations, you would expect boron | lithium to have a higher ionization energy.

5. Based on patterns of ionic charges on the periodic table, what charge would you expect an ion from a Group 15 element to have?

   a. 2+   c. 3+

   b. 2−   d. 3−

6. Which of these is a correctly written formula for the compound? Select all correct answers.

   a. aluminum bromide, $AlBr_3$

   b. strontium iodide, Sr_2I

   c. sodium fluoride, NaF

   d. barium phosphide, Ba_3P_2

   e. magnesium selenide, Mg_2Se

7. Describe Rutherford's gold foil experiment and its importance in understanding the structure of atoms.

_____

_____

_____

_____

_____

_____

_____

8. Explain how patterns in electronegativity on the periodic table can be used to predict bond formation.

_____

_____

_____

_____

_____

_____

_____

9. A water molecule, H_2O, has a bent shape. Explain how the valence electrons of the atoms cause the molecule to have this shape.

_____

_____

_____

_____

_____

_____

_____

UNIT PROJECT

Return to your unit project. Prepare your research and materials into a presentation to share with the class. In your final presentation, evaluate the strength of your hypothesis, data, analysis, and conclusions.

Remember these tips while evaluating:

- What properties of an atom were best illustrated by each type of model?
- How did you incorporate the patterns of the periodic table into your models?
- What predictions about the properties of the atom can be predicted using your models?

UNIT 4

Chemical Attractions

YOU SOLVE IT

**How Can You Change the
Properties of a Substance?**

To begin exploring this unit's concepts,
go online to investigate ways to solve a
real-world problem.

The reaction of copper and nitric acid produces
nitric oxide gas and a solution of copper nitrate.

If you ever walked past the Columbus Tower, also known as the Sentinel Building, in San Francisco, you likely noticed its unusual color. The outside of the building is covered with white tile and blue-green metal. The metal is copper. When the cladding was first added to the building in the early 20th century, it was the color of a shiny copper penny. In time, the exposure of the building's outer walls to compounds in the air changed it first to a reddish color, then black, and finally the blue-green color it has today. You might have seen similar changes in the color of a metal bicycle left out in the rain as it began to rust, or noticed a similar color on the Statue of Liberty. The formation of the patina on the Columbus Tower and rust on a bicycle adds mass to the objects.

PREDICT How can the mass of an object increase? How might this change in mass be related to a change in color?

_____

_____

_____

_____

_____

_____

DRIVING QUESTIONS

As you move through the unit, gather evidence to help you answer the following questions. In your Evidence Notebook, record what you already know about these topics and any questions you have about them.

1. How do forces between particles affect the properties of materials?
2. How can interactions between particles be modeled?
3. How does the law of conservation of mass apply to chemical reactions at both the macroscopic and subatomic scales?
4. In what ways can the changes in chemical reactions be quantified in terms of reactants and products?
5. What is solubility, and how do different factors affect it?

UNIT PROJECT

Go online to download the Unit Project Worksheet to help plan your project.

Designing Detergents

A detergent is a cleansing agent that cleans materials by combining with dirt and oil so that it can be dissolved and washed away. Investigate properties of natural and synthetic detergents. What is the difference between the two and does it affect how they work? Develop a plan to optimize a particular property of a detergent, such as environmental safety while maintaining performance.

Language Development

Use the lessons in this unit to complete the chart and expand your understanding of the science concepts.

TERM: polarity

Definition	Example

Similar Term	Phrase

TERM: hydrogen bonding

Definition	Example

Similar Term	Phrase

TERM: law of conservation of mass

Definition	Example

Similar Term	Phrase

TERM: chemical equation

Definition	Example

Similar Term	Phrase

TERM: mole

Definition	Example

Similar Term	Phrase

TERM: solution

Definition	Example

Similar Term	Phrase

TERM: solubility

Definition	Example

Similar Term	Phrase

TERM: concentration

Definition	Example

Similar Term	Phrase

The Properties of Materials

Fog rolls over the Golden Gate Bridge in San Francisco, California.

CAN YOU SOLVE IT?

Along the California coast, it is common to see fog for several days each year. In places where water resources can be scarce but fog is plentiful, some people are hoping to "harvest" water from the fog. Scientists and engineers around the world have tested different methods for collecting water from fog. When developing water-collecting technology, the properties of the materials are especially important. Some researchers have looked to nature for inspiration, studying plants and animals that collect water from the air. For example, some desert insects are able to capture water on their bodies. Understanding how living things attract water to their bodies allows scientists to develop materials that can do the same. Materials scientists look for patterns in how natural fog-collecting systems work and then investigate how these patterns can be applied to human-made systems.

PREDICT What properties do you think a material should have to collect water from fog? What criteria and constraints might be important when designing a material like this?

_____

_____

_____

_____

 Evidence Notebook As you explore this lesson, gather evidence to explain how the properties of materials at a larger scale are related to forces at the atomic scale.

Observing Properties of Compounds

FIGURE 1: Static makes a person's hair stick to a balloon.

Have you ever rubbed a balloon on your head? If so, you may have noticed that "static" makes your hair stand up. You also may have noticed that your hair sticks to the balloon, a phenomenon commonly known as "static cling."

PREDICT What do you think causes hair to stick up when rubbed on a balloon, as shown in Figure 1? Why might hair to stick to the balloon?

_____

_____

_____

_____

Forces Between Particles

FIGURE 2: Charged particles may attract or repel each other.

opposite charges attract

like charges repel

Most materials have no *overall* charge because they have equal numbers of protons and electrons. When you rub a balloon on your hair, however, electrons from atoms in your hair are transferred to atoms in the balloon. This transfer makes some atoms in your hair positively charged and some atoms in the balloon negatively charged. Because like charges repel, the positively charged strands of your hair spread far away from one another. Opposite charges attract, so the positively charged hair sticks to the negatively charged balloon. Repulsions and attractions due to electric charge are known as electric force. Another name for electric force is the Coulomb force.

 Math Connection

Calculating Force

Coulomb's law describes how to calculate electric force. This law states that the magnitude of the electric force ($F_{electric}$) between two point charges (q_1 *and* q_2) is directly related to the product of the charges and inversely related to the square of the distance (d) between them. The Coulomb constant (k_C) is a constant used in the calculation of electric force. The equation for Coulomb's law is:

$$F_{electric} = k_C \frac{q_1 q_2}{d^2}$$

 Collaborate As charge increases, electric force increases. However, if the distance between two charges doubles, electric force decreases by a factor of four. How does the equation for this law demonstrate these relationships between charge, distance, and force?

Attractive forces exist between protons and electrons in atoms. In ionic compounds, strong attractive forces hold ions tightly together, which explains why these compounds have high melting points. Molecular compounds tend to have relatively low melting points, but attractive forces can still exist between molecules.

ASK Figure 3 shows capillary action, in which a liquid moves up a narrow opening in a glass tube against the force of gravity. Write some questions you have about why water exhibits capillary action.

_____

_____

_____

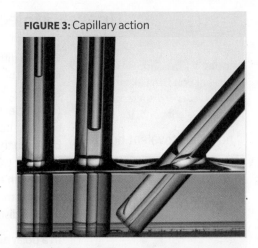

FIGURE 3: Capillary action

 Hands-On Activity

Modeling Intermolecular Forces

Models can help explain how interactions at the small scale affect properties of substances at the larger scale. In this activity, you will use magnets to model the strength of forces between molecules. Forces between molecules are known as intermolecular forces. Typically, as the strength of the forces between molecules increases, the energy required to change the state of that substance also increases.

MATERIALS

· indirectly vented chemical splash goggles

· boxes of labeled "molecules," each containing magnets of a different strength

SAFETY INFORMATION

· Wear indirectly vented chemical splash goggles during all segments of the activity.

indirectly vented chemical splash goggles

CARRY OUT THE INVESTIGATION

1. Make a table in your Evidence Notebook to record observations of the strengths of intermolecular forces between "molecules" in each of the five labeled boxes.

2. Use the magnets in each box to model the intermolecular forces between these molecules. Note the amount of force you need to pull each set of magnets apart, and record your observations.

3. Draw a scale of intermolecular force strength in your Evidence Notebook. Label the left end _Weakest_ and the right end _Strongest_. Plot the formulas and names for the five molecules you modeled in the correct order along the scale.

DRAW CONCLUSIONS

In your Evidence Notebook, rank the molecular substances you modeled from lowest boiling point to highest. Give evidence for your claim, and explain your reasoning.

Uneven Molecular Charges

FIGURE 4: In a nonpolar covalent bond, the electron cloud is evenly dispersed. In a polar covalent bond, it is not.

nonpolar covalent bond

polar covalent bond

FIGURE 5: Iodine chloride is a dipole.

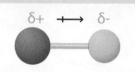

Why do different molecular compounds exhibit different intermolecular forces? The answer has to do with the type of atoms in a molecule and how they are arranged. Recall that electronegativity is the tendency of an atom to pull electrons toward itself. When two atoms of the same element form a covalent bond, such as that in Cl_2, the bonding electrons are evenly shared between the two atoms. This is known as a *nonpolar covalent bond*. When atoms of two different elements form a covalent bond, such as that in ICl, the atom with the higher electronegativity attracts the bonding electrons more strongly than does the other atom. This is known as a *polar covalent bond*. This uneven distribution of charges in a molecule is known as polarity.

In a polar molecule, such as ICl, one end of the bond has a partial negative charge, and the other end has a partial positive charge. These two ends are called poles, and a molecule with two poles is said to be a *dipole*. Magnets can be used to model dipoles because a magnet has a north pole and a south pole. In Figure 5, a model of iodine monochloride, ICl, is shown. Its dipole is represented by an arrow with a head that points toward the negative pole and a crossed tail near the positive pole. Partial charges are represented by the lowercase Greek letter delta, δ. A partial positive charge is shown as $\delta+$, and a partial negative charge is shown as $\delta-$.

The polarity of diatomic molecules such as ICl is determined by just one bond. For molecules that contain more than two atoms, polarity is determined by both the polarity of the individual bonds and the three-dimensional arrangement of the molecule. How the three-dimensional arrangement of dipoles in a molecule affects the overall polarity of the molecule is shown in Figure 6. A water molecule has two dipoles, and because the molecule is bent, the arrangement of the bonds is not symmetrical. In addition, there are two unshared electrons on the oxygen atom in a water molecule. Therefore, the water molecule is highly polar. It behaves as if it has two centers of charge, one positive and one negative. Carbon dioxide, by contrast, is nonpolar, even though it has two polar bonds. The carbon dioxide molecule is symmetrical, so the two dipoles cancel each other out.

FIGURE 6: Water and ammonia are polar molecules, whereas carbon tetrachloride and carbon dioxide are nonpolar.

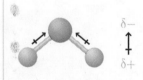

a   Water, H_2O

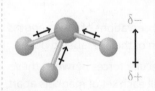

b   Ammonia, NH_3

c   Carbon tetrachloride, CCl_4

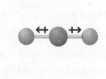

d   Carbon dioxide, CO_2

The water molecule is bent, so its bond polarities combine to give one end of the molecule a partial positive charge and the other end of the molecule a partial negative charge. Ammonia has a pyramid shape, so it is also a polar molecule.

In carbon tetrachloride and carbon dioxide, the bond polarities extend equally and symmetrically in different directions, canceling each other's effect. Therefore, these molecules are nonpolar.

Collaborate Think back to the question about why water exhibits capillary action. With a partner, make a claim for how this phenomenon is related to the polarity of water molecules.

Dipole-Dipole Forces

You have seen that in the polar molecule iodine chloride, the highly electronegative chlorine atom has a partial negative charge, causing the iodine atom to have a partial positive charge. As a result, the negative and positive ends of neighboring iodine chloride molecules attract each other. In Figure 7, these attractive forces are shown as arrows.

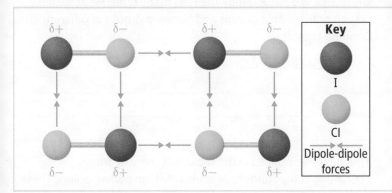

FIGURE 7: The arrows show the dipole-dipole forces between the positive and negative ends of neighboring ICl molecules. These forces can be modeled by magnets because the south pole of a magnet is attracted to the north pole of other magnets.

When a liquid is heated, energy is added to the system. The kinetic energy of the liquid's molecules increases, and they move faster. As the temperature approaches the boiling point, the molecules move fast enough to overcome the attractive forces between molecules. They pull away from each other and enter the gaseous state. Boiling point is a good measure of the attractive forces between molecules of a liquid. The stronger the forces are between molecules, the higher the boiling point will be.

APPLY Select the correct terms to complete the statement about ICl and Br_2.

ICl is a polar | nonpolar molecule, whereas Br_2 is polar | nonpolar. The boiling point of ICl is likely to be higher | lower than the boiling point of Br_2. This is due to dipole-dipole interactions between two positive | two negative | positive and negative portions of polar molecules.

A polar molecule also can induce the formation of a dipole in a nonpolar molecule by temporarily attracting the electrons in the nonpolar molecule. This results in a short-term intermolecular force. For example, the positive pole of a polar water molecule causes a temporary change in the electron distribution of an adjacent nonpolar O_2 molecule. The temporary negative pole induced in the side of the O_2 molecule closest to the water molecule is attracted to the positive pole of the H_2O molecule. This shift of electrons in the oxygen molecule then causes an induced positive pole on the opposite side of the oxygen molecule.

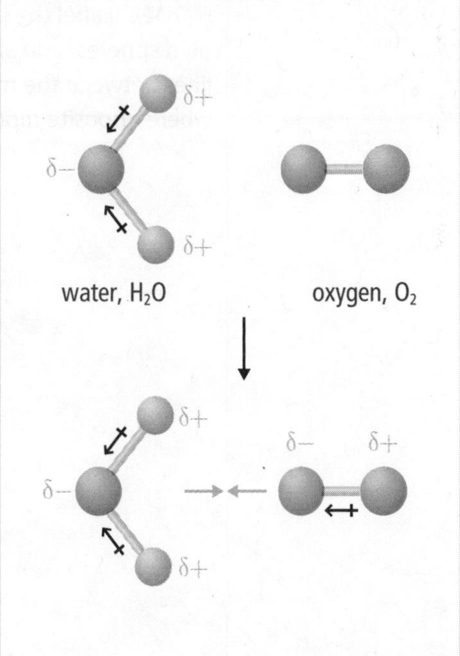

EXPLAIN Do you think a dipole-induced dipole interaction is stronger or weaker than a dipole-dipole interaction? Use evidence to support your claim.

_____

_____

_____

_____

_____

FIGURE 8: Dipole-induced dipole interaction

water, H_2O oxygen, O_2

Hydrogen Bonding

Some dipole-dipole interactions can be especially strong. For example, in some hydrogen-containing compounds such as hydrogen fluoride (HF), water (H_2O), and ammonia (NH_3), a special kind of dipole-dipole interaction exists.

Boiling Points and Bonding Types		
Bonding Type	Substance	bp (1 atm, °C)
Nonpolar-covalent (molecular)	H_2	−253
	O_2	−183
	Cl_2	−34
	Br_2	59
	CH_4	−162
	CCl_4	77
	C_6H_6	80
Polar-covalent (molecular)	PH_3	−88
	NH_3	−33
	H_2S	−60
	H_2O	100
	HF	20
	HCl	−85
	ICl	97
Ionic	NaCl	1465
	MgF_2	2239
Metallic	Cu	2567
	Fe	2861
	W	5660

GATHER EVIDENCE Study the data in the table. What patterns do you notice within groups and between groups of different bonding types?

_____

_____

_____

_____

You may have noticed in the table that some hydrogen-containing compounds have unusually high boiling points. These compounds have two things in common. First, they all contain a hydrogen atom. Second, the hydrogen atom is bonded to a highly electronegative atom that has pulled hydrogen's bonding electron almost completely away. Thus, the hydrogen atom is left with a strong partial positive charge.

Molecules that contain a hydrogen atom bonded to a highly electronegative atom—fluorine, oxygen, or nitrogen—are strongly polar. Particularly strong dipole-dipole forces exist between molecules of these compounds. The name hydrogen bonding is given to the intermolecular force in which a hydrogen atom that is bonded to a highly electronegative atom (and thus is positively charged) is attracted to a partial negative charge on a nearby molecule. A hydrogen bond is usually represented by a dotted line that connects the hydrogen-bonded hydrogen to the partial negative charge on another molecule.

MODEL Label the partial negative and partial positive charges on the water molecules. (Red spheres indicate oxygen atoms, blue spheres hydrogen atoms.) Then, draw dotted lines between the molecules to represent hydrogen bonds. Hydrogen bonds should form where opposite dipoles are near each other.

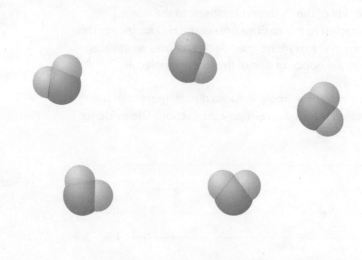

Analyzing the Properties of Water

Water is a substance with many unusual properties given its relatively small molecular mass and size. For one, it has an unusually high boiling point. In addition, water adheres, or "sticks" to surfaces such as glass. This explains why water appears to climb up narrow tubes in the phenomenon known as capillary action. Cohesion between water molecules causes water to form a bubbled-up shape when it is dropped onto some surfaces. The ability of the surface of a liquid to form a "skin" is known as surface tension. This property of water allows some smaller insects to walk easily on its surface.

FIGURE 9: Different liquids exhibit different amounts of surface tension.

EXPLAIN Explain how the formation of hydrogen bonds is related to the unique properties of water. Discuss the role of hydrogen bonds in boiling point, capillary action, and surface tension.

_____

_____

_____

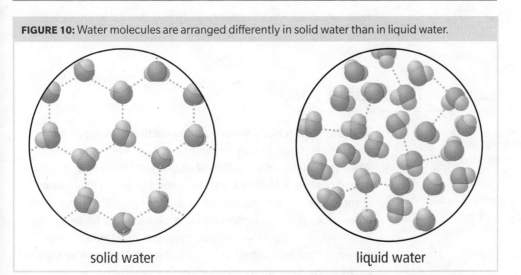

FIGURE 10: Water molecules are arranged differently in solid water than in liquid water.

solid water   liquid water

If you have ever frozen a full bottle of water, you have discovered that, unlike other substances, water expands when it freezes. Like many of water's unique properties, this is related to the formation of hydrogen bonds. When water freezes, the molecules lose kinetic energy and slow down, so more hydrogen bonds form between them. The water molecules form a network structure in which each water molecule is held away from nearby molecules at a fixed distance. Hydrogen bonds are constantly being formed and broken between molecules in liquid water. In order for liquid water to boil and become a gas, hydrogen bonds between the water molecules must be broken.

INFER Complete the statement to explain why icebergs float in liquid water.

The amount of space between molecules in solid water is less | greater than that in liquid water. As a result, the density of solid water is less | greater than that of liquid water. Because substances with lower density float | sink in substances with higher density, ice floats in liquid water. This explains why icebergs float on water and do not sink.

FIGURE 11: Icebergs float on liquid water.

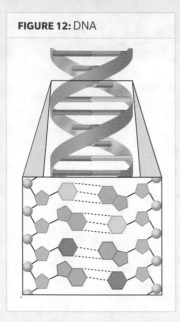

FIGURE 12: DNA

Living Systems

Hydrogen bonds play a very important role in living organisms. For example, DNA molecules are held together by hydrogen bonds. A DNA molecule looks like a long twisted ladder, with two long chains of sugar molecules and phosphate groups making up the sides of the ladder and nitrogen bases sticking into the center like steps of the ladder. These nitrogen bases are held together by millions of hydrogen bonds, which stabilize the DNA molecule. Because individual hydrogen bonds are weak, some break to allow the chains to separate during DNA replication and protein synthesis.

 Language Arts Connection Research the structure of DNA. Why is it important to have hydrogen bonds rather than ionic or covalent bonds holding the two chains of DNA together? Develop a presentation answering this question and explaining how the different types of chemical bonds in a DNA molecule relate to its structure and function.

London Dispersion Forces

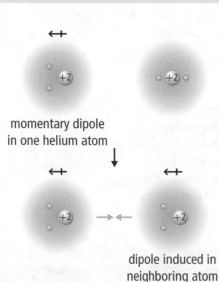

FIGURE 13: When an instantaneous, temporary dipole develops in a helium atom, it induces a dipole in a neighboring atom.

momentary dipole in one helium atom

dipole induced in neighboring atom

In all atoms, electrons are in constant motion. As a result, the electron distribution may become slightly uneven at any instant. While this uneven distribution of charge lasts for only a very short period of time, it creates a positive pole in one part of an atom or molecule and a negative pole in another part. This temporary dipole does not affect molecules or atoms that are far away, but it can induce a dipole in a nearby neighbor. The two atoms or molecules are held together for an instant by the weak attraction between the temporary dipoles. These weak intermolecular attractions that result from the constant motion of electrons are called *London dispersion forces*. All London forces are temporary because electrons are in constant motion and so quickly move to other locations. Unlike hydrogen bonds, London dispersion forces exist between atoms or molecules of any kind, including nonpolar molecules and noble gas atoms.

The strength of London forces increases as the number of electrons in the interacting atoms or molecules increases. So, London dispersion forces increase with increasing atomic or molar mass. This trend is evident in the halogen group of the periodic table. While the lightest halogens, fluorine and chlorine, are gases at room temperature, the next larger, bromine, is a liquid. The next larger still, iodine, is a solid.

 Evidence Notebook Briefly summarize each type of intermolecular force that can occur between particles. Then, make a claim about which of these forces is most likely responsible for making fog stick to a surface. Use evidence to support your claim, and explain your reasoning.

Hands-On Lab
Exploring Intermolecular Forces

Intermolecular forces can provide information about how a substance will behave. When a substance has strong intermolecular forces, it requires more energy when in the solid state to become a liquid (melt) or in the liquid state to become a gas (evaporate). As a result, melting point tends to increase and evaporation rate tends to decrease when intermolecular forces are greater. Surface tension also increases with increasing intermolecular forces.

In this lab, you will design a procedure to analyze intermolecular forces in four common household chemicals—water, acetone, isopropyl alcohol, and glycerol. The structures of these substances are shown in Figure 14. You should collect data related to the evaporation rate and surface tension of these compounds. Then, you will analyze your results to answer the research question for this lab.

Research Question: How do intermolecular forces affect the surface tension and evaporation rate of different molecular compounds?

FIGURE 14: Structures for water, acetone, isopropyl alcohol, and glycerol

Water	Acetone	Isopropyl Alcohol	Glycerol
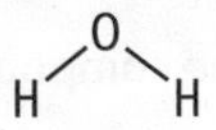	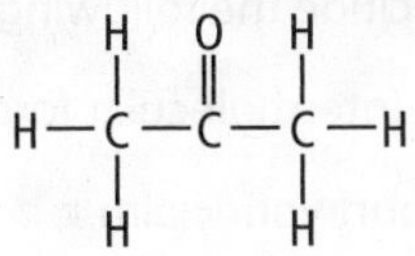	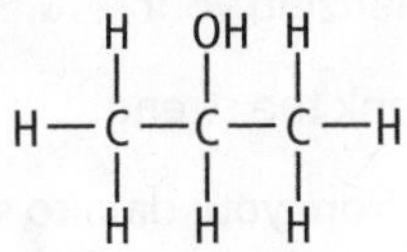	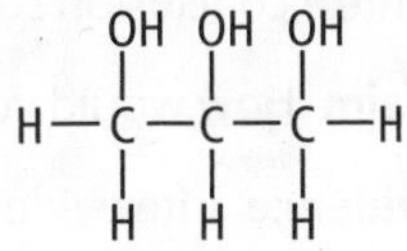
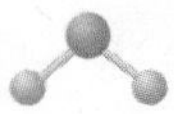	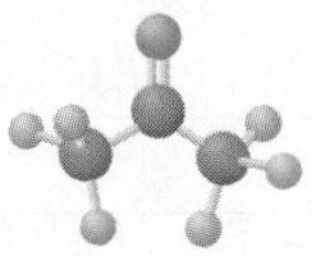	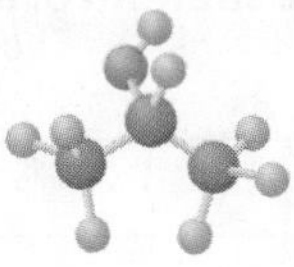	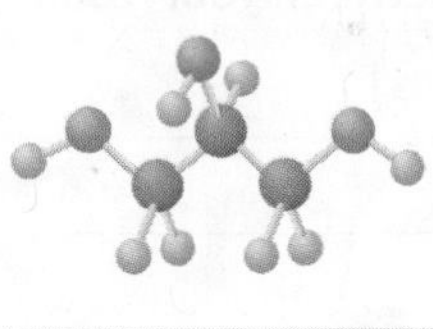

MAKE A CLAIM

In your Evidence Notebook, explain which type of intermolecular forces you think act in each substance and explain your reasoning. Then, make a prediction about the strength of the total intermolecular force in each substance.

POSSIBLE MATERIALS

- indirectly vented chemical splash goggles, nonlatex apron, and nonlatex gloves
- acetone in dropper bottle
- flasks with stoppers (4), each containing water, acetone, isopropyl alcohol, or glycerol
- glycerol in dropper bottle
- isopropyl alcohol in dropper bottle
- marker
- stopwatch or clock with second hand
- water in dropper bottle
- wax paper (1 sheet)

indirectly vented
chemical splash
goggles

SAFETY INFORMATION

- Wear indirectly vented chemical splash goggles, a nonlatex apron, and nonlatex gloves during the setup, hands-on, and takedown segments of the activity.
- All operations in which noxious or poisonous gases or flammable vapors are used or produced must be carried out in the fume hood.
- Never pour chemicals, either used or unused, back into their original container. Dispose of chemicals according to your teacher's instructions.
- Use caution when working with glassware, which can shatter if dropped and cut skin.
- Wash your hands with soap and water immediately after completing this activity.

PLAN THE INVESTIGATION

1. In your Evidence Notebook, develop a procedure and safety plan for your investigation.
2. Draw a data table in your Evidence Notebook for recording your observations and data. When designing your data table, consider what types of data would be appropriate for analyzing surface tension and rate of evaporation.
3. Have your teacher approve your plans before you begin your work. If you need additional materials to complete your procedure, discuss these with your teacher.
4. Clean up your lab area and dispose of your lab materials as instructed by your teacher.

DRAW CONCLUSIONS

Write a conclusion summarizing your results. Include the following sections:

Claim How would you rank the strength of the intermolecular forces in the compounds?

Evidence Cite evidence from your data to support your claim.

Reasoning Explain how the data you cited supports your claim. What is the connection between your results and the strength of intermolecular forces?

_____
_____
_____
_____
_____
_____
_____
_____
_____
_____
_____

 Evidence Notebook How could the knowledge you gained from this investigation be applied to the question about fog collection? What properties would a material need to have to collect water from the air, and how do these properties relate to intermolecular forces?

Materials Science and Design

Have you ever wondered how smartphone glass was developed? Engineers are always trying to improve materials. Materials science is the scientific study of the properties and applications of materials. In developing flexible phone glass, for example, scientists and engineers not only had to study the properties of the glass, but they had to find ways to deliver needed quantities of the glass to the manufacturer. Flexible glass can be delivered in rolls and then cut into pieces.

FIGURE 15: Testing the flexibility of screen glass

The Structure of Materials

Materials scientists develop new materials and optimize the performance of materials that already exist. These scientists investigate how factors at the atomic scale affect the properties of materials at the macroscopic scale. Materials are often subdivided into five major categories: metals, ceramics, semiconductors, polymers, and composites.

Metals

For thousands of years, humans have used metals for many purposes from tools to jewelry. In fact, historians talk about the transitions from the Stone Age to the Bronze or Iron Ages when discussing ancient human history. Today, materials scientists are still finding ways to make and use new metal products more efficiently. In addition, scientists can combine different metals to form alloys such as steel that have different properties from their components. All metals exhibit metallic bonding where valence electrons are shared by the entire solid. Thus, they share properties of thermal and electrical conductivity, malleability, ductility, and the ability to reflect light from their shiny surfaces. These properties allow us to develop medical implants, lighter airplanes, and better methods of communications.

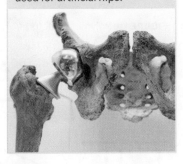

FIGURE 16: Titanium metal is used for artificial hips.

Ceramics

A ceramic is neither metallic nor organic. Most ceramics are hard and chemically non-reactive, and they usually are formed by heating other substances. Some ceramics are conductors, meaning they transmit electricity and heat, while others are not. Glass, pottery, clay, bricks, tiles, and cement are typical ceramics. They are used to make such diverse products as spark plugs, artificial joints, body armor, skis, cooktops, and race car brakes.

FIGURE 17: Porcelain or glass insulators may protect utility poles from high voltages.

EXPLAIN Recall that metals conduct electricity because metal ions exist in a "sea" of electrons, and the electrons are free to move between the ions. Based on this information, what do you know about the electrons in ceramics?

_____

_____

_____

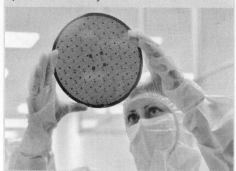

FIGURE 18: A clean room at a computer-chip production facility

Semiconductors

Semiconductors are materials that have electrical conductivity values between that of a conductor, such as copper, and an insulator, such as glass. Their resistance decreases as their temperature increases. Thus, they are not effective conductors at low temperatures, but they do conduct electrical currents at temperatures above room temperature. This property makes them valuable in advanced electronics and communications, where their conducting properties may be altered in useful ways by the controlled introduction of impurities. Silicon, the most widely used semiconductor, makes up chips in electronic devices. Chip production must be done in clean rooms under controlled conditions with low concentrations of dust particles and other unwanted impurities and at a specific humidity. Semiconductors are also used to make solar cells because they absorb light and generate a current. They are used to make lasers and LEDs because they can emit colored light when they contain certain impurities.

Polymers

Think about how many different types of plastic you use every day. They are invaluable to everyday life, but disposing of them responsibly is not always easy. Could optimizing the properties of plastics make it easier to recycle them? Most plastics are made of polymer-based materials. Polymers are compounds composed of very large molecules. These molecules are made up of smaller subunits called monomers. Polymers are everywhere—from storage containers to biomedical items such as contact lenses. DNA, spider silk, and proteins are natural polymers. The hydrocarbon monomers that make plastics come from fossil fuels. Hydrocarbons are compounds that contain only carbon and hydrogen.

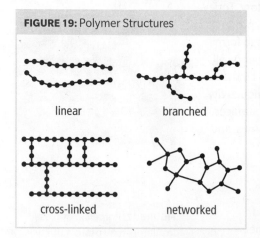

FIGURE 19: Polymer Structures

linear

branched

cross-linked

networked

The properties of different types of plastics result from their molecular structure. For example, a linear polymer is a long chain of subunits linked together. Because linear chains can stack closely together, materials made of this type of polymer, such as nylon, have relatively high densities, strengths, and melting points. Branched polymers have groups of subunits branching off from a long polymer chain. Depending on how these side chains branch off, intermolecular forces may exist between them. For example, the polymers in low-density polyethylene (LDPE) are more highly branched than those in high-density polyethylene (HDPE). As a result, the polymers in LDPE cannot stack as neatly together, and the plastic is more flexible than HDPE. However, plastics made of LDPE are not as strong as those made of HDPE.

Cross-linked polymers form long chains, either branched or linear, that develop covalent bonds between the polymer molecules. These bonds are much stronger than the intermolecular forces that hold other polymers together. Thus, cross-linked polymers such as synthetic rubber are strong and stable. Finally, network polymers, such as epoxy adhesives, form so many interconnections between chains that an entire sample of the polymer may be a single molecule. These polymers are strong and heat resistant.

Thermoplastics are polymer-based materials that melt when heated. Their properties are influenced by electrostatic forces between their molecules. Thermoplastics are formed by applying heat and pressure to the monomer subunits. The length of the polymer, which influences properties such as toughness and melt temperature, can be controlled. The melt temperature of a thermoplastic affects how easily it can be recycled.

After the polymers in thermoplastics form, the chains are like long, tangled bundles of spaghetti. There are no covalent bonds between chains, but there are weak attractive forces that exist between neighboring chains. These forces become stronger when the plastic cools and weaker when it is heated. The shape of the polymer molecules also influences the final material because it affects how densely the molecules will pack together.

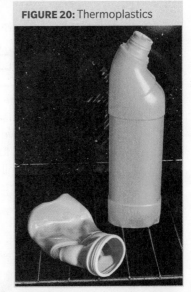

FIGURE 20: Thermoplastics

EXPLAIN Select the correct terms to complete the statement.

The greater the attractive forces are between molecules in a thermoplastic, the more flexible | tougher the material will be. Greater intermolecular forces between chains also means the plastic will melt at a lower | higher temperature. In Figure 20, the bottle with stronger intermolecular forces between its molecules is most likely the intact | melted bottle. The bottle that would be easier to recycle is most likely the intact | melted bottle. Recycling reduces pollution and the need for new materials.

Influence of Engineering, Technology, and Science

Composite Materials in Prosthetic Limbs

In a composite, different materials are combined to form a new material with its own unique properties. One component of a composite typically surrounds and binds the other component. The original materials and the new material all exist separately in the final structure. The first composite made was fiberglass, composed of glass fibers and plastic. Glass is strong but brittle. The plastic holds glass fibers together to form a light, strong, and flexible composite. Other modern composites include wood laminates used for flooring, reinforced concrete, and even waterproof clothing.

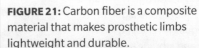

FIGURE 21: Carbon fiber is a composite material that makes prosthetic limbs lightweight and durable.

Composite materials have helped revolutionize many products, including vehicles, sports equipment, and prosthetic limbs. For example, the "blade leg" shown in Figure 21 typically contains carbon fiber material. This composite material was originally developed for use in aerospace technologies, but its use has expanded quickly due to its desirable properties. The advantages of using carbon fiber over more traditional materials include increased flexibility, greater durability and strength, and reduced weight.

Carbon fiber is made by embedding fibers made from carbon in a resin. Different forms of carbon fiber have different properties based on the orientation of the fibers and the type of resin used. Controlling these aspects of the material allows scientists to develop carbon fibers with varying degrees of strength, weight, and stiffness. The development of new composite materials is likely to keep changing the way we use materials in our daily lives.

Language Arts Connection Research composite materials used in the construction of prosthetic limbs. Make a pamphlet explaining the costs and benefits of these materials in terms of affordability, durability, and environmental impact. In addition, explain how the properties of these materials at the larger scale are related to their properties at the atomic scale.

Optimizing Material Design

As was mentioned at the beginning of this lesson, fog collectors could provide an alternative source of fresh water in dry areas. This technology works best in areas with frequent foggy periods. This includes coastal areas where fog is moved toward the land by wind, similar to many parts of California. Fog-collecting technology also has been used in other parts of the world, including Chile, Peru, and Guatemala.

FIGURE 22: These nets are part of a fog-harvesting project on East Anacapa Island in California. The material used in nets like these is usually nylon, polyethylene, or polypropylene. The density of the mesh can be varied to capture more or less water. Droplets that collect on the mesh may drip into a gutter or similar structure that channels the water into a storage tank. Dust, debris, and algae must be regularly removed from nets, and storage tanks must be maintained to prevent fungi and bacterial growth.

Researchers are taking inspiration from living things to design water-collecting materials. For example, the Namib desert beetle survives in its desert home in southern Africa by drinking water that condenses on its hard, bumpy wing covers in early morning fog. A microscopic examination of the beetle's wings shows that they are covered with tiny bumps and grooves that appear to be composed of different materials. The bumps are made of a material that attracts water from the air, and the material that makes up the grooves repels the water. Thus, the water runs along the grooves and is channeled into the beetle's mouth. Engineers have used this observation to develop a new material that mimics the way the beetle's water-gathering system works. One part of the material attracts and collects water from the air. Another part of the material repels this water, which runs off the material and can be collected.

FIGURE 23: The Namib desert beetle can harvest water from the air.

ASK What are some questions you would ask to learn more about how living things collect water from the air?

_____

_____

_____

_____

_____

Could fog collection be an answer to problems associated with water scarcity in areas such as California? This technology has many factors that must be considered before it is installed in an area. For example, fog is often seasonal, so fog may not be available year-round. The technology also works best at particular heights and slopes. In addition, it is not unusual for a person in the United States to use 80 gallons of water per day. This amount does not include the amount of water used to grow crops or manufacture products. So, it might be asked whether enough water is produced to make the process worthwhile. The water must also be transported and distributed.

ANALYZE Imagine you are designing a system that will provide irrigation water for crops in a California town. The town experiences heavy fog for four months each year. List some criteria and constraints that would be important to consider when developing this material. Then, prioritize the items according to their level of importance.

_____

_____

_____

After developing a new material, such as a water-collecting fabric, materials scientists test and analyze the material to make sure it has the desired properties. An engineer may use a decision matrix to determine how well a design meets important criteria. In a decision matrix, each criterion is given a number, or weight, based on how important that criterion is. For example, in the hypothetical decision matrix below, durability is given a weight of 4, so, it is the most important criterion. Limiting algae growth is the least important, so it has a weight of 1. Each design is rated based on how well it meets the chosen criteria. The score for each criterion in a design is then multiplied by its respective weight, and the products are totaled. Engineers may choose to take the design with the highest score to the next phase in the engineering design process, or they may choose to brainstorm new ideas if no designs meet the requirements satisfactorily.

Decision matrix for fog-collecting material				
Design Criteria	Weight	Design 1	Design 2	Design 3
Durability	4	5	1	4
Water collected	3	2	3	4
Cost	2	1	2	1
Algae growth	1	1	4	0
Total Points		29	21	30

A matrix helps engineers consider tradeoffs of different designs. Materials scientists optimize materials for efficiency. They also optimize the processes that produce those materials. After repeated testing of a material, scientists may start the design process over again. If the manufacturing process is inefficient or too costly, a new process may be developed. The optimization process constantly considers these tradeoffs.

 Evidence Notebook How would you analyze the performance of a fog-collecting material? What tests would you run, and how would you measure a successful design?

Engineering Lab

Experimenting with Polymers

You are a materials scientist who has been hired by a toy company to develop a bouncy polymer toy. The company wants the toy to bounce at least 15 cm high when dropped from a height of 30 cm onto a tile floor at room temperature. The toy should also retain a spherical shape for several bounces and be stretchy and moldable by hand. Last, the toy should be colorful and fun to look at. You will make an initial version of the polymer to be used in the toy by cross-linking polyvinyl alcohol (PVA) monomers with sodium borate. You will then test the polymer's properties and determine how to optimize it.

FIGURE 24: Sodium borate forms covalent bonds to link chains of polyvinyl alcohol.

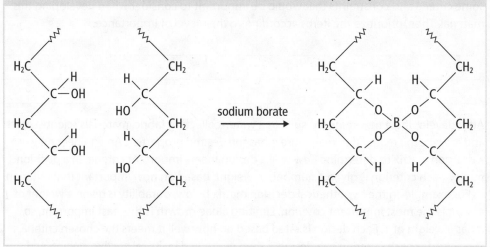

DESIGN CHALLENGE

Test and optimize a polymer toy that fulfills the company's design criteria.

CONDUCT RESEARCH

Research the polymer you will be making. How is it formed? What are its properties? As part of your research, look for information that could help you meet the criteria for a successful solution and maximize the bounciness of a toy made with this polymer.

DEFINE THE PROBLEM

Define the engineering problem you must solve in this lab. Identify the criteria and constraints for the problem.

_____

_____

_____

_____

_____

_____

POSSIBLE MATERIALS

- indirectly vented chemical splash goggles, nonlatex apron, nitrile gloves
- food coloring, assorted colors
- graduated cylinder, 50 mL
- plastic cup, 4 oz
- polyvinyl alcohol (PVA), 5% solution (30 mL)
- ruler, 30 cm
- sodium tetraborate, 4% solution (5 mL)
- wooden dowel, ¼-in. diameter (8 in. long)

SAFETY INFORMATION

- Wear indirectly vented chemical splash goggles, a nonlatex apron, and nitrile gloves during the setup, hands-on, and takedown segments of the activity.
- If you get a chemical in your eye, use an eyewash station immediately.
- All operations in which noxious or poisonous gases or vapors are used or produced must be carried out in the fume hood.
- Never pour chemicals, either used or unused, back into their original container. Dispose of chemicals according to your teacher's instructions.
- Wash your hands with soap and water immediately after completing this activity.

indirectly vented chemical splash goggles

DESIGN SOLUTIONS

Your first step is to make a polymer according to an existing recipe.

1. Use a graduated cylinder to measure 30 mL of polyvinyl alcohol. Pour the alcohol into a plastic cup.
2. Add one drop of food coloring.
3. Rapidly add 5.0 mL of sodium borate solution, and stir briskly for 2 minutes.

TEST

You now need to test how well your polymer meets the criteria and constraints of the problem you defined. In your Evidence Notebook, write the procedures you will use for testing how well the polymer meets the criteria. Make sure your teacher approves your plans before proceeding. Make a data table in your Evidence Notebook to record all your observations. Then, perform your tests. Clean up your lab station and all equipment, but do not discard your polymer.

1. Which criteria were met by the current toy design? Which criteria were not met?

_____

_____

_____

2. Did any problems arise with your testing procedure? If so, describe changes that should be made to the testing procedure. Have your teacher approve these changes, and run your tests again using the new procedure.

_____

_____

_____

OPTIMIZE

1. How do you think the recipe needs to be changed to optimize the polymer? Explain why you think these changes will result in the desired properties.

_____

_____

_____

_____

_____

_____

_____

_____

2. You now need to optimize the design solution. You will need to consider certain tradeoffs. For example, if you try to optimize how high the toy can bounce, it might not be as stretchy and moldable. You will need to decide which criterion is more important. Make a decision matrix and indicate the relative weight of each criterion. Indicate how well your first design met each criterion. As you test new designs, you will use your decision matrix to compare each different iteration.

3. Make a new polymer by adjusting the original recipe. Use your decision matrix to track your results. If time permits, continue iterating and improving your polymer.

COMMUNICATE

Make a presentation that shows how well your final design worked, how you tested the design, and how you determined if the design was successful. You should also describe what changes your design had compared with your original design. If time allows, share your presentation with your classmates.

 Evidence Notebook Explain how the properties of the polymer you designed are related to intermolecular forces. What are the components of a polymer, and what types of forces typically hold these components together?

Careers in Science

Organic Chemist

Could you use your knowledge of intermolecular forces to help develop a cure for a disease? One person who is doing just that is James Nowick, a professor and organic chemist. Organic chemistry is the field of study that focuses on the chemistry of carbon-based molecules, especially those in living things. An organic chemist may study the structure and function of proteins, carbohydrates, DNA, or lipids. A person in this field might want to learn how these molecules are produced in the body, how they interact with other molecules, or how they affect a person's health.

Understanding the structure and function of proteins is an important part of finding cures for diseases such as Alzheimer's disease. Professor Nowick studies proteins involved in Alzheimer's and other neurodegenerative diseases. His research group is developing synthetic molecules that are similar in structure and function to these proteins. The purpose of developing these synthetic proteins is to model interactions between different parts of molecules. For example, a beta-pleated sheet is a zig-zag-shaped structure found in some proteins. When two beta-pleated sheets are near each other, hydrogen bonds form between the polar carbon-oxygen and nitrogen-hydrogen groups on the two sheets.

By using synthetic proteins as models, Nowick's group is able to learn more about the forces that hold these molecules together and how changes in these interactions might lead to disease. The techniques his team uses include molecular modeling, spectroscopy, and x-ray crystallography. These tools allow the group to understand how the building blocks of proteins interact and how they could possibly manipulate those interactions. The general process Nowick's group uses typically involves making new molecules that they think will interact through hydrogen bonding and other intermolecular forces. They can then analyze how the proteins fold, interact with other molecules, and operate in the human body.

FIGURE 25: James Nowick studies a model of an organic molecule.

James Nowick has been honored many times for his teaching, mentorship, and contributions to his community. He identifies as part of the LGBTQ+ community and has worked with organizations such as the Gay and Transgender Chemists and Allies subdivision of the American Chemical Society. This group works to promote inclusion, advocacy and collaboration among LGBTQ+ chemists. Nowick's contributions to science and his community are numerous. His work will likely continue to spur other important discoveries in this field and inspire others to pursue careers in science.

Chemistry in Your Community Research a scientist who works in the field of organic chemistry or biochemistry. Develop a profile for this person that explains the topics they study, what questions they hope to answer through their research, and how they collaborate with others in their field. Discuss the real-world applications of their research, and, if applicable, explain how intermolecular forces are related to their area of study.

| APPLICATIONS OF MATERIALS SCIENCE | EVAPORATION AND INK SOLVENTS | CAREER: BIOMEDICAL ENGINEER | Go online to choose one of these other paths. |

Lesson Self-Check

CAN YOU SOLVE IT?

FIGURE 26: Areas such as San Francisco, California, have fog for several days each year.

To provide water for locations that do not have adequate amounts of rain, scientists and engineers are developing ways to harvest usable amounts of water from fog. Water-collecting methods must include ways to efficiently collect this water, store it, and then transport it to its final destination.

To design these materials and methods, scientists and engineers have learned from examples in nature where water is collected by living things. Observations of these examples aid in the design and testing of materials and systems that can be used to reclaim usable water from fog.

 Evidence Notebook In your Evidence Notebook, explain what properties a material would need to have to collect water from fog. Discuss the following in your explanation:

1. **Claim** What properties would the material need to have to collect fog? Would it need to have multiple properties in multiple areas?

2. **Evidence** Explain how the properties of the required materials are related to interactions at the atomic scale.

3. **Reasoning** Why would a material need to have the properties you described in order to collect fog from the air?

CHECKPOINTS

Check Your Understanding

1. Although xenon and neon are noble gases and therefore do not typically form bonds, weak attractive forces do exist between atoms of these substances. Choose the statement that best explains why xenon has a higher boiling point than neon.

   a. Xenon has a smaller atomic mass than neon.

   b. Xenon has more electrons than neon.

   c. Xenon forms more hydrogen bonds than neon.

   d. Xenon is more polar than neon.

2. Water (H_2O) and hydrogen sulfide (H_2S) are made up of molecules with a bent structure, but the melting point of H_2O much higher than the melting point of H_2S? Why is this?

   a. The intermolecular forces in H_2S are much greater than those in H_2O.

   b. The intermolecular forces in H_2O are much greater than those in H_2S.

   c. The three-dimensional arrangement of water makes it a polar molecule.

   d. Hydrogen sulfide has a lower molar mass than water.

3. Select the correct terms to complete this statement about polymers used in thermoplastics.

The strength of intermolecular forces between polymer chains affects the properties of the material. The greater the intermolecular forces between adjacent molecules, the more | less rigid one would expect the material to be. As the strength of attractive forces between molecules increases, more | less energy is required to melt the material. Therefore, it would be easier to recycle a plastic with relatively strong | weak intermolecular forces between its molecules as compared to other types of plastics.

4. Which statements best describe a composite material? Select all correct answers.

   a. Composites all contain carbon, which makes them lightweight.

   b. A composite may have more desirable properties than its components.

   c. Composites form hydrogen bonds, which makes them stronger than their components.

   d. A brick made of mud and straw is an example of a composite; a brick made of mud is not.

5. Select the correct terms to complete this statement about charged particles.

Like charges attract | repel, and opposite charges attract | repel. According to Coulomb's law, as the distance between two charged particles decreases, the force between the particles decreases | increases. As the magnitude of the charges decreases, the force decreases | increases.

6. A scientist is conducting an experiment to determine the melting point of a substance. They find that the melting point is about 160 °C higher than they expected based on the size and molecular mass of the compound. What would explain their results? Select all correct answers.

   a. The substance is nonpolar, so London dispersion forces exist.

   b. Dipole-induced dipole attractions strongly hold the molecules together.

   c. Temporary dipole-induced attractions form in the solid when it melts.

   d. The substance is strongly polar, so dipole-dipole attractions exist.

   e. Hydrogen bonding strongly holds the molecules together in the solid state.

CHECKPOINTS (continued)

7. Refer to Coulomb's law and explain how electric force, charge, and the distance between charges are related.

_____

_____

_____

_____

8. Explain whether HCl or HF shows the stronger intermolecular forces and how this is related to trends in the periodic table. Then, explain which of these compounds would have a higher boiling point based on differences in intermolecular forces.

_____

_____

_____

_____

9. Water striders are insects that can walk on the surface of water. Would you expect a water strider to be able to walk on the surface of acetone? Explain why or why not, and give reasons for your answer in terms of intermolecular forces.

_____

_____

_____

_____

_____

MAKE YOUR OWN STUDY GUIDE

 In your Evidence Notebook, design a study guide that supports the main ideas from this lesson:

The presence of intermolecular forces influences the properties of materials.

Materials scientists use their knowledge of molecular structure and intermolecular forces in polymers and composite materials to develop new materials with desirable properties.

Remember to include the following information in your study guide:

• Use examples that model main ideas.
• Record explanations for the phenomena you investigated.
• Use evidence to support your explanations. Your support can include drawings, data, graphs, laboratory conclusions, and other evidence recorded throughout the lesson.

Consider how different patterns in the physical properties of substances can provide evidence for the existence of intermolecular forces between the molecules of substances.

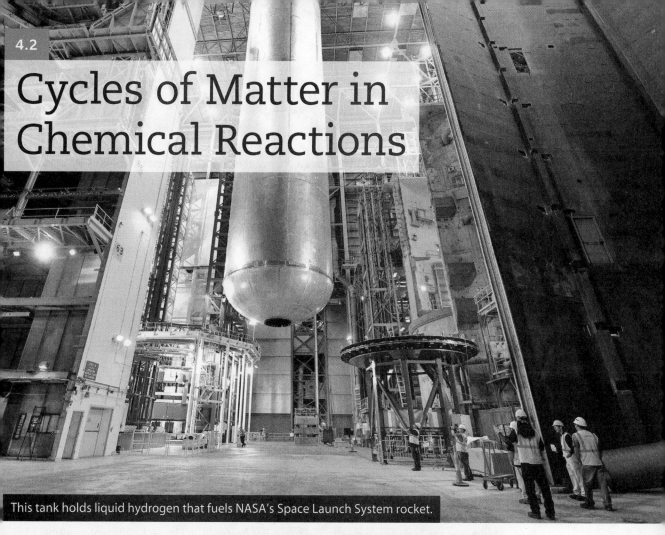

Cycles of Matter in Chemical Reactions

This tank holds liquid hydrogen that fuels NASA's Space Launch System rocket.

CAN YOU EXPLAIN IT?

Chemical reactions occur at all scales, from test tubes to rocket fuel tanks that hold millions of liters. Rockets, in contrast to vehicles like cars and airplanes, use liquid hydrogen as fuel. Hydrogen is lightweight, burns at a very high temperature, and provides more thrust per unit of volume than other fuel. Liquid oxygen is required to make the hydrogen burn. When these two reactants combine explosively inside a rocket engine, water is formed. A water molecule—H_2O—contains twice as many hydrogen atoms as oxygen atoms. Going into space isn't like driving to the store. Before launch, scientists must consider the exact proportions of substances involved in this chemical reaction to calculate the amount of fuel that is required to make the mission successful.

ANALYZE How could you determine the amount of hydrogen needed for a space flight?

_____

_____

_____

_____

 Evidence Notebook As you explore this lesson, gather evidence to explain how cycles of matter in chemical reactions can be observed and quantified.

Analyzing the Composition of Matter

Explore Online ▶

Hands-On Lab

The Composition of Hydrates
Analyze the amount of water released when copper sulfate hydrate is heated.

When matter undergoes a chemical reaction, patterns can be observed in the way the matter changes. In the late 1700s, chemist Antoine Lavoisier set out to test a theory he had about what exactly happened in a chemical reaction. His hypothesis was that any time matter reacts in a closed system, the total amount of matter before and after the reaction stays the same. This may seem logical today, but, at that time, it was not a certainty. Lavoisier carried out very precise experiments to test it. In one experiment, he flowed water through a hot metal tube, causing a metal in the tube to rust and gas to be produced. Lavoisier carefully weighed the materials before and after the experiment.

> **Collaborate** If the chemical formula for water is H_2O, what would you expect to find about the proportions of oxygen and hydrogen produced by its breakdown?

Conservation of Matter

Through further experimentation, scientists confirmed that when a chemical reaction occurs, the total amount of matter present in a system before the reaction always equals the total amount of matter present after the reaction. So, the total mass of the reactants, or starting materials, equals the total mass of the products, or ending materials. This is known as the law of conservation of mass. For example, in Figure 1, different amounts of lead and sulfur react to form lead sulfide. In each reaction, matter is conserved.

FIGURE 1: Three different combinations of lead and sulfur, which react to form lead sulfide

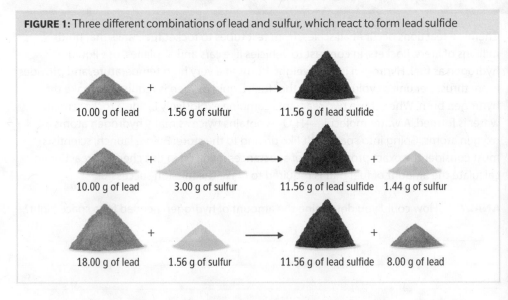

10.00 g of lead + 1.56 g of sulfur → 11.56 g of lead sulfide

10.00 g of lead + 3.00 g of sulfur → 11.56 g of lead sulfide + 1.44 g of sulfur

18.00 g of lead + 1.56 g of sulfur → 11.56 g of lead sulfide + 8.00 g of lead

GATHER EVIDENCE How do the data shown in Figure 1 support the law of conservation of mass? What other patterns do you notice in the data?

_____

_____

_____

You may have noticed that when lead and sulfur combine to form lead sulfide, certain patterns are apparent. The amount of lead sulfide produced remains the same, even when more reactant is available. Experiments with different combinations of substances led scientists to conclude that when elements combine to form compounds, they tend to do so in predictable proportions.

For example, scientists noticed that when metals were burned in air, the metals always combined with a proportional amount of oxygen. If potassium burned in oxygen, every 39.1 g of potassium combined with 8.00 g of oxygen. If calcium burned, every 40.1 g of calcium combined with 16.0 g of oxygen. These observations became known as the *law of definite proportions*. Also known as the law of constant composition, this law states that chemical compounds contain fixed, constant proportions of their constituent elements. The table shows the composition of water by mass. Consider how these data support the law of definite proportions.

Composiiton of Water by Mass		
Mass of water	Mass of oxygen	Mass of hydrogen
18 g	16 g	2 g
36 g	32 g	4 g
54 g	48 g	6 g
72 g	64 g	8g

EXPLAIN Write an explanation for how the data in the table support the law of definite proportions.

_____

_____

_____

_____

Although the ratio by mass of oxygen to hydrogen in water is 8:1, a water molecule does not have eight oxygen atoms and one hydrogen atom. We observe this 8:1 ratio because an oxygen atom is about 16 times more massive than a hydrogen atom. The masses of different elements might need to be considered when comparing numbers of atoms. You will explore this concept further in another part of this lesson.

Scientists also observed that when elements combined to form different compounds, the ratios of the masses of elements in all compounds were reducible to small, whole numbers. This is known as the *law of multiple proportions*. For example, carbon monoxide contains a different proportion of carbon and oxygen atoms than carbon dioxide. However, both compounds have ratios of carbon to oxygen that are reducible to small, whole number ratios. Scientists concluded that in chemical reactions, combinations of atoms simply rearrange. The atoms themselves, however, don't break apart.

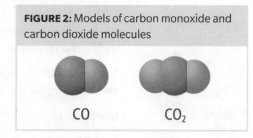

FIGURE 2: Models of carbon monoxide and carbon dioxide molecules

CO   CO₂

Evidence Notebook To launch a rocket, liquid oxygen and liquid hydrogen are combined inside the rocket engine to react explosively. How do you think scientists take into account the law of conservation of mass when they calculate the amount of fuel needed for a rocket launch?

Hands-On Lab
Analyzing Chemical Reactions

How can you quantify changes in matter that happen in chemical reactions? Observable evidence that a chemical change has occurred includes a color change, the formation of a new solid or gas, and the release of energy in the form of light, sound, or heat. Chemical reactions may also absorb energy and feel cold to the touch. But how do you quantify the amount of matter consumed and produced by a chemical reaction? In this lab, you will develop procedures for analyzing both qualitative and quantitative changes in matter.

You will perform two reactions, and each will occur in a different type of system. In the first reaction, you will burn magnesium in an open system (your classroom). In an open system, matter is able to enter and exit the system. The second reaction will take place in a closed system, where matter is not able to enter or exit. This reaction produces a gas, so you must develop a way to trap the gas using the materials provided. For each reaction, you should record both qualitative and quantitative data. These include evidence that a chemical reaction has occurred, as well as the masses of the reactants and products.

Research Question: How does the type of system in which a reaction occurs affect the measurement of reactants and products?

- -

MAKE A CLAIM

How do you think the results will differ between a reaction completed in a closed system and a reaction completed in an open system? Write a prediction in your Evidence Notebook, and explain your thinking.

- -

POSSIBLE MATERIALS

- indirectly vented chemical splash goggles, nonlatex apron, nitrile gloves
- balance
- balloon, nonlatex
- Bunsen burner
- calcium chloride (5–10 g)

- Erlenmeyer flask, 250 mL
- funnel
- graduated cylinder, 25 mL
- magnesium ribbon, 5 cm
- resealable plastic bag
- sodium bicarbonate (5–10 g)

- spoons or spatulas (2)
- tongs
- water
- weighing boats or weighing paper (4)

- -

SAFETY INFORMATION

- Wear indirectly vented chemical splash goggles, a nonlatex apron, and nitrile gloves during the setup, hands-on, and takedown segments of the activity.

- Use caution when working with Bunsen burners. This heat source can seriously burn skin and clothing. Secure loose clothing, wear closed-toe shoes, and tie back hair.

- Use tongs to handle magnesium. Never look directly at magnesium when it is burning.

- Immediately wipe up spilled liquids so they do not become a slip/fall hazard.

- Use caution when working with glassware, which can shatter if dropped and cut skin.

- Wash your hands with soap and water immediately after completing this activity.

indirectly vented chemical splash goggles

Plan the Investigation: Part I

In your Evidence Notebook, develop a procedure, safety plan, and data table for your investigation. In your data table, you should record qualitative observations, including signs that a chemical reaction occurred, and quantitative observations (masses of reactants and products). Have your teacher approve your plans before proceeding.

ANALYZE

1. What evidence is there that a chemical reaction occurred in Part I? How does this evidence relate to changes that occurred at the molecular level?

_____

_____

_____

2. When magnesium metal burns, it reacts with oxygen gas in the air to form a compound called magnesium oxide. How did the mass of the magnesium strip you started with compare to the mass of the magnesium oxide that was produced?

_____

_____

_____

3. According to the law of conservation of mass, matter cannot be created or destroyed. With this in mind, how would you explain any changes in mass you observed? How did these changes compare to what you expected to observe?

_____

_____

_____

Plan the Investigation: Part II

The reaction in Part I took place in an open system. For Part II, your task is to design a closed system that will contain all of the products, including carbon dioxide gas. The challenge comes not only from containing the gas, but also in accounting for the mass of the container in which the products are stored.

The reactants you will combine are water, calcium chloride, and sodium bicarbonate. The mass of water can be calculated indirectly by measuring its volume because the density of water is 1.00 g/mL. For example, 30.0 mL of water has a mass of 30.0 g. The products of this reaction are calcium carbonate, sodium chloride, water, and carbon dioxide.

In your Evidence Notebook, develop a procedure and safety plan for your investigation. When you write your procedure, think about how you will obtain and record the masses of the reactants and products. In addition, consider how you will account for the mass of the container when analyzing your data. Draw a diagram showing how you will carry out the reaction in a closed system. Remember to record both qualitative and quantitative data, including evidence that a chemical reaction occurred and the masses of both the reactants and products. Ask your teacher to approve your procedure and safety plan before proceeding.

ANALYZE

1. What evidence is there that a chemical reaction occurred in Part II of this lab?

_____

_____

2. How does the total mass of the reactants in Part II compare to the total mass of the products? How well did your system contain all the matter that was produced?

_____

_____

_____

3. What changes would you make to the system you designed to make it more effective at containing all the matter produced by this chemical reaction?

_____

_____

_____

DRAW CONCLUSIONS

Write a conclusion that addresses each of the points below.

Claim How do the masses of the reactants and products compare for the reaction completed in the closed system a nd the reaction completed in the open system?

Evidence Describe evidence from both experiments to support your claim.

Reasoning Explain how the evidence you cited supports your claim. In addition, discuss the law of conservation of mass and its relationship to these experiments. If matter is not created or destroyed, why does the total mass of the products sometimes appear to be different than the total mass of the reactants?

_____

_____

_____

_____

_____

_____

_____

 Evidence Notebook If a piece of metal is left outside in the rain, it may start to rust. If you measured the mass of the metal before and after it rusted, you would find that its mass increased. In your Evidence Notebook, explain why the mass of the metal appears to increase, even though atoms are not created or destroyed. How would the mass of a metal before and after rusting compare to the mass of a log before and after it was burned? Explain your reasoning.

Modeling Chemical Reactions

If you are able to predict patterns in chemical reactions, you can perform a reaction more efficiently and minimize waste. Imagine you own a company that makes ready-to-eat foods. You want to buy exactly the right amounts of ingredients to make a certain number of turkey and cheese sandwiches. For the most efficient process, you would have to know the proportions in which the ingredients combine, and to do this, you would need to model the recipe.

FIGURE 3: Making sandwiches with exact proportions of ingredients

2 pieces of bread + 4 slices turkey + 1 piece cheese → 1 sandwich

Collaborate If you needed to make 1350 sandwiches, how many pieces of turkey would you need? Explain to a partner how you determined your answer.

Writing Chemical Equations

Chemical reactions can also be modeled in order to make predictions about how much product is expected to form. Consider the burning of magnesium. Magnesium is an element, so it can be represented by its chemical symbol from the periodic table, Mg. Oxygen is also an element, but it is in a unique group of elements called diatomic elements that form molecules made up of two atoms. Therefore, the chemical formula for a molecule of oxygen is O_2. Mg and O_2 combine to yield a product called magnesium oxide, MgO.

In a chemical equation, the reactants and products are separated with plus signs and the production of a new substance is shown with an arrow. The ratio of magnesium atoms to oxygen atoms in magnesium oxide is 1:1 because a magnesium atom loses two electrons to form a 2+ charge, and an oxygen atom gains two electrons to form a 2− charge.

$$Mg + O_2 \rightarrow MgO$$

Explore Online ▶

Hands-On Activity

Modeling Chemical Reactions
Model the conservation of mass and relationships between reactants and products in a chemical reaction.

MODEL Draw a model illustrating this reaction at the molecular level. Use circles or other shapes to represent atoms. Then, use labels to show whether the reaction, as shown here, obeys the law of conservation of mass.

Chemical equations also may indicate the reactant or product's physical state. These appear as a small letter in parenthesis, such as (*g*) for gas, (*l*) for liquid, (*s*) for solid, and (*aq*) for aqueous, meaning dissolved in water. For this magnesium reaction, the equation is

$$Mg(s) + O_2(g) \rightarrow MgO(s)$$

Balancing Chemical Equations

FIGURE 4: Burning a magnesium ribbon

The chemical equation you saw for the burning of magnesium is not yet complete. In the unfinished equation, there are two oxygen atoms in the reactants and only one in the product. But, the law of conservation of mass states that matter cannot be destroyed. The equation must be balanced to show the true ratios in which the reactants combine. A balanced equation follows the law of conservation of mass.

To balance a chemical equation, you use coefficients. These are numbers placed in front of each reactant or product to indicate their amounts. When a coefficient is placed before a chemical formula with subscripts, you multiply those subscripts by the coefficient to determine the numbers of atoms. Remember that subscripts are based on patterns in the periodic table and represent ratios of atoms. So, they do not change when a chemical equation is balanced. One way to balance a chemical equation is to list each element on both sides of the equation and write the number of atoms present before and after the reaction. Then, adjust the coefficients until the number of each type of of atom is the same on both sides of the equation.

SAMPLE PROBLEM

Begin by listing the number of atoms of each element on both sides of the equation. Then, look for numbers of atoms that are not equal on both sides, such as the oxygen in this equation. Insert coefficients to balance the number of atoms, and update the list as you go. Often, it is best to balance oxygen and hydrogen atoms last. Polyatomic ions, such as SO_4^{2-}, can be listed as complete ions if it makes balancing easier.

Note that the ratio of coefficients for this equation is 2:1:2. When no coefficient or subscript is shown, it is assumed to be 1.

FIGURE 5: Balancing a chemical equation

$$Mg \quad + \quad O_2 \quad \rightarrow \quad MgO$$
Mg: 1   Mg: 1
O: 2   O: 1

$$Mg \quad + \quad O_2 \quad \rightarrow \quad 2MgO$$
Mg: 1   Mg: 1̶ 2
O: 2   O: 1̶ 2

$$2Mg \quad + \quad O_2 \quad \rightarrow \quad 2MgO$$
Mg: 1̶ 2   Mg: 1̶ 2
O: 2   O: 1̶ 2

PRACTICE PROBLEM

SOLVE Write the coefficients necessary to balance each chemical equation.

1. _____ $H_2O \rightarrow$ _____ $H_2 +$ _____ O_2

2. _____ $Al_2O_3 \rightarrow$ _____ $Al +$ _____ O_2

3. _____ $Na_3PO_4 +$ _____ $CaCl_2 \rightarrow$ _____ $NaCl +$ _____ $Ca_3(PO_4)_2$

Evidence Notebook In your evidence notebook, balance the following chemical equation and write an explanation for how you balanced it: $P + O_2 \rightarrow P_2O_5$

Patterns in Types of Reactions

Grouping reactions into categories makes it easier to understand them. The five general types of chemical reactions are shown in Figure 6. In a synthesis reaction, two or more reactants combine to form one product. In a decomposition reaction, one reactant breaks down to form two or more products. Single and double displacement reactions are those in which one or two elements, respectively, in compounds are exchanged. Combustion reactions involve the burning of typically carbon-based molecules in oxygen. The products of a complete combustion reaction are always carbon dioxide and water.

FIGURE 6: Five main types of chemical reactions

Type of Reaction	General Format	Example
Synthesis	$A + B \rightarrow AB$	$2Mg + O_2 \rightarrow 2MgO$
Decomposition	$AB \rightarrow A + B$	$2Ag_2O \rightarrow 4Ag + O_2$
Single displacement	$A + BD \rightarrow AD + B$	$Mg + 2HCl \rightarrow MgCl_2 + H_2$
Double displacement	$AC + BD \rightarrow AD + BC$	$FeS + 2HCl \rightarrow FeCl_2 + H_2S$
Combustion	$C_xH_x + O_2 \rightarrow CO_2 + H_2O$	$C_3H_8 + 5O_2 \rightarrow 3CO_2 + 4H_2O$

EXPLAIN How would you explain the difference between single displacement and double displacement reactions to someone who was unfamiliar with chemical equations?

_____

_____

_____

In the single displacement reaction shown in Figure 7a, a copper wire is placed in a solution of silver nitrate. In the double displacement reaction shown in 7b, two aqueous solutions are combined, resulting in a solid product.

FIGURE 7: Single and double-displacement reactions

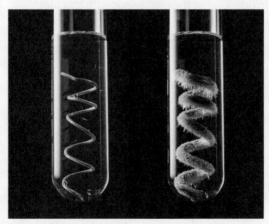

a **Single Displacement** A copper wire is placed in a solution of silver nitrate. The products are solid silver and aqueous copper(II) nitrate.

$Cu(s) + 2AgNO_3(aq) \rightarrow 2Ag(s) + Cu(NO_3)_2(aq)$

b **Double Displacement** Solutions of lead(II) nitrate and potassium iodide are combined, producing solid lead(II) iodide and aqueous potassium nitrate.

$Pb(NO_3)_2(aq) + 2KI(aq) \rightarrow PbI_2(s) + 2KNO_3(aq)$

The five types of reactions commonly occur in daily life. Have you ever left a bike or metal tool outside for a long period of time? If so, you may have observed rust forming. Rusting is a synthesis reaction in which iron metal combines with oxygen gas and water to form iron oxide. Single displacement reactions can be used to electroplate auto parts. A double displacement reaction takes place when an antacid neutralizes stomach acid.

Hydrogen can be obtained through a decomposition reaction that breaks water molecules into hydrogen and oxygen. This can be achieved through a method called electrolysis, but it is relatively expensive. Therefore, scientists and engineers are continually working to improve methods for obtaining hydrogen from water. Optimizing this process would make hydrogen fuel a more viable option for use in vehicles.

 Energy and Matter

Combustion Reactions

Explore Online ▶

FIGURE 8: A balloon filled with hydrogen explodes when ignited.

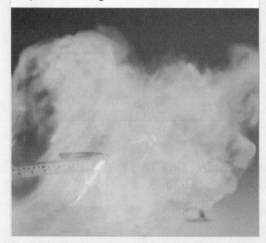

Combustion reactions are often used to provide heat and light, as they do in fireplaces and bonfires. These reactions also release large amounts of energy. You can see the results of this energy when you ignite a balloon filled with hydrogen gas and it explodes violently.

Combustion reactions provide power when compounds containing carbon burn in engines. Most automobiles, buses, and airplanes have internal combustion engines, in which a fuel containing carbon burns in oxygen to produce carbon dioxide, water, and energy. One effect of using combustion engines is that large amounts of carbon dioxide are produced and released into Earth's atmosphere. Carbon dioxide is a greenhouse gas, meaning that it absorbs energy and raises Earth's temperature. As a result, scientists are looking for alternative energy sources that do not contain carbon. Hydrogen fuel might be an alternative; the end product of its combustion is water, not carbon dioxide. One of the challenges with this fuel source is that elemental hydrogen is not found in nature like the hydrocarbons of petroleum and natural gas.

EXPLAIN How do energy and matter change form in a combustion reaction?

In a combustion reaction, thermal energy | chemical energy in the reactants is converted to thermal energy | chemical energy when the fuel is ignited. The fuel reacts with oxygen in the air to form the products carbon dioxide and water | hydrogen. Carbon dioxide is a greenhouse gas, so using combustion engines leads to a(n) decrease | increase in the amount of energy stored in Earth's atmosphere.

 Evidence Notebook Recall the reaction that takes place in a rocket engine, $H_2 + O_2 \rightarrow H_2O$. In your Evidence Notebook, discuss this equation in terms of what you have learned in this lesson. What type of reaction is this? How would you obtain the balanced form of this reaction? Why is it necessary to balance a chemical equation when considering amounts of reactants and products?

Quantifying Matter in Chemical Reactions

Think back to the ingredients needed to make sandwiches. You need four pieces of turkey for each sandwich. If you had 288 pieces of turkey, how many sandwiches could you make? You can use dimensional analysis to convert one quantity to another.

$$288 \ \text{pieces turkey} \times \frac{1 \ \text{sandwich}}{4 \ \text{pieces turkey}} = 72 \ \text{sandwiches}$$

 Collaborate Show how you would use dimensional analysis to determine the number of sandwiches you could make with 374 pieces of bread. Then compare answers with a partner.

Quantifying Moles in Chemical Reactions

Just as you can use a recipe to predict how many sandwiches you can make, you can use a chemical equation to predict how much product will be made from a certain amount of reactant. The process of calculating quantities of matter in chemical reactions is called *stoichiometry*. In stoichiometric calculations, the proportions of reactants and products is important. The coefficients in a balanced equation represent moles, the unit chemists use to quantify matter in chemical reactions. In the reaction below, two moles of magnesium combine with one mole of oxygen to produce two moles of magnesium oxide.

$$2Mg + O_2 \rightarrow 2MgO$$

Therefore, you can use the coefficients in this equation to make predictions about amounts of reactants and products. To do this, you use a conversion factor that shows the coefficients as mole quantities. A conversion factor is a ratio that by definition always equals one, so either factor can be written as the numerator. Below are some conversion factors that could be used to solve problems related to this chemical equation. The components of the conversion factor depend on what is being compared. The arrangement of the numerator and denominator depends on the needs of the problem.

Comparing magnesium to magnesium oxide:

$$\frac{2 \ \text{mol Mg}}{2 \ \text{mol MgO}} \quad \text{or} \quad \frac{2 \ \text{mol MgO}}{2 \ \text{mol Mg}}$$

Comparing oxygen to magnesium oxide:

$$\frac{1 \ \text{mol O}_2}{2 \ \text{mol MgO}} \quad \text{or} \quad \frac{2 \ \text{mol MgO}}{1 \ \text{mol O}_2}$$

MODEL Use the balanced equation for the synthesis of magnesium oxide to write the conversion factors you could use to compare moles of oxygen to moles of magnesium.

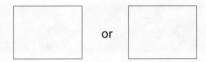

Calculating Molar Amounts

SAMPLE PROBLEM   If 45.3 moles of oxygen were available, how many moles of magnesium oxide would be produced when the magnesium was burned in oxygen?

$$2Mg + O_2 \rightarrow 2MgO$$

ANALYZE   Start with the given amount. Then, set up a conversion factor that will allow you to cancel the given unit and convert to the requested unit.

$$45.3 \text{ mol } O_2 \times \frac{\text{mol ?}}{\text{mol ?}} = \text{mol MgO}$$

SOLVE   Use the balanced equation to complete the conversion factor and solve.

$$45.3 \text{ mol } O_2 \times \frac{2 \text{ mol MgO}}{1 \text{ mol } O_2} = 90.6 \text{ mol MgO}$$

PRACTICE PROBLEMS   **SOLVE** Use the balanced equation to complete these problems.

1. How many moles of MgO are made if 0.37 moles of O_2 react with Mg?

2. If 8.2 moles of Mg are burned, how many moles of MgO are produced?

Quantifying Particles in Chemical Reactions

FIGURE 9: One mole of several substances

The concept of the mole can be used to calculate how many particles are in a certain amount of matter. *Particles* can refer to atoms, molecules, or formula units, depending on the substance. Figure 9 shows exactly one mole of five substances. Starting from the left, they are: sugar, salt, carbon, oxygen (pictured in a balloon), and copper.

 Collaborate The table below shows the number of particles in one mole of each substance in the photo. Discuss the patterns you notice with a partner. Does the chemical formula affect the number of particles in one mole of each substance? What is similar about one mole of each substance, and what is different?

Substance	Table sugar ($C_{12}H_{22}O_{11}$)	Salt (NaCl)	Carbon (C)	Oxygen (O_2)	Copper (Cu)
Particles in one mole	6.02×10^{23} molecules	6.02×10^{23} formula units	6.02×10^{23} atoms	6.02×10^{23} diatomic molecules	6.02×10^{23} atoms

Calculating Numbers of Particles

Knowing how many particles in are in one mole allows you to calculate the number of particles that should be present before or after a reaction. To convert between moles and particles, use a conversion factor that compares these two quantities. The number of particles in one mole, or Avogodro's number, is also known as "the chemist's dozen."

$$\frac{1 \text{ mol}}{6.02 \times 10^{23} \text{ particles}} \quad \text{or} \quad \frac{6.02 \times 10^{23} \text{ particles}}{1 \text{ mol}}$$

SAMPLE PROBLEM If 45.3 moles of oxygen react, how many formula units of magnesium oxide are produced?

$$2Mg + O_2 \rightarrow 2MgO$$

ANALYZE Plan out the conversion factors needed to solve for particles of MgO.

$$45.3 \text{ mol } O_2 \times \frac{? \text{ mol MgO}}{? \text{ mol } O_2} \times \frac{6.02 \times 10^{23} \text{ particles}}{1 \text{ mol MgO}} = ? \text{ particles MgO}$$

SOLVE Use coefficients from the balanced equation to complete the conversion factor and solve.

$$45.3 \text{ mol } O_2 \times \frac{2 \text{ mol MgO}}{1 \text{ mol } O_2} \times \frac{6.02 \times 10^{23} \text{ particles MgO}}{1 \text{ mol MgO}} = 5.45 \times 10^{25} \text{ particles MgO}$$

PRACTICE PROBLEM You can also determine how many moles of a substance are produced if you are given the number of particles. Consider this problem: How many moles of magnesium oxide are produced when 7.94×10^{24} particles of magnesium are burned?

ANALYZE Place the quantities in the correct locations to solve the Practice Problem.

| 2 mol MgO | 2 mol Mg | 7.94×10^{24} particles Mg |

| 1 mol Mg | 6.02×10^{23} particles Mg |

$$\boxed{} \times \frac{\boxed{}}{\boxed{}} \times \frac{\boxed{}}{\boxed{}}$$

SOLVE Use the equation you set up above to calculate the final answer.
If 7.94×10^{24} atoms of magnesium react, _____ moles of magnesium oxide will be produced.

 Evidence Notebook In your Evidence Notebook, show how you would solve this problem and then explain in words how you solved it: How many particles of magnesium oxide are produced when 5.50 moles of magnesium are burned?

Think back to the sandwich-making scenario. If you had to order sandwich supplies by mass, how would you know how much food to buy? You would need to know the mass of the ingredient you were working with. For example, if you purchased 1000.0 grams of turkey and wanted to calculate how many sandwiches you could make, you would need to know the mass of one piece of turkey. If one piece of turkey had a mass of 15.0 grams, you could use dimensional analysis to determine how many sandwiches are possible.

$$1000.0 \text{ g turkey} \times \frac{1 \text{ piece turkey}}{15.0 \text{ g turkey}} \times \frac{1 \text{ sandwich}}{4 \text{ pieces turkey}} = 16.7 \text{ sandwiches}$$

Quantifying Mass in Chemical Reactions

In the same way that you must know the mass of each item when ordering food by weight, you must consider the mass of different particles to make predictions about the amount of product made in a chemical reaction. Moles allow you to convert from a quantity that is difficult to measure, such as the number of molecules in a substance, to a quantity that is easy to measure, such as mass in grams. You know you can measure mass by putting a substance on a balance, but how do you determine the mass of one mole?

The following table shows the mass in grams of one mole of each substance.

Substance	Table sugar $(C_{12}H_{22}O_{11})$	Salt (NaCl)	Carbon (C)	Oxygen (O_2)	Copper (Cu)
Mass of one mole in grams	342.3 g	58.44 g	12.01 g	32.00 g	63.55 g

EXPLAIN Complete this statement based on the data shown in the table.

One mole of sugar has the same | a different mass than one mole of salt. This indicates that the mass of one mole of a substance depends | does not depend on the chemical makeup of the substance. However, the number of particles in one mole depends | does not depend on the identity of the substance.

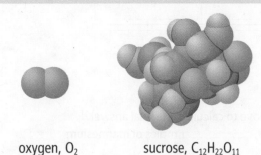

FIGURE 10: Molecular models of oxygen and sucrose molecules show how the molecular structure of these substances differs.

oxygen, O_2 sucrose, $C_{12}H_{22}O_{11}$

Why does the mass of one mole differ from one substance to another, but the number of particles in one mole does not? Consider the structure of each of the substances presented in the table. Figure 10 shows models of two of these substances—a diatomic oxygen molecule and a sucrose (sugar) molecule.

PREDICT What differences do you notice when looking at the models of an oxygen molecule and a sucrose molecule? How do you think the mass of one mole of these substances is related to their molecular structure?

The mass in grams of one mole of an element or compound is called its *molar mass*. The molar mass of a single element, such as carbon, is equivalent to its atomic mass, as listed on the periodic table, expressed in grams. So, the mole is a unit that allows you to convert from grams, which you can measure on a balance, to individual molecules or atoms.

$$\text{molar mass in grams} = 1 \text{ mole} = 6.02 \times 10^{23} \text{ particles}$$

The molar mass of a compound depends on the atomic masses of the elements that make it up and how many atoms of each element are present. For example, copper has a higher molar mass than oxygen, even though an oxygen molecule is made up of two atoms. This is because a copper atom has more protons and neutrons than an oxygen atom, so its atomic mass on the periodic table is much higher than oxygen's. Large molecules, such as sucrose, tend to have high molar masses because so many atoms are present in one particle. In the case of sucrose, one molecule contains 45 atoms!

To calculate molar mass, you first use the periodic table to find the atomic masses of the elements. Then, you multiply each atomic mass by the number of atoms indicated by the subscripts, and add the values you obtain. For example, the molar mass of sucrose, $C_{12}H_{22}O_{11}$ is calculated as follows:

C: 12.01 u $\times$ 12 atoms

H: 1.008 u $\times$ 22 atoms

O: 15.999 u $\times$ 11 atoms

So, the final molar mass is: $(12.01 \times 12) + (1.008 \times 22) + (15.999 \times 11) = 342.3$ g/mol

SOLVE Use a periodic table to calculate the following molar masses.

1. The molar mass of of $CaCl_2$ _____ g/mol.

2. The molar mass of $Mg_3(PO_4)_2$ is _____ g/mol.

Suppose you wanted to obtain one molar mass of a substance to use in a chemical reaction. You would have to measure out that mass in grams on a balance. The precision of your balance can make a big difference in your final outcome.

 Scale, Proportion, and Quantity

Molar Mass at an Industrial Scale

Correctly calculating the molar mass of a substance and correctly measuring that mass on a balance are two requirements for large-scale industrial processes. Imagine, for example, a chemical process for manufacturing a product such as aspirin tablets on an industrial scale. If a chemical engineer either miscalculated the molar mass of the ingredients or made an error in measuring their mass, the aspirin tablets would contain either too much or too little of the active ingredient. Too much active ingredient might be dangerous to a person's health, and too little might be ineffective.

FIGURE 11: This worker is manufacturing a product on an industrial scale.

 Language Arts Connection Research the chemical formula of aspirin and calculate its molar mass. Then write an explanation for why a small error in rounding or measuring could affect the production of an industrial-scale product such as medicine.

Problem Solving

Calculating Mass

If you burn 3.06 g of magnesium, how many grams of MgO will be produced?

$$2Mg + O_2 \rightarrow 2MgO$$

ANALYZE To convert from grams of magnesium to grams of magnesium oxide, you need to know the molar masses of both. You do not consider the coefficients when calculating molar mass because they will be included in another step of the solving process.

Mg: 24.31 g/mol

MgO: $(24.31 \text{ u} \times 1) + (15.99 \text{ u} \times 1) = 40.3$ g/mol

SOLVE Now, you start with the given quantity and set up conversion factors in a way that allows all the units to cancel except for the unit on your final answer.

$$3.06 \text{ g Mg} \times \frac{1 \text{ mol Mg}}{24.31 \text{ g Mg}} \times \frac{2 \text{ mol MgO}}{2 \text{ mol Mg}} \times \frac{40.3 \text{ g MgO}}{1 \text{ mol MgO}} = 5.07 \text{ g MgO}$$

Notice that the mole-to-mole ratio, shown in the middle of the three conversion factors, is always present in a stoichiometry problem. Other conversion factors can be placed before and after it, but the comparison of moles of one substance to moles of another based on the chemical reaction is vital to any stoichiometry problem.

**PRACTICE
PROBLEM** Most metallic elements are found in nature in the form of oxides. Removing oxygen is necessary to obtain the pure element as used in products like aluminum foil. How many grams of aluminum are produced in this reaction if 100.4 grams of aluminum oxide are supplied?

$$2Al_2O_3 \rightarrow 4Al + 3O_2$$

ANALYZE Calculate the molar masses of aluminum and aluminum oxide.

SOLVE Start with the given from the question, and set up the conversion factors in a way that will allow units to cancel out, leaving only the unit required for the final answer.

 Evidence Notebook The balanced reaction for the burning of hydrogen gas in a rocket engine is:

$$2H_2 + O_2 \rightarrow 2H_2O$$

In your Evidence Notebook, calculate how many particles of water will be produced if 85.2 grams of oxygen are consumed in the reaction. Show your work, and then write a general plan explaining how to solve this problem.

Limiting and Excess Matter

Consider again the reaction between magnesium and oxygen, only now imagine two different scenarios. In one, the reaction between the magnesium ribbon and oxygen takes place in the open air. In the second, the reaction occurs in a glass chamber that prevents the magnesium from reacting with any more oxygen than what happens to be present in the chamber.

FIGURE 12: When magnesium is ignited in an open system, the mass of the products is different from when it is ignited in a closed system.

a Magnesium is ignited in the open air.   **b** Magnesium is ignited inside a jar.

PREDICT Why do you think the mass of magnesium oxide produced in this reaction differs in an open system and in a closed system? How does this relate to the amount of reactants available in each scenario?

_____

_____

_____

_____

Quantifying Limiting and Excess Matter

Think about making sandwiches using this recipe.

2 pieces of bread + 4 slices turkey + 1 piece cheese → 1 sandwich

When following a recipe, it is often the case that you purchase too much of one ingredient or too little of another. In chemistry, having too much or too little reactant also occurs. If there is too little of one reactant compared to another, the reactant that runs out first is called the *limiting reactant*. The reactant that has extra left over after the reaction ends is called the *excess reactant*.

ANALYZE Select the correct terms to complete the statement.

Imagine you had 75 pieces of bread, 200 slices of turkey, and plenty of cheese to make sandwiches with. You would run out of turkey | bread | cheese first, so it is the limiting | excess ingredient. There would be cheese and turkey | bread left over when all the sandwiches are made, so these are the limiting | excess ingredients.

Problem Solving

Determining Limiting and Excess Reactants

EXAMPLE PROBLEM

To determine the limiting and excess reactant for a reaction, you must first know the quantity of each reactant that is available. Consider this problem:

If you burn 48.6 grams of magnesium in 39.0 grams of oxygen:

1. How much magnesium oxide is produced?

2. Which reactant is the limiting reactant?

3. Which is the excess reactant?

$$2Mg + O_2 \rightarrow 2MgO$$

ANALYZE

To determine how much product will actually be made, we must determine how much product each amount of reactant would produce. This means we will calculate two quantities.

$$48.6 \text{ g Mg} \times \frac{1 \text{ mol Mg}}{24.31 \text{ g Mg}} \times \frac{2 \text{ mol MgO}}{2 \text{ mol Mg}} \times \frac{40.3 \text{ g MgO}}{1 \text{ mol MgO}} = 80.6 \text{ g MgO}$$

$$39.0 \text{ g O}_2 \times \frac{1 \text{ mol O}_2}{32.0 \text{ g O}_2} \times \frac{2 \text{ mol MgO}}{1 \text{ mol O}_2} \times \frac{40.3 \text{ g MgO}}{1 \text{ mol MgO}} = 98.2 \text{ g MgO}$$

SOLVE

The amount of product that can be made is equal to the lesser amount from the two calculations. Therefore:

1. The amount of product made is equal to 80.6 g MgO.

2. Magnesium is the limiting reactant.

3. Oxygen is the excess reactant.

PRACTICE PROBLEM

ANALYZE If a sample of magnesium with a mass of 35.0 grams reacts with 35.0 grams of oxygen, how much magnesium oxide will be produced?

SOLVE In this reaction, the amount of magnesium oxide produced is _____.

The limiting reactant is _____ and the excess reactant is _____.

  Evidence Notebook In the Example Problem, the reactant that was present in a greater amount was actually the limiting reactant. Explain why this is, citing evidence from the balanced chemical equation to support your claim.

Determining Percent Yield

In the real world, chemical reactions do not always produce the expected amount of a product. Often, unpredictable side reactions take place. For example, if you ignite 0.972 g of Mg metal, you may get only 0.988 g of MgO, not the expected 1.61 g. The possible reasons for this include the fact that hot Mg metal will react with nitrogen in the air to produce magnesium nitride, Mg_3N_2. Also, the hot magnesium can react with any water vapor that might be present to give magnesium hydroxide, $Mg(OH)_2$. The products of these side reactions are called byproducts.

The amount of product that should be produced from given amounts of reactants is called the theoretical yield of a reaction. As you just learned, many reactions do not yield the theoretical amount of products. The amount of product that actually results from a reaction is called the actual yield. If the actual yield of a reaction is the same as the theoretical yield, the reaction is said to be 100% efficient. With some exceptions, reactions are not 100% efficient. The efficiency of a reaction is measured by calculating percent yield. The percent yield is the ratio of the actual yield to the theoretical yield, multiplied by 100.

$$\text{Percent yield} = \frac{\text{actual yield}}{\text{theoretical yield}} \times 100\%$$

EXPLAIN How could the sandwich analogy be applied to the concept of percent yield? Write your own scenario related to the making of sandwiches that describes the concept of percent yield.

_____

_____

_____

_____

_____

_____

Percent yield isn't important just in making sandwiches. It is also important when trying to determine how much product will actually be produced in a chemical reaction. When a chemist is considering a reaction, he or she needs to know whether the expectations about the amount of product formed is realistic.

 Data Analysis

SOLVE Returning to a previous example, suppose you burn magnesium in a limiting amount of oxygen, expecting to get 1.61 g MgO. But, you find only 0.988 g MgO after the reaction. The percent yield of this reaction is _____%

Chemical reactions take place in the real world, so the actual yield of a reaction is never quite equal to the theoretical yield. Thus, reactions are almost never 100% efficient. The factors that reduce actual yield include side reactions, reactions of a product with other substances in the surroundings, and impurities in the reactants. Even inaccurate measurements can affect the percent yield of a reaction.

Maximizing Percent Yield

FIGURE 13: Hydrogen can be made from wood chips.

Hydrogen is the cleanest-burning fuel, producing only water vapor when it is burned. But, it is not widely used at this time because it does not occur in any significant concentrations as a pure element on Earth. However, it can be chemically removed from a wide variety of abundant, naturally occurring hydrogen-containing compounds.

Hydrogen is used to power a small number of buses and automobiles as well as rocket engines. If these vehicles become more numerous, a large amount of hydrogen fuel will be needed. How will it be produced, and where will it be stored? There are many problems associated with the production and storage of large amounts of hydrogen.

One solution to producing low-cost hydrogen in quantity is to stockpile and distribute biomass such as plant material, converting it to hydrogen as needed. Unlike fossil fuels, plant material such as wood, leaves, and stalks are renewable. Chemists and chemical engineers are collaborating to develop a process that produces hydrogen from sugars in wood. Enzymes convert the sugars to hydrogen gas with a yield of two hydrogen molecules per carbon atom, the maximum possible yield. The hydrogen can then be easily separated from aqueous substances in the reaction chamber. Wood that would have normally been discarded can be used for this process.

PREDICT Describe some of the solutions that engineers might propose for maximizing the production of hydrogen from discarded wood.

_____

_____

_____

_____

_____

ANALYZE What types of criteria and constraints might engineers consider when evaluating competing solutions? Discuss issues related to technology, science, affordability, and environmental impacts.

_____

_____

_____

_____

 Evidence Notebook Write a short paragraph explaining how the proportional relationships between mass and moles can be used to increase the yield of a chemical reaction in the real world. For example, the NASA space launch rocket depends on very careful control of the proportions of fuel to oxygen to maximize the thrust of the rocket.

Hands-On Activity

Modeling Chemical Reactions

In this activity, you will develop a model to demonstrate how matter is conserved in a chemical reaction. Then, you will use your model to determine how much product is made when different amounts of reactant are available.

POSSIBLE MATERIALS

- indirectly vented chemical splash goggles, nonlatex apron
- beads, assorted colors
- chemical modeling kit
- computer
- glue
- nuts and bolts
- paper clips, assorted sizes and colors
- paper, white and assorted colors
- polystyrene-foam balls, assorted sizes and colors
- scissors
- snap-together blocks
- string
- tape
- trays, plastic (2)
- toothpicks

SAFETY INFORMATION

- Wear indirectly vented chemical splash goggles and a nonlatex apron during the setup, hands-on, and takedown segments of the activity
- Use caution when using sharp tools, which can cut or puncture skin.

indirectly vented chemical splash goggles

DEVELOP A MODEL

1. Consider the reaction in which propane is burned in oxygen to produce carbon dioxide and water. Balance the chemical equation.

$$C_3H_8 + O_2 \rightarrow CO_2 + H_2O$$

2. Write a plan describing which type of model you will use to illustrate the conservation of mass in this reaction. Think about what would work best for demonstrating proportional relationships between the reactants and products. You may use a physical, mathematical, or computer model. You will use your model to show how the amounts of reactants available affect the amounts of products that are made. If you need other materials, ask your teacher if they can be provided.

3. Have your teacher approve your balanced equation and your plan.

4. Construct your model according to your plan. Then, use your model to investigate and record what happens when different amounts of reactants are available.

5. Present your model to your classmates. Explain how it demonstrates the conservation of mass, and use it to show how changing the amount of available reactants affects the amount of carbon dioxide and water produced.

6. Clean up your workstation, dispose of waste, and wash your hands.

| GRAVIMETRIC ANALYSIS | MORE PRACTICE WITH STOICHIOMETRY | EXPLAINING STOICHIOMETRY | Go online to choose one of these other paths. |

Lesson Self-Check

CAN YOU EXPLAIN IT?

FIGURE 14: Tanks aboard NASA's Space Launch System rocket hold liquid hydrogen fuel and liquid oxygen oxidizer.

How did engineers know how large to make the tanks that hold the liquid hydrogen and oxygen in the rocket and how much fuel they would need? A thorough knowledge of the chemical reaction that will boost the rocket into space was needed. Carrying excess reactant would create extra weight without extra thrust, decreasing efficiency and increasing cost. In this lesson, you learned that hydrogen burns in the presence of oxygen to produce water. How do you think you could determine the amount of hydrogen needed for a space flight? Think about the ways stoichiometry is used to solve problems such as this one.

 Evidence Notebook Refer to your notes in your Evidence Notebook to explain how you could determine the amount of hydrogen needed for a space flight. Using this information, answer the following questions:

1. What is the equation for the reaction that takes place in the rocket engine?
2. How and why should this equation be balanced?
3. Given a certain quantity of liquid oxygen, how could you determine the amount of liquid hydrogen needed to react completely with the oxygen?
4. From these quantities, how could you determine how much water is produced?

CHECKPOINTS

Check Your Understanding

1. Select all correct answers for how the law of conservation of mass is met in a balanced equation.

☐ **a.** The same number of atoms of each element appears on both sides of the equation.

☐ **b.** Subscripts are added to balance the number of atoms of each element.

☐ **c.** Formulas of reactants are changed to ensure that the mass of elements is conserved.

☐ **d.** Coefficients are added to balance the number of atoms of each element.

☐ **e.** Formulas of products are changed to ensure that the mass of elements is conserved.

2. Write the coefficients necessary to balance the equation for the reaction between aluminum and hydrochloric acid.

_____ Al + _____ HCl → _____ $AlCl_3$ + _____ H_2

3. Match the correct description of a chemical reaction in column A with events in a model sandwich shop in Column B.

Column A:

Simpler substances are made from a complex substance. ○
A new compound is made. ○
One element replaces another. ○
Two elements are exchanged. ○

Column B:

○ Lettuce is substituted for cheese when making sandwiches.
○ Turkey is put into sandwiches labeled "cheese" and cheese is put into sandwiches labeled "turkey."
○ A new kind of sandwich—turkey and avocado—is made.
○ A sandwich is broken apart into lettuce, meat, and bread.

Sodium chloride is produced from its elements through a synthesis reaction. Use this chemical equation to answer Questions 4-7:

$$Na + Cl_2 \rightarrow NaCl$$

4. What is the correct ratio of coefficients for the balanced equation?

○ **a.** 2:2:1

○ **b.** 1:1:2

○ **c.** 2:1:1

○ **d.** 2:1:2

5. What mass of sodium would be required to produce 25.0 mol of sodium chloride?

○ **a.** 288 g Na

○ **b.** 575 g Na

○ **c.** 1150 g Na

○ **d.** 1460 g Na

6. What mass of chlorine would be required to produce 25.0 mol of sodium chloride?

○ **a.** 222 g Cl_2

○ **b.** 443 g Cl_2

○ **c.** 886 g Cl_2

○ **d.** 1772 g Cl_2

7. How many formula units are present in 25.0 mol of sodium chloride?

○ **a.** 1.51×10^{25} formula units NaCl

○ **b.** 1.60×10^{23} formula units NaCl

○ **c.** 0.428×10^{23} formula units NaCl

○ **d.** 3.52×10^{25} formula units NaCl

8. A chemist mixed sodium sulfide and cadmium nitrate solutions in a test tube. The equation is

$$Na_2S(aq) + Cd(NO_3)_2(aq) \rightarrow 2NaNO_3(aq) + CdS(s)$$

Sodium sulfide is the limiting reactant. Select the substances that are found in the test tube after the reaction has ended.

☐ **a.** Na_2S

☐ **b.** $Cd(NO_3)_2$

☐ **c.** $NaNO_3$

☐ **d.** CdS

CHECKPOINTS (continued)

9. Explain why, when performing stoichiometric calculations, it is important to use a balanced equation and consider the coefficients in the equation when converting from one quantity to another.

_____

_____

_____

10. The first step in the industrial manufacture of nitric acid is the catalytic oxidation of ammonia: $NH_3(g) + O_2(g) \rightarrow NO(g) + H_2O(g)$.

    The equation is unbalanced. The reaction is run using 824 g NH_3 and excess oxygen. How many moles of NO are formed? How many moles of H_2O are formed?

_____

_____

_____

11. Answer the following questions about theoretical yield and actual yield in stoichiometric calculations: How does one determine the theoretical yield and the actual yield? How does the value of the theoretical yield generally compare with the value of the actual yield? How can you compare the two values mathematically and why would you make this comparison?

_____

_____

_____

_____

_____

MAKE YOUR OWN STUDY GUIDE

 In your Evidence Notebook, design a study guide that supports the main ideas from this lesson:

The law of conservation of mass is the basis for writing balanced equations and applies to all chemical reactions.

The mole is the basic unit for all calculations used to determine the expected amount of product or reactant for a chemical reaction.

Reactants might be limiting or in excess.

Remember to include the following information in your study guide:

- Use examples that model main ideas.
- Record explanations for the phenomena you investigated.
- Use evidence to support your explanations. Your support can include drawings, data, graphs, laboratory conclusions, and other evidence recorded throughout the lesson.

Consider how the methods you have developed in this lesson can be used to show that the total amount of matter in all closed systems is conserved.

Intermolecular Forces in Mixtures

A solution of sodium acetate is poured onto a few crystals of sodium acetate on the table.

CAN YOU EXPLAIN IT?

Sodium acetate is a chemical that has a variety of uses, including as a food seasoning, a concrete sealant, and as an active ingredient in heating packs. The beaker in this photo contains a solution of sodium acetate at room temperature. On the table are a few small sodium acetate crystals. The clear solution flows smoothly like water when poured from the beaker. However, instead of forming a pool of liquid, as you might expect, it forms more solid crystals on top of the crystals on the table.

The temperature of the liquid has not changed, so why does the sodium acetate in the solution become solid? It only solidifies once it comes into contact with the sodium acetate crystals that are already on the table. What could be causing this change?

PREDICT Why do you think the sodium acetate in the solution changes to a solid when it is poured on top of sodium acetate crystals?

_____

_____

_____

_____

Explore Online ▶

FIGURE 1: As the sodium acetate solution is poured onto sodium acetate crystals, more crystals form on top of them.

Evidence Notebook As you explore the lesson, gather evidence about the unique properties of substances in solution and how a solution of a substance can quickly crystallize under the right conditions.

Hands-On Lab

Measuring the Electrical Conductivity of Mixtures

In this investigation, you will explore the electrical conductivity of various solutions. A solution is a homogeneous mixture in which two or more substances are uniformly dispersed at the molecular level.

Research Question: Why might some solutions be better conductors of electrical charge than others?

MAKE A CLAIM

In your Evidence Notebook, make a claim about which of the test solutions you think will conduct electricity well. Which do you think will not conduct electricity? Justify your predictions.

MATERIALS

- indirectly vented chemical splash goggles, nonlatex apron, nitrile gloves

- beaker, 100 mL (8)

- conductivity tester

- paper towels

- wash bottle

Test Solutions

- aluminum chloride, $AlCl_3$, solution, 0.05 M (50 mL)

- calcium chloride, $CaCl_2$, solution, 0.05 M (50 mL)

- distilled water (300 mL)

- ethanol, C_2H_5OH, (50 mL)

- sodium chloride, NaCl, solution, 0.05 M (50 mL)

- sugar water (50 mL)

- tap water (50 mL)

SAFETY INFORMATION

- Wear indirectly vented chemical splash goggles, a nonlatex apron, and nitrile gloves during the setup, hands-on, and takedown segments of the activity.

- Never pour chemicals, either used or unused, back into their original container. Dispose of chemicals according to your teacher's instructions.

- Use caution when working with glassware, which can shatter if dropped and cut skin.

- Tell your teacher immediately if you spill chemicals on yourself, the work surface, or floor.

PLAN THE INVESTIGATION

In your Evidence Notebook, write a procedure to test the electrical conductivity of the seven test solutions. Consider the accuracy you could achieve based on the limitations of your materials. Your procedure should also include safety considerations and any additional materials you may need. Have your procedure and safety plans checked by your teacher before you begin.

indirectly vented chemical splash goggles

COLLECT DATA

Decide what data to record for each solution, the conditions for the measurements, and how many trials you will need to complete. Develop a data table in your Evidence Notebook.

ANALYZE

Answer the following questions in your Evidence Notebook.

1. Did the result you found for distilled water match your result for tap water? Explain why the results do or do not make sense.

2. Compare the results you found for NaCl solution and sugar water. Why do you think the results were the same or different?

3. Compare your results for $AlCl_3$, $CaCl_2$, and NaCl. Why do you think the results were the same or different?

DRAW CONCLUSIONS

Write a conclusion that addresses each of the points below.

Claim Compare how well each of the solutions you tested conducted electricity. What about their physical or chemical properties could influence this ability?

Evidence Give specific examples from your data to support your claim.

Reasoning Explain how the evidence you have supports your claim. Describe, in detail, the connections between the evidence you cited and the argument you are making.

_____
_____
_____
_____
_____
_____
_____
_____
_____
_____
_____
_____
_____
_____
_____
_____
_____
_____

 Evidence Notebook Recall what you know about valence electrons, atomic structure, bonding, and electrical charge. How might these relate to the conductivity of solutions?

Describing Solutions

FIGURE 2: Cooking oil being poured into water

If you've ever looked at a bottle of oil and vinegar dressing, you probably noticed that the oil settles in a layer above the vinegar. You can mix the oil and vinegar by shaking the bottle, but they quickly settle into layers again. Regardless of how hard you try, oil and vinegar will not mix for long.

Other substances, however, mix easily. For example, both salt and sugar readily mix with water. In fact, both salt and sugar water solutions play an important role in many living things and in Earth's systems. Heating and cooling the water can often have a strong effect on each of the materials that will go into solution and the speed at which they dissolve.

 Collaborate Discuss with a partner why some substances dissolve easily while others require shaking or stirring, or may not dissolve at all. Why might heating affect the rate and amount of substance that can dissolve?

Solutions contain both a solvent and a solute. The solvent is the substance in which the solute dissolves. The solvent usually makes up the greatest amount of the solution. Solutions are described as being *homogeneous* because, at the molecular level, the solute particles are evenly distributed throughout the solvent. Solute particles may be atoms, molecules, or ions. They are so small that they maintain their even distribution without settling. One substance is *soluble* in another if it can dissolve in that substance.

The Solution Process

If you've ever looked closely enough at particles of salt, you may have seen that it is made of tiny crystals. When stirred into water, however, it does not keep this crystal shape. The crystals quickly begin to break apart. The smaller the crystals are to begin with, the easier it is to dissolve the salt in the water.

APPLY Model how the interaction of solvent particles with a large block of solute is different from the interaction of solvent particles with finely powdered solute.

Think about what happens to a single crystal of salt when placed into a volume of water. As the salt dissolves, only the particles on the surface of the crystal touch the water. The rate of dissolving depends on the surface area of the crystal. If you were to break the single salt crystal into smaller crystals before mixing, the salt will dissolve faster. The separate crystals have a greater surface area that can interact with the water.

PREDICT How might stirring, shaking, or heating a mixture help make the solute dissolve more quickly?

_____

_____

_____

_____

Suppose you stir salt into water and watch it dissolve. Then you stir in more salt, and it too dissolves. At some point, however, no more salt will dissolve. Any more that you add will remain as solid crystals in the water. There is a limit to how much of a particular solute can dissolve in a particular solvent at a certain temperature. If the system involves gases, both pressure and temperature limit the amount of solute that can dissolve in a solvent.

Explore Online ▶

Hands-On Lab

Temperature and Solubility
Investigate how temperature affects the solubility of a substance.

Let's consider more closely what happens when crystals of salt are mixed with water. Gradually the salt molecules begin to move from the crystals into the water. This is known as _dissolution_. Once dissolved by the water, however, the molecules are colliding with each other. Some of these collisions will form crystals again. This is known as _recrystallization_. Both processes are constantly occurring within the solution at the same time. Eventually, both will occur at the same rate. They will reach an equilibrium as shown in Figure 3.

FIGURE 3: When the rate of dissolution is greater than the rate of recrystallization, the solution is dissolving. When the rates are equal, the solution is at equilibrium.

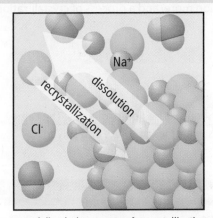

rate of dissolution > rate of recrystallization
Dissolving

rate of dissolution = rate of recrystallization
Equilibrium

Adding more solute to a solution that is in equilibrium at a given temperature will not increase the amount that is dissolved in the solvent. The amount of solute that a solvent can dissolve depends on the volume of the solvent. A solution that contains the maximum amount of dissolved solute is _saturated_. If you increase the amount of solvent in a saturated solution, the solution becomes _unsaturated_ and you can dissolve more solute. Each solution has a given ratio of solvent to solute at a given temperature.

Keep in mind, however, that the amount of solute that can dissolve depends on the temperature of the solution. For gases, it also depends on pressure. Solubility is the ability of a solute to dissolve in a solvent at a given temperature and pressure. Increasing the temperature of a solution generally increases the solubility of a solute in the solvent. Decreasing the temperature decreases the solubility, so some of the dissolved solute might come out of solution and form a solid.

Explore Online ▶

FIGURE 4: Solute in this supersaturated sodium acetate solution crystallized when a sodium acetate crystal was added.

A *supersaturated* solution contains more solute than its solubility limit. Honey, for example, is a naturally occurring supersaturated solution. Under certain conditions, you can dissolve more solute in a saturated solution by heating it, adding the extra solute, and then slowly cooling it. A supersaturated solution, however, is not stable. It will remain supersaturated only as long as it remains undisturbed. This principle explains why honey crystallizes at colder temperatures.

EXPLAIN When a small crystal of sodium acetate was added to a supersaturated solution of sodium acetate, solute in the solution crystallized, as shown in Figure 4. Why do think this happened?

_____

_____

_____

_____

_____

Any increase in temperature, tapping the solution, or even dropping a single crystal of solute into the solution, called *seeding*, can disturb the solution and cause crystals to form. The formation of one crystal disturbs the solution more, and a process of crystallization begins throughout the solution.

Factors Affecting Solubility

The solvent and solute of a solution can be either a solid, a liquid, or a gas. The same is true for the solute. The table below describes examples of solute and solvent combinations in familiar solutions.

Example	Solute State	Solvent State
oxygen in nitrogen	gas	gas
carbon dioxide in water	gas	liquid
alcohol in water	liquid	liquid
mercury in silver and tin	liquid	solid
sugar in water	solid	liquid
copper in nickel	solid	solid

Most solutions used in chemistry have liquid solvents. A solution in which the solvent is water is called an *aqueous solution*. Chemical formulas are sometimes labeled (*aq*) to identify aqueous solutions. Aqueous solutions are particularly important because water is able to dissolve many substances, which is why water is known as the universal solvent. Nearly 71% of Earth's surface is covered by water, and water is also a key component of the atmosphere. Water also accounts for about 70% of the mass of cells, so the chemistry of water is critical to all life.

Solubility and Polarity

Recall that water molecules are polar. Oxygen atoms have a slightly stronger attraction for electrons than hydrogen atoms do. The oxygen part of a water molecule therefore has a partial negative charge, labeled δ^- in Figure 5, and the hydrogen part has a partial positive charge, labeled δ^+. When crystals of an ionic solid, such as sodium chloride, NaCl, dissolve in water, these positive and negative ends separate the sodium and chloride ions. The negatively charged parts of water molecules attract and surround the positive ions of the ionic solid. The positively charged parts of water molecules attract and surround the negative ions of the ionic solid. This process is called *hydration* and is how ionic compounds dissolve.

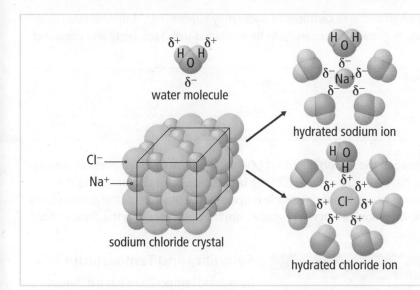

FIGURE 5: Water's polarity allows it to hydrate positive and negative ions of an ionic solid. This conceptual model shows that the partial negative charge of water is attracted to the positive ion. The partial positive charge of water is attracted to the negative ion.

INFER Complete the statement about the behavior of nonpolar solvents.

Ionic compounds would be generally   soluble | not soluble   in nonpolar solvents. The nonpolar solvents   have | do not have   the charges necessary to draw the ions out of the crystal and into solution.

Nonpolar substances, such as fats, oils, and greases, do not easily dissolve in polar liquids, because the forces between the polar molecules are stronger. This is why oil and water form layers instead of mixing. Liquids that are not soluble in each other are called *immiscible*. Nonpolar substances generally do dissolve in nonpolar liquids, such as gasoline and carbon tetrachloride. The intermolecular forces are weak in nonpolar solvents, so both solvent and solute particles can mix freely. Liquids that dissolve freely in one another in any proportion are called *miscible*.

 Collaborate A common way to remember the relationship between polarity and solubility is "like dissolves like." With a partner, explain how this description is useful for determining the solubility of substances.

Solubility and Pressure

Because the particles in liquids and solids are already very close together, pressure has little effect on the solubility of substances in these states. Changes in pressure, however, do affect the solubility of gases. Imagine you have a closed container containing a liquid and a gas, as shown in Figure 6. The liquid is the solvent and the gas above it is the solute. When the pressure on the system is increased, the gas and liquid particles collide more often than they did at the original pressure. As a result, more gas dissolves in the liquid.

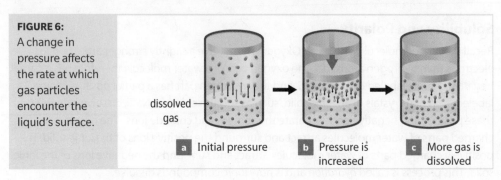

FIGURE 6: A change in pressure affects the rate at which gas particles encounter the liquid's surface.

dissolved gas

a Initial pressure   b Pressure is increased   c More gas is dissolved

APPLY An unopened bottle of carbonated water may appear "flat," but when you open it, the water fizzes. How can this observation be explained using solubility and pressure?

_____

_____

_____

_____

Carbonated beverages, those with dissolved CO_2 gas, demonstrate how pressure affects the solubility of a gas. During production of the beverage, CO_2 gas is forced into the liquid under high pressures. When the bottle is opened, the pressure of the gas suddenly decreases. The carbon dioxide can now escape from the liquid, causing the drink to fizz.

Solubility of Solids in Liquid

FIGURE 7: Effect of temperature on the solubility of a solid in a liquid

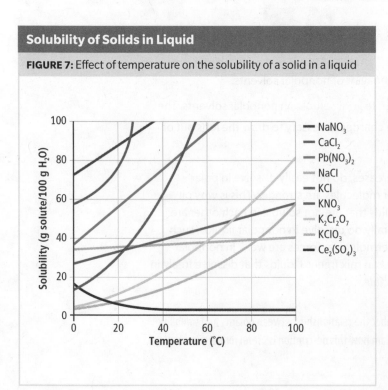

- NaNO₃
- CaCl₂
- Pb(NO₃)₂
- NaCl
- KCl
- KNO₃
- K₂Cr₂O₇
- KClO₃
- Ce₂(SO₄)₃

Solubility and Temperature

Increasing temperature has a different effect on the solubility of liquids and gases. Figures 7 and 8 show how the solubility of different gases and liquids change when the temperature is increased.

ANALYZE Based on Figure 7, what effect does temperature have on the solubility of a solid in a liquid?

○ **a.** Solubility always increases with an increase in temperature.

○ **b.** Solubility always decreases with an increase in temperature.

○ **c.** Solubility generally increases with an increase in temperature, but sometimes decreases.

○ **d.** Solubility generally decreases with an increase in temperature, but sometimes increases.

For a solid dissolved in a liquid, increasing the temperature generally increases the solubility as well. When the temperature is increased, the particles of the solution have more kinetic energy. The increased movement allows the solvent particles to surround and dissolve the solute particles more effectively.

The effect of temperature on solubility is different for a gas dissolved in a liquid. As shown in Figure 8, as temperature increases, the gas particles have more kinetic energy and are better able to escape from the liquid solvent. For all gases, increasing temperature decreases the solubility of the gas. As in liquids and solids, polarity also affects the solubility of the gas particles.

Solubility of Gases in Liquid

FIGURE 8: Effect of temperature on the solubility of a gas in a liquid

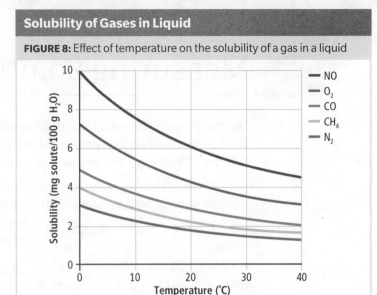

INFER Would you expect an opened can of carbonated water to go "flat" quicker if it was cold or warm? Use evidence to support your claim.

_____

_____

_____

_____

 Patterns

Colloids and Suspensions

When you add a solid to a liquid, the solid might dissolve, forming a solution. A solution, however, is not the only possible result of adding a solid to a liquid. _Suspensions_ are heterogeneous mixtures in which the solute particles are very large and settle out of the solution. An example of a suspension is a jar of muddy water. When you mix the jar, the water appears uniform and cloudy. But if left undisturbed, the soil particles will settle to the bottom of the container.

FIGURE 9: The Tyndall Effect

Colloids have particles that are smaller than the particles in a suspension but larger than those in a solution. In a jar of muddy water, when the large soil particles settle to the bottom, the water can still appear cloudy. This is because there are colloidal particles in the water. Many other colloids appear homogeneous, but the particles are actually large enough to scatter light. This effect, known as the Tyndall effect, is shown in Figure 9. This effect is not seen in true solutions because only the small, randomly moving particles in a colloid can scatter light.

 Collaborate Fog is an example of a colloid—liquid water particles dispersed in air. When driving in foggy conditions, experts say that drivers should use low-beam or fog lights but never high-beam lights. With a partner, argue whether this is good or bad advice.

Measuring Solution Composition

The concentration of a solution is the amount of solute in a given amount of solvent. Some medications are solutions—a one-teaspoon dose at the correct concentration might cure the patient, while the same dose in the wrong concentration might kill the patient.

Scientists can determine the concentration of a solution by finding the molarity of the solution. *Molarity* (*M*) is the number of moles of solute in one liter of solution.

$$\text{Molarity } (M) = \frac{\text{amount of solute (mol)}}{\text{volume of solution (L)}}$$

For example, a one-molar solution of sodium hydroxide, NaOH, contains one mole of NaOH in every liter of solution. The concentration of a one-molar solution of sodium hydroxide is written as 1 M NaOH.

SAMPLE PROBLEM An IV saline solution commonly found in hospitals contains 9.00 grams of NaCl dissolved in enough solvent to form a solution with a volume of 1.00 L. What is the molarity of the saline solution?

ANALYZE **Given:** solute mass = 9.00 g NaCl

solution volume = 1.00 L

Unknown: molarity of NaCl solution

SOLVE Use the periodic table to compute the molar mass of NaCl as 58.44 g/mol. Calculate the molarity using the molar mass of NaCl as a conversion factor.

$$\frac{9.00 \text{ g NaCl}}{1.00 \text{ L solution}} \times \frac{1 \text{ mol NaCl}}{58.44 \text{ g NaCl}} = 0.154 \text{ M NaCl}$$

PRACTICE PROBLEM SOLVE A scientist wants to test the effects of different potassium chloride, KCl, solution concentrations. Potassium chloride is sometimes used to treat conditions that result from potassium depletion, such as cardiac or kidney disease. The scientist dissolves 255 g KCl to make a 3.20 L solution. Use the space provided to calculate the molarity of the potassium chloride solution.

_____ M KCl

You may have heard of solutions being referred to as *dilute* or *concentrated*, but these are not very definite terms. *Dilute* means that there is a relatively small amount of solute in a solvent. *Concentrated*, on the other hand, means that there is a relatively large amount of solute in a solvent. It is important to note that these terms are unrelated to the degree to which a solution is saturated. A saturated solution of a substance that is not very soluble might be very dilute.

If a scientist dilutes 1.00 L of a 0.500 M NaOH solution to 2.00 L, she could find the new concentration simply by using the ratio $M_1V_1 = M_2V_2$.

$$\frac{(0.500\ M)(1.00\ L)}{(2.00\ L)} = 0.250\ M$$

Solutions are often diluted just before use because those of greater molarity take up less lab space. Chemists can have solutions of greater molarity and lower volume in stock and then dilute them to ones of higher volume and lower molarity for use.

Note that a 1 M solution is not made by adding 1 mol of solute to 1 L of solvent. Instead, 1 mole of solute is first dissolved in less than 1 L of solvent. The resulting solution is carefully diluted with more solvent to bring the total volume to 1 L.

SAMPLE PROBLEM	A 21.7 g sample of potassium chromate is needed to carry out a reaction in an aqueous solution of potassium chromate. All you have on hand is 5.00 L of a 6.00 M K_2CrO_4 solution. What volume of the solution is needed to give you the 21.7 g K_2CrO_4 needed for the reaction?
ANALYZE	**Given:** volume of solution = 5.00 L concentration of solution = 6.00 M K_2CrO_4 **Unknown:** volume of K_2CrO_4 solution in L
PLAN	The molarity indicates the moles of solute that are in 1.00 L of solution. Given the mass of solute needed, the amount in moles of solute can be found. Use the molarity and the amount, in moles, of K_2CrO_4 to determine the volume of K_2CrO_4 that will provide 21.7 g. <div align="center">grams of solute → moles solute</div> <div align="center">moles solute and molarity → liters of solution needed</div>
SOLVE	To get the moles of solute, you'll need to calculate the molar mass of K_2CrO_4. <div align="center">1 mol K_2CrO_4 = 194.2 g K_2CrO_4</div> <div align="center">21.7 g K₂CrO₄ × $\dfrac{1\ \text{mol } K_2CrO_4}{194.2\ \text{g } K_2CrO_4}$ = 0.112 mol K_2CrO_4</div> Now use the moles of solute and the molarity to find the liters of solution needed: <div align="center">0.112 mol K₂CrO₄ = $\dfrac{1L}{6.0\ \text{mol } k_2CrO_4}$</div> <div align="center">= 0.019 L of K_2CrO_4 solution</div>
PRACTICE PROBLEM	**SOLVE** To prepare a 4.20 M HCl solution that contains 655 g HCl, the volume of the solution must be _____ L.

 Evidence Notebook Review the demonstration of sodium acetate forming a crystal column as it is poured. In your Evidence Notebook, describe this solution on a molecular scale. How does the microscopic arrangement of particles affect the macroscopic behavior of the solution?

Analyzing the Behavior of Solutions

Ionic and covalent substances often behave differently when dissolved in an aqueous solution. Suppose you dissolve an ionic substance, such as sodium chloride, in a polar solvent, such as water. Sodium chloride contains ionic bonds, which means sodium ions and chlorine ions already exist before the substance is added to the water. The ionic compound dissolves as the polar water molecules surround and separate the ions in a process called *dissociation*.

Some covalent compounds, such as hydrochloric acid, also dissolve in polar solvents. Hydrogen chloride is a polar covalent bond that forms ions when dissolved in a polar compound. When dissolved in water, these ions constitute the acid hydrochloric acid. The process in which some polar covalent solute molecules from ions in solution is called *ionization*.

MODEL In the space provided, develop a model that explains the difference between dissociation and ionization. How can your model help you remember these differences?

Modeling the Dissociation of Ionic Compounds

When dissolved in a solvent, ionic compounds dissociate completely into their separate ions. For example, if you dissolve silver nitrate, $AgNO_3$, in water, the water does not actually contain $AgNO_3$. It contains only Ag^+ and NO_3^- ions. For each mole of $AgNO_3$ that you dissolve, the solution will contain a total of two moles of ions, one mole of Ag^+ ions and one mole of NO_3^- ions.

$$AgNO_3(s) \rightarrow Ag^+(aq) + NO_3^-(aq)$$

| 1 mole | 1 mole | 1 mole |

Similarly, a solution of manganese bromide, $MnBr_2$ contains the ions Mn^{2+} and Br^-. The balanced equation shows that a total of three moles of ions are produced for each mole of $MnBr_2$, one mole of Mn^{2+} ions and two moles of Br^- ions.

$$MnBr_2(s) \rightarrow Mn^{2+}(aq) + 2Br^-(aq)$$

| 1 mole | 1 mole | 2 moles |

APPLY Explain how matter is conserved on a molecular scale when ionic compounds dissociate in solution.

Even though ionic compounds dissociate completely, if the amount of compound exceeds its solubility in the solution, some of the compound will not dissociate. Some ionic compounds' solubilities are so low that they are considered *insoluble*. Through a lot of observation, chemists have developed rules that describe some general patterns of solubility for ionic compounds.

Using these patterns, we can predict whether a compound made of a certain combination of ions is soluble. For example, almost all compounds containing sodium are soluble, while most sulfides are insoluble. If a solution contains several different ions, the solubility rules help predict which combination of ions will be the first to become insoluble as their concentrations increase.

Explore Online

Hands-On Lab

Reacting Ionic Species in Aqueous Solution
Mix ionic compounds in aqueous solution to determine the solubility of the products.

PREDICT Sodium nitrate and ammonium chloride are soluble in water. Sodium chloride and ammonium nitrate are also soluble in water. On a molecular scale, describe the solution that results when solutions of sodium nitrate and ammonium chloride are mixed.

_____

_____

_____

If the mixing results in a combination of ions that forms an insoluble compound, a precipitation reaction will occur. Precipitation occurs when the attraction between the ions is greater than the attraction between the ions and surrounding water molecules. Precipitation reactions can be used for making pigments, removing salts from water in water treatment, and in classical chemical analysis.

Patterns in solubility help predict what precipitate will form when two compounds are mixed. Suppose you mix an aqueous solution of potassium iodide with an aqueous solution of lead nitrate. Both solutions are colorless, but when you mix them, a bright yellow solid forms. The precipitate could be either potassium nitrate or lead iodide. Using patterns of solubility, scientists can determine that lead iodide is insoluble, and it is therefore the yellow precipitate shown in Figure 10.

FIGURE 10: A precipitation reaction of aqueous lead nitrate and aqueous potassium iodide

 Scientific Knowledge Assumes an Order and Consistency in Natural Systems

Recycling Palladium

Dental fixtures often include precious metals because of their low reactivity. If the fixtures are removed, the metal can be recovered by dissolving the scrap in a carefully chosen solvent in which the metal precipitates. Palladium in dental scrap can be retrieved by dissolving the scrap in hydrochloric acid and using a reagent to precipitate out the palladium from the solution. This kind of recycling saves energy compared to mining and processing new raw palladium ore. It also conserves a limited valuable resource from going to a landfill.

FIGURE 11: Palladium can be recovered from dental scraps.

 Language Arts Connection Research other precipitation reactions that are used to recycle rare materials. How do these reactions offset the impacts of mining? Write a short newspaper article describing your findings.

Modeling the Ionization of Molecular Compounds

FIGURE 12: HCl completely ionizes in water. $HC_2H_3O_2$ partially ionizes in water.

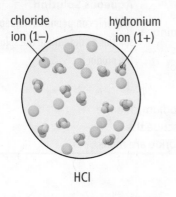

chloride
ion (1–)

hydronium
ion (1+)

HCl

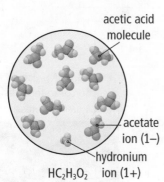

acetic acid
molecule

acetate
ion (1–)

hydronium
ion (1+)

$HC_2H_3O_2$

Water is able to ionize some polar molecular compounds. The extent to which the ionization occurs depends on the difference in strength of the solute's molecular bond and the attraction of the water molecules. If water's attraction is stronger, the covalent bond of the solute molecule breaks apart and forms ions. Hydrogen chloride completely ionizes in water because the attraction of the water molecules breaks the H–Cl bond, forming a hydrogen ion, H^+, and a chloride ion, Cl^-.

$$HCl \rightarrow H^+(aq) + Cl^-(aq)$$

Molecular compounds such as HCl that have a hydrogen atom covalently bonded to a highly electronegative atom can release H^+ ions in an aqueous solution. An H^+ ion, however, is so strongly attracted to other charged particles that it readily bonds covalently with a water molecule.

$$H_2O(l) + HCl(g) \rightarrow H_3O^+(aq) + Cl^-(aq)$$

H_3O^+ is known as a *hydronium ion*. The ionization of a compound in which an H^+ ion forms a hydronium ion is described as donating a proton (that is, an H^+ ion) to a water molecule.

Some molecular compounds have stronger bonds to their hydrogen atoms. Acetic acid (household vinegar), $HC_2H_3O_2$, ionizes less readily because hydrogen bonds more strongly to the molecule. Some acetic acid molecules ionize in water, but most remain molecules, so that both exist in solution. Some molecular compounds, such as sugar, dissolve in water but do not form ions.

EXPLAIN What determines whether a molecular compound will ionize in water?

_____

_____

_____

Strong and Weak Electrolytes

You previously tested the conductivity of different solutions. An *electrolyte* is a substance that conducts an electric current when dissolved in solution because it yields ions. A *nonelectrolyte* is a substance that does not conduct an electric current when dissolved in solution because it does not yield ions. You likely found that some electrolytes conduct electricity better than others. The strength with which substances conduct an electric current is related to their ability to form ions in solution.

APPLY Complete the statement by selecting the correct terms.

A substance such as sodium chloride dissociates completely in water. Sodium chloride conducts electricity poorly | well because all | some | none of the dissolved compound forms ions. A substance such as acetic acid only partially ionizes in water. Acetic acid would conduct electricity poorly | well because all | some | none of the dissolved compound forms ions.

Matter and Energy Your body needs electrolytes to help send the electrical impulses that tell your muscles to contract. When you work out, your body loses electrolytes through sweat. Sports drinks supply your body with additional water as well as electrolytes to replace what you've lost. Research why these drinks are so popular with athletes. Would your body replace the lost electrolytes without a sports drink?

All soluble ionic compounds are considered *strong electrolytes*. A strong electrolyte is any compound whose dilute aqueous solutions conduct electricity well. A limited number of molecular compounds, such as HCl, also yield only ions when they dissolve and are also strong electrolytes. A *weak electrolyte* forms only a few ions in water, so it is not a good conductor of electric current. Ammonia, NH_3, is an example of a weak electrolyte. When ammonia is dissolved in water, only about one out of every hundred ammonia molecules will interact with water molecules to produce ions.

Evidence Notebook Review your data from the electrical conductivity investigation. In your Evidence Notebook, use your conductivity measurements to classify each compound as a strong electrolyte, a weak electrolyte, or a nonelectrolyte.

Colligative Properties

Pure water cannot conduct electricity, freezes at 0 °C, and boils at 100 °C. Salt water does conduct electricity, freezes at a slightly lower temperature than pure water, and boils at a slightly higher temperature than pure water. What could cause the differences between these two liquids? A solution made by dissolving a solute in a liquid will have physical and chemical properties that the solvent alone did not have.

Salt can be added to icy sidewalks to melt the ice. The salt actually lowers the freezing point of the water. Therefore, ice is able to melt at a lower temperature than it normally would. This change is called *freezing-point depression*. The addition of salt also raises the boiling point of the solvent. This change is called the *boiling-point elevation*.

INFER Imagine what would happen if ocean water froze each time the temperature reached the freezing point of pure water, 0 °C. Tides and the constant movement of the water partly explain why the ocean water remains liquid. How does freezing-point depression also explain the behavior of ocean water?

_____

_____

_____

_____

_____

FIGURE 13: Ocean water remains liquid.

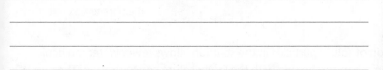

The boiling point and freezing point of a solution differ from those of the pure solvent. A nonvolatile solute, which is a substance that has little tendency to become a gas under existing conditions, raises the boiling point and lowers the freezing point of a solution. For example, adding glycol to a car's radiator increases the boiling point of water in the radiator, which prevents overheating. Adding glycol also lowers the freezing point, preventing freezing in cold weather.

The presence of solutes (either molecules or ions) affects the properties of solutions. *Colligative properties* are dependent on the concentration of solute particles, but are not dependent on the identity of the solute particles. The greater the concentration of solute particles in a certain mass of solvent, the greater the change in the colligative property.

APPLY When added to water, would you expect sodium chloride, NaCl, or calcium chloride, $CaCl_2$, to have a greater effect on the boiling-point elevation of the solution?

One mole of NaCl dissolves to give one | two | three dissolved particles per mole.

One mole of $CaCl_2$ dissolves to give one | two | three dissolved particles per mole.

Therefore, NaCl will have a lesser | greater effect than $CaCl_2$ when added to water.

Vapor pressure is the pressure caused by molecules in the gas phase that are in equilibrium with the liquid phase. Vapor pressure is a colligative property. Increasing the concentration of solute particles means fewer solvent particles are able to escape from the liquid to enter the gas phase, lowering the vapor pressure. The solution remains liquid over a larger temperature range. The change in vapor pressure affects the boiling and freezing points of the solution, making these colligative properties as well.

Figure 14 shows a U-tube containing sucrose solutions of different concentrations. The solutions are separated by a semipermeable membrane that blocks the passage of certain particles but allows others to pass through. In this case, the larger sucrose molecules are blocked, but the smaller water molecules can pass through freely. Over time, the level of the more highly concentrated sucrose solution will rise.

 Collaborate With a partner, discuss what is happening in the U-tube that would cause the level of solution to change. Why did only the more highly concentrated solution change, and not the lower? Use evidence from Figure 14 to support your ideas.

FIGURE 14:
Osmosis is the movement of solvent molecules from the solution with lower solute concentration to the solution with higher solute concentration.

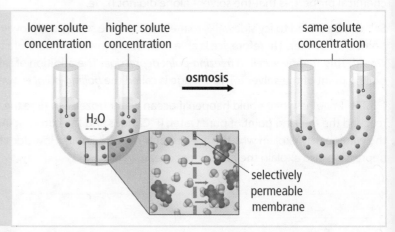

A higher concentration of solute particles in the solution allows fewer water molecules to strike the membrane than on the side with the lower solute concentration. The rate of water molecules moving into the higher concentration solution is greater than the rate moving in the opposite direction. *Osmosis* is the diffusion of a solvent through a semipermeable membrane to the side of higher solute concentration.

As the difference in the heights of the solutions increases, an increasing pressure difference will develop. Eventually, the rate of solvent molecules moving each way across the membrane will become equal. *Osmotic pressure* is the external pressure that must be applied to stop osmosis. Osmotic pressure is dependent on the concentration of solute particles, not on the type of solute particles, so it is also a colligative property.

Stability and Change

Osmosis in Living Systems

Cells are surrounded by a semipermeable membrane that regulates the movement of water and other substances into and out of the cell. Biological cells depend on the proper functioning of osmosis. Osmoregulation is the feedback mechanism by which cells control osmotic pressure.

A cell is said to be isotonic if the concentration of solute is the same both inside and outside the cell. If the concentration of solute decreases inside the cell, it becomes hypertonic and water will start to move out of the cell, causing it to shrink. If the concentration of solute increases inside the cell, it becomes hypotonic and water will start to move into the cell, causing it to swell. IV solutions given to hospital patients need to be isotonic with respect to the patients' blood for this reason.

Explore Online ▶

Hands-On Lab

Diffusion and Cell Membranes
Investigate osmosis across a semipermeable membrane.

MODEL Blood cells in three different solutions are shown below. Label each cell as either isotonic, hypertonic, or hypotonic. Then add arrows to the cells at the bottom to model the movement of water into and out of the cell.

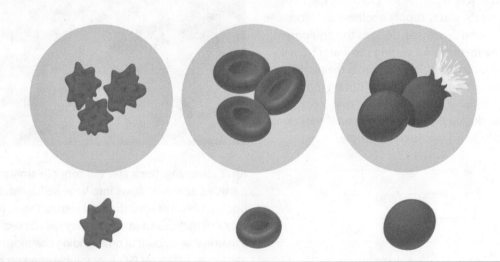

In plants, hypotonic cells enable plants to maintain an upright structure. The cell walls of plants constrain the expansion of the cells resulting in the buildup of water pressure inside the cell. This pressure causes the rigidity the plant needs to stand upright.

APPLY Complete the statement by selecting the correct terms.

A plant wilts when the cells become isotonic | hypertonic | hypotonic relative to the environment. As water flows into | out of the cell, the cell loses | gains pressure, causing it to wilt.

Evidence Notebook Sodium acetate is the sodium salt of acetic acid. Research the properties of sodium acetate, CH_3CO_2Na. What kind of solution is sodium acetate and what is it used for?

Careers in Engineering

Water Supply Engineer

When you turn on a faucet, you expect a flow of clean, drinkable water. If you are confident in the purity of your water supply, you can thank a water supply engineer. Water supply engineers identify and develop water sources, produce and maintain water purification systems, and develop water distribution systems.

One of the main challenges is developing steps for water purification. The water you drink may originate in a lake or a river, or it may come from groundwater. The water is usually pumped to the surface from drilled wells that are sometimes hundreds of feet deep.

Regardless of its source, the water must be cleaned and purified before it can be sent to homes, schools, and businesses. A water supply engineer develops the water purification processes, designs the equipment, and plans the methods for testing the water to make sure it is fit for consumption. California maintains over 24 000 water quality testing sites to obtain these data.

INFER What do you think would happen if water was not purified before it was used by people?

_____

_____

_____

_____

_____

_____

_____

_____

_____

_____

_____

_____

Screening is the first step in the process. During screening, water passes through a screen to remove larger objects such as trash, leaves, twigs, and even fish. The fish are returned to the stream beyond the intake location for the water purification plant.

FIGURE 15: A water supply engineer collecting a sample

After screening, the water still contains smaller particles, so it next flows into large sedimentation pools where this solid material settles. Often, the water contains particles so small that they will not settle out in a reasonable amount of time. Adding chemicals such as aluminum sulfate, $Al_2(SO_4)_3$, or soluble iron salts can result in a precipitate that settles out along with the particles. Unwanted ions, such as magnesium ions that cause hard water, are also precipitated out. The precipitates are removed through different filtration processes.

Water from rivers and lakes is likely to be contaminated with bacteria and so must be disinfected. This is usually the last step in water treatment before the water is piped to consumers. Chlorine gas is the cheapest and most common substance used to disinfect water on a large scale. However, it can react to form chlorine-containing organic byproducts that may cause cancer. As a result, chlorine treatment is minimized and supplemented by treatment with chloramine, NH_2Cl (g). Chloramine is also an effective disinfectant that does not form harmful byproducts.

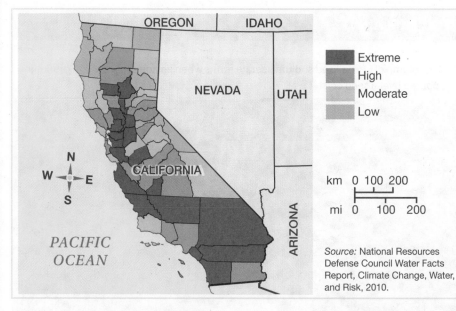

FIGURE 16: Some areas in California are at extreme risk of stressing their water supply. Water supply engineers must design ways to maintain freshwater distribution, even though water supplies will become more stressed in the coming years.

Legend:
- Extreme
- High
- Moderate
- Low

km 0 100 200
mi 0 100 200

Source: National Resources Defense Council Water Facts Report, Climate Change, Water, and Risk, 2010.

California has had several major droughts in the last century in which low precipitation levels caused decreases in surface water runoff that supplies water for basic needs. Water supply engineers must monitor water supply levels and the demand on these supplies and find ways to mitigate the stress on water resources. Figure 16 shows areas in California that are at risk of stressing water supplies.

ANALYZE What areas in California are at most risk of low water supplies? How could these areas lower their demand for water? How might a water supply engineer help reduce this stress?

_____

_____

_____

_____

_____

Water supply engineers monitor water supplies to predict when they will be insufficient. This data helps address the problem of developing and maintaining water retrieval systems from dwindling supplies.

After humans use water for a variety of domestic, agricultural, and industrial purposes, the used water needs to be cleansed before it can be released back into rivers. Cleansing of water sources helps prevent waterborne diseases, which have been a primary cause of death for more than a million people per year.

Earth has a limited supply of water that is continually recycled through natural and human-designed purification systems. Modern sanitation systems and water treatment plants have saved more lives than nearly any other improvement in our health care system. Water chemists and engineers play an essential societal role in this process.

Chemistry in Your Community Imagine you are a water supply engineer. Your task is to develop a water treatment plant for a community located away from developed areas. Write a report describing questions you would ask and steps you would take to identify and develop a suitable source of water for this community. When writing your report, consider how the diverse needs of the community might influence the water treatment system you develop. How will you address their demand for water while keeping the stress on the water resource low?

 SEPARATING SALT MIXTURES   **TESTING WATER FOR IONS**   **REVERSE OSMOSIS**   Go online to choose one of these other paths.

Lesson Self-Check

CAN YOU EXPLAIN IT?

FIGURE 17: A column of crystallized sodium acetate forms when an aqueous solution of sodium acetate is poured over a seed crystal.

A solution consists of a solute dissolved in a solvent. The sodium acetate solution in the beaker consists of the ionic compound sodium acetate, CH_3CO_2Na, dissolved in water. In the beaker, the solution is a clear liquid. Figure 17 demonstrates that when the solution is poured on top of a few crystals of sodium acetate, it forms a column of crystalline solid.

 Evidence Notebook Refer to your notes in your Evidence Notebook to explain why the sodium acetate forms a crystalline solid when it is poured instead of remaining in liquid form. Your explanation should include a discussion of the following:

1. Make a claim about the impact of solubility on the sodium acetate experiment.
2. What evidence supports your claim? Why is the seed crystal required for this phenomenon to occur?
3. Suppose you changed the temperature of the sodium acetate solution before pouring it from the beaker. Would you observe the same result if it were cooled first? Would you observe the same result if it were heated? Explain why or why not.

CHECKPOINTS

Check Your Understanding

1. Solutions are produced from each of these compounds. Which would most likely produce a solution that would conduct an electrical current? Select all correct answers.
   - ☐ **a.** aluminum chloride, $AlCl_3$
   - ☐ **b.** chromium trioxide, CrO_3
   - ☐ **c.** ethanol, C_2H_5OH
   - ☐ **d.** glucose, $C_6H_{12}O_6$
   - ☐ **e.** sodium azide, NaN_3

2. Which statement correctly describes the effect of an increase in temperature on the solubility of a solid dissolved in a liquid?
   - ○ **a.** Solubility increases for all solids.
   - ○ **b.** Solubility decreases for all solids.
   - ○ **c.** Solubility increases for most solids but decreases for some.
   - ○ **d.** Solubility decreases for most solids but increases for some.

3. Which statement correctly describes the effect of an increase in temperature on the solubility of a gas dissolved in a liquid?
   - ○ **a.** Solubility increases for all gases.
   - ○ **b.** Solubility decreases for all gases.
   - ○ **c.** Solubility increases for most gases but decreases for some.
   - ○ **d.** Solubility decreases for most gases but increases for some.

4. Which statement correctly describes the effect of pressure on the solubility of a substance?
   - ○ **a.** A decrease in pressure increases the solubility of most liquids.
   - ○ **b.** Solids experience the greatest effect from changes in pressure.
   - ○ **c.** Changes in pressure cannot increase solubility.
   - ○ **d.** Increased pressure causes more gas particles to dissolve in liquids.

5. Complete the statement.

   The freezing point of pure water is higher | lower than the freezing point when a solute is dissolved in the water. The change in the freezing point occurs because the vapor pressure of the solution is higher | lower than that of the pure water. This change in vapor pressure also causes the boiling point of the solution to be higher | lower than the vapor pressure of pure water. The change in boiling point is directly proportional to the number of | identity of the solute particles.

6. Which of the following types of compounds is most likely to be a strong electrolyte?
   - ○ **a.** a polar compound
   - ○ **b.** a nonpolar compound
   - ○ **c.** a covalent compound
   - ○ **d.** an ionic compound

7. Which statement best explains why oil and water do not mix?
   - ○ **a.** Water is carbon-based and oil is not.
   - ○ **b.** Water is polar and oil is nonpolar.
   - ○ **c.** Oil is polar and water is nonpolar.
   - ○ **d.** Oil and water both have covalent bonds and repel one another.

8. A 3.25 L solution is prepared by dissolving 285 g $BaBr_2$ in water. Use the space provided to determine the molarity.

   _____ M $BaBr_2$

CHECKPOINTS (continued)

9. A student makes a solution by dissolving $CaBr_2$ in water. Describe what happens at the particle level as the $CaBr_2$ dissolves.

_____

_____

_____

_____

_____

_____

_____

10. Three beakers filled with liquids are sitting on a table. One liquid is a solution, one is a suspension, and one is a colloid. Describe how you can use the Tyndall effect to distinguish which type of mixture is in each beaker, and explain how the particles that each beaker contains produces this effect.

_____

_____

_____

_____

_____

_____

_____

_____

MAKE YOUR OWN STUDY GUIDE

In your Evidence Notebook, design a study guide that supports the main ideas from this lesson:

A solution is a homogeneous mixture of two or more solutes dispersed throughout a solvent. Solutions in which solutes consist of charged particles can conduct an electrical current.

Remember to include the following information in your study guide:
- Use examples that model main ideas.
- Record explanations for the phenomena you investigated.
- Use evidence to support your explanations. Your support can include drawings, data, graphs, laboratory conclusions, and other evidence recorded throughout the lesson.

How do patterns of conductivity of solutions relate to the concentration of ions in the solution?

Earth Science Connection

Cycling Matter The law of conservation of matter implies that atoms on Earth are continually recycled. Carbon, nitrogen, and other elements and compounds cycle through Earth's biosphere, geosphere, atmosphere, and hydrosphere. Because chemical changes are involved in the cycling of matter, an element can be transferred between different compounds throughout a cycle.

Develop a model describing the cycling of one type of matter, such as nitrogen, oxygen, or carbon, through Earth's systems. Construct an explanation of chemical reactions that are involved in the cycle and that the total amount of matter in the system is conserved. Explain the ways large-scale chemical manufacturing and consumer habits can negatively impact the natural recycling systems and efforts to restore this balance.

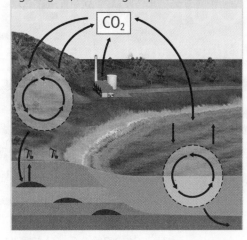

FIGURE 1: Changes in the carbon cycle occur from the interaction of chemical, geological, and biological processes .

Art Connection

Restoration Natural physical and chemical changes can degrade the original quality of artwork. A person trained in preserving and restoring paintings is called a conservator. Conservators evaluate paints and the surfaces on which they are applied. They must understand how paints age and how exposure to various chemicals and light affect the paints. Conservators must ensure that materials used in preserving and restoring paintings are compatible with the original painting and do not cause unintended reactions.

Research the ways conservators restore and preserve paintings and other works of art. Produce a multimedia presentation describing the job of a conservator and different ways they use chemistry to restore and preserve paintings.

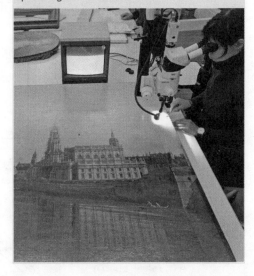

FIGURE 2: A conservator examines a painting for restoration.

Technology Connection

Barnacle Glue Barnacles attach to docks, boats, and anything they come across. Their glue sets in salt water and stays set, as anyone who has cleaned the bottom of a boat can tell you. Engineers are developing ways to make similar glues that work underwater. They're investigating using barnacle glue as a medical adhesive.

Research the properties of barnacle glue, what makes it so strong, and its ability to work underwater. How does the ability to work underwater make it useful as biomedical glue? Develop an informational pamphlet with images and diagrams about the uses of barnacle glue.

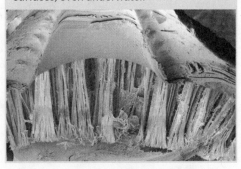

FIGURE 3: This scanning electron micrograph shows the glue threads of an acorn barnacle. These allow it to adhere to surfaces, even underwater.

A BOOK EXPLAINING COMPLEX IDEAS USING ONLY THE 1,000 MOST COMMON WORDS

RANDALL MUNROE
XKCD.COM

THE WATER IN OUR BODIES

Blood and other kinds of watery stuff inside us

Plasma, the liquid part of blood, is made up of water, salts, and protein. Blood also contains some solids, such as red blood cells, white blood cells, and platelets. What makes up the other watery substances our bodies produce?

THE STORY OF WATERY STUFF INSIDE OUR BODIES

OUR BLOOD, AND MOST OF THE WATER IN OUR BODIES, HAS THIS STUFF IN IT:

SO DOES THE SEA.

A WORLD LEADER ONCE SAID THAT THERE'S EXACTLY AS MUCH OF THAT STUFF IN OUR BLOOD AS THERE IS IN THE SEA, BECAUSE ALL LIFE CAME FROM THE SEA.

HE WAS RIGHT THAT LIFE COMES FROM THE SEA, BUT WRONG ABOUT OUR BLOOD. THERE'S MORE OF THAT WHITE STUFF IN THE SEAS THAN IN OUR BLOOD.

THANKS TO THE STUFF IN IT, THE WATER IN OUR BODIES CAN CARRY POWER. POWER MOVES THROUGH THE BODY BY PUSHING AND PULLING ON THE STUFF IN THE WATER.

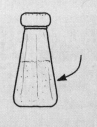

THIS WATER CAN CARRY MESSAGES IN OUR BODY THE WAY PHONE LINES CARRY VOICES, AND LETS OUR BODIES USE POWER TO PUSH AND PULL THINGS IN AND OUT OF OUR BLOOD.

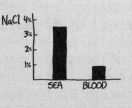

PICK UP THOSE BOOKS.

OH, GREAT. NOW MY BRAIN HAS TO SEND A LOT OF MESSAGES TO MY HAND.

SO MANY STEPS!

IT MAY NOT BE EXACTLY THE SAME AS THE SEAS THAT LIFE CAME FROM, BUT THE WATER IN OUR BODIES IS LIKE A LITTLE SEA OF OUR OWN, FULL OF HIDDEN POOLS AND TINY WONDERS.

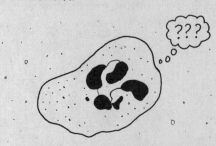
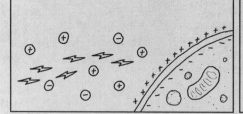

MOSTLY WATER

People often say that our bodies are mostly water, which is true. By weight, our bodies are about three parts water to two parts everything else. This water has all kinds of other things added to it. Your blood, the wet stuff in your mouth, the stuff that comes out of your eyes when you cry, and the stuff in your nose are almost all water; there's just a little other stuff in there too, and that stuff makes those kinds of water different from the normal clear water that you drink.

Since so much of our bodies are made of water, you might think that if you got a hole in your body, all your water would run out. It's true that your blood could come out—which is why people try not to get holes in them—but blood makes up only a small part of a human body's water. Most of the water is locked up in other parts of our body. Almost all the pieces we're made of have water in them—even our bones!

Most of our body parts, like all living things, are made of very tiny bags. Some of these bags hang around in our blood, while others stick together to make body parts like our hearts and skin. These bags are full of all kinds of things, but they're also full of water. If you get a hole in your body, a lot of the water is stuck in those bags—or in small spaces in between them—and won't go anywhere unless all the tiny bags break up.

WHERE IS ALL THE WATERY STUFF?

Here's what the different kinds of water in your bodies would look like if you put it in large bottles. (These are the size of bottles that people bring to parties to fill lots of people's cups from. They're often full of colorful drinks that make young people stay up all night.)

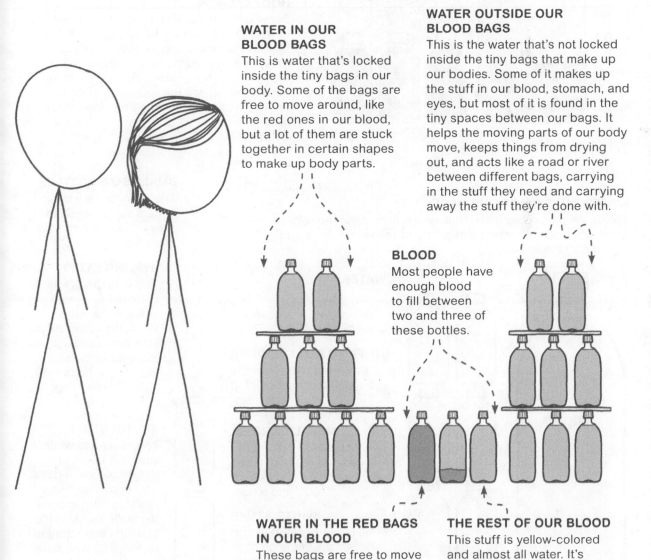

WATER IN OUR BLOOD BAGS

This is water that's locked inside the tiny bags in our body. Some of the bags are free to move around, like the red ones in our blood, but a lot of them are stuck together in certain shapes to make up body parts.

WATER OUTSIDE OUR BLOOD BAGS

This is the water that's not locked inside the tiny bags that make up our bodies. Some of it makes up the stuff in our blood, stomach, and eyes, but most of it is found in the tiny spaces between our bags. It helps the moving parts of our body move, keeps things from drying out, and acts like a road or river between different bags, carrying in the stuff they need and carrying away the stuff they're done with.

BLOOD

Most people have enough blood to fill between two and three of these bottles.

WATER IN THE RED BAGS IN OUR BLOOD

These bags are free to move around in our blood, and are what gives it that red color.

THE REST OF OUR BLOOD

This stuff is yellow-colored and almost all water. It's what things in our blood move around in.

BLOOD

WATER INSIDE OUR BAGS

This is the water that's inside the red bags in our blood. These bags are red because they have a lot of metal in them.

A big plastic bottle, the kind used to fill smaller cups

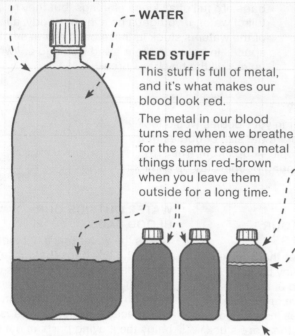

WATER

RED STUFF

This stuff is full of metal, and it's what makes our blood look red.

The metal in our blood turns red when we breathe for the same reason metal things turns red-brown when you leave them outside for a long time.

STUFF THAT STICKS TOGETHER TO COVER HOLES

If something makes a hole in your body, all your blood can fall out, which is bad. This stuff tries to fill those holes before you lose too much blood.

The hole-filling stuff is made of tiny flat circle-shaped bags. When they get near a hole, they stick together, making a thick layer that's strong enough to hold in your blood while your skin grows back over the hole.

BODY GUARDS

Some of the bags in your blood are there to keep you safe from attacks by tiny living things. Things that get into your body can make you sick. To stop them, these guards are always traveling around your body, looking for anything that's not supposed to be there. When they find something they don't like, they have all kinds of ways to mark it, attack it, and get rid of it.

SMALL-SIZE BOTTLES

These bottles are the largest size that you're allowed to carry on a flight in the US.

WATER OUTSIDE OF OUR BAGS

This is the part of our blood that's not locked up in the red bags. It's almost all water, and is kind of yellow in color if you take out all the red stuff.

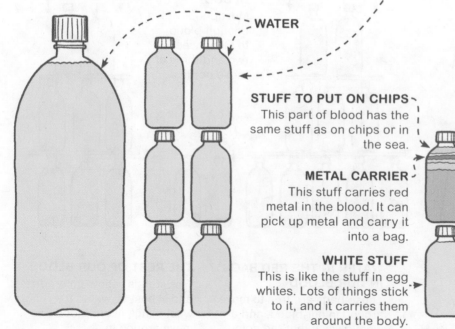

WATER

STUFF TO PUT ON CHIPS

This part of blood has the same stuff as on chips or in the sea.

METAL CARRIER

This stuff carries red metal in the blood. It can pick up metal and carry it into a bag.

WHITE STUFF

This is like the stuff in egg whites. Lots of things stick to it, and it carries them around the body.

STRONG STUFF

This is made of lots of long, thin pieces shaped like hairs. When the sticky bags in your blood are coming together to stop up a hole, these hairs help make them strong.

ROUND STUFF

This is like the white stuff, but made of bigger pieces. It does a lot of things , like carrying stuff around the body and sticking to things that shouldn't be there so your body guards can find and get rid of them.

OTHER WATERY STUFF

 Go online for more about *Thing Explainer*.

SKIN WATER

This is the water that comes out of your skin when you get too hot. As your skin dries, the water carries away heat. This water comes from the clear part of your blood.

A normal person might make this much of it in a day, but they might make a lot more if they spend time in the heat.

KINDS OF SKIN WATER

One kind of skin water keeps you cool. It comes out of your skin all over your body, and it doesn't smell like much. It's mostly water, with just a little bit of stuff in it that makes it like the sea.

Another kind of water only comes out of certain parts of the body with hair on them, like under your arms. Your body makes it when you're worried or afraid, and it's thicker and less watery than the other kind. And after it's been there for a while, it starts to smell.

A drink bottle for one person

A tiny glass, the kind that holds drinks that you drink all at once

MOUTH WATER

The water in your mouth helps food slide down your throat. It's also full of stuff that starts breaking down food as you eat it.

A normal person's mouth makes about this much water every day.

STOMACH WATER

This is the stuff in your stomach.

When you eat dinner, your stomach might fill with about this much stomach water to break down the food.

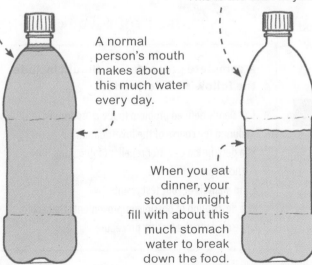

BRAIN WATER

This is the layer of water that goes around the brain. It's very much like the yellow stuff in your blood, but it's more clean and clear, so nothing gets in the brain and hurts it.

When you hit your head, this water holds your brain in place and tries to keep it from running into the bone around it.

YELLOW WATER

This stuff holds all the watery things your body is getting rid of.

It's mostly water. The main other thing in it—which got its name because it's found in yellow water—carries stuff out of the body. It's full of the kind of stuff that makes trees and grass grow.

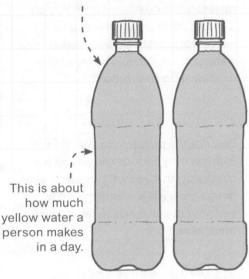

This is about how much yellow water a person makes in a day.

If you have a cold, this is how much of this stuff can fit in your nose.

NOSE STUFF

This is the stuff that comes out of your nose sometimes. It's mostly water and is a lot like the stuff that lines your throat and stomach. It helps keep the layers under it from drying out and breaking open, and catches and stops dust and things that you breathe in.

THE STUFF INSIDE YOUR EYE

This is almost completely water, but it's full of thin hairlike stuff, too small to see, which makes it thicker than water and helps the eye keep its shape.

Testing Water-Repellent Fabrics

You are working for a company that makes water-resistant materials. Water-repellent fabrics are often used in tents, garments such as coats and shoes, and tarps that protect valuable materials. Your challenge is to develop a procedure to test a fabric that repels water. Not only should the material keep water out, but it should be breathable, or allow air to flow through.

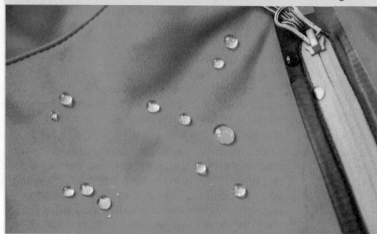

FIGURE 4: Water-repellent fabrics resist water but let air flow through.

1. DEFINE THE PROBLEM

Describe the problem you will address in this activity. Include criteria and any constraints that you will consider in your design. How will you determine how well your design repels water and how breathable it is?

2. CONDUCT RESEARCH

Research water-repellent fabrics and methods used for testing them. What is meant by the term *water-repellent*, and how is this different from waterproof? How do the adhesive and cohesive properties of water influence the way water-repellent fabrics are designed? Consider examples of plants that can also repel water and how these have influenced human-made designs.

3. CARRY OUT AN INVESTIGATION

Develop a plan for testing water-repellent fabric. Consider what materials and technology you will need, how you will safely collect and analyze data, and how you will properly dispose of waste materials.

Water Repellent Fabrics Plan an investigation to test a water-repellent fabric. Develop procedures for assessing the repellency of fabric, as well as its breathability.

4. EVALUATE DATA

Explain which parts of your testing procedure worked well and which could be improved. How might the testing procedure differ if the tests were conducted in a facility with more advanced equipment? How would you use the results of your tests to suggest further improvements to water-repellent fabrics?

5. COMMUNICATE

With your team, develop a presentation including the problem you defined, your research on water-repellent fabrics, and the results of your tests. Explain how intermolecular forces are related to the results you obtained, and suggest areas for further research.

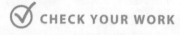 CHECK YOUR WORK

A complete presentation should include the following information:

- a clearly defined problem that was addressed during the course of the investigation
- a description of water repellent fabrics and how they work
- an analysis of your test results
- a description of possible improvements that could be made to the testing procedure

Name _____   Date _____

SYNTHESIZE THE UNIT

In your Evidence Notebook, make a concept map, other graphic organizer, or outline using the Study Guides you made for each lesson in this unit. Be sure to use evidence to support your claims.

When synthesizing individual information, remember to follow these general steps:
- Find the central idea of each piece of information.
- Think about the relationships among the central ideas.
- Combine the ideas to come up with a new understanding.

DRIVING QUESTIONS

Look back to the Driving Questions from the opening section of this unit. In your Evidence Notebook, review and revise your previous answers to those questions. Use the evidence you gathered and other observations you made throughout the unit to support your claims.

PRACTICE AND REVIEW

1. A company wants to develop a plastic with certain properties. Select the correct terms to compare different types of polymers they could use.

   Linear polymers stack together neatly, whereas branched polymers do not. Therefore, linear polymers are held together less | more tightly by intermolecular forces. As a result, linear polymers typically have lower | higher melting points than branched polymers do.

2. Consider the following unbalanced chemical equation:

   $$Al + Br_2 \rightarrow AlBr_3$$

   What mass of bromine is required to produce 125 g $AlBr_3$?

   a. 12.6 g
   b. 56.2 g
   c. 74.9 g
   d. 112 g

3. Which of these compounds would likely conduct an electrical current if dissolved in water? Select all correct answers.

   a. sulfur dioxide, SO_2
   b. magnesium bromide, $MgBr_2$
   c. gallium(III) nitrite, $Ga(NO_2)_3$
   d. carbon tetrabromide, CBr_4
   e. dinitrogen tetroxide, N_2O_4

4. Which statement correctly describes the effect an increase in pressure would have on the solubility of a substance?

   a. It would increase the solubility of a gas but have little effect on a solid or a liquid.
   b. It would increase the solubility of a gas and a liquid but have little effect on a solid.
   c. It would decrease the solubility of a solid but have little effect on a liquid or a gas.
   d. It would decrease the solubility of a solid and a liquid but have little effect on a gas.

5. A substance is dissolved in pure water, and both the freezing point and the boiling point of the liquid change. Which of these statements are true? Select all correct answers.

   a. The change in boiling point is directly proportional to the molarity of the solution.
   b. The freezing point of the pure water is higher than the freezing point of the solution.
   c. The change in the freezing point occurs because the vapor pressure of the solution is higher than that of the pure water.
   d. The change in vapor pressure causes the boiling point of the solution to be higher than the boiling point of the pure water.

6. A 3.28 L solution is prepared by dissolving 535 g $CaCl_2$ in water. What is the molarity of the solution? Though more expensive than NaCl, $CaCl_2$ can prevent water from freezing and melt ice at lower temperatures than standard road salt. Explain why this happens.

_____

_____

_____

7. Explain how hydrogen bonding is related to the properties of materials, such as water. Why is hydrogen bonding so important to biochemistry?

_____

_____

_____

_____

8. Use the concept of a mole to explain why a chemical reaction may not consume all of the reactants. Why is this idea so important in chemical manufacturing?

_____

_____

_____

_____

9. Explain why chemical equations must be balanced and how this relates to the law of conservation of mass.

_____

_____

_____

_____

UNIT PROJECT

Return to your unit project. Prepare your research and materials into a presentation to share with the class. In your final presentation, evaluate the strength of your hypothesis, data, analysis, and conclusions.

Remember these tips while evaluating:

- What structural features are common to all detergents, and how do they affect the properties of detergents?

- How can you model detergent structure to help illustrate their function?

- Why might different detergents be used for different applications?

- How do intermolecular forces facilitate the usefulness of detergents?

UNIT 5

Reaction Energy

YOU SOLVE IT

Why Use Diesel?

 To begin exploring this unit's concepts,
go online to investigate ways to solve a
real-world problem.

Chemical reactions always involve
changes in both matter and energy.

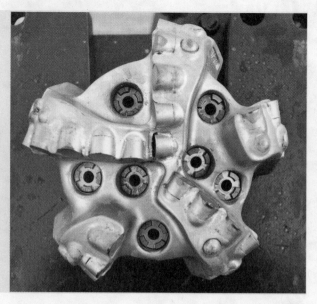

FIGURE 1: Diamond grit is a key material in this drill bit.

Until the mid-20th century, diamonds were obtained naturally from deep underground mines where they formed due to tremendous pressure and heat. Now, diamonds can also be made in laboratories. As in nature, it takes a lot of energy to make a diamond in a laboratory. Using one method, a huge press pushes on a small cylinder containing carbon at very high temperature. Synthetic diamonds are often used in industry, but some laboratories produce gemstone-quality diamonds that can be used in jewelry.

PREDICT Why do you think energy must be added to change carbon powder into a synthetic diamond?

_____

_____

_____

DRIVING QUESTIONS

As you move through the unit, gather evidence to help you answer the following questions. In your Evidence Notebook, record what you already know about these topics and any questions you have about them.

1. What is the source of energy in chemical systems and processes?
2. How can we model the patterns of energy flow in a chemical reaction?
3. How can energy be used to control chemical reactions?

UNIT PROJECT

Go online to download the Unit Project Worksheet to help plan your project.

Chemical Changes on Earth

In photosynthesis, plants use solar energy to release oxygen and build sugar molecules from carbon dioxide and water. In cellular respiration, plants and animals run this reaction in reverse. The energy released by breaking down sugars is used to fuel all life processes including growth. Research the conditions that affect the rates of these chemical reactions and how climate change can affect those rates.

Language Development

Use the lessons in this unit to complete the chart and expand your understanding of the science concepts.

TERM: exothermic reaction

Definition	Example

Similar Term	Phrase

TERM: endothermic reaction

Definition	Example

Similar Term	Phrase

TERM: enthalpy

Definition	Example

Similar Term	Phrase

TERM: Hess's law

Definition	Example

Similar Term	Phrase

TERM: collision theory

Definition	Example
Similar Term	Phrase

TERM: activation energy, E_a

Definition	Example
Similar Term	Phrase

TERM: catalyst

Definition	Example
Similar Term	Phrase

TERM: reaction rate

Definition	Example
Similar Term	Phrase

Energy in Chemical Bonds

A sparkler gives off light and heat.

CAN YOU EXPLAIN IT?

For many people, watching the brilliant flashes of light emitted by sparklers is an enjoyable part of a celebration. A sparkler is a type of small-scale firework that consists of a thin rod with one end coated in a paste. The paste contains bits of aluminum or magnesium metal. This chemical system also contains a fuel source, such as carbon or sulfur, and a compound that provides the component for it to burn—oxygen. When the sparkler is lit, heat from the reaction causes the bits of metal to become so hot that they glow, producing the bright flashes of light. Sparklers can be large or small and can emit a variety of colors, but they all follow this same basic construction.

INFER   What do you think is the source of the energy in a chemical reaction, such as the reaction that occurs when you light a sparkler?

_____

_____

_____

_____

_____

> **Evidence Notebook** As you explore the lesson, gather evidence to explain why some chemical reactions give off energy while others absorb energy.

Describing Changes in Energy

When vinegar and baking soda are mixed, the resulting chemical reaction causes bubbles to form. If you touch the container before and after the reaction, you will also notice that it feels cooler after the reaction has occurred. The sparkler got hotter when it burned. Not all chemical reactions result in such a change in temperature, however.

 Collaborate With a partner, brainstorm several examples of temperature changes that result from chemical reactions. Why do these temperature changes occur?

Analyzing Changes in Energy

The photos in Figure 1 show three examples of chemical reactions. In the first reaction, sugar combines with sulfuric acid. In the second, barium hydroxide reacts with ammonium chloride. In the third, potassium permanganate reacts with glycerin.

FIGURE 1: These reactions show how energy changes in different ways during a chemical reaction.   **Explore Online ▶**

a Reaction 1 Sugar is combined with sulfuric acid, producing black carbon and water vapor. The water is vaporized due to the increase in temperature.

b Reaction 2 When barium hydroxide reacts with ammonium chloride, the temperature in the flask decreases and the flask freezes to the wood.

c Reaction 3 When glycerin is added to a sample of potassium permanganate, the energy released by the reaction ignites the glycerin.

MODEL Draw the reactions in Figure 1. Use arrows to model the movement of energy in each reaction. Do the arrows show energy being released to the environment or absorbed from the environment?

An increase in temperature is not the only sign of energy being released during a chemical reaction. The formation of light or sound can also indicate the release of energy. Observing the absorption of energy can be more difficult. Other than a decrease in temperature, there are no observable signs of this transformation. The energy, of course, needs to go somewhere. It is transferred to the compounds.

Exothermic and Endothermic Reactions

Any reaction that releases energy in the form of heat, light, sound, electricity, or motion is known as an exothermic reaction. A reaction that absorbs energy in the form of heat is known as an endothermic reaction. A decrease of temperature in the environment is the result of energy flowing from the surroundings into the system. The feeling of cold is the result of energy being taken from the surroundings to fuel the reaction.

Explore Online

Hands-On Lab

Investigating Energy in Chemical Processes Carry out an investigation about which chemicals make the best hot and cold packs.

Energy and Matter

Using Reaction Energy

Chemical hand warmers are used to warm up your hands and feet. These warmers contain finely powdered iron in a porous envelope inside a sealed pouch. When the pouch is opened, the iron reacts with atmospheric oxygen to form iron(III) oxide, releasing energy in the form of heat.

$$4Fe + 3O_2 \rightarrow 2Fe_2O_3 + energy$$

This iron oxide reaction can also be used to produce higher temperatures, such as in MREs ("meals-ready-to-eat") used by the military. MREs include iron and magnesium, both of which react with oxygen and release energy in the form of heat. This allows military personnel to have hot meals without requiring heating equipment such as stoves.

FIGURE 2: MREs rely on chemical reactions to warm food.

This is just one example of a chemical reaction that can gently warm your hands or potentially produce enough heat to burn your skin. It is important, therefore, that the amount of energy released by the reaction be controlled. It is essential that scientists can measure the amount of energy in an entire system and be able to develop ways to control its release.

APPLY Is the chemical reaction between iron and oxygen endothermic, or is it exothermic? In your explanation, discuss how energy is transformed, and whether the products or reactants have greater chemical energy.

_____

_____

_____

_____

Enthalpy of Reaction

When using a chemical reaction for a specific purpose, such as to cook an MRE, it is extremely important to control the amount of energy released. Of course, the amount of energy released must be appropriate to warm the food to the correct temperature. However, the energy must not be too great to be contained in a reasonably portable package. Energy changes that occur during a reaction can be described in terms of enthalpy, *H*. This is a property related to the energy of a system.

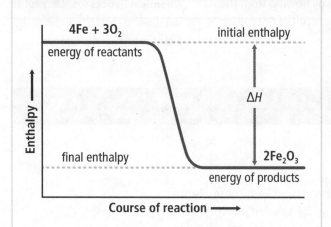

FIGURE 3: For this reaction, enthalpy of reaction is the difference in the total enthalpy of iron and oxygen and the enthalpy of iron(III) oxide.

Enthalpy, however, cannot be measured directly. Therefore, it is more useful to describe the change in enthalpy, ΔH, of a reaction. This is the energy released or absorbed as heat by a system at constant pressure. For a chemical reaction, the overall ΔH is found by subtracting the enthalpy of the reactants from the enthalpy of the products.

This change in enthalpy is known as the *enthalpy of reaction*. Enthalpy of reaction is an extensive property. This means it depends on the amount of substance involved. Chemists, therefore, usually report enthalpy of reaction in terms of moles of substances in the reaction, measured in kJ/mol.

PREDICT Would you expect the value of ΔH to be positive or negative for an endothermic reaction? Would ΔH be positive or negative for an exothermic reaction? Write a simple equation for change in enthalpy to help you determine your answers.

_____

_____

_____

_____

We cannot measure enthalpy directly because it depends on the energy of a substance's particles. All particles have some motion, some energy, so there is no absolute zero on the enthalpy scale. Because there is no absolute reference point for enthalpy, a difference in enthalpy is all that can be measured.

We can compare measuring the change in enthalpy to measuring the energy of water going over a waterfall. A sample of water rushing over the top of the waterfall has a certain amount of energy. As the water nears the bottom of the falls, it is moving faster and has more energy. Measuring the absolute energy of the water at the top and the bottom of the falls cannot be done because of all the motion involved. But, we can determine the difference in energy at the top and bottom of the falls.

Evidence Notebook Write an explanation based on evidence for whether the reaction that occurs in a lit sparkler is endothermic or exothermic. How is energy transformed in this reaction? What can you determine about the enthalpy of the reactants and products?

Measuring Changes in Energy

Earlier in this lesson you observed examples of exothermic and endothermic reactions. A lit sparkler gives off light and heat, indicating an exothermic reaction has taken place. Mixing solutions of barium hydroxide and ammonium chloride causes a chemical reaction that results in a decrease in temperature that causes the flask to "freeze" to the wood, indicating an endothermic reaction.

Modeling Changes in Energy

Modeling energy changes can help to clarify interactions that proceed during chemical reactions. Examples of such models include diagrams, graphs, and chemical equations. It simplifies matters to identify each type of reaction by whether the overall reaction absorbs or releases energy. Whether the products are warmer or cooler than the reactants does not explain the energy changes that actually happen during the course of the reaction.

You have seen a model of what happens in an exothermic reaction when you examined the diagram of its enthalpy change. How do you think this diagram compares to the diagram of the enthalpy change of an endothermic reaction?

MODEL Draw an enthalpy diagram for the endothermic reaction that occurs between barium hydroxide and ammonium chloride. Label the initial enthalpy, final enthalpy, and change in enthalpy on your diagram.

Recall that the change in energy over the course of a reaction is referred to as the enthalpy of reaction, ΔH. The value of ΔH represents the change in energy from reactants to products. Mathematically, the change in enthalpy for a reaction is defined as:

$$\Delta H = H_{products} - H_{reactants}$$

The change in enthalpy over the course of a reaction can also be modeled graphically. The x-axis represents the course of reaction, and the y-axis represents enthalpy.

FIGURE 4: Diagrams of enthalpy change provide information about energy flow in chemical reactions.

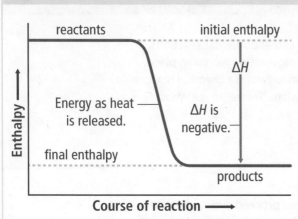

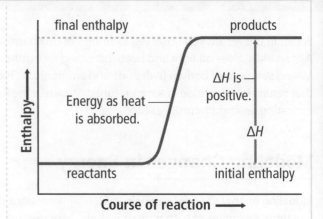

EXPLAIN Complete the statements by selecting the correct terms.

Because energy is given off in an exothermic reaction, the enthalpy of the products must be greater | less than that of the reactants. Therefore, the change in enthalpy, ΔH, for the reaction must be positive | negative. Energy is absorbed in an endothermic reaction, so the enthalpy of the products must be greater | less than that of reactants. Therefore, the change in enthalpy, ΔH, for the reaction must be positive | negative.

FIGURE 5: Changes in enthalpy provide valuable information about chemical processes.

a Burning coal is an exothermic process.

b Nitric oxide, which contributes to smog, forms in an endothermic process.

Recall that, based on enthalpy changes for a reaction, we can infer information about the properties of the substances involved in the reaction. Consider the combustion of carbon.

$$C(s) + O_2(g) \rightarrow CO_2(g) + energy$$

This reaction is exothermic, so the product has lower potential energy than the reactants and is therefore more stable than carbon or diatomic oxygen.

The synthesis of nitric oxide is endothermic so it requires energy:

$$energy + N_2(g) + O_2(g) \rightarrow 2NO(g)$$

This reaction does not occur spontaneously at typical air temperatures. But when fossil fuels are burned, nitrogen in the surrounding air reacts with oxygen, producing nitric oxide. The excess nitric oxide released is a major contributor in acid rain, ozone depletion, and smog.

Modeling Changes in Enthalpy

FIGURE 6: This military plane is dropping magnesium flares to light up the surface of the ground below.

When magnesium metal is ignited, the reaction produces an intense bright white light. For this reason, the reaction is good for use as signal flares, such as the ones shown in Figure 6. How could scientists determine how much energy is released in such a reaction?

In addition to graphing, scientists also model the change in enthalpy using a thermochemical equation. These equations look like other chemical equations but include the value of ΔH, which is usually shown to the right side of the chemical equation, and the physical states of all reactants and products. Including the physical states is important because the change in enthalpy associated with a reaction is dependent on physical state. Examine the thermochemical equation for the combustion of magnesium.

$$2Mg(s) + O_2(g) \rightarrow 2MgO(s) \qquad \Delta H = -1203 \text{ kJ}$$

Recall that enthalpy of reaction is usually reported in terms of moles of substances in the reaction and is measured in kJ/mol. Imagine that you want to find ΔH for one mole of magnesium oxide. The balanced chemical equation shows ΔH for two moles of magnesium oxide. Therefore, the coefficients in the balanced chemical equation and the value of ΔH must be divided by two to obtain the value for a single mole.

$$Mg(s) + \frac{1}{2}O_2(g) \rightarrow MgO \qquad \Delta H = -601.6 \text{ kJ}$$

SOLVE The combustion of hydrogen to form one mole of gaseous water has been experimentally determined to release 241.8 kJ of energy.

$$H_2(g) + \frac{1}{2}O_2(g) \rightarrow H_2O(g) \qquad \Delta H = -241.8 \text{ kJ}$$

Complete the thermochemical equation for the production of two moles of water.

_____ $H_2(g)$ + _____ $O_2(g)$ → _____ $H_2O(g)$ $\quad \Delta H = -$ _____ kJ

INFER The decomposition of water is the reverse process of the formation of water shown above. Given the law of conservation of energy, what is the enthalpy of reaction for the decomposition of one mole of gaseous H_2O into H_2 gas and O_2 gas?

○ **a.** +241.8 kJ/mol

○ **b.** −241.8 kJ/mol

○ **c.** +483.6 kJ/mol

○ **d.** −483.6 kJ/mol

Modeling Enthalpy as a Reactant or a Product

Thermochemical equations are occasionally written with the enthalpy of reaction represented as a reactant or a product in the reaction equation. The actual enthalpy of reaction can be shown on the graphs of the reactions.

Enthalpy Change of CO_2

FIGURE 7: The enthalpy change is negative for the formation of carbon dioxide.

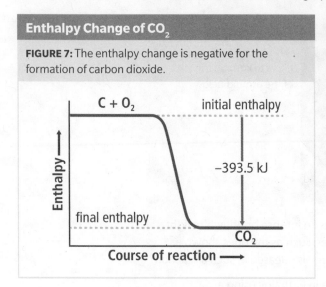

Enthalpy Change of NO

FIGURE 8: The enthalpy change is positive for the formation of nitric oxide.

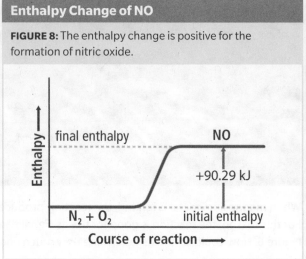

EXPLAIN Complete the statement by selecting the correct terms.

reactant   product

Because energy is generated by an exothermic reaction, the energy released by the reaction can be treated as a _____ in the equation for the reaction.

Because energy is absorbed by an endothermic reaction, the energy required by the reaction can be treated as a _____ in the equation for the reaction.

The enthalpy of reaction can also be included in the equation as a reactant or a product. For example, the formation of carbon dioxide is exothermic. The change in enthalpy for the reaction is a negative value, when written to the right of the equation as a ΔH value. However, it can also be written as a positive value as a product in the equation.

$$C(s) + O_2(g) \rightarrow CO_2(g) + 393.5 \text{ kJ}$$

On the other hand, the formation of nitric oxide is endothermic, so the change in enthalpy is a positive value. This value can be written as a positive value to the right of the equation. It can also be written as a positive value as a reactant in the equation.

$$\frac{1}{2}N_2(g) + \frac{1}{2}O_2(g) + 90.29 \text{ kJ} \rightarrow NO(g)$$

Notice that when writing change in enthalpy as a reactant or a product, a positive value is always used. If the enthalpy is written after the equation, it is shown as a positive value for endothermic reactions and a negative value for exothermic reactions.

 Evidence Notebook Draw a graph representing the change in enthalpy for the chemical reactions that occur in fireworks. Place labels for *enthalpy, products, reactants, initial enthalpy,* and *final enthalpy* on your graph. Show whether the change in enthalpy is positive or negative.

Predicting Changes in Energy

Ethanol, C_2H_5OH, is commonly added to gasoline to reduce the amount of carbon monoxide produced when the fuel is burned. While this more efficient burning is better for the environment, there are some disadvantages. The combustion of ethanol only produces about 60% as much energy per gram as the combustion of gasoline does. The presence of ethanol also causes increased water absorption in the fuel.

How do scientists know that burning ethanol is more efficient but produces less energy? The combustion of ethanol releases 235.1 kJ of energy per mole of ethanol burned. The thermochemical equation for this combustion is:

$$C_2H_5OH(g) + 3O_2(g) \rightarrow 2CO_2(g) + 3H_2O(g) + 235.1 \text{ kJ}$$

 Collaborate What information would you need to gather in order to calculate the energy released in the combustion of ethanol? How could you minimize unwanted variables in your test?

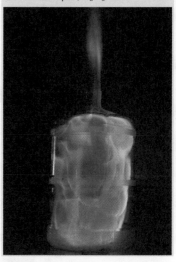

Explore Online ▶

FIGURE 9: This demonstration shows the rapid combustion of ethanol vapor, C_2H_5OH.

Changes in Enthalpy

In order to calculate and compare enthalpy changes for different reactions, scientists must have a way to standardize enthalpy values. Many enthalpies are measured at standard temperature and pressure, which is 25 °C (298 K) and 1 atm, and are often calculated based on the formation of one mole of substance. Consider the two thermochemical equations for the formation of carbon dioxide and nitric oxide:

$$C(s) + O_2(g) \rightarrow CO_2(g) \quad \Delta H = -393.5 \text{ kJ}$$
$$N_2(g) + O_2(g) \rightarrow 2NO(g) \quad \Delta H = 180.6 \text{ kJ}$$

Both reactions are examples of synthesis reactions in which a compound is produced from pure elements. Both equations also show the change in enthalpy when the compounds form in their standard states. Thermochemical data are often recorded as the enthalpies of such synthesis reactions.

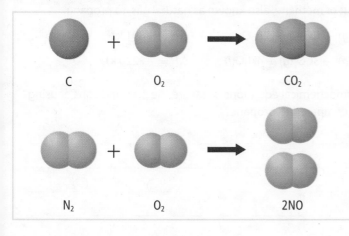

C O_2 CO_2

N_2 O_2 2NO

FIGURE 10: These models show the formation of CO_2 and NO from their elements.

Enthalpy is an extensive property; it depends on the amount of substance. In order to compare ΔH on a molar basis, both equations must result in the same amount of product. In the formation of carbon dioxide, the balanced equation already shows the production of one mole of CO_2:

$$C(s) + O_2(g) \rightarrow CO_2(g) \qquad \Delta H = -393.5 \text{ kJ}$$

The balanced equation for the formation of nitric oxide was for the production of two moles of NO. To compare the changes in enthalpy, we must adjust the equation for the formation of nitric oxide to also show the change in enthalpy for one mole of product. To do this, divide the coefficients in the equation by two. We also must divide the value of ΔH by 2 because only half as much product is being formed.

$$\frac{1}{2}N_2(g) + \frac{1}{2}O_2(g) \rightarrow NO(g) \qquad \Delta H = 90.29 \text{ kJ}$$

Energy and Matter

Combustion of Fuels

Scientists can compare the energy content of fuels by combusting them and comparing the amount of energy released. When comparing the change in enthalpy using combustion, scientists compare the energy needed to combust one mole of reactant. This is different from other measurements, which are based on the formation of one mole of product.

Enthalpy Change of Carbon-Based Compounds		
Name	Formula	ΔH (kJ/mol)
methane	$CH_4(g)$	−891
ethane	$C_2H_6(g)$	−1561
propane	$C_3H_8(g)$	−2220
butane	$C_4H_{10}(g)$	−2878

Scientists use thermochemical equations to compare the amount of energy produced by burning different types of fuels. They can also use these equations to compare the amount of carbon dioxide that each type of fuel produces when it is burned. For example, the following equations may be used to compare the energy output and the CO_2 output of methane, also known as natural gas, to propane.

$$CH_4(g) + 2O_2(g) \rightarrow CO_2(g) + 2H_2O(l) \qquad \Delta H = -891 \text{ kJ}$$

$$C_3H_8(g) + 5O_2(g) \rightarrow 3CO_2(g) + 4H_2O(l) \qquad \Delta H = -2220 \text{ kJ}$$

INFER Based on the thermochemical equations, what are the pros and cons of using methane as a fuel source compared to propane?

_____

_____

_____

_____

_____

Using Calorimeters

To understand energy flow in a chemical reaction, enthalpy change must be measured. This must be done under standard conditions, with a device that accurately measures these changes in energy. One such device is a calorimeter. There are many different types of calorimeters. However, all of them are well insulated so that they minimize any energy transferred to the calorimeter itself. They also have a way of accurately measuring the quantity of heat released or absorbed by matter when it undergoes a chemical or physical change. Two common types of calorimeters are the constant-pressure calorimeter and the bomb calorimeter. They can be used for both endothermic and exothermic reactions.

A constant-pressure calorimeter, shown in Figure 11, measures changes in enthalpy under constant pressure. Processes such as energy transfer between two substances and chemical reactions in solution occur at a constant pressure. To determine energy flow, a thermometer measures the temperature before and after such a change occurs. Constant-pressure calorimeters can be made from common household items, such as coffee cups.

A bomb calorimeter is used when chemical reactions, such as combustion, produce large amounts of gaseous products and large changes in thermal energy. When these changes are contained at a fixed volume, the pressure of the system increases. A bomb calorimeter, such as the one shown in Figure 12, has a sealed chamber that can contain high-pressure gases. Energy transfers as heat through the walls of a chamber to a surrounding liquid, such as water. Scientists use these calorimeters to determine the energy content of substances such as fuels and explosives.

PREDICT What type of calorimeter would you use to determine the energy change when water forms from a mixture of hydrogen and oxygen gases? Why is this the best type of calorimeter to use?

_____

_____

_____

_____

_____

_____

_____

_____

_____

_____

FIGURE 11: This constant-pressure calorimeter measures temperature changes as chemical and physical changes occur at a constant pressure.

Explore Online ▶

FIGURE 12: A bomb calorimeter is a constant-volume calorimeter. The bomb is the part of the calorimeter that is designed to withstand high temperatures and pressures.

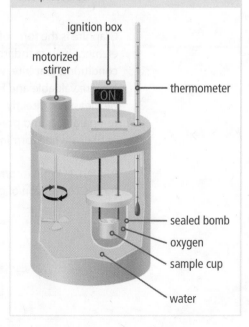

ignition box

motorized stirrer

thermometer

ON

sealed bomb

oxygen

sample cup

water

Enthalpy of Reaction

Enthalpy of reaction is the heat absorbed or released during a chemical reaction at a constant pressure. Recall that enthalpy of reaction is an extensive property. In order to compare thermochemical equations, we must adjust them to obtain enthalpy values based on the amount of substances reacting.

To calculate the total enthalpy change of a reaction, we take the sum of the change in enthalpy of the products multiplied by the amount of products formed, and subtract the sum of the change in enthalpy of the reactants multiplied by the amount of reactants consumed. We can generalize this mathematically as:

$$\Delta H = \Sigma(\Delta H_{products} \times mol_{products}) - \Sigma(\Delta H_{reactants} \times mol_{reactants})$$

where the symbol Σ means "the sum of." This principle is known as Hess's law, and it is dependent on the law of conservation of energy. Hess's law shows that the enthalpy change of a reaction is equal to the sum of enthalpy changes for the individual steps in the process.

As an example of how Hess's law is used, consider pure carbon, which can exist in multiple forms. Graphite and diamond, for example, are both examples of pure carbon. They differ from each other according to the arrangement of carbon atoms in space and the pattern of carbon-carbon bonds. These differences result in different chemical and physical properties for graphite and diamond.

FIGURE 13: Pure carbon exists in different arrangements.

a Graphite

b Diamond

Graphite is the form of carbon in its standard state. The enthalpy of formation for any element in its standard state is zero, so this value for graphite is zero. Under the right conditions, graphite, which is inexpensive and readily available, can form diamond, which is more valuable and less available. The enthalpy for the formation of diamond cannot be measured directly in most laboratories because the reaction requires extremely high temperatures and pressures. We can, however, use Hess's law to determine the change in enthalpy when forming diamond from graphite.

PREDICT What information would you need in order to calculate the change in enthalpy for the conversion of graphite to diamond?

_____

_____

_____

_____

_____

Hess's law needs one important assumption to work. It assumes that the energy difference between reactants and products is independent of the route taken to get from one to the other. This is why scientists can calculate enthalpies of reaction without actually measuring the change in enthalpy directly for each reaction. This process can be diagrammed, as shown in Figure 14. Reactants A and B can produce Product D in a single step or in two steps. The enthalpy, H_3, in the single step reaction is the same as the sum of the enthalpies H_1 and H_2 in the two-step reaction. It does not matter which path was actually taken to produce D from A and B; the change in enthalpy is the same.

Hess's law can be diagrammed with a graphical representation or as a cycle. Both diagrams emphasize that the same change in enthalpy applies to the formation of the products, no matter how many reaction steps are taken to form them. In other words, both of these diagrams show that enthalpy change is independent of the pathway taken. The law of conservation of energy supports the assumptions of Hess's law.

FIGURE 14: Hess's law can be modeled graphically or as a cycle.

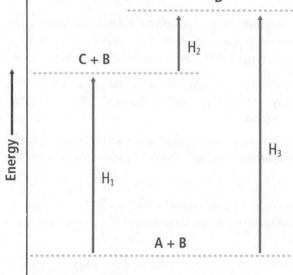
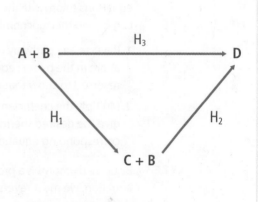

Similar diagrams can be used to model enthalpy changes of any reaction. For example, a model could show that carbon dioxide (D in the diagram) can be formed directly from carbon and oxygen (A and B in the diagram) in a single step. Or, carbon dioxide can be formed by reacting carbon and oxygen to form carbon monoxide (C in the diagram), which then reacts with more oxygen to form carbon dioxide. You could also show that carbonic acid, H_2CO_3, could be formed directly from water and carbon dioxide, or it could be formed in several steps from individual elements. Whether the path consists of one step or more, the enthalpy change is the same for each reaction.

EXPLAIN To form diamond from graphite, oxygen is first combined with the carbon in graphite. Explain how you could use a diagram similar to the ones shown in Figure 14 to model the formation of diamond from graphite.

_____

_____

_____

_____

Problem Solving

Calculating Enthalpy of Reaction

SAMPLE PROBLEM   You can think of the formation of diamond from graphite as a multi-step reaction. The first step is the formation of carbon dioxide from graphite and oxygen. This is followed by the step in which carbon dioxide decomposes into diamond and oxygen.

$$C(graphite) + O_2(g) \rightarrow CO_2(g) \rightarrow C(diamond) + O_2(g)$$

In order to calculate the change in enthalpy for this reaction, we can use the combustion reactions of the elements.

$$C(graphite) + O_2(g) \rightarrow CO_2(g) \qquad\qquad \Delta H = -393.5 \text{ kJ}$$

$$C(diamond) + O_2(g) \rightarrow CO_2(g) \qquad\qquad \Delta H = -395.4 \text{ kJ}$$

PLAN   To use such a system of equations, you must be able to add the pathway thermochemical equations to provide the overall thermochemical equation. The general principles for combining thermochemical equations ensure that matter and energy remain balanced.

1. Reverse any pathway equation necessary to provide the same reactants and products as are in the overall equation. If any reaction is reversed, the sign of ΔH also must be reversed to show that energy is conserved.

2. Multiply the coefficients of the known equations so that, when added together they give the desired thermochemical equation. Multiply the ΔH by the same factor as the corresponding equation.

ANALYZE   Because diamond is a product in the overall equation and a reactant in the pathway equation, we must reverse the combustion equation for diamond and change the sign of ΔH from negative to positive.

$$CO_2(g) \rightarrow C(diamond) + O_2(g) \qquad\qquad \Delta H = +395.4 \text{ kJ}$$

SOLVE   The thermochemical equations can now be added together using Hess's law to give the enthalpy of formation of diamond and the balanced equation.

$$C(graphite) + \cancel{O_2(g)} \rightarrow \cancel{CO_2(g)} \qquad\qquad \Delta H = -393.5 \text{ kJ}$$

$$\cancel{CO_2(g)} \rightarrow C(diamond) + \cancel{O_2(g)} \qquad\qquad \Delta H = +395.4 \text{ kJ}$$

$$\overline{C(graphite) \rightarrow C(diamond) \qquad\qquad \Delta H = +1.9 \text{ kJ}}$$

You can check your work by using Hess's law.

$$\Delta H = \Sigma(\Delta H_{products} \times mol_{products}) - \Sigma(\Delta H_{reactants} \times mol_{reactants})$$

$$\Delta H = \Sigma\left(395.4 \, \frac{\text{kJ}}{\text{mol}} \times 1 \, mol_{products}\right) - \Sigma\left(-393.5 \, \frac{\text{kJ}}{\text{mol}} \times 1 \, mol_{reactants}\right)$$

$$\Delta H = 395.4 \text{ kJ} - 393.5 \text{ kJ} = 1.9 \text{ kJ}$$

PRACTICE PROBLEM

The reaction for the formation of methane gas from graphite and hydrogen is represented by the equation:

$$C(graphite) + 2H_2(g) \rightarrow CH_4(g)$$

In order to calculate the change in enthalpy for this reaction, the steps in the process must include graphite and hydrogen as reactants and methane as a product. The following thermochemical equations contain all of the necessary substances:

1. $C(graphite) + O_2(g) \rightarrow CO_2(g)$ $\qquad\qquad\qquad\qquad$ $\Delta H = -393.5$ kJ

2. $CH_4(g) + 2O_2(g) \rightarrow CO_2(g) + 2H_2O(l)$ $\qquad\qquad$ $\Delta H = -890.8$ kJ

3. $H_2(g) + \frac{1}{2}O_2(g) \rightarrow H_2O(l)$ $\qquad\qquad\qquad\qquad$ $\Delta H = -285.8$ kJ

ANALYZE The second thermochemical equation must be reversed so that the products of the overall reaction match the products of the thermochemical equation. Complete this new equation.

_____ + _____ → _____ + _____ $\qquad\qquad$ $\Delta H =$ _____

ANALYZE The third thermochemical equation is for one mole of water, but the second equation is for two moles of water. To compare these equations, we must balance the third equation to reflect the production of two moles of water. Complete the equation by writing the coefficients and the new enthalpy.

_____ $H_2(g) +$ _____ $O_2(g) \rightarrow$ _____ $H_2O(l)$ $\qquad$ $\Delta H =$ _____ kJ

SOLVE The three reorganized thermochemical equations can now be added together and like terms can be canceled. Complete the problem by canceling the like terms and writing the enthalpies for each reaction.

$C(graphite) + O_2(g) \rightarrow CO_2(g)$ $\qquad\qquad\qquad$ $\Delta H =$ _____ kJ

$CO_2(g) + 2H_2O(l) \rightarrow CH_4(g) + 2O_2(g)$ $\qquad$ $\Delta H =$ _____ kJ

$2H_2(g) + O_2(g) \rightarrow 2H_2O(l)$ $\qquad\qquad\qquad$ $\Delta H =$ _____ kJ

$C(graphite) + 2H_2(l) \rightarrow CH_4(g)$ $\qquad\qquad\qquad$ $\Delta H =$ _____ kJ

MODEL Draw a diagram for this reaction that is similar to the diagrams in Figure 14. Use arrows to show changes in enthalpy for each pathway and for the overall reaction.

Reaction Enthalpy and Bond Energies

The overall enthalpy of a reaction reflects the difference in the energy required to break bonds in the reactants and the energy released when new bonds are formed in the products. The breaking of a bond is always an endothermic process that requires an input of energy. This means that all chemical reactions, even those that release energy, must first absorb enough energy for the reactant bonds to be broken.

Bond energies can be used to predict the stability of the products of a reaction. For an exothermic reaction, the total bond energy of the products is greater than the total bond energy of the reactants, so the products are more stable than the reactants. For an endothermic reaction, the total bond energy of the products is less than the total bond energy of the reactants, so the products are less stable than the reactants.

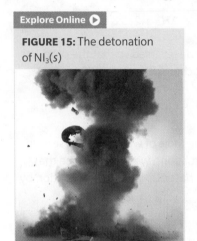

Explore Online ▶

FIGURE 15: The detonation of $NI_3(s)$

For example, nitrogen triiodide, NI_3, has a large positive change in enthalpy. For this reason, NI_3 is sensitive to shock. The explosive exothermic decomposition of the compound can be activated using just a touch.

INFER What can you conclude about the bond energies of diatomic nitrogen and iodine compared to those of nitrogen triiodide?

_____

_____

_____

Many commonly used explosives are nitrogen-containing compounds that release stable, diatomic nitrogen as well as large amounts of energy. Nitroglycerine, $C_3H_5N_3O_9$, which is used to make dynamite, is a well-known explosive. The decomposition of sodium azide, NaN_3, is used to inflate automobile air bags in as few as 40 milliseconds. Many fertilizers contain ammonium nitrate, NH_4NO_3. This compound is a cost-effective way to increase the amount of nitrogen in the fertilizer, but it also makes it extremely explosive. Manufacturers must use extreme care to keep any source of ignition away from ammonium nitrate.

As these examples show, reactions tend to proceed toward a lower-energy state. You might expect all reactions to be exothermic, but some endothermic reactions do occur with an outside influence, such as heating. Something other than enthalpy change, therefore, must help determine whether a reaction will occur.

Nature also proceeds toward increasing randomness of a system. Recall that this tendency toward randomness is called *entropy*. The change in entropy is the difference between the entropy of the products and that of the reactants. An increase in entropy has a positive value, and a decrease in entropy has a negative value. Processes in nature are driven toward *least* enthalpy and *greatest* entropy.

An ice cube melting is an example of an endothermic process. When an ice cube melts at room temperature, energy is transferred from the environment to the ice. The molecules in the ice become less ordered as it changes from the solid phase to the liquid phase. The same is true for a liquid becoming a gas. Entropy also increases when a reaction produces a greater number of moles of product than there are reactants. A system that can go from one state to another without a decrease in enthalpy does so with an increase in entropy. Both influence whether or not a reaction can or will occur and under what conditions.

 Evidence Notebook What conclusions can you draw about the changes in enthalpy for the reactions that occur when burning a sparkler?

Careers in Science

Computational Chemist

Suppose scientists want to study the thermodynamics of a volcanic eruption. They might want to know how the sulfur, sulfur dioxide, and sulfur trioxide spewed into the atmosphere combine with water to form acid rain. A great many reactions involving sulfur and oxygen take place. These reactions cannot be duplicated in such a large scale in a lab, but they can be simulated in a computer model. The chemists must break down the overall reactions into subcomponents of the system to build their model.

Computational chemists use computer simulations to help solve chemical problems by building mathematical models. In 1995, three computational chemists won the Nobel Prize in chemistry for explaining how ozone forms and decomposes in the atmosphere. Their work involved little lab experimentation. They constructed models using known thermodynamic and chemical laws. The prize-winning chemists constructed their model by examining the relationships among chemical reactions involving chlorine and bromine atoms in the atmosphere. They used this model to study how these atoms interact with reactant concentrations, wind, air temperatures, and seasonal changes in sunlight.

Computational chemists may study atoms or molecules at a sub-microscopic level. Or, they may model the properties of larger systems, such as large volumes of gases, solutions, or solids. They may try to find a starting point for a new laboratory synthesis, such as to help develop new drugs. Computational chemists can also improve the productivity and efficiency of industrial processes using computer models to predict how reacting molecules combine under different conditions. Many chemical problems cannot be solved analytically or experimentally, so mathematical models are often necessary.

FIGURE 16: Computational chemists use computers to develop models and interpret data.

For example, much about ozone depletion in the atmosphere could not be studied experimentally. Computational chemists may use supercomputers and computing clusters that require massive amounts of data. Statistical analysis is often involved.

Chemistry in Your Community Research a computational chemist whose contributions to the field were influenced by his or her community. How did his or her diverse background influence the decision to become a computational chemist? Imagine that you are such a chemist, and you have been asked to give a presentation using digital media for career night at your school. Make a presentation for your class that explains the following:

- the daily tasks of a computation chemist
- the research a computational chemist performs
- the educational background required for the position

EXPLAINING ENDOTHERMIC AND EXOTHERMIC PROCESSES

PHOTOSYNTHESIS AND RESPIRATION

 CALORIMETRY AND HESS'S LAW

Go online to choose one of these other paths.

Lesson Self-Check

CAN YOU EXPLAIN IT?

FIGURE 17: Chemical reactions produce the bright flashes of light from a sparkler.

The bright flashes of light you see from a lit sparkler are tiny bits of metal that are so hot they glow brilliantly. The chemical reaction that provides energy in the form of heat to the metal is often the reaction of a compound, such as the decomposition of potassium nitrate, forming potassium nitrite and oxygen:

$$2KNO_3(s) \rightarrow 2KNO_2(s) + O_2(g)$$

This reaction has a negative change in enthalpy, which can be found with the use of a calorimeter, an energy diagram, or Hess's law. There are many other chemical reactions that also occur when a sparkler is ignited, as evidenced by the output of energy we can see and feel.

Evidence Notebook Refer to your notes in your Evidence Notebook to explain why some chemical reactions give off energy while others absorb it. How can you use evidence from observations of a sparkler to describe the reaction's change in enthalpy and compare the bond energy and stability of the compounds?

1. What can you conclude about the change in enthalpy and a comparison of the bond energy and stability of the compounds in the potassium nitrate reaction in a sparkler?
2. What evidence from the sparkler supports your conclusion? Explain your reasoning.
3. How can you extend these concepts to explain why some chemical reactions give off energy while others absorb it?

CHECKPOINTS

Check Your Understanding

1. Determine whether each reaction description is characteristic of an endothermic or exothermic reaction.

Reaction Description	Reaction Type
absorbs heat	Endothermic | Exothermic
releases heat	Endothermic | Exothermic
warms the surroundings	Endothermic | Exothermic
cools the surroundings	Endothermic | Exothermic
product energy > reactant energy	Endothermic | Exothermic
product energy < reactant energy	Endothermic | Exothermic

2. Complete the statements.

For an exothermic reaction, ΔH is greater than | less than | equal to zero, and the products are less | more stable than the reactants. For an endothermic reaction, ΔH is greater than | less than | equal to zero, and the products are less | more stable than the reactants.

3. In which reactions are the products more stable than the reactants? Select all correct answers.

☐ **a.** a reaction in which energy is absorbed

☐ **b.** a reaction with a negative change in enthalpy

☐ **c.** a reaction with the change in energy treated as a product

☐ **d.** a reaction in which the products have less chemical energy than the reactants.

4. Hydrogen reacts with chlorine to produce hydrogen chloride, releasing 92.3 kJ/mol of energy. Complete the thermochemical equation.

$\frac{1}{2}H_2(g) + \frac{1}{2}Cl_2(g) \rightarrow HCl(g)$ $\Delta H =$ _____ kJ

5. A scientist mixes two substances in a beaker and then notices that the outside of the beaker feels colder. What can the scientist infer about this type of reaction? Choose all correct answers.

☐ **a.** It always proceeds spontaneously.

☐ **b.** It releases thermal energy.

☐ **c.** Products are more stable than reactants.

☐ **d.** It has a positive enthalpy of reaction.

☐ **e.** In its thermochemical equation, ΔH has a positive sign.

☐ **f.** The bond energy is lower in the products than the reactants.

☐ **g.** The products have more energy than the reactants.

6. Suppose you want to calculate the enthalpy change for the following reaction.

$2Al(s) + Fe_2O_3(s) \rightarrow Al_2O_3(s) + 2Fe(s)$ $\Delta H = ?$

You have the following data:

$2Al(s) + 3O_2(g) \rightarrow 2Al_2O_3(s)$ $\Delta H = -3202$ kJ

Which of the following equations would be best to combine with the equation above to yield the first equation?

○ **a.** $Fe(s) + O_2(g) \rightarrow Fe_2O_3(s)$

○ **b.** $2Fe_2O_3(s) \rightarrow O_2(g) + 4FeO(s)$

○ **c.** $Al_2O_3(s) + 6HCl(aq) \rightarrow 2AlCl_3(aq) + 3H_2O(g)$

○ **d.** $2Fe_2O_3(s) + 6C(s) \rightarrow 3CO_2(g) + 4Fe(s)$

7. Use the given enthalpies to calculate the enthalpy change for the decomposition of hydrogen peroxide.

$2H_2O_2(l) \rightarrow 2H_2O(l) + O_2(g)$ $\Delta H = ?$

$\Delta H\, H_2O_2(l) = -187.8$ kJ/mol

$\Delta H\, H_2O(l) = -285.8$ kJ/mol

$\Delta H\, O_2(g) = 0$ kJ/mol
(O_2 is an element in its standard state.)

$\Delta H =$ _____ kJ

CHECKPOINTS (continued)

8. How does the stability of the products of a reaction relate to potential energy in endothermic and exothermic reactions?

_____

_____

_____

_____

_____

_____

_____

_____

9. What is enthalpy? If you know the change in enthalpy of a reaction, can you determine whether the reaction is spontaneous? Explain.

_____

_____

_____

_____

_____

_____

_____

_____

MAKE YOUR OWN STUDY GUIDE

 In your Evidence Notebook, design a study guide that supports the main ideas from this lesson:
The enthalpy, entropy, and bond energy of reactants and products determine energy changes in a chemical reaction.

The stability of a compound depends on its bond energies.

Remember to include the following information in your study guide:

- Use examples that model main ideas.
- Record explanations for the phenomena you investigated.
- Use evidence to support your explanations. Your support can include drawings, data, graphs, laboratory conclusions, and other evidence recorded throughout the lesson.

Consider how changes in energy and matter during an exothermic or endothermic reaction affect the stability of the products of the reaction.

Reaction Rates

Light sticks glow brighter in warm water **than** in cold water.

CAN YOU EXPLAIN IT?

When you crack and shake a light stick, it begins to emit light. The light is evidence that a chemical reaction is occurring inside the tube. This reaction is similar to the reaction that occurs in fireflies and other bioluminescent organisms. Light sticks are common decorations often used in festive settings. They can also serve as emergency light sources or distress signals in both military and civilian settings. Notice the difference in the light intensity emitted by the light sticks in the photograph. The light stick in the beaker of warm water on the left shines more brightly than the light stick in the beaker of ice water on the right.

PREDICT Why would changing the temperature of a light stick affect the intensity of the light that it emits? Consider what is occurring at the molecular scale that would affect the rate of the reaction. Which of these light sticks do you think would stop glowing first?

_____

_____

_____

_____

_____

Evidence Notebook As you explore the lesson, gather evidence to explain the factors that affect the rate of a chemical reaction.

Hands-On Lab
Observing Reaction Rates

The rate of a chemical reaction is not a constant value. There are several factors that can change a reaction's rate. The usefulness of a chemical reaction does not just depend on what change takes place. It also depends on controlling the reaction so that it is not too fast or too slow for a particular application. Chemists often speed up or slow down reactions to optimize certain outputs for a variety of safety, economic, and environmental reasons.

Research Question: Why would scientists want to control the speed of a chemical reaction?

MAKE A CLAIM

In your Evidence Notebook, predict how you think the changes in each of the four separate experiments will affect the rate of the reaction. Consider what the variable is and what is kept constant in each experiment.

MATERIALS

- indirectly vented chemical splash goggles, nonlatex apron, nitrile gloves
- beaker, 250 mL (3)
- Bunsen burner
- copper foil strip
- effervescent antacid tablet (3)
- graduated cylinder, 10 mL
- HCl solution, 0.1 M
- hot plate
- ice
- magnesium ribbon
- matches
- sandpaper
- steel wool
- test tube, 16 × 150 mm (6)
- tongs
- water
- zinc strip

SAFETY INFORMATION

indirectly vented chemical splash goggles

- Wear indirectly vented chemical splash goggles, a nonlatex apron, and nitrile gloves during the setup, hands-on, and takedown segments of the activity.

- Use caution when working with Bunsen burners, because this heat source can seriously burn skin and clothing. Secure loose clothing and tie back hair.

- Use caution when working with hot plates, which can cause skin burns or electric shock.

- Use caution when working with glassware, which can shatter if dropped and cut skin.

- Never pour chemicals, either used or unused, back into their original container. Dispose of chemicals according to your teacher's instructions.

PLAN THE INVESTIGATION

In your Evidence Notebook, develop procedures for the following investigations. Make sure your teacher approves your procedures and safety plans before proceeding.

Part 1 Test how different metals (magnesium, zinc, and copper) react when placed in 0.1 M HCl. Determine whether the reaction rate was different between each metal. What did you test in this experiment that caused the rate of the reaction to change?

Part 2 Test how fast a small, tightly balled sample of steel wool burns in a flame compared to a loosely balled sample of steel wool. What did you test in this experiment that caused the rate of the reaction to change?

Part 3 Test how a strip of magnesium reacts in different concentrations of vinegar. You can make different concentrations of vinegar by adding water to the solution. What did you test in this experiment that caused the reaction rate to change?

Part 4 Test how the temperature of water affects the rate at which an effervescent antacid tablet dissolves. What did you test in this experiment that caused the reaction rate to change?

DRAW CONCLUSIONS

Write a conclusion that addresses each of these points.

Claim For each experiment, explain how each factor you tested affected the reaction.

Evidence Give specific examples from your data to support your claim.

Reasoning Explain how the evidence you gave supports your claim. Describe, in detail, the connections between the evidence you cited and the argument you are making.

_____

_____

_____

_____

_____

_____

_____

_____

_____

_____

_____

_____

_____

_____

_____

_____

_____

EXTEND

Develop a Model During a chemical reaction, atoms, ions, or molecules interact with one another. Choose one factor you explored. In your Evidence Notebook, make a drawing that shows how changing the factor affects a chemical reaction on the molecular scale. What are the limitations of your 2-dimensional model?

 Evidence Notebook In the light stick example, what factor was changed to cause them to glow with different intensities?

Collision Theory

As it burns, charcoal reacts with oxygen in the air. When you burn charcoal in a grill, it burns slowly without a noticeable flame, like the charcoal sample shown in a cylinder of air in Figure 1a. The cylinder in Figure 1b shows charcoal burning in pure oxygen. In pure oxygen, the reaction is much faster and burns with a flame.

FIGURE 1: Charcoal burns differently in air than in pure oxygen.

a Charcoal in air

b Charcoal in pure oxygen

MODEL Draw sketches that compare how the charcoal samples in Figure 1 will look after 10, 20, and 60 minutes. Assume that there is a constant supply of air or oxygen. If the charcoal is completely burned, how will the total amount of energy released in the two setups compare?

Understanding Chemical Reactions

Chemical reactions involve the energy-*absorbing* breaking of bonds in the reactants and the energy-*releasing* forming of new bonds in the products. Collision theory states that, in order for a chemical reaction to occur, particles must collide. The collisions break the bonds in the reactants and get the different particles to interact. But not every collision will result in a reaction. The colliding particles must have sufficient energy and the correct orientation. Several factors increase the chances of collisions being effective.

EXPLAIN Using Figure 2, complete the statement by selecting the correct terms.

When concentration is increased, for example by using pure oxygen instead of air to burn charcoal, the number | energy of collisions between reactant particles increases | decreases. As a result, the rate of a chemical reaction increases. This is due to an overall increase | decrease in the number of effective collisions.

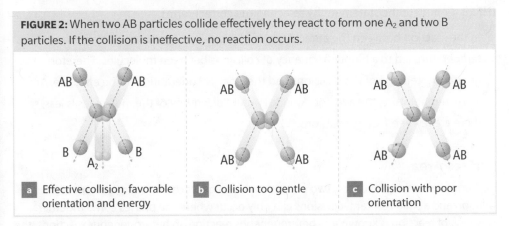

FIGURE 2: When two AB particles collide effectively they react to form one A_2 and two B particles. If the collision is ineffective, no reaction occurs.

a Effective collision, favorable orientation and energy

b Collision too gentle

c Collision with poor orientation

During a chemical reaction, reactant particles are constantly colliding. When a collision has sufficient energy and proper orientation, a reaction may occur between the colliding particles. However, if the collision does not have enough energy or if the colliding particles are not correctly oriented to cause a change, it will fail to cause a chemical reaction. The reaction rate of a chemical reaction is measured as the change in concentration of reactants per unit of time as the reaction proceeds.

Increasing Reaction Rates

Reaction rate is essentially a measure of the frequency of effective collisions. Any change in conditions that affects these collisions affects the reaction rate. There are several factors that can be modified in order to change the rate of a chemical reaction.

Concentration

Though there are exceptions, almost all reactions increase in rate when the concentration of the reactants are increased. Figure 3 is a simple model showing that, as the concentration increases, the number of total collisions between particles, represented by a line, increases. At lower concentration, there may be only one effective collision out of many. At medium concentration, this number may rise to four. And at even higher concentration there are more than twenty. Increasing the number of collisions increases the likelihood that effective collisions—those with the correct orientation and energy—will occur. These effective collisions increase the reaction rate.

ANALYZE Complete the statement by selecting the correct terms.

In the reaction between HCl and magnesium, increasing the concentration of acid increased | decreased | did not change the overall rate of collisions between particles. Higher concentration caused an increase in effective | ineffective | all collisions between reactants. An increase in the number of effective | ineffective | all collisions led to an increase in the rate of reaction.

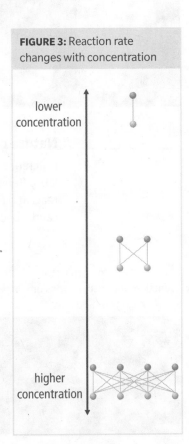

FIGURE 3: Reaction rate changes with concentration

lower concentration

higher concentration

Temperature

Temperature is a measure of the average kinetic energy of the particles in a substance. As the temperature increases, particles move faster and have more energy. Therefore, as temperature increases, the number of collisions having enough energy to cause a reaction increases. A greater number of effective collisions increases the reaction rate.

INFER Complete the statement by selecting the correct terms.

> In the reaction between the antacid tablet and water, a decrease | an increase in temperature led to a higher frequency of collisions between molecules. Therefore, a greater percentage of the collisions had the energy | orientation to be effective. At a lower temperature, the average kinetic | potential energy of the molecules is less, so there are fewer effective collisions.

Surface Area

In chemical reactions involving two phases, such as a gaseous and solid reactant or a solution and a solid reactant, collisions can only occur where the phases come together. This type of reaction is known as a heterogeneous reaction. In heterogeneous reactions, the reaction rate depends on surface area, the area of contact between the two phases.

FIGURE 4: Crushed marble reacts more vigorously in hydrochloric acid than a solid piece of marble.

EXPLAIN When a piece of marble, primarily calcium carbonate, is dropped into hydrochloric acid, a few bubbles form. An equal mass of powdered marble, however, reacts rapidly, forming many gas bubbles. Why?

○ **a.** The marble powder has a coating of oxygen atoms from the air, which causes the bubbles.

○ **b.** The marble powder has much more surface area, so the acid comes into contact with more calcium carbonate.

○ **c.** The marble powder has more atoms than the solid marble, so the powder reaction proceeds faster.

○ **d.** The marble powder has a different molecular structure that is more reactive than a solid piece of marble.

Nature of Reactants

Different substances can vary greatly in their tendencies to react. As you observed in the lab, different metals react differently with acid. Even substances that seem very similar can react at different rates. For example, a beeswax candle burns more slowly than a paraffin candle because the waxes have different chemical structures.

FIGURE 5: Once started, the reaction between magnesium and oxygen continues.

Investigating the Reaction Process

Many chemical reactions do not occur spontaneously. For example, magnesium is a metal that is quite stable when exposed to air. Add thermal energy from a lighted match, however, and it burns rapidly, releasing heat and bright light. Recall that, according to collision theory, an effective collision must involve enough energy to cause the reaction to occur. The collision between two particles must provide enough energy to get past the repulsion of their electron clouds and bring the atoms close enough to one another to form a new chemical bond. The heat provides this energy.

For a chemical reaction to occur, existing chemical bonds must break before new bonds can form. The breaking of bonds is always an endothermic process, requiring an energy input. Bond formation is an exothermic process. Even when the overall process of a chemical reaction is exothermic, an input of energy must occur to start the reaction.

Figure 6 shows what must happen for a reaction to occur. The minimum energy required for the collision of reactant particles to result in a reaction is called the activation energy, E_a. This is the "hill" on the graph. Once started, the reaction proceeds spontaneously. The reaction releases energy as it proceeds. The chemical potential energy of the reactants is higher than that of the products, so the forward reaction is exothermic.

An endothermic reaction would appear as the reverse image of the reaction in Figure 6. The reactant molecules have a lower potential energy level than the product molecules. The activation energy of the reverse reaction is designated by the symbol E_a'. Notice the "hill" is larger. The energy of the activated complex is the same for both the forward and reverse reactions of a reversible reaction.

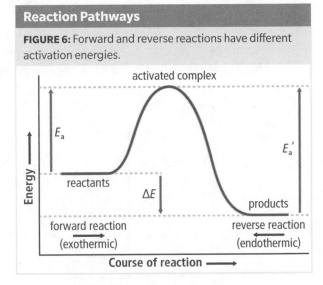

Reaction Pathways

FIGURE 6: Forward and reverse reactions have different activation energies.

The overall energy change in the reaction, ΔE, is the same in either direction, as predicted by the law of conservation of energy. The change in energy is negative for the exothermic direction and positive for the endothermic direction.

Energy and Matter

Transition States

At the peak of the Reaction Pathways graph, there is a brief interval between the time that the reactant bonds are broken and product bonds are formed. This transitional structure is called an *activated complex*, and it exists for only a brief period of time. Just because the activated complex forms does not necessarily mean products will form. It may return to the original reactants. Increasing the temperature of the reaction causes more particles to have sufficient energy to form the activated complex on collision. That is why reaction rate increases as temperature increases. Increasing temperature increases the opportunities for products to form.

APPLY How does concentration affect the formation of the activated complex?

_____

_____

_____

_____

_____

_____

Calculating Energy Requirements

SAMPLE PROBLEM

MODEL Label the reactants, products, ΔE, E_a, and E_a'. Determine the value of $\Delta E_{forward}$, $\Delta E_{reverse}$, E_a, and E_a' on the energy diagram.

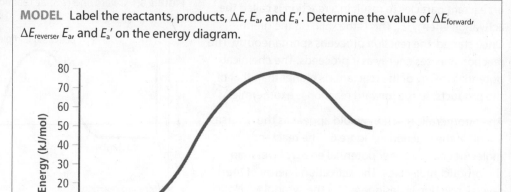

SOLVE Figure 7 shows a completed energy diagram. The energy level of reactants is shown to the left and that of the products to the right on an energy curve. Total energy change, ΔE, is the difference between these two levels. Activation energy, the minimum energy for an effective collision, differs in the forward and reverse directions. E_a is the difference between the *reactant* energy level and the peak. E_a' is the difference between the *product* level and the peak.

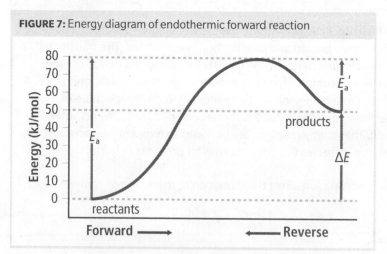

FIGURE 7: Energy diagram of endothermic forward reaction

$\Delta E_{forward}$ = energy of products − energy of reactants
$\Delta E_{forward}$ = 50 kJ/mol − 0 kJ/mol = 50 kJ/mol

$\Delta E_{reverse}$ = energy of reactants − energy of products
$\Delta E_{reverse}$ = 0 kJ/mol − 50 kJ/mol = −50 kJ/mol

E_a = energy of activated complex − energy of reactants
E_a = 80 kJ/mol − 0 kJ/mol = 80 kJ/mol

E_a' = energy of activated complex − energy of products
E_a' = 80 kJ/mol − 50 kJ/mol = 30 kJ/mol

MODEL On the energy diagram, label the following values: $\Delta E_{forward}$, $\Delta E_{reverse}$, E_a, and E_a'.

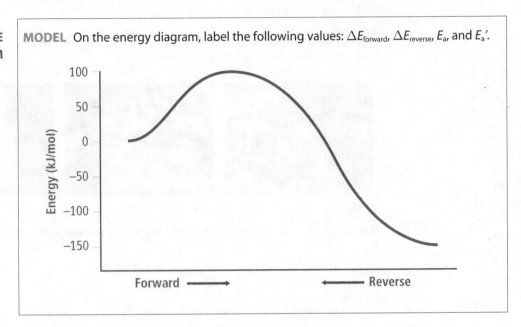

SOLVE Use the diagram you completed above to answer the following questions. Show your work in the space provided.

1. What is the value of $\Delta E_{forward}$? _____

2. What is the value of $\Delta E_{reverse}$? _____

3. What is the value of E_a? _____

4. What is the value of E_a'? _____

5. Is the forward reaction exothermic or endothermic in the diagram above? Use evidence from your calculations to support your claim.

_____
_____
_____
_____
_____

Lowering Activation Energy

Hydrogen peroxide decomposes to form water and oxygen gas in a very slow chemical reaction. When dish soap is added to hydrogen peroxide, we can see the reaction results as bubbles in the soap. If a small amount of sodium iodide is added to the mixture, the bubbles form very rapidly, as shown in Figure 8.

FIGURE 8: When sodium iodide is added to a hydrogen peroxide and dish soap solution, the reaction occurs very quickly.

Explore Online ▶

ASK What questions do you have about the role of sodium iodide in this reaction?

_____

_____

When sodium iodide was added, foam formed rapidly, bubbling out of the flask. The sodium iodide acted as a catalyst. A catalyst is a substance that changes the rate of a chemical reaction without being consumed during the reaction. For this reason, catalysts do not appear among the final products in the chemical equation of the reaction. Catalysts provide an alternate energy pathway or reaction mechanism having a lower energy barrier between reactants and products. A lower activation energy is required to start the reaction. Many reactions inside living things, such as photosynthesis and cellular respiration, use a catalyst so they can proceed rapidly at relatively low temperatures.

ANALYZE The energy diagram for the decomposition reaction of hydrogen peroxide is shown below. Draw a line representing the energy of this reaction when the sodium iodide catalyst is added. Use evidence to support your drawing.

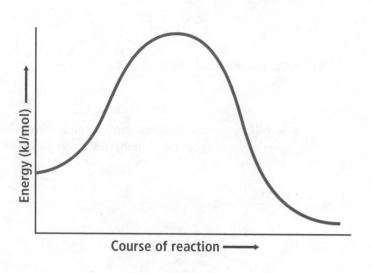

Engineering
Catalyzing Changes

Think about all of the things you use that are made of plastic: shopping bags, packaging materials, bottles, wrapping film, and many others. Plastic is convenient, but it can also be a big problem. Plastic materials, such as polyethylene bottles, do not break down in the environment for a very long time. Plastic sits in landfills, resulting in mountains of plastic waste.

FIGURE 9: Mountains of plastic waste have accumulated around the world.

Scientists are now studying a process that uses two catalysts to convert waste plastic into diesel fuel. Their conversion is a two-step process using polyethylene, the most common plastic material in use. Polyethylene, $(C_2H_4)_n$, is commonly produced from the catalytic polymerization of ethylene, which comes from petrochemicals. Polyethylene is made up of a long chain of carbon atoms, each attached to two hydrogen atoms. The first catalyst speeds up a reaction that removes the hydrogen atoms from these long chains. As the hydrogen is removed, double bonds form between carbon atoms of the giant polyethylene molecules. Carbon chains with double bonds react much more readily with other compounds than do chains with only single bonds.

Although the double bonds provide a site for reactions that break apart the chain, those reactions are not fast enough to be practical for handling large volumes of plastic. This is where a second catalyst comes into play. This catalyst reduces the activation energy and helps break apart the plastic at the double bonds. The result is a mixture of hydrocarbon chains of various lengths. The catalysts continue to break apart the long hydrocarbon chains until they are short enough to be recycled for other purposes, such as fuel.

The catalyst molecules for this process are expensive to produce. They contain expensive metals, such as iridium and rhenium. To make the process cost-effective, the catalysts are recovered and reused. Each molecule of catalyst can promote the conversion of polyethylene molecules over and over again.

ANNOTATE Annotate the text to find evidence that the catalysts change the rate of the chemical reaction used to break down polyethylene. Then explain why the catalysts can be used more than once.

_____

_____

_____

_____

_____

_____

 Evidence Notebook Draw an energy diagram for the light stick reaction, and identify the activation energy of the reaction. Which factor affected the light sticks to make one brighter than the other? Use evidence from this lesson to support your claim.

The Rate Law

FIGURE 10: A series of controlled explosions break apart rocks at a quarry.

An explosion at a quarry is an impressive example of a chemical reaction. Explosive materials, such as nitroglycerin, trinitrotoluene (TNT), and dynamite are primarily organic substances. They contain mostly carbon, hydrogen, oxygen, and nitrogen atoms held together by relatively weak bonds.

These materials undergo rapid decomposition. The released elements immediately react to form gaseous N_2, CO, CO_2, and NO_2. The bonds in these molecules are much stronger than those in the original explosive material, so an enormous amount of energy is released. In addition, the sudden formation of gaseous material causes a tremendous increase in pressure that provides the force to demolish an unwanted building or break apart rocks for building roads.

PREDICT How could scientists determine the reaction rate of an explosive reaction?

_____

_____

_____

_____

Relating Concentration and Reaction Rate

We can experimentally determine the rate of a reaction by measuring the rate reactants are consumed or products are formed. It is often important to know and control the rate of a chemical reaction. For example, in an industrial process, equipment must be designed to handle a certain rate of production. If the reaction rate is too slow, then the product may cost too much. If the reaction rate is too fast, gaseous products and energy may be produced too rapidly. This can damage equipment or even cause a dangerous explosion.

The relationship between reaction rate and concentration is determined by keeping the temperature of the system constant and varying the concentration of a single reactant at a time. By running a series of such experiments, changing one reactant at a time, a chemist can determine how the concentration of each reactant affects the reaction rate.

For example, nitrogen monoxide gas reacts with hydrogen gas to produce nitrogen gas and water vapor as shown in the equation:

$$2NO(g) + 2H_2(g) \rightarrow N_2(g) + 2H_2O(g)$$

A series of experiments were performed to measure the rate of this reaction. First, scientists measured how changing the H_2 concentration affected the reaction rate when the NO concentration was held constant. Then, the scientists ran another series of experiments to measure the effect of the NO concentration while the H_2 concentration was held constant. When determining the rate of a reaction, it is important to only change the concentration of one reactant at a time. Otherwise, scientists would not be able to determine the effect of the reactants on the rate.

Experimental Reaction Rates Data		
Concentration of NO	Concentration of H_2	Change in Rate
Initial	Initial	R
Initial	Doubled	$2R$
Initial	Tripled	$3R$
Doubled	Initial	$4R$
Tripled	Initial	$9R$

Math Connection

Identifying Rate Relationships

We can represent the relationship of rate to concentration mathematically. If R represents reaction rate and [A] is the concentration of reactant A, the mathematical relationship is $R \propto$ [A] when the ratio of rate to concentration is linear. The "$\propto$" symbol means "is proportional to."

ANALYZE Use the Experimental Reaction Rates Data to determine the relationship of reactants to reaction rate. Select all correct answers.

- [ ] **a.** $R \propto [H_2]$
- [ ] **b.** $R \propto [H_2]^2$
- [ ] **c.** $R \propto [NO]$
- [ ] **d.** $R \propto [NO]^2$
- [ ] **e.** $R \propto [H_2][NO]$
- [ ] **f.** $R \propto [H_2][NO]^2$

A rate law is an equation that expresses the dependence of reaction rate on the concentrations of the reactants. The general form of a rate law is

$$R = k[A]^n[B]^m$$

where R represents the reaction rate, k is the specific rate constant, and [A] and [B] represent the molar concentrations of reactants A and B. The powers to which the concentrations are raised in calculating the rate law are represented by n and m. The rate law is applicable for a specific reaction at a given set of conditions. The value of k must be determined experimentally after the exponents have been determined experimentally.

In the example of the hydrogen gas and nitrogen monoxide gas reaction, we can replace the proportionality symbol, $\propto$, with the constant k to write the rate law:

$$R = k[H_2][NO]^2$$

Based on the experiment, you can determine that the rate is directly proportional to the concentration of hydrogen gas. So, the n in this rate law is 1, which is not written. The rate is also directly proportional to the square of the nitrogen monoxide concentration. So, the m in this rate law is 2.

The specific rate constant does not change over the course of the reaction if conditions other than concentration of reactants and products are constant. A change in the temperature of the reaction mixture, however, does change the value of k.

Determining the Rate Law

SAMPLE PROBLEM Fluorine gas reacts with chlorine dioxide gas according to the following equation:

$$F_2(g) + 2ClO_2(g) \rightarrow 2FClO_2(g)$$

Use the following experimental data to write a rate law for this reaction.

Experiment	Concentration of F_2	Concentration of ClO_2	Rate (mol/L·s)
1	0.10 M	0.10 M	1.1×10^{-3}
2	0.20 M	0.10 M	2.2×10^{-3}
3	0.10 M	0.20 M	2.2×10^{-3}
4	0.20 M	0.20 M	4.4×10^{-3}

ANALYZE To write the rate law, first examine the data to see how the rate of reaction changes as the concentrations of the reactants change.

When $[F_2]$ doubles and $[ClO_2]$ remains constant, the rate of reaction doubles from 1.1×10^{-3} mol/L·s to 2.2×10^{-3} mol/L·s, So, the rate is directly proportional to $[F_2]$, or $R \propto [F_2]$.

When $[ClO_2]$ doubles and $[F_2]$ remains constant, the rate of reaction also doubles from 1.1×10^{-3} mol/L·s to 2.2×10^{-3} mol/L·s. So, the rate is directly proportional to $[ClO_2]$, or $R \propto [ClO_2]$.

SOLVE Because the rate is proportional to both $[F_2]$ and $[ClO_2]$, you can write the rate law $R = k[F_2][ClO_2]$. The data from Trial 4 help confirm the rate law because when both $[F_2]$ and $[ClO_2]$ double, the rate increases by a factor of four, from 1.1×10^{-3} mol/L·s to 4.4×10^{-3} mol/L·s.

PRACTICE PROBLEMS **SOLVE** Nitrogen monoxide and oxygen react to produce nitrogen dioxide according to the following equation:

$$O_2(g) + 2NO(g) \rightarrow 2NO_2(g)$$

Experiment	Concentration of O_2	Concentration of NO	Rate (mol/L·s)
1	1.20×10^{-2} M	1.40×10^{-2} M	3.30×10^{-3}
2	2.40×10^{-2} M	1.40×10^{-2} M	6.60×10^{-3}
3	1.20×10^{-2} M	2.80×10^{-2} M	1.32×10^{-2}

Based on the reaction rate data, what is the rate law for this reaction?

 Evidence Notebook In your Evidence Notebook, consider the rate law for the reaction occurring in a light stick. What information would you need in order to set up an experiment to determine the rate law?

Engineering

Chemical Kinetics

Industrial explosives are used to break apart rock in mines and quarries, to clear paths for new roads, and even demolish buildings. During the explosion of these materials, matter moves very rapidly—several kilometers per second—and with a lot of force. It is important to direct this force only where it is needed. Because many of these reactions occur so rapidly, it can be difficult to study exactly how these chemical changes occur.

There are many forms of explosives used in mining, each with unique properties and reactions. Mining explosives are designed to be stable and safe to handle for long periods of time, but they also provide the maximum amount of energy when they are used. Because they provide so much energy, it is important that engineers understand how they will react to prevent accidental explosions.

Scientists and engineers process data from test explosions to model exactly what is occurring during the brief reaction. By calculating the rate of reaction under different conditions and the amount of energy released, they can determine the best design for an explosive system that performs the task safely.

In addition to using an understanding of the reactions to design better applications, understanding chemical kinetics helps in the design of safer materials. For example, a simple mechanical impact on an explosive can result in localized heating. This can cause mechanical deformation and possibly fracturing or fragmenting of the material. One section may ignite, and as the ignition spreads, the energy released could lead to anything from slow combustion of the material to violent detonation of the whole explosive device. Chemists who specialize in kinetics, materials scientists, and engineers work together to predict explosive sensitivity and design new materials that do not accidentally detonate.

FIGURE 11: A detonation test for a mining explosive

The behavior of explosives is a challenging topic because the reactions themselves are very complex, and they occur extremely rapidly. Modern sensors and computer models allow engineers to determine reaction rates with more precision than in the past. This allows them to design explosive materials and direct forces in a way that maximizes productivity and safety.

Language Arts Connection Research more information about chemical kinetics and engineering in a field other than explosives manufacturing, such as pharmaceuticals. Consider the following questions to guide your research:

- What is the engineer trying to discover through chemical kinetics?

- How are the data and conclusions from chemical kinetics experiments used in this field?

- Why is an understanding of kinetics important in process design?

Write a blog post that summarizes your findings about this field of research.

ENADERS
| ENZYMES | REACTION MECHANISMS | CLOCK REACTIONS | Go online to choose one of these other paths.

Lesson Self-Check

CAN YOU EXPLAIN IT?

FIGURE 12: Temperature affects the rate of the reaction in the light sticks.

Light sticks consist of two nested tubes. The tough plastic outer tube is filled with a solution of a reactant and a dissolved dye. A thin inner tube made of glass or brittle plastic holds a solution of a second reactant. When the tube inside a light stick is broken, the two reactants mix and start reacting. The reaction releases energy that is absorbed by the dye. Energy released by the reaction causes the dye to glow. As the reactants are used up and their concentration decreases, the light stick gradually becomes dimmer.

 Evidence Notebook Refer to your notes in your Evidence Notebook to explain why changing the temperature of a light stick affects the intensity of the light that it emits. Your explanation should include a discussion of reaction rates. Consider the following when constructing your explanation:

1. Make a claim about how temperature affects the brightness of a light stick.
2. What evidence supports your claim? How do chemical reaction rates apply to the brightness of a light stick? What is happening in the light stick on the molecular scale?
3. How does the evidence about chemical reactions support your claim?

CHECKPOINTS

Check Your Understanding

1. Complete the statement.

The rate of a chemical reaction depends on a number of different factors. When the temperature of the reaction mixture increases, the reaction rate decreases | increases | is not affected. When particles have more energy, the number of effective activations | collisions | transitions increases. At a higher concentration of reactants, the reaction rate decreases | increases | is not affected, along with the overall frequency of collisions.

2. According to collision theory, which variables affect the rate of a chemical reaction? Select all correct answers.

☐ **a.** concentrations of dissolved reactants
☐ **b.** chemical properties of reactants
☐ **c.** size of crystals of solid reactants
☐ **d.** shape of the container holding reactants

3. Complete the statement.

For a particular chemical reaction, an effective collision can only occur when molecules have the correct orientation | shape and sufficient concentration | energy. If those two conditions are not met, a collision | reaction will not occur.

Use the table for Questions 4 and 5.

Energy values of a chemical reaction	
Chemical Species	Energy (kJ/mol)
Reactants	0
Products	−110
Activated complex	45

4. Complete the statement.

During the reaction described in the table, the overall energy of the reaction is −110 kJ/mol | 110 kJ/mol, indicating that the reaction is endothermic | exothermic. The energy required to cause effective collisions between particles is 45 kJ/mol | 110 kJ/mol.

5. Which statements correctly describe the reaction described in the table? Select all correct answers.

☐ **a.** The activation energy of the reverse reaction is −45 kJ/mol.
☐ **b.** The change in energy of the reverse reaction is +110 kJ/mol.
☐ **c.** The forward reaction releases energy, so no energy must be added to start it.
☐ **d.** The forward reaction may continue spontaneously once the activation energy is added.

Use the table for Questions 6 and 7.

Reaction rates for chemical reaction: A(aq) + B(aq) → C(aq)			
Experiment	[A]	[B]	Rate (M/s)
1	0.150 M	0.300 M	0.013
2	0.150 M	0.600 M	0.052
3	0.300 M	0.300 M	0.026

6. Complete the statement.

doubles   quadruples   remains unchanged

Based on the data in the table, when the concentration of reactant A doubles, the reaction rate _____ and when the concentration of reactant B doubles, the reaction rate _____.

7. What is the rate law for the reaction between A and B?

○ **a.** $R = k[A][B]$ ○ **c.** $R = k[A][B]^2$
○ **b.** $R = k[A]^2[B]$ ○ **d.** $R = k[A]^2[B]^2$

CHECKPOINTS (continued)

8. Describe two ways to make a chemical reaction proceed faster, and explain why the rate increases according to collision theory.

_____

_____

_____

9. Use collision theory to explain why a candle cannot start burning until a flame is brought to the wick, but it continues burning once started.

_____

_____

_____

_____

10. When vinegar and baking soda are mixed together in an aqueous solution, the solution becomes colder as the reaction proceeds. How does an endothermic reaction continue without the addition of energy from outside the solution system? What can you conclude about the activation energy of the reaction?

_____

_____

_____

_____

_____

MAKE YOUR OWN STUDY GUIDE

 In your Evidence Notebook, design a study guide that supports the main ideas from this lesson:

The rate of a chemical reaction can be measured, and it can vary depending on the nature of the reactants, surface area, temperature, concentration, and the presence of a catalyst.

According to collision theory, a reaction can occur when particles collide with sufficient energy and in a favorable orientation.

The rate law of a reaction describes the correlation between the concentration of each reactant and the reaction rate.

Remember to include the following information in your study guide:
- Use examples that model main ideas.
- Record explanations for the phenomena you investigated.
- Use evidence to support your explanations. Your support can include drawings, data, graphs, laboratory conclusions, and other evidence recorded throughout the lesson.

Consider how collision theory builds a relationship between patterns of behavior of particles in chemical reactions to explain observable phenomena on a larger scale in the world around you.

Life Science Connection

Bioluminescence Even on the brightest day, sunlight is absorbed before it reaches the deep ocean. However, even far below the surface, it is not all dark. Many deep ocean organisms produce light. This light, called bioluminescence, comes from chemical reactions which release energy as light. Many organisms in the ocean and on land use bioluminescent signals to communicate, to hunt for prey, to attract mates, and to scare off predators.

> Produce a short video about one aquatic organism and one terrestrial organism that use bioluminescence. Explain how these organisms control chemical reactions to produce light energy and discuss the function of the bioluminescent signals.

FIGURE 1: Some organisms produce light.

Technology Connection

Smelting Most metals exist in nature as ores, which are rocks containing compounds of the metal and other elements, often oxygen. The smelting process extracts the metal from the ore. During smelting, ores are heated to provide energy for the chemical reactions that separate the metal from oxygen. The amount of energy needed to separate metal atoms varies with the metal and the type of ore. The most important advances in ancient metallurgy found ways to make hotter fires to refine metals.

> Write a short report about the history of smelting in ancient cultures as well as modern smelting processes. When did different metals come into production? How has the necessary temperature for smelting been achieved, both historically and in modern industry?

FIGURE 2: The process of making pure metals, such as iron, from ores is an important industrial process.

Health Connection

Time Release Pharmacokinetics is the study of interactions between medications and chemicals inside the body. Understanding how a medication affects a person is important for determining correct dosages. Given the many differences between individuals, scientists are developing more individualized medications. Researchers can decide whether to allow a slow, steady release, or immediate exposure to the full dose.

> Write a medical pamphlet that discusses why different timed releases are important for modern medical treatment. Also discuss how differences between individuals can affect the way the medication interacts with processes in the body.

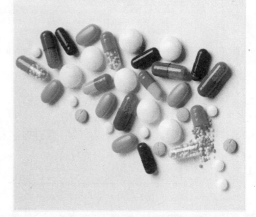

FIGURE 3: Pharmacokinetics helps scientists develop medications that interact with the body at different rates.

A BOOK EXPLAINING
COMPLEX IDEAS USING
ONLY THE 1,000 MOST
COMMON WORDS

ENERGY

How much is stored in things and how much it takes to do stuff

It is a fundamental law of science that the total amount of energy remains the same before and after a change. Energy cannot be destroyed or created. Take a look at some ways of measuring all that energy.

RANDALL MUNROE
XKCD.COM

THE STORY OF HOW ENERGY HELPS US KEEP TRACK OF THINGS

ENERGY ISN'T A REAL THING. THAT IS, IT'S NOT A THING YOU CAN HOLD OR TOUCH. IT'S MORE LIKE A WAY OF KEEPING TRACK OF THINGS. IT'S KIND OF LIKE MONEY.

YOU CAN CHANGE YOUR MONEY FROM PAPER TO PIECES OF METAL TO NUMBERS ON A COMPUTER, BUT IT DOESN'T CHANGE HOW MUCH YOU HAVE.

EVEN THOUGH YOU DON'T HOLD ON TO ANY OF THE SAME STUFF, HOW MUCH YOU HAVE STAYS THE SAME.

CAN YOU MAKE CHANGE?

SURE!

...AS LONG AS I COUNTED RIGHT!

ENERGY IS LIKE THAT. IT'S NOTHING BUT A NUMBER THAT HELPS US KEEP TRACK OF THINGS. IT ALWAYS STAYS THE SAME — IT JUST MOVES FROM ONE THING TO ANOTHER. AND KNOWING HOW MUCH ENERGY SOMETHING HAS TELLS US ABOUT HOW MUCH IT CAN DO.

KEEPING TRACK OF ENERGY HELPS US KNOW HOW FAR WE CAN DRIVE A CAR, HOW HIGH WE CAN LIFT SOMETHING, AND HOW LONG YOUR PHONE WILL LAST BEFORE IT TURNS OFF.

POP

BOOM

KEEPING TRACK OF ENERGY CAN ALSO HELP US LEARN NEW THINGS. IF WE COUNT HOW MUCH ENERGY IS GOING INTO SOMETHING, AND HOW MUCH IS COMING OUT, SOMETIMES THOSE NUMBERS DON'T MATCH UP. THAT TELLS US THAT WE'RE MISSING SOMETHING, AND WE SHOULD LOOK AT EVERYTHING MORE CAREFULLY. THERE MIGHT BE SOMETHING BIG TO DISCOVER.

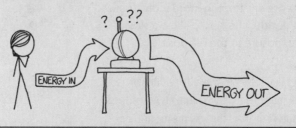

ENERGY IN

ENERGY OUT

HOW MUCH ENERGY THINGS TAKE

These pictures show how much energy is stored in things and how much energy it takes to do things.

1 PIECE OF ENERGY

You can use different kinds of numbers to talk about how much energy is stored in something, just like how you can use different kinds of numbers to say how tall you are. Lots of countries got together and agreed to use one size of number for energy to make things less confusing. Each of these squares is "1" using that size.

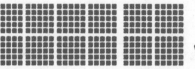

CLIMBING A TREE

This is how much energy a small animal uses to climb a tree.

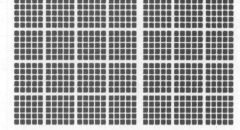

WHITE FOOD

This is how much energy is in one tiny piece of white food.

WATCH

This is how much energy is held in those silver circles that make small things like old watches run.

BIGGER BOXES

To show things with more stored energy, let's add a new kind of box that's as big as ten hundred of the old ones.

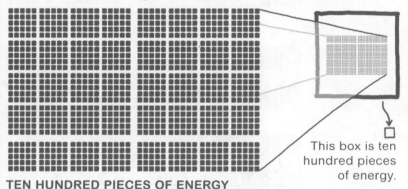

This box is ten hundred pieces of energy.

TEN HUNDRED PIECES OF ENERGY

GOING UP A FEW STAIRS

One of these bigger boxes is as much energy as it takes for a person to climb a short set of stairs.

GOING UP A FLOOR

Climbing enough stairs to go up one floor in a building takes about two of these boxes.

(That's only six of those pieces of white food!)

1 FOOD-ENERGY

On the sides of food boxes in the US, they tell you how much energy is in the food. "1" using their numbers is the same as three of these boxes.

"AA" POWER BOX

A PHONE

The energy stored in a small phone or hand computer

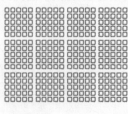

THE ENERGY STORED IN A SMALL COMPUTER

These hold about as much energy as those things people throw at each other during wars.

THE ENERGY STORED IN THESE THINGS YOU STAND ON AND RIDE AROUND

These things have a name that makes it sound like they can fly, but they can't.

They're fun to ride around on, but they need so much energy that sometimes, if their power boxes aren't very well made, they catch fire.

MORE ENERGY

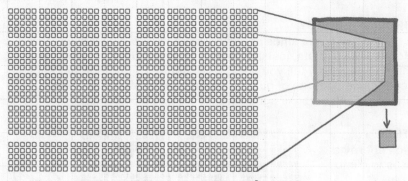

EVEN BIGGER BOXES
To show things that carry more energy, each of the boxes in this part of the page hold as much energy as ten hundred of the boxes on the page before this one.

Here's how you write this much energy: 10^6 J.

HAIR DRYER (10 MINUTES)
The energy used by a hair dryer in ten minutes

CAR STARTER
The energy in the power box that starts a car

OLD LIGHT (1 DAY)
The energy used by an old light in one day

NEW LIGHT (1 DAY)
The energy used by a new light in one day

FOOD (NORMAL PERSON)
The energy in the food a normal person eats in one day

FOOD (THE ROCK)
The energy in the food The Rock eats in a day. ("The Rock" is the name of a very strong man who acts in movies.)

$1 OF POWER
The energy you would get from your wall if you paid $1 to the power company

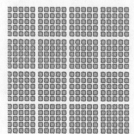

CAR THAT USES WALL POWER
This is how much energy is stored in the power box used by the kind of new car that doesn't burn anything.

STORM FLASH HITTING SAND
The energy that goes into the ground and turns sand to rock and air when the ground is hit by a flash of light from a big storm

ONE LARGE BOOK
If you burned a big book for its heat, this is how much energy you'd get.

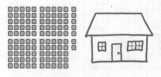

A HOUSE FOR A DAY
The energy used by a normal house in the US in one day

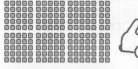

A CAR FOR A DAY
The energy used by a normal car in the US in one day

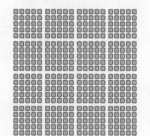

THE ENERGY USED TO MAKE A PAIR OF BLUE PANTS
This is how much energy is used by one pair of blue pants during its life. This counts the sun's light needed to grow the stuff the pants are made of and the energy to run the machines that keep the pants clean.

WAY MORE ENERGY

 Go online for more about *Thing Explainer*.

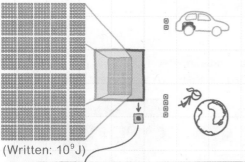

(Written: 10^9 J)

ENERGY IN A CAR
The energy in a normal car when you fill it up before a long drive

GOING TO SPACE
This is how much energy it takes to lift a person to space (if you don't throw away energy on extra stuff along the way like a rocket does).

THE ENERGY IT WOULD TAKE TO DRIVE A CAR AROUND THE WORLD
(if there were a road running around the middle of the Earth)

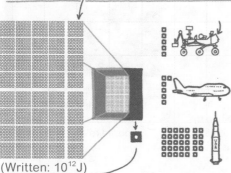

(Written: 10^{12} J)

BOX OF HEAVY METAL
The energy in a box of heavy metal powering a space car.

SKY BOAT
The energy in a sky boat that carries people across the sea

MOON BOAT
The energy in one of the space boats we flew in to visit the moon

A BIG OCEAN-CROSSING BOAT
The energy a big boat uses when carrying stuff across our biggest body of water

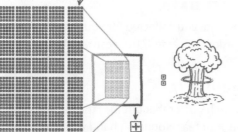

(Written: 10^{15} J)

CITY-BURNING MACHINE
The energy that would come out if we set off one of our war machines—the kind that flies around the world, blows up, and burns a city

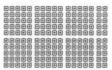

ONE SECOND OF SUN
The energy from all the sun's light that hits the Earth in one second

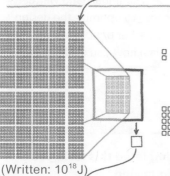

(Written: 10^{18} J)

A BIG CIRCLE STORM
The energy from all the winds, from start to end, in the kind of big circle storm that forms over warm seas

US WALL POWER
The energy all the people in the US use in a year (only counting the kind of power carried by power lines)

US ENERGY USE (ALL KINDS)
The energy used by the US in a year, adding together all the stuff we get power from

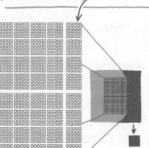

(Written: 10^{21} J)

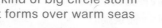

ONE DAY OF SUN
The energy in the sun's light that hits Earth every day

ENERGY IN THE GROUND
The energy we could get if we dug up all the stuff in the ground we can burn for power

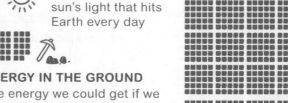 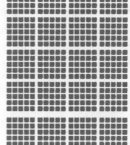

SPACE ROCK OF DEATH
Long ago, one of these hit Earth and killed most of the animals in the family birds are from. This is how much energy it let out when it hit.

Optimizing Heat Packs

There are many different types of heat packs available, but what is the difference between them? Research heat packs and the different ways they release energy in the form of heat. Your engineering challenge is to build a hand warmer and optimize it by increasing the temperature or making it last longer.

1. DEFINE THE PROBLEM

Decide which engineering challenge to investigate. What criteria and constraints need to be considered in your final design? Are there any tradeoffs to consider when developing a solution to this problem?

2. CONDUCT RESEARCH

Investigate three to four different kinds of hand warmers and develop a decision matrix to help you weigh the pros and cons of each style. Consider what situations or environments each kind of hand warmer is designed to work within. How did these considerations influence each design?

3. CARRY OUT AN INVESTIGATION

With a small group, build a homemade hand warmer.

Explore Online ▶

🧪 **Hands-On Lab**

Design a Hand Warmer Many hand warmers rely on simple chemical reactions to produce heat. Develop a homemade hand warmer, then optimize your design.

4. PLAN AN INVESTIGATION

With your team, optimize your hand warmer to either produce more heat or to last longer. Consider which of the materials in the hand warmer are most important for the design challenge you chose to investigate. Then, write a plan about how you will adjust your hand warmer to build a successful solution. Consider what data you will collect and how you will measure success.

FIGURE 4: Hand warmers can use physical or chemical changes to release energy in the form of heat.

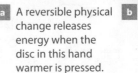

a A reversible physical change releases energy when the disc in this hand warmer is pressed.

b An irreversible chemical reaction releases energy when this hand warmer is exposed to air.

5. EVALUATE DATA

Evaluate the data you collected for your hand warmer. Was your design successful? How can you tell?

6. COMMUNICATE

Make a research poster that outlines the background information your team found on hand warmers and the design challenge your team investigated. Your poster should display the data on your initial hand warmer. Then, explain how you chose to optimize the design and the data that shows whether or not your solution was effective. Finally, explain how you evaluated your design process.

✓ CHECK YOUR WORK

Once you have completed this task, you should have the following:

- a problem statement that was addressed in the final presentation
- data on the performance of the initial design
- a presentation explaining how your hand warmer works and the process used to optimize it
- data on the performance of the final design
- an evaluation of the effectiveness of the design solution process

Name _____   Date _____

In your Evidence Notebook, make a concept map, other graphic organizer, or outline using the Study Guides you made for each lesson in this unit. Be sure to use evidence to support your claims.

When synthesizing individual information, remember to follow these general steps:

- Find the central idea of each piece of information.
- Think about the relationships among the central ideas.
- Combine the ideas to come up with a new understanding.

Look back to the Driving Questions from the opening section of this unit. In your Evidence Notebook, review and revise your previous answers to those questions. Use the evidence you gathered and other observations you made throughout the unit to support your claims.

1. Complete the statement about the change in enthalpy during the combustion of carbon.

   Carbon and oxygen react by combustion to form carbon dioxide in an endothermic | exothermic reaction. The enthalpy change during the reaction is negative | positive so the chemical bonds of the products have less | more energy than the chemical bonds of the reactants. The products are less | more stable than the reactants.

2. According to collision theory, which variables affect the rate of a chemical reaction? Select all correct answers.

   ☐ **a.** concentration of reactants
   ☐ **b.** temperature of reaction mixture
   ☐ **c.** volume of reaction vessel
   ☐ **d.** chemical structure of the reactants
   ☐ **e.** interaction with a catalyst

3. Propane is easily liquefied and stored in large tanks to heat homes, or stored in portable tanks for outdoor grills. It reacts with oxygen in an exothermic reaction that produces 2219 kJ/mol of thermal energy. Complete the thermochemical equation for this reaction.

   $$C_3H_8 + 5O_2 \rightarrow 3CO_2 + 4H_2O$$

   $\Delta H =$ _____ kJ

4. For the reaction:

   $$A(g) + B(g) \rightarrow C(g)$$

   when $[A] = [B] = 0.250$ M, $R = 1.5 \times 10^{-4}$ M/s
   when $[A] = 0.500$ M and $[B] = 0.250$ M,
   $R = 3.0 \times 10^{-4}$ M/s
   when $[A] = 0.250$ M and $[B] = 0.500$ M,
   $R = 6.0 \times 10^{-4}$ M/s

   What is the rate law for the reaction between A and B?
   ○ **a.** $R = k[A][B]$
   ○ **b.** $R = k[A]^2[B]$
   ○ **c.** $R = k[A][B]^2$
   ○ **d.** $R = k[A]^2[B]^2$

5. An enzyme is a catalyst that is used by an organism and that controls the reaction rate of biological reactions. Which of these could be a function of an enzyme in a cell? Select all correct answers.

   ☐ **a.** To cause a reaction to occur at a lower temperature than outside the cell.
   ☐ **b.** To increase the reaction rate of a reaction that would otherwise be too slow for the cell to function.
   ☐ **c.** To shift a reversible reaction in the direction of the products.
   ☐ **d.** To reduce the concentration of reactants needed to form a given amount of products.

6. What is the effect of increasing temperature on the reaction rate, the rate law, and on the specific rate constant of a chemical reaction?

_____

_____

_____

_____

_____

_____

7. Explain how the activation energy and the energy of the activated complex of an endothermic reaction compare to the activation energy and the energy of the activated complex of its reverse reaction.

_____

_____

_____

_____

_____

_____

_____

8. Explain why there is a danger of explosion in places such as coal mines, sawmills, and grain elevators, where large amounts of dry, powdered combustible materials are present.

_____

_____

_____

_____

_____

_____

_____

UNIT PROJECT

Return to your unit project. Prepare your research and materials into a presentation to share with the class. In your final presentation, evaluate the strength of your hypothesis, data, analysis, and conclusions.

Remember these tips while evaluating:

- Clearly define the purpose and goals of your research.

- Use scientific principles in evaluating your findings and using them to explain phenomena.

- Make a clear claim about how your evidence supports a claim about a phenomenon.

- Relate patterns of change in matter and energy to your explanation of the specific changes you are addressing.

Human Activity and Earth's Atmosphere

YOU SOLVE IT

Can You Design a Battery?

 To begin exploring this unit's concepts,
go online to investigate ways to solve a
real-world problem.

Energy for lighting can sometimes
blur the distinction between day
and night.

FIGURE 1: Massive solar projects are capturing renewable energy from the sun.

Fossil fuels provide energy for most electricity, transportation, and manufacturing in the United States. The combustion of fossil fuels produces greenhouse gases which contribute to climate change. To slow climate change, scientists are developing and optimizing renewable energy sources. These sources produce little to no greenhouse gases when generating energy. However, some renewable energy technologies have limitations that can make them less practical, or more costly, than fossil fuels. For example, large solar farms are only efficient in sunny locations. They also take up large amounts of land and can impact local ecosystems.

PREDICT What do you think are some of the challenges for solutions that could decrease the use of fossil fuels and make renewable energy sources more practical to use?

_____

_____

_____

DRIVING QUESTIONS

As you move through the unit, gather evidence to help you answer the following questions. In your Evidence Notebook, record what you already know about these topics and any questions you have about them.

1. How is energy obtained from different sources stored, transported, and used?
2. How do scientists and engineers use their knowledge of climate science and chemistry to develop energy system solutions that optimize conservation and minimize pollution at different scales?
3. How has California addressed environmental problems related to energy use?

UNIT PROJECT

Go online to download the Unit Project Worksheet to help plan your project.

Build a Wind Turbine

Build, test, and optimize the blade design for a wind turbine that generates electrical energy. What criteria and constraints are important to consider when developing a wind turbine?

Language Development

Use the lessons in this unit to complete the chart and expand your understanding of the science concepts.

TERM: efficiency

Definition	Example

Similar Term	Phrase

TERM: renewable energy

Definition	Example

Similar Term	Phrase

TERM: energy budget

Definition	Example

Similar Term	Phrase

TERM: feedback loop

Definition	Example

Similar Term	Phrase

TERM: acid

Definition	Example

Similar Term	Phrase

TERM: base

Definition	Example

Similar Term	Phrase

TERM: pH

Definition	Example

Similar Term	Phrase

TERM: acid precipitation

Definition	Example

Similar Term	Phrase

Human Populations and Energy Use

An oil pumpjack operates near homes in a California neighborhood.

CAN YOU SOLVE IT?

You might have seen structures around your community that are used for collecting, transporting, or burning fuel. The oil pumpjack near these homes in California pumps crude oil from Earth's crust. After the oil is extracted, it is separated into its components, which are used to make various products. Some products may be burned to produce electricity or move vehicles, or they may be used to make new materials such as plastics. There are benefits to using fossil fuels, such as their convenience and relatively low cost. However, using these fuels can also be hazardous to the environment and human health. As a result, scientists and engineers are working together to find solutions to our society's energy needs. Every energy source has pros and cons that should be evaluated.

PREDICT Imagine you are developing an energy plan for a town in California. The plan must reduce environmental impacts, provide for the town's energy needs, and fit within the town's budget. What types of pros and cons might you need to consider when evaluating different energy sources, such as oil, gas, solar, and wind?

_____

_____

_____

 Evidence Notebook As you explore this lesson, gather evidence to explain the benefits and costs of using different energy sources.

Analyzing Energy Consumption

Modern life is based on the use of energy for almost every task. Energy is used for cooking, lighting, air conditioning, and transportation. The energy to make this happen usually comes from fossil fuels, such as oil and gas, but it may also come from other sources, such as solar energy. In the same way that a car needs fuel to move, your body needs fuel to maintain and repair itself. When you eat, energy in the food is released and transformed to allow cells to carry out the functions needed for life. Whether it is the food we eat or the gas we put in our cars, fuel contains stored energy that can be used to carry out tasks.

 Collaborate With a partner, make a list of things you do every day that consume energy. For each item on the list, identify the source of energy.

FIGURE 1: Wonderwerk Cave is a site where early hominins left evidence of using fires as early as one million years ago.

Combustion: The Original Energy Resource

People have been using the combustion of fuel for heating and cooking ever since early human ancestors started using fire. Wood is a common fuel used for fires. Wood and other plant matter is made largely of cellulose. Cellulose is composed of glucose molecules linked together to form long chains. Burning wood is a combustion reaction in which glucose, $C_6H_{12}O_6$, reacts with oxygen to produce carbon dioxide and water with the release of energy.

$$C_6H_{12}O_6(s) + 6O_2(g) \rightarrow 6CO_2(g) + 6H_2O(l) + energy$$

Systems and System Models

When glucose in wood is burned in a fire, energy is released quickly, and a large portion of that energy is in the form of heat. When living organisms break down glucose, the same amount of energy is released, but the process occurs through many enzyme-regulated steps. By slowing down the process of breaking down glucose, living organisms can release the energy in small amounts and use it for cell processes. *Metabolism* is the chemical process that occurs in living organisms that breaks down glucose from food and releases usable energy. The chemical equation for metabolism is:

$$C_6H_{12}O_6(s) + 6O_2(g) \rightarrow 6CO_2(g) + 6H_2O(l) + energy$$

EXPLAIN Compare and contrast the burning of wood and the metabolism of glucose in your cells. How are they similar, and how are they different?

_____

_____

_____

Data Analysis

Population and Carbon Emissions

Humans depended mainly on burning wood as their primary energy source up until the nineteenth century. Coal and oil have since replaced wood as a primary energy source because they are more efficient fuel sources for an industrialized world. The small amount of carbon dioxide (CO_2) released when early human ancestors burned wood in fires was not a problem for the atmosphere to recycle. Earth's population, however, has substantially increased. The average amount of energy used by each individual has also increased. People now burn much larger amounts of fossil fuels for heating and cooling, in the production of electricity, and for powering vehicles. As a result, carbon emissions have increased significantly.

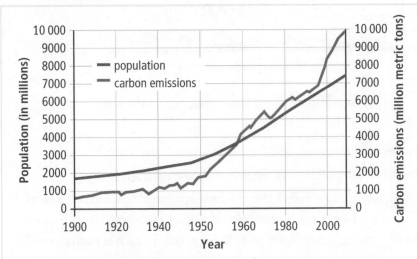

World Population and Carbon Emissions

FIGURE 2: This graph shows global human population and carbon emission levels from 1900 to the early 21st century. Carbon emissions are expressed in millions of metric tons. One metric ton is equivalent to 1000 kg.

Credit: Adapted from World Population Prospects 2017 by United Nations, Population Division. Copyright © 2017 by United Nations. Adapted and reproduced by permission of the United Nations.
Credit: Adapted from Historical Population data by Netherlands Environmental Assessment Agency. Copyright © 2018 by Netherlands Environmental Assessment Agency. Adapted and reproduced by permission of Netherlands Environmental Assessment Agency.
Source: Carbon Dioxide Information Analysis Center. Global, Regional, and National Fossil-Fuel CO_2 Emissions. DOI: 10.3334/CDIAC/00001_V2017

ANALYZE Describe patterns you see in the graph. How have both population and carbon emissions changed?

_____

_____

_____

_____

_____

Today, Earth has over 7 billion people, and the number is expected to reach 11 billion by the year 2100. This trend correlates with a steep increase in fossil fuel usage, but individual energy use is also a factor. *Per capita consumption* of resources refers to the average amount an individual uses. Between 1980 and 2014, the world per capita consumption of oil increased by over 30 percent.

Biomass fuels, such as wood, were the dominant source of energy in the early history of the U.S. Coal became an important energy source during the Industrial Revolution (1712–1850). The next new energy sources, introduced in about 1900, were petroleum and natural gas. Nuclear energy, as well as renewable energy sources such as hydroelectric, solar, and wind, became more widely used in the twentieth century.

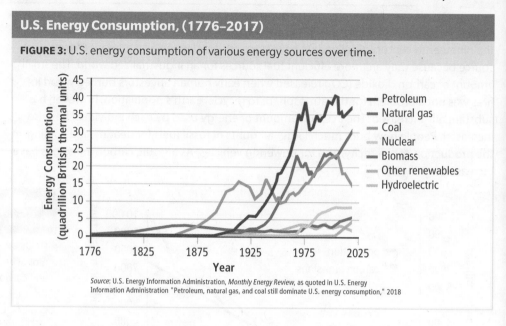

U.S. Energy Consumption, (1776–2017)

FIGURE 3: U.S. energy consumption of various energy sources over time.

Source: U.S. Energy Information Administration, *Monthly Energy Review*, as quoted in U.S. Energy Information Administration "Petroleum, natural gas, and coal still dominate U.S. energy consumption," 2018

EXPLAIN Complete the statement about the data shown in the graph.

From 1950 to 1975, the consumption of petroleum and natural gas increased | decreased. In the early 2000s, the consumption of coal and petroleum increased | decreased while the consumption of natural gas increased | decreased. At the same time, the consumption of other forms of energy, such as hydroelectric and other renewable resources, increased | decreased as societies progressed into the 21st century.

The growing population's use of fossil fuels since the start of the Industrial Revolution has rapidly increased the concentration of carbon dioxide in Earth's atmosphere. As a result, the lower atmosphere and surface are rapidly warming, snow and ice are melting, and sea level is rising. Therefore, reducing carbon emissions is a critical step in protecting the health of our planet for future generations. In order to decrease carbon emissions, the consumption of fossil fuels must decrease. Scientists and engineers are working diligently to develop solutions that will help people use energy more efficiently and make using renewable energy sources more practical and affordable.

 Collaborate Using energy more efficiently conserves resources and reduces pollution. With a partner, discuss some ways you could conserve energy in your daily life.

 Evidence Notebook Describe some of the challenges you can see with trying to reduce global carbon emissions. What questions would you ask to better define this problem?

Evaluating Energy Sources

Every energy source has benefits and costs. Some are convenient to use but have negative effects on the environment. Some have fewer environmental impacts but are costly. A cost-benefit analysis is one way to compare energy solutions. Part of this analysis includes a cost-benefit ratio, which is the present value of all a solution's benefits divided by the present value of all its costs. A solution is generally considered worthwhile if this ratio is greater than 1.

Evidence Notebook As you read about each energy source, use a graphic organizer to summarize its benefits and costs. Consider how each source is obtained, transported, and used, as well as its power output, effects on the environment, and effects on human health.

Using Fossil Fuels

Fossil fuels include coal, petroleum, and natural gas. These fuels formed over millions of years and are buried in Earth's crust. Fossil fuels are nonrenewable resources, meaning they are not being replenished as fast as they are used. They will eventually either run out or become no longer economically feasible to extract.

Coal

Millions of years ago, swamps containing abundant plants covered many areas of Earth. As the plants died, their remains built up, forming thick layers of dead organic matter. Over time, heat and pressure from being buried chemically changed the organic matter into dense coal. Today, coal is mined as an energy source. Subsurface coal mining involves drilling through Earth's surface, removing coal, and transporting it to the surface. This method of mining can be dangerous for workers and have long-term effects on their health. Prolonged exposure to coal dust can impair lung function. Another method for extracting coal is surface mining, which strips away the overlying rock to expose the coal. This method is easier than underground mining, but surface mining operations can cause pollution and destroy natural habitats.

FIGURE 4: Coal miners work in difficult and dangerous conditions to break up and remove coal in mines.

When burned, coal releases energy as well as impurities that were part of the original plants, such as sulfur, aluminum, mercury, and lead. These impurities pollute the air, water, and soil in ecosystems. Humans and other organisms rely on healthy functioning ecosystems. Due to strict laws in the state of California, only one coal-fired power plant still operates there. The state receives some energy from out-of-state coal power plants, but these sources are being phased out.

Language Arts Connection In the process of mine reclamation, land that was previously used for mining is restored to a more natural state. Research mine reclamation and make an infographic to show how it reduces negative impacts on the environment.

Petroleum

Petroleum, also called crude oil, is composed of the remains of ancient marine organisms. Burning petroleum releases 40–60 percent more energy per gram than coal. Petroleum formed when ancient marine organisms died, and their matter built up and was quickly buried on the ocean floor. Rather than hardening into a solid such as coal, the organic matter turned to liquid carbon over millions of years. The liquid rose up through rock layers and became trapped in geologic structures, producing pools of petroleum. Today, wells are drilled into the pools and petroleum is pumped out of the ground.

Because petroleum is a liquid, it is easier to distribute and use than coal. However, petroleum must be processed, or refined, to make products such as gasoline. In order to reduce carbon emissions and pollution from petroleum, California requires that vehicles use special blends of gasoline and imposes a relatively high gasoline tax.

 Matter and Energy

Refining Petroleum

Petroleum is a mixture of hydrocarbons that are separated during refining. In a process called fractional distillation, heat is applied to the petroleum, causing the hydrocarbons to evaporate. The vapors pass into a tall column, which is hot at the bottom and cool at the top. Condensers are placed at different heights in the column, allowing materials to be separated by boiling point. Each hydrocarbon has unique properties. The smallest hydrocarbons (1 to 4 carbon atoms) are used as light fuels, as gasoline additives, and in plastics manufacturing. Heavier hydrocarbons (5 to 18 carbon atoms) are used as fuels, such as gasoline, diesel, and heating oil. The heaviest hydrocarbons (more than 18 carbon atoms) are used as lubricants, waxes, paraffin, asphalt, and coke—a fuel used in the manufacture of steel.

INFER Complete the statement about fractional distillation.

The hydrocarbons with the fewest carbon atoms rise to the top of a petroleum fractionating tower. These hydrocarbons have the lowest | highest boiling points. The hydrocarbons with the most carbon atoms are collected from the bottom of a fractional distillation column. These hydrocarbons have the lowest | highest boiling points and flow less | more easily than other hydrocarbons in the column.

FIGURE 5: Concern about oil spills from the Dakota Access Pipeline led to a 2016 protest by the Standing Rock Sioux.

Crude oil is refined into many different hydrocarbons, and some are used as fuels. This fuel is transported from the refinery to users through pipelines, by truck, and by train. The transport of fuels requires the use of additional fuel and carries risks, such as spills and explosions. Most pipelines run underground and cross both remote and urban areas throughout the U.S. The construction of pipelines fragments habitat and affects human property. While generally safe, pipelines eventually leak and sometimes rupture. Whether from oil tanker accidents, oil well accidents, or pipeline leaks, spilled oil pollutes water and land and harms organisms. For example, spills from drill sites on land can seep into the ground or into rivers and lakes and contaminate the drinking water of many communities. Modern drilling methods are reducing some risks of spills, but other challenges still remain.

Natural Gas

The same process that formed petroleum from ancient marine organisms also formed natural gas. Natural gas is made up primarily of the lightest hydrocarbon, methane (CH_4). It is used as an energy source for cooking and heating in homes, and it is burned to generate electricity. Natural gas burns completely, making it a cleaner fuel than coal or petroleum. Because it is a gas, it does not contain the same impurities found in petroleum or coal, so it does not cause the same kind or amount of pollution. Burning natural gas does still produce carbon dioxide, but the output is 30 percent less than petroleum and 43 percent less than it is for coal.

FIGURE 6: Natural gas burns completely.

Hydraulic Fracturing

Hydraulic fracturing, commonly called fracking, is a method used to increase the extraction of petroleum and natural gas from deep underground. Fracking involves injecting water, sand, and other substances–such as detergents, salts, acids, alcohols, lubricants, and disinfectants–into rock under very high pressure. This causes the rock to fracture and release petroleum and natural gas, which are then pumped out of the ground along with the water. The water must be separated from the petroleum and gas before they can be refined. The water is contaminated with chemicals from the injection mixture and with toxic substances from underground, so it must be handled as hazardous waste.

FIGURE 7: Fracking is a method used to extract fossil fuels, such as natural gas and petroleum, from rock underground.

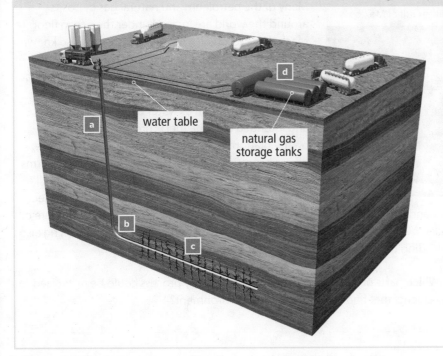

water table

natural gas storage tanks

a A well is drilled into the shale that potentially contains natural gas. A steel pipe called a casing is inserted into the well to keep the well open.

b The well is drilled vertically and then extended horizontally into the shale that contains the natural gas.

c Explosive charges make holes in the well casing and fracture the surrounding rock. Sand, water, and chemicals are pumped into the cracks at high pressure to fracture the rock further. Gas escapes through the fissures propped open by sand particles and into the well casing.

d When fracking is complete, gas flows to the surface where it can be collected and stored.

ANALYZE There is growing concern about the effects of fracking on soil and water quality, as well as the link between fracking and earthquakes. Which parts of the fracking process do you think are related to these problems? Explain your reasoning.

_____

_____

_____

_____

Fracking has experienced increasing use since the 1990s due to the development of new methods for extracting natural gas. The increase in the injection of chemicals into the ground has led to an increase in contamination of soil as well as groundwater and surface water—both sources of drinking water—in areas where it has been used extensively. The chemicals used in fracking can cause health problems for many human body systems. In addition, the returned fluids contain other harmful substances picked up during the process. They are hazardous waste and must be handled carefully.

Another concern with natural gas is what happens when it leaks. Although it burns more cleanly than other fossil fuels, unburned methane has a much stronger effect on Earth's atmosphere than carbon dioxide. In 2014, California passed a law requiring gas companies to make data about methane leaks available to the public. Since then, methane emissions by utility companies have decreased. The worst methane leak in U.S. history occurred near Los Angeles, California. The Aliso Canyon gas leak released over 97 000 metric tons of methane into the atmosphere and forced the evacuation of 8000 homes.

EXPLAIN How would you describe the benefits and costs of using natural gas to a person who was concerned about climate change and their family's health?

_____

_____

_____

FIGURE 8: An offshore drilling rig in the Gulf of Mexico

Many of the petroleum and natural gas deposits around the world are located under the ocean floor. To reach these reservoirs, offshore platforms, also known as oil rigs, are used for drilling and extraction. These platforms may be anchored to the ocean floor or float on the surface. The design of the platform depends on many factors such as water depth, platform size, and intended use. The fuel is processed and stored on the platform until it can be transported to shore, where it is refined and distributed. Offshore platforms often include living facilities for workers, as well. Like other extraction methods, offshore drilling is subject to accidents and spills. In 2010, the Deepwater Horizon oil spill occurred at an offshore oil rig and spilled over 200 million gallons of crude oil into the Gulf of Mexico. The oil rig also exploded, leading to the loss of life and many injured workers.

PREDICT Which parts of the offshore drilling and delivery process could be optimized to minimize accidents that harm humans and the environment?

_____

_____

_____

Tar Sands and Oil Shales

Tar sands and oil shales are petroleum resources that have only recently become economical to extract. Like surface coal mining, surface mining for tar sands and oil shale causes habitat loss, increased erosion, and runoff of polluted water. The extraction process is expensive and requires a considerable amount of water and energy. As in fracking, the waste water is highly contaminated and must be handled as hazardous material.

Transforming Energy

Today, most electricity is produced through burning fossil fuels. Fossil fuels are primary energy sources because they occur naturally. Secondary energy sources are made from primary energy sources. Electricity is a common secondary energy source that can be produced from many different primary energy sources.

Explore Online ▶

FIGURE 9: Internal combustion engine

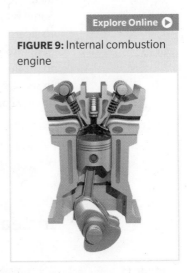

Most vehicles currently use internal combustion engines. This type of engine converts the energy released from combustion reactions into mechanical energy, which can be used to do work. In the internal combustion engine, the reaction is confined within a chamber that contains a movable piston. Gas is admitted into the chamber, compressed by the piston, and then ignited by a spark. The sudden, significant increase in pressure from the exploding high-temperature gases forces the piston outward. Connecting the piston to a spinning crankshaft allows this mechanical energy the gases produce to do work. It might turn the wheels of a vehicle or the rudders of ship.

The chemical energy in fossil fuels can also be used to produce electrical energy. In a coal-fired electric power plant, the process begins by burning coal in a furnace and using the heat to turn water into steam in a boiler. The powerful jet of steam then turns a turbine to produce mechanical energy. The turbine spins a shaft connected to a generator. The generator contains magnets that generate a magnetic field. When the magnets move relative to coils of wire, they produce an electric field. This is called electromagnetic induction. Thus, the generator spins and transforms the mechanical energy of the spinning shaft into electrical energy through electromagnetic induction. The steam is cooled, and the water is returned to the original water source.

FIGURE10: A coal-fired power plant burns coal to produce electricity.

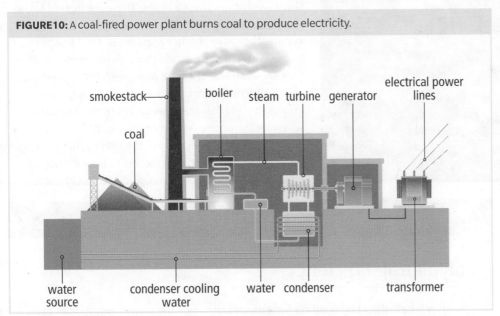

MODEL Draw a flow chart to show how energy changes form at each step in a coal-fired power plant.

Not all of the heat released from the combustion of coal is used to generate electricity. In fact, most of the heat is wasted, meaning it becomes unavailable for producing electricity. Some is lost with the exhaust gases from the furnace. Other heat is lost as the water turns to steam. Still, other energy is lost through friction in the spinning turbine and in the generator, further reducing the amount of chemical energy from the coal that is used to produce electricity. Additional energy is required for the operation of the plant itself. In short, each conversion has a loss of energy associated with it. The greater number of energy conversions, the greater amount of energy is wasted.

 Collaborate Discuss this question with a partner: What steps of electricity generation should an engineer focus on if they want to make electricity production more efficient?

Increasing Efficiency

FIGURE 11: Plugs in a powerstrip generate heat when they are plugged in. This thermogram shows the areas of highest temperature as white, red, and orange. The more efficient plugs produce less heat, meaning more of the useful energy is output for their respective devices.

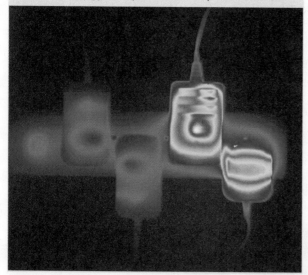

During any energy conversion, some energy is wasted and is therefore not usable. The efficiency of an energy conversion is calculated as the ratio between the useful energy produced and the energy input to the system. Efficiency is often reported as a percent value. For example, a coal-fired power plant loses energy in many stages of the energy conversion process. The efficiency rate for a coal-fired power plant is about 33 to 38 percent. Additional losses occur during the transmission of electricity from resistance in the wires. Once electricity enters a home, there are further losses due to electric conversions in heating and cooling systems, lights, and other appliances. Heat inside the house is lost to the outside through poor insulation. Cars are even less efficient. Most vehicles convert only about 12 to 30 percent of the energy from gasoline into usable mechanical energy. Energy is wasted when fuel is incompletely burned. Further losses occur during the operation of the engine, the cooling system, and the electrical systems to operate the air conditioner, lights, computer, and ignition system.

 Problem Solving

Calculating Efficiency

Efficiency is calculated by dividing the energy output by the energy input. The result is multiplied by 100 to express efficiency as a percentage.

$$\text{Efficiency} = \left(\frac{\text{energy output}}{\text{energy input}} \right) \times 100$$

SOLVE A car engine produces 604 kJ of mechanical energy from fuel capable of producing 2416 kJ of energy. The efficiency of the engine is _____%.

Alternative Energy Sources

As you have observed, the use of fossil fuels has known drawbacks. Not only do they produce pollutants when used, but also extracting them from the ground has potentially damaging effects on ecosystems. In addition, their increased use has resulted in increased levels of carbon dioxide in the atmosphere. Fossil fuels are also nonrenewable and will eventually run out. Scientists, policymakers, and concerned citizens are therefore looking for alternative energy sources, including nuclear power and renewable energy resources. Renewable resources are those that can be replenished as they are used. Such sources include wind, solar, geothermal, water, and biomass.

Nuclear Power

Most energy-releasing reactions are chemical reactions, which do not affect atomic nuclei. Nuclear reactions involve changes in nuclei, during which small amounts of matter are changed to huge amounts of energy. Just as in a coal power plant, this energy can be used to power steam turbines, so they can generate electrical energy. Although nuclear energy produces no atmospheric pollutants, the processes for mining and refining radioactive materials require large amounts of energy. Nuclear fuel is radioactive, and major concerns surround the disposal of used, or "spent," nuclear fuel. These fuels are extremely toxic and are known carcinogens. Their negative impacts on organisms and ecosystems are long-lived and difficult to mitigate. Accidents at power plants, such as the nuclear disaster at the Fukushima power plant in Japan in 2011, have added to concerns over the safety and reliability of nuclear power solutions.

FIGURE 12: The Diablo Canyon nuclear power plant in San Luis Obispo County

The dependence on nuclear energy has decreased in California in recent years. It has become a less-desirable energy source as the cost of natural gas and renewable energy sources has dropped and nuclear safety concerns remain. In January of 2018, the California Public Utilities Commission decided to close California's last nuclear power plant by 2025. This power plant is the Diablo Canyon Power Plant in San Luis Obispo County, shown in Figure 12. The power company itself asked the commission to close it down. Its federal license to operate expires in 2025. The power plant, however, is a major employer, and so the shutdown may not be easy for some.

 Language Arts Connection Economics is a major concern with closing down the Diablo Canyon Power Plant. As the fourth-largest employer in the county, the plant supports the local economy through the approximately $1 billion a year it pays its 1500 employees, most of whom will have to search for new jobs. A proposal to spend $85 million in the community over the next several years to help with the transition was not approved. Many people, including some legislators, believe that the county and its residents deserve to be compensated for the impacts on the community when the plant shuts down. Write a statement explaining whether you agree with requiring compensation for the losses suffered by the community when the plant shuts down. Support your answer with examples and evidence. Other than these community members, who might be affected either positively or negatively by the plant's closure?

FIGURE 13: The Topaz Solar Farm in San Luis Obispo County is a 550-megawatt photovoltaic power station, one of the world's largest solar farms.

Solar Energy

Solar energy, which is energy from the sun, can be used to produce electricity. Photovoltaic cells are devices that convert the energy in visible light directly into electrical energy. Photovoltaic cells are connected in panels to produce electricity that may be used at that site. Excess electricity can be sent back to the electrical grid for distribution and use at other locations.

In regions that do have consistent sunlight, huge solar energy "farms" produce energy for entire communities. 25.6 square kilometers of land near the location of the Diablo Canyon nuclear power plant is now covered with a solar energy farm. This is just one of many such farms that dot the California landscape. At the end of 2016, California was the highest solar-power generating state in the United States, and its capacity for producing solar power is only expected to increase.

FIGURE 14: The San Gorgonio Pass wind farm is located in the rugged mountains that surround the Los Angeles Basin.

Wind Energy

Energy from the movement of air in the form of wind can be harnessed to make electricity. Wind generators come in many different sizes. While small windmills produce only a modest amount of electricity, large wind turbines, over 100 m tall, used in groups called wind farms can deliver much more power. They are often situated on hilltops, open plains, shorelines, or in mountain gaps—places that generally experience steady winds. Wind farms need to be in areas with a minimum annual average wind speed of about 20 km per hour. Of course, the wind speed has to be high enough to turn the blades, but winds that are too strong can damage the blades. When wind speeds are too high, turbines must be shut down temporarily and the blades locked in place.

While not unusual to see a private windmill providing energy to an individual home or business, most wind energy is commercial. Wind energy accounted for 39 percent of the renewable energy produced in California in 2016. At that time, this was enough electricity to provide power to more than 2 million households in California. More importantly, the cost of this wind energy was approximately one-fourth of the cost it had been in the 1980s. Most of the wind farms in California are located in Altamont, East San Diego County, Pacheco, Solano, San Gorgonio, and Tehachapi.

APPLY Solar and wind energy are both intermittent resources that cannot be relied upon for a constant stream of energy production. Explain why developing better ways to store energy is an important part of making these energy sources more practical to use.

_____

_____

_____

_____

Geothermal Energy

Geothermal energy is heat that comes from below Earth's surface. Similar to the other examples, geothermal energy takes steam from underground sources and uses it to turn a turbine. As an energy source, it is clean, renewable, and produces no greenhouse gases. In addition, unlike the sources of solar energy and wind energy, its source is not variable. If geothermal energy is available at all in a region, it is available consistently. In 2016, geothermal energy provided almost 6 percent of California's energy needs.

California generates the largest amount of geothermal energy in the United States. After all, California is located on the "ring of fire," which is the volcanically active region surrounding the Pacific Ocean. Just as magma near Earth's surface produces volcanoes, it provides heat in Earth's crust that can be tapped to provide geothermal energy. California has 25 geothermal resource areas, many of which are used to harness geothermal energy. The largest concentration of geothermal plants is in the Geysers Geothermal Resource Area in Lake and Sonoma Counties. This facility, shown in Figure 15, is located north of San Francisco and has been producing electricity since the 1960s.

FIGURE 15: The Geysers geothermal power plant is the largest producer of geothermal electricity in the world

Energy from Water

Hydroelectric energy is electricity that is produced from moving water. The movement of water causes a turbine to spin, which produces electricity that is distributed to the power grid. Electricity can be generated from the movement of river water or ocean water. A major drawback of generating hydroelectric power from a river is the need for a dam. Dams are expensive to build and change the natural flow of water. Carbon dioxide and methane may also form in the water behind the dam and be emitted into the atmosphere. For these reasons, some dams have been decommissioned. California has more than 250 hydroelectric facilities. Electricity produced by running water and used by California in 2017 totaled nearly 21 percent of the state's total system power.

Regions like California, which has a long ocean shoreline, are prime candidates for using ocean energy. Although ocean energy can be used in many different ways, the most common forms of usage are tidal power, wave power, and ocean thermal energy conversion. The tidal differences found in California are not large enough to make tidal power a viable energy source there. California is much more likely to use wave energy as a power source along its Pacific coastline. Wave energy conversion is similar to tidal power in that energy in water movement is harnessed to turn turbines. Wave energy conversion units are installed underwater or on the water's surface. These may pose threats to boats if they cannot detect them and collide with them.

 Collaborate Discuss this question with a partner: Why is it important to consider the geography of a place like California when considering developing new energy sources?

 Evidence Notebook California has enacted many laws and regulations to decrease carbon emissions. Propose another step that could be taken to make energy use safer, more efficient, and/or less harmful to the environment. Which groups of people should be consulted before enacting your proposal? What are some of the tradeoffs you would have to make to enact it?

Analyzing the Effects of Carbon Emissions

As world population grows, so does demand for energy. As the graph in Figure 16 shows, the global consumption of coal, natural gas, and liquid fuels is expected to continue to increase for decades into the future. One major factor that drives this increase is changes that are occurring in countries such as China and India. In these countries, per capita energy use is currently much lower than it is in countries such as the U.S. or Australia. However, as technology advances and the standard of living increases, energy consumption will also increase. Many countries around the world are undergoing rapid changes, and the impact of these changes is expected to be substantial.

World Energy-Related Carbon Dioxide Emissions by Fuel Type, with Projections to 2040

FIGURE 16: As the use of fossil fuels increases, carbon emissions also increase.

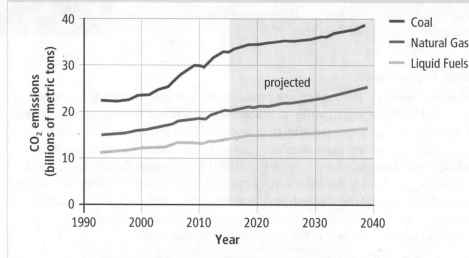

Source: U.S. Energy Information Administration, *International Energy Outlook 2017*, "Executive Summary."

 Collaborate With a partner, talk about how patterns in fossil fuel consumption might vary in different locations due to differences in geography, technology, and lifestyles.

As the use of fossil fuels increases, carbon emissions also increase. Burning fossil fuels has steadily raised the levels of CO_2 in the atmosphere since 1850. In 2015, about 33.9 billion tons of CO_2 were released into the atmosphere from burning fossil fuels. This amount is expected to continue to increase. Currently, CO_2 is building up faster than natural processes can remove it from the atmosphere. Evidence shows that this excess CO_2 changes the way energy flows on Earth, and these changes are resulting in an increasing global temperature, sea level rise, and shifting climate patterns.

PREDICT How do you think scientists use projections of future carbon emissions to predict how these emissions will change the flow of energy on Earth?

_____

_____

_____

Hands-On Lab

Modeling the Effect of Carbon Dioxide on Temperature

In this lab, you will use a model to investigate how adding carbon dioxide to a closed system affects energy flow. In a closed system, such as Earth, matter does not enter or exit the system, but energy is free to move through the system boundary. Your task is to construct two model systems - one experimental setup and one control setup. The gas in the control setup should be the same gas as is found in Earth's lower atmosphere. The gas in the experimental setup should have a higher concentration of carbon dioxide than in the control. One way to produce carbon dioxide is to add effervescent tablets to water.

Research question: How does the presence of increased carbon dioxide change the way energy flows in a closed system?

MAKE A CLAIM

Write a prediction in your Evidence Notebook for how you think the temperature of the air in the experimental setup will compare to that of the control setup. Explain your thinking.

MATERIALS

- indirectly vented chemical splash goggles, nonlatex apron
- bottles, empty, 2 L (2)
- colored pencils
- effervescent tablets (3)
- graph paper
- heat lamp, 100 W with bulb holder and clamp
- rubber stoppers with hole in the center (2)
- thermometers (2)
- timer
- water, 2 L

SAFETY INFORMATION

- Wear indirectly vented chemical splash goggles and a nonlatex apron during the setup, hands-on, and takedown segments of the activity.
- Use caution when working with heat lamps, which can cause skin burns.
- Use only GFI protected circuits when using electrical equipment, and keep away from water sources to prevent shock.

indirectly vented chemical splash goggles

PLAN THE INVESTIGATION

1. Write a procedure and a safety plan in your Evidence Notebook for carrying out your experiment. You should include a control setup and an experimental setup. In the control setup, add 1 liter of water and no effervescent tablets. In the experimental setup, add 1 liter of water and 3 effervescent tablets. In your procedure, outline the variables you will keep constant between the two setups. In addition, explain how often you will collect data.

2. Construct a data table in which to record your data.

3. Construct a graph on which you will plot your data for both systems.

4. Have your teacher approve your procedure and safety plan before you begin. As you gather data, be sure to record it in your data table and construct your graph.

ANALYZE

1. Describe the trends shown in the graph of your data. How did the temperature change differ for the two systems?

_____

_____

_____

_____

2. What are some of the strengths and limitations of the model you used? What changes would you make to gather more precise data?

_____

_____

_____

_____

3. What types of models do you think scientists use to make predictions about the effect of carbon dioxide on air temperature in a closed system?

_____

_____

_____

_____

DRAW CONCLUSIONS

Write a conclusion that addresses each of the points below.

Claim Explain how increased carbon dioxide affects the flow of energy in a closed system.

Evidence Describe examples from your data that support your claim.

Reasoning Explain how the evidence you cited supports your claim.

_____

_____

_____

_____

_____

_____

_____

_____

_____

Energy Absorption and the Behavior of Molecules

Why does adding carbon dioxide to a system make the temperature of air in the system increase? The reason has to do with how energy is absorbed by different gases. When energy from sunlight enters Earth's atmosphere, it is in the form of electromagnetic radiation. The sun's radiation is made up of mostly visible light, but it ranges from long-wavelength infrared radiation to short-wavelength ultraviolet radiation.

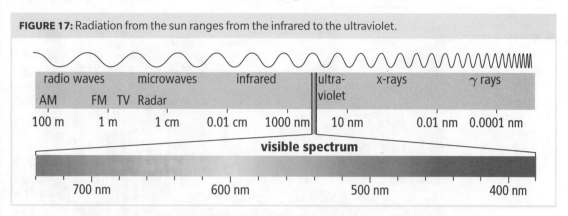

FIGURE 17: Radiation from the sun ranges from the infrared to the ultraviolet.

Some sunlight is reflected by Earth, and some is absorbed. As energy from sunlight is absorbed by land, air, and water, their temperatures increase. These materials then give off, or emit, energy as *infrared radiation*. This is the same type of radiation that is produced by a heat lamp. When molecules in the atmosphere absorb infrared radiation, their molecular vibrations increase.

Molecules can vibrate in multiple directions along their bonds. For example, carbon dioxide exhibits symmetrical stretching, asymmetrical stretching, and bending vibrations along the bonds between its carbon atom and its two oxygen atoms. Gases such as carbon dioxide, methane, and water vapor all exhibit these complex vibrational motions. Collisions between these energized molecules transfer energy among all the molecules. As a result, the molecules' average thermal energy increases and the temperature of the atmosphere increases.

The primary components of Earth's atmosphere, nitrogen (N_2) and oxygen (O_2) are each made up of two atoms that are the same and therefore do not exhibit complex vibrational motion.

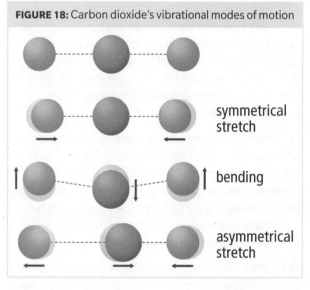

FIGURE 18: Carbon dioxide's vibrational modes of motion

symmetrical stretch

bending

asymmetrical stretch

MODEL Draw a simple flow chart to show how energy is transferred from sunlight to carbon dioxide molecules in Earth's atmosphere.

Evidence Notebook Describe, on a molecular level, how methane (CH_4) absorbs infrared radiation. Then, explain why the emission of methane into Earth's atmosphere from a natural gas leak would have a significant effect on average global temperature.

Engineering

Reducing Emissions from Vehicles

FIGURE 19: Most vehicles on the road today burn fossil fuels such as gasoline or diesel. In order to lessen the environmental impacts of transportation, vehicles must be engineered to have greater fuel efficiency and give off fewer pollutants.

Increased concern about climate change has spurred efforts to find methods to reduce carbon emissions. Because the combustion of fossil fuels has such a strong effect on climate through the emission of carbon dioxide, one approach is to increase the efficiency at which the fuels are used.

Fuel efficiency is a measure of the amount of energy a fuel releases during combustion. When applied to vehicles, a key factor in fuel efficiency is a vehicle's average miles per gallon (mpg). The United States sets fuel efficiency standards for vehicles. Fuel shortages in 1973 initiated a widespread effort to increase efficiency as a way to reduce fuel consumption.

The 1975 Energy Policy and Conservation Act set these plans in motion and established a goal for typical cars to have an average fuel efficiency of 27.5 mpg by 1985. The Environmental Protection Agency (EPA) set a goal of 34.1 mpg by 2016. Levels vary depending on the size and type of vehicle, but the goal set by the EPA for 2025 is about 54.5 mpg. Like all laws, these laws are subject to change as governments change.

Other countries have also set fuel efficiency mandates for vehicles. Because cars are made in many different places and sold around the world, these laws could influence car makers to develop cars with even higher efficiencies than those required in the U.S.

PREDICT What are some of the criteria and constraints an engineer might consider when attempting to increase the fuel efficiency of a vehicle? How might factors such as vehicle performance, maintenance, and cost be factored in?

_____

_____

_____

_____

In addition to setting guidelines for fuel efficiency, government regulations also set constraints on the emissions of fuels used in vehicles. In 1970, Congress passed the Clean Air Act that established goals for reducing atmospheric pollutants.

In response, the first catalytic converters were installed in vehicles in 1975. These devices, and later improved versions, use chemical reactions to reduce some of the harmful emissions from vehicle exhaust, such as unburned hydrocarbons, carbon monoxide, and nitrogen oxides. The Clean Air Act has been successful in reducing tailpipe pollutants in passenger vehicles by up to 99 percent as well as eliminating lead and reducing sulfur content of fuels.

The EPA's 2016 regulations on fuel efficiency also set a limit on average carbon dioxide emission by vehicles of 250 grams per mile, and the current 2025 goal is 163 grams of carbon dioxide per mile.

Each time the efficiency standards and constraints on carbon dioxide emissions of fuels increase, manufacturers work to design and construct new vehicles that will meet the requirements.

Manufacturers have developed various technologies to meet these regulations. Because less fuel usage means greater fuel efficiency, one approach is to reduce the weight of cars and improve their aerodynamics. Manufacturers have also improved tires to decrease resistance and improved engine performance so that fuels burn more efficiently with less waste. Hybrid vehicles that are partially battery powered have also decreased fuel usage.

ANALYZE What are some ways vehicle makers could decrease the weight of vehicles and make them more aerodynamic? What are some of the tradeoffs that engineers might have to make to decrease the weight of a vehicle and the air resistance it encounters?

_____

_____

_____

_____

_____

Another way to increase fuel efficiency is to educate the public about simple techniques that will improve the fuel efficiencies of their cars. For example, keeping tires properly inflated reduces the drag on the car. Properly maintained engines burn fuel more efficiently. Reducing unnecessary trips and avoiding sudden starts and stops can also reduce fuel consumption.

EXPLAIN Describe some steps you and your family could take to reduce your use of vehicles and/or increase the fuel efficiency of the vehicles you use.

_____

_____

_____

_____

_____

Another factor that often influences decisions about fuel efficiency is the cost of gasoline. When the cost of gas is low, people are not as concerned about the fuel efficiency of their vehicles. For this and other reasons, California imposed a gasoline tax that is one of the highest in the country. The extra cost deters drivers from making unnecessary trips.

As gas prices remain low, interest in fuel-efficient and low-emissions vehicles can stagnate. However, some countries, such as China and France, have set ambitious goals to eventually eliminate fossil-fuel-burning vehicles all together.

The goal of all of these standards and regulations is to decrease carbon emissions and offset the effects of climate change. Reducing the use of fossil fuels by increasing the use of more environmentally friendly energy resources is one of the solutions that all nations must keep exploring in order to protect the future of our planet.

Language Arts Connection Research how California has taken the lead in efforts to increase fuel efficiency and reduce harmful emissions. Write a blog entry detailing your research. Explain how the California Air Resources Board has used incentives for fuel conservation, initiated research into zero emission vehicles and low-carbon fuels, and set regulations to improve fuel efficiency and lower emissions that are more stringent than national requirements.

| CALIFORNIA PETROLEUM | ALISO CANYON GAS LEAK | GENERATING NATURAL GAS FROM BIOMASS | Go online to choose one of these other paths. |

Lesson Self-Check

CAN YOU SOLVE IT?

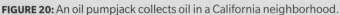

FIGURE 20: An oil pumpjack collects oil in a California neighborhood.

As the human population has increased, so has the need for energy. Most of our energy comes from burning fossil fuels, such as oil and gas. The extraction, transport, and use of these fuels have benefits and costs. Burning fossil fuels produces carbon dioxide, which increases Earth's average global temperature. This, in turn, causes sea level rise, ocean acidification, and other phenomena which negatively affect human health and the environment. Emissions from burning fossil fuels also produce pollution, which decreases water and air quality. Therefore, many countries have started developing plans for moving away from fossil fuels and relying solely on renewable energy sources. However, even renewable energy sources can have negative impacts. Scientists and engineers have a very important role in developing solutions for these impacts.

 Evidence Notebook Refer to your notes in your Evidence Notebook to explain how you would weigh the pros and cons of different energy sources to develop a plan that reduces environmental impacts and provides for all of a location's energy needs.

1. **Claim** What are the main factors that should be considered when deciding which combination of energy sources should be used in a certain area?
2. **Evidence** Describe specific examples of costs and benefits associated with different fuel sources. Include information related to effects on the environment, effects on human health, effects on societies and their economies, and financial considerations.
3. **Reasoning** Explain why you think the factors you described should be considered when developing solutions and how they might affect the implementation of a specific solution.

CHECKPOINTS

Check Your Understanding

1. What type of energy change occurs in the combustion of coal at a power plant?
   - ○ **a.** kinetic energy to potential energy
   - ○ **b.** chemical energy to thermal energy
   - ○ **c.** thermal energy to mechanical energy

2. What is a way that hydraulic fracturing can endanger the environment?
   - ○ **a.** chemically hazardous waste water
   - ○ **b.** large areas of damaged vegetation
   - ○ **c.** production of large amounts of radioactive waste
   - ○ **d.** emission of carbon dioxide to the atmosphere

3. Which of these are drawbacks of using solar and wind energy?
   - ○ **a.** These energy sources give off large quantities of carbon emissions.
   - ○ **b.** They have several negative impacts on the environment and human health.
   - ○ **c.** These energy sources are only available in certain places and at certain times.

4. Which of these are environmental costs of using nuclear energy? Select all correct answers.
   - ☐ **a.** A significant amount of carbon emissions is given off.
   - ☐ **b.** The waste generated is hazardous and must be disposed of.
   - ☐ **c.** Nuclear material can be spilled into the ocean if reactors are near the coast.
   - ☐ **d.** A large amount of cold water is generated, which must be stored somewhere.

5. The release of what compound is the greatest danger to the environment in the extraction and delivery of natural gas?
   - ○ **a.** methane
   - ○ **b.** water vapor
   - ○ **c.** nitrogen gas
   - ○ **d.** carbon dioxide

6. Put the sentences in order to show how electrical energy is produced at a coal-fired electric power plant.
   - _____ **a.** The turbine spins a shaft connected to a generator.
   - _____ **b.** Coal is burned in a furnace through combustion.
   - _____ **c.** Kinetic energy is converted to electrical energy.
   - _____ **d.** Pressurized steam is used to spin a turbine.
   - _____ **e.** Heated water is vaporized inside a boiler.

7. Calculate the efficiency of a car engine if the motor produces 1070 kJ of mechanical energy using a fuel that is capable of producing 3220 kJ of energy.

   The efficiency of the engine is

   _____ %.

8. Select the correct terms to complete the statement.

   Gases such as carbon dioxide and methane have few | many vibrational modes of motion. They contribute to climate change because they are better able to absorb infrared | ultraviolet radiation.

CHECKPOINTS (continued)

9. Imagine you are developing an energy plan for a school. The school administration wants to minimize carbon emissions and save money on energy. What types of criteria and constraints do you think a school must consider when budgeting money for energy? Write a list of questions that you would ask to define and delimit this problem.

_____

_____

_____

_____

_____

_____

10. Although natural gas is often branded as a "cleaner burning fuel," it does come with costs to the environment and human health. Explain why this is, based on the methods used to extract natural gas and also based on the molecular structure of methane.

_____

_____

_____

_____

_____

_____

MAKE YOUR OWN STUDY GUIDE

 In your Evidence Notebook, design a study guide that supports the main ideas from this lesson:

Energy sources have different benefits and costs, which must be considered when developing solutions to the world's energy needs.

The extraction and delivery of energy can have harmful effects on the environment and humans.

Actions by humans have contributed to increasing carbon dioxide levels in the atmosphere.

Some gases absorb more energy than others and therefore have a stronger effect on Earth's temperature. Examples include carbon dioxide and methane.

Remember to include the following information in your study guide:
- Use examples that model main ideas.
- Record explanations for the phenomena you investigated.
- Use evidence to support your explanations. Your support can include drawings, data, graphs, laboratory conclusions, and other evidence recorded throughout the lesson.

Consider how the costs and benefits of different energy sources are taken into account when developing solutions to a society's energy needs.

6.2

Energy Flows and Feedback in the Earth System

One effect of a drought in San Jose, California

CAN YOU EXPLAIN IT?

This reservoir near San Jose, California, was once filled with water used by local homes and businesses. However, during a drought it dried up completely. California suffered from severe drought conditions from 2012 through 2016. The drought has lessened somewhat since 2017, but some areas are still experiencing dry conditions. As a result, it is important to understand the causes and effects of droughts. In addition, scientists want to understand how Earth system interactions, including climate change, affect the intensity and frequency of extreme weather conditions such as drought.

PREDICT How could global climate change be related to the drought in California, which is a more local weather phenomenon?

_____

_____

_____

_____

_____

_____

 Evidence Notebook As you explore the lesson, gather evidence to explain how global climate change relates to drought in California.

Matter and Energy in the Earth System

One characteristic of Earth that makes it suitable for life is its temperature. Earth is warmer than most planets, and its temperature stays relatively steady. The air temperature at Earth's surface ranges from about −88 °C to 58 °C (−126 °F to 136 °F). In contrast, the atmosphere of the moon ranges from about −233 °C to 123 °C (−387 °F to 253 °F) during a single period of day and night.

FIGURE 1: The moon's atmosphere is much thinner than Earth's atmosphere is.

 Collaborate Discuss these questions with a partner: How does the temperature range at Earth's surface differ from that at the moon's? How do you think the composition of Earth's atmosphere is related to this phenomenon?

Earth as a System

A system is *closed* if no matter enters or leaves the system. In most cases, the Earth system is considered a closed system. This is because exchanges of matter between Earth and space are small in scale, or rare, such as the case of large meteorites colliding with Earth.

FIGURE 2: The Earth system consists of interacting subsystems.

Energy can enter and leave a closed system, and energy enters and leaves the Earth system through Earth's atmosphere. The atmosphere is a subsystem made up of gases that surround Earth. Earth's atmosphere contains mostly nitrogen and oxygen, with smaller amounts of water vapor and carbon dioxide. Earth is warm and maintains this warmth due to the volume and composition of its atmosphere. Earth's atmosphere is thick and plentiful compared to that of the moon.

The atmosphere interacts with Earth's other subsystems when energy and matter flow between systems. In fact, all the subsystems within the Earth system interact with each other. The other subsystems include the hydrosphere, which includes all water on Earth; the biosphere, which contains all living organisms; and the geosphere, the rocky, solid part of Earth.

Scientists may define the geosphere, atmosphere, hydrosphere, and biosphere slightly differently, based on what they study. For example, the frozen part of the hydrosphere—including glaciers, ice sheets, and loose snow—is sometimes separated out as the *cryosphere*. The part of Earth constructed or modified by humans—including cities, farms, mines, reservoirs, landfills, and pollutants—is sometimes referred to as the *anthrosphere*.

EXPLAIN Describe an example of the atmosphere interacting with each of these systems: biosphere, hydrosphere, and anthrosphere.

_____

_____

_____

The Cycling of Matter in the Earth System

Living things and physical processes are both involved in how matter cycles in the Earth system. This movement of matter involves processes such as the carbon cycle, the water cycle, and the nitrogen cycle. None of these cycles is isolated. They are all interconnected. For example, changes in the carbon cycle can affect the water cycle by altering the way energy flows through Earth's systems. If an increase in the concentration of CO_2 in the atmosphere causes higher temperatures, the water cycle can be affected because there may be an increase in evaporation of water from Earth's surface into the atmosphere.

FIGURE 3: The carbon cycle involves interactions between all of Earth's systems.

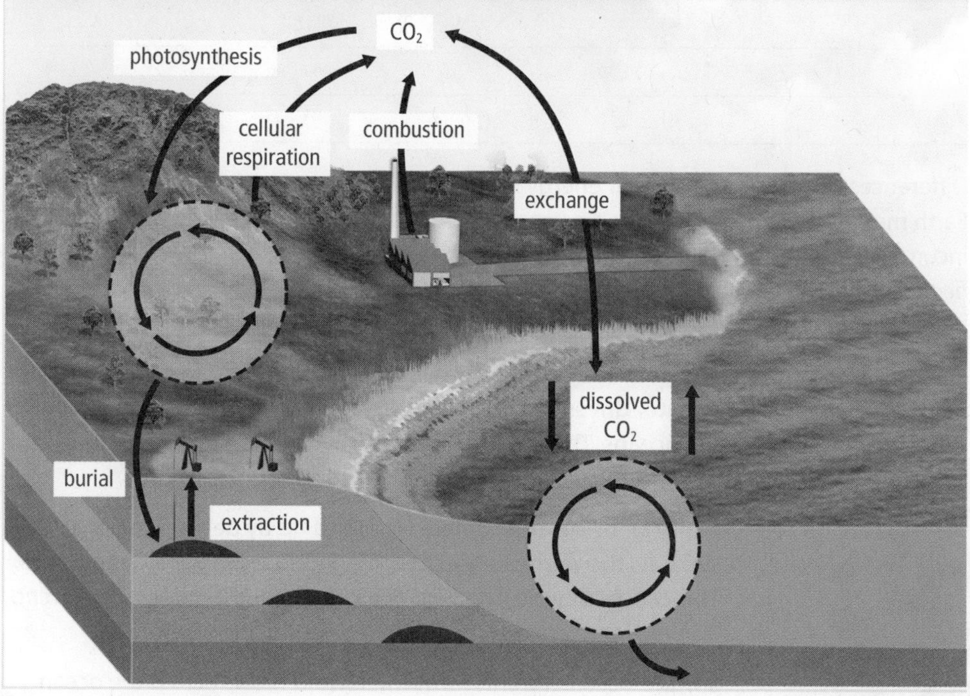

ANALYZE Complete the statements about how human activities affect the carbon cycle.

As humans extract fossil fuels, the amount of carbon in Earth's geosphere decreases | increases. As fossil fuels are burned, the amount of carbon dioxide in Earth's atmosphere decreases | increases. As a result, the amount of CO_2 that is dissolved in Earth's oceans should decrease | increase as fossil fuel consumption increases.

The Flow of Energy in the Earth System

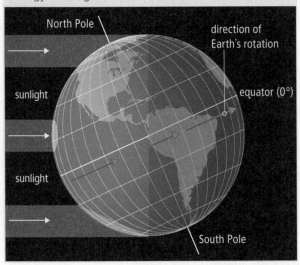

FIGURE 4: Earth's shape and tilt determine the amount of energy each region of Earth receives.

North Pole

direction of Earth's rotation

sunlight

equator (0°)

sunlight

South Pole

Almost all the energy input to the Earth system comes from the sun. Energy from Earth's interior also contributes, but only a very small amount. Energy from the sun powers chemical changes such as photosynthesis and physical processes such as the water cycle.

In Figure 4, you can see that sunlight is not distributed evenly. Because of Earth's spherical shape, regions near the equator receive more energy than polar regions do. Because of the tilt of Earth's axis, the Northern Hemisphere receives more sunlight and has longer days than other regions on Earth for half of the year. This orientation is shown in Figure 4. Halfway through another revolution when the southern part of the axis points toward the sun, the Southern Hemisphere receives more energy, and the Northern Hemisphere receives less. These changes cause Earth's seasons.

PREDICT Different parts of Earth receive different amounts of sunlight. How do you think conduction, convection, and radiation redistribute incoming solar energy? Try to think of one example for each process.

_____

_____

_____

_____

Differences in the amount of solar energy received and reflected in different regions of Earth mean that some regions are warmer than others. The difference in the amount of incoming solar energy and the amount of energy radiated back to space is called *net heating*. Near the equator there is a net energy surplus, and in the polar regions there is a net energy deficit.

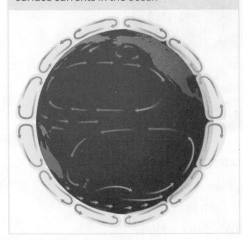

FIGURE 5: Convection currents in the air and surface currents in the ocean

The net heating imbalance between the poles and areas near the equator drives a circulation system in both the atmosphere and the oceans. The net flow of energy in both of these circulation systems is from equatorial regions toward polar regions.

Warm air in the atmosphere is pushed up by denser, cooler air that sinks. As the warm air rises, it cools, increases in density, and sinks. This causes a cyclical pattern of motion called a *convection current*. Convection currents transfer energy in the atmosphere.

Surface ocean currents form when wind blows across the ocean surface. Convection currents also form in the ocean when dense water sinks and becomes a deep current below the ocean surface. Surface currents and convection currents transfer energy from one part of Earth to another in the ocean.

The Greenhouse Effect

The net flow of energy in the Earth system from the equatorial regions to the polar regions is not the only process that affects Earth's surface temperatures. Another important factor is the chemistry of some of the trace gases in the atmosphere.

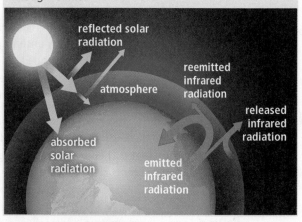

FIGURE 6: The greenhouse effect keeps Earth warm enough for life.

When solar energy warms Earth's surface, that energy is radiated into the atmosphere from the surface in the form of infrared radiation, which is a form of longwave radiation. This is the type of radiation that comes from a heat lamp. This longwave radiation flows through the atmosphere, and if it is not absorbed in the atmosphere, it flows back out into space.

Most of the gases in the atmosphere do not absorb longwave radiation, but there are trace gases in the atmosphere that do. When energy is absorbed in this way, Earth's surface and lower atmosphere are warmed because the gases that absorb the longwave radiation radiate some of it back toward the surface.

The warming of the surface and the lower atmosphere that occurs when trace gases absorb and radiate longwave radiation is called the greenhouse effect. The trace gases responsible for the greenhouse effect are called *greenhouse gases*. Examples include water vapor, carbon dioxide, and methane.

If the concentration of greenhouse gases increases, more of Earth's emitted radiation is absorbed and radiated back into the Earth system. This energy remains in the Earth system longer than it would have had the energy gone directly to space. This causes Earth's average temperature to increase.

EXPLAIN Select the correct terms to complete the statements about how carbon emissions by humans affect the flow of energy in Earth's atmosphere.

As humans burn fossil fuels, such as coal and petroleum, the amount of carbon dioxide in Earth's atmosphere decreases | increases. Because carbon dioxide is a greenhouse gas, its molecules absorb | reflect longwave energy and then radiate it back into the Earth system. So, adding carbon dioxide to Earth's atmosphere faster than it can be removed causes Earth's average temperature to decrease | increase.

Some greenhouse gases, such as carbon dioxide and methane, have rapidly increased in concentration because of human activities and practices. This is causing what is called the *enhanced greenhouse effect* and carbon dioxide emissions are a major contributor to it. Other greenhouse gases come exclusively from human activities. Some of these include fluorinated compounds such as chlorofluorocarbons, perfluorocarbons, and sulfur hexafluoride. Some of these human-made greenhouse gases have lifetimes of hundreds or thousands of years in the atmosphere, so the effect they have on Earth's atmosphere will be quite long as well.

 Collaborate With a partner, use what you have learned about the moon and Earth to infer what surface temperatures on Mercury and Venus are like. Mercury is the planet closest to the sun and has a very thin atmosphere. Venus is the second planet from the sun and has a thick atmosphere that is about 96% carbon dioxide.

Earth's Energy Budget

After energy comes into the Earth system from the sun, it flows in different ways through all of Earth's subsystems. Energy is transferred from place to place, and it can be transformed into different forms of energy, but energy cannot be destroyed. Even though energy can remain in the Earth system for different periods of time, eventually, the same amount of energy entering the Earth system flows back into space. These flows of energy into and out of the Earth system are known as Earth's energy budget. For Earth's temperature to be stable long-term, the energy budget must remain balanced. The energy budget is balanced when energy input equals energy output.

Figure 7 shows an overall view of Earth's energy budget. Some of the energy that comes into the Earth system is reflected right back into space. But much of the energy from the sun is absorbed and flows through Earth's subsystems. This energy drives photosynthesis, the water cycle, wind, and many more processes. Eventually, this energy flows back into space in the form of longwave radiation.

FIGURE 7: Earth's energy budget is balanced.

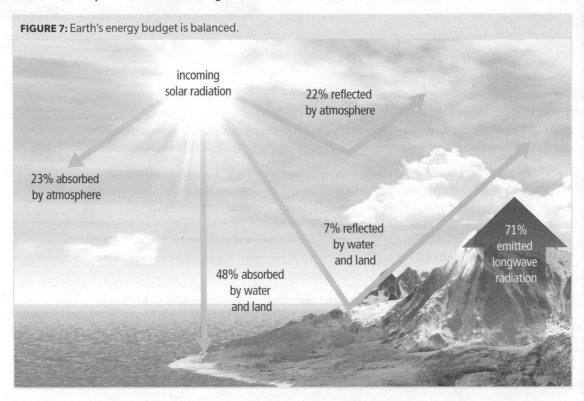

SOLVE Use Figure 7 to complete the table about Earth's energy budget.

Energy input	%
Enters Earth system but is reflected back into space right away	_____
Absorbed in the Earth system	_____
Total =	100%

Energy output	%
Reflected into space by the atmosphere	_____
Reflected into space by water and land	_____
Emitted after transfers and transformations in Earth system	_____
Total =	100%

Measuring Energy Flow

How do scientists gather data about energy inputs and outputs to analyze Earth's energy budget? Almost all the energy that enters the Earth system comes in the form of sunlight, or solar energy. One way this can be measured is by instruments in space. For example, NASA has placed an instrument called the Total and Spectral Solar Irradiance Sensor (TSIS-1) on the International Space Station. This instrument measures and records the total amount of solar energy it receives, and those data can be used to calculate the total amount of solar energy that is received by Earth. Another instrument, the Spectral Irradiance Monitor (SIM), measures the different types of electromagnetic radiation in incoming solar energy.

The output of energy from the Earth system is all the energy that leaves the Earth system and flows back into space. About 30% of this is solar energy—mostly shortwave radiation—that is reflected back into space by Earth's atmosphere and surface, and about 70% is longwave radiation that is emitted back into space after having first been absorbed by various parts of the Earth system.

Explore Online ▶

| a | Emitted Longwave Radiation |
| b | Reflected Solar Radiation |

FIGURE 8: The output of longwave radiation from Earth is shown on the left. Orange areas show areas of greater energy output. The output of shortwave radiation is shown on the right. Lighter areas show areas of greater energy output. The combination of these two sets of data enable scientists to calculate Earth's energy output.

Figure 8 shows data from CERES instruments, which are part of NASA's Clouds and the Earth's Radiant Energy System. These instruments are aboard satellites and spacecraft to measure energy leaving the Earth system. Scientists can analyze these data to understand how properties of the surface such as snowpack and properties of the atmosphere such as cloud cover affect Earth's energy budget. The CERES data also show changes in the output of energy from the Earth system over time, which helps scientists study climate events such as El Niño and model future climate conditions.

 Language Arts Connection Research technologies used to measure energy flows on Earth. What does each type of technology measure? How are the data used by scientists?

 Evidence Notebook Energy is constantly entering and leaving the Earth system, but as greenhouse gas concentrations increase, more energy remains in the Earth system for a longer period of time. This raises the average global temperature. How are human activities related to this phenomenon?

Human Impacts on Earth's Climate

Imagine a light shining into a glass fish tank. The light is an energy input for the system of the fish tank, which includes the tank, water, fish, and rocks. Energy leaves the system through the uncovered top of the tank. Eventually, the system reaches a stable temperature as the incoming and outgoing energy are balanced. The water temperature will remain stable unless there is a change in energy flow, such as a change in the intensity of the light or the addition of a tank cover. Now consider the sun as an energy input to the Earth system. When Earth's incoming energy and outgoing energy are the same, the energy budget is balanced, and global temperature stays relatively stable. If this balance is upset, global temperatures either rise or fall.

Factors that Affect Earth's Energy Budget

FIGURE 9: A large volcanic eruption is one example of a natural phenomenon that causes climate changes by unbalancing the energy budget.

Many factors can change Earth's energy budget. Natural factors that force such changes over thousands of years include small changes in Earth's orbit or the tilt of Earth's axis, as well as changes in the sun's brightness. The energy budget can also be disrupted by sudden natural events, including volcanic eruptions.

PREDICT Large explosive eruptions send ash, sulfur dioxide, water vapor, and carbon dioxide high into the atmosphere. How might volcanic eruptions disrupt Earth's energy budget?

_____

_____

_____

_____

Human activities can also upset Earth's energy budget. For example, deforestation decreases the amount of CO_2 that is removed from the atmosphere. The combustion of fossil fuels releases CO_2 and other greenhouse gases into the atmosphere.

Analyzing Changes in Earth's Energy Budget

It can be helpful to consider how energy flows in and out of the Earth system at three different levels. The lowest of these levels is Earth's surface. This is the area where most solar heating takes place. The uppermost level is the top of the atmosphere, where solar energy enters the system. Between this and the surface is Earth's atmosphere. Analyzing energy flow at each of these levels helps scientists understand the interactions that affect Earth's climate and climate change.

Energy Flow at Earth's Surface

Changes on Earth's surface affect the absorption of incoming solar energy and change the flow of energy in the Earth system. Generally, dark surfaces absorb more solar energy than light surfaces. The reflectiveness of a surface is referred to as its *albedo*. A surface with a high albedo reflects more sunlight than a surface with a low albedo. For example, snow has a higher albedo than grass, but grass has a higher albedo than dark pavement.

FIGURE 10: Soot and greenhouse gases are released by the burning of fossil fuels. Soot that is deposited on snow and ice changes the albedo of these surfaces.

Recall that land and water absorb about 48 percent of incoming solar energy and reflect about 7 percent. As humans use land for roads, buildings, and agriculture, the albedos of surfaces change. In turn, this disrupts Earth's energy balance.

MODEL   Draw a diagram to show how the flow of energy at Earth's surface would be affected by the accumulation of soot on snow and ice. In your diagram, illustrate how the relative amounts of energy absorbed and reflected at Earth's surface would change.

 Evidence Notebook In your Evidence Notebook, make a claim based on evidence to answer this question: In drought conditions, the amount of dust present in the air may increase. How would an increase in dust during a drought affect the flow of energy in an area that is covered by snow for part of the year? Explain your reasoning.

Factors that Affect Climate
Determine whether land or water absorbs heat faster. Then, construct an explanation for how the properties of land and water affect climate.

For the energy budget to balance at Earth's surface, land and water must transfer the energy that is absorbed. The transfer happens in three ways: by convection, by radiation, and when evaporation takes place on Earth's surface.

Figure 11 shows that about 25 percent of the energy in Earth's energy budget leaves Earth's surface during evaporation. Solar energy is absorbed by liquid water, and some water molecules enter the air as water vapor. As the water vapor condenses, energy is released to the atmosphere as thermal energy. Evaporation from ocean water and the resulting release of thermal energy into the atmosphere are major factors in the energy budget near Earth's surface.

About 5 percent of energy in Earth's energy budget leaves the surface through convection. Air in direct contact with warmer parts of Earth's surface gains energy and becomes less dense than the surrounding air. Energy then flows in a convection current. The remaining 17 percent of energy is emitted as thermal radiation.

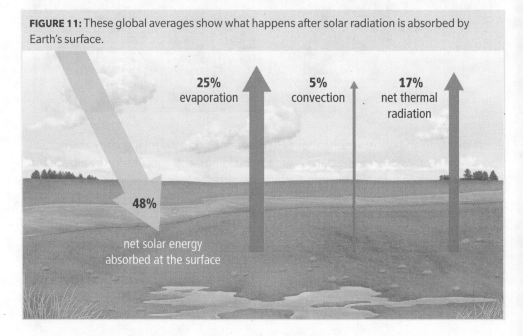

FIGURE 11: These global averages show what happens after solar radiation is absorbed by Earth's surface.

25%
evaporation

5%
convection

17%
net thermal
radiation

48%

net solar energy
absorbed at the surface

INFER Which of these are the most likely effects of a decrease in the overall ice and snow cover on Earth's surface? Select all correct answers.

☐ **a.** More energy would be absorbed by Earth's surface.

☐ **b.** Less energy would be transferred by convection.

☐ **c.** More energy would be reflected by Earth's surface.

☐ **d.** Less energy would be transferred by radiation.

Energy Flow in Earth's Atmosphere

Energy from Earth's surface is transferred to Earth's atmosphere and to space. About 17 percent of the energy budget is emitted from the surface as thermal infrared radiation. However, only about 12 percent of this energy ever directly reaches space. What happens to the remaining 5 percent of the energy? It is absorbed and emitted by greenhouse gases in the atmosphere.

When matter absorbs energy, the energy is transferred in the form of kinetic energy and the atoms and molecules in the matter move more quickly. As the average kinetic energy of the particles increases, the temperature of the matter increases. This is what occurs when thermal radiation is absorbed by greenhouse gases. The particles move faster, and the temperature of the gases—and thus the atmosphere—increases.

The absorption of energy by greenhouse gases has other effects in addition to warming the atmosphere. Because these gases radiate this energy in all directions, some of the radiated energy is absorbed by Earth's surface. Then Earth's surface becomes warmer.

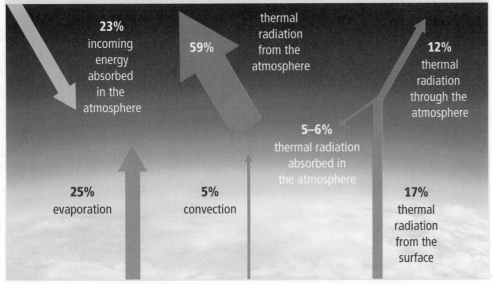

FIGURE 12: The atmosphere gets its energy in several ways. The atmosphere absorbs 23% of incoming solar energy. Energy from the surface is transferred to the atmosphere by evaporation (25%) and convection (5%). Finally, the atmosphere absorbs energy emitted by the surface (5–6%). Totaled, this is 58–59%. This equates to the percentage that is eventually emitted by the atmosphere as thermal radiation, as shown by the largest arrow.

23% incoming energy absorbed in the atmosphere

59% thermal radiation from the atmosphere

12% thermal radiation through the atmosphere

5–6% thermal radiation absorbed in the atmosphere

25% evaporation

5% convection

17% thermal radiation from the surface

ANALYZE Select the correct terms to complete the statements about how greenhouse gases such as carbon dioxide affect the flow of energy in Earth's atmosphere.

When greenhouse gas molecules absorb energy, they move more quickly | slowly. This leads to a(n) decrease | increase in the temperature of the gas. The molecules radiate energy in all directions, and some of this energy is absorbed by Earth's surface. Thus, as the concentrations of greenhouse gases in Earth's atmosphere increase, the amount of energy that is absorbed and re-emitted by Earth's atmosphere will decrease | increase, and Earth's average global temperature will decrease | increase.

What overall changes does the increase in greenhouse gases have on Earth's climate? The greenhouse gases that have been released by humans and are currently in the atmosphere create an energy imbalance that affects Earth's climate, now and in the future. According to current scientific data, the average surface temperature of Earth has risen between 0.6 °C and 0.9 °C in the last century. Until greenhouse gases are stabilized, temperatures will continue to rise in response to the current imbalance in Earth's energy budget. If the concentration of greenhouse gases stabilizes, then Earth's temperature, and thus its climate, will again reach equilibrium. However, the temperature at this new equilibrium will be higher than it was before the additional greenhouse gases were released into the atmosphere.

Analyzing Weather Patterns

To learn more about weather and climate, scientists study many types of data, including precipitation and temperature. Figures 13 and 14 show precipitation and temperature trends for the wet season in California. The wet season has been studied because this is when the majority of rain falls in California's Mediterranean climate.

California's Average Wet Season Precipitation Amounts, 1896–2017

FIGURE 13: Total precipitation each year, October through March

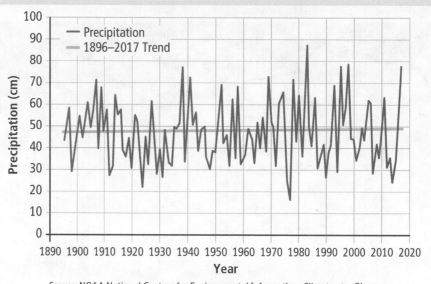

Source: NOAA National Centers for Environmental Information, Climate at a Glance: Statewide Time Series, published March 2018.

California's Average Wet Season Temperatures, 1896–2017

FIGURE 14: Average temperature each year, October through March

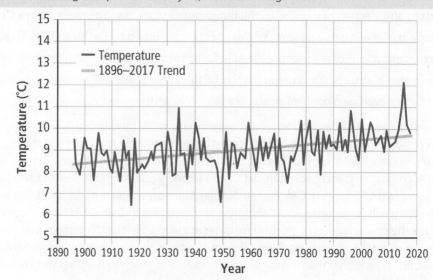

Source: NOAA National Centers for Environmental Information, Climate at a Glance: Statewide Time Series, published March 2018.

ANALYZE Which of these claims are best supported by the data shown in Figures 13 and 14? Select all correct answers.

☐ a. The overall trend for precipitation shows a decrease over time.

☐ b. The overall trend for precipitation indicates it stayed relatively steady or increased slightly over time.

☐ c. The overall trend for temperature shows a decrease over time.

☐ d. The overall trend for temperature indicates it stayed relatively steady.

☐ e. The overall trend for temperature shows an increase over time.

Droughts cause a decrease in soil moisture and a decrease of water supplies at the surface and in groundwater reservoirs. Droughts cause water supply shortages compared to the needs of society for agriculture, industry, power generation, and personal use of water. For these reasons, scientists study factors related to drought and the effects of a drought on the Earth system.

EXPLAIN Use the data shown in Figures 13 and 14 to answer the following questions:

1. Many places in California have experienced drought due to higher evaporation rates, less precipitation falling as snow, and snow melting earlier in the year. Which graph might explain these observations? Explain.

_____

_____

_____

_____

_____

_____

_____

2. How might human activities be related to the drought conditions? What other types of data would further support this claim?

_____

_____

_____

_____

_____

_____

It is important to understand that a drought is not necessarily defined by rainfall amounts. Recall the graph showing how precipitation amounts have remained steady in California over recent history. Yet, California has experienced major droughts in recent history. Now recall the graph of increasing temperatures, which have caused more evaporation, less precipitation to fall as snow, earlier snow melt, and less water reaching places where people need it during the summer.

Studying Climate History

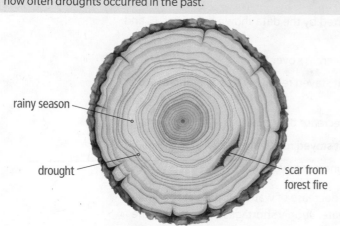

FIGURE 15: Scientists can study patterns in tree rings to learn about how often droughts occurred in the past.

rainy season

drought

scar from forest fire

Direct measurements of temperatures in the Earth system have been made for less than 200 years, so how do scientists know what Earth's climate was like before that? This information comes from paleoclimate data found in tree rings, the rock and fossil record, and ice cores.

For example, ice cores can be analyzed to determine Earth's atmospheric composition and temperature history for hundreds of thousands of years in the past. Scientists can conclude that, although Earth has experienced different climate cycles in the past, these cycles were more gradual or less extreme than those occurring today. Another example of paleoclimate data is the location and age of coal beds because coal forms in tropical, swampy environments.

An additional source of paleoclimate data is the study of tree rings. If the rings are close together, the tree did not grow much, and it can be inferred that climate conditions did not favor growth during that time. If the rings are farther apart, rainfall and temperature were favorable. Patterns in tree rings can also indicate events such as drought, which allows scientists to study the way droughts have occurred in Earth's past. To better understand the history of drought in California, scientists have studied ring patterns in trees such as juniper and redwood.

APPLY What tree ring pattern would you expect during several consecutive years of drought conditions?

○ **a.** The tree rings would be far apart.

○ **b.** The tree rings would be close together.

○ **c.** There would be no rings.

Case Study: Recent California Drought

During a drought, the input of water is less than the output of water. Examples of inputs are precipitation, runoff, and snowmelt. Examples of outputs are use by humans and evaporation. As you saw in the graphs, precipitation has remained steady but temperatures have increased in California since 1896. Higher temperatures result in increased evaporation, drier soils, loss of vegetation, and more precipitation falling as rain rather than snow. Less snow, in addition to earlier snow melt, results in less water reaching areas where people need it during the summer months. This is when the demand for water is highest in California.

 Collaborate Talk with a partner about how drought or other extreme weather conditions have affected your community. How did the conditions affect your daily life, environment, and health? Has your community implemented any solutions to better predict extreme weather and/or prevent its harmful effects? If so, do you think the solutions have achieved the intended result? If not, what solutions might you suggest?

During droughts, there is increased risk of heat waves and wildfires, and if wildfires occur, water is limited for fighting them. Animal and plant species may be lost because of a lack of available water. Consistently dry land can lead to dust storms, soil erosion, and loss of vegetation. When it does rain, large amounts of water saturating areas with little vegetation can result in landslides and mudslides. Human health is also affected by poor air and water quality and heat stress. Examine Figure 16, which shows drought conditions in California from 2012 to 2018.

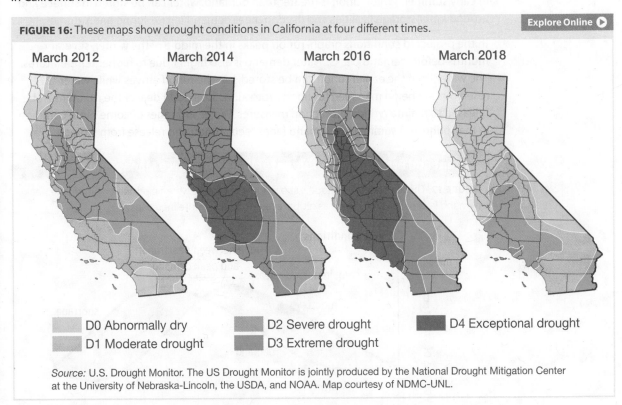

FIGURE 16: These maps show drought conditions in California at four different times.

Explore Online ▶

March 2012   March 2014   March 2016   March 2018

D0 Abnormally dry   D2 Severe drought   D4 Exceptional drought
D1 Moderate drought   D3 Extreme drought

Source: U.S. Drought Monitor. The US Drought Monitor is jointly produced by the National Drought Mitigation Center at the University of Nebraska-Lincoln, the USDA, and NOAA. Map courtesy of NDMC-UNL.

GATHER EVIDENCE What patterns do you notice in the data? Which areas are more prone to drought? How did the severity of drought change from year to year?

_____

_____

_____

_____

Drought conditions in California depend on more than just the amount of rainfall received. Approximately 30 percent of the freshwater used in the state comes from the winter snows that fall in the Sierra Nevada mountains. During the summer and fall, the snow melts and feeds into rivers and lakes. This water is essential during months when there is little or no rainfall.

EXPLAIN Complete the statements about the connection between global surface temperature and snowpack.

As Earth's average global temperature increases, less | more snow melts during the winter in some places. This decreases | increases snowpack—the amount of snow that accumulates over the winter.

Using Models to Make Predictions

Recall that higher temperatures in California have resulted in snow melting earlier in the year, and therefore, runoff is entering streams and reservoirs earlier in the year. The conceptual models in Figure 17 show the timing of water runoff and demand in California. Under current conditions, runoff peaks in early spring, a few months before demand peaks in early summer. When runoff is greater than demand, water can be stored in surface and groundwater storage facilities and used to meet demand in late spring and summer.

In the projected conditions graph, runoff peaks in the middle of the winter, several months before demand peaks. Water demand is also higher due to higher temperatures. The water from the earlier runoff can be stored, but the runoff arrives while water reservoirs are being managed for flood protection. So, a good deal of the runoff must be released to maintain flood protection measures. Water shortages become more common in the spring and summer, as demand far exceeds runoff and release from storage.

Current and Projected Conditions for Water Resource Management

FIGURE 17: These conceptual models show how the time between peak water runoff and peak demand is expected to change as global average temperature increases.

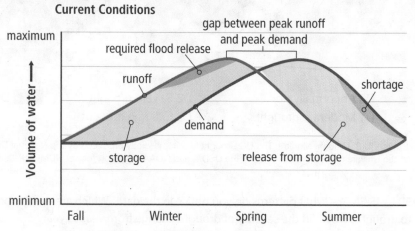

Source: California Department of Water Resources, California Climate Science and Data for Water Resources Management, June 2015.

Source: California Department of Water Resources, California Climate Science and Data for Water Resources Management, June 2015.

Using Computational Models

Computational modeling uses mathematics and computer programming to simulate physical processes and analyze the behavior of complex systems. Scientists use advanced computational models to study Earth's systems, such as the atmosphere and oceans. A global climate model is a computational model that simulates major climate system components, such as the atmosphere, land surface, sea ice, and oceans. These models allow scientists to make predictions about how human activities might affect the flow of energy and cycling of matter in the Earth system.

Future conditions, such as global temperature increase and sea-level rise, can be predicted by scientists using climate-modeling software. They can also predict trends in more localized factors, such as changes in currents or in reservoir levels. No model can be used for every scenario. Often, several models are used so that the constraints of one model are covered by the attributes of a different model. Modeling factors in the Earth system helps scientists and governments understand current situations and plan for future conditions.

ASK Write a list of questions you could investigate using a global climate model.

_____

_____

_____

_____

_____

_____

_____

 Language Arts Connection Research global climate models and how they are used. Select one model or group of models to focus on, and prepare a report describing the model(s) you researched. Your report should address the following questions:

• How was the model developed?

• How does the model simulate complex interactions within and between Earth systems?

• How is this model used to make predictions about the effects of human activities on Earth's systems?

• What are the strengths and limitations of this model?

• How have predictions based on this model been used in practical applications?

In your report, cite specific text evidence from reliable sources. Describe your findings in your own words, and synthesize the information in a way that is easy to understand. Include a list of sources with your final report.

 Evidence Notebook Explain the different effects of California's increasing temperatures and how they relate to drought.

Feedback Systems

FIGURE 18: Ice loss is part of a feedback loop.

Human-caused increases in greenhouse gases are changing Earth's temperature. This, in turn, causes other changes such as sea-level rise. When one change in a system causes one or more other changes to occur, it is called feedback. One example of feedback is the loss of Earth's polar ice. Losing polar ice makes Earth's surface less reflective, and less energy is reflected back into space. More energy is absorbed by Earth's surface, making temperatures warmer. The increased temperature, in turn, further increases the rate of ice loss. When feedback factors combine to lead back to the starting point of the process, a feedback loop forms.

Balancing Feedback

When a change occurs in a system, feedback may counteract or reinforce that change. In *balancing feedback*, the initial change in the system is counterbalanced, returning the system to its previous state. This is also known as negative feedback.

Figure 18 shows an example of balancing feedback. Higher concentrations of greenhouse gases lead to an increase in global average temperature, which then causes an increase in evaporation. Water vapor rises, cools, and condenses into clouds. Because clouds are white, they have a high albedo, which leads to more solar energy reflected into space. Less energy is absorbed by Earth, counteracting the initial change.

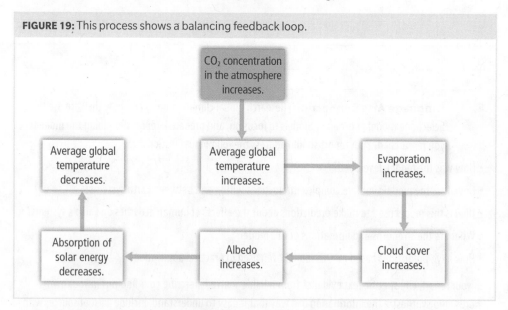

FIGURE 19: This process shows a balancing feedback loop.

EXPLAIN Sweating helps keep your body temperature stable. Explain how this is an example of balancing feedback. Discuss the role of evaporation in this process.

_____

_____

_____

Reforestation and Climate Change

Reforestation refers to renewing forest cover on land that formerly had trees on it. The initial forest may have been cut down, or the trees might have been victim to some natural disaster such as forest fire or blight. Reforestation can occur by natural seeding, or it might involve humans planting young trees or sowing seeds.

Many countries support reforestation because of its benefits to living things and the environment. Planting trees restores habitats, which helps increase biodiversity. It also helps prevent erosion and desertification, preserving valuable land. Reforestation promotes healthy ecosystems, which provide "services" we depend on. For example, as runoff flows through a forest, abundant soil and plants can filter pollutants from the water. Plants can provide food, shade, medicine, and building materials.

FIGURE 20: People can take part in reforestation.

Another benefit of reforestation is that it leads to an increase in photosynthesis, which removes carbon dioxide from the atmosphere. However, research shows that there is too much carbon dioxide in the air to be counteracted by simply increasing photosynthesis. To fully counteract excess carbon dioxide in the atmosphere, an incredibly large area of land would have to be reforested.

There are drawbacks to reforestation as well. In some cases, it takes a tremendous effort to reforest areas, especially if the soil has been degraded or removed. Reforestation also makes areas inaccessible for mining, growing crops, and construction.

ANALYZE Answer these questions about reforestation.

1. Explain why reforestation should be combined with other efforts in order to reduce the effects of human activities on Earth's climate.

_____

_____

_____

2. How might a scientist use a global climate model to analyze the effects of reforestation on the cycling of matter and flow of energy in Earth's systems? Describe specific examples of questions a scientist might investigate using this type of model.

_____

_____

_____

_____

_____

_____

Reinforcing Feedback

Recall that in balancing feedback, the initial change in the system is counteracted. But sometimes, feedback causes the initial change to become more intense. This feedback is part of a *reinforcing feedback loop*. This is also known as a positive feedback loop.

Refer to Figure 21, and think about how increasing global temperatures could result in even more greenhouse gases in the atmosphere. Permafrost is frozen soil that is found in polar regions. Trapped within permafrost are greenhouse gases, such as methane and carbon dioxide. Increasing global temperatures are melting permafrost in some areas.

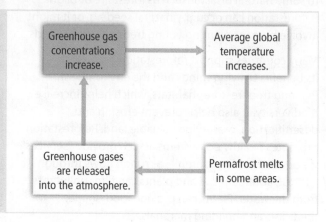

FIGURE 21: In a reinforcing feedback loop, the feedback becomes more intense with each cycle.

 Language Arts Connection Desertification is a process that can occur when feedback causes initial changes in soil and vegetation to worsen over time. Research this phenomenon and make an infographic explaining how positive feedback loops are related to desertification. Include factors that can influence this process, such as changes in soil quality, changes in climate, increased soil erosion, and decreased vegetation.

Feedback Systems and Drought

One example of a reinforcing feedback loop is related to drought. As drought persists in California, the land there becomes dustier. Some of that dust lands on the snowpack in the Sierras. When the snow becomes dusty, its albedo is decreased. The snow reflects less solar energy and absorbs more energy. This absorbed energy makes the snow melt faster.

When snow melts faster, the meltwater from the snow flows downhill earlier than usual in the spring. Early in the year, reservoirs are full of water from winter rains. Less water arrives when it is needed during the summer. A long, dry summer produces yet more dust that will settle on the snowpack and intensify the cycle.

MODEL Draw a diagram showing how the presence of dust on California's snowpack would result in a positive feedback loop.

In the Airborne Snow Observatory plane, monitoring equipment is flown over snowpacks, making measurements of their sizes and albedos. This project is a joint venture between NASA and the California Department of Water Resources.

FIGURE 22: A monitoring plane from the Airborne Snow Observatory collects snowpack data.

Data show that global winds have carried dust from as far away as the deserts in the Middle East and North Africa to the snowpacks in California. Scientists have also discovered that reducing albedo is not the only effect this dust has on weather and climate.

A dust particle in a cloud can provide a surface on which water can condense and form a raindrop or a snow crystal. To provide needed rain, humans sometimes spread particles in clouds in a process known as *cloud seeding*. Dust particles from natural sources are a form of natural cloud seeding. Data on the effect of cloud seeding by dust particles have shown as much as a 40 percent increase in precipitation over California from clouds that contain these dust particles.

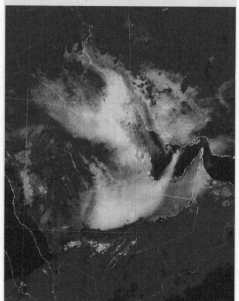

FIGURE 23: This satellite image shows a dust storm over Iraq and Saudi Arabia.

Scientists are now studying changes in the amount of dust brought into California from other regions by analyzing satellite images. Newer satellite images allow researchers to see dust much better than they could in the past. They not only want to know how much dust is present, but they also want to know how those amounts have changed over time.

Scientists have hypothesized that recent droughts in the Middle East and North Africa are increasing the amount of natural cloud seeding by dust in the Sierras. If data support this hypothesis, it would mean that, although the water supply in California has decreased, the water supply could at the same time be increased by climate change elsewhere in the world.

Even if this dust from faraway sources is promoting precipitation in California, the amount of increase is not enough to end California's water shortage. One explanation for this phenomenon is that much natural cloud seeding results from particles of marine bacteria or sea salt. These materials are lighter in color than dust is, so dust is more likely to make resulting snow melt faster due to loss of albedo.

 Engineering

Developing Solutions to Climate Change

Climate and climate models are complex because so many interrelated factors affect climate. Models have to consider how factors within a system interact and how systems and factors affect each other, both positively and negatively. For example, information from a climate model might indicate that dust that exacerbates a drought in California can seed clouds and bring precipitation to that same region.

In addition, scientists and engineers from different fields must work together to develop effective models. The contribution of each field is essential for collecting and analyzing data and predicting the effects of changes in the atmosphere.

EXPLAIN Describe an example of how climate models could help scientists, engineers, and governments establish the criteria and constraints for a solution to climate change.

_____

_____

_____

_____

_____

 Evidence Notebook Which type of feedback loop do you think applies most to the drought problem in California? Cite evidence to support your claim, and explain your reasoning.

Careers in Science

Climatologist

A climatologist is someone who studies Earth's climate. When you think of climate, you might think of temperature and precipitation in a region. You probably know that a tropical climate is warm and wet, and a desert climate is hot and dry. It is easy to see that climatology involves the analysis of weather. Both climatologists and meteorologists study causes and effects of weather and its patterns. But they each study weather over different periods of time.

A meteorologist studies short-term weather, such as what the precipitation and temperature will be tomorrow or next week. Climatologists study weather factors on a long-term basis. Climatologists want to understand long-term changes in variables such as temperature and precipitation. They want to study what causes these changes and what might be done to predict and mitigate changes in climate.

What is involved in being a climatologist? This career field is full of possibilities. A climatologist might conduct research on how feedback loops bring about changes in climate or how greenhouse gases foster climate changes. Depending on what they are studying, they might collect data directly, or they might rely on mathematical and computer modeling. They might work in a university, a research facility, or a government or private agency. They can do field work, office work, lab work, or any combination of these choices.

Climatologists confer with other scientists and climatologists. Data collected by one climatologist might help another climatologist support his or her predictions on climate change. A climatologist studying the climate of a specific region can contribute to the knowledge of a climatologist studying global climate changes. A climatologist studying the effect on climate of changes in ocean currents might have to

FIGURE 24: Scientists in Antarctica use a weather station to gather data related to climate change.

draw on the expertise of oceanographers, physicists, and geologists. A meteorologist might call on a climatologist to help make more accurate weather predictions.

Not only must climatologists confer with others in their field or in related fields, they must communicate clearly with them. Climatologists might make presentations at conferences and seminars, and they might present new findings in scientific journals or other publications.

Climatologists can use their expertise to inform societal decisions about laws, policies, and manufacturing processes. And climatologists can encourage governments and civic organizations to enact laws to mitigate the effects of climate change.

Chemistry in Your Community Scientists from diverse backgrounds are responsible for many advances in the field of climate science. Research a climatologist whose career interests you. What topics do they study? How does their research benefit science and society? Make a pamphlet describing the person you researched, what their research entails, and how they have influenced the communities they are a part of.

| MODELING EARTH'S ENERGY BUDGET | INVESTIGATING EXTREME WEATHER | MICROCLIMATES | Go online to choose one of these other paths. |

Lesson Self-Check

CAN YOU EXPLAIN IT?

FIGURE 25: This dried-up reservoir is the result of a drought in California.

In California, periods of intense drought have brought issues such as water availability to the forefront. Scientists want to understand how Earth system interactions, including rising temperatures, relate to extreme weather conditions such as California's recent drought. To do this, scientists gather and analyze data and use climate models to draw conclusions about how changes in climate relate to local weather phenomena.

 Evidence Notebook Refer to your notes in your Evidence Notebook to construct an explanation for how global climate change could be related to the drought in California, which is a more local weather phenomenon.

1. What is the relationship between global climate change and the occurrence of drought conditions in California?
2. Describe specific examples of scientific evidence that support your claim. Are there certain trends or patterns in climate data that support your claim?
3. Explain how the evidence you cited supports your claim.

CHECKPOINTS

Check Your Understanding

1. Which of these is true of the Earth system?
   - ○ **a.** Energy rarely enters or leaves the system.
   - ○ **b.** Matter rarely enters or leaves the system.
   - ○ **c.** Matter easily enters the system but cannot leave the system.
   - ○ **d.** Energy easily enters the system but cannot leave the system.

2. Which of these processes removes carbon from Earth's atmosphere?
   - ○ **a.** cellular respiration
   - ○ **b.** combustion of fossil fuels
   - ○ **c.** photosynthesis
   - ○ **d.** extraction of fossil fuels

3. Even though Earth's South Pole receives no sunlight during winter in the Southern Hemisphere, the area is not totally without heat. Explain this phenomenon.
   - ○ **a.** Energy is reflected to that area.
   - ○ **b.** The dark region has stored energy from when it was in sunlight.
   - ○ **c.** Increased levels of carbon dioxide make the area warmer.
   - ○ **d.** Energy is carried from one part of Earth to another by convection currents.

4. What happens to solar energy that enters the Earth system? Select all correct answers.
   - ☐ **a.** It is absorbed by the atmosphere.
   - ☐ **b.** It is reflected back into space.
   - ☐ **c.** It is completely used up by environmental processes.
   - ☐ **d.** It is completely absorbed by surfaces that have high albedo.
   - ☐ **e.** It is absorbed by Earth's surface.

5. How might a scientist use a computer model of current effects of greenhouse gases on climate to predict future effects of greenhouse gases on climate?
   - ○ **a.** Assume that future effects will be the same as current effects.
   - ○ **b.** Study the pattern of causes and effects, and extend them to predict future effects.
   - ○ **c.** Predict that established patterns will be reversed.

6. Which of the following statements is true about the diagram shown here? Select all correct answers.

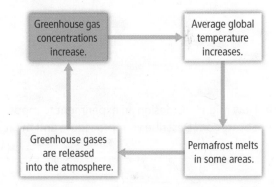

   - ☐ **a.** It shows an example of balancing feedback.
   - ☐ **b.** It shows how a change in a system can cause further changes in the system.
   - ☐ **c.** It shows a positive feedback loop.
   - ☐ **d.** It shows an example of a negative feedback loop.
   - ☐ **e.** It shows a reinforcing feedback loop.

7. Select the correct terms to explain how burning fossil fuels affects the flow of energy in Earth's atmosphere.

   As humans burn fossil fuels for transportation and energy, the amount of carbon dioxide in Earth's atmosphere decreases | increases. Carbon dioxide is a greenhouse gas, so adding this gas to Earth's atmosphere causes global temperatures to decrease | increase.

CHECKPOINTS (continued)

8. Draw a diagram to show how a decrease in sea ice could lead to a reinforcing feedback loop. Indicate how a change in albedo would have effects that would reinforce the initial change.

9. Explain why Earth has a relatively high temperature compared to some other planets. How is this phenomenon related to the greenhouse effect?

_____

_____

_____

_____

10. How might you design an experiment to model the effects of albedo on energy absorption? Describe your procedure and the results you would expect.

_____

_____

_____

_____

MAKE YOUR OWN STUDY GUIDE

In your Evidence Notebook, design a study guide that supports the main ideas from this lesson:

Earth is a closed system made up of smaller, interconnecting systems.

Earth's energy budget consists of inputs and outputs.

Natural changes and human activities can disrupt the balance of Earth's energy budget.

Models can be used to study past climate conditions on Earth and to predict future climate.

Models can illustrate feedback loops that show factors that affect Earth's climate.

Remember to include the following information in your study guide:

- Use examples that model main ideas.
- Record explanations for the phenomena you investigated.
- Use evidence to support your explanations. Your support can include drawings, data, graphs, laboratory conclusions, and other evidence recorded throughout the lesson.

Consider how climate change is an effect resulting from numerous, interacting causes.

Solutions to Environmental Problems

Acid precipitation has destroyed plant life on Mt. Mitchell in North Carolina.

CAN YOU SOLVE IT?

The trees in this image were not damaged by fire or disease; they were damaged by rain. Rain water is naturally slightly acidic due to the presence of carbon dioxide in the air. Carbon dioxide reacts with water to form carbonic acid. Life on Earth is adapted to this amount of acidity, and it does not harm Earth's organisms. However, some human activities and natural events can cause the release of certain gases that make water in the atmosphere become more acidic, causing *acid precipitation*. For example, sulfur dioxide gas from the eruption of Kilauea in Hawaii formed acid precipitation when it reacted with water in the atmosphere. The trees in the image, however, are not near an active volcano, so what caused the acid precipitation? In industrialized nations, most acid precipitation is the result of human activity. The extraction and combustion of fossil fuels releases carbon dioxide, nitrogen oxides, and sulfur oxides into the atmosphere where they react with water, making the rain water more acidic.

ANALYZE How do you think human activities cause acid precipitation? What types of solutions do you think can solve this problem at the local and global levels?

_____

_____

_____

 Evidence Notebook As you explore the lesson, gather evidence to explain how solutions to environmental problems such as acid precipitation are developed.

Acids and Bases in the Earth System

Acid precipitation harms ecosystems and damages human infrastructure. To develop solutions to this problem, scientists and engineers must understand acids. The properties of an acid depend on its specific chemical makeup, but all acids share some common properties. The same is true for an acid's opposite: a base.

PREDICT What properties do you think of when you think of the term "acidic"? How might acids differ from bases?

_____

_____

_____

Properties of Acids and Bases

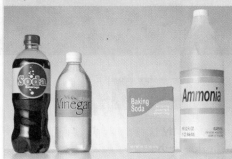

FIGURE 1: Many items that you use every day are acidic or basic.

Acids and bases are all around us. They are in the foods we eat, the beverages we drink, and the products we use. Citric acid in limes and grapefruits gives these fruits their sour taste. Milk, yogurt, and sour cream contain lactic acid. Sulfuric acid is in most car batteries. Acids react with bases and some metals. Acid molecules generally contain one or more hydrogen atoms. When they are added to water, most acids ionize, forming ions in the water. The ionization of most acids leads to the release of hydrogen ions (H^+) into a solution. For example, hydrochloric acid (HCl) forms the following ions in water:

$$HCl(g) \xrightarrow{H_2O} H^+(aq) + Cl^-(aq)$$

Common bases include ammonium hydroxide (NH_4OH), a household cleaning product, and sodium hydroxide (NaOH), used in drain cleaner. Bases taste bitter and feel slick—the slick feel of some soaps is the result of the presence of a base. Bases react with acids, but they do not react with metals. Some bases contain a hydroxide ion (OH^-). When added to water, these bases dissociate, releasing hydroxide ions into the solution. For example, sodium hydroxide dissociates in water to form sodium ions and hydroxide ions:

$$NaOH(s) \xrightarrow{H_2O} Na^+(aq) + OH^-(aq)$$

ANALYZE Categorize each compound as an acid or a base based on its chemical formula.

| H_2SO_4 | LiOH | KOH | H_3PO_4 | $Ca(OH)_2$ | HF |

Acid	Base
_____	_____
_____	_____
_____	_____

Hydrogen ions released from the ionization of an acid are attracted to negatively charged areas on water molecules, forming hydronium ions (H_3O^+). The following chemical equation represents the formation of hydronium ions when hydrochloric acid is added to water:

$$HCl(g) + H_2O(l) \rightarrow H_3O^+(aq) + Cl^-(aq)$$

Because a hydrogen atom is made up of one electron and one proton, a positive hydrogen ion is simply a proton. Therefore, when HCl is in water, we say that a proton is transferred from the acid to the water. Thus, one way to define an acid is a substance that donates protons in solution.

FIGURE 2: Hydrochloric acid, sometimes called muriatic acid, is used to treat the water in swimming pools.

FIGURE 3: This molecular model shows that when hydrochloric acid is added to water, a proton is transferred to water, forming hydronium ions and chloride ions.

$$H\ Cl\ +\ H\ O\ H \rightarrow\ O\ H\ H\ +\ Cl$$

EXPLAIN Select the correct terms to complete the statement.

Nitric acid has the chemical formula HNO_3. When nitric acid interacts with water, protons are transferred to | from nitric acid to | from water, which produces hydroxide | hydronium ions.

While many acids contain hydrogen atoms and ionize in water to form hydronium ions, not all acids behave this way. Some acids donate protons (hydrogen ions) to solvents other than water. Another way to classify acids is as any substance that accepts a pair of electrons from another substance.

When ions are formed in an acidic solution, the solution has the capacity to conduct electricity. Therefore, an acid such as HCl is also an electrolyte. Some acids, known as *strong acids*, ionize or dissociate completely in solution and are therefore strong electrolytes. Other acids, known as *weak acids*, do not ionize or dissociate completely in solution and are therefore weak electrolytes. The strength of an acid is not related to its concentration. A strong acid can be dilute, and a weak acid can be concentrated. The strength of an acid is a measure of the degree to which it ionizes or dissociates.

Some human activities result in excess acid in the atmosphere. This leads to acid precipitation and initiates a series of cause-and-effect changes that affect the stability of natural systems. Two strong acids found in acid precipitation are sulfuric acid (H_2SO_4) and nitric acid (HNO_3). When precipitation containing these acids mixes with soil, it leaches nutrients from the soil and causes the release of toxic substances such as aluminum. Excess aluminum ions (Al^{3+}) in soil interfere with plants' ability to grow, take up water, and absorb nutrients. Acidic fog and clouds can damage plants' leaves, decreasing their ability to carry out photosynthesis.

When water from acid precipitation runs off into lakes and other bodies of water, aquatic organisms are negatively affected by the increased acidity, aluminum, and nutrients.

Evidence Notebook In your Evidence Notebook, make a model to show what happens when nitric acid and sulfuric acid mix with water in the atmosphere. Using your model, demonstrate how these acids cycle from the atmosphere into the biosphere. Then explain why the presence of these acids harms ecosystems.

FIGURE 4: Sodium hydroxide is a key ingredient in many drain cleaners.

Like acids, bases can be reactive. One example is sodium hydroxide (NaOH), a common ingredient in drain cleaner. Unlike acids, bases such as NaOH do not react with metals. Therefore, it reacts with and dissolves materials that clog metal pipes, but will not react with the pipes themselves. Sodium hydroxide dissociates completely in water to form sodium ions and hydroxide (OH^-) ions:

$$NaOH(s) \xrightarrow{H_2O} Na^+(aq) + OH^-(aq)$$

Ammonia, another base, interacts with water to form ammonium ions and hydroxide ions:

$$NH_3(aq) + H_2O(l) \rightarrow NH_4^+(aq) + OH^-(aq)$$

APPLY Select the correct terms to complete the statement about ammonia.

When ammonia is mixed with water, a proton is transferred to | from
ammonia to | from water, which produces hydroxide | hydronium ions.

A base can be described as a substance that produces hydroxide ions in solution and accepts hydrogen ions (protons). Many bases, therefore, are metal hydroxides, such as sodium hydroxide, potassium hydroxide, and aluminum hydroxide. Ammonia, NH_3, is an example of a base that is a proton acceptor.

Similar to acids, bases can be described as strong or weak based on the degree to which they dissociate or ionize. Strong bases ionize or dissociate completely in aqueous solution. Weak bases ionize or dissociate only to a small degree. Weak bases produce few hydroxide ions or accept few protons when added to water. Ammonia is an example of a weak base. For every 100 ammonia molecules that dissolve, only one forms ions. Ninety-nine molecules remain as ammonia. The strength of an aqueous base depends on the number of hydroxide ions it produces in solution, not on the number of hydroxide ions in the base.

EXPLAIN A student uses a conductivity meter to analyze two solutions of equal volume and concentration. One solution contains a weak base, and the other contains a strong base. Make a claim based on evidence for which solution will have a higher conductivity, and explain your reasoning.

_____

_____

_____

_____

The pH Scale

Acids form aqueous solutions containing excess hydronium ions, and bases form solutions containing excess hydroxide ions. A solution that contains neither excess hydronium ions nor excess hydroxide ions is said to be *neutral*.

INFER Complete the statements defining acidic and basic solutions in terms of hydronium and hydroxide ion concentrations.

| < | > | = |

In a neutral solution, $[H_3O^+]$ _____ $[OH^-]$.   In an acidic solution, $[H_3O^+]$ _____ $[OH^-]$.

In a basic solution, $[H_3O^+]$ _____ $[OH^-]$.

The concentrations of H_3O^+ and OH^- in aqueous solutions are generally very small, requiring scientific notation to be expressed succinctly. For example, the hydronium ion concentration of a certain acid might be 0.00043 M, which could be expressed as 4.3×10^{-4} M. In order to simplify calculations involving concentrations of acids and bases, scientists use the pH scale. This scale is convenient because it removes the need for scientific notation. A solution's pH is defined by the equation

$$pH = -\log[H_3O^+]$$

The equation for pH is an example of a logarithmic function. The common logarithms (log) of a number is the power to which 10 must be raised to equal the number. Therefore, $\log(10^7)$ is 7. When calculating pH, you take the negative of the log. So, if the hydronium ion concentration of a solution is 10^{-4} M, the log is -4. The pH is then $-(-4)$, or 4.

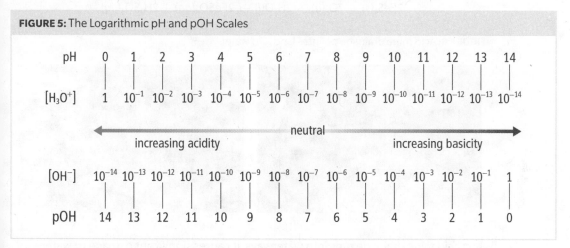

FIGURE 5: The Logarithmic pH and pOH Scales

Every unit change in pH represents a change of 10 units in hydronium ion concentration. The hydronium ion concentration of a solution with a pH of 3 is $10 \times 10 \times 10$, or 10^3 times greater than that of a solution of pH 6. The hydronium ion concentration of a solution of pH 1 is ten trillion (10×10^{12}) times greater than that of a solution of pH 14! The pH scale allows scientists to model these large changes in concentration on a more manageable scale.

You can also describe solutions in terms of their pOH, or hydroxide ion concentration. This scale also relies on logs:

$$pOH = -\log[OH^-]$$

If either pH or pOH is known, the following equation allows you to determine the other. This value varies slightly with changes in pressure or temperature, but is very near 14 at 1 atm and 25 °C:

$$pH + pOH = 14$$

ANALYZE Categorize each item as describing an acidic, basic, or neutral solution.

pH = 9 $[H_3O^+] = 1 \times 10^{-7}$ $[H_3O^+] = [OH^-]$ $H_3O^+ = 1 \times 10^{-13}$ $[H_3O^+] > [OH^-]$

$[H_3O^+] = 1 \times 10^{-2}$ pH = 7 $[H_3O^+] < [OH^-]$ pH = 5

Acidic	Neutral	Basic

Cause and Effect
Acid Runoff

Many of the objects you use every day are manufactured from raw materials that come from mines. As you've learned, however, mining presents some serious environmental problems. One is acid mine drainage, or when water seeping out of a mine becomes acidic. In addition to coal or metal ores, many mines contain sulfur compounds, such as pyrite, FeS_2. When exposed to air and water, FeS_2 forms sulfuric acid:

$$2FeS_2(s) + 7O_2(g) + 2H_2O(l) \rightarrow 2FeSO_4(aq) + 2H_2SO_4(aq)$$

FIGURE 6: Acid mine drainage pollutes land and water.

When acid mine drainage runs into waterways, it causes significant damage to water quality and aquatic habitats. As a result, many of the aquatic organisms in a waterway polluted by acid mine drainage do not survive. Some organisms can withstand slight changes in acidity, but as pH decreases, more and more species are affected. Figure 7 shows the pH some organisms can withstand before being critically affected. Water that appears clear and colorless can still contain below normal, wildlife-threatening pH levels.

FIGURE 7: Critical pH levels for aquatic organisms

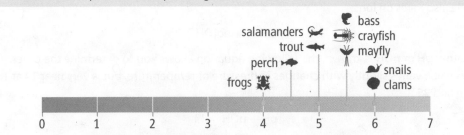

Acidic runoff problems do not stop when a mine closes. Mining companies are required by law to return the mine to a natural state. However, the waste materials brought up from deep inside Earth can continue to cause acid runoff into the future.

Language Arts Connection Can land affected by acid mine drainage be reclaimed? What can be done to prevent future acid mine drainage? Prepare a presentation answering these questions for a mining company that wants to know how to treat and prevent acid mine drainage. What recommendations can you give them to find a better balance between economic constraints and environmental systems?

Hands-On Lab
Analyzing Acids and Bases

Have you ever heard the term *acid* referenced in a movie or television show? If so, the acid was probably very strong and highly corrosive. It could have been powerful enough to eat through metal or dissolve evidence of a crime. Although these extreme applications of acids may be common on the screen, acids and bases are actually common in everyday household items. But how can you tell when you're using, or even eating or drinking, something acidic or basic? In this lab, you will design a procedure to determine whether several household substances are acidic or basic in solution based on the pH scale. Then, you will analyze what happens when you combine a strong acid and a strong base.

Research Question: Are there patterns to the way we use acids and bases in household products? Are acids better suited to certain tasks, and bases to other tasks?

- -

MAKE A CLAIM

In your Evidence Notebook, predict whether each household substance will be acidic or basic. What do you think will happen when you combine a strong acid and a strong base?

- -

MATERIALS

- indirectly vented chemical splash goggles, nonlatex apron, nonlatex gloves
- chalk (contains calcium carbonate)
- conductivity probe
- deionized water in wash bottle
- droppers
- HCl solution, 0.1 M, in dropper bottle
- NaOH solution, 0.1 M, in dropper bottle
- pH paper and pH probe
- well plate
- household substances in solution: baking soda, coffee, glass cleaner, lemon juice, milk of magnesia, seltzer water, soapy water, vinegar

- -

SAFETY INFORMATION

- Wear indirectly vented chemical splash goggles, a nonlatex apron, and nonlatex gloves during the setup, hands-on, and takedown segments of the activity.

- Never taste any substance or chemical in the lab. Tell your teacher immediately if you spill chemicals on yourself, the table, or floor.

Part I: Analyzing Household Substances

- -

PLAN THE INVESTIGATION

1. Review the appropriate safety rules for handling acids and bases.

2. Write a procedure and safety plan in your Evidence Notebook explaining how you will determine whether each household substance is acidic or basic. Consider properties such as pH, reactivity, and electrolytic behavior. With your group, discuss the order in which you should make observations and how to best conserve time and materials. For example, if you placed 10 drops of lemon juice in a well plate, how could you most effectively perform multiple tests on the same 10 drops of this solution?

3. Make a data table in your Evidence Notebook in which to record your observations.

4. Have your teacher approve your procedure and safety plan before you begin your work. If you need additional materials, discuss these with your teacher.

5. Clean up your lab area and dispose of your lab materials as instructed by your teacher.

indirectly vented chemical splash goggles

DRAW CONCLUSIONS

Claim Which of the solutions you tested were acidic, and which were basic?

Evidence Cite evidence from your data to support your claim.

Reasoning Explain how the data you cited supports your claim. What is the connection between the properties you observed and the way you categorized each substance?

_____

_____

_____

_____

_____

_____

_____

_____

_____

_____

Part II: Combining Acids and Bases

PLAN THE INVESTIGATION

1. Review the appropriate safety rules for combining acids and bases.

2. Write a procedure in your Evidence Notebook for how you will determine the pH of a strong acid (HCl), a strong base (NaOH), and the solution produced when they are combined in equal parts. With your group, discuss appropriate procedures for safely making a solution composed of equal parts 0.1 M hydrochloric acid and 0.1 M sodium hydroxide. How will you make the solution, and how will you safely measure its pH?

3. Make a data table in your Evidence Notebook to record your observations. You should record the pH of hydrochloric acid, sodium hydroxide, and the solution made up of equal parts acid and base.

4. Have your teacher approve your procedure, safety plans, and data table before you begin your work. If you need additional materials to complete your procedure, discuss these with your teacher.

5. Clean up your lab area and dispose of your lab materials as instructed by your teacher.

CONSTRUCT AN EXPLANATION

Answer the following questions in your Evidence Notebook.

1. What were the pH values for each solution you tested? What does this tell you about the hydronium ion concentration in each solution?

2. What did you notice about the pH of the solution made up of equal parts acid and base? What types of molecular-scale interactions might account for your observations?

3. How do you think the results would have been different if you had combined a weak acid with a strong base, or a strong acid with a weak base? Explain your answers.

Neutralization Reactions

You might think that combining a strong acid and a strong base would result in an even more reactive compound. However, if you combine HCl and NaOH (assume equal volumes and concentrations), the resulting solution is relatively unreactive, or chemically stable, and has a neutral pH. How can this be? Recall that strong acids and bases exist as ions in aqueous solutions. The following reactions occur when HCl and NaOH are added to water:

$$HCl(g) + H_2O(l) \rightarrow H_3O^+(aq) + Cl^-(aq)$$

$$NaOH(s) + H_2O(l) \rightarrow Na^+(aq) + OH^-(aq)$$

When these solutions are mixed, the hydronium and hydroxide ions react with each other. The hydronium ion donates a hydrogen ion to the hydroxide ion, forming two water molecules—one from the reaction between the ions and one left over after the hydronium ion donates the hydrogen ion.

$$H_3O^+(aq) + OH^-(aq) \rightarrow 2H_2O(l)$$

The chloride and sodium ions remain in the solution as ions.

 Collaborate With a partner, discuss why you might treat an acid spill with a base or a base spill with an acid.

The resulting solution now contains sodium and chloride ions dissolved in water, forming sodium chloride (NaCl). Any reaction between a strong acid and a strong base is similar to this acid-base reaction. When a strong acid and a strong base react, a *neutralization* reaction occurs. NaCl is often referred to as "salt," but all neutralization reactions produce a substance called a salt. A *salt* is the compound formed from the cation (positive ion) from the base and the anion (negative ion) from the acid. For example, when potassium hydroxide (KOH) reacts with sulfuric acid (H_2SO_4), the salt formed is potassium sulfate (K_2SO_4).

FIGURE 8: Emergency spill kits in the lab are used to clean up acidic or basic spills.

While mixing equal volumes and concentrations of a strong acid with a strong base results in a neutral solution, what happens when you combine a weak acid and a strong base, or a strong acid and a weak base? Think about the degree to which each of these forms ions in solution. Strong acids and bases completely ionize or dissociate in solution, whereas weak acids and bases do not.

EXPLAIN Select the correct terms to complete the statements about acids and bases. Assume equal volumes and concentrations of each.

A strong acid forms many | few hydronium ions in solution, and a weak base produces many | few hydroxide ions in solution. Therefore, when these are combined, there will be an excess of hydronium | hydroxide ions, so the solution will be slightly acidic | basic. A strong base produces many | few hydroxide ions in solution, and a weak acid produces many | few hydronium ions. When these are combined, there will be an excess of hydronium | hydroxide ions, so the solution will be slightly acidic | basic.

 Evidence Notebook Carbonic acid formed from dissolved carbon dioxide is present in normal rainwater. Acid precipitation contains acids such as nitric acid and sulfuric acid. What can you infer about the strengths of these acids based on their environmental effects?

Engineering

Solutions to Acid Precipitation

If you were to measure the pH of normal precipitation—rain, sleet, or snow—you might expect it to be neutral, with a pH of 7. You would find, however, that normal precipitation is slightly acidic. Depending on where it has fallen, it has a pH from 5 to 7 because the carbon dioxide in the air combines with water in the atmosphere to form carbonic acid.

If the pH of precipitation falls below 5, it is considered to be acid precipitation. Acid precipitation forms when sulfur and nitrogen oxide gases formed from burning fossil fuels combine with precipitation to form sulfuric and nitric acids. Both of these acids are strong acids, so they ionize completely, producing many hydronium ions.

Explore Online ▶

Hands-On Lab

Effects of Acid Rain on Plants
Design and conduct an experiment to determine how acid rain affects the growth of plants.

Acid precipitation can lower the pH of soil and water. Such changes affect both animal and plant life because organisms require a narrow range of pH for survival or optimal growth. As a result, life in lakes and ponds can be adversely affected if the pH decreases too much. Soil pH also affects where plants can grow. A decrease in soil pH can disturb native populations of plants that are adapted to a more neutral pH. Acid precipitation also damages buildings and statues made from marble or limestone. These two kinds of rock are forms of calcium carbonate, which is a base and so reacts with acids.

 Collaborate With a partner, discuss why you think most organisms can only live within a narrow pH range.

Many industrial processes and the burning of coal, oil, gasoline, and diesel fuel produce oxides of nonmetals such as SO_2, SO_3, NO, and NO_2. Oxides form when another element chemically combines with oxygen. These particular oxides come from the oxidation of sulfur in the fuels or nitrogen in the air. When sulfur dioxide, SO_2, enters the atmosphere, it reacts with oxygen to produce sulfur trioxide, SO_3. When sulfur trioxide reacts with rainwater, a strong acid called sulfuric acid (H_2SO_4) forms.

$$SO_3(g) + H_2O(l) \rightarrow H_2SO_4(aq)$$

The oxides of nitrogen also react in the atmosphere to produce nitrous acid, HNO_2, and nitric acid, HNO_3. Acid precipitation emissions in the United States have markedly decreased over recent decades due to increased regulation and decreased use of sulfur-containing coal. Increasing sulfur dioxide emissions are still a problem in other countries.

MODEL Draw a model that explains how matter cycles through the atmosphere, hydrosphere, and biosphere when acid precipitation occurs.

FIGURE 9: Observe the damage that is caused by acid precipitation.

a Statue damaged by acid rain

b Forest killed by acid precipitation

c Fish killed by acidified water

DEFINE What questions could be asked about acid precipitation that might help an engineer offer possible solutions from the scale of individual actions to societal systems?

_____

_____

_____

_____

In response to acid precipitation and other forms of air pollution, the United States amended the Clean Air Act in 1990 to mandate a reduction in the emissions of sulfur and nitrogen oxides. Such mandates not only must set goals for certain deadlines, they also must face the challenges of developing ways of accomplishing them.

Almost all sulfur dioxide (SO_2) emissions come from the generation of electricity in coal-fired power plants. Engineers and scientists faced the challenges of meeting the requirements established by laws. As a result of the Clean Air Act, SO_2 emissions from power plants in the United States decreased by 73% from 2006 to 2015. There was also a 32% decrease in coal-fired electricity generated over that period.

POLLUTION CONTROL SYSTEMS

In developing ways to control gases that cause acid precipitation, engineers dealt with the problem on both collective and individual levels. For example, the amount of pollution released in car exhaust is small compared to that produced by a factory. But the pollution caused by millions of cars is significant. One of the main ways engineers addressed this challenge was to develop and install catalytic converters into cars' exhaust systems.

Recall that a catalyst speeds up or enables a chemical reaction without itself being permanently changed by the reaction. A catalytic converter uses metal catalysts to change the gases coming from the engine into less harmful gases. Catalytic converters tend to be very expensive because precious metals, such as rhodium, platinum, and sometimes palladium, are used. The metal catalysts work at temperatures above 260 °C. This means that before the car engine reaches this temperature, harmful gases still are released into the air. The catalytic converter design could be improved by developing catalysts that work at lower temperatures.

Most catalytic converters change nitrogen oxides into nitrogen gas and oxygen gas, carbon monoxide into carbon dioxide, and unburned or partially burned hydrocarbons into carbon dioxide and water. Although carbon dioxide is a greenhouse gas that contributes to climate change, it is nontoxic and less damaging than carbon monoxide. Overall, car emissions produced when using a catalytic converter are much less harmful than those produced by a car that does not have this device. The millions of cars with catalytic converters are now producing a small fraction of the pollutants that could potentially cause acid precipitation.

PREDICT What tradeoffs might be considered if a country decided to require all vehicles to have catalytic converters? Explain your answer.

_____

_____

_____

FIGURE 10: Electric cars need to be periodically recharged at electric charging stations.

Another way to reduce acid precipitation is to change power sources to those that do not burn fossil fuels. For example, electric cars do not burn fossil fuels, so they do not directly produce air pollution. Although electric cars do not directly produce air pollution, they may still cause environmental problems. Often the electricity used to charge the battery comes from a power plant that burns fossil fuels. For electric cars to not contribute to carbon dioxide emissions, they need to be charged on sources of electricity such as solar, wind, nuclear, or hydropower, which do not produce carbon dioxide.

INFER Electric cars do not produce local air pollution, so they are said to have a "long tailpipe." Explain what you think the "long tailpipe" analogy means.

_____

_____

_____

The use of pollution-control equipment by power plants and the use of low-sulfur coal has helped to decreased SO_2 emissions. This was done in order to comply with the federal Mercury and Air Toxics (MATS) law, which factories were required to comply with by 2015. This pollution-control equipment often includes "scrubbers," which remove SO_2 from power-plant exhaust gas.

The most common scrubber consists of a tower with nozzles, shown in Figure 11. The nozzles spray a semi-liquid mixture, which contains a compound that reacts with the SO_2 gas in the exhaust gas. The reaction produces a solid, thus removing most of the SO_2 from the output. One commonly used mixture is made from limestone, $CaCO_3$:

$$CaCO_3(s) + SO_2(g) \rightarrow CaSO_3(s) + CO_2(g)$$

Recall that, although a catalytic converter removes carbon monoxide from car exhaust, it releases carbon dioxide into the atmosphere. A similar tradeoff exists in using scrubbers. Carbon dioxide, a greenhouse gas, is produced while the toxic SO_2 pollutant is removed from the output gas.

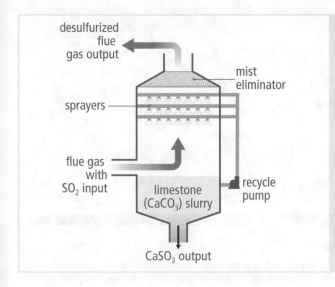

desulfurized
flue
gas output

mist
eliminator

sprayers

flue gas
with
SO_2 input

limestone
($CaCO_3$) slurry

recycle
pump

$CaSO_3$ output

FIGURE 11: In a scrubber absorber tower, power plant exhaust gas is passed through a series of sprayers. The mixture in the sprayers contains a compound that reacts with sulfur dioxide in the gas, forming a solid that can be removed.

ANALYZE The use of desulfurization techniques has been described using the term *clean coal*. Based on your observations, do you think this is a legitimate description? Explain your answer.

_____

_____

_____

_____

_____

Some innovations have been developed to make the scrubber process more profitable. Additional processing steps can convert the $CaSO_3$ output into $CaSO \cdot 2H_2O$ (gypsum) that can be used to make wallboard and other products. Another innovation has been the use of seawater to scrub the output gases. The SO_2 is absorbed by the water, forming sulfite ions and hydronium ions. The hydronium ions react with natural carbonates in the seawater to form CO_2, which is released.

One partial solution to SO_2 emissions involves another fossil fuel. Some of the observable decrease in SO_2 emissions in the recent past has been due to an increased use of natural gas to generate electricity. Because natural gas contains only trace amounts of sulfur, less SO_2 was emitted over time. Because of the abundance of coal, however, there is a current push back to coal use. As coal use increases globally, additional challenges to keep SO_2 levels under control arise.

ACID PRECIPITATION ON THE GLOBAL SCALE

The acid precipitation problem in the United States has been largely reduced, but it continues to be a global problem. Some countries rely on coal-powered plants to produce large amounts of their electricity. For example, both China and India rely heavily on coal as an energy source. Thus, SO_2 emissions continue to pollute the air in these countries. In fact, severe haze and other air-quality issues are major health concerns in China and India. Emission patterns in these countries are also affected by changes in their economies, environmental regulations, and population demographics.

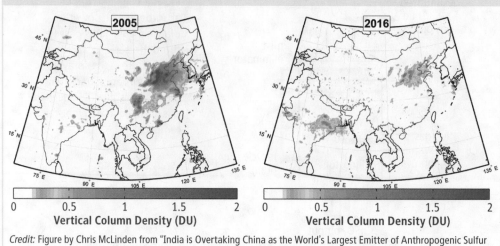

FIGURE 12: SO$_2$ Emissions in China and India, 2005 and 2016

Credit: Figure by Chris McLinden from "India is Overtaking China as the World's Largest Emitter of Anthropogenic Sulfur Dioxide" by Can Li, et al, from *Scientific Reports*, November 9, 2017. Reprinted by permission of the authors.

EXPLAIN The maps in Figure 12 show low SO$_2$ emissions as white and high emissions as purple. What patterns do you see in SO$_2$ emissions in India and China during this time?

_____

_____

_____

Most of the SO$_2$ emissions produced by China and India come from coal-fired power plants and factories. As the maps indicate, China implemented changes in recent years that greatly decreased its SO$_2$ emissions. However, emissions in India have increased. In India, about 33 million people now live in areas that are heavily polluted with SO$_2$. Sulfur dioxide causes not only acid precipitation but also haze and human health problems.

Despite improvements in China, haze remains a serious problem, and the country still must reduce emissions of pollutants other than SO$_2$. In India, problems with haze have not been as bad as in China because the areas where the most emissions occur are not heavily populated. However, as the demand for electricity increases in India, a growing number of people will be adversely affected by the effects of burning coal.

Language Arts Connection Research how countries around the world have been affected by acid precipitation and what they have done to fix the problem. Choose one country to study further. Use these questions to guide your research:

- What methods are used to help reduce acid precipitation? Where are these methods used?
- What data support how effective these methods are?
- Are methods that are effective in one region likely to be effective in another region? Why?
- Why is acid precipitation also considered an international, global-scale problem?

Present your findings in a short video that could be used on a chemistry classroom webpage.

Evidence Notebook Describe the reduction of acid precipitation in the United States. How does the problem continue to be an issue on a global scale? How do you think switching to alternative energy resources, such as renewable resources or nuclear energy, could impact SO$_2$ emissions?

Energy Storage Solutions

When fossil fuels are used to generate electricity, power plants adjust the reactions to produce more energy at peak times, when the energy is needed. One of the biggest challenges to renewable energy sources, such as wind and solar energy, is capturing and storing energy when it is produced so it can be used later. For example, solar energy may produce an excess of electricity in the daytime, but it cannot produce it at night.

INFER What is required for a practical device that stores electrical energy? Select all correct answers.

☐ **a.** It stores energy only when energy is not being produced.

☐ **b.** It stores energy only from renewable energy sources.

☐ **c.** Energy must be able to move from the storage unit to where it is needed.

☐ **d.** Its design takes into account getting energy to the unit and storing energy there.

☐ **e.** It is competitive in cost compared to other sources of energy.

To be useful, electricity must be available when it is needed. Several technologies exist for storing energy from renewable resources. However, there are technical, scientific, and economical barriers that must be overcome in order to implement these technologies on a larger scale.

Generating Electric Current

Most batteries work by converting chemical energy into electrical energy. This is done using a reaction called an oxidation-reduction reaction. In this type of reaction, electrons are transferred from one substance to another. Recall that atoms gain or lose electrons in reactions forming a stable octet in their outer energy level. More electronegative atoms tend to gain electrons, and less electronegative atoms tend to lose electrons.

Consider a strip of zinc metal in a copper(II) sulfate solution. The zinc loses electrons to the copper(II) ions in the solution. When the copper(II) ions gain electrons, they fall out of solution as copper atoms. This can be seen as a layer of copper on the zinc bar in the beaker on the right in Figure 13. As electrons are transferred between zinc atoms and copper(II) ions, energy is released as heat.

FIGURE 13: The blue color of the copper sulfate solution is due to the presence of the copper(II) ion. The solution becomes lighter in color as copper ions in the solution are replaced by zinc ions. The copper atoms replace zinc atoms on the zinc bar.

The overall reaction for this demonstration is:

$$Zn(s) + CuSO_4(aq) \rightarrow Cu(s) + ZnSO_4(aq)$$

We can simplify this by only modeling the changes in the zinc and copper species:

$$Zn(s) + Cu^{2+}(aq) \rightarrow Cu(s) + Zn^{2+}(aq)$$

Using this simplified equation, we can see that the zinc atom lost electrons, gaining a positive charge. Zinc is said to have been oxidized, and this portion of the reaction is called oxidation. The copper(II) ion gains electrons, and its charge decreases. Copper is said to have been reduced, and this portion of the reaction is called reduction. Note that the process of *reduction*, while involving a gain in electrons, results in a reduced charge.

Each of the paired reactions in an oxidation-reduction reaction can be written as a *half-reaction*, representing the change in charge of the reactants and the movement of electrons. In a half-reaction, the electrons transferred between species are written as either a product or reactant, depending on whether the electrons were gained (reduction) or lost (oxidation). Half-reactions help scientists follow the flow of electrons. Knowing the number of electron transfers helps in balancing oxidation-reduction reactions because charge, like atoms, must be conserved in a chemical reaction.

SOLVE Write each chemical species in its correct location to complete the half-reactions.

$$Zn(s) \quad Cu(s) \quad Zn^{2+}(aq) \quad Cu^{2+}(aq)$$

Oxidation: [ ] → [ ] $+ 2e^-$

Reduction: [ ] $+ 2e^- \rightarrow$ [ ]

A mnemonic device is an aid to assist remembering certain information. A common mnemonic device to remember the transfer of electrons in oxidation-reduction reactions is "OIL RIG." In this statement, OIL stands for "Oxidation Is Loss" and RIG stands for "Reduction Is Gain."

APPLY In the space provided, write your own mnemonic device about oxidation-reduction reactions. You do not have to use the same letters as OIL RIG. Your device should be something that will be easy for you to remember.

_____

_____

_____

If the substance that is being oxidized is separated from the substance that is being reduced, as shown in Figure 14, the electron transfer is accompanied by a transfer of electrical energy instead of energy as heat. This is how an *electrochemical cell* operates, which is the simplest part of a battery. This name comes from the transformation from chemical energy to electrical energy that occurs in the cell. Inside an electrochemical cell are two electrodes—the negative anode and the positive cathode. Each electrode is in contact with an electrolyte.

One means of separating oxidation and reduction reactions is by separating them with a porous barrier, or salt bridge. This barrier prevents the metal atoms of one half-reaction from mixing with the ions of the other half-reaction. Ions in the two solutions can move across the salt bridge, which keeps a precipitate from building up on the electrodes, as you saw in Figure 13. Electrons can be transferred from the anode to the cathode through an external connecting wire.

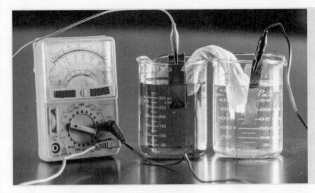

FIGURE 14: A voltaic cell generates electricity, which can be measured using a galvanometer.

MODEL Electric current moves in a closed loop path, or circuit. Analyze the circuit in Figure 14. Draw a diagram explaining the movement of electrons and ions. How does the charge within the system remain balanced?

Figure 14 shows a voltaic cell, also called a galvanic cell. These types of electrochemical cells use spontaneous reactions to convert chemical energy into electrical energy. Most batteries are voltaic cells. In this voltaic cell, the half-cell on the right is composed of a zinc anode submerged in a solution of zinc sulfate ($ZnSO_4$). The half-cell on the left is composed of a copper cathode submerged in a solution of copper sulfate ($CuSO_4$).

Explore Online ▶

Hands-On Lab

Designing and Using Voltaic Cells Compare the efficiency of voltaic cells using different materials.

EXPLAIN Select the correct terms to complete the statement explaining how electrons and ions move in a voltaic cell.

Electrons | Ions spontaneously flow through the connecting wire from the anode to the cathode. The anode is oxidized | reduced, and the cathode is oxidized | reduced. Electrons | Ions in the solution move across the salt bridge, which is a paper towel in this example. If the half-cells were not separated, current would continue to flow | stop flowing.

A voltaic cell is sometimes referred to as a wet cell battery because the electrolyte is a liquid. However, the voltaic cells most commonly used to power everyday electronics are dry cell batteries. Dry cell batteries use a paste electrolyte instead of a liquid. Batteries can also vary in the number of electrochemical cells they contain. For example, the dry cell batteries used in a flashlight contain only one electrochemical cell. Other batteries, such as small 9-volt batteries and most 12-volt car batteries, contain several electrochemical cells in series.

Collaborate Discuss this question with a partner: Based on what you know about acids and bases, why do you think these substances are commonly found in batteries?

Harnessing Chemical Energy

There are several different types of batteries, most of which are based on the same principles as the voltaic cell. These batteries vary in strength based on the materials they contain and the number of cells included. Unlike electrical power produced from fossil fuels, current from a battery produces no greenhouse gases or gases that cause acid precipitation. There are, however, certain environmental concerns with using batteries, including their manufacturing and disposal. Three of the most common types of batteries are alkaline, lead storage, and lithium ion.

FIGURE 15: Alkaline batteries are commonly used in household items.

Alkaline Batteries

Alkaline dry-cell batteries are common "disposable" batteries, such as the AA batteries you might use in a remote or the 9V battery you might use in a smoke detector. In these batteries, zinc metal and manganese dioxide (MnO_2) transfer electrons. A base, such as potassium hydroxide (KOH) or sodium hydroxide (NaOH), forms ions that allow current to flow. The base gives these batteries their name—*alkaline* is a term used to describe basic substances. As with most spontaneous chemical reactions, the reaction in the battery no longer continues when one of the reactants is used up.

Alkaline batteries used to contain mercury, so it was illegal to dispose of them in a landfill. Today, most alkaline batteries do not contain mercury, so many states now allow them to be thrown away. Does that mean these items have no environmental impact in landfills? Not necessarily. Many alkaline batteries still contain small amounts of metals that could be recycled. They also will not break down in a landfill. Many states do not have a cost-effective recycling program for these kinds of batteries. However, some states will still recycle these batteries during larger waste collection events. California is one of the few states where it is illegal to throw away alkaline batteries.

 Language Arts Connection Some experts even claim that accumulating batteries to be recycled could be more harmful than throwing them in the trash. Research this claim and other claims about the pros and cons of recycling or throwing away alkaline batteries. What data support or refute claims that these batteries can be thrown in a landfill?

One way to reduce the number of batteries that enter landfills is to buy rechargeable batteries instead. Rechargeable alkaline batteries can have current applied to the battery, reversing the reaction and producing the original reactants. These reactants can again react and produce current.

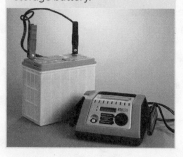

FIGURE 16: Car batteries are a common example of a lead storage battery.

Lead Storage Batteries

Lead storage batteries are commonly used as automotive batteries. In this type of battery, the electrolyte is a mixture of water and sulfuric acid. Lead and lead dioxide, PbO_2, transfer electrons, producing a current. A typical 12-volt automotive battery has six, 2-volt connected cells in series. Within each cell, as the products of the chemical reaction form, reactants eventually run out. Applying a current to the products returns reactants into solution, allowing the reaction to run again. The ability to recharge a lead storage battery makes it extremely useful to power vehicles.

Each time a lead storage battery is charged or discharged, not all of the reactants are used. Over time, the battery will no longer produce a current. Lead storage batteries contain both lead and sulfuric acid. If they are not disposed of correctly, the acid they contain can pollute soil and water. Most businesses that sell these batteries will take old batteries and recycle them. In the United States, most unusable lead storage batteries are recycled.

ASK How do you think the design of lead storage batteries could be optimized so the battery has less of an impact on the environment? If you were an engineer tasked with this challenge, what questions would you ask about lead storage batteries?

_____

_____

_____

_____

Lithium Ion Batteries

Most rechargeable electronic devices have one thing in common: they are powered by a lithium-ion battery. In these batteries, charged lithium ions move between graphite (a form of carbon) and a lithium compound, generating a current.

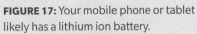

FIGURE 17: Your mobile phone or tablet likely has a lithium ion battery.

These batteries store many times more energy than other rechargeable batteries per weight. Lithium ion batteries can be recharged many times without changing the amount of energy they store, and they do not lose their charge as fast as other rechargeable batteries. A disadvantage of lithium ion batteries is that they need a control circuit to monitor the battery use to prevent them from overheating and possibly exploding.

DEFINE What are some important criteria for batteries that are used in cell phones or computers?

_____

_____

_____

_____

Battery Research

Battery technology has developed several batteries that are an improvement over previous batteries. Because so many devices depend on batteries, engineers and scientists are trying to develop even better batteries. These improved batteries may have more power, be smaller and lighter, charge faster, be cheaper than current batteries, and be easier to recycle. One potential new battery is a lithium-air battery.

Lithium is one of the lighter elements, which contributes to the light weight of the battery. The lithium-air battery would use oxygen from air, so there is no need for an electrolyte solution. In theory, this type of battery would be able to hold 40 times (per unit weight) the charge of a lithium ion battery, making the battery lighter and able to hold more energy than current batteries. Each new type of battery comes with its benefits and risks. For example, lithium is a finite resource that is already in great demand. Increasing the production of lithium could have environmental consequences.

Storing Renewable Energy

Much of our energy comes from burning fossil fuels. Although these fuels are relatively inexpensive and readily available, they produce gases that contribute to climate change and acid precipitation. Some states, such as California, are committing to increased use of renewable energy sources, which are cleaner forms of energy. Recall that many renewable energy sources do not supply a steady flow of energy. It is important to store the energy from these sources as it is produced, so it can be supplied to customers when it is needed. Batteries are one possible solution to this engineering challenge.

PREDICT How might criteria and constraints differ for batteries that store energy from renewable sources from those that power cell phones?

_____

_____

_____

FIGURE 18: This battery farm stores renewable energy.

To meet the demands of energy storage, large-scale battery storage farms are being developed to hold large amounts of energy for later use. The batteries in these farms must be able to recharge quickly and be recharged many times without degrading the battery. Lithium-ion batteries could fulfill these criteria, but lithium is extremely scarce. Sodium-ion batteries are a potential alternative to lithium-ion because sodium is more readily available. A downside to sodium-ion batteries is that they are heavier than lithium-ion batteries. This is less of a challenge for battery farms because the batteries do not need to be portable.

These types of batteries can be charged while excess energy is being produced, and then that energy can be fed back into the system when energy is needed. Using batteries can also provide an energy reserve to add energy to the system during times of peak use.

Currently, California is the only state that is dealing with excess energy from solar power. The problem is not that there is too much solar power—there is inadequate storage for the excess power. This power needs to be available during times that solar power is not being produced, such as at night. Power companies have struggled with using batteries to store this power because batteries have always been quite expensive.

For the expense of battery storage to decrease, it must become more common. Beginning in 2016, several "battery farms" have been built in California, and more are planned. As more battery farms are built, costs will likely continue to fall. Batteries that store electricity from solar energy might become a major step in making our society less dependent on fossil fuels and mitigate environmental problems.

Evidence Notebook Suppose you were asked to provide information about battery development as part of a project to increase renewable energy use. Based on what you have read, how would you prioritize criteria and account for tradeoffs for selecting batteries for energy storage?

Engineering Lab

Storing a Charge

You are probably familiar with the batteries used to power devices such as calculators, watches, and toys. These batteries are most likely zinc-carbon batteries, alkaline batteries, or mercury batteries. In this experiment, you will design an unusual battery that uses common household items to produce electricity. However, it relies on the same principles as other batteries.

The common household item that you choose to use for this experiment acts as a voltaic cell. In the case of a lemon or other citrus fruit, the oxidation and reduction reactions take place as the metals come in contact with the acidic solution in the fruit. Electrons are lost during oxidation, which occurs at the electrode called the *anode*. Electrons are gained during reduction, which occurs at the electrode called the *cathode*. There is a flow of electrons from the anode to the cathode that can be measured or observed. This flow of electrons is electric current. Attaining a good current depends on selecting the appropriate pairing of materials for the cathode and anode that facilitates the oxidation-reduction reaction.

Design Challenge: What combination of household materials produces the best battery in terms of voltage and battery life?

DEFINE THE PROBLEM

Which combination of materials do you think will make the best battery and why? How will you determine whether your battery design is better than others?

_____

_____

_____

_____

_____

_____

POSSIBLE MATERIALS

- indirectly vented chemical splash goggles, nonlatex apron, nonlatex gloves
- aluminum foil
- apple
- clock, battery removed
- copper strip, 1 mm × 1 cm × 5 cm
- copper wire
- grapefruit
- lemon
- lime
- magnesium strip, 1 mm × 1 cm × 5 cm
- orange
- pennies
- potato
- scalpel
- thermometer, battery removed
- voltmeter
- zinc strip, 1 mm × 1 cm × 5 cm

indirectly vented
chemical splash
goggles

SAFETY INFORMATION

- Wear indirectly vented chemical splash goggles, a nonlatex apron, and nonlatex gloves during the setup, hands-on, and takedown segments of the activity.
- Never taste any substance or chemical in the lab.
- Use caution when using sharp tools, which can cut or puncture skin.
- Follow your teacher's instructions for disposing of all waste materials.
- Wash your hands with soap and water immediately after completing this activity.

DESIGN SOLUTIONS

1. Write a procedure in your Evidence Notebook for determining which combination of materials results in the best battery. The factors that make a battery desirable over others include greater voltage and a longer battery life. When developing your plan, consider whether your procedure can be completed during the time your teacher has allotted for this lab. As you plan the procedure, make the following decisions:
   - Decide what methods and/or materials you will test.
   - Decide how you will measure or determine if a test is successful.
   - Select the materials and technology that you will need for your experiment from those that your teacher has provided.
   - Decide what your control(s) will be.
   - Decide what safety procedures are necessary.

2. Make a data table in your Evidence Notebook in which to record your observations.

3. Have your teacher review your procedure, safety plan, and data table before starting the investigation. If necessary, adjust your plans based on your teacher's suggestions.

TEST

1. Obtain your materials and set up any apparatus you will need.
2. Take appropriate safety precautions.
3. Make observations while you perform your tests.
4. Collect data and organize them into appropriate tables and/or graphs. Be certain that the graphs and tables are properly constructed and labeled. Compare the amounts of voltage achieved and the duration of battery use to determine which battery is best.
5. Create a labeled diagram of your prototype, including any measurements.
6. Share your results with other teams. Elicit their feedback on your design.
7. Optimize your design and test it again.
8. Clean all apparatus and your lab station. Return equipment to its proper place. Follow your teacher's instructions for discarding materials. Wash your hands thoroughly after all work is finished and before you leave the lab.

ANALYZE

In your Evidence Notebook, make a diagram to describe how your battery design works. How did you settle on your final design, and how did you choose your materials? Then, use your diagram to explain how your combination of materials works together to generate a current.

COMMUNICATE

Answer the following questions in your Evidence Notebook.

1. Summarize your findings and observations. How did feedback from your classmates affect your final design? Did your design perform as you predicted?

2. Describe how the different outcomes of your classmates were influenced by different variables within the designs. Were there any patterns that were evident? Explain.

3. Share your results with your classmates. Which battery setup was the best? Which battery lasted the longest? Which battery provided the best voltage reading?

DRAW CONCLUSIONS

Write a conclusion that addresses each of the points below.

Claim Which combination of materials resulted in the best battery?

Evidence Cite evidence from the results of your group and your classmates to support your claim.

Reasoning Explain how the evidence you gave supports your claim. Describe, in detail, the connections between the evidence you cited and the argument you are making.

_____

_____

_____

_____

_____

_____

_____

_____

_____

_____

_____

_____

_____

_____

_____

_____

_____

EXTEND

Was your experiment a good model for a long-lasting and effective battery? In your Evidence Notebook, explain why or why not, and give examples of what might be missing from your model.

 | **EFFECTS OF ACID RAIN ON PLANTS** | **ACIDS AND BASES IN FOOD** | **VOLCANOES AND ACID PRECIPITATION** | Go online to choose one of these other paths.

Lesson Self-Check

CAN YOU SOLVE IT?

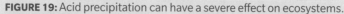

FIGURE 19: Acid precipitation can have a severe effect on ecosystems.

As you look at the image in Figure 19, you can see that environmental problems such as acid precipitation can be remedied. The damaged trees are still damaged, but early steps of forest recovery are visible. Fresh, green groundcover blankets the forest floor around the trees. What needs to be done to keep the forest in recovery and prevent further damage by acid precipitation? By understanding the human and natural causes of acid precipitation and its effects, scientists and engineers can use models, and collect and analyze data to address the problem. Then, both collectively and individually, we can do what is needed to minimize acid precipitation and its environmental effects.

 Evidence Notebook Refer to your notes in your Evidence Notebook to describe some possible solutions to acid precipitation. Include a discussion of what problems exist and what possible solutions might be. Consider the following when writing your explanation:

1. How is acid precipitation formed, and how can it be eliminated, or at least reduced? What are some individual choices you can make to reduce acid precipitation?
2. What evidence supports your proposed solutions to the problem?
3. How does this evidence support your claim?

CHECKPOINTS

Check Your Understanding

1. Potassium hydroxide, KOH, is a strong base. Hydrofluoric acid, HF, is a weak acid. Equal volumes and concentrations of each is involved in a neutralization reaction. What are the results of this reaction? Select all correct answers.

   ☐ **a.** The reaction produces a salt and water.

   ☐ **b.** The salt solution is neutral.

   ☐ **c.** The results have a pH > 7.

   ☐ **d.** The salt formed is KF.

   ☐ **e.** The results have a pH < 7.

2. Determine whether each description is a property of an acid, a base, or both.

Solution Description	Solution Type
forms OH⁻ in solution	acid | base | both
tastes sour	acid | base | both
feels slippery	acid | base | both
has a pH less than 7	acid | base | both
forms ions in solution	acid | base | both
has a pH greater than 7	acid | base | both
can be strong or weak	acid | base | both
reacts in a neutralization reaction	acid | base | both
forms H_3O^+ in solution	acid | base | both

3. Complete the statements about the pH scale.

   The pH of a solution is a measure of the concentration of the hydroxide | hydronium ions it contains. The pH can be calculated by finding $\log[H_3O^+]$ | $\log[OH^-]$ | $-\log[H_3O^+]$ | $-\log[OH^-]$. The pH of milk is about 6.6, so milk is acidic | basic | neutral. The pH of soapy water is about 12, so soapy water is acidic | basic | neutral.

4. Which type of region is most likely to produce the most acidic precipitation?

   ○ **a.** agricultural regions

   ○ **b.** housing developments

   ○ **c.** industrial areas

   ○ **d.** tropical rainforests

5. Acid precipitation is a global problem. What are regions with high levels of acid precipitation most likely to have in common?

   ○ **a.** large wind and solar farms

   ○ **b.** a high reliance on coal as an energy source

   ○ **c.** increased use of natural gas as an energy source

   ○ **d.** geothermal energy as an energy source

6. Although the batteries in "electric" cars are different, most cars still use lead storage batteries. Which statements are true about a lead storage battery? Choose all correct answers.

   ☐ **a.** It is rechargeable by reversing the reaction that occurs in it.

   ☐ **b.** It contains graphite and lithium.

   ☐ **c.** It is also referred to as a dry cell battery.

   ☐ **d.** It is a series of electrochemical cells.

   ☐ **e.** It is a type of voltaic cell.

   ☐ **f.** Chemical reactions occur in the battery.

   ☐ **g.** It is used to store excess energy from solar panels.

7. Why is the development of a battery system essential for the effective use of wind power?

   ○ **a.** Windmills require batteries to turn them.

   ○ **b.** Batteries supply power for transporting electricity from one place to another.

   ○ **c.** Batteries store excess power for use when the wind does not blow.

   ○ **d.** Battery farms use less land than wind farms commonly do.

CHECKPOINTS (continued)

8. The owner of a copper mine has depleted the supply of copper ore and has abandoned the mine. Describe what might happen to the land surrounding the mine over the next several years. What could be done to avoid any damage to the environment around the mine?

_____

_____

_____

_____

9. Explain how the development of energy storage systems can help solve the environmental problems caused by acid precipitation.

_____

_____

_____

_____

10. Suppose a nearby pond is acidic, and its acidity is increasing. Propose two solutions to bring the water in the pond back to neutral. Justify your solutions.

_____

_____

_____

_____

_____

MAKE YOUR OWN STUDY GUIDE

In your Evidence Notebook, design a study guide that supports the main ideas from this lesson:

Scientific concepts, such as the behavior of acids and bases, can be applied to solve problems, such as acid precipitation.

Causes to problems must be examined in order to determine solutions.

Remember to include the following information in your study guide:
- Use examples that model main ideas.
- Record explanations for the phenomena you investigated.
- Use evidence to support your explanations. Your support can include drawings, data, graphs, laboratory conclusions, and other evidence recorded throughout the lesson.

Engineers and scientists continuously strive to solve environmental problems, such as acid precipitation, by analyzing and weighing relative costs and risks versus benefits. They develop methods of remediation that involve applying scientific principles to technological systems.

Physical Science Connection

Energy Efficiency Better energy efficiency means reducing the amount of energy needed to do something. Car makers redesigned engines and bodies so that today's cars travel much farther on a given amount of fuel. Most new appliances use much less energy than those made even a few years ago. Better energy efficiency and developing renewable sources increase sustainability of energy use and reduce pollution.

> Research how engineers increase the energy efficiency of a vehicle, appliance, or other device. Choose a modern appliance or machine and compare its efficiency to past options. Make a pamphlet that informs consumers about changes that improve energy efficiency. Include calculations of the annual energy savings of the more efficient design.

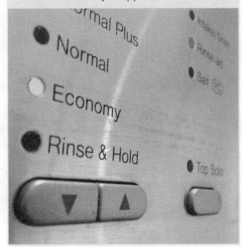

FIGURE 1: Energy settings help consumers increase efficiency of appliances.

Health Connection

Pollution Risks Coal-fired power plants are a major source of pollution, such as soot, greenhouse gases, and toxic gases and metals. These pollutants can enter the air and water sources, causing health problems such as heart disease, lung disease, and cancer. Due to wind or water currents, communities located away from these sources can still suffer from health concerns.

> Choose a power source, such as coal, natural gas, or nuclear energy, and research health concerns for people living near the plant. Find out what measures are being taken to reduce pollution and protect human health. Write a fictional interview between you and a doctor to explain the effects of pollution on human health.

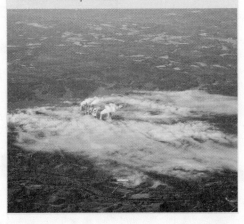

FIGURE 2: Many coal-fired power plants produce soot and toxic gases, which can cause health problems.

Environmental Connection

Determining Past Climate How could you learn about the climate thousands of years ago to better understand current trends? By studying patterns in data, scientists determined that methane is released from undersea sources more often when global temperatures are higher. Scientists are also seeing a pattern of increased methane bubbles from sources such as the La Brea tar pits, supporting claims that global temperatures are increasing.

> Climate researchers often collect data from thousands, or hundreds of thousands, of years ago. Investigate a climate project that you find interesting and prepare a multimedia presentation to demonstrate the links between researchers' data and their conclusions using visuals.

FIGURE 3: Methane bubbles increase with rising global temperatures.

THING **EXPLAINER** BY RANDALL MUNROE

A BOOK EXPLAINING COMPLEX IDEAS USING ONLY THE 1,000 MOST COMMON WORDS

CLOUD MAPS
How maps that help us guess the future are put together

You've seen weather maps on TV or online. Scientists use weather data and weather patterns to help predict and forecast the weather. How are all these data gathered?.

THING EXPLAINER
COMPLICATED STUFF IN SIMPLE WORDS

RANDALL MUNROE
author of *What If?* and creator of xkcd

RANDALL MUNROE
XKCD.COM

THE STORY OF MAPS THAT SHOW RAIN, WIND, AND STORMS

HIGHS AND LOWS

These lines show how hard the air is pressing down on different areas of the map—which is sort of a strange idea, but important for understanding rain and wind.

These maps are a lot like maps used to show the shape of mountains. The lines join areas where the air is pressing down with the same weight, and the middles of circles are areas where air is especially heavy or light. They're marked "Heavy" and "Light" (or "High" and "Low") to help you know which is which.

LOWS (RAIN MAKERS)

Areas with lighter air over them are called "lows." Air moves across the ground toward those areas, and—just like water moving toward a hole in the bottom of a pool—it goes faster and starts moving in a circle.

Air usually rises up in these "light" areas, which makes rain. As the air rises, the water in the air cools down and turns into little drops, just like water on the side of a glass with a cold drink in it.

This area will have heavy rain (or snow, if it's cold enough).

COLD AIR

This area will be cold and clear.

This area will have strong, cold winds and heavy rain.

This area will have light wind and light rain.

COOL AIR

Low

COOL AIR

This area will be cool.

The dark areas on this map show where it will rain.

WARM AIR

This area will be clear and warm for now.

HIGHS (CLEAR AREAS)

In a "heavy" (or "high") area, air is pressing down hard, which keeps wet air from rising and keeps clouds and rain from forming. These areas usually have clear skies and not very much wind.

HIGH

This area may see flashes of light in the sky and winds strong enough to blow away a house.

Low

GREAT CIRCLE STORMS

These storms are a kind of "low" powered by the heat carried by sea water as it turns to air and rises from the surface when warmed by the Sun. They have very strong winds in a circle near the center, but right *in* the center it's calm—and can even be clear. People call this clear area the "eye" of the storm.

When these storms come in from the sea, they bring the sea with them. Their winds push water ahead of them, and it can make the sea come up onto the land and cover whole cities. They can also make so much rain that rivers rise and wash away people, cars, and houses.

Thanks to computers, we've gotten a lot better at guessing where circle storms are going to go, which helps us to tell people to get out of the way.

CLOUD MAPS

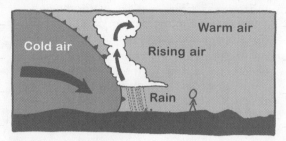

COLD AIR COMING IN
This line shows where cold air is coming in. This can mean there will be wind, and then flashes of light, sounds from the clouds, and very, very heavy rain, but it doesn't last long.

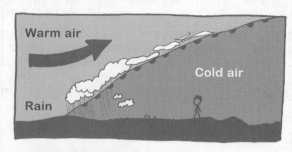

WARM AIR COMING IN
This line means warm air will be moving into an area. This can mean there will be clouds ahead of the warm air, sometimes a few days before it gets there, and rain as it moves in.

Around here, the air stops getting colder as you go higher, so warm air stops rising.

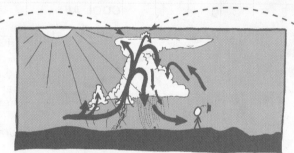

This piece of cloud sticking up means warm air is rising so fast that it shoots up above where it would normally stop. It means the storm is very strong.

VERY BIG SUMMER STORMS
Sometimes, on hot days, air heated by the sun rises up very fast, then cools and pours down rain. These storms can make spinning wind that blows away houses.

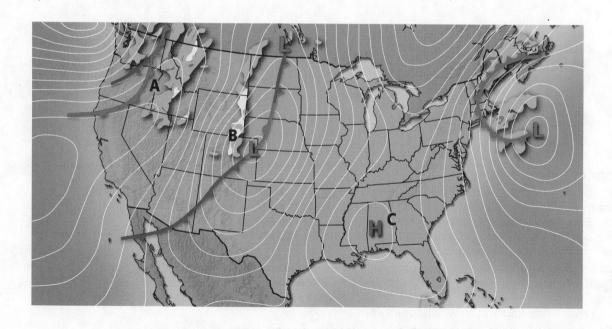

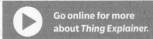
THINGS YOU SEE ON RADIO MAPS AND WHAT THEY MEAN

Sky-watching stations point radio waves at clouds. If there are big drops of water in the clouds, the radio waves hit them and come back. By pointing the radio in different directions, the people in the stations can make a map of all the rain and snow in clouds around them.

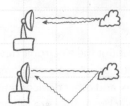

Here's how to understand some of the shapes you see on those maps:

RAIN

Big shapes like this mean rain. It will probably last a while and be light sometimes and heavy other times.

SOUND STORM

This shape means a storm is coming, which may bring light, sound, and strong wind.

WIND STORM

This shape means a storm with lights and sound is coming, and the wind ahead of it might be even stronger than normal.

SPINNING WIND

This shape, like a bent finger, means a spinning cloud is touching the ground, and may be tearing up trees and houses.

Sometimes, if you look at the shapes made by the radio, you can see the stuff the storm has picked up. It looks like a small ball in the middle of the bent finger shape.

SKIN BIRDS

This circle shape isn't rain—it's hundreds and hundreds of little skin birds all flying out of a big hole to eat flies when the Sun sets.

Sometimes other animals, like normal birds or flies, show up on these maps too.

TREES

When there's no rain to see, sometimes the map shows little lines of noise from the radio waves hitting the tops of trees and houses.

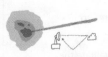

GROUND

This shape happens when the radio waves hit clouds, then a pool of water on the ground, then come back. That makes them take longer, so it looks like there's rain far away.

Recycling "e-waste"

Think about the electronic devices you or your community used to own. Computers, printers, cellular phones, and other devices tend to become outdated very quickly. As they are replaced, the older devices join a stream of electronic waste, or e-waste. The electronic components and the batteries in these devices contain metals and other materials that can be toxic to the environment. The plastic parts degrade very slowly, if at all. Recycling and reusing materials helps reduce pollution. How do the problems associated with e-waste influence other decisions about alternative energy sources?

FIGURE 4: E-waste is an increasing disposal problem.

1. DEFINE THE PROBLEM

What information will your team need in order to propose a solution to the problems of e-waste?

2. CONDUCT RESEARCH

Research how e-waste is currently recycled. What problems are associated with disposal and what efforts are already underway to resolve the problems? Collect quantitative data to support your proposed solution. Consider how the engineering design process can help optimize technologies such as batteries, and reduce the impact of e-waste on the environment.

3. ANALYZE DATA

Organize the data that you collected. How effective are the current recycling solutions? How would you improve an existing solution, or what other ideas does your team have to reduce e-waste? Analyze the quantitative data you collected to determine how a proposed solution could be evaluated.

4. DESIGN A SOLUTION

Brainstorm new or revised solutions to the problem of e-waste. Choose a solution and identify what changes would be involved to implement it and the expected results. What community members or organizations would need to be involved? What are some of the costs to implement your plan? How does your plan optimize short- and long-term costs and benefits for local and global economies, as well as ecology?

5. COMMUNICATE

Make a presentation for your class that explains which e-waste solution you and your team think is most effective. Include your research, the quantitative data you collected, and any visuals that will help support your claim.

 CHECK YOUR WORK

A complete presentation should include the following information:

- a clearly defined problem with supporting questions that are answered in the final presentation
- relevant data that are explained in the final presentation
- a proposed solution to eliminate or reduce electronic waste
- a set of criteria and constraints to evaluate the solution

Name _____   Date _____

SYNTHESIZE THE UNIT

In your Evidence Notebook, make a concept map, other graphic organizer, or outline using the Study Guides you made for each lesson in this unit. Be sure to use evidence to support your claims.

When synthesizing individual information, remember to follow these general steps:

- Find the central idea of each piece of information.
- Think about the relationships among the central ideas.
- Combine the ideas to come up with a new understanding.

DRIVING QUESTIONS

Look back to the Driving Questions from the opening section of this unit. In your Evidence Notebook, review and revise your previous answers to those questions. Use the evidence you gathered and other observations you made throughout the unit to support your claims.

PRACTICE AND REVIEW

1. Which of the energy sources produce carbon dioxide emissions as they produce energy? Select all correct answers.

- ☐ **a.** coal
- ☐ **b.** natural gas
- ☐ **c.** nuclear
- ☐ **d.** petroleum
- ☐ **e.** solar

2. Consider the source for each of the types of electrical energy production. Which of the following sources are renewable? Select all correct answers.

- ☐ **a.** wind
- ☐ **b.** nuclear
- ☐ **c.** petroleum
- ☐ **d.** solar
- ☐ **e.** tidal

3. How would a global increase in the amount of dark material deposited on snow and ice affect the flow of energy through Earth's systems? Select all correct answers.

- ☐ **a.** More solar radiation would be reflected.
- ☐ **b.** Earth's albedo would decrease.
- ☐ **c.** More solar radiation would be absorbed.
- ☐ **d.** The snow and ice would remain solid, even at higher temperatures.

4. Complete the statement.

During the combustion of fossil fuels, hydrocarbons in fossil fuels combine with carbon dioxide | nitrogen | oxygen to form water and carbon dioxide | nitrogen | oxygen. In this reaction, energy is absorbed | released.

5. Complete the statement about acids and bases.

Acids form aqueous solutions containing excess hydronium | hydroxide ions and bases form solutions containing excess hydronium | hydroxide ions. A neutral solution, which is neither acidic nor basic, has a pH that is equal to 0 | 1 | 7 | 10. When crushed limestone is added to a lake that has become acidic, the limestone causes a decrease | an increase in pH as acid is neutralized.

6. Complete the statement about energy sources.

Based on trends that have been established, use of nonrenewable | renewable | both renewable and nonrenewable energy is predicted to increase in the next few decades. Increasing use of renewable energy sources to power automobiles could reduce the increase of coal | petroleum fuels but it is likely to require significant expansion of electrical transmission | pipeline infrastructure.

7. Natural gas has become a major source of electrical energy as the price decreases and its availability increases. Combustion of natural gas produces less carbon dioxide than the combustion of coal when you compare equivalent units of electrical energy. Explain why using natural gas to generate energy still involves tradeoffs in terms of climate change.

_____

_____

_____

_____

_____

_____

8. Scientists have undertaken extensive research projects to model past climates on Earth. How could this data provide information that is useful today? Provide a specific example to support your answer.

_____

_____

_____

_____

_____

_____

9. How does acid precipitation form, and why is it an environmental concern?

_____

_____

_____

_____

_____

UNIT PROJECT

Return to your unit project. Prepare your research and materials into a presentation to share with the class. In your final presentation, evaluate the strength of your proposal, data, analysis, and conclusions.

Remember these tips while evaluating:

- How does your proposal incorporate factors such as economic and environmental considerations?

- What are the costs and benefits of your proposed solution?

- What tradeoffs might be involved in your proposed solution?

- How does your proposal relate to a real-world problem?

Chemical Equilibrium Systems

YOU SOLVE IT

How Can You Increase Ammonia Production?

 To begin exploring this unit's concepts, go online to investigate ways to solve a real-world problem.

Waves of changing equilibrium move across a solution.

Hydrangeas are unique plants with blooms ranging from pink to blue, including all shades of lavender, violet, and purple. Unlike other plants that come in different colors, the color of hydrangeas can be controlled. These blooms do not have different colored pigments. Instead, they have a red pigment that reacts with aluminum in the soil. In acidic soil, aluminum ions are mobile and can be taken up into the plant. The aluminum ions react with the red pigment, resulting in blue blooms. In basic soil, the aluminum ions form compounds with other ions. These compounds cannot be taken into the plant, so no interaction occurs with the pigment and the blooms are pink.

PREDICT Why do you think changing the acid level in soil affects the amount of aluminum that is available to the roots of a hydrangea plant?

_____

_____

_____

DRIVING QUESTIONS

As you move through the unit, gather evidence to help you answer the following questions. In your Evidence Notebook, record what you already know about these topics and any questions you have about them.

1. What cause and effect mechanisms explain how a reaction proceeds?
2. What scale is used to rate the strengths of acids and bases?
3. What predictable patterns happen when chemical equilibrium is disturbed?
4. How can matter cycles and energy flows in chemical equilibrium processes be used to address ecological and economic concerns?

UNIT PROJECT

Go online to download the Unit Project Worksheet to help plan your project.

Investigating the Solvay Process

The Solvay process produces sodium carbonate, which is used in a variety of applications, including to soften water, as a food additive, and to make glass. Research the Solvay process and how it is used in manufacturing. Then, prepare a presentation that explains how controlling and optimizing equilibrium reactions is an essential part of this process.

Language Development

Use the lessons in this unit to complete the chart and expand your understanding of the science concepts.

TERM: reversible reaction

Definition	Example

Similar Term	Phrase

TERM: chemical equilibrium

Definition	Example

Similar Term	Phrase

TERM: equilibrium constant

Definition	Example

Similar Term	Phrase

TERM: acid-base indicator

Definition	Example

Similar Term	Phrase

TERM: titration

Definition	Example

Similar Term	Phrase

TERM: buffer

Definition	Example

Similar Term	Phrase

TERM: ocean acidification

Definition	Example

Similar Term	Phrase

TERM: Le Châtelier's principle

Definition	Example

Similar Term	Phrase

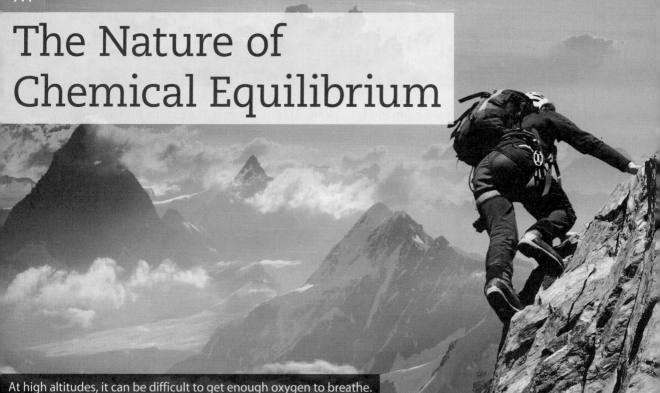

The Nature of Chemical Equilibrium

At high altitudes, it can be difficult to get enough oxygen to breathe.

CAN YOU EXPLAIN IT?

If you have ever been somewhere that is at a high altitude, you may have felt like it was becoming difficult to breathe. As you reach higher and higher altitudes, air pressure decreases, which makes it more difficult to take in enough oxygen. At very high altitudes, many people experience what is called "altitude sickness." The symptoms of altitude sickness include headache, dizziness, and shortness of breath. Interestingly, some people are able to withstand the conditions at high altitudes and do not experience altitude sickness. This trait can be especially helpful when climbing tall mountains.

In order to understand how people adapt to high altitudes, it is helpful to understand how oxygen binds to molecules in our blood. Oxygen enters our lungs when we breathe in air. Oxygen in the inhaled air passes into tiny blood vessels that surround the air sacs within the lungs. Oxygen then attaches to hemoglobin molecules in red blood cells, and the circulatory system transports the oxygenated blood to the body's cells. Where oxygen is needed, it is released to cells for use in chemical reactions such as cellular respiration. The deoxygenated blood is then transported back to the lungs.

INFER How might people's bodies be adapted to high-altitude conditions where oxygen availability is low?

_____

_____

_____

_____

 Evidence Notebook As you explore this lesson, gather evidence to explain how chemical reactions reach a state of equilibrium.

Explaining Equilibrium

When wood burns in a fire, chemical reactions occur that change the molecular arrangement of the atoms in the wood. Atoms in molecules such as cellulose are rearranged to form new products, such as carbon dioxide and ash. Burning a log is not a reversible process, however. The wood cannot be remade from ash. Unlike the chemical reactions that occur when wood is burned, some reactions can proceed in both forward and reverse directions.

 Data Analysis

Analyzing Amounts of Reactants and Products

What types of evidence might indicate that a reaction can proceed in both the forward and reverse directions? And, when this happens, does the reaction ever come to a stop? Consider nitrogen dioxide, NO_2, a common component of polluted air, which is a reddish-brown gas. Two molecules of this gas react to form the gas dinitrogen tetroxide, N_2O_4. N_2O_4 is colorless and such a strong oxidizing agent that its has been used as a rocket propellant.

The table shows possible data we might see if we allowed 0.0500 mol NO_2 to react to form N_2O_4 in a closed system. The data show the amount of each compound in moles over time as the reaction proceeds.

Amounts of NO_2 and N_2O_4 as Reaction Proceeds	
Amount of NO_2	Amount of N_2O_4
0.0500 mol	0.0000 mol
0.0428 mol	0.0036 mol
0.0320 mol	0.0090 mol
0.0220 mol	0.0140 mol
0.0154 mol	0.0173 mol
0.0120 mol	0.0190 mol
0.0106 mol	0.0197 mol
0.0102 mol	0.0199 mol
0.0100 mol	0.0200 mol
0.0100 mol	0.0200 mol
0.0100 mol	0.0200 mol

ANALYZE Based on the data in the table, what can you say about the amount of reactant and product present when the reaction reaches a stable state? What do you think is occurring at the molecular level when the reaction reaches this state?

_____

_____

_____

_____

_____

_____

_____

_____

_____

_____

_____

_____

We see that the reaction that forms dinitrogen tetroxide reaches a stable state where the ratio of the two gases is 0.0100 mol/0.0200 mol. Although it might seem as if the reaction has stopped at this point, the gases are still reacting. Nitrogen dioxide is still forming dinitrogen tetroxide. Dinitrogen tetroxide is also decomposing to form nitrogen dioxide. The rates of both reaction are equal. We use a double arrow to show the reaction.

$$2NO_2(g) \rightleftharpoons N_2O_4(g)$$

Reversible Reactions

A chemical reaction in which the products can react to reform the reactants is called a reversible reaction. Another example of a reversible reaction involves copper sulfate pentahydrate, a common fungicide and herbicide. The *hydrate* means water molecules are present in the copper sulfate crystal, and its formula is $CuSO_4 \cdot 5H_2O$.

FIGURE 1: Forward and reverse reactions

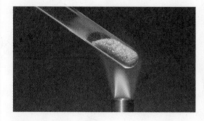 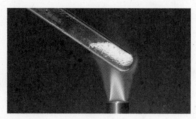 

a Blue crystals of copper sulfate pentahydrate are placed over a hot flame.

b Water is released from the compound, leaving white crystals of copper sulfate.

c Water is added back to the copper sulfate, and the crystals turn blue.

 Collaborate With a partner, discuss how the images in Figure 1 support the claim that this is a reversible reaction. What might a chemical equation for this reaction look like?

 Stability and Change

Reversible and Irreversible Reactions

FIGURE 2: The combustion of candle wax is effectively a one-way reaction.

Many of the reactions we see in our daily lives are irreversible in practical terms. When you bake a cake, you cannot reverse the reactions that occurred to get back the eggs, flour, and milk. When you burn a candle, you cannot rebuild the candle out of compounds in the air. It was once believed that all chemical reactions were irreversible. That changed when a chemist saw salts forming around the edges of lakes and inferred from his observations that the reaction forming the salts must be reversible.

 Evidence Notebook When solid ammonium chloride is placed in a test tube and held over a flame, the gases ammonia and hydrogen chloride are produced. As the reaction proceeds, some solid crystals can be observed forming on the glass at the top of the test tube. Make a claim for whether this reaction is reversible or irreversible and explain your reasoning.

Chemical Equilibrium

You can represent the concentration changes during a reversible chemical reaction on a graph. Consider again the chemical reaction:

$$2NO_2(g) \rightleftharpoons N_2O_4(g)$$

The graph in Figure 3 shows changes in the concentrations of the reactant and product as the reaction progresses. As the graph shows, the amounts of product and reactant present at specific conditions eventually stabilize. At this point, called chemical equilibrium, the forward reaction is occurring at the same rate as the reverse reaction. Although the rates of the forward and reverse reactions are the same at equilibrium, the concentrations of the products and reactants are generally different.

NO_2 and N_2O_4 Concentrations Over Time

FIGURE 3: As the reaction progresses, chemical equilibrium is reached.

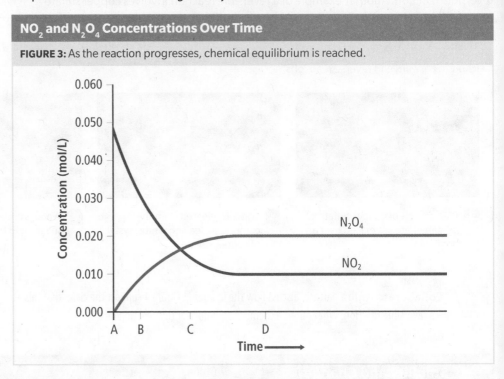

ANALYZE Which of the following statements about this reaction are true? Select all correct answers.

- ☐ **a.** At Time B, the reaction has not yet reached chemical equilibrium.
- ☐ **b.** Chemical equilibrium for this reaction occurs at Time C.
- ☐ **c.** At equilibrium, the concentrations of NO_2 and N_2O_4 are equal.
- ☐ **d.** At Time D, the reaction has reached chemical equilibrium.
- ☐ **e.** The concentrations of NO_2 and N_2O_4 differ when chemical equilibrium is reached.

You are probably familiar with instances of equilibrium. For example, a state of solution equilibrium exists above the liquid in a closed soda bottle. Carbon dioxide gas is both dissolved in the liquid, making the drink fizzy, and in the gas above the liquid. When the bottle is closed tightly, carbon dioxide constantly moves between the liquid and the gas.

 Collaborate With a partner, discuss the limitations of models such as the graph shown in Figure 3 in representing what is happening in chemical equilibrium. What kind of model could be used to represent the process more completely?

The rate of a chemical reaction depends on many different conditions, including the concentration of the reactants. In a reversible reaction, the forward and reverse reactions proceed independently and continually. The rate of each reaction changes over time as concentrations change. Consider a generalized reaction where two reactants, A and B, react to form two products, C and D.

$$A + B \rightleftharpoons C + D$$

Before the overall reaction approaches equilibrium, the forward and reverse reactions happen at different rates. At equilibrium, the forward and reverse reactions occur at the same rates. The graph in Figure 4 represents this process.

FIGURE 4: The graph shows how the rates of the forward and reverse reactions change as a hypothetical chemical reaction reaches equilibrium.

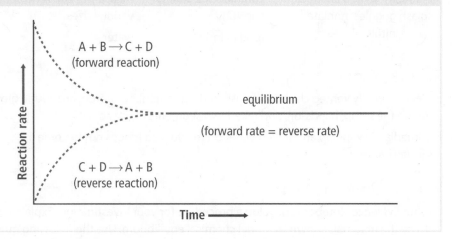

EXPLAIN Use the graph in Figure 4 to complete the statement.

As the reaction proceeds, the rate of the forward reaction increases | decreases while the rate of the reverse reaction increases | decreases. This occurs because, as the concentration of reactants increases | decreases, the concentrations of the products increases | decreases. When the chemical reaction reaches equilibrium, the rate of the forward reaction is greater than | equal to | less than the rate of the reverse reaction.

When the reaction begins, the rate of the forward reaction is high because the concentrations of A and B are high. The rate of the reverse reaction is initially low because concentrations of C and D are low. As concentrations change, the rate of the forward reaction decreases, and the rate of the reverse reaction increases. At equilibrium, the rates of each reaction are the same.

This type of equilibrium is called a *dynamic equilibrium* because the system is in a constant, but balanced, state of change. Forward and reverse reactions continue to take place, but no noticeable change in concentrations occurs because the reaction rates are the same.

 Language Arts Connection Write an analogy that could be used to describe chemical equilibrium. Your analogy should address the idea that, at chemical equilibrium, the rates of the forward and reverse reactions are the same, but the concentrations of the products and reactants are often different. Explain your analogy to a partner, and have your partner explain their analogy to you.

Hands-On Activity
Modeling Chemical Equilibrium

There are different ways to model chemical equilibrium for a reversible reaction. In this activity, you will develop a model of equilibrium using water and measuring cups.

Research Question: How can you use a physical model to model chemical equilibrium?

MATERIALS

- indirectly vented chemical splash goggles, nonlatex apron, nitrile gloves
- containers, 2-3 liters each (2)
- food coloring
- measuring cups and spoons, various sizes
- water

SAFETY INFORMATION

- Wear indirectly vented chemical splash goggles, a nonlatex apron, and nitrile gloves during the setup, hands-on, and takedown segments of the activity.
- Immediately wipe up any spilled water on the floor so it does not become a slip/fall hazard.

PLAN THE INVESTIGATION

In your Evidence Notebook, develop a procedure for your investigation. Explain how you will use the materials shown to model chemical equilibrium. Use the following questions to guide your planning: How will you model the formation of products and reactants? How will you show how the rate of each reaction changes as equilibrium is reached? Make sure your teacher approves your plans and safety precautions before proceeding.

indirectly vented
chemical splash
goggles

CONSTRUCT AN EXPLANATION

1. Explain how your model illustrated the concept of a chemical reaction progressing toward equilibrium.

_____

_____

_____

_____

2. Which parts of this model worked well, and which could be improved? Explain how you could improve on this model.

_____

_____

_____

 Evidence Notebook Think back to the question about how some people are adapted to high altitudes. In your Evidence Notebook, answer these questions: Do you think the reaction that allows oxygen to bind to hemoglobin in blood cells is a reversible or irreversible reaction? How do you think equilibrium might be related to this phenomenon? Explain your answers.

Measuring Equilibrium

You know that when a reversible reaction reaches equilibrium, the forward and reverse reactions are occurring at the same rate. But how can you predict the amounts of products and reactants that will be present at equilibrium? Consider the synthesis of hydrogen and iodine to form hydrogen iodide. Iodine gas is dark purple and hydrogen gas is colorless. When iodine and hydrogen are mixed in a closed flask, they react to form hydrogen iodide, a colorless gas. The reaction is represented by the equilibrium equation:

$$H_2(g) + I_2(g) \rightleftharpoons 2HI(g)$$

As the reaction proceeds, hydrogen and iodine molecules break apart and form HI molecules. At the same time, some of the HI molecules begin to break apart, reforming hydrogen and iodine molecules. When the system is at equilibrium, the gas in the flask is a violet color, indicating a mixture of all three gases.

FIGURE 5: Hydrogen (left) reacts with iodine (right) to form hydrogen iodide.

 Collaborate For a reversible reaction, how do you think chemists determine the amounts of reactants and products that will be present at equilibrium? Discuss with a partner.

The Equilibrium Constant

When a chemical reaction reaches equilibrium, each reactant and product will have a certain concentration. These concentrations can be compared mathematically to make predictions about future reactions. Consider the general reaction:

$$3A + 4B \rightleftharpoons 2C + 1D$$

The concentrations of the reactants and products can be compared using a ratio. This relationship is referred to as the chemical equilibrium expression and is represented by the value K_{eq}, known as the equilibrium constant. The equilibrium constant indicates the relative amounts of products and reactants that exist when the reaction reaches equilibrium at a given temperature. The numerator in an equilibrium expression is the mathematical product of the concentrations of the products. The denominator is the mathematical product of the concentrations of the reactants. Each concentration is raised to a power equal to the coefficient of that substance in the chemical equation. For the equation above, the chemical equilibrium expression is:

$$K_{eq} = \frac{[C]^2[D]^1}{[A]^3[B]^4}$$

ANALYZE Explain why, based on this expression, an increase in the concentration of A would have a greater effect on K_{eq} than an increase in the concentration of D.

_____

_____

_____

Constructing an Equilibrium Expression

SAMPLE PROBLEM

Write the equilibrium expression for the reversible reaction between nitrogen gas and hydrogen gas to produce gaseous ammonia.

$$N_2(g) + 3H_2(g) \rightleftharpoons 2NH_3(g)$$

SOLVE

The product becomes the numerator of the ratio, and the reactants are the denominator. The concentration of each substance is raised to a power equal to its coefficient. If the coefficient is 1, you do not need to write the power.

$$K_{eq} = \frac{[NH_3]^2}{[N_2][H_2]^3}$$

PRACTICE PROBLEM

Consider the reversible reaction between hydrogen and iodine gases.

$$H_2(g) + I_2(g) \rightleftharpoons 2HI(g)$$

SOLVE Write the chemical equilibrium expression for this reaction.

Even though concentrations are given in moles per liter, units are not used in calculating the equilibrium constant. By convention, the value of K_{eq} is a ratio without a unit. The equilibrium constant is always stated for a specific temperature. The equilibrium constant for a particular reaction is always the same at a given temperature, but it varies as temperature varies.

Some reactions, called heterogeneous reactions, involve matter in two or more phases. In calculating the equilibrium constant, the concentrations of pure solids and liquids are considered constant and do not appear in equilibrium calculations.

An example is calcium carbonate heated in a sealed container:

$$CaCO_3(s) \rightleftharpoons CaO(s) + CO_2(g)$$

The point of equilibrium is determined only by the carbon dioxide concentration. Therefore, the equilibrium expression for this reaction is $K_{eq} = [CO_2]$.

ANALYZE Write the equilibrium expression for this heterogeneous equilibrium reaction.

$$Fe_3O_4(s) + 4H_2(g) \rightleftharpoons 3Fe(s) + 4H_2O(g)$$

Analyzing the Equilibrium Constant

Because the equilibrium constant is calculated as a ratio of products to reactants, the value of K_{eq} reflects the extent to which the reaction favors product formation. If K_{eq} is much greater than 1, the reaction equilibrium will have large concentrations of products compared to reactants. It will nearly reach completion.

If K_{eq} is much less than 1, the reaction will reach equilibrium when only a small amount of reactants have become products. The scale of the equilibrium constant represents the proportion of products to reactants in a system at equilibrium. As K_{eq} approaches zero, the equilibrium state is almost all reactants; as K_{eq} approaches infinity, the equilibrium state contains almost all products.

FIGURE 6: Reaction direction compared to K_{eq}

K_{eq}	Composition of system at equilibrium
2×10^{-9}	negligible products
0.02	reactants dominate
0.2	
1	reactants and products present in equal amounts
5	
50	products dominate
5×10^{8}	negligible reactants

(left axis, top to bottom: reactants favored → products favored)

EXPLAIN How does the mathematical expression of K_{eq} relate to the relative concentrations of reactants and products for a high value of K_{eq} compared to a low value of K_{eq}?

_____

_____

_____

_____

Stability and Change

Chemical Change and the Reaction Quotient

The equilibrium constant, K_{eq}, relates the concentrations of products to reactants at equilibrium, when their concentrations are stable. K_{eq} is referred to as a *constant* because, under the same conditions, a given equilibrium reaction will always end up with a specific ratio of product to reactant concentrations. At any time during a reaction, the ratio of product to reactant concentrations can be measured and expressed in terms of a reaction quotient, Q. Consider the general chemical equation:

$$aA + bB \rightleftharpoons cC + dD$$

Q is calculated in the same way as K_{eq}. For the above general equation, Q would be:

$$Q = \frac{[C]^c[D]^d}{[A]^a[B]^b}$$

Over the course of a reaction, the concentration of the products increases and the concentration of the reactants decreases. When the reaction reaches equilibrium, $Q = K_{eq}$. Before the reaction reaches equilibrium, comparing Q and K_{eq} tells you what must happen for a reaction at that point to reach equilibrium. If $Q > K_{eq}$, more reactants must form for it to reach equilibrium. On the other hand, if $Q < K_{eq}$, more products must form for the reaction to reach equilibrium.

Problem Solving
Quantifying Equilibrium

Equilibrium constants cannot be predicted. They must be determined experimentally by analyzing the components of the equilibrium mixture. Consider again the equilibrium expression for the synthesis of hydrogen iodide:

$$K_{eq} = \frac{[HI]^2}{[H_2][I_2]}$$

If the concentrations of the reactants and products are known, K_{eq} can be calculated. If K_{eq} and the concentration of some reactants or products are known, the concentration of the other chemical species can be determined.

The table shows typical results from analyzing equilibrium mixtures containing H_2, I_2, and HI. Calculations show that at 425 °C, the equilibrium constant for this equilibrium reaction system has an average value of 54.34. The more trials that are performed, the closer the average of the calculated K_{eq} values will get to 54.34. Because temperature affects the collision rates of molecules, it affects the value of K_{eq}, so you would get a different value at a different temperature.

Trial	[H₂]	[I₂]	[HI]
1	0.4953×10^{-3}	0.4953×10^{-3}	3.655×10^{-3}
2	1.141×10^{-3}	1.141×10^{-3}	8.410×10^{-3}
3	3.560×10^{-3}	1.250×10^{-3}	1.559×10^{-2}
4	2.252×10^{-3}	2.336×10^{-3}	1.685×10^{-2}

EXAMPLE PROBLEM   Calculate the value of K_{eq} based on the results of Trial 1.

SOLVE   Use the concentration values from the table to calculate K_{eq}.

$$K_{eq} = \frac{[3.655 \times 10^{-3}]^2}{[0.4953 \times 10^{-3}][0.4953 \times 10^{-3}]} = 54.46$$

PRACTICE PROBLEMS   SOLVE Complete the following calculations.
1. Calculate the value of K_{eq} for Trial 2.

2. Calculate the value of K_{eq} for Trial 3.

 Evidence Notebook The value of K_{eq} depends on the temperature at which the reaction occurs. When you exercise, your body temperature increases. How do you think this increase in temperature might affect the equilibrium and K_{eq} for oxygen and hemoglobin?

Language Arts

Carbon Monoxide Poisoning

Every year, more than 400 people in the United States die from carbon monoxide poisoning, and another 20 000 people require hospital treatment for this exposure. What causes carbon monoxide, CO, to be an environmental hazard, and what causes its toxic effects in the human body?

Carbon monoxide is a product of the incomplete combustion of carbon-containing fuels, including coal, petroleum products, and natural gas. When these fuels burn in pure oxygen, most of the carbon atoms are converted to CO_2. However, when oxygen is a limiting factor, some CO often forms as part of the combustion products.

Inside homes, fuel-burning furnaces are designed to vent the CO-containing exhaust gases into the atmosphere. During power outages, some people use portable fuel-fired heaters and generators that are not vented. When these devices are used incorrectly, they can release exhaust into the home, leading to CO poisoning. In addition to ensuring that such devices are operated properly, carbon monoxide detectors may be used in the home to alert people when CO levels become dangerous. Incidents of CO poisoning increase sharply during events that cause disruption of electrical or natural gas service, such as natural disasters.

Inside the human body, oxygen is absorbed by blood as it passes through the lungs. The oxygen moves through the body by binding to hemoglobin molecules in the blood. Each hemoglobin molecule can bind to four oxygen molecules in a reversible reaction, forming oxyhemoglobin $Hb(O_2)_4$.

$$Hb(aq) + 4O_2(g) \rightleftharpoons Hb(O_2)_4(aq)$$

Hb represents a hemoglobin molecule. If a person inhales air that contains carbon monoxide, CO molecules bond to hemoglobin in place of oxygen to form carboxyhemoglobin.

$$Hb(aq) + 4CO(g) \rightleftharpoons Hb(CO)_4(aq)$$

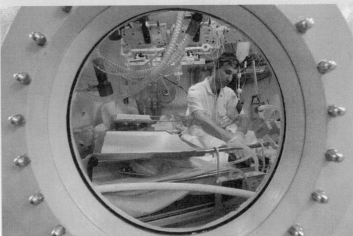

FIGURE 7: A hyperbaric oxygen chamber can be used to treat CO poisoning.

Carbon monoxide bonds to hemoglobin much more strongly than oxygen does. The equilibrium constant for the production of $Hb(CO)_4$ is about 200 times higher than the equilibrium constant for the formation of $Hb(O_2)_4$. As a result, oxygen is blocked from reaching the cells, and the person becomes ill and may die. The most effective way of treating CO poisoning is to replace the CO with O_2 using the following equilibrium reaction.

$$Hb(CO)_4(aq) + 4O_2(g) \rightleftharpoons Hb(O_2)_4(aq) + 4CO(g)$$

Increasing the pressure (concentration) of O_2 will force this equilibrium to the right. Patients are treated in a hyperbaric chamber where they can breathe pure oxygen at pressures greater than normal atmospheric pressure.

Language Arts Connection Research the risk of CO poisoning in homes, and develop a pamphlet that will help people recognize the risks of carbon monoxide poisoning. Explain where people might encounter high CO levels in the air and what events might cause the production of CO. Explain the reason that CO is dangerous in terms that someone who has not studied chemistry could understand.

CALCULATING EQUILIBRIUM CONCENTRATIONS

EXPLAINING EQUILIBRIUM

Go online to choose one of these other paths.

Lesson Self-Check

FIGURE 8: At high altitudes, the pressure of atmospheric oxygen decreases.

At high altitudes, atmospheric pressure is much lower than at sea level, which affects the ability of hemoglobin in our blood to bind to oxygen. As a result, some people experience altitude sickness at these pressures. Some people, however, are adapted to high altitudes and do not experience these symptoms when oxygen availability is low. This trait can be especially helpful when climbing tall mountains.

The reaction that allows oxygen to bind to hemoglobin is a reversible reaction. Every hemoglobin molecule binds four oxygen molecules and transports them to the body's cells. This process can be represented by the following chemical equation:

$$\text{Hb}(aq) + 4\text{O}_2(g) \rightleftharpoons \text{Hb(O}_2)_4(aq)$$

Research has revealed that some groups of people who are adapted to high altitudes have an especially high concentration of hemoglobin molecules in their blood. An example is those who live in the Andes mountains in South America, as their ancestors have done for thousands of years. This unique evolutionary adaptation has given them the ability to live at high altitudes without getting altitude sickness.

 Evidence Notebook Refer to your notes in your Evidence Notebook to construct an explanation for these questions: Why is it important that this reaction be reversible? What does it mean for this reaction to be at equilibrium? Why does a higher concentration of hemoglobin allow a person to obtain sufficient oxygen at high altitudes?

1. Make a claim that answers the questions above.
2. Use evidence and examples to support your claim.
3. Explain how the evidence and examples you cited support your claim.

CHECKPOINTS

1. When a reversible chemical reaction is at equilibrium, the forward and reverse reactions

- ○ **a.** come to a stop.
- ○ **b.** proceed at the same rate.
- ○ **c.** fluctuate but average the same rate.

2. Sulfur trioxide and sulfur dioxide are two common components of the acid rain that results from the burning of coal. In a closed system with oxygen, they establish an equilibrium state.

$$2SO_3(g) \rightleftharpoons 2SO_2(g) + O_2(g)$$

Select the correct terms to complete the statements.

If a sample of pure SO_3 is placed in a closed container, the forward | reverse reaction will begin immediately. Once the system reaches equilibrium, the amount of oxygen in the system will remain constant | steadily increase.

3. What must happen when a reversible reaction occurring in a closed container is NOT in a state of equilibrium? Select all correct answers.

- ☐ **a.** The forward and reverse reactions proceed at different rates until equilibrium is reached.
- ☐ **b.** The forward reaction rate increases, and the reverse reaction rate decreases.
- ☐ **c.** The amount of products and reactants keeps changing until equilibrium is established.
- ☐ **d.** One reaction stops, and the other continues until they reach equilibrium.

4. What is the equilibrium expression for the reaction shown?

$$2NO_2(g) \rightleftharpoons N_2O_4(g)$$

- ○ **a.** $K_{eq} = \dfrac{[NO_2]}{[N_2O_4]}$
- ○ **b.** $K_{eq} = \dfrac{[NO_2]^2}{[N_2O_4]}$
- ○ **c.** $K_{eq} = \dfrac{[N_2O_4]}{[NO_2]}$
- ○ **d.** $K_{eq} = \dfrac{[N_2O_4]}{[NO_2]^2}$

5. Complete the following statement about equilibrium constants.

The value of K_{eq} indicates which reaction is favored. If K_{eq} is very large, the forward | reverse reaction is favored, and the reactants | products are present at a higher concentration.

6. What is the equilibrium expression for the reaction shown?

$$PbCrO_4(s) \rightleftharpoons Pb^{2+}(aq) + CrO_4^{2-}(aq)$$

- ○ **a.** $K_{eq} = [Pb^{2+}][CrO_4^{2-}]$
- ○ **b.** $K_{eq} = \dfrac{1}{[Pb^{2+}][CrO_4^{2-}]}$
- ○ **c.** $K_{eq} = \dfrac{[Pb^{2+}][CrO_4^{2-}]}{[PbCrO_4]}$
- ○ **d.** $K_{eq} = \dfrac{[PbCrO_4]}{[Pb^{2+}][CrO_4^{2-}]}$

7. Nitrogen and hydrogen react to form ammonia by the following equilibrium reaction.

$$N_2(g) + 3H_2(g) \rightleftharpoons 2NH_3(g)$$

The concentrations in the reaction vessel are

$[N_2] = 0.0280$
$[H_2] = 0.0100$
$[NH_3] = 0.0120$

What is the value of K_{eq} under these conditions?

_____

8. Which of the following are true of a chemical reaction at equilibrium? Select all correct answers.

- ☐ **a.** The forward and reverse reactions proceed at the same rate.
- ☐ **b.** The concentrations of the reactants and the products are the same.
- ☐ **c.** The rate of the forward reaction is greater than the rate of the reverse reaction.
- ☐ **d.** The concentrations of the reactants may differ from those of the products.

CHECKPOINTS (continued)

9. Consider the generic reaction: A + B ⇌ C + D. Explain what happens as this reaction reaches equilibrium. How do the rates of the forward and reverse reactions change as the reaction progresses? What can be predicted about the concentrations once the reaction reaches equilibrium? Does the reaction ever stop completely?

_____

_____

_____

_____

_____

_____

_____

10. Explain how you can use the value K_{eq} to infer information about an equilibrium reaction. What does it mean if the value of K_{eq} is relatively large? What does it mean when it is relatively small? Explain your answers.

_____

_____

_____

_____

_____

_____

_____

_____

MAKE YOUR OWN STUDY GUIDE

 In your Evidence Notebook, design a study guide that supports the main ideas from this lesson:

Reversible reaction systems form a state of equilibrium when the forward and reverse reactions occur at the same rate.

The equilibrium constant, K_{eq}, shows the relationship of reactant and product concentrations at equilibrium.

Remember to include the following information in your study guide:
- Use examples that model main ideas.
- Record explanations for the phenomena you investigated.
- Use evidence to support your explanations. Your support can include drawings, data, graphs, laboratory conclusions, and other evidence recorded throughout the lesson.

Consider how chemical equilibrium constants explain the stability and change of a system involving a reversible chemical reaction.

Equilibrium Systems

The white crust in parts of the Mojave desert contains borax.

CAN YOU EXPLAIN IT?

In and around Death Valley in the Mojave Desert, there are places where the ground is covered by white mineral deposits. These deposits have a high concentration of a mineral known as sodium borate, also called borax. The deposits formed when water evaporated from lakes and pools, and they are an important part of the history of the area. In the late 1800s, mining companies sprang up around the deposits to collect the valuable material, first using mule teams and then railroads. Sodium borate is used to produce boric acid, which was an important ingredient in many cleaning products. This material is also useful for making solutions needed for a number of chemical and medical analyses. Boric acid can be combined with other substances to make what is called a buffer. Buffers keep the pH of a solution within a certain range. The sodium borate buffer stabilizes pH in ranges between 8 and 10.

PREDICT Based on what you know about acids, bases, and equilibrium, how do you think buffers keep pH levels within a certain range?

_____

_____

_____

_____

 Evidence Notebook As you explore this lesson, gather evidence to explain how chemical equilibrium in a system can be manipulated and maintained.

Acid-Base Equilibrium Systems

Scientists and engineers may need to control equilibrium in a system for many different reasons. A chemist might want to keep conditions within a certain range while conducting a precise chemical analysis. An engineer might alter equilibrium in a system in order to remove impurities from drinking water.

At any point during an acid-base reaction, an equilibrium exists that determines the pH. Manipulating this equilibrium allows scientists to control pH. Controlling equilibrium in acid-base systems is often necessary because changes in pH can cause new, unwanted changes. For example, many reactions that involve enzymes must occur within a narrow pH range to avoid changing the structure and function of the enzymes.

EXPLAIN Recall that pH reflects the hydronium ion concentration in a solution. Complete these statements about how hydronium ion concentration is related to pH.

The transfer of a proton (H^+) from | to a water molecule results in the formation of a hydronium ion, (H_3O^+). The more hydronium ions there are in an aqueous solution, the lower | higher the pH will be.

FIGURE 1: Universal indicator can be used to determine pH. Each color corresponds to a different pH.

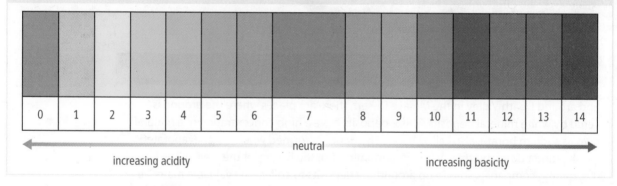

| 0 | 1 | 2 | 3 | 4 | 5 | 6 | 7 | 8 | 9 | 10 | 11 | 12 | 13 | 14 |

neutral

← increasing acidity   increasing basicity →

As an acid-base reaction progresses, an acid-base indicator can be used to monitor the changes in equilibrium by measuring the pH at a particular point. Acid-base indicators are compounds whose color is sensitive to the pH of a solution. Universal indicator contains several chemicals that change color at different pH values. Figure 1 shows the colors of universal indicator that correspond to different pH values. In a neutral solution, universal indicator will appear green. As a solution becomes more acidic, the color gradually changes to red. As a solution becomes more basic, the neutral green color gradually changes to purple.

FIGURE 2: In a solution of milk of magnesia, universal indicator turns purple.

Figure 2 shows what happens when universal indicator is combined with an antacid called milk of magnesia, which has long been used to treat such ailments as upset stomach and heartburn. Milk of magnesia is a solution of magnesium hydroxide, $Mg(OH)_2$, and it causes the indicator to turn purple.

INFER Select the correct terms to complete the statements.

The color of the indicator shown in Figure 2 indicates that this is a(n) acidic | basic solution. Therefore, this solution has a relatively low | high concentration of hydronium ions as compared to a neutral solution.

When hydrochloric acid (HCl) is added to the milk of magnesia solution, the indicator changes colors in a repeating cycle of reds, greens, and blues.

FIGURE 3: The color of the solution changes after the HCl has been added.

Explore Online ▶

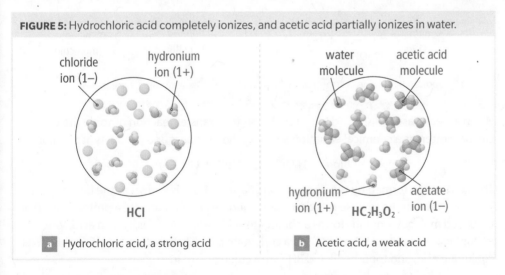

Collaborate Why do you think the color of the solution oscillates after HCl is added to the milk of magnesia solution? How might this observation relate to chemical equilibrium?

Acids and Bases in Solution

When analyzing equilibrium in acid-base reactions, it is important to remember that not all acids and bases are the same. Figure 4 shows what happens when calcium carbonate, $CaCO_3$, is placed in hydrochloric acid, shown in the left beaker, and vinegar, or acetic acid ($HC_2H_3O_2$), in the right beaker. Figure 5 shows how strong acids, such as HCl, ionize completely in water. All of the HCl ionizes to form H_3O^+ and chloride (Cl^-) ions. In weak acids, such as $HC_2H_3O_2$, hydrogen atoms are bound more tightly, so fewer H_3O^+ ions are present in the solution. Recall that a substance that already exists as ions is said to *dissociate* in solution. A substance that forms ions in solution *ionizes*.

FIGURE 4: Reactions of $CaCO_3$ with HCl and $HC_2H_3O_2$ solutions

FIGURE 5: Hydrochloric acid completely ionizes, and acetic acid partially ionizes in water.

chloride ion (1–)   hydronium ion (1+)

HCl

a   Hydrochloric acid, a strong acid

water molecule   acetic acid molecule

hydronium ion (1+) $HC_2H_3O_2$ acetate ion (1–)

b   Acetic acid, a weak acid

ANALYZE Make a claim for why $CaCO_3$ reacts more vigorously with HCl than with $HC_2H_3O_2$. Use evidence from Figure 5 to support your claim, and explain your reasoning.

_____

_____

_____

Strong acids ionize completely in water. For example, HCl ionizes into H^+ and Cl^- in water, and no HCl molecules remain. Weak acids do not ionize completely. Thus, when a weak acid is combined with water, some amount of reactant is still present at equilibrium. The behavior of a weak acid can be written in the form of a chemical equation. In this equation, HA represents a weak acid, such as acetic acid. The negative ion (A^-) formed in solution is known as that acid's *conjugate base*. In the reverse reaction, the conjugate base can accept a proton, like bases would.

$$HA(aq) + H_2O(l) \rightleftharpoons H_3O^+(aq) + A^-(aq)$$

EXPLAIN Select the correct terms to complete the statement about this equation.

For a reversible reaction at equilibrium, the rate of the forward reaction is less than | equal to | greater than the rate of the reverse reaction. Because a weak acid does not ionize completely, there will | will not be both products and reactants present at equilibrium. The concentrations of the reactants and products are | are not always equal at equilibrium and depend on the degree to which an acid forms ions.

Strong bases dissociate completely in water. When weak bases dissolve in water, however, some of the base stays in its molecular form. Figure 6 shows how a strong base, such as sodium hydroxide, NaOH, dissociates completely in water. A weak base, such as ammonia, NH_3, does not ionize completely and produces few hydroxide ions in solution.

FIGURE 6: Strong bases produce more hydroxide ions in solution than weak bases.

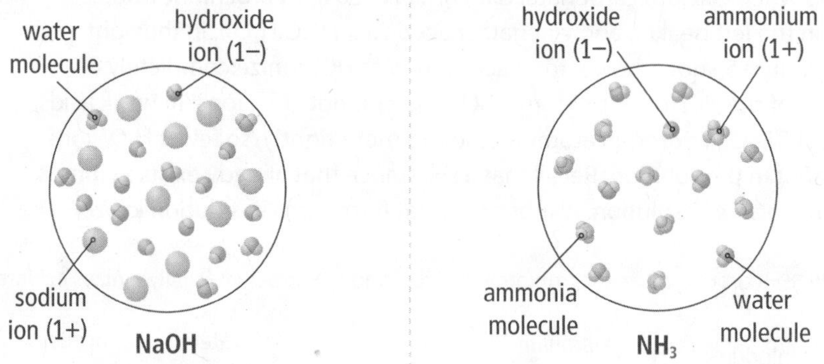

water molecule
hydroxide ion (1−)
sodium ion (1+)
NaOH

a   Sodium hydroxide, a strong base

hydroxide ion (1−)
ammonium ion (1+)
ammonia molecule
water molecule
NH₃

b   Ammonia, a weak base

When a weak base is dissolved in water, the proton-transfer reaction of some molecules can be written as a chemical equation showing the reactants and products at equilibrium:

$$B(aq) + H_2O(l) \rightleftharpoons BH^+(aq) + OH^-(aq)$$

The positive ion formed by the dissociation of a weak base is known as the base's *conjugate acid*. In the reverse reaction, the conjugate acid can donate a proton. Each pair of related molecules or ions forms a conjugate acid-base pair. Thus, HA, an acid, forms A^-, its conjugate base, and HA and A^- are a conjugate pair. Likewise, B, a base, forms BH^+, its conjugate acid, and together B and BH^+ are a conjugate pair.

Very strong acids and very strong bases are quite reactive, but their conjugates are only slightly reactive. Therefore, a strong acid or base will ionize or dissociate completely. However, when the reactants are weak acids or weak bases, an equilibrium system is established. The conjugate base of a weak acid or the conjugate acid of a weak base is reactive enough to reverse the proton transfer, reforming the original molecule.

Equilibrium Expressions for Acids and Bases

You can write an equilibrium expression for an aqueous solution of a weak acid or base. This equilibrium expression represents the relationship between each of the components within the solution. Recall that in an equilibrium expression, the products of the reaction are placed in the numerator, and the reactants are placed in the denominator.

MODEL Complete the equilibrium expressions for weak acids and weak bases.

$$[HA] \qquad [B] \qquad [A^-] \qquad [BH^+]$$

$$HA(aq) + H_2O(l) \rightleftharpoons H_3O^+(aq) + A^-(aq)$$

$$K_{eq} = \frac{[H_3O^+]\ \boxed{}}{\boxed{}\ [H_2O]}$$

$$B(aq) + H_2O(l) \rightleftharpoons BH^+(aq) + OH^-(aq)$$

$$K_{eq} = \frac{\boxed{}\ [OH^-]}{\boxed{}\ [H_2O]}$$

Each of the equilibrium constant equations that you constructed above includes the concentration of water. However, water is a solvent, so the concentration of liquid water in the solution is high enough that it can be assumed to be constant. Because the concentration does not change, water can be removed from the equilibrium constant, K. For the reaction of the acid HA, the equation becomes

$$K_a = \frac{[H_3O^+][A^-]}{[HA]}$$

The new equilibrium constant, K_a, relates the relative concentrations of the acid and its ions in solution. For example, citric acid ($C_6H_8O_7$) is a weak acid with a K_a of 7.41×10^{-4} at 25 °C. This acid is present in fruits, such as oranges, limes, and lemons. It is also a natural preservative and is used to add a sour taste to foods and drinks.

FIGURE 7: These foods contain citric acid, a weak acid.

APPLY Complete the statements about citric acid.

The K_a value for citric acid indicates that the reactants | products are favored in this reaction. Therefore, most of the acid molecules do | do not ionize in water.

The equilibrium constant for a weak base can be written in a similar way to that of a weak acid. The base is a reactant, so it is placed in the denominator of the equilibrium expression. The conjugate acid and hydroxide ions are the products, so they form the numerator of the expression. Thus, for the reaction of the base B, the equation becomes

$$K_b = \frac{[BH^+][OH^-]}{[B]}$$

The equilibrium constant, K_b, relates the relative concentrations of the base and its ions in solution. For a weak base, K_b is small, indicating that most of the base molecules do not form ions. As with other equilibrium constants, the value of K_a or K_b is constant at a specific temperature. At a different temperature, the values will be different.

K_a Values for Weak Acids at 25 °C		
Acid	Formula	K_a
chlorous acid	$HClO_2$	1.15×10^{-2}
hydrofluoric acid	HF	6.31×10^{-4}
nitrous acid	HNO_2	5.62×10^{-4}
acetic acid	$HC_2H_3O_2$	1.75×10^{-5}
hydrocyanic acid	HCN	6.16×10^{-10}

K_b Values for Weak Bases at 25 °C		
Base	Formula	K_b
methylamine	CH_3NH_2	4.57×10^{-4}
ammonia	NH_3	1.78×10^{-5}
pyridine	C_5H_5N	1.70×10^{-9}
aniline	$C_6H_5NH_2$	7.41×10^{-10}
urea	$(NH_2)_2CO$	1.30×10^{-14}

ANALYZE Use the K_a and K_b values in the tables to complete the statements.

According to the data, acetic acid has a smaller | larger K_a value than nitrous acid. Therefore, acetic acid ionizes to a lesser | greater extent than nitrous acid. Methylamine has a smaller | larger K_b value than ammonia, so methylamine dissociates to a lesser | greater extent than ammonia.

 Stability and Change

Acid and Base Salts

In a neutralization reaction, an acid reacts with a base, producing water and a salt. When a salt dissolves in water, it produces cations of the base from which it was formed and anions of the acid from which it is formed. Even though salts are formed from neutralization reactions, their solutions are not necessarily neutral. The pH of a salt solution depends on interactions between its ions and water molecules.

FIGURE 8: Universal indicator in these solutions shows that salt solutions do not all have a neutral pH.

Salts that form from the neutralization of a strong acid and a strong base, such as NaCl, dissolve to produce neutral solutions. This is because the ions that form when the salt dissolves (Na^+ and Cl^-) do not react with water.

The aqueous solution of salts formed from a strong base and a weak acid are slightly basic. This is because the anions from the weak acid accept a proton from water, forming the weak acid and hydroxide ions. The cations from the strong base do not react with water because a strong base is already ions in solution. The opposite occurs for a strong acid and a weak base. The cations from the weak base donate a proton to water, increasing the hydronium ion concentration, resulting in a slightly acidic solution.

 Collaborate How do you think the salt formed by the combination of a weak acid and a weak base would be different than one formed by the combination of a strong acid and strong base?

 Evidence Notebook The sodium borate that you saw at the beginning of this lesson is a salt that has a basic pH in solution. What does this tell you about the acid and base that form this salt?

Measuring pH

Monitoring pH can be very important in chemical reactions. For many lab experiments and manufacturing processes, conditions must be in a certain range for success. Chemical reactions in which one or more reactants are acids or bases can be sensitive to changes in pH. Also, industrial equipment can be damaged by materials that are too acidic or too basic. Ways to measure pH include indicator solutions, indicator strips, and pH probes.

Acid-Base Indicators

Acid-base indicators change color when pH changes. Indicators are color-sensitive to changes in a solution's hydronium ion (H_3O^+) concentration. Each row in Figure 9 contains solutions of a single indicator. Each column represents a different pH level of 1 through 10. Good indicators show strong color changes as pH changes and are generally used at low concentrations in a reaction mixture.

Notice that each indicator shows a color change at particular pH levels and may remain at one color for much of the pH range. It is important to consider this characteristic when choosing an indicator for a specific application.

EXPLAIN Universal indicator is a mixture of several indicators. Why would this mixture be more useful in some applications than one of the individual indicators shown in Figure 9?

FIGURE 9: Each row shows a different indicator in solutions from pH 1 at the left to pH 10 at the right.

_____

_____

_____

Acid-base indicators are weak acids or bases themselves. These indicators exist in equilibrium in the solution to which they are added. For example, an indicator that is a weak acid will be one color in acidic conditions, and its conjugate base will be a different color in basic conditions. Phenolphthalein, shown in the last row of the photo in Figure 9, is a commonly used indicator. It is also a weak acid. In acidic and neutral solutions, phenolphthalein is colorless. When a base is added, the equilibrium shifts towards the conjugate base, which has a magenta color. So, phenolphthalein turns basic solutions pink.

In labs, pH is most often measured with a pH meter. A pH meter has two electrodes and measures the voltage between the electrodes when they are in a solution. The solution behaves as an electrolyte, so it conducts electricity. The measured voltage is a function of the hydronium ion activity of the solution, so it can be used to accurately measure pH. A change in the concentration of hydronium ions affects both pH and the measurement read by the meter.

FIGURE 10: Using a pH meter

Testing pH Measurement Tools

Sometimes, it is necessary to precisely determine the exact pH of a solution. At other times, an estimate is acceptable. The precision of tools used to measure pH varies. For example, some pH meters can measure with a precision of a hundredth of a pH unit. Other tools, such as an indicator strip, which is a paper strip soaked in an indicator solution and dried, may have a precision of a full pH unit or more. Choosing the right tool for a certain application requires that one consider factors such as cost, convenience, and precision. In this lab, you will test different types of pH measurement tools and make a claim about which is most appropriate for different situations.

The tools available include an indicator made with red cabbage, which, like many plant pigments, changes color at different pH values. Specifically, red cabbage turns red, purple, or violet in the presence of an acid and turns anywhere from blue to yellow-green in the presence of a base. This indicator can be prepared by blending red cabbage in water and straining out the plant matter. pH paper is a strip that incorporates a mixture of several indicators and is typically compared to a color guide on the package. It is important to use the correct guide because indicator strips can be made of different mixtures of indicators. A pH probe usually has a digital read-out and, depending on the type of probe, the reading may take some time to stabilize.

Research Question: What are the benefits and drawbacks of using different pH measurement tools?

FIGURE 11: Color guide for red cabbage indicator

pH	acidic			basic		
	2	4	6	8	10	12
Color	red	pink	purple	blue	blue-green	green-yellow

MAKE A CLAIM

In your Evidence Notebook, make a claim about which pH measurement tool you think will provide the most precise measurements. Which tool will be the easiest to use?

MATERIALS

- indirectly vented chemical splash goggles, nonlatex apron, nitrile gloves
- beakers, 250 mL (9)
- droppers (9)
- pH testing tools: pH paper, pH probe, red cabbage indicator
- test substances: ammonia, lemon juice, fruit juice, milk, liquid detergent, soft drink, antacid tablet (crushed and dissolved in water), baking soda, vinegar
- well plate
- white paper (1 sheet)

SAFETY INFORMATION

· Wear indirectly vented chemical splash goggles, a nonlatex apron, and nitrile gloves during the setup, hands-on, and takedown segments of the activity.

· Never taste any substance or chemical in the lab.

· Immediately clean up any liquid spilled on the floor so it does not become a slip/fall hazard.

· Wash your hands with soap and water immediately after completing this activity.

indirectly vented
chemical splash
goggles

PLAN THE INVESTIGATION

1. Write a procedure in your Evidence Notebook for testing the pH of the substances using the different measurement tools provided. When developing your procedure, consider the order in which you should test each tool. Note any safety precautions you need to take while conducting your investigation.

2. Make a data table for recording your data. You should include the pH measurements you make using each tool for each test substance and observations about the precision of different tools.

3. Have your teacher approve your procedure, safety plans, and data table before you begin testing substances.

ANALYZE

Obtain the actual pH values for the test substances from your teacher. How do your data compare to the known values for each substance? If your values were different, what do you think are possible sources of error?

_____

_____

_____

_____

_____

_____

CONSTRUCT AN EXPLANATION

Answer the following questions in your Evidence Notebook.

1. Of the tools tested, which gave the most precise pH readings? In what type of situation would you need this level of precision or higher when testing for pH?

2. Which tool could be most easily obtained from common household items? When might homeowners want to test the pH of something around their home?

3. When might pH paper be preferable over a pH probe? What are some of the benefits and drawbacks for each of these tools?

The tools and techniques used to measure pH depend on the situation. Different pH indicators exist for measuring different parts of the pH scale. Some have only two colors—one for acidic conditions and one for basic conditions.

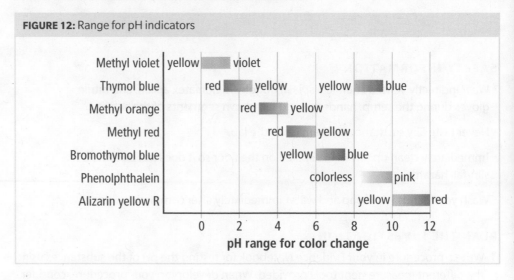

FIGURE 12: Range for pH indicators

Methyl violet: yellow → violet
Thymol blue: red → yellow, yellow → blue
Methyl orange: red → yellow
Methyl red: red → yellow
Bromothymol blue: yellow → blue
Phenolphthalein: colorless → pink
Alizarin yellow R: yellow → red

pH range for color change (0 2 4 6 8 10 12)

ANALYZE If a chemist were testing the pH of a set of materials that ranged in pH from 3 to 5, which indicator would be most appropriate?

○ **a.** phenolphthalein   ○ **c.** methyl orange

○ **b.** bromothymol blue   ○ **d.** methyl violet

Titration

Because indicators change color in specific equilibrium positions, they can be used to analyze acidic and basic solutions by a process called titration. Titration is the addition of a measured volume of a solution of known concentration to find the concentration of an unknown solution. Acid-base titration involves adding an acid or base of known concentration to an acid or a base of unknown concentration to reach neutralization.

During the titration of an acid solution by a base, the incremental addition of base slowly changes the equilibrium amount of hydronium ions. In Figure 13, students are using a burette to add drops of base to an acidic solution containing phenolphthalein.

Eventually, the phenolphthalein indicator in the flask will start to turn pink. Swirling the solution returns it to colorless at first, but in time, the right amount of base makes the solution turn and stay pink. This is called the equivalence point. An indicator or pH probe can be used to find the point where enough base has been added to reach the equivalence point. This volume and the known base concentration can then be used to calculate the number of moles of base that neutralized the solution. This value reflects the number of moles of acid in the unknown solution and can be used to calculate its concentration. Titration of a base by a known concentration of acid follows the same process.

FIGURE 13: Students doing an acid-base titration

 Collaborate Explain to a partner how to carry out an acid-base titration. Then have your partner explain to you why a titration would be necessary.

In a titration, the solution of unknown concentration is the *analyte* and the solution of known concentration, the standard solution, is the *titrant*. At the equivalence point, the analyte and titrant are present in chemically equivalent amounts. The number of moles of hydronium ions from the acid equals the number of moles of hydroxide ions from the base. This is true whether the acid is the titrant or analyte.

The pH of the solution changes rapidly as the equivalence point is approached, making it appear as an almost vertical segment of a graph of the pH of a titration. If the indicator changes color on that part of the graph, the color of the solution will change right at the equivalence point, so the concentration of the analyte can be calculated stoichiometrically.

The pH of the equivalence point for an acid-base reaction is used to find the most suitable indicator. When the titrant and the analyte are a strong acid and a strong base (either order), the equivalence point pH is 7. At that point, the change in pH is large and sudden. The typical indicator for this titration is phenolphthalein. When the analyte is a weak acid and the titrant is a strong base, the equivalence point pH is greater than 7. When the analyte is a weak base and the titrant is a strong acid, the equivalence point pH is less than 7. Generally, weak acids or bases are not used as titrants.

Titrating an Eggshell
Determine the amount of calcium carbonate in an eggshell by acid-base titration.

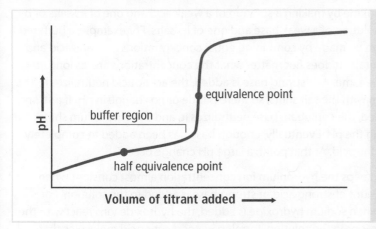

FIGURE 14: Titration curve of a weak acid by a strong base

INFER Which statements are true of a titration curve? Select all correct answers.

☐ **a.** The pH of the equivalence point is always greater than 7.

☐ **b.** The pH changes very quickly near the equivalence point.

☐ **c.** The indicator should have a color change near the equivalence point pH.

☐ **d.** The pH of a solution always increases during a titration.

☐ **e.** The concentration of the titrant must be a known value.

When the analyte is a weak acid or a weak base, the pH curve shows a gradual change before the equivalence point. The range in which this gradual change occurs is known as the buffer region. The midpoint of the buffer region is called the half-equivalence point. At this point, enough titrant has been added to convert exactly half of the analyte to its conjugate, and the concentration of the acid is equal to the concentration of the conjugate base. There is no buffer region when both acid and base are strong.

In a laboratory, a pH meter is often used to measure pH during a titration. Indicators, however, must change color over a pH range that includes the equivalence point. The point in a titration at which an indicator changes color is called the indicator's end point.

Buffers

The gradual change in pH leading up to the equivalence point of the weak acid-strong base titration is caused by *buffering*. The equilibrium between the weak acid and its salt buffers the solution against rapid pH changes. A solution that resists changes in pH due to addition of hydronium ions or hydroxide ions is called a buffered solution, or a buffer.

EXPLAIN In Figure 15, universal indicator shows how pH changes when an acid is added to a buffer solution and to pure water. How can you tell that the solution on the left is buffered? Explain your reasoning.

_____

_____

_____

_____

A buffer is made by making a solution of a weak acid and one of its salts or by making a solution of a weak base and one of its salts. For example, a buffered solution can be made by combining equal concentrations of acetic acid and sodium acetate. It does not matter what the concentrations are, as long as they are the same. As a strong base is added, the acetic acid neutralizes it. The equilibrium with the salt shifts, so there is little or no change in pH. If a strong acid is added, the conjugate base neutralizes it, and the equilibrium shifts, maintaining the pH. Eventually, enough base has been added to completely neutralize the acid. At that point, a large pH change occurs.

The buffer keeps the hydronium ion concentration almost constant when a small amount of strong acid or strong base is added to the solution. For example, when sodium hydroxide is added, the hydroxide ions react with the hydronium ions in the solution, forming water. Acetic acid molecules then ionize, mostly replacing the hydronium ions neutralized by the base:

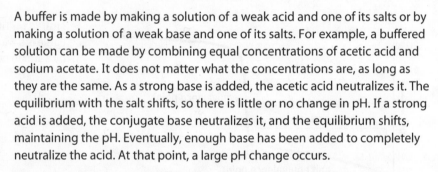

$$HC_2H_3O_2(aq) + H_2O(l) \rightleftharpoons H_3O^+(aq) + C_2H_3O_2^-(aq)$$

When hydrochloric acid is added to the buffer solution, its hydronium ions combine with acetate ions, forming acetic acid molecules, restoring the hydronium ion to form acetic acid molecules:

$$H_3O^+(aq) + C_2H_3O_2^-(aq) \rightleftharpoons HC_2H_3O_2(aq) + H_2O(l)$$

In both cases, there is very little change in the hydronium ion concentration and, therefore, very little change in the pH.

APPLY Which of these statements is true about how a buffer made from acetic acid and acetate minimizes changes in pH?

○ **a.** The addition of a strong acid does not change the pH of the buffer at all.

○ **b.** When an acid is added to the buffer, the concentration of acetate ions increases.

○ **c.** When a strong base is added to the buffer, the pH increases slightly.

○ **d.** The addition of a base causes the equilibrium to shift in favor of acetic acid.

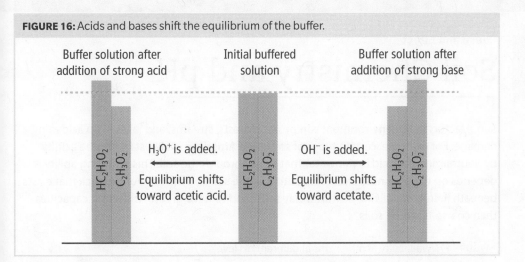

FIGURE 16: Acids and bases shift the equilibrium of the buffer.

Buffer solution after addition of strong acid

Initial buffered solution

Buffer solution after addition of strong base

H_3O^+ is added.

Equilibrium shifts toward acetic acid.

OH^- is added.

Equilibrium shifts toward acetate.

$HC_2H_3O_2$ $C_2H_3O_2^-$

ANALYZE Use the graph shown in Figure 16 to complete the statements about the acetic acid/acetate buffer system.

When a base is added to the buffer system, hydroxide ions from the base combine with protons from acetate | acetic acid, and the equilibrium position shifts toward acetic acid | acetate. When an acid is added to the system, hydrogen ions from the acid combine with acetate | acetic acid, and the equilibrium position shifts toward acetic acid | acetate.

Recall that buffers can be made of either a weak acid and its salt or a weak base and its salt. An example of a buffer system made of a weak base and its salt is the one made using ammonia and ammonium chloride. When a strong base, such as sodium hydroxide, is added to the ammonia/ammonium buffer, ammonium ions react with hydroxide ions, and the pH changes very little:

$$NH_4^+(aq) + OH^-(aq) \rightleftharpoons NH_3(aq) + H_2O(l)$$

When a strong acid is added to the ammonia/ammonium buffer, ammonia molecules react with hydronium ions to form ammonium ions and decrease the hydronium ion concentration almost to its original value:

$$H_3O^+(aq) + NH_3(aq) \rightleftharpoons NH_4^+(aq) + H_2O(l)$$

Buffers function best when the K_a of the conjugate weak acid is close to the desired range of the hydronium ion concentration of the buffer.

Many consumer medical products are buffered to protect the body from potentially harmful pH changes. For example, aspirin (acetylsalicylic acid) is sometimes buffered to avoid irritation of the stomach lining. The pH of gastric acid is about 1.5 to 3.5. Aspirin is buffered by adding the salts of a weak acid to it. The anions of the salts react with hydronium ions released by the aspirin in the body as it dissolves.

 Language Arts Connection Buffering is important in living things. For example, blood is buffered by the bicarbonate ion, HCO_3^-. Research these questions about the bicarbonate buffering system in blood and make an infographic to illustrate your findings: Why is buffering important in blood? How does this buffering system work?

Cause and Effect

Soil Chemistry and pH

Some factors in the environment can protect forests, streams, and lakes from acid rain damage. For example, certain types of soil in the American Midwest buffer the acidity by neutralizing the acid in rainwater that flows through the soil. This buffering ability depends on the thickness and composition of the soil and the type of bedrock that exists beneath it. In general, fine-textured clay soils tend to have greater buffering capacities than coarse-textured soils.

FIGURE 17: Availability of metal ions at different pH levels

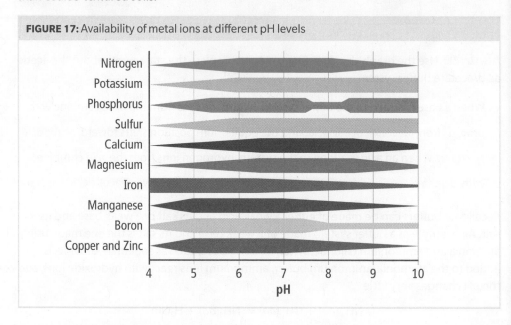

PREDICT According to Figure 17, how does the availability of different metal ions change as soil pH decreases? How do you think these changes affect plants?

_____

_____

_____

_____

The pH of soil is very important to plants because pH affects the availability of metal ions in the soil. Acid rain reduces the availability of plant nutrients, such as potassium and calcium, in the soil. In addition, heavy metals, such as copper and zinc, begin to ionize and dissolve when the soil pH decreases. These and other heavy metals are toxic to plants.

Melting snow and heavy rain can result in what is known as episodic acidification. Bodies of water that do not normally have a high acid level may become acidic temporarily when the soil cannot buffer it. This short burst of high acidity can stress the ecosystem and cause harm to a variety of organisms.

 Evidence Notebook Consider what you know about buffer solutions. If you wanted to make a buffer solution using sodium borate, what other type of compound would you need to make the buffer? Explain your answer.

Solubility Equilibria

Just as a weak acid in solution has an equilibrium state, an ionic compound in solution also has as an equilibrium state. Solubility is the amount of solute that can be dissolved in a solvent, such as water. Knowing the degree of solubility of ionic compounds in water provides information that can be used to control the concentrations of these compounds.

FIGURE 18: Shells are made up of mostly $CaCO_3$. When crushed, they can be used to filter water.

For example, water purification methods can be designed to remove hazardous metal ions from drinking water. Most people in the United States receive water from a municipal water supply. In general, this water undergoes a purification process that removes bacteria, heavy metals, and other harmful pollutants. This technological process is expensive, though, and is therefore not affordable in many places around the world. Therefore, scientists and engineers are developing new ways to design more affordable purification methods. For example, researchers in Vietnam have developed a system of filtering water using crushed seashells as the filtration medium. The shells are made mostly of calcium carbonate ($CaCO_3$), which is slightly soluble in water. This filtration process helps produce safe, drinkable water by removing certain hazardous metal ions.

PREDICT How might filtering water though crushed seashells help remove metal ions?

_____

_____

_____

_____

Analyzing Solubility

The solubility of compounds varies widely. Some compounds are more soluble than others. It is important to note that solubility comparisons of different salts are only meaningful when conditions, particularly temperature, are the same. Conventionally, solubilities of salt compounds are compared by the maximum amount of the salt (solute) that can be dissolved in 100 g of water at 25 °C. These solutions are said to be saturated. Recall that a saturated solution is not necessarily a concentrated solution.

In general, a substance is said to be soluble if the solubility is greater than 1 g per 100 g of water, and slightly soluble if less than that. Higher solubility means that the solute forms ions more completely.

Name of Salt	Formula	Solubility at 25 °C in g/100 g of water
silver chloride	AgCl	0.000192
calcium carbonate	$CaCO_3$	0.0014
lead(II) sulfate	$PbSO_4$	0.0044
lead(II) chloride	$PbCl_2$	1.08
sodium chloride	NaCl	36
sodium acetate	$NaC_2H_3O_2$	50.4
cobalt(II) chloride	$CoCl_2$	52.9
potassium iodide	KI	148
silver nitrate	$AgNO_3$	234

 Evidence Notebook Draw a diagram showing how solutions containing these salts would differ: AgCl, $PbCl_2$, NaCl, and $AgNO_3$. Use the solubility values in the table to infer the degree to which each compound will form ions in solution.

The Solubility Product

FIGURE 19: Solid calcium fluoride forms an equilibrium with the solution.

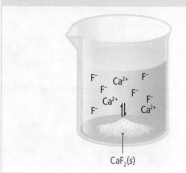

$CaF_2(s)$

Salts that are only slightly soluble still dissociate in solution to some extent. The degree of a substance's solubility is described with an equilibrium constant known as the solubility product, or K_{sp}. Knowing the solubility product for a salt allows one to make inferences about the behavior of the salt ions in solution. For example, chemists use K_{sp} to predict whether a precipitate will be formed in certain situations. They can then use this knowledge to optimize processes such as water purification.

Consider calcium fluoride (CaF_2). At standard conditions, some calcium fluoride will remain a solid, and some will dissociate in solution, breaking into positive calcium ions (Ca^{2+}) and negative fluoride ions (F^-).

SAMPLE PROBLEM   Calculate K_{sp} for the ionization of calcium fluoride, which is represented by the equation:

$$CaF_2(s) \rightleftharpoons Ca^{2+}(aq) + 2F^-(aq)$$

ANALYZE   Remember that a solid substance in a heterogeneous reaction is not included in its equilibrium expression. So, only the ions are represented in the expression. Based on the balanced equation, we can see that each mole of CaF_2 that dissolves produces 1 mole of Ca^{2+} and 2 moles of F^- ions. The coefficient of 2 for F^- in the equation above means that the concentration of fluoride ion in the K_{sp} expression must be squared:

$$K_{sp} = [Ca^{2+}][F^-]^2$$

Now we can use solubility data from the table of solubility values to calculate molar concentrations of the ions in solution. The solubility of CaF_2 is 1.6×10^{-3} g/100 g of water. Use dimensional analysis to find the moles of CaF_2 that dissolve in 1 L of water:

$$\frac{1.6 \times 10^{-3} \text{ g CaF}_2}{100 \text{ g water}} \times \frac{1 \text{ g water}}{1 \text{ mL water}} \times \frac{10^3 \text{ mL}}{1 \text{ L}} \times \frac{1 \text{ mol CaF}_2}{78.1 \text{ g CaF}_2} = 2.05 \times 10^{-4} \frac{\text{mol}}{\text{L}} \text{ CaF}_2$$

SOLVE   We can now use molar concentrations to calculate K_{sp}. Substitute the concentrations into the K_{sp} expression. The concentration of CaF_2 must be doubled to get $[F^-]$.

$$K_{sp} = [Ca^{2+}][F^-]^2 = [2.05 \times 10^{-4}][2 \times 2.05 \times 10^{-4}]^2 = 3.45 \times 10^{-11}$$

PRACTICE PROBLEM   Calculate K_{sp} for lead(II) chloride, $PbCl_2$. The solubility of this compound at 20 °C is 1.08 g/100 g of water. The ionization of lead chloride is represented by this equation:

$$PbCl_2(s) \rightleftharpoons Pb^{2+}(aq) + 2Cl^-(aq)$$

ANALYZE   Write the K_{sp} expression for this equation. Then, use dimensional analysis to convert the solubility value to moles of $PbCl_2$.

SOLVE   Use the molar concentration to calculate K_{sp}.

Calculating the K_{sp} value for a salt allows you to draw conclusions about the degree to which the salt dissociates in solution. Figure 20 shows solubility and K_{sp} values for several salts. Note the relationship between solubility and K_{sp}.

FIGURE 20: Solubility and K_{sp} Values for Various Ionic Compounds

Name of Salt	Formula	Solubility at 25 °C in g/100 g of water	K_{sp}
silver chloride	$AgCl$	0.000192	1.8×10^{-10}
calcium carbonate	$CaCO_3$	0.0014	3.4×10^{-9}
lead(II) sulfate	$PbSO_4$	0.0044	2.5×10^{-8}
lead(II) chloride	$PbCl_2$	1.08	1.7×10^{-5}
sodium chloride	$NaCl$	36	(Solubility products are usually not reported for compounds classified as soluble—greater than 1 g/100 g water at 20 °C.)
sodium acetate	$NaC_2H_3O_2$	50.4	
cobalt(II) chloride	$CoCl_2$	52.9	
potassium iodide	KI	148	
silver nitrate	$AgNO_3$	234	

INFER Use the table in Figure 20 to complete the statement.

As the solubility of a salt decreases, K_{sp} generally increases | decreases. For example, lead(II) sulfate has a higher | lower solubility than lead(II) chloride, and it has a higher | lower K_{sp} value. Therefore, when equal amounts of these salts are placed in equal amounts of water, there will be more | fewer ions present in the lead(II) sulfate solution than in the lead(II) chloride solution.

FIGURE 21: In the beaker on the left, copper(II) carbonate hydroxide, $Cu_2CO_3(OH)_2$, also known as the mineral malachite, is combined with water. In the beaker on the right, copper(II) sulfate, $CuSO_4$, is combined with water.

EXPLAIN Based on what you see in in Figure 21, what can you conclude about the solubility and K_{sp} values of copper(II) carbonate hydroxide and copper(II) sulfate? How do they compare? Explain your reasoning.

_____

_____

_____

_____

Think back to the question about why adding crushed seashells to contaminated water helps purify the water. Pollution from industrial waste, landfills, mines, and other sources can contaminate water with heavy metal ions such as lead, copper, nickel, and zinc. When people consume water contaminated with high concentrations of heavy metals, the metals can damage the nervous system, which can lead to mental and motor dysfunction.

In order to combat this problem, researchers have tested the effect of adding crushed shells, such as discarded clam shells, to contaminated water. Adding seashells to water has been shown to cause lead carbonate to precipitate out of the water. Lead replaces the calcium in calcium carbonate, and the lead carbonate can be filtered out of the water.

ANALYZE The solubility product of lead(II) carbonate is 7.4×10^{-14}. The solubility product of calcium carbonate is 3.4×10^{-9}. Explain which of these compounds is more soluble in water. Then explain why this difference makes sense, given the results researchers obtained when they added calcium carbonate to water contaminated with heavy metals.

The Common-Ion Effect

An extremely powerful method of removing specific ions from a solution is to treat water with calcium carbonate to cause other, less soluble compounds, like lead carbonate, to precipitate out. To understand this, consider what occurs when the soluble salt sodium chloride (NaCl) is added to a saturated solution of silver chloride (AgCl). Both compounds form ions in solution. For example, AgCl dissociates to form Ag^+ and Cl^- ions:

$$AgCl(s) \rightleftharpoons Ag^+(aq) + Cl^-(aq)$$

Sodium chloride is also a soluble salt and dissociates in solution:

$$NaCl(s) \rightleftharpoons Na^+(aq) + Cl^-(aq)$$

In a saturated AgCl solution, the concentrations of Ag^+ and Cl^- ions are in a one-to-one ratio. When additional chloride ions from NaCl get introduced, what must happen to the Ag^+ concentration in order for K_{sp} to maintain its value?

$$K_{sp} = [Ag^+][Cl^-] = 1.8 \times 10^{-10}$$

As the concentration of Cl^- ions increases, the product of the concentrations of Ag^+ and Cl^- ions becomes higher than the value of K_{sp}. This causes additional AgCl to form a precipitate and come out of solution. The precipitation occurs until the solution reaches a new equilibrium. The addition of NaCl to a saturated solution of AgCl illustrates the common-ion effect. The common-ion effect can be summarized in this way: When a saturated solution of one compound is combined with a second compound having an ion in common with the first compound, the less soluble compound will precipitate.

In the case of the compounds NaCl and AgCl, the common ion is Cl^-. Adding NaCl solution increases $[Cl^-]$. This also reduces the solubility of AgCl because more chloride ions are already present in solution. Equilibrium is reestablished in the only way possible: precipitation of AgCl. This reduces the concentration of both ions until the product of the two is once again equal to K_{sp}. In the resulting solution, the silver ion concentration is reduced.

 Collaborate Silver is toxic at high concentrations. With a partner, discuss how you could use the common-ion effect to remove silver ions from water.

Engineering
Water Softeners

Many parts of the country have water that is described as "hard water." This water has a high mineral content. The image shows what can happen to a shower head over time as hard water flows through it. The most common source of hardness is a combination of the ions Ca^{2+} and Mg^{2+}. The carbonates of these cations, $CaCO_3$ and $MgCO_3$, are only slightly soluble. Most forms of limestone are made up mostly of $CaCO_3$ with a small amount of $MgCO_3$. Underground water that flows through limestone beds dissolves these carbonates from the rock around them, forming a saturated solution of the two compounds. Additional carbonate ions can form in the water as CO_2 dissolves from the atmosphere and becomes carbonic acid, H_2CO_3.

FIGURE 22: Slightly soluble carbonates have deposited on this showerhead.

A slight change in conditions can increase the carbonate ion concentration and cause carbonates to precipitate in household water pipes, water heaters, and showerheads. Besides being unsightly, the precipitates can clog flow. Hard water also prevents soap from forming a thick, foamy lather.

ASK Imagine you were asked to design a solution to problems associated with hard water. What are some questions you would ask to define the problem? How would you delineate the criteria and constraints?

_____

_____

_____

_____

_____

_____

_____

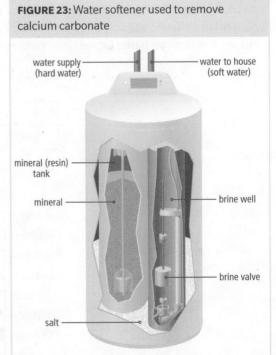

FIGURE 23: Water softener used to remove calcium carbonate

water supply (hard water) — water to house (soft water)

mineral (resin) tank

mineral — brine well

— brine valve

salt

In many municipal water systems, hard water is "softened" by adding slaked lime, a common name for calcium hydroxide, $Ca(OH)_2$. When this compound is added to a saturated solution of $CaCO_3$, some of the calcium carbonate precipitates out of the solution due to a common-ion effect. $Ca(OH)_2$ is more soluble than $CaCO_3$. This "lime softening" technique also removes Mg^{2+} ions, but in a different way. Addition of $Ca(OH)_2$ raises the pH, which means it raises the OH^- concentration. $Mg(OH)_2$ is less soluble than $MgCO_3$, so the hydroxide precipitates. In this way, the two main causes of water hardness have been removed.

Evidence Notebook In your evidence notebook, summarize what you have learned about the solubility product constant and the common-ion effect. Then, explain how these concepts can be used to purify drinking water.

Language Arts

Acid-Base Indicators in Foods

Previously, you used an indicator extracted from red cabbage to determine the pH of substances. Many common pH indicators are compounds that are found in plants or that are modifications of natural compounds. In some cases, the plants themselves can provide information about the pH of the soil they are growing in. Certain types of hydrangea bushes have blooms that are blue when the plant is growing in acidic soil and red when the same plant is growing in alkaline soil. Gardeners can add substances to modify the pH of the soil and get the color of blooms they prefer.

There are a number of foods that you can use to make your own pH indicators. These include beets, cherries, turmeric, onion, tomato, and turnips. Even some teas can be used as pH indicators. The chart in Figure 24 shows some of the color changes associated with common food-based indicators.

EXPLAIN What food-based indicator would you use if you wanted to determine whether the pH of a cleaning solution was strongly basic? Explain your reasoning.

_____

_____

_____

FIGURE 25: Food items containing cyanidin

Most of the strongly colored foods that can be used as pH indicators contain one or more compounds from a group of pigments called anthocyanins. This group of compounds also gives violets, roses, and autumn leaves their color. In addition to making the landscape and our foods more colorful, anthocyanins are important ingredients of a healthy diet. They protect people against many diseases.

One common anthocyanin pigment is cyanidin. Cyanidin is the reddish-purple pigment found in red cabbage as well as in many types of red fruits and vegetables. Among these are grapes, blackberries, cherries, and red onions. Extracts from these foods may display different color changes than the red cabbage extract. That is due to the presence of compounds in addition to cyanidin that change color based on pH.

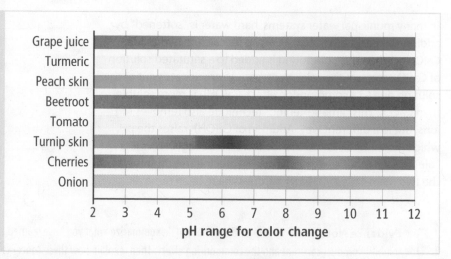

FIGURE 24: pH indicators from the kitchen

Grape juice
Turmeric
Peach skin
Beetroot
Tomato
Turnip skin
Cherries
Onion

2 3 4 5 6 7 8 9 10 11 12

pH range for color change

a Positive ion at acidic pH

b Neutral molecule at neutral pH

c Negative ion at basic pH

Cyanidin has a strong reaction to pH changes. In acidic solutions, it is bright red, but as the solution approaches neutral, the color shifts to violet-blue. The structural changes of cyanidin in acidic, neutral, and basic solutions are shown in Figure 26. As the pH increases from acidic to neutral, the cyanidin loses a hydrogen ion, changing from a positively charged ion to a neutral molecule. This altered structure absorbs light differently, resulting in the color change from bright red to violet-blue. If you add base to a neutral solution containing the indicator, the cyanidin molecule loses a second hydrogen ion. As this structural change occurs, cyanidin appears blue or blue-green.

An indicator that is a weak acid changes color when its structure changes as a result of losing a hydrogen ion. This can be modeled as the chemical equation:

$$HIn \rightleftharpoons H^+ + In^-$$

where HIn represents the acidic structure of the indicator and In⁻ represents its conjugate base structure. Acid-base indicators dissociate at different rates, according to the relative activity of the indicator and the conditions under which it is being used, such as the temperature and the pH of the solution. Thus, each indicator will have its own dissociation constant and a distinctive pH at which the color transition between HIn and In⁻ occurs.

For cyanidin, the neutral molecule is the conjugate base of the positive cyanidin ion. In acidic solutions, the positive ions and neutral molecules are in equilibrium. As pH increases, the positive ions lose a hydrogen ion, forming the neutral molecule.

When the equilibrium shifts towards the neutral molecule, the color of the solution changes from red to violet. As the pH continues to increase, a second hydrogen ion is lost from cyanidin. Another equilibrium shift occurs, this time in favor of the negative ion. This shift causes the color of the solution to change from violet to blue.

Why does cyanidin change color when it loses a hydrogen ion? The molecule has three ring structures containing double bonds. The electrons in this type of ring structure tend to absorb visible light at various frequencies. The side groups attached to the rings affect what frequency is absorbed.

Language Arts Connection Research a food that can be used to make an acid-base indicator. Then, write an instruction booklet that a person could use to make the indicator and understand how it works on a molecular level. Answer the following questions in your booklet:

- What pH range does the indicator work within?

- Is the indicator an acid or a base?

- What is the molecular structure of the indicator?

- What is the chemical equilibrium system of the indicator?

- How can you explain the changes in structure and equilibrium in a way that the average person could understand?

If time allows, present your "recipe" to your peers.

USING SHELLS TO TREAT WATER THE BUFFER IN LEMONADE SOLUBILIITY PRODUCT CONSTANT Go online to choose one of these other paths.

Lesson Self-Check

FIGURE 27: In parts of the Mojave Desert, borax can be mined at the surface.

The mineral deposits seen as a crust on the surface of this part of the Mojave Desert contain the salt sodium borate, also known as borax, left behind by the evaporation of ancient lakes. Borax, is used to make buffer solutions that are important in analytical chemistry and medical applications, among other uses. A borate buffer can be made by combining sodium borate with boric acid. Boric acid does not ionize to form hydrogen ions the way many acids do. Instead, boric acid functions as an acid because it has a strong attraction for hydroxide ions. Although the chemistry of a borate-boric acid buffer is more complex than that in some buffer systems, the same general principles still apply. A borate buffer maintains a pH between a narrow range (8–10), even when acids or bases are added to the solution.

 Evidence Notebook Refer to your notes in your Evidence Notebook to construct an explanation for how a buffer helps keep pH within a certain range.

1. **Claim** How does a buffer minimize pH changes? How is this related to equilibrium?
2. **Evidence** Describe evidence and specific examples from the lesson to support your claim.
3. **Reasoning** Explain how the evidence you cited supports your claim.

CHECKPOINTS

Check Your Understanding

1. The K_a value of nitrous acid, HNO_2, is 4.0×10^{-4}. Which statement about nitrous acid is true?

   ○ **a.** Nitrous acid dissociates completely in aqueous solution.

   ○ **b.** Nitrous acid does not dissolve in water.

   ○ **c.** Nitrous acid is a strong electrolyte.

   ○ **d.** Nitrous acid is as a weak acid.

Use the illustration to answer question 2.

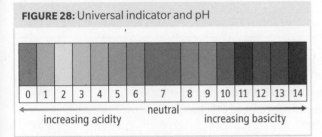

FIGURE 28: Universal indicator and pH

increasing acidity — neutral — increasing basicity

0 1 2 3 4 5 6 7 8 9 10 11 12 13 14

2. The following solutions were tested using universal indicator, and the observed colors were recorded. Place the solutions in order from the solution with the highest hydronium ion (1) concentration to the solution with the lowest hydronium ion concentration (6).

   _____ **a.** 1.0 M hydrogen chloride, red

   _____ **b.** 0.5 M sodium chloride, dark green

   _____ **c.** 0.01 M borax, light blue

   _____ **d.** 0.1 M potassium acetate, dark blue

   _____ **e.** lemon juice, yellow

   _____ **f.** vinegar, light green

3. Which of these shows an acid followed by its conjugate base?

   ○ **a.** HSO_4^-, H_2SO_4

   ○ **b.** HCl, $NaCl$

   ○ **c.** HCO_3^-, CO_3^{2-}

   ○ **d.** H_2O, H_3O^+

4. Which of these statements about a buffer made with a weak acid, such as acetic acid, are correct? Select all correct answers.

   ☐ **a.** The buffer contains both the acid and a salt of the acid.

   ☐ **b.** The addition of an acid to the buffer causes a decrease in its pH.

   ☐ **c.** The K_a of the buffer is always equal to its pH.

   ☐ **d.** The pH of the buffer changes gradually as a strong base is added to it.

5. Lead sulfate is often seen in the electrodes of car batteries, as it is formed when the battery is discharged. The K_{sp} of lead sulfate, $PbSO_4$, is 2.5×10^{-8}. Which of the following statements are correct? Select all correct answers.

   ☐ **a.** Lead sulfate dissociates completely when combined with water.

   ☐ **b.** Lead sulfate in solution is at equilibrium with crystals of undissolved lead sulfate.

   ☐ **c.** Lead sulfate will precipitate if a solution of soluble lead nitrate is added to a saturated solution of lead sulfate.

   ☐ **d.** Lead sulfate will precipitate if a solution of barium sulfate ($K_{sp} = 1.1 \times 10^{-10}$) is added to a saturated solution of lead sulfate.

   ☐ **e.** Additional lead sulfate will dissolve if a solution of sodium sulfate is added.

6. Select the correct terms to complete the statement.

   Urea is the main nitrogen-containing substance in the urine of mammals. The K_b of urea is 1.5×10^{-14}, and the K_b of ammonia is 1.8×10^{-5}. Based on those values, ammonia dissociates to a lesser | greater degree than urea. Therefore, the hydrogen ion | hydroxide ion concentration is higher in an ammonia solution, if the two solutions have the same concentration. The ammonia | urea solution has a higher pH.

CHECKPOINTS (continued)

7. How could you use the common ion effect to isolate a valuable metal that is in solution?

_____

_____

_____

8. Phosphoric acid, H_3PO_4, is a weak acid, whereas hydrochloric acid, HCl, is a strong acid. Explain how the degree of ionization differs for these two acids and how this difference affects their properties at the larger scale.

_____

_____

_____

_____

9. A pH meter is used to monitor the titration of a weak base with a strong acid. In the buffer zone, the meter shows that, when one drop of acid is added, the pH falls to a lower value and then rises until it is nearly the same as it was before the drop was added. Explain what equilibrium shift causes this pattern of pH change.

_____

_____

_____

_____

MAKE YOUR OWN STUDY GUIDE

 In your Evidence Notebook, design a study guide that supports the main ideas from this lesson:

Strong acids ionize, and strong bases dissociate almost completely in solution. Weak acids and bases have only partial ionization or dissociation.

There are several ways to measure pH, including indicators, test strips, and probes. Each method has advantages and disadvantages.

Buffers maintain relatively stable pH when acid or base is added due to the equilibrium shift between an acid and its conjugate base.

Remember to include the following information in your study guide:
- Use examples that model main ideas.
- Record explanations for the phenomena you investigated.
- Use evidence to support your explanations. Your support can include drawings, data, graphs, laboratory conclusions, and other evidence recorded throughout the lesson.

Consider how equilibrium between acids and bases can cause the pH of a buffer to be stable.

Disrupting Equilibrium in the Ocean

Pteropod shells degrade when oceanic carbon dioxide levels increase.

CAN YOU EXPLAIN IT?

Pteropods, a group of sea snails, and other marine organisms, such as corals, build shells and skeletons of calcium carbonate. Calcium and carbonate ions in the ocean water provide the raw material for these structures. The amount of carbonate ions in the water depends on a series of equilibrium reactions that rely on atmospheric carbon dioxide dissolving in the ocean. There is a balance between dissolved carbon dioxide and carbonate ions. Human activity produced dramatic increases in the concentration of carbon dioxide in the atmosphere over the last 50 to 100 years. More carbon dioxide has dissolved in the ocean, disrupting the equilibrium balance. The calcium carbonate structures of marine organisms, such as the corals in Figure 1, are degrading or disappearing in response to this shift.

PREDICT Why do you think increasing atmospheric carbon dioxide levels cause marine organisms to lose calcium carbonate from their shells and skeletons?

_____

_____

_____

FIGURE 1: Coral with a calcium carbonate skeleton (above) and without (below)

Evidence Notebook As you explore the lesson, gather evidence to explain the ways chemical equilibrium can be shifted to favor products or reactants.

Hands-On Lab
Modeling Ocean Acidification

The oceans cover approximately 71% of Earth's surface and contain 90% of Earth's biosphere. The huge surface area interface between the atmosphere and the hydrosphere, and the fact that carbon dioxide is soluble in water, means that oceans are the single largest "sink" for Earth's increasing concentration of human-generated carbon dioxide.

Increased atmospheric carbon dioxide from human activity, such as burning fossil fuels, means more carbon dioxide dissolves in the ocean. The ocean is normally at a pH around 8. When carbon dioxide dissolves, it chemically reacts with water to form carbonic acid as shown in the equilibrium equation:

$$CO_2 + H_2O \rightleftharpoons H_2CO_3$$

Carbonic acid in aqueous solution ionizes to form hydrogen ions and bicarbonate ions according to the equilibrium equation:

$$H_2CO_3 \rightleftharpoons H^+ + HCO_3^-$$

Bicarbonate ions then ionize to form hydrogen ions and carbonate ions according to the equilibrium equation:

$$HCO_3^- \rightleftharpoons H^+ + CO_3^{2-}$$

All three of these reactions occur constantly in the ocean. The balance of the products and reactants of each reaction affects the other reactions. As Figure 2 shows, when more carbon dioxide dissolves in the ocean, more hydrogen ions are produced.

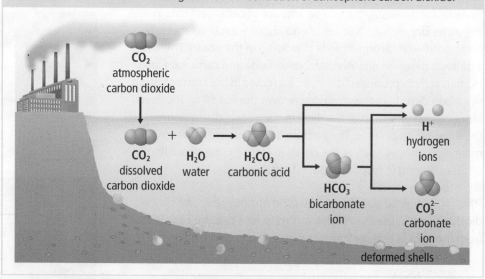

FIGURE 2: The equilibrium among carbon dioxide, carbonic acid, bicarbonate ions, and carbonate ions is sensitive to changes in the concentration of atmospheric carbon dioxide.

The additional hydrogen ions decrease the pH of the solutions that make up ocean water. While the pH of the ocean may not be less than 7, it is becoming *less basic*. Any reduction in the pH of the ocean is known as ocean acidification.

Research Question: What other ways can ocean acidification affect Earth's ecosystems?

Part 1: Testing the pH of Water

In the first part of this lab, you will explore the effect of increased concentration of dissolved carbon dioxide on the pH of water.

MAKE A CLAIM

In your Evidence Notebook, describe the relationship between carbon dioxide concentration and pH. How does this relationship affect the equilibrium of the bicarbonate reaction in the ocean?

MATERIALS

- indirectly vented chemical splash goggles, nonlatex apron, nitrile gloves
- beaker, 200 mL
- bromothymol blue indicator solution (50 mL)
- drinking straw

SAFETY INFORMATION

- Wear indirectly vented chemical splash goggles, a nonlatex apron, and nitrile gloves during the setup, hands-on, and takedown segments of the activity.

- Only exhale through the straw in this investigation. Do not inhale or ingest the bromothymol blue solution.

- Immediately wipe up any spilled liquid on the floor so it does not become a slip/fall hazard.

- Wash your hands with soap and water when you are finished handling chemicals.

CARRY OUT THE INVESTIGATION

As cells oxidize glucose to release energy, they produce carbon dioxide as one of the products. As part of your metabolism, your body must remove carbon dioxide through your circulatory and respiratory systems. When you breathe out, the air from your lungs contains an increased level of carbon dioxide relative to the air you breathe in. In this investigation, you will allow this air to pass through water that contains a pH indicator and make observations about any changes that occur.

The indicator that you will use is called bromothymol blue. When the pH of the indicator solution is above 7, it has a blue color. Before beginning the investigation, check to be sure that the solution you are using is blue.

indirectly vented chemical splash goggles

1. Pour 50 mL of indicator solution into a beaker. Observe and record the color of the indicator in your Evidence Notebook.
2. Place the end of the straw in the indicator solution. Exhale gently through the straw, causing bubbles to come up through the solution. Do not breathe in through the straw. Observe and record the color of the solution as you exhale.

3. After the color has changed, stop exhaling into the solution and record the color.

ANALYZE

Answer the following questions in your Evidence Notebook.

1. Using an indicator chart for bromothymol blue, explain how the pH of the solution was affected by the carbon dioxide in the air you exhaled.

2. Analyze the information shown in the Carbon Dioxide and pH graph. Make a claim about the relationship between atmospheric carbon dioxide concentration and the carbon dioxide concentration of seawater.

Carbon Dioxide and pH

FIGURE 3: This graph shows changes in atmospheric carbon dioxide concentrations, seawater carbon dioxide concentrations (pCO_2), and seawater pH since 1999.

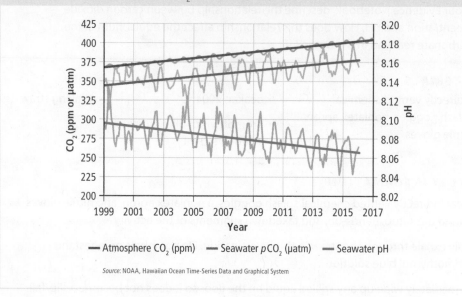

Source: NOAA, Hawaiian Ocean Time-Series Data and Graphical System

3. Consider what you discovered about the effects of dissolved carbon dioxide in water during your investigation. Examine the graph in Figure 3 and explain how your investigation supports the information shown.

Part 2: Modeling the Effects of pH Changes

In the next part of this investigation, you will model how the change in pH of ocean water affects organisms with calcium carbonate shells. Because the change is relatively slow compared to the time available for your investigation, you will model the effects using vinegar, which is more acidic than ocean water. You can also use chalk, which is made of calcium carbonate but is less dense than most seashells.

POSSIBLE MATERIALS

- indirectly vented chemical splash goggles, nonlatex apron, nitrile gloves
- beaker, 250 mL (2)

- chalk
- distilled vinegar
- hand lens

- pH indicator or probe
- seashells
- water

SAFETY INFORMATION

- Wear indirectly vented chemical splash goggles, a nonlatex apron, and nitrile gloves during the setup, hands-on, and takedown segments of the activity.

- Immediately wipe up any spilled water on the floor so it does not become a slip/fall hazard.

indirectly vented
chemical splash
goggles

PLAN THE INVESTIGATION

Design your own investigation that safely models the effects of pH change on the shells of marine organisms. Think about how you can model ocean acidification and what kinds of observations would indicate a change in calcium carbonate. Write a procedure for your investigation, develop a data collection plan, write a safety plan, and list all the materials you will need. Identify your control, variables, and how you will measure change in your investigation. Your teacher must approve your plans before you begin.

ANALYZE

In your Evidence Notebook, explain whether you think your investigation accurately tested the effects of pH on calcium carbonate. Explain why or why not, citing evidence from the investigation. How could you improve your investigation?

CONSTRUCT AN EXPLANATION

Using evidence from your investigation, explain why a decrease in pH results in a change in the carbonate equilibrium system.

When shells are exposed to acid, their carbonate ions become part of an equilibrium reaction, represented by the equilibrium equation: $HCO_3^- \rightleftharpoons H^+ + CO_3^{2-}$. The pH decreases when the bicarbonate | carbonate | hydrogen ion concentration increases. As a result, the equilibrium shifts toward the reactants | products, which causes the bicarbonate | carbonate | hydrogen ion concentration in solution to decrease.

DRAW CONCLUSIONS

Claim Make a claim explaining why the calcium carbonate shells and skeletons of marine organisms deteriorate with increased levels of atmospheric carbon dioxide.

Evidence Use evidence from the two parts of this investigation to support your claim.

Reasoning Describe how the evidence you gave supports your claim. What would happen if a marine organism affected by ocean acidification were placed into ocean water with normal pH? Would its shell grow back?

_____

_____

_____

_____

_____

_____

_____

_____

 Evidence Notebook Think about the results of the two parts of your investigation. How do your observations help explain what is happening in the images of the pteropod shells and coral skeletons?

Shifting Equilibrium Concentration

As in the example of carbon dioxide in water, many chemical systems in nature and industrial chemistry involve systems of chemical reactions in equilibrium. The equilibrium states are "dynamic," meaning they can be shifted to form more or less products. Let's consider another equilibrium system as a model for the principles of chemical equilibrium. Adding water or hydrochloric acid to a cobalt(II) chloride, $CoCl_2$, solution causes the color of the solution to change. The ions and molecules in solution are constantly reacting in forward and reverse reactions. The $CoCl_2$ equilibrium system is modeled by the equation:

$$[Co(H_2O)_6]^{2+}(aq) + 4Cl^-(aq) \rightleftharpoons [CoCl_4]^{2-}(aq) + 6H_2O(l)$$

Pink   Blue

When the solution has a higher concentration of $[Co(H_2O)_6]^{2+}$ ions, it appears pink. When the solution has a higher concentration of $[CoCl_4]^{2-}$ ions, it appears blue. Figure 4 shows the color changes when hydrochloric acid and water are added.

FIGURE 4: The cobalt(II) chloride solution changes color when HCl and water are added. **Explore Online ▶**

a   Initially, the solution is pink.

b   After HCl is added the solution turns blue.

c   Adding water turns the solution pink again.

GATHER EVIDENCE Using evidence from Figure 4, explain what happens to the product and reactant concentrations when hydrochloric acid or water is added to the system.

_____

_____

_____

Adding Reactants or Products

The cobalt(II) chloride equilibrium reaction is reversible. Figure 4a shows that when the solution is in equilibrium, it is pink. In Figure 4b hydrochloric acid is added. This adds chloride ions, a reactant, to the solution. This disrupts the equilibrium and causes it to shift. As a result, the solution turns blue, indicating that there are more $[CoCl_4]^{2-}$ ions, a product. In Figure 4c water, a product, is added. Again the equilibrium is disrupted and shifts. The solution turns from blue back to pink. This indicates that the solution now contains more $[Co(H_2O)_6]^{2+}$ ions, a reactant.

EXPLAIN Why does adding more reactant or product to an equilibrium system cause the equilibrium concentrations to shift?

Adding more reactant increases the frequency of collisions between product | reactant particles, which shifts the reaction in favor of the products | reactants. Adding more product increases the frequency of collisions between product | reactant particles, which shifts the reaction in favor of the products | reactants.

Figure 5 shows that the cobalt(II) chloride system reaches equilibrium when the forward and reverse reactions occur at the same rate. The concentrations do not change at equilibrium, so the graph shows a straight, horizontal line. Water is not shown in Figure 5 because the concentration of water remains approximately constant.

Addition of HCl to the CoCl₂ System

FIGURE 5: The concentrations in the cobalt(II) chloride equilibrium system change with the addition of hydrochloric acid.

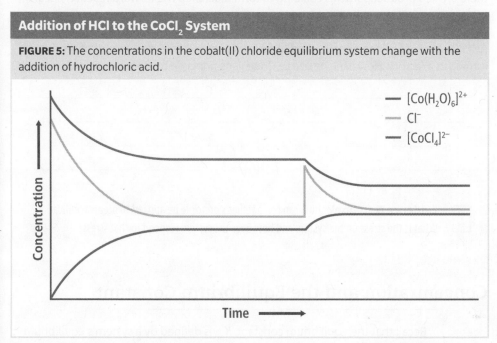

— $[Co(H_2O)_6]^{2+}$
— Cl^-
— $[CoCl_4]^{2-}$

Concentration

Time

The sharp increase in the Cl^- line indicates when hydrochloric acid was added. The system is no longer in equilibrium, and the forward reaction occurs at a faster rate than the reverse reaction, producing more product. This continues until new equilibrium concentrations are established, modeled as straight, horizontal lines on the graph.

ANALYZE Why is at least one reactant species not completely consumed during the reaction? Use evidence from the graph and reaction rates to support your claims.

_____

_____

_____

_____

During an equilibrium reaction, as some reactants are converted to products, some products are also being converted to reactants. Adding a reactant increases the collisions between reactant particles, so the rate of the forward reaction increases. This disrupts the dynamic equilibrium. As more reactants are converted to products, the forward reaction will slow because there are less reactant particles colliding. At the same time, because the concentration of product particles increases, the rate of the reverse reaction will increase. Eventually, the rates will equalize at a new equilibrium position. The opposite shift occurs with the addition of a product.

Removing Reactants or Products

The disruption of an equilibrium system places stress on the system. Le Châtelier's principle states that when an equilibrium system is stressed, the equilibrium will shift in a way that reduces the stress on the system. In the same way adding a reactant or product puts stress on a system, removing a reactant or product also puts a stress on the system. According to Le Châtelier's principle, the system will respond to reduce that stress.

When a reactant is removed from the system, the forward reaction slows, but the reverse reaction occurs at the same rate. This results in more reactants being formed. When a product is removed, the opposite effect is observed. The reverse reaction slows, because there are less product particles colliding to form reactants. The forward reaction occurs at the same rate, so more product is formed.

APPLY A chemical engineer is asked to find a way to increase the amount of product formed in a factory. How can she use Le Châtelier's principle to meet these new demands?

_____

_____

_____

_____

 Evidence Notebook How can Le Châtelier's principle be applied to ocean acidification? What is the stress on the system and how does the system respond to that stress?

Concentration and the Equilibrium Constant

FIGURE 6: Equilibrium concentrations may change, but K_{eq} is constant with constant temperature.

Recall that the equilibrium constant, K_{eq}, is defined by a system's equilibrium expression, represented by the ratio of the concentrations of the reaction's products over its reactants. For the reaction $aA + bB \rightleftharpoons dD + eE$,

$$K_{eq} = \frac{[D]^d[E]^e}{[A]^a[B]^b}$$

The reaction equation for the cobalt(II) chloride equilibrium system is

$$[Co(H_2O)_6]^{2+}(aq) + 4Cl^-(aq) \rightleftharpoons [CoCl_4]^{2-}(aq) + 6H_2O(l)$$

The equilibrium expression for this reaction is written as:

$$K_{eq} = \frac{[[CoCl_4]^{2-}]}{[[Co(H_2O)_6]^{2+}][Cl^-]^4}$$

Recall that water is not included in the expression because the concentration is approximately constant.

 Collaborate Using the equilibrium equation, explain how the concentrations of reactants and products will change when the concentration of chloride ions increases. With a partner, discuss what happens during the forward and reverse reactions when the concentration changes. Why does K_{eq} remain the same?

Le Châtelier's principle can be modeled mathematically using the equilibrium expression. Changing concentrations does not change the value of K_{eq}. When the concentration of one reactant is increased, the concentration of the other reactant decreases as the particles collide. This increases the concentration of the products. These changes result in the same value of K_{eq}. Increasing the concentration of a product causes the concentration of other products to decrease as they react to form reactants. This increases the concentration of reactants. The value of K_{eq} does not change.

Measuring Ocean pH

To learn more about ocean acidification, scientists must study how concentrations of hydrogen ions and other molecules change over time. These scientists need to collect data over a long period of time in order to observe trends. It is also valuable to have data from many locations collected simultaneously and frequently. Because it is not possible to visit the sites and collect samples physically, ocean researchers use buoys to monitor pH changes. The buoy's outer housing contains a self-operating laboratory, and it is anchored to the sea floor so it does not move. Devices in this portable lab sample the water from the ocean, analyze the results, and send a report to the home base. Computers combine this data from multiple sampling stations with other types of environmental tests. Scientists then draw conclusions about changes in the ocean and their causes based on this evidence.

FIGURE 7: Although this research buoy looks like a navigation buoy, it has a very different purpose.

Along coasts around the world, including the coast of California, you can see these floating labs. They do not always look much different from other buoys used for purposes such as navigation, but their designs are very different. A buoy used for monitoring the ocean environment must house sensitive instruments, as well as their power sources and communication systems. Salt water can be very corrosive, so special considerations must be taken when choosing the materials to build the buoys. The data they collect must be extremely precise and accurate. A pH change of 0.1 units in ocean water can have a significant effect on the carbonate cycle because this indicates nearly a 30% increase in acidity. In addition to the pH measurement itself, the instruments must accurately record the water temperature because temperature variations can affect the measured pH value.

DESIGN What are some of the criteria and constraints that an engineer would have to consider when designing a buoy to house an ocean pH lab?

_____

_____

_____

 Evidence Notebook Make a claim about how a change in the concentration of carbonate ions in ocean water could affect the calcium carbonate shells of marine organisms.

Changes in Pressure

Nitrogen dioxide, a brown gas, and dinitrogen tetroxide, a colorless gas, exist in an equilibrium system as modeled by the equation:

$$2NO_2(g) \rightleftharpoons N_2O_4(g)$$

Nitrogen dioxide gives the system its color. When more nitrogen dioxide is present, the gas is a darker reddish-brown. When more dinitrogen tetroxide is present, that means less nitrogen dioxide is present, so the gas is a very light brown color.

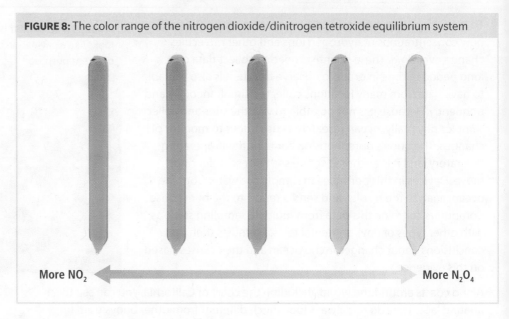

FIGURE 8: The color range of the nitrogen dioxide/dinitrogen tetroxide equilibrium system

More NO$_2$ ⟷ More N$_2$O$_4$

Gas Kinetics and Equilibrium

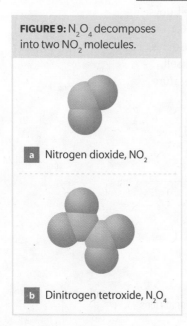

FIGURE 9: N$_2$O$_4$ decomposes into two NO$_2$ molecules.

a Nitrogen dioxide, NO$_2$

b Dinitrogen tetroxide, N$_2$O$_4$

Figure 9 shows the NO$_2$ and N$_2$O$_4$ molecules. When a molecule of NO$_2$ collides with another NO$_2$ molecule, a molecule of N$_2$O$_4$ may form. In the equilibrium system, N$_2$O$_4$ continuously decomposes into two molecules of NO$_2$. Increasing or decreasing the pressure on the system puts a stress on the system. Le Châtelier's principle predicts that the equilibrium will shift in a way that counteracts this stress.

Recall that, for any gas at a given temperature and pressure, the same number of molecules occupies the same volume. And volume and pressure are inversely related. So decreasing the volume of a gas or gas mixture at constant temperature increases the pressure of a system because the gas molecules collide more frequently with the container they are in.

Nitrogen dioxide and dinitrogen tetroxide form an equilibrium system that contains both gases. When the NO$_2$/N$_2$O$_4$ equilibrium system is sealed in a syringe at room temperature and atmospheric pressure, the gas appears light brown. Compressing the syringe causes the gas color to initially darken as the concentration increases and then return to the light-brown color as the equilibrium is reestablished. Figure 10 shows this change.

FIGURE 10: The color changes in the NO_2/N_2O_4 gaseous equilibrium system within a syringe

Explore Online ▶

| a Initial pressure | b Compressed—initial | c Compressed—final | d Return to initial pressure |

MODEL Make a drawing that shows what is happening inside the syringe on a molecular level. For each stage, show the relative concentrations of each species and how they are changing or staying the same.

In the initial state, Figure 10a, the two gases are at equilibrium. When the syringe is initially compressed in Figure 10b, the ratio of the gases remains the same, but the mixture appears darker. This is because the concentration of NO_2, the source of the color, has increased. However, NO_2 molecules now react faster than they are formed, producing more N_2O_4. Eventually, a new equilibrium is established, shown in Figure 10c. The lighter color indicates the equilibrium shifted to produce more product, N_2O_4.

PREDICT When the plunger is drawn back in the syringe, why does the equilibrium shift back towards the reactant, NO_2?

_____

_____

_____

Gas Concentrations and Equilibrium

The concentrations of nitrogen dioxide/dinitrogen tetroxide change when the pressure changes from an initial pressure, P_1, to a new pressure, P_2. At the instant the pressure increases to P_2, the concentrations of both gases increase before the equilibrium shifts. Then, the gas concentrations stabilize at the new equilibrium position associated with P_2.

FIGURE 11: The concentrations of the NO_2/N_2O_4 equilibrium system change when the pressure on the system changes.

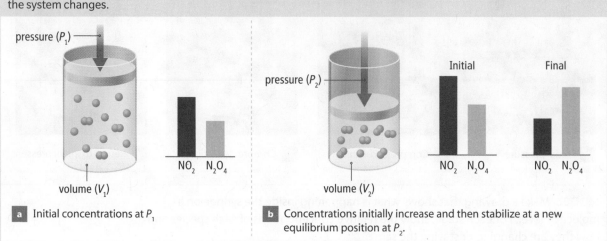

a Initial concentrations at P_1

b Concentrations initially increase and then stabilize at a new equilibrium position at P_2.

APPLY What can you conclude about the changes that occur in the nitrogen dioxide/dinitrogen tetroxide equilibrium system when the pressure on the system changes?

○ **a.** An increase in pressure results in a shift toward NO_2 because the reverse reaction increases the number of NO_2 particles in the container.

○ **b.** An increase in pressure does not change the ratio of NO_2 and N_2O_4 because the system remains in equilibrium when the number of particles is constant.

○ **c.** An increase in pressure results in a shift toward N_2O_4 because the forward reaction reduces the number of particles in the container.

For every molecule of N_2O_4 there are two molecules of NO_2 in the balanced chemical equation. Increasing the pressure of the system increases the partial pressures of both gases, increasing their concentrations. This results in particles colliding more frequently with one another and with the sides of the container. As the rate of collisions increases, the rate of the forward reaction increases. This means more NO_2 particles react, shifting the equilibrium toward the product, N_2O_4. This causes the color of the system to change from dark to light brown.

EXPLAIN Complete the statements by selecting the correct terms.

When pressure increases, the equilibrium shifts toward the side of the reaction with a greater | fewer number of moles of gas. This is because more reaction collisions occur on the side of the reaction equation with a greater | fewer number of moles of gas.

When a gaseous equilibrium system has an unbalanced number of moles in the reactants and products, a change in pressure will change the forward and reverse reaction rates. At higher pressures, the side of the reaction with more particles has more frequent molecular collisions and proceeds at a faster rate. This increases the number of moles of gas on the opposite side of the reaction. This shift continues until the forward and reverse rates are balanced and equilibrium is reached.

Equilibrium in the Earth System

Scientists are able to measure past levels of carbon dioxide in the atmosphere by determining the concentration of carbon dioxide in air bubbles trapped in ice cores. Figure 12 shows that, over the past 400 000 years, carbon dioxide levels fluctuated within a relatively stable range. In the last century, however, carbon dioxide in the atmosphere increased significantly. Human combustion of fossil fuels and destruction of vegetation altered the equilibrium of carbon dioxide in the atmosphere and the hydrosphere.

Historical Carbon Dioxide Levels

FIGURE 12: Atmospheric carbon dioxide levels fluctuated in the past, but increased significantly in recent years.

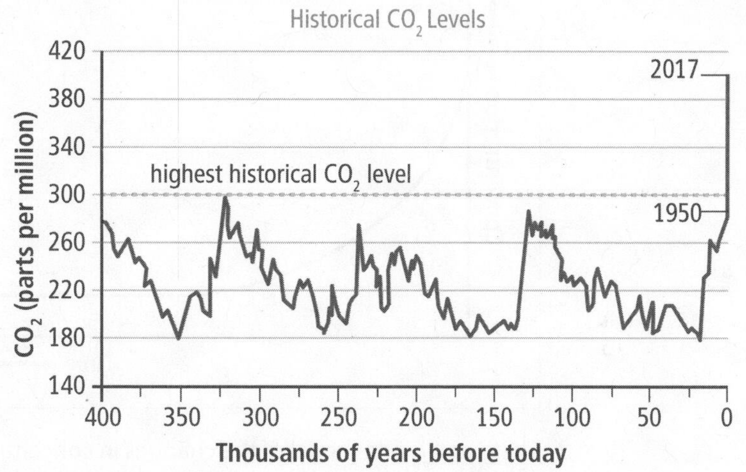

Earth is a closed system. There is no significant gain or loss of matter between Earth and outside sources. Although the total amount of matter on Earth does not change, it does cycle within various parts of the system. Some carbon dioxide fluctuations over long periods of time could be the result of carbon dioxide levels in the ocean and atmosphere cycling as temperatures vary on the planet. Other carbon dioxide fluctuations may be the result of changes in the biosphere or massive volcanic eruptions. The recent increase outside the historical range is due to a change in human activity. As humans burn fossil fuels, large amounts of carbon previously bound beneath Earth's surface are released into the atmosphere as carbon dioxide.

GATHER EVIDENCE Which statements are supported by evidence shown on the graph? Select all correct answers.

☐ **a.** The level of CO_2 was constant until the past century.

☐ **b.** There are patterns in historical CO_2 levels.

☐ **c.** The recent change in CO_2 levels represents an increase that is unlikely to drop.

☐ **d.** The recent increase in CO_2 levels indicates a stress on the equilibrium system.

EXPLAIN How is the change in carbon dioxide level in the atmosphere related to ocean acidification? How does the graph support the fact that ocean acidification is a problem caused by humans?

_____

_____

_____

_____

_____

Gas Concentrations and the Equilibrium Constant

Changing pressure affects the equilibrium of gaseous systems by affecting the reactant and product concentrations. The graph below shows the abrupt change in concentrations in the NO_2/N_2O_4 equilibrium system when the pressure on the system is increased.

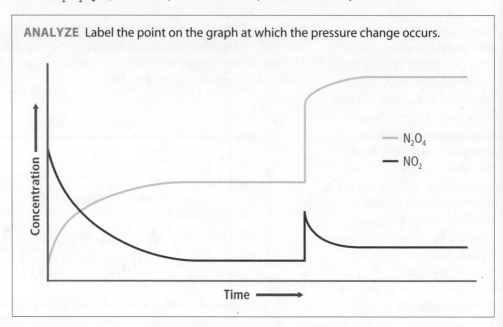

ANALYZE Label the point on the graph at which the pressure change occurs.

The graph is one model of the changes in concentration in the equilibrium system. Another model of the system is the equilibrium expression that describes the equilibrium state of the system:

$$K_{eq} = \frac{[N_2O_4]}{[NO_2]^2}$$

EXPLAIN Using the graph and the equilibrium expression, explain how a change in pressure results in an equilibrium shift.

An increase in the pressure on the system causes a decrease | an increase in the concentrations of NO_2 | N_2O_4 | both gases in the system. However, the change in concentration of NO_2 results in a positive | negative change in the denominator of the equilibrium expression, shifting the equilibrium system in favor of NO_2 | N_2O_4 .

Other Equilibrium Systems Involving Gases

Gaseous equilibrium systems are not limited to those containing gases alone. Many systems also involve liquids and solids. Syngas is a fuel-gas mixture made of hydrogen gas and carbon monoxide. It is used in combustion engines and as an intermediate in the production of many other chemicals. It is even used as an intermediate in the production of synthetic natural gas.

Syngas can be produced when water vapor comes into contact with red-hot carbon. The following equilibrium is established:

$$H_2O(g) + C(s) \rightleftharpoons H_2(g) + CO(g)$$

SOLVE Complete the equilibrium expression for the reaction by writing the correct variables in the equation.

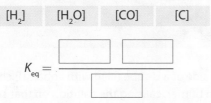

$[H_2]$ $[H_2O]$ $[CO]$ $[C]$

$$K_{eq} = \frac{\boxed{}\ \boxed{}}{\boxed{}}$$

FIGURE 13: A coke oven produces syngas, a mix of hydrogen and carbon monoxide.

PREDICT How do you think changes in pressure affect the syngas equilibrium system?

_____

_____

_____

Pure liquids and solids are not included in an equilibrium expression because their concentrations are not affected by a change in pressure. An increase in pressure on the syngas reaction system will shift the equilibrium toward the reactants. A decrease in pressure will shift the equilibrium toward the products.

 Collaborate With a partner, discuss what will happen if an inert gas is introduced to a gaseous equilibrium system and the volume is kept constant.

Adding an inert gas to a reaction vessel increases the overall pressure on the system but does not cause a shift in the equilibrium when the volume of the system is kept constant. As the inert gas increases the total pressure, the partial pressures of each gas in the system are unchanged. Therefore, the concentrations of the reacting gases are unchanged. For this reason, no shift in reaction concentrations results from the addition of an inert gas to a gaseous equilibrium system.

 Evidence Notebook Increasing the amount of carbon dioxide in the atmosphere increases the carbon dioxide pressure as a fraction of the overall atmospheric pressure. Do you think this pressure change affects the concentration of dissolved carbon dioxide in the ocean?

Changes in Temperature

The temperature on one side of a U-tube filled with cobalt(II) chloride solution was increased using a Bunsen burner, causing the solution on that side to turn blue.

FIGURE 14: Energy in the form of heat is applied to the cobalt(II) chloride solution.

Explore Online ▶

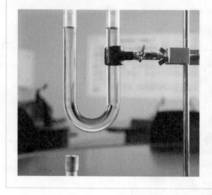 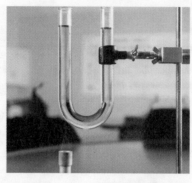 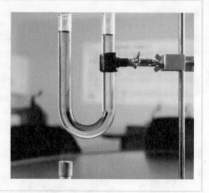

👥 **Collaborate** With a partner, discuss what is happening on a molecular scale to cause the color on one side of the U-tube to change when the temperature increased.

Temperature and Reversible Reactions

FIGURE 15: Endothermic and exothermic equilibrium systems

 The $CoCl_2$ system is endothermic.

b The NO_2/N_2O_4 system is exothermic.

The cobalt(II) chloride equilibrium reaction is endothermic:

$$\text{energy} + [Co(H_2O)_6]^{2+}(aq) + 4Cl^-(aq) \rightleftharpoons [CoCl_4]^{2-}(aq) + 6H_2O(l)$$

As shown in Figure 15a, when the temperature increases in this reaction, the solution turns blue. When the temperature decreases, the solution turns pink.

The nitrogen dioxide/dinitrogen tetroxide equilibrium system is an exothermic reaction:

$$2NO_2(g) \rightleftharpoons N_2O_4(g) + \text{energy}$$

As shown in Figure 15b, when the temperature increases in this reaction, the system turns darker brown. When the temperature decreases, the system becomes lighter.

APPLY How does equilibrium shift when energy is added?

For an endothermic reaction, adding energy in the form of heat shifts the reaction towards the products | reactants. In the $CoCl_2$ system, adding energy formed more $[CoCl_4]^{2-}$ | $[Co(H_2O)_6]^{2+}$, causing the solution to turn blue.

For an exothermic reaction, adding energy shifts the reaction towards the products | reactants. In the NO_2/N_2O_4 system, adding energy formed more NO_2 | N_2O_4.

The effect of adding or removing energy as heat from an equilibrium system can be predicted by considering energy as a product or reactant. For an endothermic reaction, energy can be modeled as a reactant. Adding energy has the same effect as increasing the concentration of a reactant. Le Châtelier's principle predicts this will shift the equilibrium in favor of the products. Removing energy, like removing a reactant, shifts the reaction in favor of the reactants.

For an exothermic reaction, energy can be modeled as a product. Adding energy has the same effect as increasing the concentration of a product. The equilibrium shifts in favor of the reactants. Removing energy, like removing a product, shifts the equilibrium in favor of the products.

Temperature and the Equilibrium Constant

Modifying the temperature of a system changes the average kinetic energy of the particles. This changes the number of effective collisions between molecules in the system. Recall that K_{eq} is temperature-dependent. Adding or removing energy in the form of heat establishes a new equilibrium position. The new position is described by the equilibrium constant associated with the new temperature.

Changing the Temperature of CoCl$_2$

FIGURE 16: The cobalt(II) chloride solution is initially at room temperature. Changing the temperature of the solution causes a change in the equilibrium concentrations.

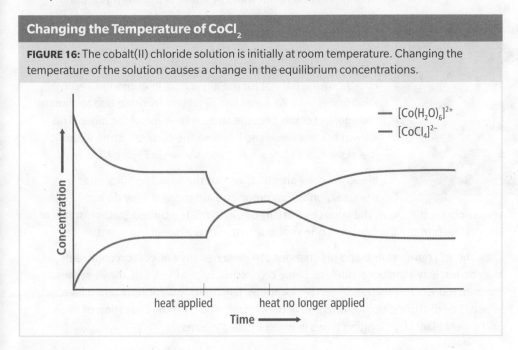

ANALYZE Based on the graph which of the following statements are true? Select all correct answers.

☐ **a.** While heat is applied, a new equilibrium position is established.

☐ **b.** The equilibrium constant does not change during the experiment.

☐ **c.** Increasing the temperature shifts the equilibrium toward $[CoCl_4]^{2-}$.

☐ **d.** When heat was no longer applied, the equilibrium returned to its original state.

Adding energy increases the concentration of $[CoCl_4]^{2-}$ in the solution. The reaction mixture changes from pink to blue. This new equilibrium position can be maintained only as long as energy is added. When the solution is no longer heated, it changes from blue back to pink as it returns to its original temperature. When energy is allowed to dissipate, the equilibrium system shifts back to its original position associated with the original K_{eq}.

The equilibrium position, along with the value of K_{eq}, was continuously changing while heat was being applied until it reached a new stable equilibrium position. The equilibrium position and its associated K_{eq} also changed constantly when heat was no longer being applied until it reached its original room temperature state. Then the concentrations returned to their original equilibrium.

 Collaborate Photochemical smog is a type of air pollution often seen in the Los Angeles basin. Nitrogen oxides, including nitrogen dioxide, are key components of smog. Nitrogen dioxide is responsible for the characteristic brown color of smog. With a partner, research photochemical smog. What effect does temperature have on smog? How does smog affect human health?

 Stability and Change

Temperature and Changing Oceans

FIGURE 17: Bleached coral

Changes in pH are not the only effect of increasing carbon dioxide in the atmosphere on ocean life. Most corals display a range of colors, including brown, orange, red, yellow, and occasionally blue or green. The color comes not from the coral polyps, but from algae that live in the reef community. The corals provide habitat for the algae and, in exchange, receive food from them. As water temperatures increase due to climate change, the corals become stressed and expel the algae. This is known as *coral bleaching* because the coral structure without the algae has a stark white color, shown in Figure 17.

Bleached coral are still alive, but the bleaching increases the stress on the community even more. If they do not reincorporate the algae, the corals eventually die. In 2005, the United States lost half of its coral reefs in the Caribbean in one year due to a massive bleaching event.

Even though temperature and pH changes can have negative effects on coral reefs, they do not leave the ocean lifeless. Some organisms, such as jellyfish, thrive in these warmer, more acidic waters. In certain locations, jellyfish populations reached levels at which they disrupted ecosystems and actually interfered with the operation of ships and power plants by clogging pipes in water intake systems.

EXPLAIN How do increasing global temperatures due to climate change affect the natural equilibria between Earth's atmosphere, hydrosphere, and biosphere? How do human activities need to change to keep these equilibria in balance?

_____

_____

_____

 Evidence Notebook Discuss how an equilibrium system responds to changes in concentration, pressure, and temperature, as well as how each type of change affects the value of K_{eq}. How might changes in concentration and temperature affect the shells of marine organisms?

Engineering
Catalysts and Equilibrium

Ammonia is produced industrially by reacting nitrogen and hydrogen:

$$N_2(g) + 3H_2(g) \rightleftharpoons 2NH_3(g)$$

Ammonia is one of the top industrially produced, inorganic chemicals in the world. The majority of it is used directly or indirectly as agricultural fertilizer to increase crop yields. Without ammonia-based fertilizers, mass starvation would be more common. Under normal conditions, the reaction that produces ammonia proceeds too slowly to obtain a significant amount of product. Scientists and engineers need a way to increase the rate of this reaction.

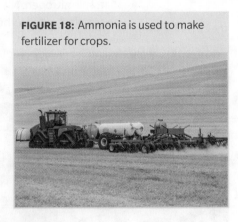

FIGURE 18: Ammonia is used to make fertilizer for crops.

REACTION RATES AND CONCENTRATION

The mechanism of a reaction can be altered by adding a *catalyst*, a substance that changes the rate of the reaction without being consumed or changed significantly. The addition of a catalyst speeds up the overall rate of a reaction for both the forward and the reverse reactions in an equilibrium system. The graph below shows that equilibrium is reached faster in the presence of a catalyst.

MODEL Draw two additional lines showing how the equilibrium reaction will proceed when a more efficient catalyst is present.

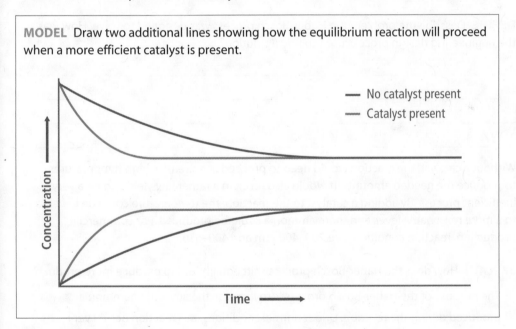

— No catalyst present
— Catalyst present

Concentration

Time ➝

INFER How does a catalyst affect an equilibrium system? Each answer choice may be used more than once. Some answer choices may not be used at all.

| increases | decreases | does not change |

The addition of a catalyst to an equilibrium system _____ the rate of the forward reaction and _____ the rate of the reverse reaction. The equilibrium concentration of each product and reactant _____ with the addition of a catalyst to an equilibrium system.

MAXIMIZING AMMONIA PRODUCTION

Nitrogen compounds are an essential part of fertilizer for agriculture because nitrogen is needed by plants to grow. Despite its abundance in the atmosphere, relatively few organisms are able to extract and chemically break apart the strongly triple-bonded, diatomic nitrogen. Nitrogen is therefore a limiting reactant for plant growth and must be supplemented in human agriculture.

FIGURE 19: Chemical plants worldwide produce over 140 million metric tons of ammonia per year.

The German chemist Fritz Haber developed the method for converting hydrogen and nitrogen to ammonia by using high pressure and catalysts. Knowing how to control the reaction was not enough, though. In order to satisfy the demand for ammonia, a large-scale process was needed. Another German chemist, Carl Bosch, engineered the production facilities needed to produce ammonia in sufficient amounts.

The Haber-Bosch process was the first industrial chemical process to use high pressure for a chemical reaction. Nitrogen from the air is combined with hydrogen under extremely high pressures and high temperatures. Ammonia is removed as soon as it is formed to shift the equilibrium toward the product.

DEFINE Describe the problem the Haber-Bosch process was designed to solve. How was the engineering design process used to find a solution?

_____

_____

_____

_____

Without a catalyst, the reaction would need to proceed at extremely high temperatures to produce the needed amounts. It would also result in a rather low yield and be a very inefficient process. By adding a catalyst to the reaction, the temperature could be lowered to a more reasonable level, and more ammonia could be produced. For commercial production, reaction conditions are 200–400 atm and 400–650 °C.

EXPLAIN How does the Haber-Bosch process shift equilibrium to produce more product?

The purpose of the Haber-Bosch process is to increase the amount of ammonia produced during the reaction. Under normal conditions, this reaction occurs very slowly | quickly. A catalyst is added to decrease | increase the rate of the equilibrium reaction. By decreasing | increasing the pressure of the reaction system, the equilibrium shifts in favor of ammonia production. Ammonia is added to | removed from the system as it is produced to shift the equilibrium reaction in favor of producing more ammonia.

 Evidence Notebook How can catalysts be used to shift an equilibrium reaction? Explain how this knowledge helped engineers develop the Haber-Bosch process and solve a global challenge.

Careers in Science

Environmental Chemist

Human activities can cause changes in the environment. Environmental chemists study the causes and effects of these changes at both the molecular and societal scales, and recommend solutions when those changes are detrimental. They study the effects of human pollution on systems as small as the area around a manufacturing plant and as large as the atmosphere and oceans. Environmental chemists work with other scientists and engineers to identify and solve environmental problems.

FIGURE 20: Environmental chemists help clean oil spills.

Environmental chemists study the impact human pollution has on plants, animals, and ecosystems. They are often called upon during environmental emergencies to test water, air, or soil samples and determine the extent of the damage. This information helps contain the emergency, such as a ship leaking oil in the ocean or a spill of industrial or agricultural chemicals. Environmental chemists also help determine the procedure for containing the emergency and neutralizing or minimizing the damage.

Projects involving environmental chemistry extend beyond response to a single event. Over the last few decades, the air quality in many large cities in the United States has improved significantly. An understanding of the chemistry of the atmosphere and of the interactions between the atmosphere and contaminants from burning fossil fuels led to many practices that reduced pollution. Environmental chemists played a large role in developing that understanding.

Chemists play a key role in marine environmental studies as well. The complex chemical interactions within and between the atmosphere and the hydrosphere are only partially understood, and there is still much more to learn. Environmental chemists work to understand the natural processes within these environmental systems and to determine the effect of human activities on Earth's systems.

While some environmental chemists may spend a lot of time in the field or at sea, collecting samples, they also work in a laboratory analyzing data and drawing conclusions from their findings. For a given project, problem, or even large-scale environmental disaster, environmental chemists use a scientific approach to find an explanation.

Environmental chemistry does not only focus on reacting to environmental pollution, but it aims to proactively prevent future problems. Environmental chemists seek to develop sustainable methods to reduce, reuse, and recycle matter, conserve energy, and reduce pollution by aligning human-engineered systems with natural systems.

Chemistry in Your Community Research an environmental chemist from a diverse background who studies environmental issues in California. If possible, conduct a personal interview with the scientist. Learn about the scientist's background, what experiences influenced the chemist's decision to work in environmental chemistry, and how the chemist's work affects California communities.

CARBON RESERVOIRS | EQUILIBRIUM IN THE HUMAN BODY | SHIFTING EQUILIBRIUM | Go online to choose one of these other paths.

Lesson Self-Check

CAN YOU EXPLAIN IT?

FIGURE 21: The shells of pteropods and other marine organisms deteriorate with increasing atmospheric carbon dioxide levels.

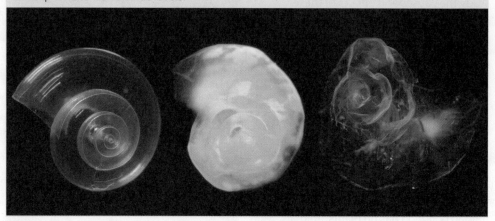

Dramatic changes can occur to marine organisms when they are not able to build or maintain their calcium carbonate shells or skeletons. This phenomenon has been observed in many species of marine organisms from around the world. The deterioration of shells has increased dramatically as the concentration of carbon dioxide in the atmosphere has increased over time, and it appears to be accelerating.

There is a strong correlation between the increase in atmospheric carbon dioxide and the damage to coral colonies. Scientists have established that there is a clear cause-and-effect relationship between the human production of carbon dioxide and the decline of coral reefs around the world. When carbon dioxide levels increase, marine organisms are not able to add to their carbonate shells. These organisms are also losing the carbonate ions that are in their shells, causing the deterioration shown in Figure 21.

 Evidence Notebook Refer to your notes in your Evidence Notebook to construct an explanation describing why increasing atmospheric carbon dioxide levels causes marine organisms to lose calcium carbonate from their shells and skeletons. Your explanation should include a discussion of the equilibrium chemistry of the ocean carbonate cycle. Using this information, answer the following questions:

1. How could the change in carbon dioxide in the atmosphere affect the ability of marine organisms to build calcium carbonate shells?
2. What evidence supports your claim? How can a change in atmospheric composition affect the chemistry of the ocean?
3. How does the interaction of the atmosphere and the ocean support your explanation for the loss of calcium carbonate in the shells and skeletons of marine organisms?

CHECKPOINTS

Check Your Understanding

1. Increasing the concentration of a reactant in an equilibrium system
   - a. shifts the equilibrium toward the products.
   - b. shifts the equilibrium toward the reactants.
   - c. does not shift the equilibrium.

2. Decreasing the concentration of a reactant in an equilibrium system
   - a. shifts the equilibrium toward the products.
   - b. shifts the equilibrium toward the reactants.
   - c. does not shift the equilibrium.

3. Increasing the temperature of an exothermic equilibrium system
   - a. shifts the equilibrium toward the products.
   - b. shifts the equilibrium toward the reactants.
   - c. does not shift the equilibrium.

4. Decreasing the temperature of an endothermic equilibrium system
   - a. shifts the equilibrium toward the products.
   - b. shifts the equilibrium toward the reactants.
   - c. does not shift the equilibrium.

5. Why does adding a catalyst to an equilibrium system not change the concentration of reactants or products? Select all correct answers.
   - a. The reaction rates for the forward and reverse reactions do not change.
   - b. The forward reaction rate increases.
   - c. The reverse reaction rate increases.
   - d. The forward reaction rate decreases.
   - e. The reverse reaction rate decreases.

6. Which of the following would result in a change in the value of K_{eq}? Select all correct answers.
   - a. increasing temperature
   - b. increasing the concentration of a product
   - c. decreasing temperature
   - d. decreasing the concentration of a reactant
   - e. increasing the pressure on a gaseous equilibrium system
   - f. adding a catalyst

7. The reaction between hemoglobin (Hb), and oxygen, O_2, in red blood cells is responsible for transporting O_2 to body tissues. This process can be represented by the equilibrium reaction:

$$Hb(aq) + O_2(g) \rightleftharpoons HbO_2(aq)$$

What will happen to the concentration of oxygenated hemoglobin, HbO_2, at high altitude, where the pressure of oxygen is 0.1 atm instead of 0.2 atm, as it is at sea level?

   - a. The concentration of HbO_2 will be more than it is at sea level.
   - b. The concentration of HbO_2 will be less than it is at sea level
   - c. The concentration of HbO_2 will not change.

Use the following information to answer Questions 8 and 9.

Historically, sulfur dioxide (SO_2) generated from the burning of coal has been a major precursor to acid precipitation by way of its conversion to sulfur trioxide (SO_3), and its subsequent reaction with water.

Imagine you have a sealed vessel containing the following equilibrium system:

$$2SO_3(g) \rightleftharpoons 2SO_2(g) + O_2(g)$$

8. How will the equilibrium shift under the following conditions?

   Decreasing the pressure of the container will produce more $SO_3 \mid SO_2 \mid O_2 \mid SO_2$ and O_2.

   Decreasing the volume of the container will produce more $SO_3 \mid SO_2$.

9. If the pressure is increased by adding neon gas to the container, this addition will
   - a. produce more SO_3.
   - b. produce more SO_2 and O_2.
   - c. not affect the equilibrium concentrations.

CHECKPOINTS (continued)

10. Using collision theory and Le Châtelier's principle, explain how ammonia production can be increased by increasing the pressure on the reaction mixture.

_____

_____

_____

_____

11. According to Le Châtelier's principle, how will changes in temperature and changes in pressure affect the equilibrium of the following reaction?

$$CO(g) + 3H_2(g) \rightleftharpoons CH_4(g) + H_2O(g) + energy$$

_____

_____

_____

_____

12. Why is it unlikely that adding dissolved calcium carbonate to the ocean could reverse the effects of carbon dioxide on marine ecosystems?

_____

_____

_____

_____

MAKE YOUR OWN STUDY GUIDE

 In your Evidence Notebook, design a study guide that supports the main ideas from this lesson:

Le Châtelier's principle states that an equilibrium system responds to a stress by shifting the equilibrium in order to relieve that stress.

Stress on the system can be caused by a change in pressure, temperature, or concentration of reactants or products. A catalyst does not shift equilibrium, but it increases the rate of the forward and reverse reactions.

Remember to include the following information in your study guide:
- Use examples that model main ideas.
- Record explanations for the phenomena you investigated.
- Use evidence to support your explanations. Your support can include drawings, data, graphs, laboratory conclusions, and other evidence recorded throughout the lesson.

Consider how the models for equilibrium you have developed in this lesson can be used to analyze the stability and change of many different types of systems.

Engineering Solutions to Ecosystem Disruption

Many organisms in marine ecosystems are affected by ocean acidification.

CAN YOU SOLVE IT?

As oysters form their shells on top of layers of older shells, they form a reef that provides shelter and feeding places for fish, crabs, and other species. Oyster reefs also protect coastlines from storms and tides. Eelgrass growing in the oyster beds stabilizes the bottom of the beds. It also provides additional habitat for organisms in the ecosystem. Oysters filter particles out of the water, which allows light to reach the eelgrass, promoting a healthy ecosystem.

As you observed, increased atmospheric carbon dioxide decreases the pH of ocean water, making oceans more acidic. Oysters are key organisms in their ecosystem. When they are unable to build and maintain their calcium carbonate skeletons, the entire ecosystem may suffer. The effect of ocean acidification on oysters also affects many people that farm oysters as a career. Due to these potential ecological and economical effects, engineers and other groups are developing ways to slow or reverse the effects of ocean acidification.

PREDICT How could you use the engineering design process to develop local and global solutions to reduce the damage happening to oyster beds? What engineering solutions, individual changes, or larger societal changes can be made to mitigate the effects of ocean acidification?

_____

_____

_____

_____

 Evidence Notebook As you explore the lesson, gather evidence to explain how engineering solutions to ecosystem disruption are developed and implemented.

Aquatic Disruptions

Ocean water is slightly basic but decades of observations show that the water is becoming more acidic. The pH scale is logarithmic, so even a small pH change relates to a large change in water chemistry.

 Collaborate With a partner, make a list of questions about the relationship between ocean acidification and ecosystems that depend on oyster beds. What are some possible criteria and constraints to be considered when designing a solution to ocean acidification?

Recall that the engineering design process includes steps to develop or improve technology: defining the problem, defining criteria and constraints, developing solutions, choosing and modeling the most promising ideas, and optimizing solutions. The process relies on continual testing and retesting of results to develop a solution that meets all the constraints.

Local Solutions

FIGURE 1: Kelp can reduce acidification by using carbon dioxide for photosynthesis.

Solutions to ocean acidification can occur on different scales. At the local scale, a coastal community may try various methods to increase ocean pH in their area. These solutions might rely on technologies, or they may rely on something that has been around much longer—photosynthetic organisms. These organisms use carbon dioxide during photosynthesis to form glucose. They use the glucose for energy, or convert it into larger molecules. During photosynthesis, carbon dioxide is removed from the water, shifting the chemical equilibrium and raising the pH.

Growing new or reestablishing beds of kelp or eelgrass can have relatively quick, positive effects on ocean acidification and marine ecology. Even though this solution has benefits, it has some limitations, and even risks. Invasive species can be a problem in water as well as on land. Aquatic organisms must be carefully selected that will enhance, and not disrupt, the local ecosystems, and that will absorb the most carbon dioxide.

APPLY Which statements about biological solutions to ocean acidification are true? Select all correct answers.

- ☐ **a.** Biological solutions have no cost because photosynthetic organisms grow by themselves.

- ☐ **b.** Carbon dioxide is a reactant in photosynthesis, so this solution reduces CO_2 concentration in the atmosphere.

- ☐ **c.** Any photosynthetic organism can be used as part of a solution to ocean acidification.

- ☐ **d.** Carefully chosen species can enhance the environment beyond the effect on ocean acidification.

- ☐ **e.** Planting kelp or eelgrass to reduce ocean acidification also increases habitat.

Ocean acidification can also be addressed using chemical solutions. For example, adding calcium carbonate—limestone—to the ocean causes an increase in the pH of water, making it less acidic. It also increases the ability of the ocean to absorb carbon dioxide from the atmosphere. A major limitation of this solution is that it would take a lot of limestone and a long time to cause a major change in pH. Limestone also must be mined, and mining activities can add carbon dioxide to the atmosphere. It is possible that more carbon dioxide could be added to the atmosphere through mining than the limestone will absorb from the ocean.

FIGURE 2: Limestone is quarried from deposits and transported away for use.

EXPLAIN What effects does calcium carbonate have on ocean acidification? What are potential drawbacks of using calcium carbonate as a solution?

Adding a basic compound, such as calcium carbonate, to acidified water causes a neutralization | precipitation | synthesis reaction that decreases | increases the pH of the water. Drawbacks of the technique include forming areas in water that are too basic for some organisms, and the possibility of reducing the carbon dioxide | oxygen | water level too far. As with other solutions, the effectiveness of chemical treatment is limited by the size | temperature of the ocean.

Another way to increase carbonate in the water is to add ground-up seashells to the ocean. As with limestone, these shells dissolve slowly and neutralize acid. They also provide a surface that oyster larvae and other marine animals can cling to. However, like limestone, it would take a tremendous amount of shells to neutralize acid in large areas.

Unfortunately, even the best engineering solutions to ocean acidification have drawbacks. Consider the size of the open ocean compared to areas near the coasts. Water circulates and moves throughout the ocean, so it must be continually treated. Treatment must be ongoing because the ocean is in equilibrium with the atmosphere. As the concentration of carbon dioxide in the atmosphere continues to increase, the amount of carbon dioxide available for absorption by the ocean also continues to increase.

ARGUE Even a very expensive solution may be the best option if it is a permanent solution. Why would the proposed solutions discussed so far not be permanent solutions?

_____

_____

_____

_____

EVALUATE Why is slowing the rate of or preventing future acidification of the ocean critical, regardless of remediation efforts?

_____

_____

_____

_____

Global Considerations

Ocean acidification is a global, system-level problem that involves the interaction of the atmosphere, hydrosphere, lithosphere, biosphere, and human activities. Ocean water around the world is affected as it interacts with the atmosphere and circulates. Although local solutions to acidification play an important role in protecting or restoring specific ecosystems, engineers must consider the greater problem of pH in the entire ocean in order to design a truly effective solution. Scientists, engineers, and citizens need to think and act both locally and globally.

FIGURE 3: This model shows current oceanic pH levels and predicted pH levels if people reduce or do not reduce atmospheric CO_2 levels.

Explore Online ▶

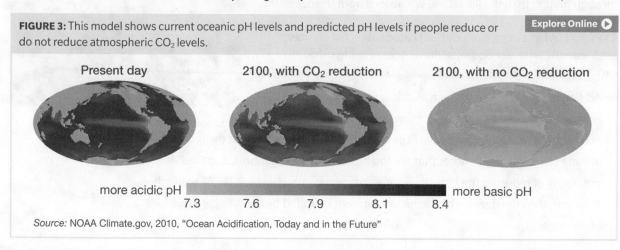

Present day | 2100, with CO_2 reduction | 2100, with no CO_2 reduction

more acidic pH ▬▬▬▬▬▬▬▬▬▬▬▬▬▬ more basic pH

7.3   7.6   7.9   8.1   8.4

Source: NOAA Climate.gov, 2010, "Ocean Acidification, Today and in the Future"

Scientists use known and expected levels of carbon dioxide in the atmosphere to make computer models that project these changes over time. From this and other data, they can determine the pH levels of the ocean. Figure 3 shows a projection of how pH in the ocean might change if humans reduce carbon dioxide emissions significantly, and if emissions continue at the current rate. Because the pH scale is logarithmic, the third map indicates a change in acidity that is three times the current level.

INFER What conclusions can you draw based on data from the model of pH levels? Select all correct answers.

☐ **a.** Adding calcium carbonate to the entire ocean is the only way to increase pH.

☐ **b.** Ocean acidification is a global problem and will require a global solution.

☐ **c.** Continuing carbon dioxide emissions at current levels, with no increase, is a feasible solution to reduce ocean acidification.

☐ **d.** By the end of the century, marine organisms with calcium carbonate shells and skeletons are likely to be stressed throughout the ocean.

☐ **e.** According to Figure 3, the problems shown at the end of the century are inevitable.

FIGURE 4: Upwelling brings water from the deep ocean to the surface.

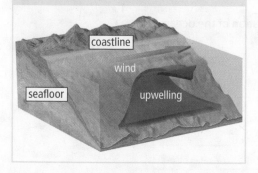

The movement of ocean water also makes ocean acidification a particularly difficult global challenge. Any solution treating ocean water must be applied continuously, because currents move the water between different depths and different locations. For example, winds off the west coast of the United States push warm surface waters away from the coastline, and cold water surges upward from the deep ocean in a process called *upwelling*. Research has indicated that this cold water is also bringing acidified water to the surface, very close to the western coast. Having this acidic water near the shore could help explain observations of changes in the calcium carbonate shells of marine organisms, such as oysters.

Because of ocean currents, such as the ones shown in Figure 5, one city, state, or even a single country will not have the same impact as a global initiative to address the cause of ocean acidification. Once carbon dioxide dissolves in the ocean and the pH lowers, that acidic water can then travel around the world through these ocean currents. So, even if a country is not the cause of carbon dioxide emissions and ocean acidification, they will still have to address the effects of these problems.

FIGURE 5: Carbon dioxide, absorbed by warm surface water, is carried by ocean currents.

Explore Online ▶

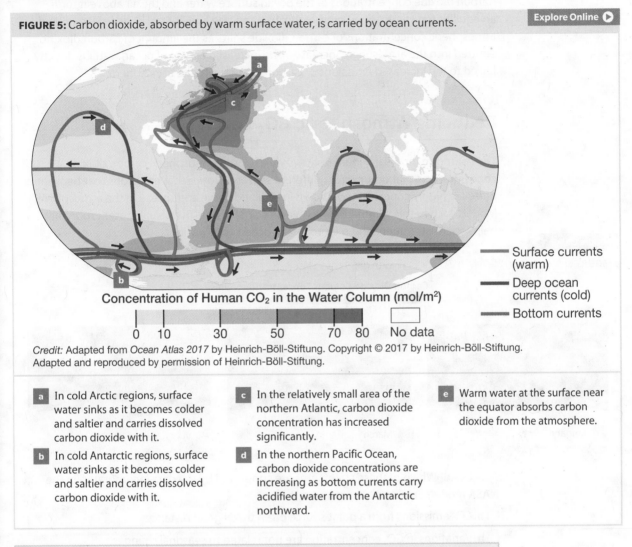

Concentration of Human CO_2 in the Water Column (mol/m²)

0   10   30   50   70 80   No data

— Surface currents (warm)
— Deep ocean currents (cold)
— Bottom currents

Credit: Adapted from *Ocean Atlas 2017* by Heinrich-Böll-Stiftung. Copyright © 2017 by Heinrich-Böll-Stiftung. Adapted and reproduced by permission of Heinrich-Böll-Stiftung.

a In cold Arctic regions, surface water sinks as it becomes colder and saltier and carries dissolved carbon dioxide with it.

b In cold Antarctic regions, surface water sinks as it becomes colder and saltier and carries dissolved carbon dioxide with it.

c In the relatively small area of the northern Atlantic, carbon dioxide concentration has increased significantly.

d In the northern Pacific Ocean, carbon dioxide concentrations are increasing as bottom currents carry acidified water from the Antarctic northward.

e Warm water at the surface near the equator absorbs carbon dioxide from the atmosphere.

 Collaborate With a partner, discuss how the movement of water in ocean currents makes ocean acidification a global problem. Use evidence from the map to support your claims.

A global problem covers the entire Earth and affects people in many different countries. A solution to a global problem, such as ocean acidification, climate change, or pollution by plastic, becomes increasingly effective as more nations participate in the solution. Because the problems are so vast, solutions must be implemented on a global scale. In addition, different countries have different priorities, so achieving such cooperation can be a difficult task.

 Evidence Notebook How does the combination of local and global solutions relate to specific problems such as damage to oyster beds along the western coast of the United States?

Atmospheric Disruptions

Carbon dioxide concentrations of the ocean surface water and the air above it form an equilibrium state. As you previously observed, the equilibrium between ocean and atmospheric concentrations of carbon dioxide shifts as the amount of carbon dioxide emitted into the atmosphere increases. The increased acidity of ocean water is directly linked to the increased emissions of carbon dioxide into the atmosphere.

Reducing Atmospheric CO_2 Levels

The computer model in Figure 6 shows variations in atmospheric carbon dioxide concentrations that occur across different seasons. Notice that emissions that begin at one place are highly concentrated (shown in red) and move and spread in the atmosphere. Models such as this summarize massive amounts of data in a visual presentation that helps scientists understand the process of ocean acidification.

Explore Online ▶

FIGURE 6: Atmospheric levels of CO_2 change with different seasons. Red indicates higher CO_2 concentration.

Carbon Dioxide Column Concentration [ppmv]

377 379 381 383 385 387 389 391 393 395

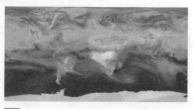

a January   b March   c July

ANALYZE Which of these statements are supported by the data incorporated in the NASA model? Select all correct answers.

☐ **a.** CO_2 emissions from a point source often travel great distances.

☐ **b.** Variations in CO_2 concentration are not related to seasonal changes.

☐ **c.** The highest widespread concentrations of CO_2 occur in the arctic.

☐ **d.** CO_2 concentrations are greatest in areas close to the emission source.

Because carbon dioxide is a greenhouse gas and it affects ocean acidity, reducing carbon dioxide emissions is an important part of mitigating ocean acidification. One method engineers have developed to lower carbon dioxide emissions is through carbon capture and storage (CCS). Most CCS processes capture carbon dioxide produced by burning fossil fuels, such as natural gas and oil. A pipeline is used to move the carbon dioxide into rock several kilometers below the ground.

Good locations for carbon dioxide storage include oil and gas fields (where underground pipes already exist), saline formations where the gas can be absorbed by saltwater, and porous rock formations, such as basalt. Basalt is volcanic rock that includes a number of different minerals. Over time, the carbon dioxide reacts with other molecules in the basalt, forming calcite, dolomite, and other materials. These reactions keep carbon "stored" underground and out of the atmosphere.

CCS has been demonstrated to be an effective way to keep carbon dioxide from being emitted into the atmosphere. There are, however, disadvantages to clean coal technology using CCS. Carbon dioxide is not the only harmful substance released in the combustion of fossil fuels. Even if carbon dioxide is contained, combustion still produces sulfur and nitrogen oxides, as well as releasing heavy metals and other contaminants. The process is very expensive, which limits its application. Another concern is that carbon dioxide stored underground might cause earthquakes, releasing the stored carbon dioxide.

FIGURE 7: Sample of basalt rock

ARGUE Do you think that clean coal technology using capture and storage of carbon dioxide is a feasible solution to problems related to ocean acidification? Why or why not?

_____

_____

_____

_____

Reaching Global Agreements on Climate Change

One of the most difficult parts of addressing global challenges, such as climate change or ocean acidification, is reconciling the interests of many different countries. Solutions to these problems require many nations to work together.

The Kyoto Protocol is an international agreement that sets internationally binding emission reduction targets. During the first commitment period, 2008–2012, a total of 37 countries and the European Community committed to reduce greenhouse gas emissions by an average of 5% compared to the 1990 levels. During the second period, 2013–2020, parties committed to reduce emissions to at least 18% below 1990 levels. The Protocol established a credit trading system that allows countries that exceed these goals to sell credits to countries that do not. The Kyoto Protocol is seen as an important first step towards emission reduction. However, some of the countries responsible for the most greenhouse gas emissions, including the United States, have not agreed to the treaty.

The Paris Agreement is another example of an international agreement that aims to reduce greenhouse gas emissions and climate change. The central aim of the treaty is to strengthen the global response to the threat of climate change. It does this by keeping the change in global temperature below 2 °C above pre-industrial levels. It limits the amount of greenhouse gases emitted by human activity to the same levels that trees, soil, and oceans can absorb naturally, beginning at some point between 2050 and 2100. The agreement went into effect in 2016. By 2017, 178 parties had ratified the agreement.

Language Arts Connection Research the Kyoto Protocol and the Paris Agreement. Prepare a report that explains what they are trying to do, and how countries are trying to achieve the goals. What happens when countries do not participate or fail to meet their goals? How are countries held accountable and how are emission levels monitored?

Identifying Interest Groups

International agreements are the first step toward a global solution to global problems. Because there is a limit to the ability of one country or group of countries to enforce these agreements with others, compliance with international agreements is essentially voluntary. The effectiveness of the agreements depends on a commitment, not only of the governments of the participating countries, but also of their citizens, businesses, and institutions. These parties, or interest groups, are directly affected by the changes that must be made to meet the commitments of international agreements.

FIGURE 8: Involved citizens can urge governments to find solutions.

Solutions must consider all interested parties, including businesses, people whose jobs might be affected, farmers, taxpayers, and the general public. While engineers and policy makers may be able to design a solution to meet the goals of the agreement, such a solution will not help unless it is implemented. Individual citizens making informed consumer and voting choices, including ones that take future generations into account, are a critical part of any solution strategies. There will always be tradeoffs in finding solutions that consider the needs of all interested parties.

 Evidence Notebook Who might be involved in a decision to restrict oyster harvesting for a period of time to allow the oyster population to stabilize from ocean acidification? Write an argument from the position of opposing interest groups that would benefit from or be harmed by such a decision. What tradeoffs might be considered to please both parties?

A solution that reduces carbon dioxide emissions must consider the interests of many parties. For example, companies that generate energy but also produce carbon dioxide emissions have a direct interest in the solution. So do users of the energy, such as manufacturing, transportation, and other industries as well as individuals. Environmental groups and other concerned citizens have a stake in the solution. Farming, fishing, travel, and other sectors of the economy are also interest groups in these solutions. For any given decision, some stakeholders may gain economically and others may lose economically.

 Influence of Engineering, Technology, and Science on Society and the Natural World Individuals are also responsible for increased carbon emissions. Find a carbon footprint calculator and use it to investigate carbon emissions on a larger scale. How do your daily choices affect Earth's carbon budget? What can you do to reduce carbon emissions? Consider ways to use less fossil fuels and to increase the efficiency of the fuels we do use. How can we create win-win solutions for ecology and economics from the individual scale to the international scale?

Explore Online ▶

Hands-On Lab

Identifying Sources of Pollution Investigate common sources of pollution in your home and find ways to mitigate their effects.

Carbon dioxide emissions are not the only form of air pollution. Many cities have frequent episodes of smog, which can cause severe health problems. In the past, smog consisted mainly of particles from smoke mixed with fog, giving the pollution its name. The smog that is currently a problem in cities such as Los Angeles, is a mixture of many different compounds that form when sunlight interacts with nitrogen oxides and other pollutants from the combustion of fossil fuels. Smog becomes worse when temperature conditions trap air over a city for days at a time. During these periods, smog can build and become highly toxic to humans, causing severe sickness.

Smog is a major concern because it can cause a number of health problems. In particular, people with asthma and other chronic illnesses, pregnant women, the very young, and the very old are especially at risk from exposure to smog. In the California south coast area, regulations have reduced smog and ozone levels, reducing the health risk to citizens of southern California. Air pollution remains a problem, as the graph in Figure 9 shows. In the last few years, pollution has actually begun to increase again.

Number of Days that Ozone Exceeds Standards

FIGURE 9: Overall, there has been a significant decrease in pollution over the last half century.

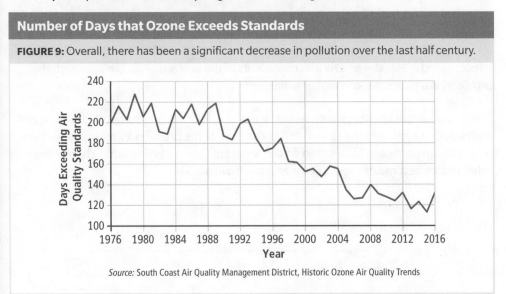

Source: South Coast Air Quality Management District, Historic Ozone Air Quality Trends

EXPLAIN What kinds of interest groups would be affected by a state, such as California, further reducing the amount of air pollution that is considered acceptable?

_____

_____

_____

_____

_____

FIGURE 10: Smog in the atmosphere above Los Angeles

Much of the improvement in air quality is a result of emission standards that apply to cars and other motor vehicles, for which California has led the nation for decades. There are, however, many other potential sources of air pollution that contribute to smog. These include manufacturing industries, oil refineries, diesel trucks, railroads, and ships. Ozone and many other components of smog are not emitted directly. These components form through photochemical reactions in the atmosphere when contaminants are exposed to sunlight. This makes it difficult to determine exactly where the original contaminants came from.

Regulation of air pollution is a complicated process because there are many stakeholders, with many different interests. Solutions do not affect all interested parties the same way. Policymakers and legislators have to balance all of these interests, as well as those of future generations, when they decide on solutions to the problem.

 Evidence Notebook How do increasing atmospheric levels of carbon dioxide influence ocean acidification and marine ecosystems?

Engineering
Designing Solutions

Using the engineering design process, develop one or more possible solutions or strategies that will mitigate the effects of ocean acidification on oyster beds. There are many different ways to approach a solution—the goal is to have a solution that is effective, and meets the criteria and constraints of the problem. You can approach the problem on a local scale or a global scale.

PLAN Brainstorm possible solutions to the ocean acidification-oyster problem. Note how each solution addresses the criteria and constraints of the problem by making a decision matrix to compare each idea. Based on the results of your decision matrix, choose the solution that best meets these criteria and constraints.

_____

_____

_____

_____

FIGURE 11: Engineering design is often most effective as a group endeavor.

DEVELOP A MODEL

Scientists often develop models or prototypes to help them test their designs. The purpose of the model is to test the solution and determine if it is likely to be successful, before proceeding to implementation. Models can be working prototypes of a device, but there are other types of models. Scientists and engineers often use computer simulations as models. A more basic model is a sketch of a design or device that shows how it operates. If the solution is a process, the model could be a flowchart that shows how different parts of the process are related and where decision points occur.

MODEL Determine what type of model is most appropriate for your solution. For example, you can make a sketch, build a physical model, or make a computer model. Brainstorm what your model will accomplish in the space provided.

_____

_____

_____

_____

DEVELOP A TEST

An important part of designing a solution is testing it to obtain data that can be used to optimize the solution. For large engineering solutions, such as mitigating water acidification in a bay, the first test occurs on a small scale. The data generated by this initial test will help guide scientists and engineers as they move to a full-scale project. Undertaking a major project without testing data can lead to very expensive solutions that do not work.

Correlation vs. Causation

People naturally try to find patterns when analyzing data. A graph that shows a relationship between two variables, forming a pattern of direct or inverse relationship, demonstrates a *correlation*. But correlation does not necessarily show that one variable is the cause of the other. You may see arguments that climate change data are coincidence—correlation without causation. How can you tell which it is? In order to establish *causation*, you need multiple lines of evidence and you need to understand how one variable is related to another.

For example, scientists determined that fossil fuel combustion contributes to climate change. The link between fossil fuels and carbon dioxide emission is well-established based on measured data from many sources. The greenhouse effect has been confirmed by many investigations. Additionally, the kinetic molecular theory explains the simple observations that all fluids (including water) expand when they are heated. When ice on land melts, it increases the volume of liquid water in the hydrosphere. The combination of these reliable lines of research, theory, and observations establishes the causation.

The kinds of tests you perform with your model will depend on the type of design you proposed. If the proposal is to add something to the bay to change the pH, you could measure the pH of real or simulated seawater before and after treatment. Then repeat the test to be sure results are reproducible. If you are designing a global solution, you may need to design a test that models input and output digitally rather than doing a physical test.

FIGURE 12: Many designs can be tested in a lab by simulating actual conditions.

ARGUE Based on your test results, make a claim about whether you think your solution will solve the stated design problem. Use evidence to support your evaluation. Give particular attention to the large-scale implementation of your solution, and both the economical and ecological implications.

_____

_____

_____

_____

_____

 Evidence Notebook Make a report or presentation including your problem statement, your model, testing plan, and test results. Explain how your solution would restore damaged oyster beds. If your tests indicate that the solution would not work, explain what changes you could make to improve it.

Engineering

Designing Freshwater Treatment Systems

FIGURE 13: Some forms of water pollution are easily observed, while others are harder to detect.

One of the enduring problems throughout the history of California is providing adequate and safe supplies of water for drinking, sanitation, irrigation, and other activities. During periods of drought, the problem becomes even harder to manage. Even when supplies are abundant, there are challenges to maintaining water quality and fair distribution. Delivering clean water for homes, businesses, agriculture, and the environment is a challenge that must be addressed at scales from personal decisions to state-wide policy. A variety of local challenges are the result of human activities and natural processes. While some pollution sources remain from past mining and water management activities, many sources are ongoing and others may not have been identified yet. While water treatment can address many of the problems of water quality, the most cost-effective solution is nearly always preventing pollution from occurring in the first place.

DEFINE Research a problem related to freshwater resources in your community. The problem can be related to either supply or quality of water relative to the overall demand.

_____

_____

_____

Solutions to large-scale problems can often start at the individual level. For example, something as simple as using a refillable water bottle reduces environmental pollution by single-use plastic bottles. Waste chemicals, such as used oil or herbicides quickly become pollution if they are poured out near a street with a storm drain. Being mindful of the environmental impact of different chemicals is a step toward protecting water resources.

PLAN Identify one action you could personally take that could help with the problem you defined. How could you enlist others to be part of your solution?

_____

_____

_____

_____

At the town or county level, different interest groups have different stakes in an issue. For example, building development and farming are activities that may affect water quality. Local environmental groups have an interest in pursuing activities that can protect water supplies, such as buying land near bodies of water. The municipal or county government may work with these interest groups to find solutions that work for each group's needs. However, solutions often do not meet all the needs of each interest group.

REVISE Adjust your solution and adapt it so that it could be implemented at the county level. If your solution is not suited for this level, propose a different solution.

_____

_____

_____

At the state level, the solutions to a problem exist on a larger scale than that of a town or a county. The state of California manages vast supplies of water and controls much of the distribution network. Interest groups can be politically powerful and well-funded. Statewide organizations of developers or farmers have greater resources to address a problem than individuals. At the state level, water quality efforts may include large investments in infrastructure to protect water. State water quality regulations are often intended to prevent pollution rather than to clean it up.

FIGURE 14: Water treatment can occur at scales extending beyond a town or county.

ASK Consider what the water quality needs of the state of California are. How would you change your engineering solution or problem to address needs at the state level?

_____

_____

_____

At the national level, the states themselves are interest groups. Other interest groups could include large business organizations, municipal and county governments, national and international environmental groups, Native American groups, and even other countries. The federal government can become involved with water management when it flows between multiple states. For example, the Colorado River flows through a number of states with dry climates. The federal government is involved in determining how much water can be withdrawn from the system, what level of water is held in reservoirs, and issues related to water quantity and quality.

EVALUATE How well do you think the United States handles water resources? Where do you think there could be improvements in our engineering design solutions?

_____

_____

_____

Chemistry in Your Community Research community organizers and their role in water treatment decisions. How do communities handle their water supplies? How do the needs of a community influence the solutions to water problems that the community adopts?

| ENVIRONMENTAL AWARENESS | | WATER QUALITY TESTING | | ANALYZING PARTICULATE POLLUTION | Go online to choose one of these other paths. |

Lesson Self-Check

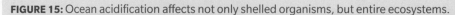

CAN YOU SOLVE IT?

FIGURE 15: Ocean acidification affects not only shelled organisms, but entire ecosystems.

In many parts of the world, oysters and other shell-forming organisms are not thriving in environments where they once did. Their larvae have trouble forming protective shells. This makes them vulnerable to predators and to disease. As these organisms disappear, the entire ecosystem in the area can be disrupted. The changes have been linked to a decrease in the pH of the water. Evidence shows that this pH change has occurred throughout the world and that all of the changes are linked.

 Evidence Notebook Refer to the notes in your Evidence Notebook to explain how the engineering process could be used to develop a solution to ocean acidification. What types of considerations would need to be made to develop a solution that works at the local scale, and takes global factors into account? Your explanation should include a discussion of solving problems using the engineering process as well as the following:

1. Make a claim about what has caused the change in pH in ocean water.
2. Where has the pH change in the ocean been observed? What chemical process regulates ocean pH?
3. How does the evidence you cited support your claim about the cause of the change in ocean pH?

Check Your Understanding

1. Which statements about ocean acidification are true? Select all correct answers.

   ☐ **a.** Ocean acidification is a local issue and can be fixed by treating water in small areas.

   ☐ **b.** Ocean acidification only occurs in shallow waters near land.

   ☐ **c.** The level of ocean acidification varies in different parts of the ocean.

   ☐ **d.** Part of the decrease in the pH of ocean water is caused by runoff of farm chemicals.

   ☐ **e.** Ocean acidification is a global problem and the main solution is to reduce carbon emissions on a global scale.

2. Explain how eelgrass can be used as a solution to ocean acidification.

   Eelgrass can be planted in acidic water as part of a biological | chemical treatment for the problem of ocean acidification. This is an example of a global | local solution. As the grass grows in the water, it removes carbon dioxide | hydrogen | oxygen from the water through the process of photosynthesis.

3. The term carbon capture and storage usually refers to which process?

   ○ **a.** isolating carbon dioxide from industrial processes and storing it underground

   ○ **b.** removing carbon dioxide from the atmosphere and storing it underground

   ○ **c.** removing carbon dioxide from ocean water and storing it underground

   ○ **d.** crushing coal to remove impurities, reducing the amount of carbon dioxide released from burning coal

4. What process is responsible for moving acidified water from the poles to other areas of the ocean?

   ○ **a.** surface winds

   ○ **b.** surface currents

   ○ **c.** deep currents

   ○ **d.** upwelling

5. You are working with a group of interested parties to develop an engineering design solution to a water quality problem. Place these steps of the design process in the most likely order that you would proceed.

   _____ **a.** test the solution

   _____ **b.** brainstorm possible solutions

   _____ **c.** analyze data

   _____ **d.** develop a problem statement

   _____ **e.** construct a model

6. Which of the following would be interest groups in a project involving the reduction of ocean acidity? Select all correct answers.

   ☐ **a.** consumers of seafood

   ☐ **b.** oyster larvae

   ☐ **c.** conservation organizations

   ☐ **d.** sea otters

   ☐ **e.** oyster harvesters

7. When trying to reduce ocean acidification in a local area, why might it be more beneficial to add ground up shells to the water instead of limestone? Select all correct answers.

   ☐ **a.** There is a greater abundance of shells than limestone, making it easier to treat large sections of water.

   ☐ **b.** Limestone must be mined, which releases carbon dioxide into the atmosphere. This could cancel out the amount of carbon dioxide the limestone can absorb.

   ☐ **c.** In addition to absorbing carbon dioxide, the shells can also serve as a habitat to encourage new oyster beds to grow.

   ☐ **d.** The shells absorb more carbon dioxide more quickly than limestone, meaning the water will not need to be treated as often.

CHECKPOINTS (continued)

8. Explain why a local solution to ocean acidification is not likely to be permanent.

_____

_____

_____

_____

9. Why would engineers use a model of a global solution to ocean acidification as part of the engineering design process?

_____

_____

_____

_____

_____

10. Discussions about ocean acidification often focus on shelled organisms, such as oysters, sea snails, and crabs. But it can also affect fish and whales that feed on these organisms. What other interest groups might one day be affected by ocean acidification, even if they are not affected now?

_____

_____

_____

_____

_____

_____

_____

_____

MAKE YOUR OWN STUDY GUIDE

 In your Evidence Notebook, design a study guide that supports the main ideas from this lesson:

Carbon dioxide emissions are the cause of increased acidity in the ocean.

The roles of interest groups should be considered in developing an engineering solution.

Remember to include the following information in your study guide:

- Use examples that model main ideas.
- Record explanations for the phenomena you investigated.
- Use evidence to support your explanations. Your support can include drawings, data, graphs, laboratory conclusions, and other evidence recorded throughout the lesson.

Consider how some solutions can only be accomplished as large-scale projects by many interest groups.

Technology Connection

Monitoring Pollution Semipermeable membrane devices (SPMDs) sample pollutants in ocean water along the California coast and in other parts of the ocean. The membranes in the devices collect organic compounds, such as pesticides, that don't completely mix with water and occur in such small quantities that they are hard to study. SPMDs collect the pollutants, then concentrate them for easier measurement.

Prepare a presentation explaining how technologies used to monitor pollution work and what types of data they collect. How do scientists use that data to understand the effects of human activities on equilibrium systems in air, water, or land? In your presentation, discuss the potential impacts of this technology on society and the environment.

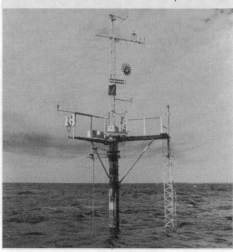

FIGURE 1: A buoy equipped with specialized instruments monitors air and sea pollution.

Social Studies Connection

Human Population The human population of an area may be stable for a long time, or it might change at a predictable rate. Different factors can change this equilibrium state, such as a change in birth or death rates, a large employer moving in or away, or many people moving in or out. These factors could cause shortages or oversupply of related resources. Over time, a new equilibrium is reached.

Build a timeline of the history of your community and label significant events that affected the population. What events caused sudden or long-term changes to its size or makeup? Include text and media comparing the changes to the concept of dynamic chemical equilibrium. How is this a good or poor analogy for chemical equilibrium?

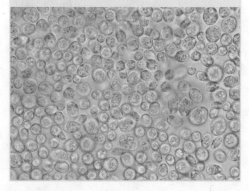

FIGURE 2: Changes in human populations lead to changes in needed resources.

Environmental Science Connection

Acidophiles Populations of living organisms exist in a state of equilibrium with their environments, and any significant change disrupts that equilibrium. However, microorganisms known as acidophiles have adapted to thrive in environments that may be a wasteland for other life forms. These bacteria, archaea, and algae can live in places with a pH as low as 0. They are sometimes used as an indicator of mine drainage when pH has been lowered.

What do scientists hope to learn from acidophiles? Make a pamphlet explaining how scientists are using this information to improve technologies, such as wastewater treatment systems.

FIGURE 3: This green algae thrives in highly acidic conditions.

A BOOK EXPLAINING COMPLEX IDEAS USING ONLY THE 1,000 MOST COMMON WORDS

THING EXPLAINER
COMPLICATED STUFF IN SIMPLE WORDS

RANDALL MUNROE
author of *What If?* and creator of *xkcd*

RANDALL MUNROE
XKCD.COM

EARTH'S SURFACE

All about Earth and what happens at its surface

Transferring a curved surface to a flat map results in a distorted image of the curved surface, so cartographers have developed several ways to do it. On the following pages are cylindrical projections of Earth.

THE STORY OF MAPPING OUR ROUND EARTH

THE EARTH'S SURFACE IS SPECIAL, AS FAR AS WE KNOW. IT'S THE ONLY PLACE WHERE WE'VE FOUND SEAS OF WATER, AND THE ONLY PLACE WHERE THE LAND IS MADE OF SHEETS OF ROCK THAT MOVE AROUND.

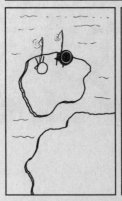

THERE ARE A LOT OF INTERESTING THINGS HERE.

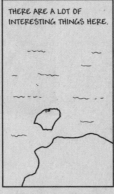

MAPS OF EARTH'S SURFACE SHOW WHERE SOME OF THEM ARE.

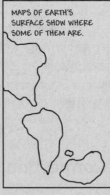

EARTH IS A ROUND BALL, SO TO FIT ITS SURFACE ON A PAGE, IT HAS TO BE STRETCHED OUT.

HEY, DID YOU KNOW THAT STRETCHING IS REALLY GOOD FOR YOU?

THIS CHANGES THE SHAPES AND SIZES OF SOME AREAS.

VERY FUNNY.

ON THIS MAP, IT MAKES THE LAND AT THE TOP AND THE BOTTOM LOOK MUCH BIGGER THAN IT REALLY IS, AND SOME OF THE PLACES NEAR THE SIDES LOOK STRETCHED OUT.

???

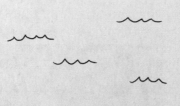

There's no way around this problem. Every paper map of a round world is wrong about size, shape, or the direction from one place to another. The shape chosen for this map tries to keep all these things in mind, not stretching any one part too much or making any area look too wrong.

PLACES WHERE THERE ARE A LOT OF TREES

PLACES WHERE THE ROCKS ARE OLD

■ As old as the first big animals   ■ As old as the earliest life

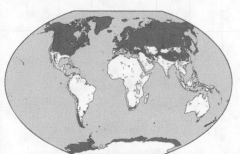

PLACES WHERE IT SNOWS

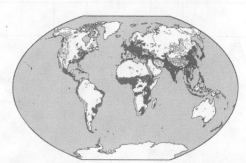

PLACES WHERE A LOT OF PEOPLE LIVE

PLACES WHERE THE EARTH SHAKES A LOT

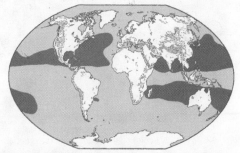

SEAS WITH BIG WARM CIRCLE STORMS

PLACES WITH LOTS OF FLASHING SKY LIGHTS

PLACES WHERE LONG SPINNING CLOUDS REACH DOWN FROM STORMS AND BLOW AWAY HOUSES

■ Sometimes   ■ A lot

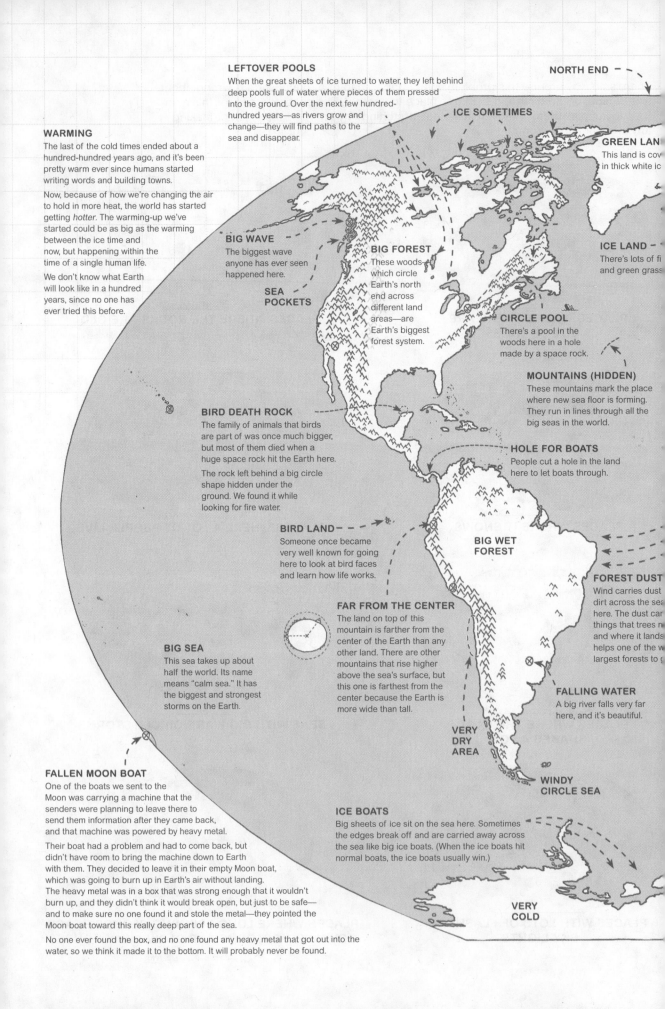

LEFTOVER POOLS
When the great sheets of ice turned to water, they left behind deep pools full of water where pieces of them pressed into the ground. Over the next few hundred-hundred years—as rivers grow and change—they will find paths to the sea and disappear.

NORTH END

ICE SOMETIMES

GREEN LAN
This land is cov in thick white ic

WARMING
The last of the cold times ended about a hundred-hundred years ago, and it's been pretty warm ever since humans started writing words and building towns.

Now, because of how we're changing the air to hold in more heat, the world has started getting *hotter*. The warming-up we've started could be as big as the warming between the ice time and now, but happening within the time of a single human life.

We don't know what Earth will look like in a hundred years, since no one has ever tried this before.

BIG WAVE
The biggest wave anyone has ever seen happened here.

SEA POCKETS

BIG FOREST
These woods—which circle Earth's north end across different land areas—are Earth's biggest forest system.

ICE LAND
There's lots of fi and green grass

CIRCLE POOL
There's a pool in the woods here in a hole made by a space rock.

MOUNTAINS (HIDDEN)
These mountains mark the place where new sea floor is forming. They run in lines through all the big seas in the world.

BIRD DEATH ROCK
The family of animals that birds are part of was once much bigger, but most of them died when a huge space rock hit the Earth here.

The rock left behind a big circle shape hidden under the ground. We found it while looking for fire water.

HOLE FOR BOATS
People cut a hole in the land here to let boats through.

BIRD LAND
Someone once became very well known for going here to look at bird faces and learn how life works.

BIG WET FOREST

FOREST DUST
Wind carries dust dirt across the sea here. The dust car things that trees n and where it lands helps one of the w largest forests to g

FAR FROM THE CENTER
The land on top of this mountain is farther from the center of the Earth than any other land. There are other mountains that rise higher above the sea's surface, but this one is farthest from the center because the Earth is more wide than tall.

BIG SEA
This sea takes up about half the world. Its name means "calm sea." It has the biggest and strongest storms on the Earth.

FALLING WATER
A big river falls very far here, and it's beautiful.

VERY DRY AREA

FALLEN MOON BOAT
One of the boats we sent to the Moon was carrying a machine that the senders were planning to leave there to send them information after they came back, and that machine was powered by heavy metal.

Their boat had a problem and had to come back, but didn't have room to bring the machine down to Earth with them. They decided to leave it in their empty Moon boat, which was going to burn up in Earth's air without landing. The heavy metal was in a box that was strong enough that it wouldn't burn up, and they didn't think it would break open, but just to be safe—and to make sure no one found it and stole the metal—they pointed the Moon boat toward this really deep part of the sea.

No one ever found the box, and no one found any heavy metal that got out into the water, so we think it made it to the bottom. It will probably never be found.

WINDY CIRCLE SEA

ICE BOATS
Big sheets of ice sit on the sea here. Sometimes the edges break off and are carried away across the sea like big ice boats. (When the ice boats hit normal boats, the ice boats usually win.)

VERY COLD

DEEPEST HOLE
Some people made a deep hole here to learn about the inside of the world. They stopped after a while because the inside of the world turned out to be too hot. The hole is still there, but they put a cover over it.

HOT ROCKS AND THE GREAT DYING
Before the time of the great bird animals, hot rocks rose from the ground here and covered the land. Fires burned, and smoke poured out across the Earth. The rocks cooled in a great sheet across the land and much of it is still there.

At the same time the hot rocks covered the land, nearly all life died out. People who learn about the past call this the Great Dying; more kinds of life disappeared from Earth than at any other time.

Most people think the fire, rocks, and clouds of smoke were what *caused* the Great Dying, but we're still figuring out how it happened. It was so long ago that many of the rocks from that time are lost or hidden deep in the ground.

MORE OF THAT BIG FOREST

This is the deepest water that's not a sea.

RING OF FIRE
(Real name)

SAND SEA

SAND SEAS
These areas are hot and dry. Wind pushes big waves of sand across them like moving mountains.

EARTH'S BIGGEST MOUNTAIN

DEEP PART
This is the deepest part of the sea. The distance from the sea surface down to the bottom here is a little farther than the distance up to the top of the highest mountain.

MOUNTAIN BUILDING
This land crossed the sea and is in the middle of running into the larger land to the north. This has pushed up the world's tallest mountains.

LOST LAND
Over a hundred years ago, hot rock coming out of the Earth made a mountain sticking up from the sea blow up, sending huge waves of water over all the land around it.

FALLING WATER
A big river falls very far here, and it's beautiful.

LAND BREAKING
The land here is slowly breaking in half. One day this one big area of land will become two.

BIG ANIMALS WITH POCKETS

WINDY CIRCLE SEA

BIRDS IN SUITS

WINDY CIRCLE SEA

VERY COLD

VERY COLD

SOUTH END

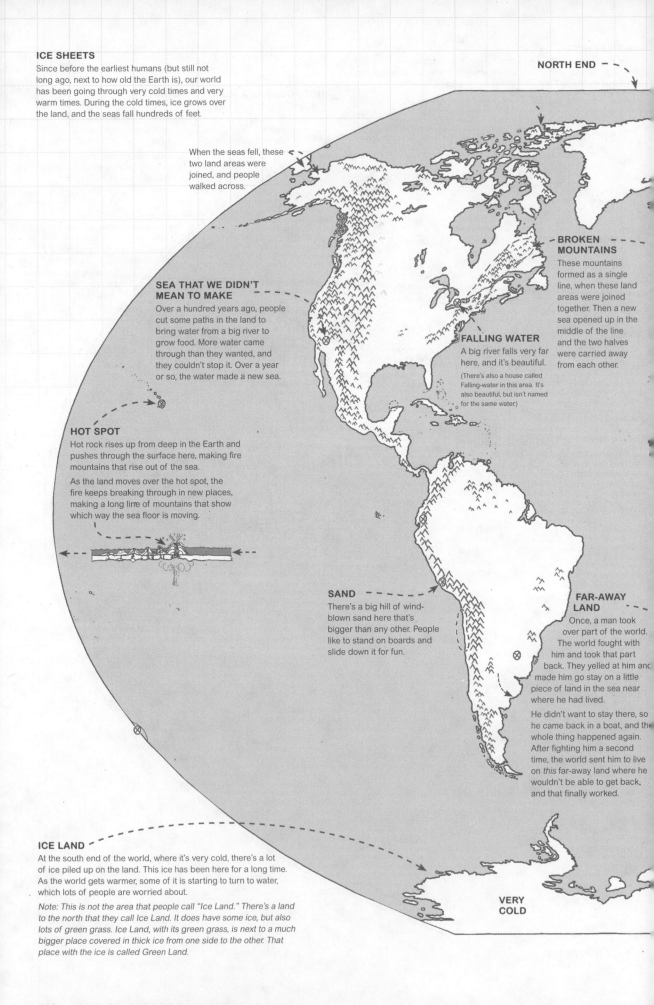

ICE SHEETS

Since before the earliest humans (but still not
long ago, next to how old the Earth is), our world
has been going through very cold times and very
warm times. During the cold times, ice grows over
the land, and the seas fall hundreds of feet.

When the seas fell, these
two land areas were
joined, and people
walked across.

**BROKEN
MOUNTAINS**

These mountains
formed as a single
line, when these land
areas were joined
together. Then a new
sea opened up in the
middle of the line
and the two halves
were carried away
from each other.

**SEA THAT WE DIDN'T
MEAN TO MAKE**

Over a hundred years ago, people
cut some paths in the land to
bring water from a big river to
grow food. More water came
through than they wanted, and
they couldn't stop it. Over a year
or so, the water made a new sea.

FALLING WATER

A big river falls very far
here, and it's beautiful.

(There's also a house called
Falling-water in this area. It's
also beautiful, but isn't named
for the same water.)

HOT SPOT

Hot rock rises up from deep in the Earth and
pushes through the surface here, making fire
mountains that rise out of the sea.

As the land moves over the hot spot, the
fire keeps breaking through in new places,
making a long line of mountains that show
which way the sea floor is moving.

SAND

There's a big hill of wind-
blown sand here that's
bigger than any other. People
like to stand on boards and
slide down it for fun.

**FAR-AWAY
LAND**

Once, a man took
over part of the world.
The world fought with
him and took that part
back. They yelled at him and
made him go stay on a little
piece of land in the sea near
where he had lived.

He didn't want to stay there, so
he came back in a boat, and the
whole thing happened again.
After fighting him a second
time, the world sent him to live
on *this* far-away land where he
wouldn't be able to get back,
and that finally worked.

ICE LAND

At the south end of the world, where it's very cold, there's a lot
of ice piled up on the land. This ice has been here for a long time.
As the world gets warmer, some of it is starting to turn to water,
which lots of people are worried about.

*Note: This is not the area that people call "Ice Land." There's a land
to the north that they call Ice Land. It does have some ice, but also
lots of green grass. Ice Land, with its green grass, is next to a much
bigger place covered in thick ice from one side to the other. That
place with the ice is called Green Land.*

**VERY
COLD**

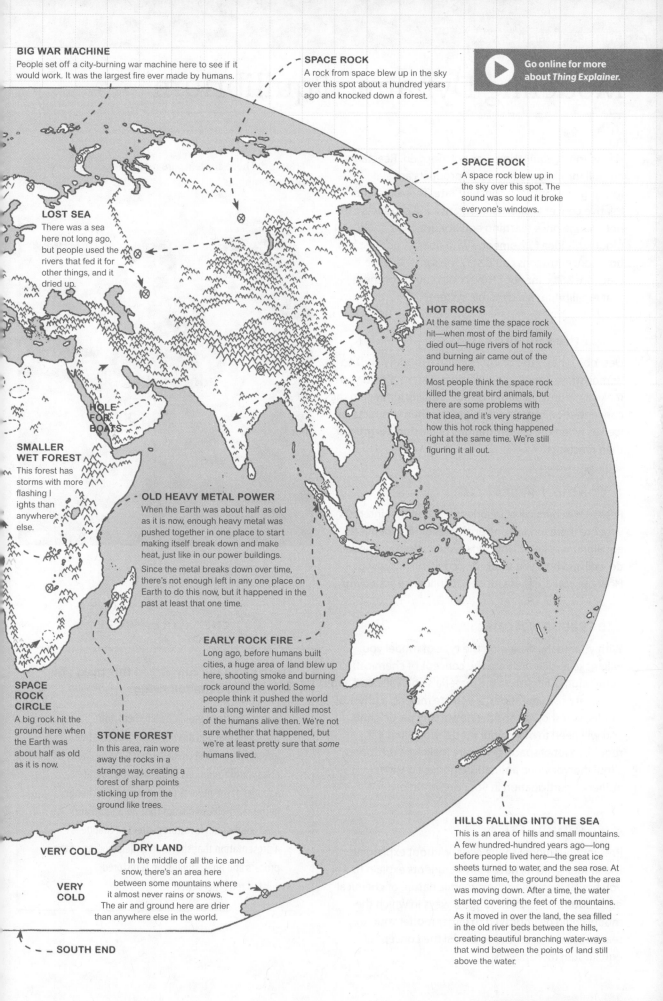

BIG WAR MACHINE
People set off a city-burning war machine here to see if it would work. It was the largest fire ever made by humans.

SPACE ROCK
A rock from space blew up in the sky over this spot about a hundred years ago and knocked down a forest.

▶ Go online for more about *Thing Explainer*.

SPACE ROCK
A space rock blew up in the sky over this spot. The sound was so loud it broke everyone's windows.

LOST SEA
There was a sea here not long ago, but people used the rivers that fed it for other things, and it dried up.

HOT ROCKS
At the same time the space rock hit—when most of the bird family died out—huge rivers of hot rock and burning air came out of the ground here.

Most people think the space rock killed the great bird animals, but there are some problems with that idea, and it's very strange how this hot rock thing happened right at the same time. We're still figuring it all out.

HOLE FOR BOATS

SMALLER WET FOREST
This forest has storms with more flashing l ights than anywhere else.

OLD HEAVY METAL POWER
When the Earth was about half as old as it is now, enough heavy metal was pushed together in one place to start making itself break down and make heat, just like in our power buildings.

Since the metal breaks down over time, there's not enough left in any one place on Earth to do this now, but it happened in the past at least that one time.

EARLY ROCK FIRE
Long ago, before humans built cities, a huge area of land blew up here, shooting smoke and burning rock around the world. Some people think it pushed the world into a long winter and killed most of the humans alive then. We're not sure whether that happened, but we're at least pretty sure that *some* humans lived.

SPACE ROCK CIRCLE
A big rock hit the ground here when the Earth was about half as old as it is now.

STONE FOREST
In this area, rain wore away the rocks in a strange way, creating a forest of sharp points sticking up from the ground like trees.

HILLS FALLING INTO THE SEA
This is an area of hills and small mountains. A few hundred-hundred years ago—long before people lived here—the great ice sheets turned to water, and the sea rose. At the same time, the ground beneath the area was moving down. After a time, the water started covering the feet of the mountains.

As it moved in over the land, the sea filled in the old river beds between the hills, creating beautiful branching water-ways that wind between the points of land still above the water.

VERY COLD

VERY COLD

DRY LAND
In the middle of all the ice and snow, there's an area here between some mountains where it almost never rains or snows. The air and ground here are drier than anywhere else in the world.

SOUTH END

Modeling Dynamic Equilibrium

A reaction at equilibrium has not stopped. Reactants are still forming products, and products are still forming reactants at a constant rate. Therefore, the relative concentrations of reactants and products do not change once reaching equilibrium. How could you model this idea for someone who doesn't understand how concentrations could stay the same, but the reactions still continue? How could you show them that equilibrium is a dynamic system?

FIGURE 4: These students are modeling equilibrium using pompoms.

1. DEFINE THE PROBLEM

Describe what types of information a model needs to demonstrate about an equilibrium system. Could you make a model that demonstrates equilibrium when the concentration of reactants is greater than products, as well as when the concentrations of products is greater than reactants?

2. CONDUCT RESEARCH

Research a chemical equilibrium reaction that interests you. Are there models and analogies of this chemical equilibrium system? Note what you think these models do well and how you think they could be improved. How can you use these models to influence your own?

3. DEVELOP A MODEL

With your team, decide on the type of model you will make to demonstrate the concept of chemical equilibrium. Determine the materials you will need and any safety considerations. If you are making a physical model, you should consider how many participants you will need to make your model work, and if it requires a lot of space. If you are making a computer simulation or video animation model, consider audience participation in your presentation.

4. COMMUNICATE

Present your model to the class. Without explaining the model to them, have fellow students explain to you how it is showing the dynamic nature of chemical equilibrium. Have them suggest ways in which the model could be improved to either model your reaction more clearly, or to model the concept of equilibrium more clearly.

 CHECK YOUR WORK

Once you have completed this task, you should have the following:

- a clearly defined problem statement with questions that you answer in the presentation
- information on the chemical reaction you chose and typical conditions under which it operates
- a model of the process that shows how a change in the reaction can disrupt the equilibrium and how equilibrium is restored after the change.
- a presentation that shows an understanding of the process and how equilibrium is restored
- a list of references cited

Name _____   Date _____

SYNTHESIZE THE UNIT

In your Evidence Notebook, make a concept map, other graphic organizer, or outline using the Study Guides you made for each lesson in this unit. Be sure to use evidence to support your claims.

When synthesizing individual information, remember to follow these general steps:

- Find the central idea of each piece of information.
- Think about the relationships among the central ideas.
- Combine the ideas to come up with a new understanding.

DRIVING QUESTIONS

Look back to the Driving Questions from the opening section of this unit. In your Evidence Notebook, review and revise your previous answers to those questions. Use the evidence you gathered and other observations you made throughout the unit to support your claims.

PRACTICE AND REVIEW

1. Phosphorus pentachloride decomposes into phosphorus trichloride and chlorine. In a closed system, the reaction reaches equilibrium:

$$PCl_5(g) \rightleftharpoons PCl_3(g) + Cl_2(g)$$

Complete the statement about the reaction.

If a sample of pure PCl_5 could be isolated and placed in a closed container, the forward | reverse reaction would begin immediately. Once the system reaches equilibrium, the amount of chlorine gas in the system will remain constant | steadily increase. At equilibrium, the forward and reverse reactions stop completely | continue to occur.

2. The K_{sp} of zinc carbonate, $ZnCO_3$, is 1.4×10^{-11} at 25 °C. Which of the following statements are correct? Select all correct answers.

   ☐ **a.** Zinc carbonate is slightly soluble in water.

   ☐ **b.** Zinc carbonate in solution is at equilibrium with undissolved zinc carbonate in the container.

   ☐ **c.** Zinc carbonate will precipitate if a solution of zinc hydroxide ($K_{sp} = 3.0 \times 10^{-17}$ at 25 °C) is added to a saturated solution of zinc carbonate.

   ☐ **d.** Zinc carbonate will precipitate if a solution of soluble zinc nitrate is added to a saturated solution of zinc carbonate.

   ☐ **e.** Additional zinc carbonate will dissolve if a solution of sodium sulfate is added.

3. Consider the equilibrium reaction:

$$CO(g) + 3H_2(g) \rightleftharpoons CH_4(g) + H_2O(g) + \text{energy}$$

How will increasing the temperature affect the equilibrium of the reaction?

   ○ **a.** The equilibrium shifts to the right because there is more energy available.

   ○ **b.** The equilibrium shifts to the right because the rate of collisions increases.

   ○ **c.** The equilibrium shifts to the left because there are fewer molecules on the left.

   ○ **d.** The equilibrium shifts to the left because the rate of the reverse reaction increases.

4. Which of these changes to an equilibrium system causes a change in the value of K_{eq}? Select all correct answers.

   ☐ **a.** increasing the temperature of the system

   ☐ **b.** increasing the concentration of a reactant

   ☐ **c.** adding a catalyst

   ☐ **d.** decreasing the concentration of a product

   ☐ **e.** decreasing the reaction temperature

5. Increasing the concentration of a reactant in an equilibrium system

   ○ **a.** shifts the equilibrium toward the products.

   ○ **b.** shifts the equilibrium toward the reactants.

   ○ **c.** does not shift the equilibrium.

6. Imagine a factory that produces paint was found to be polluting a local stream with excess chemicals from production. What interest groups might be involved in deciding how to control the pollution in the stream and pass legislation to prevent future pollution?

_____

_____

_____

_____

_____

7. In a reversible reaction, the forward and reverse reactions both occur. Why does the forward reaction in an equilibrium system never go to completion? Explain in terms of reactants and products.

_____

_____

_____

_____

_____

8. In a manufacturing process, the product of the forward reaction is continually removed. A catalyst is added, increasing the rates of both the forward and reverse reaction. How will adding a catalyst affect the production of the process?

_____

_____

_____

_____

_____

UNIT PROJECT

Return to your unit project. Prepare your research and materials into a presentation to share with the class. In your final presentation, evaluate the strength of your hypothesis, data, analysis, and conclusions.

Remember these tips while presenting:

- Include a clear statement of the problem that is being addressed and sources cited.

- Use graphics or multimedia tools to explain solutions to problems and how scientific principles are applied.

- Present your findings in a clear and organized way.

- Include criteria and constraints that drive process decisions.

- Incorporate the concepts of stability and change in your explanation of processes.

Index

Page numbers for definitions are printed in **boldface type**.
Page numbers for illustrations, maps, and charts are printed in *italics*.

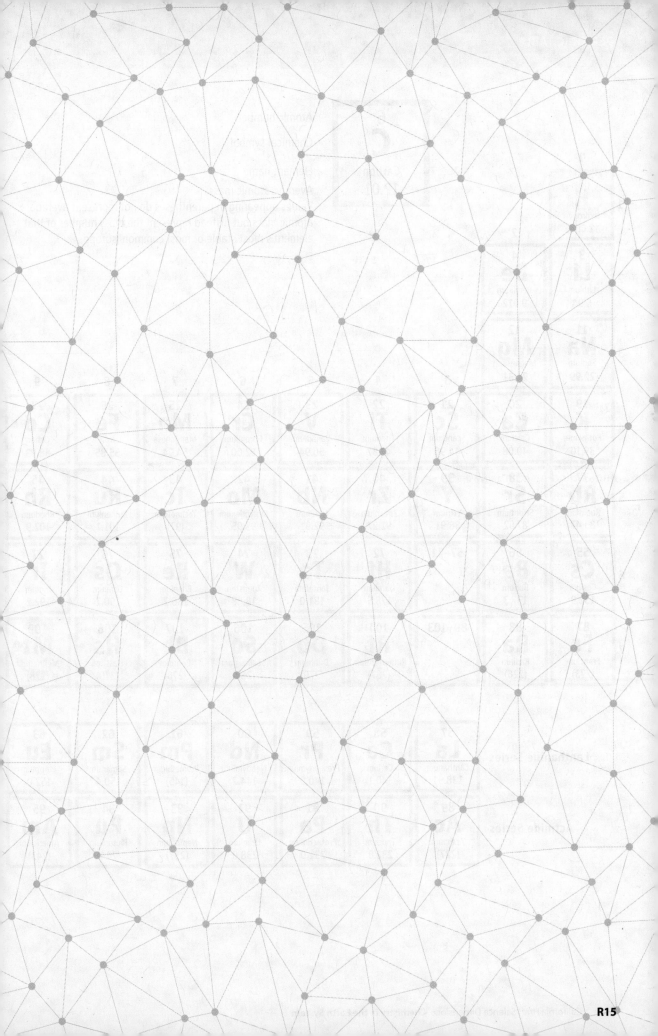

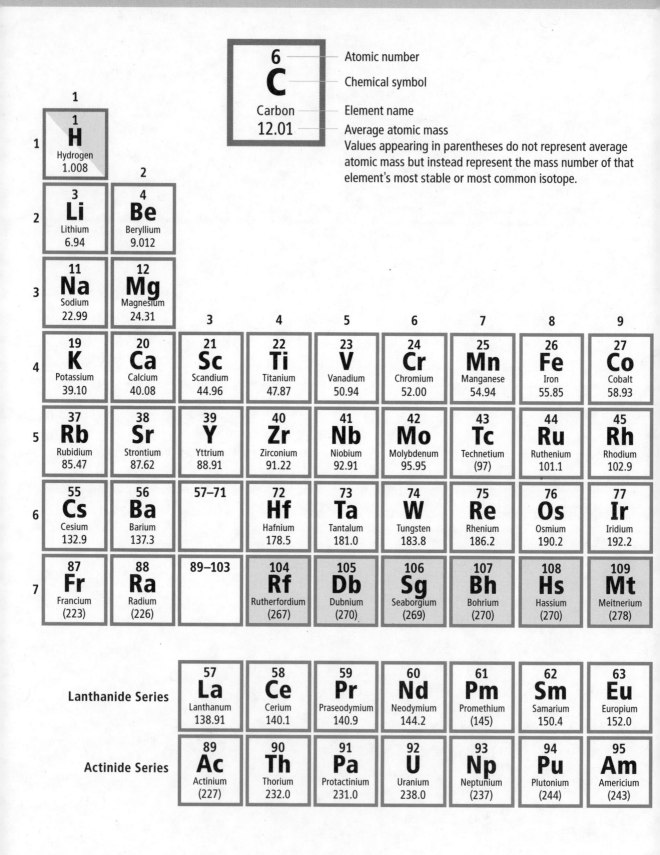

6
C
Carbon
12.01

Atomic number
Chemical symbol
Element name
Average atomic mass

Values appearing in parentheses do not represent average atomic mass but instead represent the mass number of that element's most stable or most common isotope.

Lanthanide Series

| 57 La Lanthanum 138.91 | 58 Ce Cerium 140.1 | 59 Pr Praseodymium 140.9 | 60 Nd Neodymium 144.2 | 61 Pm Promethium (145) | 62 Sm Samarium 150.4 | 63 Eu Europium 152.0 |

Actinide Series

| 89 Ac Actinium (227) | 90 Th Thorium 232.0 | 91 Pa Protactinium 231.0 | 92 U Uranium 238.0 | 93 Np Neptunium (237) | 94 Pu Plutonium (244) | 95 Am Americium (243) |

Metals Metalloids Nonmetals

State of Element at STP

Solid Liquid

Gas Not yet known

	18
	2 **He** Helium 4.003

13	14	15	16	17
5 **B** Boron 10.81	**6** **C** Carbon 12.01	**7** **N** Nitrogen 14.007	**8** **O** Oxygen 15.999	**9** **F** Fluorine 19.00	**10** **Ne** Neon 20.18

13	14	15	16	17
13 **Al** Aluminum 26.98	**14** **Si** Silicon 28.085	**15** **P** Phosphorus 30.97	**16** **S** Sulfur 32.06	**17** **Cl** Chlorine 35.45	**18** **Ar** Argon 39.95

10	11	12	13	14	15	16	17	18
28 **Ni** Nickel 58.69	**29** **Cu** Copper 63.55	**30** **Zn** Zinc 65.38	**31** **Ga** Gallium 69.72	**32** **Ge** Germanium 72.63	**33** **As** Arsenic 74.92	**34** **Se** Selenium 79.0	**35** **Br** Bromine 79.90	**36** **Kr** Krypton 83.80
46 **Pd** Palladium 106.4	**47** **Ag** Silver 107.9	**48** **Cd** Cadmium 112.4	**49** **In** Indium 114.8	**50** **Sn** Tin 118.7	**51** **Sb** Antimony 121.8	**52** **Te** Tellurium 127.6	**53** **I** Iodine 126.9	**54** **Xe** Xenon 131.3
78 **Pt** Platinum 195.1	**79** **Au** Gold 197.0	**80** **Hg** Mercury 200.6	**81** **Tl** Thallium 204.38	**82** **Pb** Lead 207.2	**83** **Bi** Bismuth 209.0	**84** **Po** Polonium (209)	**85** **At** Astatine (210)	**86** **Rn** Radon (222)
110 **Ds** Darmstadtium (281)	**111** **Rg** Roentgenium (281)	**112** **Cn** Copernicium (285)	**113** **Nh** Nihonium (286)	**114** **Fl** Flerovium (289)	**115** **Mc** Moscovium (289)	**116** **Lv** Livermorium (293)	**117** **Ts** Tennessine (293)	**118** **Og** Oganesson (294)

64 **Gd** Gadolinium 157.3	**65** **Tb** Terbium 158.9	**66** **Dy** Dysprosium 162.5	**67** **Ho** Holmium 164.9	**68** **Er** Erbium 167.3	**69** **Tm** Thulium 168.9	**70** **Yb** Ytterbium 173.1	**71** **Lu** Lutetium 175.0
96 **Cm** Curium (247)	**97** **Bk** Berkelium (247)	**98** **Cf** Californium (251)	**99** **Es** Einsteinium (252)	**100** **Fm** Fermium (257)	**101** **Md** Mendelevium (258)	**102** **No** Nobelium (259)	**103** **Lr** Lawrencium (262)

Elements with atomic numbers of 95 and above are not known to occur naturally, even in trace amounts. They have only been synthesized in the lab. The physical and chemical properties of elements with atomic numbers 100 and above cannot be predicted with certainty.